LEGAL PRAC

KU-050-519

INTERNATIONAL INSOLVENCY LAW

Markets and the Law

Series Editor:
Geraint Howells
Lancaster University, UK

Series Advisory Board:
Stefan Grundmann – Humboldt University of Berlin, Germany
Hans Micklitz – Bamberg University, Germany
James P. Nehf – Indiana University, USA
Iain Ramsay – York University, Canada
Charles Rickett – University of Queensland, Australia
Reiner Schulze – Münster University, Germany
Jules Stuyck – Katholieke Universiteit Leuven, Belgium
Stephen Weatherill – University of Oxford, UK
Thomas Wilhelmsson – University of Helsinki, Finland

Markets and the Law is concerned with the way the law interacts with the market through regulation, self-regulation and the impact of private law regimes. It looks at the impact of regional and international organizations (e.g. EC and WTO) and many of the works adopt a comparative approach and/or appeal to an international audience. Examples of subjects covered include trade laws, intellectual property, sales law, insurance, consumer law, banking, financial markets, labour law, environmental law and social regulation affecting the market as well as competition law. The series includes texts covering a broad area, monographs on focused issues, and collections of essays dealing with particular themes.

Other titles in the series

Electronic Consumer Contracts and International Private Law
Lorna Giles

Environmental Product Policy
Rosalind Malcolm

Central European Product Liability Regimes
Magdalena Sengayen

The Yearbook of Consumer Law 2008
Edited by Christian Twigg-Fleshner, Deborah Parry,
Geraint Howells and Anette Nordhausen

Fairness in Consumer Contracts
Chris Willett

International Insolvency Law

Themes and Perspectives

Edited by

PAUL J. OMAR
Sussex Institute,
University of Sussex, UK

UNIVERSITY OF WOLVERHAMPTON
LEARNING & INFORMATION
SERVICES

ACC. NO.
2437273

CLASS
LPC 321

CONTROL NO.
0754624277

346.
078

DATE
-7. MAR. 2008

SITE
LPC

INT

ASHGATE

© Paul J. Omar 2008

All rights reserved. No part of this publication may be reproduced, stored in a retrieval system, or transmitted in any form or by any means, electronic, mechanical, photocopying, recording or otherwise without the prior permission of the publisher.

Paul J. Omar has asserted their right under the Copyright, Designs and Patents Act, 1988, to be identified as the editor of this work.

Published by
Ashgate Publishing Limited
Gower House
Croft Road
Aldershot
Hampshire GU11 3HR
England

Ashgate Publishing Company
Suite 420
101 Cherry Street
Burlington, VT 05401-4405
USA

Ashgate website: http://www.ashgate.com

British Library Cataloguing in Publication Data
International insolvency law : themes and perspectives. -
    (Markets and the law)
    1. Bankruptcy
    I. Omar, Paul J.
    346'.078

Library of Congress Cataloging-in-Publication Data
International insolvency law : themes and perspectives / edited by Paul J. Omar.
    p. cm. -- (Markets and the law)
    Includes bibliographical references and index.
    ISBN: 978-0-7546-2427-1
    1. Bankruptcy. 2. Business failures--Law and legislation. 3. International business
enterprises--Law and legislation. I. Omar, Paul J.

    K1370.I559 2008
    346.07'8--dc22

                                                                    2007035659

ISBN: 978-0-7546-2427-1

Printed and bound in Great Britain by TJ International Ltd, Padstow, Cornwall.

Contents

Notes on Contributors   vii
List of Figures and Tables   ix
Table of Cases   xi
Table of Statutory Materials   xvii
Table of International Materials   xxxvii
Editorial Preface   xxxix

PART I: GENERAL PRINCIPLES OF INSOLVENCY LAW

1. The Culture of Bankruptcy
    Harry Rajak   3

2. Cross-Border Insolvency Law: Where Private International Law and
    Insolvency Law Meet
    Rosalind Mason   27

3. The Law and Economics of Corporate Insolvency – Some Thoughts
    Armin J. Kammel   61

PART II: THE RESCUE AND FRESH START CONCEPTS

4. The Commencement of the Company Rescue: How and When Does
    it Start?
    Colin Anderson and David Morrison   83

5. A Comparative Analysis of the Administration Regimes in Australia
    and the United Kingdom
    Andrew Keay   105

6. Consuming Passions: Benchmarking Consumer Bankruptcy
    Law Systems
    Donna McKenzie Skene and Adrian Walters   135

PART III: INTERNATIONAL INSOLVENCY INITIATIVES

7. Coming to Terms with the COMI Concept in the European Insolvency
    Regulation
    Paul Torremans   173

8. The Dominance of Main Insolvency Proceedings under the European
    Insolvency Regulation
    Margreet B. De Boer and Bob Wessels   185

PART IV: FINANCE AND SECURITY ISSUES

9. Bank Insolvency and the Problem of Non-Performing Loans
    Andrew Campbell   211

10. *In Re: Spectrum Plus* – Less of a Bang than a Whimper?
    Sandra Frisby   237

PART V: INNOVATIONS IN INSOLVENCY

11. A Plea for the Development of Coherent Labour and Insolvency
    Principles on a Regional Basis in SADC Countries
    Stefan van Eck and André Boraine   267

12. Widening the Insolvency Lens: The Treatment of Employee Claims
    Janis Sarra   295

13. The Claim Against an Insolvent for Environmental Damage
    Leonie Stander   335

14. Reducing Collateral Damage in Franchisor Insolvency
    Jenny Buchan   367

Index   *403*

Notes on Contributors

Dr. Colin Anderson is a Senior Lecturer in the Griffith Business School at the Gold Coast Campus of the Griffith University, Queensland, Australia. E-mail: <colin.anderson@griffith.edu.au>.

André Boraine is a Professor in the Department of Procedural Law in the Law Faculty at the University of Pretoria, South Africa. E-mail: <andre.boraine@up.ac.za>.

Jenny Buchan is a Lecturer in the School of Business Law and Taxation within the Australian School of Business at the University of New South Wales in Sydney, Australia. E-mail: <jm.buchan@unsw.edu.au>.

Andrew Campbell is the Reader in International Business Law and Director of the Centre for Business Law and Practice in the School of Law at the University of Leeds, United Kingdom. E-mail: <a.campbell@leeds.ac.uk>.

Margreet B. De Boer is a Lecturer in Law at the University of Leiden, The Netherlands. E-mail: <mbdeboer@planet.nl>.

Dr. Sandra Frisby is the Baker & McKenzie Lecturer in Company and Commercial Law in the Law School at the University of Nottingham, United Kingdom. E-mail: <sandra.frisby@nottingham.ac.uk>.

Dr. Armin J. Kammel is an expert in banking law and capital markets, working for the Austrian Association of Investment Fund Management Companies (VOEIG) in Vienna, Austria. E-mail: <armin.kammel@voeig.at>.

Andrew Keay is the Professor of Corporate and Commercial Law in the Centre for Business Law and Practice in the School of Law at the University of Leeds, United Kingdom. E-mail: <A.R.Keay@leeds.ac.uk>.

Donna McKenzie Skene is a Senior Lecturer in the School of Law at the University of Aberdeen, United Kingdom. E-mail: <d.w.mckenzie@abdn.ac.uk>.

Dr. Rosalind Mason is a Professor and Head of School of the School of Law at the Queensland University of Technology in Brisbane, Australia. E-mail: <rosalind.mason@qut.edu.au>.

Dr. David Morrison is a Senior Lecturer in the TC Beirne School of Law at The University of Queensland in St Lucia, Australia. E-mail: <d.morrison@uq.edu.au>.

Harry Rajak is Professor Emeritus in the Sussex Law School at the University of Sussex in Brighton, United Kingdom. E-mail: <h.h.rajak@sussex.ac.uk>.

Janis Sarra is the Associate Dean and Professor in the Faculty of Law at the University of British Columbia in Vancouver, Canada as well as Director of the National Centre for Business Law. E-mail: <sarra@law.ubc.ca>.

Leonie Stander is a Professor in the Law Faculty at the Potchefstroom Campus of the North-West University, South Africa. E-mail: <Leonie.Stander@nwu.ac.za>.

Paul Torremans is the Professor of Intellectual Property Law in the Law School at the University of Nottingham, United Kingdom. He is also a member of the Department of Private International Law at the Faculty of Law in the University of Ghent, Belgium. E-mail: <paul.torremans@nottingham.ac.uk>.

Stefan van Eck is a Professor in the Department of Mercantile Law in the Law Faculty at the University of Pretoria, South Africa. E-mail: <stefan.vaneck@up.ac.za>.

Adrian Walters is Geldards LLP Professor of Corporate and Insolvency Law in the Nottingham Law School at Nottingham Trent University, United Kingdom. E-mail: <adrian.walters@ntu.ac.uk>.

Bob Wessels is the Professor of Commercial Law in the Law Faculty at the Vrije University in Amsterdam, The Netherlands. He is also the Distinguished Adjunct Professor of Comparative and International Insolvency Law at St. John's University School of Law, New York, United States. E-mail: <bwessels@bobwessels.nl>.

List of Figures and Tables

Figures

10.1	Profile of Appointors	250
10.2	Profile of Financing Arrangements in Administrative Receivership	252
10.3	Profile of Financing Arrangements in Administration	253
10.4	Returns to 'Secured Creditors' in Receivership	254
10.5	Returns to 'Secured Creditors' in Administration	255
10.6	Returns to Receivables Financiers in Receivership	255
10.7	Returns to Receivables Financiers in Administration	256

Tables

2.1	The Universalism-Territoriality Paradigm	49
3.1	Corporate Insolvency Laws and their Creditor-Debtor-Orientation	66
3.2	The Payoff System	72
5.1	Administration Procedures	108
5.2	Post-Enterprise Act Administration Procedures	110
5.3	Creditors' Voluntary Liquidation Procedures	132
14.1	Contractual Commitments of Franchisee	373
14.2	Survey of Assets in a Franchise System	375
14.3	The Monetary Cost of Assets	376
14.4	Franchisee Interests in Real Property	378
14.5	Stakeholders Recognised in Business Failure Laws	383
14.6	Possible Categorisation of Franchisees in Franchisor Insolvency	391

Table of Cases

Australia

Australian Competition & Consumer Commission v Ewing [2004] FCA 5   401
Australian Competition & Consumer Commission v Simply No-Knead
     (Franchising) Pty Ltd [2000] FCA 1365   384
Australian Competition & Consumer Commission v Trayling [1999]
     FCA 1133   384
Australasian Memory Pty Ltd v Brien (2000) 200 CLR 270; (2000)
     34 ACSR 250   117, 124-125
Beatty v Brashs Pty Ltd (1998) 26 ACSR 685   96
Brash Holdings Ltd v Katile Pty Ltd (1994) 13 ACSR 505   124
Burger King Corporation v Hungry Jack's Pty Limited [2001] NSWCA 187   384
Cadwallader v Bajco Pty Ltd & Ors [2002] NSWCA 328   87
Cawthorn v Keira Constructions Pty Ltd (1994) 13 ACSR 337   117-118
Crimmins v Glenview Home Units Pty Ltd [2001] NSWSC 699   92
Dallinger v Halcha Holdings Pty Ltd (admr apptd) (1995) 18 ACSR 835   97
Dallinger v Halcha Holdings Pty Ltd (1996) 14 ACLC 263   131
Deputy Commissioner of Taxation v Pddam Pty Ltd (1996) 19 ACSR 498   131
Deputy Commission of Taxation v Portinex (No1) [2000] NSWSC 99;
     (2000) 156 FLR 453   126
Deputy Commissioner of Taxation v Portinex Pty Ltd (2000) 34 ACSR 391   133
DCT v Foodcorp Pty Ltd (1994) 113 ACSR 796   96
Federal Commissioner of Taxation v Just Jeans Pty Ltd 87 ATC 4373;
     18 ATR 775   379
Foxcraft v The Ink Group Pty Ltd (1994) 15 ACSR 203   113
Hagenvale Pty Ltd v Depela Pty Ltd (1995) 17 ACSR 139   131
Ibbco Trading Pty Ltd v HIH Casualty and General Insurance Ltd (2001)
     19 ACLC 1093   394
Krakos Investments Pty Ltd v Federal Commissioner of Taxation 95 ATC 4369;
     (1995) 30 ATR 506   379
Lam Soon Australia Pty Ltd v Molit (No 55) Pty Ltd (1996) 14 ACLC 1737   113
McDonald's Australia Holdings Ltd & Anor v Industrial Relations Commission
     of NSW & 2 Ors [2005] NSWCA 286   384
Miba v Nescor Industries [1996] 834 FCA 1 (17 September 1996)   384
Neilson Investments (Qld) P/L & Ors v Spud Mulligan's P/L & Ors [2002]
     QSC 258   379
Otrava Pty Ltd & Ors v Mail Boxes Etc (Australia) Pty Ltd; Mail Boxes Etc
     (Australia) Pty Ltd v Otrava Pty Ltd & Ors [2004] NSWSC 1066   384
Ranoa Pty Ltd v BP Oil Distribution Ltd & Anor (1989) 91 ALR 251   379

Re Alfred Shaw and Co Ltd (1897) 8 QLJ 93   40
Re Bartlett Researched Securities Pty Ltd (1994) 12 ACSR 707   131
Re Centaur Mining & Exploration Ltd (in Liq) (Receivers and Managers
    Appointed) [2005] VSC 367   124
Re Cobar Mines Pty Ltd (1998) 30 ACSR 125   96-97
Re Depsun Pty Ltd (1994) 13 ACSR 644   96, 123
Re Greg Sewell Forgings Pty Ltd (1995) 13 ACLC 1172   117
Re Intag International Limited and the Corporations Law [1999] NSWSC 571   96
Re James Developments Pty Ltd (1999) 17 ACLC 291   114
Re Nardell Coal Corporation Pty Limited [2004] NSWSC 281   96
Re Origin Internet Solutions Pty Ltd [2004] FCA 382   114
Re Pan Pharmaceuticals Ltd [2003] FCA 855   126
Re Ricon Constructions Pty Ltd (1998) 16 ACLC 76; (1998) 26 ACSR 655   114
Re Vouris (2004) 22 ACLC 822   114
Regie National des Usines Renault SA v Zhang (2002) 210 CLR 491   41
Sanders v Glev Franchises Pty Ltd [2002] FCA 1332   384
St Leonards Property Pty Ltd v Ambridge Investments Pty Ltd (2004)
    210 ALR 265   127
Tolcher v National Australia Bank (2004) 22 ACLC 397   392
Wallace-Smith v Thiess Infraco (Swanston) Pty Ltd [2005] FCAFC 49   386

Austria

Collins & Aikman Products GmbH Leoben Court (judgment of
    31 August 2005) NZI 2005, 646   196, 200

Belgium

Tribunal de Commerce de Charleroi (16 July 2002),
    Me Hertsens v. SARL Bati-France [2004]
    Tijdschrift voor Belgisch Handelsrecht 811   173-174, 178-179
Rechtbank van Koophandel Tongeren (20 February 2003),
    Voorlopige bewindvoerders van de SPRL C v. SPRL C [2004]
    Tijdschrift voor Belgisch Handelsrecht 70   173-174, 179

Canada

Country Style Food Services Cases:
    Country Style Food Services Inc. v. 1304271 Ontario Ltd
    (Ontario Superior Court of Justice, Chapnik J., Judgment of
    11 February 2003)   398
In the matter of the Companies Creditors Arrangement Act., RSC 1985 C c-36,
    as amended AND In the matter of the Courts of Justice Act RSO 1990 c-43,
    as amended AND in the matter of a plan of compromise or arrangement of
    Country Style Food Services Inc, Country Style Food Services Holdings Inc,
    Country Style Realty Limited, Melody Farms Specialty Foods and Equipment

Limited, Buns Master Bakery Systems Inc and Buns Master Bakery Realty Inc
(15 April 2002, Court of Appeal for Ontario Docket M28458,
unreported decision) 398
Magnetic Marketing Ltd v Print Three Franchising Corp. et al. (1991)
38 CPR (3d) 540 397

European Community

Eurofood IFSC Ltd (Case C-341/04) [2006] BCC 397 179, 181-183

France

CA Versailles (4 September 2003) ISA Daisytek SAS et alia v. Me Valdman
et alia [2004] Tijdschrift voor Belgisch Handelsrecht 820 173, 180

Germany

ISA Deutschland GmbH Düsseldorf Court (judgment of 9 July 2004) ZIP 2004,
1514; NZI 2004, 628 195

Ireland

Irish Supreme Court (judgment of 27 July 2004) In the Matter of Eurofood IFSC
Ltd and in the Matter of the Companies Acts 1963 to 2001 173, 179

South Africa

Bareki NO and Another v Gencor Ltd and Others 2006 1 SA 432
(T) 440 349, 355
Canadian Superior Oil Ltd v Concord Insurance Co Ltd (formerly INA
Insurance Co Ltd) 1992 4 SA 263 (W) 361
Coetzee v Attorneys' Insurance Indemnity Fund 2003 1 SA 1 (SCA) 364
Coetzee (Coetzee v Vrywaringsversekeringsfonds vir Prokureurs)
2000 2 SA 262 (O) 364-365
David Trust and others v Aegis Insurance Co Ltd and others
2000 3 SA 289 (HCA) 362, 366
Director: Mineral Development, Gauteng Region and Sasol Mining (Pty) Ltd
v Save the Vaal Environment and others 1999 (2) SA 709 (SCA) 719 346
Foodgrow, a Division of Leisurenet Ltd v Keil 1999 20 ILJ 2521 (LAC) 274
Gypsum Industries Ltd v Standard General Insurance Co Ltd 1991
1 SA 718 (W) 362
Lascon Properties (Pty) Ltd v Wadesville Investment Company (Pty) Ltd
and another [1997] 3 All SA 433 (W) 347, 350
Le Roux v Standard General Versekeringsmaatskappy Bpk 2000
4 SA 1035 (HCA) 363

National Education Health & Allied Workers Union v University of
    Cape Town & Others 2003 24 ILJ 95 (CC)   275
NULW v Barnard NO (Vittmar Industries (Pty) Ltd) 2001
    9 BLLR 1002 (LAC)   274
Porteous v Strydom NO 1984 (2) SA 489 (D)   350
Przybylak v Santam Insurance Ltd 1992 1 SA 588 (K)   361
SA Municipal Workers Union & Others v Rand Airport
    Management Co (Pty) Ltd & Others 2005 26 ILJ 67 (LAC)   274-275, 277
Schutte & Others v Powerplus Performance (Pty) Ltd & Another 1999
    20 ILJ 655 (LC)   274
Smith & Another v Parton NO 1980 (3) SA 724 (D)   350
Success Panel Beaters & Services Centre CC v NUMSA 2000
    6 BLLR 635 (LAC)   274
Supermarket Haasenback (Pty) Ltd v Santam Insurance Ltd 1989
    SA 790 (W)   360
Supermarket Leaseback (Elsburg) (Pty) Ltd v Santam Insurance Ltd
    1989 2 SA 790 (W)   360-362
Supermarket Leaseback (Elsburg) (Pty) Ltd v Santam Insurance Ltd 1991
    1 SA 410 (A) 360 Thorne v The Master 1964 (3) SA 38 (N)   351
Vrywaringsversekeringsfonds vir Prokureurs v Coetzee 2001 4 SA 1273 (O)   364
Woodley v Guardian Assurance Co of SA 1976 1 SA 758 (W)   359, 362

United Kingdom

Agnew v Commissioner of the Inland Revenue [2001] UKPC 28,
    [2001] 2 AC 71 238-239   245, 248, 251
Barclays Bank plc v Homan [1993] BCLC 680   37-38
Buchler v Talbot [2004] UKHL 9   240
Cripps & Son v Wickenden [1973] 1 WLR 944   223
Dearle v Hall (1828) 3 Russ 1   257
Ex parte Pinochet [2000] AC 119 (HL)   191
Felixstowe Dock and Railway Co v US Lines Inc [1989] QB 360   46
Foley v Hill (1848) 2 HL Cas 28   212
Heather & Son v Webb (1876-77) LR 2 CPD 1   150
In the Matter of HIH Casualty and General Insurance Ltd [2006]
    EWCA Civ 732   34
Joachimson v Swiss Bank Corporation [1921] 3 KB 110   212
Macmillan Inc v Bishopsgate Investment Trust plc [1996] 1 WLR 387   41
Nicol's Tr v Nicol 1996 GWD-10-531   158
Order of the High Court of Justice (Chancery Division Birmingham),
    13 June 2005 (Order in MG Rover Nederland BV)   203
Orion Finance Ltd v Crown Financial Management Ltd [1996] 2 BCLC 78   250
Phillips v Hunter (1795) 2 HBl 402; 126 ER 618   30, 58
R v Lord Chancellor, ex parte Lightfoot [2000] QB 597   164
Re AMCD (Property Holdings) Ltd (High Court for England and Wales, 15
    June 2004) (unreported)   122

Re Atlantic Computer Systems plc [1992] Ch 505   113
Re Ballast plc [2004] EWHC 2356 (Ch); [2005] 1 WLR 1928; [2005] BCLC
    446; [2005] BCC 96   129-130
Re BCCI (No 10) [1997] 2 WLR 172   50, 52
Re Blithman (1866) LR 2 Eq 23   40
Re Brightlife Ltd [1987] Ch 200   246
Re Byford (deceased) [2003] BPIR 1089   153
Re Chancery plc [1991] BCC 171   128
Re ISA Daisytek SAS et alia (16 May 2003) [2004] Tijdschrift voor Belgisch
    Handelsrecht 813   173, 180
Re GHE Realisations Ltd [2005] EWHC 2400 (Ch); [2006] BCC 139   130
Re Griffin Hotel Co Ltd [1941] Ch 129   246
Re Keenan Bros Ltd [1986] BCLC 242   243
Re Landau [1998] Ch 223   153
Re Lewis Merthyr Consolidated Collieries Ltd [1929] 1 Ch 498; [1929] 1 Ch 498
    246-247
Re Logitext.uk Ltd [2004] EWHC 2899; [2005] 1 BCLC 326   116, 122
Re Maxwell Communications Corp plc (No 2) [1992] BCC 757   37
Re ML Design Group Ltd [2006] All ER (D) 75 (Jan)   126
Re NS Distribution Ltd [1990] BCLC 169   126
Re Preston & Duckworth [2006] BCC 133   130
Re Simoco Digital UK Ltd [2004] EWHC 209; [2004] 1 BCLC 541   122
Re Spectrum Plus [2004] EWCA Civ 670;
    [2005] UKHL 41   237, 238-239, 241-246, 248, 250, 257, 260, 263-264
Re T & D Industries plc [2000] All ER 333   126
Re TT Industries Ltd [2006] BCC 372   126
Re Woodroffes (Musical Instruments) Ltd [1986] Ch 366   246
Rouse v Bradford Banking Co [1894] AC 586   223
Scruttons Ltd v Midland Silicones Ltd [1962] AC 446   373
Siebe Gorman & Co Ltd v Barclays Bank [1979]
    2 Lloyd's Rep. 142   238, 242-243, 245, 259

United States

Dymocks Franchise Systems v Bilgola Enterprises Ltd 8 TCLR 612   399
Equal Employment Opportunity Commission v Arabian American Oil Co 111
    S Ct 1227 (1991)   39
In re UAL Corp. 428 F 3d 677 (7th Cir 2005)   327
Interpool Ltd v Certain Freights of M/V Venture Star 102 Bankr 373
    (DNJ 1988) 878   51
Local Loan Co v Hunt 292 US 234 (1934)   156
Maxwell Communication Corporation plc v Société Generale 170 BR 800
    (Bankr SDNY 1994), affirmed 186 BR 807 (SDNY 1995)   38
Maxwell Communication Corporation plc v Société Generale 93 F 3d 1036
    (2nd Cir 1996)   38-39
Sturges v Crowninshield (1819) 4 Wheat. 122   15-16

United States v Fleet Factors (1990)   342
United States v Maryland Bank & Trust (1986)   342

Table of Statutory Materials

Ancient Rome

Twelve Tables (c 450 BCE)   8, 11
    Table 3   9, 11

Australia

(i) Federal Legislation (Acts and Bills)

Bankruptcy Act 1966   385, 392
    s29   51
    s58   31
    ss115-116   31
    s269   31

Corporations Amendment (Insolvency) Bill 2007   96, 99-100, 106

Corporate Law Reform Act 1992   109

Corporations Act 2001   315-316, 385, 392
    Chapter 5   89
    Part 5.3A   89, 97, 109, 111, 117, 124-125, 387
    Part 5.8   334
    s9   101
    s95A   89, 101, 387
    s411   108
    s435A   97, 111
    s435C(1)   89
    s435C(2)(b)   128
    s435C(2)(c)   128
    s435C(3)(a)   128
    s435C(3)(b)   128
    s435C(3)(e)   128
    s435C(3)(g)   128
    s436A   89, 109, 114
    s436A(2)   95
    s436B   89, 94-95, 99, 109
    s436B(1)-(2)   114
    s436B(2)   95, 123

s436C	89, 101, 109, 114
s436C(2)	101
s436E(2)	117-118
s436E(10)	118
s437A	113, 386, 392
s437B	112
s438D	131
s439A	123, 392
s439A(4)(b)	127
s439A(6)	117, 123
s439B(2)	117
s439C	85, 118, 121, 128
s439C(c)	129
s440B	123
s440D	112, 394, 400
s441D(2)	123
s441H(2)	123
ss442A-F	392
s442A	112
s442C(1)	124
s446A(1)-(4)	129
s446A(5)	129
s447A	114, 117-118, 120-121, 124-126, 132-133
s447C(2)	124
s447D	125
s447D(1)	124
s447E	123
s449B	124
s449C(6)	124
s450A	115
s459P	387
s468(4)	386
s471(2)	394
s471B	386, 400
s477	97
s482	96
s496(1)	96
s497	96
s500(1)	386
s500(2)	386
s556	315
s556(1)	316
s558	387
s560	317
s568(1)	392
s581	51

s588FGA   33
s588G   31, 127-128
s588H(5)   128
s588H(6)(a)   128
s596A   334
s601CL   52

Corporations Law Amendment (Employee Entitlements) Act 2000   316

Insolvency (Tax Priorities) Legislation Amendment Act 1993   33

Trade Practices Act 1974   368
    Part IV   385
    Part IVA   384-385
    Part IVB   385
    Part V   384-385
    Part VC   385
    s51AC   371, 384
    s51AD   384
    s52   384
    s75AU   385
    s75AYA   385
    s75B   385

(ii) State Legislation (Acts and Bills)

Contracts Review Act 1980 (NSW)   384

Fair Trading Act 1987 (NSW)   384

Industrial Relations Act 1996 (NSW)   384
    s106   371, 384

(iii) Regulations

Corporations Regulations 2001
    Regulation 5.3A.02   127

Franchising Code of Conduct   368, 401
    Part 4   393
    s4   369

Trade Practices (Industry Codes - Franchising) Regulations 1998   368
    s5(3)   384

Austria

Bankruptcy Act 1914   78

Business Restructuring Act 1997   77-78

Settlement and Recomposition of Debts Act 1914   78

Botswana

Employment Act (29 of 1982)   288, 293
    Part III   290
    s25   290
    s27   289
    s28   288, 290
    s29   290
    s91   291-292

Employment (Amendment) Act (14 of 2003)   288

Insolvency Act 1929   290
    s38   290
    ss82-88   291
    s82   291-292
    s83   291
    s84   291
    s85   290-292
    s85(1)-(2)   291
    s85(3)   290, 292
    s85(4)   290, 292
    s87   292
    s88   292

Brazil

Bankruptcy and Restructuring Law (Federal Law No. 11.101)   307

Canada

Bankruptcy and Insolvency Act 1992   54, 308-309
    s14.06   354
    s36(1)(b)   309
    s36(2)   309
    s81.3   309
    s81.4   309
    s121(1)   355

s136(1)(d) 309

Bill C-62 2007 309, 323

Companies Creditors Arrangements Act 1985 54, 308

Employment Insurance Act 1996 322

Wage Earners Protection Program Act 2005 (Statutes of Canada 2005,
    Chapter 47) 54, 308
        s6(2) 321
        s7(1) 322
        s21 323
        s21(1) 323
        s21(1)(e) 323

China

Enterprise Bankruptcy Law 320
        Article 32 320
        Article 37 320

European Union

(i) Treaties

EC Treaty
        Article 36 191
        Article 100 344
        Article 130 344

(ii) Regulations

Council Regulation (EC) No 1346/2000 of
29 May 2000 (OJ 2000 L160/1) 52, 55-56, 58, 115, 151, 173-184, 185-208
        Chapter III 185, 187
        Recital no. 2 193
        Recital no. 3 187-188, 193
        Recital no. 12 188
        Recital no. 13 58, 174, 179, 181
        Recital no. 14 175, 178
        Recital no. 15 178
        Recital no. 16 178
        Recital no. 20 185, 188, 194, 196, 202
        Recital no. 21 188
        Article 2(h) 186

Article 3	182-183
Article 3(1)	58, 173-180, 183, 189
Article 3(2)	186-187, 190, 207
Article 3(3)	192
Article 4	186
Article 4(1)	182
Article 4(2)(c)	189
Article 5	189, 197
Article 7	189
Article 16	189
Article 16(2)	186
Article 17	186
Article 18	188-189
Article 18(1)	189-190, 191-192, 207
Article 18(2)	190
Article 18(3)	190, 192
Article 19	189
Article 20	188
Article 26	199
Article 27	187
Article 28	186
Article 29	188
Articles 31	195, 207
Article 31(1)	185, 188, 192-194, 207
Article 31(2)	185, 188, 193-194, 207
Article 31(3)	185, 188, 195, 207
Article 32	187
Article 32(1)	194, 199
Article 32(2)	188, 199
Article 32(3)	188
Article 33	186, 195-198, 206-207
Article 33(1)	188, 196-197, 199-200, 202, 208
Article 33(2)	188, 196, 201-202, 208
Article 34	186, 193, 195, 202, 207-208
Article 34(1)	188, 202-205, 208
Article 34(2)	202, 205-206
Article 34(3)	188, 202, 206, 208
Article 35	188, 204
Article 44(k)	186
Annex B	187, 197, 205

(iii) Directives

Directive 75/117/EC of 10 February 1975	268
Directive 76/207/EC of 9 February 1976	268

Directive 77/187/EC of 14 February 1977   269

Directive 80/987/EC of 20 October 1980   269, 272, 302
     Section II   303
     Article 3(2)   303
     Article 4   304
     Articles 4(2)-4(3)   303
     Article 4(3)   304
     Article 5   304

Directive 91/533/EC of 14 October 1991   268

Directive 94/19/EC of 30 May 1994   228

Directive 98/59/EC of 20 July 1998   268, 303

Directive 2000/78/EC of 27 November 2000   268

Directive 2001/23/EC of 12 March 2001   269, 273, 275
     Article 3   273
     Article 4   273, 277
     Article 5(1)   273
     Article 5(2)(b)   273
     Article 7   273

Directive 2002/74/EC of 23 September 2002   269, 272, 302

Finland

Wage Guarantee Fund Act no. 53/1993   318

France

(i) Codes

Employment Code
     Article L. 143-10   318
     Article L. 143-11-4   318

Commercial Code
     Article L. 625-8   317
     Article L. 625-9   318
     Article L. 626-20   318
     Article L. 631-17   333

(ii) Laws

Law no. 2004-391 of 4 May 2004   317

Law no. 2005-845 of 26 July 2005   317

(iii) Decrees

Decree no. 85-1388 of 27 December 1985   174

Germany

Gesetz zur Verbesserung der Betrieblichen Altersversorgung 1974   329
    §§7-15   329
    §7(1)-(2)   330
    §10   329

Insolvenzordnung 1999   320

India

Companies Act 2002   308
    s529   308

Companies (Second Amendment) Act 2002   308

Employees' State Insurance Act 1948   308

Indonesia

Labour Law 2003   306

Ireland

Anti-Discrimination Pay Act 1974   313

Employment Equity Act 1977   313

Protection of Employees (Employers' Insolvency) Act 1984   313
    s6   313

Italy

Law no. 1115 of 5 November 1968   319

Law no. 164 of 20 May 1975   319

Law no. 675 of 12 August 1977   319

Law no. 223 of 23 July 1991   319

Japan

Bankruptcy Law 1922 (Law 71 of 1922)
    Article 3 (Principle of Territoriality)   43

Employees Pension Insurance Law 1942   331

Namibia

Companies Act (61 of 1973)
    s339   283
    s348   283
    s352(1)   283

Insolvency Act (61 of 1936)   288, 292
    s2   283
    s38   283-285
    s44   286
    s44(1)   286
    ss96–102   286
    s96(1)   287
    s96(2)   287
    s97(2)-(3)   287
    s98(1)-(2)   287
    s99(1)(a)-(e)   287
    s100   285-287
    s100(1)   286-288
    s100(2)   286
    s100(3)   286
    s100(4)   286
    s102   287
    s103   287
    s106   286

Labour Act (6 of 1992)   281

Labour Act (15 of 2004)   281, 288, 292
    Part B   285
    Part F   284
    Chapter 2   281
    Chapter 3   281

Chapter 4   281
Chapter 5   281
Chapters 6-7   281
s1   285
s11(1)   285
s30   284
s31(1)   284
s31(1)(a)   284
s31(2)   284
s31(3)   284, 285-287
s33   282
s33(1)(a)   282
s33(1)(d)   282
s33(4)   282
s33(6)   282
s34   285

Netherlands

Faillissementswet
Chapter Six (Scheme for a Composition)   203
Article 5(3)   197
Article 6(1), third sentence   205
Article 7   190
Article 69   192
Articles 138-172   203
Article 138   203
Article 153(2)(4°)   205
Article 172a   203
Article 225   190
Article 252   203
Article 272(2)(5◦)   205
Article 281(2)   203
Article 290   190
Article 329   203
Article 333a   203
Article 338(2), second sentence   205
Article 361(2)   197

Netherlands Code of Procedural Law
Article 426   197

New Zealand

Insolvency (Cross-Border) Act 2006   54

South Africa

Basic Conditions of Employment Act (75 of 1997)
    s35 — 279
    s41 — 279-280
    s41(2) — 280

Close Corporations Act (69 of 1984)
    s66 — 359

Companies Act (61 of 1973)
    s21 — 356-357
    s353(1) — 351
    s339 — 359
    s386(3)-(4) — 351

Constitution of the Republic of South Africa 1996 — 344
    s8(2) — 346
    s24 — 345-347
    s24(a) — 345-347
    s24(b) — 345, 347
    s232 — 344
    s233 — 345

Cross-Border Insolvency Act (42 of 2000) — 54

Environment Conservation Act (73 of 1989)
    s31A — 348

Insolvency Act 1936 (24 of 1936) — 275, 278, 280, 352-353
    s38 — 276-279
    s38(3) — 279
    s38(5) — 276
    s38(7) — 276
    s38(9) — 277
    s38(10) — 279
    s38(11) — 278-280
    s89(1) — 351
    s89(4) — 351
    s89(5) — 351
    ss96-103 — 278
    s98A — 279
    s98A(1)(a)(iv) — 278, 280
    s99 — 279
    s100(1) — 278
    s106 — 280

s156   335, 359-366

Income Tax Act (58 of 1962)   279

Judicial Matters Second Amendment Act (122 of 1998)   278

Labour Relations Act (66 of 1995)   273, 276
    s187(1)(g)   273, 277
    s197   274, 277
    s197(2)   273-274
    s197(6)   273-274
    s197A   274, 276-277
    s197A(1)   275
    s197A(1)(a)-(b)   277
    s197A(2)   275
    s197A(2)(a)   275-277
    s197A(2)(c)   275

Labour Relations Amendment Act (12 of 2002)   276

Marine Pollution (Control and Civil Liability) Act (8 of 1981)   338
    s9(2)(b)(ii)   338

Mineral and Petroleum Resources Development Act (28 of 2002)
    ss37-38   348, 350

National Environmental Management Act (107 of 1998)
    s2(4)(p)   348
    s28   348, 349
    s28(1)   349, 355
    s28(2)   349, 355
    s28(8)   349
    s28(11)   349

National Environmental Management: Air Quality Bill (B62-2003)   350

National Environmental Management: Biodiversity Act (10 of 2004)
    s7   348, 350

National Water Act (36 of 1998)
    s19   348

National Nuclear Regulator Act (47 of 1999)
    s30   348, 350

Occupational Diseases in Mines and Works Act (78 of 1973)   279

Occupational Injuries and Diseases Act (130 of 1993) 279

Security by Means of Movable Property Act (57 of 1993)
    s1(2) 279
    s1(4) 279

Unemployment Insurance Act (63 of 2001) 276, 310

Unemployment Insurance Contributions Act (4 of 2002) 279

United Kingdom

(i) Legislation (Acts and Bills)

Bankruptcy Act 1542 4, 12, 58

Bankruptcy Act 1623 33

Bankruptcy Act 1831 14

Bankruptcy Act 1861 14

Bankruptcy Act 1883 14

Bankruptcy Act 1914 14

Bankruptcy (Scotland) Act 1985 141
    s2(4) 158
    s3(1) 158
    s5(2)-(2B) 165
    s5(2) 165
    s5(2B) 148
    s7 165
    s18 158
    s31(1) 153
    s32(2) 154-155
    s32(2A) 155
    s32(3) 155
    s32(6) 153
    s33(1) 142, 149
    s33(1)(a)-(aa) 153
    s34 153
    s35 153
    s36 153
    ss36A-F 153

s37   151
ss54-55   146
s54(3)   147
s55(2)   146
s55(2)(e)   158
s55(3)   147
s56   146
s61   153
s64(1)   158
Schedule 2A   158
Schedule 4   146
Schedule 5   142
            Paragraph 6   142
            Paragraph 7   142

Companies Act 1862   8

Companies Act 1985   8, 87
s395   245
s425   85, 87, 108
s459   123

Companies Act 2006   67
s1282   240

Companies (Consolidation) Act 1908
s107(1)   247

Company Directors' Disqualification Act 1986   147, 157
s11   147

Consumer Credit Act 2006   140

County Courts Act 1984
Part VI   142
s112(5)   143
s112(6)   143
s117   143

Debtors Act 1869   14, 17

Employment Rights Act 1996   314

Enterprise Act 2002   23-24, 65, 73, 88, 99, 102, 105, 109-110, 112, 133, 137,
                           142, 144, 147-149, 153, 157, 159, 161, 238, 241, 247, 257
s248   107

s37	151
ss54-55	146
s54(3)	147
s55(2)	146
s55(2)(e)	158
s55(3)	147
s56	146
s61	153
s64(1)	158
Schedule 2A	158
Schedule 4	146
Schedule 5	142
Paragraph 6	142
Paragraph 7	142
Companies Act 1862	8
Companies Act 1985	8, 87
s395	245
s425	85, 87, 108
s459	123
Companies Act 2006	67
s1282	240
Companies (Consolidation) Act 1908	
s107(1)	247
Company Directors' Disqualification Act 1986	147, 157
s11	147
Consumer Credit Act 2006	140
County Courts Act 1984	
Part VI	142
s112(5)	143
s112(6)	143
s117	143
Debtors Act 1869	14, 17
Employment Rights Act 1996	314
Enterprise Act 2002	23-24, 65, 73, 88, 99, 102, 105, 109-110, 112, 133, 137, 142, 144, 147-149, 153, 157, 159, 161, 238, 241, 247, 257
s248	107

Occupational Injuries and Diseases Act (130 of 1993)   279

Security by Means of Movable Property Act (57 of 1993)
      s1(2)   279
      s1(4)   279

Unemployment Insurance Act (63 of 2001)   276, 310

Unemployment Insurance Contributions Act (4 of 2002)   279

United Kingdom

(i) Legislation (Acts and Bills)

Bankruptcy Act 1542   4, 12, 58

Bankruptcy Act 1623   33

Bankruptcy Act 1831   14

Bankruptcy Act 1861   14

Bankruptcy Act 1883   14

Bankruptcy Act 1914   14

Bankruptcy (Scotland) Act 1985   141
      s2(4)   158
      s3(1)   158
      s5(2)-(2B)   165
      s5(2)   165
      s5(2B)   148
      s7   165
      s18   158
      s31(1)   153
      s32(2)   154-155
      s32(2A)   155
      s32(3)   155
      s32(6)   153
      s33(1)   142, 149
      s33(1)(a)-(aa)   153
      s34   153
      s35   153
      s36   153
      ss36A-F   153

s251 239
ss265-268 147

Enterprise Bill 2002
Chapter 10 109

Environmental Protection Act 1990
s78A 342

Insolvency Act 1986 14, 23, 67, 87, 107-108, 127, 314
Part I 87
Parts I-VII 14
Parts VIII-XI 14
Part VIII 141, 159
Part IX 141
Parts XII-XIX 15
ss1–251 14
s1A 87
s9(1) 107
s14(3) 126
s29(2) 73, 107, 111, 250
s45 239
s72A 102
s72A(4) 241
s175 239
s176A 240-241, 257
s176A(2)(a) 121
s214 31, 127
ss238-245 127
s239 127
s251 241, 245
ss252–385 14
s252 159
s253 141
s253(1) 141
s256(1)(a) 141
s256A 159
s256A(3) 141
ss257-258 141
s258(2)-(5) 148
s259 141
s260 141
s261 142
s262 141
s263(3)-(5) 141
ss263A-G 142

s264(1)(c)	148
s276	148
s279	147
s279(3)-(4)	146
s281	146
s281(2)	146
s281A	157
s283(1)	152
s283(2)	152
s283A	153
s284	152
s285(3)	151
s289(1)	156
s289(2)	156
s306	152
s307	152
s308	152
ss310-310A	150, 154
s310(2)	155
s310(7)-(9)	154
s310A	159
ss339-344	152
s360	31
s382(1)(a)	146
s382(4)	146
ss386–444	15
s426	51, 151
Schedule A1	87
Schedule B1	88, 111, 119, 121
Paragraph 2	88
Paragraph 3	98, 111, 125
Paragraph 3(1)(a)	121, 240
Paragraph 3(1)(b)	121, 240
Paragraph 3(1)(c)	240
Paragraph 3(2)	113
Paragraph 8	95
Paragraph 8(1)(b)	103
Paragraphs 10-12	107
Paragraph 11	88, 98
Paragraph 12	98
Paragraph 12(1)	110
Paragraph 12(1)(a)-(c)	114
Paragraph 12(1)(c)	116
Paragraph 12(4)	116
Paragraph 14	88, 102, 109, 113-114, 116, 241
Paragraph 14(3)	88, 102

Paragraph 15	102
Paragraph 19	115
Paragraph 22	88, 109, 113-115
Paragraph 23	114
Paragraph 26	88, 100, 115
Paragraph 27	88
Paragraph 27(1)	115
Paragraph 28(2)	115
Paragraph 30	115
Paragraph 31	115
Paragraph 35	114
Paragraph 36	116
Paragraph 36(1)(b)	116
Paragraph 37	95, 98, 103, 116
Paragraph 38	95-96, 98, 117
Paragraph 43	112, 262
Paragraph 44	112
Paragraph 44(2)-(4)	113
Paragraph 49(5)(b)	117
Paragraph 51(2)	118
Paragraph 51(2)(a)	119
Paragraph 51(2)(b)	119
Paragraph 52(1)	121
Paragraph 52(2)	120-121
Paragraph 53(1)(a)	125
Paragraph 53(3)	125
Paragraph 55	124, 126
Paragraph 55(2)	129
Paragraph 56(1)	120-121
Paragraph 58(1)	121
Paragraph 61	112
Paragraph 62	121
Paragraph 63	125-126
Paragraph 65(2)	239
Paragraph 68(2)	126
Paragraph 68(3)	126
Paragraph 69	112
Paragraph 70	240
Paragraph 70(3)	240
Paragraph 71	124
Paragraph 72(1)	262
Paragraph 72(3)	262
Paragraph 74	123
Paragraph 74(1)(a)	240
Paragraph 74(4)(d)	129
Paragraph 75	124

Paragraph 76   113
Paragraph 76(2)(a)   113, 126
Paragraph 76(2)(b)   113
Paragraph 77   114
Paragraph 77(1)(b)   126-127
Paragraph 79   124, 126, 129
Paragraph 79(1)   113
Paragraph 80   128
Paragraph 80(2)   119
Paragraph 80(3)   113
Paragraph 81   129
Paragraph 81(1)   113
Paragraph 82   129
Paragraph 82(3)(a)   113
Paragraph 83   129
Paragraph 83(1)   129
Paragraph 83(3)-(5)   129
Paragraph 83(6)(a)   113
Paragraph 84   130
Paragraph 84(2)   130
Paragraph 84(4)   113
Paragraph 88   124
Paragraph 88(1)   120
Paragraph 92   120
Paragraph 93(1)   120
Paragraph 94(1)   120
Paragraph 95   124
Paragraph 97   120
Paragraph 99(3)   240
Paragraph 107   119
Paragraph 108   119
Paragraph 111   245, 262
Schedule 4   97
Schedule 4A   157

Insolvency Act 2000   23-24, 141
s3   159
Schedule 3   159

Joint Stock Companies Acts 1844   7-8

Limited Liability Act 1855   8

Pensions Act 2004   328

Preferential Payments in Bankruptcy Act 1888
s1   239

Preferential Payments in Bankruptcy (Amendment) Act 1897   246

Welfare Reform and Pensions Act 1999
s11   153
s12   153
s13   153

(ii) Legislation (Acts and Bills): Devolved

Bankruptcy and Diligence etc
(Scotland) Act 2007   138, 144, 146-147, 153, 158, 160, 166
s2   158
s19(2)   153

Debt Arrangement and Attachment (Scotland) Act 2002   153
Part I   143, 165

Tribunals, Courts and Enforcement Bill   162, 164

(iii) Statutory Instruments

Cross-Border Insolvency Regulations 2006 (SI 2006/1030)   54, 151

Insolvency Rules 1986 (SI 1986/1925)
Rule 2.114(1)(3)   126
Rule 4.90   242
Rule 5.23   141

Occupational and Personal Pension Schemes (Bankruptcy) (No 2) Regulations
2002 (SI 2002/836)   153

(iv) Statutory Instruments: Devolved

Debt Arrangement Scheme (Scotland) Regulations 2004 (SSI 2004/468)
Regulation 22(1)   143
Regulation 26(1)   143

Debt Arrangement Scheme (Scotland) Amendment Regulations 2007
(SSI 2007/262)   149

United States

Banking Act 1933   228

Bankruptcy Act 1800   16, 18

Bankruptcy Act 1841   16

Bankruptcy Code 1978
    Chapter 7   73, 90, 94-95, 147, 169
    Chapter 11   23-25, 37, 84, 90-91, 93-95, 99, 105, 112-113,
                                              118, 122, 326-327
    Chapter 13   170
    Chapter 15   54
    s101   90
    s109   90
    s301   90, 93
    s303   90, 93
    s304   51
    s304(c)   51
    s365(n)   395
    s507(a)(4)   309
    s523   147
    s706   95
    s706(a)   95
    s727   147
    s727(8)   147
    s1112   95
    s1112(b)   90
    s1113   327

Employee Retirement Income Security Act 1974   326
    s4041 (29 USC §1341)   327
    s4042 (29 USC §1342)   327
    s4042a (29 USC §1342a)   327

Federal Deposit Insurance Act 1950
    s1821(d)(11)(ii))   229

Tax Code
    s401(k)   324

Table of International Materials

Civil Liability Convention of 29 November 1969   337

Convention on Jurisdiction and the Enforcement of Judgments in Civil and
    Commercial Matters of 27 September 1968 (Brussels Convention)   55

Convention on the Protection and Use of Transboundary Watercourses and
    International Lakes of 17 March 1992
        Article 2(5)   344-345

Convention on the Protection of the Marine Environment of the Baltic Sea
    Area of 9 April 1992
        Article 3(4)   344

European Convention on Certain International Aspects of Bankruptcy of
    5 June 1990 (Istanbul Convention)   52, 55, 186

European Bankruptcy Convention of 23 November 1995   174, 176-177

Hague Convention on Choice of Court Agreements of 30 June 2005   54

International Convention on Oil Pollution Preparedness, Response and
    Cooperation of 30 November 1990   345
        Preamble   345

ILO Protection of Wages Convention (Convention 95 of 1949)
        Article 11   302

ILO Protection of Workers' Claims (Employer's Insolvency)
    Convention (Convention 173 of 1992)   271, 273, 277-278
        Part II   271, 277, 280, 285, 288, 290-291
        Part III   271-272, 285, 290
        Article 5   271
        Article 6   271, 302
        Article 7   272, 287
        Article 8   272
        Article 9   272
        Article 12   272, 302

ILO Termination of Employment Convention (Convention 158 of 1982)
    Article 11   302

Lugano Convention of 16 September 1988   342

Southern African Development Community Code on HIV and
    Employment 1997   268

Southern African Development Community Charter of
    Fundamental Social Rights of 26 August 2003   267-268, 270
        Article 4   267
        Article 6   267
        Article 7   267
        Article 8   267
        Article 9   267
        Article 10   267
        Article 13   267, 270

Southern African Development Community Draft Code on Social
    Security 2004   268

Southern African Development Community Treaty of 17 August 1992
    Article 5   267

UNCITRAL Model Law on Cross-Border Insolvency of
    30 May 1997   29, 52, 59, 151
        Article 1(2)   55
        Article 2(b)   56
        Article 16(3)   56, 58
        Article 17(2)   56
        Article 19   56
        Article 19(2)   56
        Article 20   57
        Article 20(2)   57
        Article 20(3)   56
        Article 20(4)   57
        Article 25   57
        Article 28   57
        Article 29   57

Editorial Preface

Insolvency is a subject that has gained considerable standing as an object of academic study and professional attention since its beginnings as an offshoot of company law or, in the case of the bankruptcy of individuals, procedural law affecting claims in relation to debt or the estates of natural persons. Insolvency may claim, like its parent subjects, to contain facets of almost every other area of the law. This may be seen because of the impact of insolvency on the organisation of commercial life, the underpinning of business relations and the fulfilment of obligations arising through contract. Also, insolvency generates penal and civil liabilities because of the mismanagement of assets and is the source of sanctions affecting the ability to conduct business. Furthermore, insolvency alters the relationship between classes of participants in business life, including the State, whose interests in maintaining economic stability are most at stake in periods of insolvency. Insolvency is, nevertheless, not just a legal discipline but also one that includes the study of economics, management and business relations and in which these interdisciplinary elements have a great role to play.

International insolvency is a more recently established branch of the study of insolvency that owes much to the phenomenon of cross-border incorporations and the conduct of business in more than one jurisdiction. It is, like insolvency, also a study of law and economic rules, to which is added the extra complication of private international law and the conflict of legal rules because of the involvement of more than one legal order. International insolvency is, however, a subject that has had more than its fair share of coverage, notably because of the insolvencies that have occurred in the international business and financial sectors. The scale and magnitude of these events have prompted the attention of commentators, drawn from both academic life and practice, resulting in a considerable number of learned publications, to which this text is designed to add.

Furthermore, the intention behind the present text is that it will form an up to date account of themes, developments and perspectives in the field of insolvency law, and particularly in relation to its comparative and international aspects. Aimed at a worldwide academic and practitioner audience, the collection of essays delivers cutting edge material, thus increasing awareness of the impact of insolvency law within domestic, regional and global contexts. This is done so as to ensure that the audience for this text receives timely notice of developments in jurisdictions representing all legal traditions and in which the improvement and reform of insolvency laws and frameworks are issues of concern to judges, practitioners and academic commentators alike. Submissions for this book have come from prominent academics and researchers in the field representing a number of jurisdictions from common law, civilian and mixed traditions. All contributions have been peer-reviewed by members of a review panel representing distinguished proponents of and contributors to the development of insolvency law. This has ensured that the contents of the research and analyses included in this text are of the highest quality and will be useful and thought-provoking. Furthermore, contributions to this text specifically address and emphasise developments in the law where the articulation of insolvency with other areas of law occurs and where insolvency is a catalyst for developments of application in general law. Essays for inclusion in this text generally present three characteristics: they deal with insolvency, in its widest sense to include both procedural and substantive matters; they are international in that essays are not limited to purely domestic themes but contain comparative material and, lastly, they are innovative, in that the material may not have been treated before or that a new interpretation is being placed on hitherto available material. It is hoped that this will render the contributions here as well as the further references they contain of great value for researchers in the field.

In summary, I would like to express my appreciation to all those who have assisted in making the project a success, not least the contributors themselves, but also the members of the review panel as well as the editorial team at Ashgate. If not otherwise noted by the contributors, the law is stated as at 16 June 2007.

Paul J. Omar

of Gray's Inn, Barrister
Senior Lecturer, Sussex Law School, University of Sussex
E-mail: <paulo@sussex.ac.uk>.

PART I
GENERAL PRINCIPLES
OF INSOLVENCY LAW

Chapter 1

The Culture of Bankruptcy

Harry Rajak

Introduction – The Meanings of Bankruptcy[1]

Bankruptcy has a wide range of metaphorical[2] and literal meanings, but, in this article, is restricted in meaning to the institution of this name, invariably found in almost all legal systems.[3] Three features would seem to be essential to this institution, first, bringing to an end or otherwise subjecting to external control, a debtor's freedom to continue to enter into credit-related transactions. Secondly, a collective process, subjecting all the creditors' claims against that debtor to a single regime under which the debtor's assets are partially or totally removed from the debtor's control. Thirdly, the debtor should be discharged from all debts and restored as a full financial citizen. The bankruptcy process might well effect the sale of the debtor's assets and the distribution of the proceeds among all the creditors, but a major modern refinement for a commercial – as opposed to a consumer – bankrupt, is the use of the bankruptcy process to attempt a rescue so that the business or part of the business survives intact and continues trading in the market place.[4] With a successful rescue the business may, but will not necessarily continue under the same management as prior to the onset of the bankruptcy.

It is likely that the term, bankruptcy, derives from *banco rotto* (Italian: broken bench),[5] describing, quite literally, the condition of the bench in the market

---

1   This is a revised version of two different public lectures, the first presented at the University of Sussex in 1999 and the second at the University of Texas in 2006.
2   For a choice illustration – with bankruptcy as metaphor – note the criticism of the former French President, Jacques Chirac as 'transforming France into an autocracy, using his presidency with 'political and judicial irresponsibility, as a debtor without scruples, uses his insolvency' (*New York Times*, 29 October 2006), quoting from the biography of the President by Hervé Gattegno.
3   English speaking jurisdictions also use the word 'insolvency' and some (England and Wales, for example) have used the two terms to distinguish between the two broad categories of persons, individuals (bankruptcy) and corporations or companies (insolvency). This is not, however, a technical distinction and I take these two terms to be synonymous. Mostly, I shall use bankruptcy; see further below.
4   The important modern phenomenon of business rescue is considered below.
5   Latin: *Bancus ruptus.*

place of a banker no longer able to meet his debts.[6] Given that the bench was the place where the business was conducted, the breaking of the bench graphically illustrates the first of the essential feature of bankruptcy described above. As for the second feature, there is some evidence of this collective regime in early Greek and Slavic Law, as well as in the Law Merchant which may have influenced its introduction into England in medieval times.[7] In fact, what is regarded as the first English Bankruptcy Act was passed in 1542, a mix of criminalizing 'absconding debtors' and summary collection or realization of the debtor's assets and distribution of the proceeds for the benefit of all the creditors.[8] Earlier statutes passed in the 1280s in the reign of Edward I provided for summary execution against the goods of the debtor, but this was a remedy for a single creditor (i.e. this was not a collective process).[9] But it was not until modern times that we find the third of what we would now consider these essential aspects of a bankruptcy regime, namely the discharge of the debtor.

Bankruptcy, of course, is intimately linked to indebtedness, the latter being a necessary, if not sufficient, condition of bankruptcy. Indebtedness as a contract comprising a loan by the creditor to the debtor certainly goes back to a time 'beyond which the memory of man runneth not'. Its longevity and ubiquity can be seen in early examples which predate even the coinage economy.[10] The further step required to convert an indebtedness into bankruptcy, is the initiation of the legal process by one or more creditors – or by the debtor – resulting in the greater or lesser disempowerment of the debtor from engaging in legal transactions and the subjection to collective control of all claims and enforcement procedures against the debtor. In many jurisdictions this step requires the judgment of a court to the effect that the debtor is thus made 'bankrupt'. A useful definition of bankrupt adopted by the law is such indebtedness as not to be able to pay all debts as they fall due.[11]

The term 'bankruptcy' is used by the law in two senses. The wider meaning describes a condition in which a person's assets are worth less than his or her liabilities. As the law puts it, that person is unable to meet all debts in full as they fall due. This, of course, is a common condition, suffered by many people a good deal of the time. Borrowing money to tide oneself over until the next salary

---

6   For an alternative derivation, see Levinthal, L., 'The Early History of English Bankruptcy' [1919] 67 *University of Pennsylvania Law Review* 1 at 2.

7   Ibid., at 6–8.

8   Ibid., at 14. See also the Cork Report (1982) Cmnd 8558 at 16 (paragraph 35).

9   Ibid., at 7–9.

10 See Hesiod's *Works and Days* (8th century BCE), line 350 ('Take fair measure from your neighbour and pay him back fairly with the same measure, or better, if you can; so that if you are in need afterwards, you may find him sure'. Perseus project, <www.perseus.tufts.edu/cgi-bin/ptext?doc=Perseus%3Atext%3A1999.01.0132> (last viewed 31 May 2007). See also the Hebrew Bible, Deuteronomy, 15, 1–2 (probably 7th century BCE).

11 See Fletcher, I.F., *The Law of Insolvency* (3rd ed) (2002, Oxford University Press, Oxford) at 1 (paragraph 1–001).

payment may well be an illustration of bankruptcy in this sense, but done sensibly, rarely takes one to the next stage, which is the second, narrower use, by the law, of 'bankrupt' and 'bankruptcy'.

Here, bankruptcy describes the legal process by which a debtor is dispossessed of, or in some other meaningful way, separated from, his or her assets – they might be placed in the possession of a trustee in bankruptcy whose duty is the sale (lawyers often call this the realisation) of the assets and the distribution of the proceeds among the creditors, or the bankrupt might be placed under legal restraints as to what he or she or it may do with these assets. With the initiation of the bankruptcy process, the debtor becomes the bankrupt.

The contract under which the indebtedness was incurred will, initially, be governed by the general principles of contract which apply in whichever is the appropriate legal jurisdiction. More than likely these principles will provide creditor remedies of enforcement and execution against the debtor's assets, where the debtor fails to discharge the indebtedness in accordance with the terms of the contract. Yet, if bankruptcy does ensue, these remedies are most likely to be suspended under that jurisdiction's bankruptcy process, at least to ensure the fair distribution of the proceeds of the sale of the debtor's assets among all the creditors. It may well be, however, that the bankruptcy regime encourages a rescue and rehabilitation of the debtor, resulting in the lengthy postponement of all creditor enforcement remedies.

It, therefore, follows that choices can be made as to the nature of the bankruptcy regime; to put it crudely, a bankruptcy regime may be more favourable to the debtor than the creditor or *vice versa*. These choices can, in turn, be influenced by quite different conceptions of the condition of bankruptcy. Until comparatively recently in the United Kingdom, for example, a popular conception of bankruptcy was of a system comprising two very different evils. First, from the debtor's point of view, the misery and degradation of enslaving debt, coupled with imprisonment in inhuman conditions, the destruction of family life and so on. The second evil, from the creditor's point of view, was of a system which enabled, indeed encouraged, fraud on the part of unscrupulous debtors making it impossible to recover debts, even where assets were available.

Yet, such popular conceptions might be quite misleading and might serve to conceal some of the benefits – to both debtors and creditors – of the bankruptcy process. Many a debtor has passed from the condition of bankruptcy into the legal process of bankruptcy with relief. An order of a court declaring a debtor bankrupt immediately brings a halt to the pursuit of that debtor by his or her quite possibly dozens, even 100s of creditors. It begins a process which in suitable circumstances may lead to the rescue and rehabilitation of the bankrupt, the earlier or later discharge of the bankruptcy order, the discharge of the bankrupt's debts and the re-incorporation of the bankrupt within the commercial community.

The declaration of bankruptcy also brings order to what might have developed into a chaotic scramble among creditors, with some seeking to out-manoeuvre the others in the hunt for payment out of ever-dwindling assets. It is one of the many fascinations of bankruptcy that what starts out as a contest between debtor and creditor often turns into a contest between creditor and creditor, an inversion which might be illustrated by the simple tale of two people walking in a forest. They spot a lion coming towards them at a gathering pace and turn and run. One says to the other: 'I hope I can run faster than the lion'. The other replies: 'I only hope that I can run faster than you'.

Bankruptcy, then, is a multi-faceted institution. In its overall purpose of managing the conflict of interests between the creditors inter se, between the creditors and the debtor and, quite possibly between these private parties and the state, it can be fashioned in various ways. And as with all important legal institutions, the wider social, political and economic context is likely to be influential as to how each country's bankruptcy regime is created, interpreted and applied. Choices need to be made in relation to a whole host of issues and it is not surprising that there are popular (and often superficial) conceptions of particular bankruptcy regimes as pro-debtor and pro-creditor. This paper seeks to explore some of these 'cultural' issues, beginning with a whistle-stop vertical history, which is both superficial and lacking in breadth. Before doing so, however, it may be helpful to the general reader to indicate the significance of the distinction between individual and corporate bankruptcy.

The Subjects of Bankruptcy

As a general rule, most legal systems recognize only the acts of those who are defined as 'persons'. Typical 'acts' from the point of view of the legal system would be entering into a contract or concluding a marriage or owning something or acting as a litigant in a court of law. The category, 'persons' obviously includes individual human beings, although in some cases human beings may have only limited recognition by the law. Thus a person who is mentally incapable, may have someone appointed to represent him or her and manage his or her affairs, in which case the law will – again as a general rule – recognize the acts of that representative and not of the mentally incapable person. The acts of children below a certain age, may, similarly, enjoy only limited legal recognition and it may be illuminating to recall that in societies where slavery was – and maybe still is – carried on, slaves would often be treated as the objects rather than the subjects of the law. Thus a slave would be the thing owned or the subject matter of the contract, rather than the owner or the person whose contract the law would recognize and uphold.

And just as the category of 'person' can be defined to exclude some human beings, either wholly or in part, so it can be defined to include certain entities which are not human beings. Indeed the legal system will generally do more than simply define this extension to the 'person' category; it will also lay down the steps to be followed by individual human beings so as to create that entity which the law will then recognize as a person. The obvious example is a group of people who agree to act together to achieve some commercial purpose. If they had simply entered into an agreement to go into business together, they will be recognized as having established a 'partnership', which in many legal systems will not be recognized as a person for the purposes of the law. If, however, they go further and follow the steps laid down by a law for the creation of an entity which the law does recognize as a person, then by definition a new, non-human legal person will have come into existence. The steps laid down will invariably include the presentation of appropriately completed forms and the payment of a fee and will lead to the official registration of the new entity, which in the United Kingdom and Commonwealth countries, at least, is then known as a company registered under the appropriate statute. In the United States, the entity it is more commonly called a corporation.

We can thus regard bankruptcy as applying to either an individual human being or a company. Either can reach a condition where he or she or it is unable to pay his or her or its debts as they fall due. He or she or it may then voluntarily or involuntarily enter the legal institution of bankruptcy. In theory, the bankruptcy will follow the same course whoever the bankrupt is – the assets will be realized, the claims against the bankrupt determined, and the proceeds of the realization distributed among the creditors in accordance with the established order of distribution.

In practice, however, there is a profound difference. A company or corporation will most frequently have been created in such a way as to confer on all the human beings who are its members (shareholders) at the time of the bankruptcy, the protection of limited liability – in effect shielding them from any liability in relation to the company's debts. On one level, this is theoretically satisfying – the debts, after all, are those of the company and not of the shareholders. On another level it is jarring – the company has incurred those debts at the instance of its shareholders, generally acting through their representatives, the directors. Thus a partner of a partnership may lose all his or her property where the partnership (in theory all the partners, given that the law does not recognize the existence of the partnership) is bankrupt, whereas a director of a company is protected from such loss by the principle of limited liability.

The company first became readily available in the United Kingdom as a form of business organization with the passage of the Joint Stock Companies Act in 1844. This Act was the first to lay down the process by which any seven[12] or more individuals might seek the creation of a registered company. What had previously been an expensive, complicated operation effected either by charter issued by the Crown or ad hoc statute passed by Parliament, was now a much simpler and more straightforward process. And with the advent of limited liability for shareholders in 1855, the company registered under the Joint Stock Companies Act quickly replaced the partnership (which as pointed out above lacked legal recognition and also could not protect its partners against personal loss for the debts incurred in the course of the partnership business) as the organization of choice for commercial enterprise. In the United States, the corresponding facilities if registered corporation and limited liability were conferred by separate state statutes and arose around the same time as in the United Kingdom.

---

12 Later reduced to 2 (in 1900) and then 1 (in 1990).

The Joint Stock Companies Act of 1844 and the Limited Liability Act of 1855 (plus other relevant legislation) were consolidated in 1862 into what is regarded as the first United Kingdom Companies Act. And it was this Act and all succeeding Companies Acts up to the Companies Act 1985 which contained almost all the statutory provisions relating to the insolvency of companies incorporated under the Companies Acts. It is probably this history of the development of companies legislation which accounts for the fact that the United Kingdom and most Commonwealth countries have, until very recently, had separate statutes for the bankruptcy principles which apply to individuals (called individual bankruptcy) and for those which apply to companies (often called corporate insolvency). Other countries – the United States and most European countries – have tended to distinguish their bankruptcy principles between commercial and consumer debtors.

A Brief History of Bankruptcy

Ancient Greece and Rome

It is clear from the sources that debt was a powerful and frequently troublesome factor in ancient society. There is ample evidence of lending and borrowing in Ancient Greece. Hesiod speaks of the loan of seeds and implements between peasants,[13] other authors speak of small borrowings to cope with unforeseen crises and substantial loans among the wealthy to support an elite lifestyle. Solon's famous reforms in Ancient Greece around 590 B.C. included the shaking off of burdens, described in some sources as a cancellation of all debts. The reforms not only abolished the state of servitude from which the original obligation sprang, they also banned all future enslavement for debt. We have what is thought to be Solon's own account of this particular reform:

> I brought back to Athens, their god-founded fatherland, many who had been sold, some unjustly, some justly, some exiled through the compulsion of debt, no longer speaking the Attic language, so widely had they been wandering; others here, who were enduring shameful slavery and trembled before the whims of their masters, I made free.[14]

Although Ancient Athens is said to have been successful in maintaining the reform of abolishing debt bondage, it is clear that this phenomenon was rife throughout the rest of the Greek and Roman world. The earliest known codification of Roman Law – the Twelve Tables of around 450 BCE – deals with the problem

---

13 Above note 10.
14 See Solon (fr. 24 Diehl = fr. 36 West), quoted by Aristotle, *Constitution of Athens*, XII, 4 (and included in Austin, M.M. and Vidal-Naquet, P., *Economic and Social History of Ancient Greece, An Introduction* (1st English ed) (1977, University of California Press, Berkeley CA) at 211.

of a debtor unable to pay his debts.[15] Thus, if a debt for which judgment was given remained unpaid for 30 days, the debtor was given in private bondage to the creditor. If the debt remained unpaid for a further 60 days, the creditor was entitled to put the debtor to death (*partis secanto*, cut into pieces!) or to sell him in slavery across the Tiber.[16] This was a regime notorious for its harshness, but it does represent an early attempt to reduce the violence and disturbance to which the problem of debt could give rise, by subjecting it to a court process.

It has to be said that this system also left something to be desired as far as the creditor was concerned. The enormous power given to a creditor to put a debtor to death was not the best method for recovery of the debt and this was clearly recognized by creditors. At some stage it was replaced by a regime which made much greater commercial sense, namely giving the debtor during his bondage an opportunity to work off the debt. There thus emerged in archaic Rome the relationship of *nexum*, which represented from both the creditor's and the debtor's point of view a marked improvement on enslavement or death. Under this relationship, the debtor could work off his indebtedness and although *nexum* was abolished in 326 BCE, it seems to have been replaced by *addictio*, which was not much different.[17] For all its negative connotations, there are suggestions that in some instances at least, the debtor used this relationship to raise capital. The economic advantages of this relationship to the creditor are obvious and it was reproduced elsewhere in the ancient world.

It is clear that debt is often linked to violent political and social conflict in the Roman Republic.[18] The famous Catilinian conspiracy of 63 BCE, denounced by Cicero as a threat to the Roman Republic, drew much of its strength from followers who were deeply in debt and campaigned for widespread debt relief.[19] In the Rome

---

15 See Table 3.
16 See Buckland, W.W., *A Textbook of Roman Law* (3rd ed) (1963, Cambridge University Press, Cambridge) at 618–620 for a clear (and chilling) description of this process (known to the Roman as *manus iniectio*, literally, throwing [the debtor] into the [creditor's] hands.
17 See Frederikson, M.W., 'Caesar, Cicero and the Problem of Debt' (1966) 56 *Journal of Roman Studies* 128 at 129 (an article of exceptional interest); see also Buckland, above note 16 at 643 and Jolowicz, H.F., *Historical Introduction to Roman Law* (2nd ed) (1952, Cambridge University Press, Cambridge) at 224.
18 Livy's *History of Rome* is awash with references to the problems of debt and its interaction with social and political unrest throughout the 4th century BCE, see 6.11, 6.14, 6.18, 6.18, 6.27, 6.31–6.36, 7.21, 8.28 (the last of these references deals with the abolition in 326 BCE of the law which permitted the creditor to imprison the debtor); for the later Republic, see Andreau, J., *Banking and Business in the Roman World* (1999, Cambridge University Press, Cambridge) at 102, referring to severe debt and liquidity crises in 193–2, the 80s, 63 and 49 BCE. For an excellent account, see Brunt, P.A., *Social Conflicts in the Roman Republic* (1971, Chatto & Windus, London) at 21–22, 55–59, 129–131.
19 See Cicero's second speech against Catiline, especially at 2.4, 2.8, 2.10–2.11, 2.18–2.21; see also *Lucky City*, an illuminating review by Mary Beard of Everitt, A., *Cicero,*

of the later Republic and into the Empire a system of bankruptcy developed which we can readily recognize, with the forfeiture and sale by public auction of the debtor's property, and the distribution of the proceeds among the creditors. The earliest references to this process seem to be Cicero in the first century BCE.[20] Our other sources are much later, from the second century CE onwards, so it may be assumed that this bankruptcy process developed in the period between the late Republic and the early Roman Empire.

Many questions remain unanswered, for example what the status of conditional debts was and how debts were proved (did each creditor, for example, have to obtain a separate judgment against the debtor?).[21] Even where we do have the answer to modern bankruptcy-related questions, for example that secure and privileged claims were recognized and protected, the authority is late[22] and therefore gives little clue as to the origin and development of such rights. This 'bankruptcy' process is also open to the criticism that it was apparently necessary even where the debtor had sufficient assets to meet the debt. No lesser process seems to have been available enabling the creditor to attach part only of the debtor's property.[23] This may be not unrelated to a more general illiquidity problem in the Roman Republic, discussed by Livy.[24]

The condition of bankruptcy also had considerable personal significance in Roman society. The debtor was rendered '*infamis*' and thereby susceptible to imprisonment for debt and formally banned from the Senate and from the various magistracies and the law-courts. *Infamia*, in effect, was tantamount to political death. From the time of either Julius or Augustus Caesar, however, this necessary link between the commercial and the political was severed by a law which enabled the debtor to avoid the declaration of *infamia* if he made a voluntary surrender of his property to his creditors. Most fascinating and tantalizing is the comment that this means of escaping the taint of *infamia* was 'probably [closed] not only to those whose insolvency was due to their own fault, but also to those who had no property worth the mention to hand over to their creditors'.[25]

A Turbulent Life (2003, Random House, New York NY) in London Review of Books, 23 August 2004 (Volume 23, No. 16).

20 *Pro Quinctio* 15.50, cf Jolowicz, above note 17 at 223–4, who postulates that this procedure originated in relation to debts to the state and also in relation to debtors who sought to hide their assets.

21 Buckland, above note 16 at 644 implies that dispensing with the requirement that each creditor had to obtain his own judgment against the debtor, may only have been brought in by Justinian, i.e. in the 6th century CE.

22 Gaius (whose Institutes probably date from the latter half of the 2nd century CE) Inst, 2.155, 3.79 and Justinian's Codification in the 6th century, D 42.4.7.1, 42.5.16.5, 42.5.24.2.

23 Jolowicz, above note 17 at 225.

24 *History of Rome* 7.21.

25 Jolowicz, above note 17 at 226, who concedes that there is 'very little direct evidence for either of these exceptions', but argues that there must have been exceptions

There is no doubt that in the development of creditors' execution remedies, Roman Law was conscious of, and responsive to, the need to leave the debtor with the necessities of life. This emerges under the earlier, harsher regime laid down by the Twelve Tables regarding the treatment of a debtor committed in person to the creditor.[26] But it seems to have been the case that the idea of a discharge from unpaid or only partly paid debts never became part of Roman Law.[27] This need not surprise us. The permanent discharge is a comparatively novel idea even in our times and regular and persistent imprisonment for debt is a common feature in nineteenth century England.[28] Indeed it might be suggested that the failure of Roman society to develop a form of relief for unfortunate and oppressed debtors, may at least claim the excuse that the society did not have the example of the limited liability company which perforce provided a full and permanent discharge from personal debt.

England, the United Kingdom and the United States

Early English society reveals indebtedness arising through feudal relationships where the landlord might look for payment from his tenants of rent and other services; this gave rise to the landlord's power to distrain against the tenant's property, that is to seize and hold the tenant's property until the debt was paid or secured. This power emerged from the fact of ownership of the land and its special fascination lies in the landlord's ability to exercise this power of distraint virtually at will. As Pollock and Maitland in their magisterial History of English Law so disarmingly put it:

> In England the transition from judicial to extra-judicial distress was in this case easy, because our law admitted that every lord had a right to hold a court of and for his tenants. Probably in the twelfth century most landlords had courts of their own ... A right to distrain a man into coming before your court to answer why he has not paid his rent may in favourable circumstances become a right to distrain him for not paying his rent ...[29]

A second set of legal relationships through which indebtedness arose in early English society was that of merchant trading. Here, the source of debt recovery law came from a Europe-wide body of laws and customs based principally

---

otherwise all debtors would have enjoyed this benefit while we know that imprisonment for debt survived long beyond the date of this legislative change.

26 Twelve Tables, 3.3; as to this being the regime under later Roman Law, see Jolowicz, above note 17 at 226.

27 Gaius 2.155; Inst 4.6.40; D. 42.3.4, 6, 7; C. 7.72.10. 1a (see Buckland, above note 16 at 403, 644).

28 See below.

29 See Pollock, F. and Maitland, W., *A History of English Law* (x ed., ed. Milsom) (1968, Cambridge University Press, Cambridge) in Volume XX at XX.

on the mercantile law of Italy and known as the Law Merchant. Not surprisingly, it was influenced by the laws and institutions of Roman Law and, for some modern scholars, it represents a precedent for a commercial legal system of the European Community. Local courts were established in the jurisdictions of various independent states throughout Europe and were empowered to apply the principles developed by the Law Merchant. And these principles included the various bankruptcy regimes which were based largely on the institutions developed in the later Roman Empire.

It was not until 1542, that the first English Bankruptcy Act was passed. The mischief addressed was the fraud of which debtors were seen to be capable. The Act was aimed against 'absconding debtors', persons who:

> ... craftily obtaining in their own hands great substance of other men's goods, do suddenly flee to parts unknown, or keep their houses, not minding to pay or restore to any their creditors their duties, but at their own wills and pleasures consume debts and the substance obtained by credit of other men, for their own pleasure and delicate living, against all reason, equity and good conscience.

This gives a very clear idea of where the problem was thought to lie. Debtors were not to be thought of as unfortunate or exploited or even abused. They were, in short, criminals – a perception which was to persist until relatively recent times. Legislation later in the sixteenth century created one of the cornerstones of all modern bankruptcy regimes, namely the seizure of the bankrupt's assets, its forced sale and the distribution of the proceeds of sale among the creditors in proportion to the amount each was owed.

Other features which today are considered essential to any bankruptcy regime – the potential for the discharge of the debtor, the ability of the debtor to present his or her own bankruptcy petition (it must be remembered that however stigmatised being bankrupted might be, it did at least bring all proceedings by creditors to an end) and the power to conduct an orderly investigation into the financial affairs of the debtor – were only brought about much later following widespread agitation in the Victorian period against imprisonment for debt and against the widely perceived inadequacy and inefficiency of the system.

Much of the protest against this system we know from the great novels of the eighteenth and nineteenth centuries,[30] but there was no shortage of

---

30 Charles Dickens, whose father was imprisoned for debt, was, of course, one of the greatest, if not the greatest of these novelists; many of his novels depict poverty, debt and personal degradation, see, for example, *Dombey & Son, The Old Curiosity Shop* and his portrait of a debtors' prison in *Little Dorrit*. There is also no shortage of secondary literature analyzing the politics of Dickens' novels, see, for example, Engel, M., 'The Politics of Dickens's Novels', (1956) 71(5) *Proceedings of the Modern Language Association of America* 945. For other examples, see Henry Fielding's *Amelia* and the very useful discussion by Stephens Jnr, J.C., 'The Verge of the Court and Arrest for Debt' (1948) 63(2) *Modern Language Notes* 104.

pamphleteering by reformers at least as early as the seventeenth century much of which is collected and analysed in Donald Veall's outstanding Popular Movement for Law Reform 1640–1660.[31] The Levellers' Large petition, for example, urged relief for:

> ... all such prisoners for debt as are altogether unable to pay, that they may not perish in prison through the hard-heartedness of their creditor; and that all such who have any estates may be enforced to make payment accordingly and not shelter themselves in prison to defraud their creditors.[32]

And Thomas Grantham, a curate in Northamptonshire in the seventeenth century, asserted that imprisonment was 'against the gospel, against the good church and commonwealth'. Imprisonment was, he urged, approved by the scriptures for 'blasphemy, sabbath-breaking, sedition, attempted suicide, a quarreller, a prodigal, and a rover but not for debt'. To imprison a man when his neighbours proclaimed that he had not the means to pay, was, according to the curate 'superdiabolical'.

By the nineteenth century, much information coming out of official sources supported the novelists' depiction of this grotesque and, in economic terms, purposeless system. Lord Bowen, one of the greatest of the Victorian commercial judges described the Victorian bankruptcy system in the following terms:

> The leading idea of the law in the case of the ordinary insolvent was to seize his person. The principle of the law of bankruptcy with reference to a trader is to confiscate his property for the benefit of creditors. But during the first thirty years of the [nineteenth] century, the English bankruptcy law had been, and at the beginning of the present reign [of Queen Victoria] still was a discredit to a great country whose fleets covered the seas and whose commerce ranged the globe. Scotland and several continental nations were far in advance of us. England alone among her commercial rivals still kept to the mischievous doctrine that mercantile insolvency was to be rooted out as if it were an offence against society ... To the honest insolvent the bankruptcy court was a terror. To the evildoer it afforded means of endlessly delaying his creditors, while the enormous expense of bankruptcy administrations rendered it the interest of few to resort to the remedy except with the object of punishing the fraudulent or vexing the unfortunate.[33]

---

31 1970, Clarendon Press, Oxford.

32 Ibid., at 146.

33 See 'Progress in the Administration of Justice During the Victorian Period', in Committee of the Association of American Law Schools (ed.), *Select Essays in Anglo-American Legal History* (1907, Little Brown and Co, Boston MA) in Volume 1, 516 at 545.

Although not included in Lord Bowen's list of best practitioners, Ireland by the nineteenth century had a sophisticated system by which a jury of independent and impartial neighbours of the debtor fixed the amounts and dates for debts to be paid by instalments and reported a much better rate of debt recovery than did England.

The virtually complete control enjoyed by creditors over their debtors in the United Kingdom was reduced by an Act of 1831 which created the office of Official Assignee,[34] the beginning of the exercise of some form of public control over the fate of debtors. A further feature of the system until 1861 was the restriction of the bankruptcy regime – and therefore the relief which it could confer on debtors oppressed by their creditors – to traders. An innocent, but unfortunate, non-trader could be pursued by a single creditor and imprisoned at the latter's behest despite the preparedness of all other creditors to agree to a plan for the payment of all the debts.[35]

Further reform came eight years later when the powers of the courts to imprison debtors were drastically curtailed by the Debtors Act of 1869. Finally in 1883, with the passage of a wholly new consolidated Bankruptcy Act, the then President of the Board of Trade, Joseph Chamberlain was able to claim a law which met the claims of various interests:

> 'Every good bankruptcy law', he said while moving the second reading of the Bill:
> 'must have in view two main, and at the same time, distinct objects. First the honest administration of bankrupt estates, with a view to the fair and speedy distribution of the assets among the creditors whose property they were; secondly, following the idea that prevention was better than cure, to do something to improve the general tone of commercial morality, to promote honest trading, and to lessen the number of failures. In other words, Parliament had to endeavour, as far as possible, to protect the salvage and also to diminish the wrecks'.

Thus did the United Kingdom progress to the dawn of the twentieth century. It should be noted that the 1883 Act dealt only with individual bankruptcy, the bankruptcy of human beings, a pattern long established and continued with the successor Bankruptcy Act of 1914 and even of the Insolvency Act of 1986. Even though the latter is a full code for both individual and corporate bankruptcy, it has three distinct parts, the first covering corporate bankruptcy,[36] the second individual bankruptcy,[37] and the much smaller, final part which covers matters common to

---

34 Afterwards – and still – the Official Receiver.
35 24 & 25 Vict. c. 134 (An Act to amend the law relating to bankruptcy and insolvency in England).
36 Parts I to VII (sections 1–251).
37 Parts VIII to XI (sections 252–385).

both – such as the creation and operation of the newly created insolvency practitioner profession.[38]

What of the United States? Although the early colonists would seem to have brought with them the (quite possibly religiously inspired) conception of the moral opprobrium of indebtedness, the first part of the development of bankruptcy law in the United States is dominated by two themes, the transformation of the idea of bankruptcy from one of moral failure to one of economic failure, and secondly the conflict between those who favoured and those who opposed the passage of a Federal Bankruptcy Act.[39]

The first of these themes was largely accomplished by state law,[40] in particular, in the progressive abolition of imprisonment for debt. It is clear that in the early days of the Republic, imprisonment for debt was common,[41] but between 1821 and 1842, Kentucky, Vermont, New York, Ohio, Michigan, Alabama, Tennessee, New Hampshire, Pennsylvania, Connecticut, Maine, Massachusetts and South Carolina enacted laws abolishing imprisonment for debt (in some cases the abolition applied only to cases where the debts was below USD 30) and in 1839, the United States abolished imprisonment for debt for all people in federal courts in states which had acted to do so. The Supreme Court upheld the constitutionality of such laws and by 1857, practically all states had so acted. The Massachusetts law of 1857 declared that 'imprisonment for debt except in cases of fraud is abolished forever'.[42]

The second of these themes, of course, raised the important constitutional issue of the relative power of the individual states as against the federation. Like most constitutional conflicts, it arose from a more direct clash of interests, in this case between commercial and agrarian interests, with the latter fearing the ability of the former to expropriate their property (essentially their farms) and the hard work that had gone into working the land.

For commercial interests, of course, a Federal Bankruptcy Act would remove state borders, and, perhaps even more significantly, state laws. The former could impede an attempt to follow a debtor and his assets in pursuit of the repayment of a loan, and the latter might raise legal obstacles by way of a clash of legal systems between those of the state of the creditor and the debtor, thereby complicating the creditor's lawsuit for judgment against the debtor.

---

38 Parts XII to XIX (sections 386–444).

39 See Coleman, P.J., *Debtors and Creditors in America: Insolvency, Imprisonment for Debt and Bankruptcy 1607–1900* (1974, State Historical Society of Wisconsin, Madison WI); Mann, B.H., *Republic of Debtors, Bankruptcy in the Age of American Independence* (2003, Harvard University Press, Cambridge MA).

40 The Supreme Court decided in *Sturges* v. *Crowninshield* 4 Wheat. 122 (1819), that the constitutional disposition that the Federal Government had the power to enact legislation on bankruptcy did not preclude the states from legislating on bankruptcy, unless precluded from doing so.

41 See Warren, C., *Bankruptcy in United States History* (1935, Harvard University Press, Cambridge MA) at 13–15, 16–17 and 22.

42 Ibid., at 52.

Federal statutes did indeed come in nineteenth century America, but they also went.[43] Twice only, before the Civil War, were Federal Bankruptcy Acts passed – in 1800 and 1841 – and neither lasted longer than four years.[44] And this staccato-like effect in the matter of the Federal Bankruptcy legislation was in no small measure due to the clash between commercial and agrarian interests. Commerce not only flourishes when restrictions on its movement – including political boundaries – are removed; it also has a tendency to grow and be seen as a threat to the livelihood and way of life of traders, tradesmen and women, farmers and those who wish to be independent and self-sufficient.

The latter, of course, preferred state bankruptcy laws. As a class they were much more likely to be debtors than creditors, and could look to state legislatures which were proving their pro-debtor credentials by abolishing imprisonment for debt.

'State insolvency laws', as Friedmann puts it,[45] 'heavily favored debtors. There were usually more debtors than creditors and that meant they had many more votes'.

There was, however, a ticklish constitutional issue which needed to be resolved. Since the United States Constitution authorized the federal government '[t]o establish ... uniform laws on the subject of bankruptcies throughout the United States'[46] did this not, by implication, prohibit state legislation on bankruptcy matters? This issue was resolved by the Supreme Court in *Sturges* v. *Crowninshield*.[47] The plaintiff was attempting to recover payment under two bills of exchange and was met by the defence that his debt was discharged under the provisions of a New York statute passed 'for the benefit of insolvent debtors and their creditors'. The plaintiff rejoined that the New York statute was rendered unconstitutional by the United States Constitution. The Supreme Court held, however, that the authorisation by the constitution for federal bankruptcy legislation did not preclude or invalidate state legislation in this area. Nevertheless, the plaintiff was successful, because the Supreme Court went on to hold that the invalidation of debts incurred prior to the enactment of the New York statute (as had been the debts in this case), was, in fact, unconstitutional.

While state legislatures were, with good reason, favoured by the debtor class, they were not unmindful of the position of creditors, even if this concern

---

43 While the American constitution had given authority 'to establish uniform laws on the subject of bankruptcy throughout the United States', the American Congress showed a marked reluctance to do so.

44 The Act of April 4, 1800, was repealed on December 19, 1803 and the Act of August 19, 1841 was repealed on March 3, 1843 – see Friedmann, L.M., *A History of American Law* (3rd ed) (2005, Simon & Schuster, New York NY) at 198 (the author incorrectly gives only two and a half – instead of three and a half - years life to the Act of 1800).

45 Ibid., at 202.

46 United States Constitution, Article 1.8.

47 4 Wheat. 122 (1819).

might only have derived from an awareness that debtors had to be able to get capital and this made creditors indispensable. Thus:

> ... legislatures also enacted lien laws, which favored creditors. And they were careful to preserve some forms of creditors' rights, in lean years as well as in fat. State governments were poor and constricted. They did not indulge, in those days, in the lavish powers of subsidy and tax. But they did have power to bind and to loose, to create legal rights and impose legal duties. This power was often a substitute for direct intervention with money. Debtors desperately needed capital. This meant that the law had to be friendly to creditors too – only not too much. As a consequence the law wobbled and vacillated; it often seemed to be of two minds at once, Similarly, in times of crisis, there was immense pressure to do something for debtors – but again, not too much nor in such a way as to do permanent damage to the economy. At every point, laws of insolvency and creditors' rights reflected this push and pull of interests.[48]

United States and United Kingdom Bankruptcy – A Comparison

Comparing the development of bankruptcy principles in the United States with that of the United Kingdom is a tantalizing exercise. I shall attempt to make a few tentative observations on this through two stages of the bankruptcy developments of both countries, first the early period of the American republic, and, secondly, by reference to the approach of both countries to the modern phenomenon of business rescue.

The early colonists brought with them many important aspects of their old world heritage, but also their antagonism to that heritage. We have seen that imprisonment for debt was widespread, but equally that it was abolished during the nineteenth century. The United Kingdom was also edging towards this position. The Debtors Act passed by the United Kingdom legislature in 1869 substantially reduced the power of the courts to imprison debtors,[49] although in 1873 it could be still reported that:

> [h]aving examined the existing laws and the application of them the [Parliamentary Select] Committee conclude that the administration of the law is both unequal and uncertain. They found cases where insufficient evidence of the means of payment of the debtor was gathered and suggest that there should be more credit checks. The large number of debtors being sent to prison entails a huge cost to the taxpayer and the large number of debtors imprisoned indicates that prison is [sic – the word 'not' is obviously incorrectly omitted from this official report] acting as a

---

48 Ibid.
49 See Cohen, J., 'The History for Imprisonment for Debt and its relation to the Development of Discharge in Bankruptcy' [1982] 3 *Journal of Legal History* 153.

deterrent. There is an inequality in the law as regards small sums of money and large with the penalties for small sums unduly severe. The law in Scotland should be considered where there is no imprisonment for civil debt under 8l. 6s. 8d. [about GBP 8.33 or USD 17.00] ... The power of imprisonment for debt by County Court Judges should be abolished and there should be a period of time before the new Act is passed to allow tradesmen etc to alter their existing system of credit to comply with it ...[50]

Constitutionally, there was obviously a very different development in the bankruptcy jurisdiction in the United States from that of England and the United Kingdom. Given their different constitutional dispensations, their respective ages and their mutual antagonism, this is hardly surprising. The early experience of the United States was one of lurching towards and away from a Federal Bankruptcy Act under the influence of a strong internal conflict. In the case of England and the United Kingdom, on the other hand, there seems to have been a harmonious progression from the stigmatisation of debtors unable to pay their debts, as feckless and immoral, to a recognition that creditors' interests would be best served by affording some protection to debtors so as to lessen the number of failures. There was no constitutional complication of tension between federation and state and the debtor interest was so under-represented as rarely to disturb the harmonious legislative progress.

In that strange, maybe unique English way, debtors were represented by their antagonists, the creditors, and got their benefit if and when it suited creditors best to confer it. The mood never went beyond doing what was best for the creditors, but there was a willing acceptance that this might necessitate decent treatment for debtors, at least in the circumstances where this might lead to some financial recovery and therefore a greater likelihood that debts would be paid.

In the United States, on the other hand, there was a much stronger sense of an even-handed battle between debtors and creditors. Perhaps memories of commercial oppression and the flight to freedom were powerful stimulants in the early Republic. Moreover, the two countries had substantially different political conditions in the eighteenth century and their social composition was hardly comparable.

Yet, surprisingly or not, early attempts to secure a Federal Bankruptcy Act in the United States leant heavily on the experience of the United Kingdom.[51] In the Federal Bankruptcy Act of 1800, the then current United Kingdom Act was followed in two important and limiting respects – first, only merchants could be made bankrupt and, secondly, only a creditor could initiate the bankruptcy proceedings. The fact that bankruptcy brought much needed relief to a beleaguered debtor was evident from the practice of engaging a friendly creditor to bring

---

50 The House of Commons Select Committee on Imprisonment for Debt set up 'to inquire into the subject of imprisonment for debt by County Court Judges', available at: <www.bopcris.ac.uk/bopall/ref6728.html> (last viewed 31 May 2007).

51 At least as far as the commercial interests were concerned, see Warren, above note 41 at 7, 13–14; Skeel, above note 39 at 2; Mann, above note 39 at 221ff.

bankruptcy proceedings and much of the criticism of the Federal Bankruptcy Act was based on its unavailability to non-commercial debtors.

Reliance on British legislation may have had something of the grudging obeisance shown by a child for its parent, but there were also good practical reasons for the imitation by United States lawmakers of certain of the bankruptcy principles and institutions of the United Kingdom. Creditor commercial interests in the United States were unlikely to differ much from their English counterparts and there were likely to be close connections between some merchants in both countries. Despite the differences between the two countries – which may be said to have derived from the strength and representation of the debtor interest – it is clear that there were always convergent strains in the Bankruptcy principles and institutions of the two countries.

During this period, both countries saw the growth of large corporations, the extension to investors of limited liability and, remarkably, the development of a common law based receivership, which exploited the principles of equity and contract, and which provided what statute did not or could not, namely a regime for the reorganization of bankrupt corporations. There were, undeniably, many differences between the equity receivership of the United States and the United Kingdom's receivership regime translated as it was from land management to the management of bank loans to failing companies. Yet each country found its way to a common law solution to a huge problem – no less than the failure of large industrial enterprise which despite the capitalist system, could not be forced out of existence. Both systems, too, developed active capital markets through widespread investment in large corporations of private funds, inspired, of course by the common availability of the limited liability company.

Those who invested their wealth by taking shares in a company were one source of the capital required by companies, what we know today as equity financing. Another source of company finance was, however, on the increase and was, in time, to become of enormous significance in the United Kingdom world of credit and security. This was, of course, the provision of money by loan rather than investment, what we have come to call debt financing. It is here, where we find in the United Kingdom, the development of instruments of credit and security which greatly emphasised the differences between its bankruptcy system and that of the United States. It is also here where we can pick up the issue of business rescue, which is the second theme where I believe a comparison between the United States and the United Kingdom to be fruitful.

Debt financing is essentially a limited form of investment which provides the lender with interest rather than profits, by way of a return on the investment. The amount invested by way of loan is all that can be lost if the business fails. Like equity financing it shields the investor from any loss beyond the amount invested. But this loss might become significant where a lender makes a number of such loans and as the United Kingdom banks through their flexible overdraft system eased themselves into a more and more dominant position as lenders to industry and commerce, they sought ways to avoid what could be sizeable losses where the borrowers' businesses failed and companies declined into insolvency. While no problem of unlimited liability arose with this form of investment, given its increasing scale, the banks needed to find a way in which they might protect the investment, especially where there might, in a depression, be widespread failure.

The answer to this conundrum lay in the exploitation of the concept of security. Security, even in the mid-nineteenth century was a common idea, of vital importance to a creditor faced with a bankrupt debtor, but only available by agreement with the debtor when first advancing a loan or delivering goods or services on credit. It is here that we find a divergence in practice between United Kingdom and United States credit and security practices.

In the United Kingdom, a strong banking system developed the flexible overdraft for their entrepreneurial customers thereby enabling the latter to take just the amount of capital which was necessary from time to time in the course of the running of their businesses. Increased dependency on bank loans through the overdraft system, enabled the banks to stipulate for a form of security covering the flexible loan and, in particular, the specific form of security known as the floating charge. This not only took up from the point where the debtor had no further real or fixed security in the form of land or other chargeable assets to offer as security for the indispensable loan, it also developed into a relationship under which the bank creditor could use the receivership system to take over the debtor's business – either to effect a sale of the business, or part of the business or, indeed, to continue it under new management.

Prior to 1870, security had been conceived of as having to be fixed, immovable, a house or a factory or a warehouse, something which satisfied two essential demands of both the lender and the borrower. First it needed to be something which could simultaneously protect the lender and be of use to the debtor in generating an income. It was obviously in the interests of both lender and borrower that the loan should be serviced and repaid. Secondly, given the system of registration or at least documentation which was essential to all dealings in fixed property, the lender could be sure that the protection would not be overridden by the borrower selling the property which constituted the security. If the borrower tried to do so, the proposed transferee, who had access to the appropriate register or documents describing the fact of the security, would know that the property was charged to the proposed transferor's creditor.

Movable property, on the other hand, could not so easily perform these functions. It could not both be used by the borrower and remain in existence as security for the lender. The success of the business depended on using, changing and using up the movable goods. Of course, the purchase money loan security in the United States and the regimes of hire purchase and lease financing offered some secured protection to lenders but only in relation to specific, restricted loans. These were of little use to a general loan by a bank seeking to finance the business as a whole.

The great breakthrough came with the realisation that the lender had no need for security while the business was successful. The need for security only arose when the borrower defaulted. Thus a form of security could be granted over all the debtor's assets, movable as well as immovable, but could be suspended – so as not to clog up the running of the business – until the security actually became necessary, that is to say on the failure of the borrower. At that point, the security could be brought into effect so as to confer on the lender complete control over all the debtor's property. Just as the traditional security had been called a fixed charge – fixed, of course because the subject matter of the charge was fixed, immovable property, also fixed because the subject matter could not be moved without the secured creditor's consent – so the new security became called a floating charge. It floated, as it were, ineffectually while the borrower's business was a successful going concern, but was converted into a fixed security when the business failed. The origin of the floating charge can be traced to common law developments in the United Kingdom chancery court in the 1870s.[52]

From the lender's point of view, the added security of a floating charge was welcome and certainly of great assistance in enabling more and more profitable loans to be made. But there was another possibly even greater benefit which this new instrument of security yielded. As we have seen, when the business went insolvent, the floating charge was converted into a fixed charge (a process which became described as crystallisation) giving the secured creditor complete control over all the debtor's assets. The question then became: What was to be done with these assets? They could be sold of course, just like any property which constituted security, might be sold. But such a sale might well not yield sufficient money for the repayment of the loan – and the inevitably spiralling costs. Might the business be continued by the creditor if the latter believed that the business might be more successfully run by someone other than the original borrower? The affirmative answer to this question paved the way for the development of receivership to ensure that the lender had this full flexibility when the loan failed.

Receivership was not a new institution, It had a long and in the eyes of some, a distinguished history in enabling landlords to manage their estates as profitably as possible. The law had been fashioned so as to give landlords, who used receivership, a remarkable immunity from suit at the hands of their tenants. Now, in the case of security for a loan, with suitable wording in the contract by which the loan was made and the security conferred, the power to have a receiver appointed to run the business (as well as all the other powers, such as to sell the debtor's assets) was slotted into place alongside the floating charge, which of course, would be drafted so as to cover all the debtor's assets. The appointed receiver would have the power – under the original agreement – to run the business, shut it down, sell it or effect a combination of some or all of these powers. The receiver, in effect, became a substitute board of directors of the now insolvent company.

This concentration of power in the hands of the lender had been effected by a simple exploitation of the fundamental principles of contract and property. In the contract under which the borrower conferred on the lender the security, the power would be given to the lender to appoint a receiver, as well as giving the receiver,

---

52 See Pennington, R., 'The Genesis of the Floating Charge' [1960] 23 *Modern Law Review* 630 and the authorities cited in note 1.

when appointed, wide powers of management. When the floating charge crystallised, as it did automatically on the appointment of the receiver, the borrower – in effect the board of directors of the borrowing company – lost the right to deal with all the company's property and the receiver assumed this right. The lender, invariably the bank, had achieved a position of virtually unassailable power *vis-à-vis* the debtor and, more importantly, all other creditors.

No system that was so self-serving could have survived for so long without being of benefit to other interests. Its proponents long claimed for receivership that it was a godsend in times of trouble, offering salvage, rescue and rehabilitation and there can be no doubt that such claims had, and still have, a measure of accuracy. The Report of the Cork Committee on Insolvency Law and Practice – probably the most important official report on insolvency law and practice for 100 years – described receivership in the following terms:[53]

> There is ... one aspect of the floating charge which we believe to have been of outstanding benefit to the general public and to society as a whole; we refer to the power to appoint a receiver and manager of the whole property and undertaking of a company. The power is enjoyed by the holder of any well-drawn floating charge, but by no other creditor. Such receivers and managers are normally given extensive powers to manage and carry on the business of the company. In some cases, they have been able to restore an ailing enterprise to profitability, and to return it to its former owners. In others, they have been able to dispose of the whole or part of the business as a going concern. In either case, the preservation of the profitable parts of the enterprise has been of advantage to the employees, the commercial community, and the general public.

It is not so surprising that receivership has been of benefit to interests beyond those of the lender. Turning around a business from failure to success is a talent but by no means a unique or a rare talent. So a receiver might effect such a change for the benefit of the lender and the borrower – and thus for the borrower's other creditors – and, of course for the receiver himself. And there is a further point. Some businesses require immediate attention if they are to be turned around. Even a 24-hour delay may make the difference between life and death. The autocracy of the lender ensures the speed and secrecy that may be necessary for a lifesaving appointment of a receiver. All that is needed for the appointment of the receiver is a signature on a document under the provisions of a private agreement. In its purest form, receivership is triggered by the creditor with the floating charge and no intervention by a court or other independent agency is required.

The institutions of the floating charge and receivership were exported by the United Kingdom to Commonwealth countries which inherited its banking practices and its Common Law. It flourished in Australia and New Zealand as it did in the United Kingdom, but not in South Africa, where the legal system was not simply the English Common Law but a mixture of the Common Law and the Roman-Dutch

---

53 (1982) Cmnd 8558 at 117 (paragraph 495).

legal system. Of potentially greater interest is the fate of the floating charge and receivership in Canada. Here it has been accepted in its pure form in some provinces, but not in others. In the latter, the appointment has to be made by a court and this may be due to the influence of the United States, where the notion of a major if open-ended reconstruction of a debtor company is closely associated with supervision by the court. It is, of course, a truism, that the institutions of the floating charge and receivership have never been accepted in the United States.

The near-absolute power in the hands of the receiver and lender could, of course, be capable of abuse. The power to sell the assets or part of the assets of the insolvent business may be used simply to yield sufficient for the repayment of the loan, arrears of interest and the receiver's costs, regardless of the destructive effects this might have on the business. Doing this quickly may suit the private interests of lender and receiver more than a longer term strategy which would preserve and rehabilitate the business. Insofar as receivership is claimed as a rescue and rehabilitation regime in the interests of the public, it has to be conceded that its administration, left as it is to private initiative, creates what might be described as a conflict of interest and duty.

There can be no doubt that receivership dominated the world of the insolvent company in the United Kingdom in the twentieth century. When the Insolvency Act of 1986 sought to break the mould by creating two statutory, court-based business rescue regimes – Administration and the Corporate Voluntary Arrangement – the Legislature had to bow to the banks and the insolvency practitioners and make these new regimes subject in status to receivership.

Yet unease at its private nature and potential for abuse was palpable even at the time of the Cork Committee's paean of praise recited above. A government committee in 1993 unanimously recommended the extension of the role of the Corporate Voluntary Arrangement such that it would clip the wings of receivership, but the bank lobby ensured that the recommended reforms got nowhere. And there was a growing side wind – receivership sat uncomfortably with other bankruptcy regimes of all the other member states of the European Union where receivership was unknown and where the idea that so important and public a task as attempting the rescue of a bankrupt businesses, a task involving the preservation of business potential and limiting unemployment, should be entrusted to private initiative, was greeted with incomprehension.

But reform did come – in two mighty bursts, first in the Insolvency Act 2000 and then in the Enterprise Act 2002. Both were clearly designed to change, substantially, the balance as between receivership on the one hand and the statutory based regimes – Administration and Corporate Voluntary Arrangement – on the other. The intended changes will still take some years to achieve their full effects, but they have already brought British business rescue right into line with what has been virtually a worldwide phenomenon beginning with Chapter 11 of the United States Bankruptcy Code of 1978.

All rescue regimes pursue the same goal and face the same problem – trying to ensure that protection is given only in suitable cases, where there is a good chance of recovery and rehabilitation. Giving a business the benefit of the rescue regime means preventing the enforcement by creditors of their claims and this is a serious infringement of rights which are fundamental to creditors in any capitalist society. This moratorium carries the added risk of being abused by no-hopers simply seeking a further few months of being kept alive on the equivalent of a life support machine despite already being in a terminal condition. Creditors are obviously prepared to tolerate interference with their rights where their debtor recovers because then their claims will be paid in full – and the debtor will be available for further business in the future. But an artificially protected debtor that does not make it out of the hospital is very likely to leave an even smaller estate than would have been available had the debtor company gone straight into liquidation.

Different countries tackle this problem of selection in different ways. The most fascinating variations concern first the process by which the business is selected for protection and, secondly, how the business is managed while under that protection. In relation to both these issues, the United Kingdom and the United States apparently represent polar opposites. In the United States, any business may assume the protection of Chapter 11, simply by filing an appropriate notice at its local bankruptcy court. The protection operates instantaneously. No discretion is invoked, the protection is automatic and entirely at the instance of the debtor.

At first blush this seems a remarkably cavalier approach to the interference with fundamental commercial rights. It even carries with it the possibility of a non-bankrupt business assuming the protection for ulterior motives, for example to seek to alter its labour contracts with its employees. This cut and dried approach to the problem is, however, short-lived. It is supplemented by that great staple of American democracy – litigation – as different interest groups challenge the right of the business to its protection. In the United States, business rescue comes with a big bang. In the United Kingdom, the approach is careful, considered; selection for protection is made by a judge after argument by lawyers based on documents prepared by accountants.

A similar contrast can be seen in the two countries' approach to the question who will manage the business during the period of protection. In the United States, the business may well continue as before with the same controllers; in the United Kingdom, the professionals move in. In the United Kingdom, only qualified insolvency practitioners – a new profession, dominated by people originally trained as accountants – may act as administrators under the court-based business rescue regime of administration.[54] In the United States, lawyers facilitate the process while the business people run the bankrupt business. In the United Kingdom accountants play a major role in the running of the bankrupt business.

The changes to the United Kingdom system brought by the Insolvency Act 2000 and the Enterprise Act 2002 is likely to shift the practice of business rescue further in the direction of the American process. But the more fascinating

---

54 Indeed, the same is true of receivers.

similarities in the two systems are those which might be detected from within, from similarities of practice rather than from legal principles and institutions.

Research into Chapter 11, for example, revealed that in a high proportion of cases, the board of directors of the debtor either changed just before, or immediately upon, the onset of the Chapter 11 process. True, this relates almost entirely to big business and the shift is from one set of businesspeople to another set of businesspeople, whereas in the case of the United Kingdom, the shift is the replacement of businesspeople by professionals.

Yet this obvious difference, too, needs deconstructing. While there is no doubt that under receivership or administration, the insolvency practitioner takes charge on appointment, there are many examples – elusive and difficult to quantify given the intensely personal nature of the phenomenon – of close collaboration between insolvency practitioner and debtor in the rescue process. There can be little doubt that good – and maybe even the best – business rescues in the United Kingdom have been the result of this collaboration.

Conclusion

I have attempted to use the comparison between United Kingdom and United States bankruptcy to suggest that while different systems have evolved, they each seek similar ends and reflect much of their particular culture, whether that of the nineteenth century when they were at markedly different stages of political development or that of the late twentieth century in relation to the specific issue of business rescue. Superficially they may seem poles apart, although I have tried to suggest that below the surface they sometimes resemble each other quite closely. More significantly, however, through bankruptcy regimes we can, I believe see how local culture has influenced the shape of the particular institutions.

Chapter 2

Cross-Border Insolvency Law: Where Private International Law and Insolvency Law Meet

Rosalind Mason*

Introduction

> Merchants have no country. The mere spot they stand on does not constitute so strong an attachment as that from which they draw their gains. (Thomas Jefferson)

While merchants have engaged in trade and commerce across political borders for centuries, the accelerated growth in international trade[1] and investment and globalised production and distribution of goods and services in recent decades have had an effect at the level of national economies.

This internationalization of national economies has caused them to become more open and increasingly linked, resulting in greater interdependence. In its *2006 World Development Indicators*, the World Bank reported:

> In an era of uncertain alliances and global fears, it is striking that the world economy continues to become more integrated. Celebrated by some, deplored by others, globalization has been loudly debated over the past decade. But globalization is not a single process. It proceeds as

---

* The author acknowledges the helpful comments of Dr Reid Mortensen, University of Queensland, on an earlier version of this work. The assistance of the University of Queensland is also acknowledged as some of the research for this chapter was undertaken while the author was a Visiting Professor at the School of Law and a Visiting Fellow of their Centre for Public, International and Comparative Law.

1 World trade figures disclose an unparalleled sustained growth in international trade since the 1960s although global economic growth decelerated in 2005, following its peak in 2004, attributed mainly to weaker economic activity in Europe, the United States and a number of emerging markets: World Trade Organization, International Trade Statistics 2006, available at: <www.wto.org/english/res_e/statis_e/its2006_e/its06_general_overview_e.pdf> (last viewed 31 May 2007).

people and institutions seek profits and competitive advantage through expanding trade in goods and services and cross-border flows of financial resources and people. It has been propelled by cheaper and faster transportation, more innovative information technology, fewer or lower trade barriers, and better economic management'.[2]

The vast majority of national economies, particularly since the decline of the centrally planned economies in former communist bloc countries, are market economies which provide the opportunity for risk-taking enterprises to profit from their successes.[3] Fundamental to such a system is that businesses risk failure, whether through internal problems such as poor management and inefficient production of goods and services or because of external factors such as changes in government regulation.[4] In the context of increasing operational reliance upon credit, failure means that businesses will be unable to meet their financial obligations as they fall due.[5]

Creditors who manage the risk of such failure through obtaining an interest in the debtor's property to secure the latter's obligations may proceed to exercise their rights and enforce the security. Unsecured creditors may pursue the debtor through legal proceedings and subsequent execution of judgment. However, where financial obligations ultimately cannot be satisfied, there is a general default by the debtor. Individual debt recovery by creditors may then be eclipsed by a collective insolvency administration.[6] The majority of legal systems 'provide a legal mechanism to address the collective satisfaction' of outstanding creditor claims from the debtor's assets.[7]

This chapter introduces some of the essential features of insolvency administrations and their regulation before elaborating on the issues that may arise in a multi-state[8] insolvency, as occurred for example in the Maxwell case. Next it

---

2   World Bank, 2006 World Development Indicators, available at: <devdata.worldbank.org/wdi2006/contents/Section6_1.htm> in Chapter 6 (last viewed 31 May 2007).

3   See Flaschen, E.D. and DeSieno, T.B., 'The Development of Insolvency Law as Part of the Transition from a Centrally Planned to a Market Economy' (1992) 26(3) *The International Lawyer* 667; Baird, D.G., 'A World without Bankruptcy' (1987) 50(2) *Law and Contemporary Problems* 173 at 183.

4   See Argenti, J., *Corporate Collapse: The Causes and Symptoms* (1976, McGraw Hill, London).

5   United Kingdom Insolvency Law Review Committee, Report on Insolvency Law and Practice (1982, HMSO, London) [Cm 8558] at 54.

6   See Virgós, M., 'The 1995 European Community Convention on Insolvency Proceedings: an Insider's View' (1998) 25 *Forum Internationale* 1.

7   United Nations Commission for International Trade Law ('UNCITRAL') Legislative Guide on Insolvency Law (2004) at 9.

8   The term 'multi-state' is used to signify an insolvency that crosses borders between legal systems. The term 'state' is used to refer to a law area where one system of

outlines the private international law dimension of multi-state insolvency and places various insolvency law theories within the context of these private international law concepts. Finally it highlights the private international law questions that are addressed and those that remain unanswered by the UNCITRAL Model Law on Cross-Border Insolvency. This instrument has recently been adopted by a number of significant economies and will no doubt influence the future development of cross-border insolvency law within municipal statute and case law.

Some Essential Features of Insolvency Administrations and their Regulation

Insolvency is a collective issue. In its *Legislative Guide on Insolvency Law*, the United Nations Commission for International Trade Law ('UNCITRAL') notes that it is 'a generally accepted principle of insolvency law that collective action is more efficient in maximizing the assets available to creditors than a system that leaves creditors free to pursue their individual remedies'.[9]

Of increasing importance globally are administrations or reorganizations aimed at facilitating the rescue of businesses or their viable components.[10] Predicating this approach is 'the basic economic theory that greater value may be obtained from keeping the essential components together rather than breaking them up and disposing of them in fragments'.[11] Yet, where this is not a practical or legal option, insolvency law provides the 'bottom line', which is a liquidation administration that results in the sequestration of the debtor's estate for the benefit of the general body of creditors.[12]

Whether as a liquidation or a reorganization, collective insolvency administrations exhibit certain essential features. The first essential element is the orderly identification[13] and, in the case of sequestration, collection of the debtor's divisible property. Typically, initiation of the administration imposes a moratorium

---

private law prevails: Sykes, E.I. and Pryles M.C., *Australian Private International Law* (3rd ed) (1991, Law Book Company, Sydney) at 5.

9   UNCITRAL, above note 7 at 136.

10 See Goode, R., *Principles of Corporate Insolvency Law* (3rd ed) (2005, Sweet & Maxwell, London) at [2–01], [2–18]. Another option not considered here are informal voluntary restructurings developed by the banking sector as an alternative to formal reorganization proceedings under insolvency law: UNCITRAL, above note 7 at 21.

11 UNCITRAL, above note 7 at 11.

12 The term 'liquidation' is used throughout to signify such a sequestration and distribution of the debtor's estate – whether of an individual or corporate debtor – even though some jurisdictions use the term 'bankruptcy' for some or all of these administrations.

13 Delimiting the debtor's divisible property is a central feature of any insolvency proceeding: Rasmussen, R.K., 'A New Approach to Transnational Insolvencies' (1997) 19 *Michigan Journal of International Law* 1 at 12.

on creditor action with the debtor's estate, the divisible property available for distribution, being administered in the interests of the creditors collectively, often by a specialist insolvency officeholder.[14]

Second, it is essential that there is an orderly identification and verification of creditors' claims and distribution of the debtor's divisible property in satisfaction of those claims. Fundamental to the liquidation process is that the property is distributed among the body of creditors, typically according to a statutory regime. A longstanding principle proclaimed to apply to this process is that of equal or *pari passu* distribution. In *Phillips v Hunter*,[15] the court stated: 'The great principle of the bankrupt [sic] laws is justice founded on equality'.[16] Yet this notion of *pari passu* distribution is in fact more honoured in the breach than the observance. Secured creditors typically retain the benefit of their contractual and property rights.[17] Also, distribution regimes prefer certain classes of creditor who receive priority in the division of realised funds.[18] Thus it is more correct to say that 'creditors of equal standing share equally within their rank'.[19] In comparison, reorganizations normally allow for some flexibility in the manner of distribution. Subject to creditors' approval, they may propose distribution priorities that are different to those applicable to a liquidation.[20]

A supplementary feature of insolvency regulation is the promotion of commercial morality. It seeks to encourage honest trading and to lessen the number of business failures.[21] This is evident in the voidable antecedent transaction provisions, which may set aside certain transactions entered into during a set

---

14   The office holder or administrator is granted certain powers of investigation to help identify the property (UNCITRAL, above note 7 at 179) and powers of realisation to assist with its collection.

15   (1795) 2 HBl 402 at 405; 126 ER 618 at 620.

16   Bankruptcy and liquidation were originally administered by the Court of Chancery and this principle may reflect an equitable maxim that 'equity is equality'. This maxim 'expresses in a general way the object both of law and equity, namely to effect a distribution of property and losses proportionate to the several claims or the several liabilities of the persons concerned': Pettit, P., *Halsbury's Laws of England* (4th ed, reissue) (1991, Butterworths, London) in Volume 16 at [747], cited in Meagher, R.P., Heydon, J.D. and Leeming, M.J., *Meagher, Gummow and Lehane's Equity: Doctrines and Remedies* (4th ed) (2002, LexisNexis Butterworths, Sydney) at [3–145].

17   On the importance of corporate insolvency law recognising rights accrued prior to liquidation, see Goode, above note 10 at [2–16] and [3–02].

18   A second crucial aspect of any insolvency law is determining the relative priority of claimants to the debtor's divisible property: Rasmussen, above note 13 at 13.

19   For a discussion of the pari passu principle and its relationship with other methods of insolvency distribution, see Mokal, R.J., *Corporate Insolvency Law: Theory and Application* (2005, Oxford University Press, Oxford) in Chapter 4.

20   UNCITRAL, above note 7 at 274.

21   United Kingdom Insolvency Law Review Committee, above note 5 at 19.

'suspect period' before the insolvency adjudication.[22] In addition, certain behaviour either prior to or during an insolvency administration has been classified as criminal or quasi-criminal activity. For example, an individual who obtains credit while an undischarged bankrupt without disclosing his or her bankrupt status may commit an offence.[23] A director of a company who fails to prevent it incurring debt when it is insolvent, in circumstances where the director had reasonable grounds to suspect the company's insolvency, may contravene corporate insolvency law.[24]

These features of collective administrations indicate some of the particular characteristics of their regulation. In insolvency, all claims against the debtor will not be satisfied. Thus predictability and transparency of regulation are even more important than usual[25] in order to minimize and resolve disputes with the least possible delay and expense.[26] Yet insolvency administrations frequently involve court proceedings, especially on the extent of the divisible property and provable claims, as parties seek to improve their relative positions *vis-à-vis* the deficient estate.[27] In the case of reorganizations, litigation often surrounds the approval of the plan, for example through challenges to the voting process. The additional complexity where there is a multi-state dimension increases the importance of cooperation across jurisdictions in order to maximize the value of the estate and to lessen delay and expense.

The sequestration of a debtor's property is a complex procedure that has an inherent integrity through the unity of the estate being realized and distributed.[28] Not only is the actual administration complex and integrated, but also the various aspects of insolvency law which apply to an administration are interconnected.[29]

---

22 An insolvency adjudication is the order commencing an insolvency administration. Examples of voidable antecedent transactions are preference payments to select creditors and disposals of property at uncommercial values.

23 Bankruptcy Act 1966 (Cth), section 269 (Australia); Insolvency Act 1986, section 360 (United Kingdom).

24 That is, the Australian insolvent trading provisions Corporations Act 2001 (Cth), section 588G (Australia). See Insolvency Act 1986, section 214 (United Kingdom) for a similar wrongful trading provision.

25 UNCITRAL, above note 7 at 13 and 31. Predictability in insolvency law is important for facilitating the provision of credit and the development of financial markets.

26 On the importance of saving costs in the insolvency context, see Balz, M., 'The European Union Convention on Insolvency Proceedings' (1996) 70 *American Bankruptcy Law Journal* 483 at 528.

27 See Wood, P.R., *Principles of International Insolvency* (1995, Sweet & Maxwell, London) at 1.

28 On the European notion of the 'unity' of the estate, see below notes 127–128.

29 For example, in an Australian personal bankruptcy, the provision on commencement of the bankruptcy is intrinsically connected to the provision on property divisible among creditors and thus the relation back doctrine. This doctrine is also subject to the voidable transaction provisions: Bankruptcy Act 1966 (Cth), sections 58, 115–116.

Yet, insolvency law does not determine all legal issues within an insolvency administration. It is interwoven with other areas of law that shape its implementation.[30] As Dalhuisen states:

> as bankruptcy is at the same time a creditor's remedy as well as a substantive device and as such a complicated, composite procedure, intertwined with many other areas of the law, like personal law, company law, law of securities and priorities, contract law and sometimes also criminal and public law, it is all the more difficult to rely on a general approach without regard to the particular situation, the nature of the rules involved, and areas of the law affected.[31]

These other laws determine the pre-existing rights and interests of debtors and creditors at the time of the adjudication, which commences a liquidation. The application of insolvency law to ascertain divisible property and provable claims may require consideration of other laws. It may be necessary to refer to property and security law where a third party claims an interest in the debtor's property.[32] Contract or torts law may be relevant to determining the validity of an unsecured claim.

Liquidation transforms individual private rights of parties into an opportunity to participate in a collective administration.[33] In a reorganization, these private rights affect a creditor's position in the collective approval of a plan, for example determining their voting rights or class, or the creditor's share in any distribution under the plan finally implemented.

While debtor and creditor law emphasizes party autonomy, insolvency law features the notion of collective impartiality. Upon commencement of an insolvency administration, there is a moratorium on creditor action and proceedings and a consolidation of the conduct of litigation. Individual claims are addressed through the collective administration, which balances the disparate interests of the various parties, based on statutory provisions applicable to liquidation or reorganization (although the latter may allow for more flexibility and

---

30 See Anton, A.E., 'Note of Reservations by Mr A E Anton' in United Kingdom Bankruptcy Convention Advisory Committee, Report on the EEC Preliminary Draft Convention (1976, HMSO, London) [Cm 6602] at 120: insolvency law is not 'easily severable from the remaining rules of the legal system'.

31 See Dalhuisen, J.H., *Dalhuisen on International Insolvency and Bankruptcy* (1984, Matthew Bender, New York NY) Vol. 1, Part III, at §2.03[2]. UNCITRAL, above note 7 at 13 lists the following examples of non-insolvency laws that may affect the conduct of an insolvency proceeding: 'labour law; commercial and contract law; tax law; laws affecting foreign exchange, netting and set-off and debt for equity swaps; and even family and matrimonial law'.

32 On the protection of ownership and security rights in an insolvency, see Goode, above note 10 at [3–02] to [3–06].

33 Ibid., at [3–06].

negotiation). Insolvency poses a problem of 'collective action' rather than a private ordering based on private initiative.[34]

Thus a 'range of interests needs to be accommodated' by an insolvency law, with the parties affected including:

> the debtor, the owners and management of the debtor, the creditors who may be secured to varying degrees (including tax agencies and other government creditors), employees, guarantors of debt and suppliers of goods and services, as well as the legal, commercial and social institutions and practices that are relevant to the design of the insolvency law and required for its operation. Generally, the mechanism must strike a balance not only between the different interests of these stakeholders, but also between these interests and the relevant social, political and other policy considerations that have an impact on the economic and legal goals of insolvency proceedings.[35]

Thus the community at large has an interest in the development of insolvency law.[36] '[T]he plurality of interests' it balances include the 'general public interest through the maintenance of high standards of probity and responsibility in association with the giving and receiving of credit'.[37] This public dimension is reflected in the categories of priority creditors, which frequently include public revenue authorities.[38] In key sectors such as banking and insurance, for which public confidence is crucial, local depositors and policyholders are often

---

34 Virgós, above note 6. See also United Kingdom Insolvency Law Review Committee, above note 5 at 60; and Goode, above note 10 at [1–04] and [2–23] on the collective nature of insolvency proceedings.

35 UNCITRAL, above note 7 at 9.

36 This is reflected in recitals to early English insolvency statutes: for example, the Bankruptcy Act 1623 (21 James 1 c 19) referred to 'the general hurt of this Realm' caused by the increasing numbers of bankrupts.

37 See Fletcher, I.F., *Conflict of Laws and European Community Law* (1982, North Holland Publishing, Amsterdam) at 197.

38 While many jurisdictions in recent times have removed this priority, for example in Australia through the Insolvency (Tax Priorities) Legislation Amendment Act 1993 (Cth), the revenue authorities may still receive special treatment, for example in Australia through additional remedies against directors under the Corporations Act 2001 (Cth), section 588FGA. On the protection of public revenue through allocating a priority to government tax claims, see UNCITRAL, above note 7 at 273.

accorded priority in the event of insolvency.[39] The investigative processes in insolvency reflect society's interest in upholding commercial morality.[40]

In the past decade, insolvency laws have become recognized as essential to the regulation of market economies.[41] During the World Bank's consultation process leading to its Principles and Guidelines for Effective Insolvency and Creditors' Rights Systems, the bank stated:

> The creation of ... a framework [for an insolvency system], and its integration within the wider context of the established legal process, are vital to the maintenance of social order and stability in the fullest sense: all parties in interest need to be in a position to anticipate their legal rights in the event of the debtor's inability to pay, or to pay in full, whatever is due to them in consequence of their dealings and relationship. This in turn enables them to make calculations regarding the economic implications of such default by the debtor, and hence to estimate risk.[42]

According to Australian research, insolvency policy is more significant than might be expected, given the relatively small proportion of businesses which exit because of business failure.[43] Regulatory provisions for business insolvency affect more than just those related to the failing business. They 'affect economic incentives more broadly by changing the willingness of people to lend money to businesses, and the level of prudence adopted by entrepreneurs'.[44] They also affect the number of businesses that become insolvent and they can 'partly determine the extent of reorganization of resources in an economy over time, with potential long run impacts on overall business dynamism and productivity'.[45]

---

39   Wood, above note 27 at 24; Martin, J., 'Distribution Complexities in the Winding Up of an Insurance Company in Australia' (2002) 10 *Insolvency Law Journal* 80–94. For a recent case on the special rules applying to the distribution of assets to Australian creditors of an insurance company being wound up in Australia, see *In the Matter of HIH Casualty and General Insurance Ltd* [2006] EWCA Civ 732.

40   United Kingdom Insolvency Law Review Committee, above note 5 at 62.

41   Evidence for this can be found in the steps being taken by UNCITRAL (Legislative Guide on Insolvency Law), the World Bank (Principles and Guidelines for Effective Insolvency and Creditors' Rights Systems), the International Monetary Fund (Report of the Working Group on International Financial Crises), Asian Development Bank (Promoting Regional Cooperation in the Development of the Insolvency Law Reforms) and others to promote reform of insolvency systems.

42   World Bank, 'Draft Background Paper: Building Effective Insolvency Systems: Toward Principles and Guidelines', Paper presented to the Conference on Insolvency Systems in Asia: An Efficiency Perspective (1999, Sydney) at 1.

43   See Bickerdyce, I. et al., Business Failure and Change: An Australian Perspective (2000, Productivity Commission Staff Research Paper, Ausinfo, Canberra).

44   Ibid., at 76.

45   Ibid., at 77.

The 'close relationship between economic results and legal solutions' in the field of insolvency[46] is evident in that insolvency law finally allocates the losses in the event of financial failure of a business. It underpins the commercial and financial dealings in a market economy and the choices it makes are also a crucial indicator of the attitudes and fundamental values of the state's legal system.[47] Nevertheless, insolvency law is not merely of economic significance to the community.[48]

It is intimately linked to the commercial, financial and social fabric of a state,[49] being an important contributor to the state's commercial and economic processes and an important component of the state's general commercial laws.[50] UNCITRAL's Legislative Guide states that whatever design is chosen for an insolvency law, it should:

> be complementary to, and compatible with, the legal and social values of the society in which it is based and which it must ultimately sustain. Although insolvency law generally forms a distinctive regime, it ought not to produce results that are fundamentally in conflict with the premises upon which laws other than the insolvency law are based.[51]

Multi-State Insolvency Administrations

The embedding of insolvency law in the commercial, financial and societal culture of a state together with the complex interaction of the range of laws relevant to an insolvency administration[52] tend to militate against harmonisation between states of the resolution of multi-state insolvency issues.[53]

---

46 See Burman, H.S., 'Harmonization of International Bankruptcy Law: A United States Perspective' (1996) 64 *Fordham Law Review* 2543 at 2548.

47 Wood, above note 27 at 1.

48 See Warren, E., 'Bankruptcy Policy' (1987) 54 *University of Chicago Law Review* 775; Gross, K., *Failure and Forgiveness: Rebalancing the Bankruptcy System* (1997, Yale University Press, New Haven).

49 See Fletcher, I.F., 'Cross-Border Cooperation in Cases of International Insolvency: Some Recent Trends Compared' (1991-1992) 6/7 *Tulane Civil Law Forum* 171 at 175.

50 See the guiding principles adopted in the Australian Law Reform Commission, General Insolvency Inquiry (Report No 45) (1988, AGPS, Canberra) Volume 1 at paragraph 33. The World Bank's Principles on the Legal Framework for Corporate Insolvency state they should 'integrate with a country's broader legal and commercial systems': World Bank, Principles and Guidelines for Effective Insolvency and Creditors' Rights Systems (2001) at Principle 6.

51 UNCITRAL, above note 7 at 10.

52 United Kingdom Insolvency Law Review Committee, above note 5 at 116.

53 Fletcher, above note 49 at 175.

While harmonization may be problematic at state level, economic pressures on debtors and creditors to resolve these issues have produced novel pragmatic commercial solutions in a number of major multi-state insolvencies. These solutions based around protocols approved by the courts have been aimed at maximizing returns to creditors, typically through reorganization rather than liquidation. However, these solutions have not addressed the inherent complexities[54] caused by states' differing insolvency and private international laws. Such an economic rather than legal approach[55] to resolving the competing debtor and creditors' claims in an insolvency does not necessarily take account of the public interest dimension. Also it does not provide sufficient predictability for creditors at the time they are initially contracting with the debtor on whether their claims will be enforceable in the event of subsequent debtor default.[56]

The growing internationalisation of economic activity increases the likelihood that these effects of an insolvency will not be confined to the one state. In such instances, a state's private international law becomes relevant in determining how it resolves a foreign element in any legal dispute arising out of the insolvency. Differences in laws may permit, even encourage, debtors, their creditors and insolvency administrators to seek redress for those disputes in more than one state.

These commercial solutions to managing multi-state insolvencies, for example through court approved governance protocols coordinating concurrent administrations, rely on economic incentives, heightened by legal uncertainty, to bring the parties to the negotiating table. Even then, many interests that would otherwise be protected by state insolvency or private international law may be unrepresented. Also while major issues of jurisdiction and recognition may be addressed in such a protocol, during the administration choice of law issues and issues with third parties may arise that result in litigation. The following case study illustrates the fundamental private international law issues in a multi-state corporate insolvency.

Maxwell Case Study

The Maxwell Communications Corporation plc (MCC) multi-state insolvency is a prime example of a commercial approach to harmonising insolvency systems for the benefit of the debtor and its creditors. It resulted essentially in a 'bilateral treaty', an Order and Protocol approved by the courts in the United States and

---

54   Fletcher, above note 37 at 189.
55   Dalhuisen, above note 31 in Volume 1, Part I, at §3.10.
56   Kipnis comments on the significance of *ex ante* information about bankruptcy rules leading to a more efficient determination of the price of credit, for which see Kipnis, A.M., 'Beyond UNCITRAL: Alternatives to Universality in Transnational Insolvency' (3 July 2006), available at: <ssrn.com/abstract=913844> (last viewed 31 May 2007).

England.[57] A reorganization resulted within 16 months,[58] acknowledged as being relatively expeditious resolution for a case of that size.[59]

At the time of its collapse in 1991, the MCC multinational group consisted of some 400 public companies intertwined with 400 Maxwell private companies.[60] MCC itself was an English holding company with more than 400 subsidiaries worldwide engaged primarily in information services and electronic publishing, language instruction and general and consumer publishing.[61] Assets were located across numerous states, such as Israel, Bulgaria, Germany, Kenya and Canada, which represented a broad spectrum of legal systems.[62]

The group's principal assets were situated in the United States – some USD 700 million to 1 billion compared to its non-United States' assets estimated at less than GBP 100 million[63] – whereas England was the holding company's place of incorporation and the group's place of central management and control. Other significant MCC connections with England were that it traded on the London Stock Exchange, kept its corporate books in pounds sterling and owed most of its USD 2.4 billion debt to British banks and London branches of foreign banks.[64]

Two concurrent principal insolvency proceedings were instigated by the MCC Board. On 16 December 1991, they applied in the United States for a debtor-in-possession administration that provided for a creditor moratorium while management structured a Chapter 11 reorganization. On the following day they sought an administration order in England, which would provide a similar stay on creditor action and avoid insolvent trading liability on the part of the directors.[65]

---

57 See Flaschen, E.D. and Silverman, R.J., 'The role of the examiner as facilitator and harmonizer in the Maxwell Communication Corporation international insolvency', Chapter 25 in Ziegel, J.S. (ed.), *Current Developments in International and Comparative Corporate Insolvency Law* (1994, Clarendon Press, Oxford) at 629.

58 A Debtor's Chapter 11 Plan of Reorganization for Maxwell Communication plc was confirmed by the United States Bankruptcy Court on 14 July 1993 and a (mutually dependent) Scheme of Arrangement was sanctioned by the English High Court on 21 July 1993.

59 The approach was not without its problems however, see Brozman, T., 'A Perspective from a US Judge' (1995) 4 *International Insolvency Review* 16 at 20.

60 See Carrington, P. and Smith, H., 'Reconciling UK Administration and US Chapter 11 after Maxwell' (1992) 11(7) *International Financial Law Review* 20.

61 Flaschen and Silverman, above note 57 at 41.

62 See Clarke, T., 'Case Study: Robert Maxwell: Master of Corporate Misfeasance' (1993) 1(3) *Corporate Governance* 141 at 147 (diagram).

63 *Barclays Bank plc v Homan* [1993] BCLC 680 at 683 [*sub nom Re Maxwell Communications Corp plc (No 2)* [1992] BCC 757].

64 See Chittenden, C.M., 'After the Fall of Maxwell Communications: Is the Time Right for a Multinational Insolvency Treaty?' (1993) 28 *Wake Forest Law Review* 161 at 163 citing Sloan, A., 'Give Us Your Broke, Indebted Messes Yearning To Be Solvent' (Connecticut Law Tribune, 30 December 1991) at 29.

65 This sequence was apparently chosen because of 'cultural' differences in that United States creditors may have viewed an administration as a pre-cursor to liquidation and

An administration order was granted in England on 20 December, the court appointing administrators requested by the major bank creditors rather than management.[66] On the same day, the United States court appointed an Examiner to MCC, not to displace management but rather with powers to attempt to harmonize the concurrent proceedings and to facilitate the possibilities for rehabilitation and reorganization.[67] As a result of discussions between the Examiner and the Joint Administrators, the unique 'Order and Protocol' was proposed and approved by the English High Court on 31 December 1991 and the United States Bankruptcy Court on 15 January 1992.

Despite the Protocol assisting in the insolvency administration, issues still arose for litigation by claimants, one of the more significant being over an allegedly voidable transaction with connections to both the United States and England.[68] Shortly before the administrators were appointed in England, MCC had repaid over USD 30 million to Barclays Bank plc (Barclays) from the sale proceeds of an American asset. Barclays sought an injunction in England to prevent the administrators from taking recovery action in the United States. They argued that the action should be determined in England in accordance with English law (under which a defence was available –something not open to them under American avoidance laws).

The English Court of Appeal[69] refused the injunction and upheld the primary judge's decision that where the foreign proceedings were not vexatious or oppressive it was for the foreign court to decide whether or not it was the appropriate forum. When the preference action was instituted in the United States, the Bankruptcy Court[70] held that, as a foreign debtor had made a preferential transfer to a foreign transferee and the centre of gravity of that transfer was

---

it may also have jeopardized the voluntary petition in the United States for a debtor-in-possession administration: Carrington and Smith, above note 60.

66   Flaschen and Silverman, above note 57 at 624.

67   See Brozman, T., Final Supplemental Order Appointing an Examiner and Approving Agreement between Examiner and Joint Administrators dated 15 January 1992, cited in Flaschen and Silverman, above note 57 at 636.

68   The Second Circuit appeal court noted that the scheme and plan approved by the courts did not clearly address the choice of law and choice of forum questions generated by the relevant litigation and so the courts were required to resort to principles of comity and choice of law: *Maxwell Communication Corporation plc v Société Générale* 93 F 3d 1036 at 1053 (2nd Cir 1996).

69   *Barclays Bank plc v Homan* [1993] BCLC 680. See Mason, R., 'Local Proceedings in a Multistate Liquidation: Issues of Jurisdiction' (2006) 30(1) *Melbourne University Law Review* 145 at 182ff on the use of anti-suit injunctions in multi-state insolvencies.

70   *Maxwell Communication Corporation plc v Société Générale* 170 BR 800 (Bankr SDNY 1994) affirmed 186 BR 807 (SDNY 1995) and 93 F 3d 1036 (2nd Cir 1996). Not only Barclays but also other banks including Société Generale were involved in the litigation.

overseas, the presumption against extraterritoriality[71] prevented the local preference section avoiding the transfer.[72] The Second Circuit Court of Appeals declined to consider the question of extraterritoriality, basing its decision instead on the doctrine of international comity precluding the application of the American avoidance law to transfers in which England's interest had primacy.[73]

   This case scenario exemplifies the fundamental legal issues that arise in a multi-state insolvency. They concern jurisdiction, the applicable law and the recognition and effect accorded foreign insolvency proceedings.[74] On the question of whether a local court should exercise jurisdiction in an insolvency which has a foreign element, the MCC Order and Protocol effectively ceded jurisdiction in certain areas to one or other of the United States and England and in other matters preserved dual jurisdiction.[75] On what law should apply to resolving the issue(s) before the court in a multi-state insolvency, the United States courts in the MCC voidable transaction case against Barclays were of the view that English law applied, assuming that the United States court had had jurisdiction to deal with it. Finally the extent, if any, to which a local court should recognize or give effect to a foreign order or judgment was central to the concurrent primary proceedings in the MCC case. It was resolved through local and foreign court approval of the Order and Protocol.

Private International Law Analysis of Multi-State Insolvency Issues

Analyses of multi-state insolvency according to the insolvency law theories have been essentially about which states have jurisdiction to adjudicate in liquidation, or more recently on reorganization. Such approaches have left issues about the applicable law largely unaddressed[76] as the law of the forum has typically been applied once jurisdiction is exercised. There has been little recognition of foreign

---

71   *Equal Employment Opportunity Commission v Arabian American Oil Co* 111 S Ct 1227 at 1230 (1991).

72   Thus the court dismissed the proceedings - although it then went on to examine choice of law in respect of the avoidance action. In the circumstances, it held that English law would apply and, on the basis of comity, decided it should also dismiss the proceedings on that ground. (English avoidance law provided a good defence on the facts as agreed.) The Second Circuit appeal court also chose to defer to the courts and laws of England according to the doctrine of international comity: *Maxwell Communication Corporation plc v Société Generale* 93 F 3d 1036 (2nd Cir 1996).

73   *Maxwell Communication Corporation plc v Société Generale* 93 F 3d 1036 at 1055 (2nd Cir 1996).

74   See Nygh, P.E. and Davies, M., *Conflict of Laws in Australia* (7th ed) (2002, LexisNexis Butterworths, Sydney) at 6–7.

75   Brozman, above note 67 at 20.

76   Dalhuisen, above note 31 in Volume 1, Part III, at §2.03[3] in note 48. Also see Goode, above note 10 at [14–18] in note 63.

proceedings or laws except to the extent that, under certain approaches, a state defers to the exercise of jurisdiction in, and the municipal insolvency law of, the debtor's domicile,[77] place of incorporation[78] or seat.

Private international law adopts a more comprehensive theoretical approach to multi-state issues. The fundamental legal issues which arise in a multi-state legal problem are (i) choice of forum, (ii) the recognition and effect accorded foreign insolvency proceedings and (iii) choice of law.[79]

First, choice of forum raises questions of jurisdiction – whether a court can and will hear and determine the matter. This requires examination of the connection with the jurisdiction of the parties or the dispute. In an insolvency resulting in a sequestration of the debtor's estate rather than a reorganization,[80] typically the initial matter for determination by the court is the order, which results in the bankruptcy of an individual or the liquidation of a corporation. During the course of such a local insolvency administration, other litigious issues may arise. These may involve foreign elements, such as assets or examinable corporate officers in another state. Also while a foreign insolvency administration is in progress, issues may come before the local court, which must then determine the effect, if any, of the foreign administration upon whether it can and will hear them.

Second, recognition and enforcement[81] of foreign judgments raise questions concerning the court that issued the judgment, the type of judgment and the effect of the judgment. Approaches to this issue that are not integrated with the approach to jurisdiction and the applicable law are incomplete. A comprehensive multi-state insolvency system should link the exercise of jurisdiction with its recognition and enforcement and address the applicable law in the process.

Third, having determined that it will hear a matter, a court may then have to decide upon the law to apply. In a common law system such as Australia or

---

77   *Re Blithman* (1866) LR 2 Eq 23. Also see Smart, P. StJ., *Cross-Border Insolvency* (2nd ed) (1998, Butterworths, London) at 140, 144-6.

78   *Re Alfred Shaw and Co Ltd* (1897) 8 QLJ 93.

79   Nygh and Davies, above note 74 at 6-7; McLean, D. and Beevers, K., *Morris: The Conflict of Laws* (6th ed) (2005, Sweet & Maxwell, London) at [1–008]; Scoles, E.F. *et al.*, *Conflict of Laws* (3rd ed) (2000, West Publishing, St Paul) at 3.

80   The commencement of the process for a reorganization may be less likely to involve a court. For example, the voluntary administration process in Australia may be commenced by resolution of the debtor company's board of directors. Thus jurisdiction becomes more a matter of which companies (e.g. locally incorporated companies only or foreign registered or unregistered companies as well) may be subject to the collective administration procedure.

81   The specific term 'recognition' is used to refer to the conclusive or *res judicata* effect of a judgment. 'Enforcement' refers to the execution of a judgment – the defendant's compliance with its terms: Hartley, T.C., 'The recognition of foreign judgments in England under the Jurisdiction and Judgments Convention', in Lipstein, K. (ed.), *Harmonisation of Private International Law by the EEC* (1978, Institute of Advanced Legal Studies, University of London, London) at 105.

England, choice of law issues only arise if the parties invoke them. They are optional in the sense that the law of the forum will apply unless one or more parties seek to invoke foreign law. This will naturally only occur where it is to that party's advantage to apply the foreign law.[82] The approaches to choice-of-law have been classified into three general categories: the substantive law approach, the unilateral approach and the multilateral approach.[83]

The substantive law approach seeks 'the creation of rules of decision that directly govern multi-state transactions'.[84] Such a substantive or 'super law' approach to the problem of multi-state corporate insolvency would appear to be illusory given the diversity of states' insolvency laws and the way in which insolvency laws are intricately interwoven with so many other areas of local law and legal culture. They also involve more than balancing the interests of the immediate private parties of the debtor and petitioning creditor and include the collective body of creditors as well as matters of public interest.[85]

The unilateral approach determines 'the personal and territorial reach'[86] of the potentially applicable local municipal law. Reliance upon such an approach, which adopts an inherently parochial stance, ignores the challenges that globalisation presents to laws affecting a state's participation in international trade and commerce.

The multilateral approach provides a choice-of-law rule that selects a legal system to apply to the transaction and this system then determines the dispute. This requires a court first to characterise the issue before the court; next to select the rule of conflict of laws which lays down a connecting factor for the issue in question; and finally to identify the system of law which is tied by the relevant connecting factor to the issue as characterised.[87] Given the multidimensional aspects to legal problems that arise in an insolvency with foreign elements, an advantage of this approach is that it allows more flexibility in arriving at a suitable solution.

---

82   Under English and Australian civil procedure, parties are required to plead and prove foreign law. Where foreign law is not proved, the courts have presumed it to be the same as the law of the forum: *Regie National des Usines Renault SA v Zhang* (2002) 210 CLR 491. Thus 'the rules of choice of law, that a certain issue is to be governed by a specified foreign law ... apply only if one or other of the parties chooses to raise the point in the pleadings'. McLean and Beevers, above note 79 at [1–015].

83   See Juenger, F.K., *Choice of Law and Multistate Justice* (1993, Martinus Nijhoff, Dordrecht) at 45.

84   Ibid., at 45.

85   See Keay, A., 'Balancing Interests in Bankruptcy Law' (2001) 30(1) *Common Law World Review* 206.

86   Juenger, above note 83 at 45.

87   *Macmillan Inc v Bishopsgate Investment Trust plc* [1996] 1 WLR 387 (CA) (per Staughton LJ) at 391-2.

Multi-State Insolvency Law Theories

The analysis of multi-state insolvency issues within insolvency law scholarship has traditionally been undertaken using the two theoretical extremes of universalism and territoriality.[88] These terms are sometimes used interchangeably with the terms, unity and plurality, however the distinct (though connected) issues require separation.[89] 'Unity' and 'plurality' relate to jurisdiction and the number of courts which have jurisdiction to open insolvency proceedings over a debtor. 'Universalism' and 'territoriality' relate to the multi-state effects[90] of the insolvency proceedings.[91]

Under the principle of 'unity', there is one set of insolvency proceedings in respect of the one debtor, while 'plurality' has more than one set of proceedings in progress concurrently in different states. 'Universalism' refers to the extraterritorial effect of one set of proceedings in every other jurisdiction, while 'territoriality' refers to the limitation of the effects of a set of proceedings to its place of origin.[92]

Territoriality

Territoriality addresses choice of forum by permitting a court to exercise jurisdiction over any debtor that satisfies local insolvency law requirements. Choice of law follows the forum, in that the law of the forum applies to all aspects of the insolvency.[93] The strictly territorial approach claims no extraterritorial reach to a local insolvency order. Thus each state which accords itself jurisdiction over a debtor has authority to administer the debtor's estate within its jurisdiction. However, there are few states that adhere to the strict territorial approach. Even those which refuse to recognize a foreign adjudication will nevertheless often accord their own insolvency orders extraterritorial effect by claiming foreign property as part of a local administration.[94] The territorial approach also permits no

---

88   See Omar, P., 'The Landscape of International Insolvency Law' (2002) 11 *International Insolvency Review* 173.

89   See Fletcher, I.F., 'Future developments' (1991) 3 *Journal of International Banking Law* 89 at 92.

90   'Multi-state effects' encompasses in general terms both recognition and enforcement of foreign orders.

91   See Kayser, N., 'A Study of the European Convention on Insolvency Proceedings' (1998) 7 *International Insolvency Review* 95 at 100.

92   See Fletcher, I.F., *The Law of Insolvency* (3rd ed) (2002, Sweet & Maxwell, London) at 684-5.

93   Choice of forum is therefore likely to be outcome-determinative because insolvency laws differ between states: Westbrook, J.L., 'Theory and Pragmatism in Global Insolvencies: Choice of Forum and Choice of Law' (1991) 65 *American Bankruptcy Law Journal* 457 at 471.

94   See Trautman, D.T. et al., 'Four Models for International Insolvency' (1993) 41 *The American Journal of Comparative Law* 573 at 577. Nevertheless, in the absence of

local recognition of foreign orders or claims.[95] Thus there may be as many administrations or proceedings as there are states with the authority and power to exercise insolvency jurisdiction over the debtor.

Territoriality derives from the doctrine of state sovereignty[96] – the notion that the authority of one state, including its insolvency laws and proceedings, should be confined to the territory of that state.[97] To the extent that an insolvency order is characterized as a creditors' remedy, there is a territorial limitation of any such order. Confiscation or expropriation has traditionally been considered a sovereign state act without extraterritorial effect.[98] In describing arguments in favour of territoriality of liquidation adjudications, Story referred to the relationship between the doctrine of sovereignty and the notion of comity, and that comity should not impair the remedies or lessen the securities of a state's own residents.[99]

A unilateral approach is adopted in determining the personal and territorial reach of local laws, which reach is limited to the local law area. Therefore proceedings in one state do not affect creditors or assets in another:

> The opening, the conduct and the closing of [an insolvency] proceeding depend upon, and are intimately interwoven with, a judicial proceeding. The effects of such sovereign acts, however, do not reach further than the sovereign power from which they emanate. In other words, their effects are limited to the territory of the State, the court or administrative

---

treaties or conventions, these claims rely on recognition from the foreign states for enforcement over foreign assets: LoPucki, L.M., 'The Case for Cooperative Territoriality in International Bankruptcy' (2000) 98 *Michigan Law Review* 2216 at 2218.

95   A past example was the 1922 insolvency law in Japan: Bankruptcy Law 1922 (Law 71 of 1922), Article 3 (Principle of Territoriality) cited in Takeuchi, K., 'Treatment of International Insolvency Issues in Japan', Chapter 5 in Leonard, E.B. and Besant, J.W. (eds), *Current Issues in Cross-Border Insolvency and Reorganizations* (1994, Graham and Trotman and International Bar Association, London) at 73 in note 22. For a discussion of Japan's ongoing substantive preference for territoriality under the new Japanese bankruptcy law, see Kipnis, above note 56 in note 37.

96   See Robertson, R.N., 'Enforcement and Other Problems in International Insolvencies' in *The Meredith Lectures* (1985, McGill University, Montreal) at 267.

97   See Glosband, D.M. and Katucki, C.T., 'Claims and Priorities in Ancillary Proceedings under section 304' (1991) 17 *Brooklyn Journal of International Law* 477 at 480.

98   Dalhuisen, above note 31 in Volume 1, Part III, at §2.03[3] and §2.03[1] in note 1.

99   See Story, J., *Commentaries on the Conflict of Laws* (1883) at §414. Another argument (at §412) in favour of territoriality was that an insolvency sequestration was a statutory not a voluntary assignment.

> authority of which has opened, conducted or terminated the proceedings.[100]

Differences between the approach of states to insolvency regulation and to its underlying concepts[101] as well as the need to preserve the integrity of the local insolvency law system[102] are cited in favour of a territorial approach.[103] It permits a state to give effect to its policies on distributional priority to the maximum extent of its sovereignty.[104]

While territoriality is promoted because of the simplicity, effectiveness and certainty in having separate local proceedings,[105] it is also argued that this plurality is inefficient and increases costs to the parties and the courts.[106] A significant cost for creditors may be the need to file, perhaps to re-litigate, a claim in each state.[107] On the other hand, territoriality may arguably contain costs through courts dealing only with domestic assets and applying domestic laws.[108] Some commentators assert that it promotes predictability,[109] however others argue to the contrary, contending a territorial regime adds to the risk and thus the cost of international transactions.[110]

An overriding concern for local creditors (and arguably the protection of the state's economy in general) underpins this territorial theory.[111] Territoriality allows local creditors to prove locally and have their claims dealt with under familiar local

---

100 See Drobnig, U., 'Cross-Border Insolvency: General Problems' (1993) 19 *Forum Internationale* 9 at 12.

101 Dalhuisen, above note 31 in Volume 1, Part III, at §2.03[3].

102 Thus local laws and policies regarding the recognition, treatment and prioritisation of claims are protected: Glosband and Katucki, above note 97 at 480; Westbrook, J.L., 'Global insolvencies in a world of nation states', in Clarke, A. (ed.) *Current Issues in Insolvency Law* (1991, Stevens and Co, London) at 28-29.

103 Yet a debtor may then be faced with inconsistent results in the multiple proceedings as a result of these differences: Dalhuisen, above note 31 in Volume 1, Part III, at §1.01.

104 See LoPucki, L.M., 'Cooperation in International Bankruptcy: A Post-Universalist Approach' (1999) 84 *Cornell Law Review* 696 at 760; Bang-Pedersen, U.R., 'Asset Distribution in Transnational Insolvencies: Combining Predictability and Protection of Local Interests' (1999) 73 *American Bankruptcy Law Journal* 385.

105 Dalhuisen, above note 31 in Volume 1, Part III, at §2.03[3]. Its simplicity may save costs: Westbrook, J.L., 'Choice of Avoidance Law in Global Insolvencies' (1991) 17 *Brooklyn Journal of International Law* 499 at 514.

106 Glosband and Katucki, above note 97 at 481.

107 LoPucki, above note 104 at 761.

108 Kipnis, above note 56 at 19–23.

109 Glosband and Katucki, above note 97 at 480; LoPucki, above note 104 at 760.

110 See Panuska, T.A., 'The Chaos of International Insolvency – Achieving Reciprocal Universality under section 304 or MIICA' (1993) 6 *The Transnational Lawyer* 373 at 383; Westbrook, above note 93 at 29.

111 Thus foreign claims may not be recognized: Dalhuisen, above note 31 in Volume 1, Part III, at §2.03[3] and §2.03[1] in note 10.

insolvency law.[112] Nevertheless critics refer to the generally accepted insolvency principle of equality of creditors – both local and foreign – and so reject the theory as contravening this equality and promoting the race of the swiftest. The potential exists for unfair or uneven treatment of creditors[113] depending upon their knowledge, resources and ability.[114] As a local insolvency order does not reach foreign property,[115] the debtor might transfer property to a foreign state to the disadvantage of local creditors.[116]

While the territorial approach to multi-state insolvency issues avoids the complications inherent in any form of international cooperation,[117] it is arguably inconsistent with the general trend towards facilitating multi-state transactions.[118]

Universalism

Universalism involves two aspects. First, the 'active' aspect means that an insolvency proceeding opened in the insolvent debtor's domicile, place of incorporation or seat claims to comprise all the assets of the debtor, including those located in other states. Second, the 'passive' aspect means that if an insolvency proceeding is opened abroad in the insolvent debtor's domicile, place of incorporation or seat, it will be given full local effect in each state that has adopted universalism.[119]

---

112 Dalhuisen, above note 31 in Volume 1, Part III, at §2.03[3]. For example it ensures protection for local rules of priority. There are also benefits for creditors in litigating in a closer and more convenient forum: Kipnis, above note 56 at 19–23.

113 'Claims in one jurisdiction may receive a greater distribution because of the fortuitous presence of more assets within that jurisdiction': Glosband and Katucki, above note 97 at 481.

114 See Huber, U., 'Creditor Equality in Transnational Bankruptcies: The United States Position' (1986) 19 *Vanderbilt International Law Journal* 741 at 745; Westbrook, above note 102 at 28-9; Gross, M., 'Foreign Creditor Rights' (1991) 12 *University of Pennsylvania Journal of International Business Law* 125 at 129.

115 This property may itself be the subject of foreign attachment: Huber, above note 114 at 745. Also see Knecht, M.E., 'The 'Drapery of Illusion' of section 304' (1992) 13 *University of Pennsylvania Journal of International Business Law* 287 at 289.

116 If the local creditors wish to attach foreign property, they must go to a foreign court to do so: Knecht, above note 115 at 289-290; Glosband and Katucki, above note 97 at 481; Honsberger, J.D., 'Conflict of Laws and the Bankruptcy Reform Act of 1978' (1980) 30 *Case Western Reserve Law Review* 631 at 635.

117 Westbrook, above note 105 at 514.

118 See Harding, S.K., 'Re Sefel Geophysical Ltd' (1989) 12 *Dalhousie Law Journal* 412 at 439. However, there is support for the notion of territoriality in the context of bank insolvency: Baxter Jnr, T.C. et al., 'Two Cheers for Territoriality: An Essay on International Bank Insolvency Law' (2004) 78 *American Bankruptcy Law Journal* 57.

119 Drobnig, above note 100 at 13. See Blom-Cooper, L.J., *Bankruptcy in Private International Law* (1954, Eastern Press, London) at 14: 'A single adjudication depends for its efficacy upon acceptance of that adjudication by foreign countries, in

Choice of forum under the universal approach is based on an individual debtor's country of domicile, or in the case of a company, its place of incorporation or seat. The doctrine accepts the universal extraterritorial effect of an insolvency adjudication made in such a forum. The law of the forum then governs the insolvency administration, including its foreign effects.[120] As with territoriality, choice of forum is therefore likely to be outcome – determinative because of the differences in states' insolvency laws.[121]

Universalism has been justified on a number of bases generally linked to different analyses of a liquidation adjudication. To the extent that it is characterized as a 'general assignment' in favour of creditors, it is argued that because title to all assets vests in one entity, the law of the state in which the entity is situated should govern everything.[122] This reflects a multilateral approach to choice of the applicable law. A problem with basing the theory on this characterisation is that not all states purport to make such an assignment upon insolvency, or do so for individual debtors only and not for corporations.

A 'judgment' approach emphasizes the declaratory nature of the liquidation order.[123] Thus its effect as far as multi-state issues is concerned is more a matter of the recognition and enforcement of foreign judgments. Judgments may be characteriszed as judgments *in personam,*[124] judgments *in rem*[125] or a third category which affects the debtor's status and dealings with third parties as well as administration of the debtor's property.[126] A sequestration (bankruptcy) order has been described as a judgment which affects the status of the individual debtor and,

---

order to allow the appointed trustee ... to collect all the assets, thereby bringing about an equal distribution amongst all the creditors'.

120   This choice of law of the forum is an implicit assumption of universalism: Westbrook, above note 102 at 29.

121   Westbrook, above note 93 at 471.

122   Harding, above note 118 at 419. The emphasis in this approach to insolvency is on the transfer of property: Robertson, above note 96 at 267.

123   Harding, above note 118 at 418.

124   Judgments 'which impose a personal obligation on the debtor, such as judgments for damages for breach of contract or in tort or decrees for specific performance or an injunction': Nygh and Davies, above note 74 at [9.2].

125   That is either a judgment (i) which affects the status of a person or corporation or (ii) which affects or creates an interest in property: Nygh and Davies, above note 74 at [9.2]. However, Nygh and Davies include personal bankruptcy as an action *in rem*. Also, there is American authority that bankruptcy is an action *in rem*. 'The nature of the jurisdiction is *in rem*: The *res*, the estate of the debtor created by the commencement of the bankruptcy [liquidation] or reorganization case is viewed as a single entity to be dealt with in a single proceeding': Judge Buschman, cited by Hirst J in *Felixstowe Dock and Railway Co v US Lines Inc* [1989] QB 360 at 368.

126   Sykes and Pryles, above note 8 at 21 do not include bankruptcy or winding up of companies as actions *in rem* - rather as proceedings which must be distinguished from actions *in personam* and which are subject of special jurisdictional rules.

if declared in the state whose laws govern the debtor's status, is universally effective.[127]

Universalism has also been defended on the basis of the unity of the debtor's estate;[128] the unity of the body of creditors and the universal effect of the incapacity of the debtor.[129] The concept of 'unity' in insolvency:

> basically would imply the unity of administration, unity of procedure, unity of distribution of the assets and proceeds and unity of the applicable law, which would principally mean the application of the law of the country where the insolvency proceedings were opened.[130]

Certainly if insolvency is to be effective as a rehabilitative procedure, any discharge of debts should be recognized universally as a relief from all creditors' claims (local and foreign).[131]

As occurs with territoriality, arguments are made in favour of universalism[132] on the basis of simplicity, economy (for example, greater efficiency in judicial resources)[133] and speed.[134] Bebchuk and Guzman[135] have elaborated on these efficiency arguments. Guzman analysed the position of various

---

127　See Nadelmann, K.H., 'The Recognition of American Arrangements Abroad' (1942) 90 *University of Pennsylvania Law Review* 780 at 791; Sykes and Pryles, above note 8 at 734.

128　'In the French doctrine, another justification for the 'unity and universality' model seems to have been that it respects the fundamental principle of *unicité du patrimoine*. This means that a person can only have one patrimony, which cannot be divided. However this seems to be irrelevant nowadays': Kayser, above note 91 at 103, citing Trochu, M., *Conflits de lois et conflits de jurisdictions en matière de faillite* (1967, Sirey, Paris) at 19.

129　These three concepts have derived from Continental Europe. See Dalhuisen, above note 31 in Volume 1, Part III, at §2.03[3]. An argument put in favour of universalism is that 'the just and equal distribution of all the funds of that class of debtor becomes the common concern of the whole commercial world': Story, above note 99 at §405.

130　See Hanisch, H., 'Universality' versus Secondary Bankruptcy: A European Debate' (1993) 2 *International Insolvency Review* 151 at 153.

131　For a preliminary discussion on recognition of a foreign discharge, see Westbrook, J.L., 'Chapter 15 and Discharge' (2005) 13(2) *American Bankruptcy Institute Law Review* 503. Also see Grossman, A., 'Conflict of Laws in the Discharge of Debts in Bankruptcy' (1996) 5 *International Insolvency Review* 1.

132　Arguments in favour of universalism are longstanding. See Lowell, J., 'Conflict of Laws as applied to Assignments for Creditors' (1888) 1 *Harvard Law Review* 259.

133　See Bigelow, M., 'Public Policy Concerns Prevent Application of Comity to Foreign Bankruptcy Proceedings that Discriminate against Tax Obligations owed to the United States Government' (1991) 24 *Vanderbilt Journal of Transnational Law* 571 at 579.

134　Dalhuisen, above note 31 in Volume 1, Part III, at §2.03[3].

135　See Bebchuk, L.A. and Guzman, A.T., 'An Economic Analysis of Transnational Bankruptcies' (1999) 42 *Journal of Law and Economics* 775.

classes of creditor[136] under universalism and territoriality, concluding that the efficiency arguments for universalism remain strong.[137] However, Westbrook is cautious about overstating the efficiency arguments.[138]

In theory it would eliminate forum shopping problems.[139] However, uncertainty arises from the different bases for the proper exclusive forum.[140] This is particularly the case with companies, given differences between common law and civil law systems in allocating a company's domicile or seat.[141] For universalism to operate, it is important that the 'home state'[142] can be identified and that a debtor is not able to change its home state in an opportunistic manner.[143] Amongst other things, the laws of this state will determine creditor priorities, validity of pre-insolvency transfers and adjudicate creditor claims.[144] In response, it is argued that the identity of the home state will be obvious in most cases.[145]

The active aspect of universalism requires a state to abandon its right to control local assets[146] and to promote 'worldwide equity' at the potential expense of its own local creditors. The theory therefore lacks support in practice because of the potential for local creditors to receive particular advantages under the local law.[147] They may suffer geographical and linguistic inconvenience through proving in another forum or hardship caused by the application of unfamiliar insolvency laws. Also parties' reasonable expectations may not be met insofar as they may have contracted on the basis of local priority rules and then find that a foreign law

---

136 Guzman uses the terms 'adjusting' and 'non-adjusting' creditors borrowed from Bebchuk, L.A. and Fried, J.M., 'The Uneasy Case for the Priority of Secured Claims in Bankruptcy' (1996) 105 *Yale Law Journal* 857.

137 See Guzman, A.T., 'International Bankruptcy: In Defense of Universalism' (2000) 98 *Michigan Law Review* 2177.

138 See Westbrook, J.L., 'A Global Solution to Multinational Default' (2000) 98 *Michigan Law Review* 2276 at 2326.

139 Knecht, above note 115 at 291.

140 Also see Anton, above note 30 at 107.

141 Fletcher, above note 49 at 172.

142 'Home state' is traditionally the state that comprises an individual debtor's domicile or a corporate debtor's place of incorporation or 'seat'.

143 LoPucki, above note 94 at 2234–2237.

144 Ibid., at 2224–2225.

145 Guzman, above note 137 at 2207; Rasmussen, above note 13 at 12; Westbrook, above note 105 at 529. In an era of globalisation, however, multi-state business is increasingly complex: LoPucki, above note 94 at 2227. Also see Tung, F., 'Is International Bankruptcy Possible?' (2001) 23 *Michigan Journal of International Law* 31 at 71–2, 76 and 98 on problems with identification of the 'home state'.

146 See Nadelmann, K.H., 'The National Bankruptcy Act and the Conflict of Laws' (1946) 59 *Harvard Law Review* 1025.

147 Knecht, above note 115 at 291; Westbrook, above note 93 at 471.

applies.[148] Tung has questioned universalism from the perspective of its political plausibility.[149]

Its passive aspect likewise causes difficulty, as universalism is dependent upon foreign cooperation for the effectiveness of its claim to extraterritorial application of the forum's insolvency law.[150] This may be seen as violating the foreign state's sovereignty,[151] particularly as insolvency laws are often viewed as an extension of state policy.[152] Also an insolvency officeholder must in the end rely upon the sanctions of criminal law, which are inherently territorial in their application.[153]

Thus both theoretical extremes, territoriality and universalism, have been rejected in practice – with most jurisdictions adopting a stance on choice of forum and recognition and enforcement which combines elements of both theories, as shown by the following table.

Table 2.1   The Universalism-Territoriality Paradigm

Exercise of Jurisdiction → Recognition and Enforcement of Principal Administration↓	**Unity**	**Plurality**
Universal	*Universalism* *Modified Universalism*	*Secondary Insolvency*
Territorial	[Administration with no multi-state elements]	*Cooperative Territoriality* *Territoriality*

Source: Own Design.

---

148   Glosband and Katucki, above note 97; Anton, above note 30 at 112.
149   Tung, above note 145. He largely bases his argument on the application of elementary game theory and international relations theory.
150   Knecht, above note 115 at 291.
151   Huber, above note 114 at 744; Gaa, T.M., 'Harmonization of Bankruptcy Law and Practice: Is it Necessary? Is it Possible?' (1993) 27(4) *The International Lawyer* 881 at 887.
152   See Castel, J.G., *Canadian Conflict of Laws* (2nd ed) (1986, Butterworths, Toronto) at 520. It may also violate local social policy to import home state social policy: Tung, F., 'Fear of Commitment in International Bankruptcy' (2001) 33 *George Washington International Law Review* 555 at 573.
153   Anton, above note 30 at 122–123.

Qualified Territoriality and Universalism

Scholars have proposed various models that modify these theoretical extremes, some of which can be found in current state or convention practice.[154] The qualifications often involve concurrent proceedings, which recognize home state insolvency administrations to greater or lesser degree. In a multi-state insolvency, judicial orders are typically required in more than one state in order to control the debtor's assets. These concurrent proceedings may take the form of ordinary civil litigation,[155] enforcement of foreign judgments obtained during the principal administration,[156] specific aid and assistance for a foreign principal administration or separate insolvency administrations.

Concurrent insolvency administrations often comprise a liquidation adjudication or a reorganization that purports to be the 'main' administration[157] and similar adjudications in other jurisdictions with lesser claims to significance in the debtor's affairs. These 'non-main' administrations typically take one of two forms. First, proceedings may be primarily to aid the 'main' administration and not amount to a sequestration of the debtor's assets. For example, they involve a local moratorium on creditor action and assistance for the foreign administrator in realising local assets. Second, local administrations may be instituted, albeit ones which recognize the 'main' proceeding and cooperate to greater or lesser extent with it. Various terms are used for these forms of 'non-main' administrations. In American terminology, the former are known as 'ancillary proceedings' and the latter are 'parallel proceedings'.[158] English and Australian case law[159] tends instead to use the term 'ancillary' for local non-domiciliary (non-main) administrations. Insolvency-related proceedings brought to assist a foreign administration, not being a local bankruptcy or liquidation, do not have an established nomenclature.

The term 'ancillary administration' is used in this chapter for a local administration that recognizes and collaborates with a concurrent 'principal administration'. A principal administration is ordered in the debtor's 'home state'. The term 'auxiliary proceedings' refers to those which fall short of a local

---

154   For support for a traditional approach, see Perkins, L., 'A Defense of Pure Universalism in Cross-Border Corporate Insolvencies' (2000) 32 *Journal of International Law and Politics* 787.

155   This is often between the administrator of the debtor's estate and various creditors or third parties holding property allegedly part of the debtor's estate.

156   'Principal administration' means an insolvency administration in the debtor's home state, which may be either in a foreign or the local jurisdiction.

157   There may be more than one administration which is claimed by each officeholder to be the debtor's home state proceeding.

158   American Law Institute, Transnational Insolvency Project, cited in Westbrook, above note 138 at 2300.

159   See *Re BCCI (No 10)* [1997] 2 WLR 172 and English and Australian cases cited therein.

insolvency administration but the purpose of which is nevertheless to assist the 'principal administration'.[160]

Modified universalism accepts the central premise of universalism that there should be a single administration which deals with assets on a worldwide basis. This is modified by reserving to the local forum the discretion 'to evaluate the fairness of the [foreign home state] procedures and to protect the interests of the local creditors'.[161] In the exercise of the discretion, matters to be considered include that compliance will not alter the entitlement of parties and that it will not offend the forum's public policy.[162] It is undertaken when a foreign administration is claimed as the home state administration such that local proceedings should be stayed and all property and claims dealt with by the foreign office holder. Local proceedings are therefore merely auxiliary proceedings. Where the discretion is exercised against assisting the foreign home state administration, then a local insolvency administration may be instituted. Local insolvency law will therefore apply.[163]

Cooperative territoriality is a system in which each state administers the assets, over which it has jurisdiction,[164] as a separate estate, distributing the assets under local insolvency law. None of the proceedings are principal, ancillary or auxiliary, rather each constitutes a separate administration.[165] The system however acknowledges the multi-state dimension by providing for cooperation in the administration of the separate estates. LoPucki suggests cooperation in the form of procedures to reduce the burden of filing in multiple jurisdictions; the sharing of

---

160 Often, these are brought under Insolvency Act 1986 (UK), section 426; Bankruptcy Act 1966 (Cth), section 29 and Corporations Act 2001 (Cth), section 581 (Australia). The English provision refers to courts that 'assist' each other and the Australian provisions refer to courts that act 'in aid of and auxiliary to' each other.

161 Westbrook cites the former United States Bankruptcy Code section 304 as the leading example of this approach: Westbrook, above note 105. The now-repealed section 304 provided for a local proceeding which aided the court in the foreign main administration. However, local assistance was not automatic and depended on the American court's assessment of what would best assure an economical and expeditious administration of the estate. Their assessment was to be guided by six factors ranging from comity through to the protection of American creditors against prejudice and inconvenience in the processing of their claims in the foreign proceedings: Bankruptcy Code, section 304(c).

162 LoPucki, above note 94 at 2221.

163 See the Australian-United States case, *Interpool Ltd v Certain Freights of M/V Venture Star* 102 Bankr 373 (DNJ 1988) 878.

164 LoPucki argues that such jurisdiction depends upon having de facto power over the assets, including through multi-state agreement with respect to intangibles. That is, it would only include property that the state had sovereign power to marshal without the assistance of other states: LoPucki, above note 104 at 743.

165 Ibid., at 742.

information regarding distributions; the joint sale of assets; and the seizure and return of assets subject to avoidance action.[166]

He argues that this system provides predictability for lenders, subject to their knowing the location of assets and the distribution priorities in those states.[167] He also argues that its implementation would require minimal change in current practice.[168] Its disadvantages include that creditors may need to file and prosecute claims in all administrations; the possibility of strategic removal of assets;[169] and the need for the protection of foreign involuntary creditors such as tort claimants against discrimination.[170]

Secondary Bankruptcy[171] or to use the broader term, *Secondary Insolvency*,[172] is currently practised in various forms. Under some municipal laws, it is mandated in statute[173] and judge-made law[174] and it also appears in various multilateral conventions and international solutions.[175] One such solution, the UNCITRAL Model Law on Cross-Border Insolvency is elaborated upon below. Its approach to allocating jurisdiction develops concepts from various European conventions, in particular relying on a 'centre of main interests' to identify the 'home state' rather than the insolvent debtor's domicile, place of incorporation or seat as under universalism. Until recently, scholars have typically described the phenomenon rather than proposed it as a theory and placed it within the theoretical framework of universalism and territoriality.[176]

In a 'secondary insolvency' system, insolvency administrations proceed concurrently in each state in which a debtor has a substantial presence.[177] In common with modified universalism, it recognizes a home state 'main'

---

166   Ibid., at 750.
167   Ibid., at 751.
168   Ibid., at 753.
169   The strategic removal of assets could be addressed through treaties on repatriation of assets or, in the case of large creditors, through monitored debtor covenants: Ibid., at 758.
170   Ibid., at 753-759 on problems with cooperative territoriality and ways of addressing them. Kipnis supports cooperative territoriality while suggesting methods of dealing with the claims process and fraudulent asset transfers: Kipnis, above note 56.
171   Ibid., at 732.
172   See Anderson, K., 'The Cross-Border Insolvency Paradigm: A Defense of the Modified Universal Approach Considering the Japanese Experience' (2000) 21 *University of Pennsylvania Journal of International Economic Law* 679 at 692.
173   Australia: Corporations Act 2001 (Cth), section 601CL.
174   England: *Re BCCI (No 10)* [1997] 2 WLR 172.
175   Council of Europe Bankruptcy Convention; European Insolvency Regulation; UNCITRAL Model Law on Cross Border Insolvency.
176   See Hanisch, H., 'Survey over some laws on cross-border effects of foreign insolvency procedures on the European continent', Chapter 11 in Fletcher, above note 37 at 159; Westbrook, above note 105 at 516, although see Westbrook, above note 138; Anderson, above note 172 at 172.
177   LoPucki, above note 104 at 732.

administration with which other states cooperate. However, it differs in that the local proceedings are 'ancillary administrations' rather than 'auxiliary proceedings'. Local assets are realised and distributed to locally secured and priority claims.[178] Any remaining assets are then remitted to the primary administration for distribution.[179]

Its advantage according to LoPucki is that it gives effect to local public policy, including those reflected in the distribution rankings. Its main disadvantage is that the exception for the local secured and priority creditors is likely to exhaust the local assets. Even if there are surplus local assets, there is likely to be a delay between the opening of the local bankruptcy administration and the availability of the assets for distribution in the principal administration.[180]

UNCITRAL Model Law on Cross-Border Insolvency

Perhaps the greatest hope for progress in terms of multilateral cooperation in multi-state insolvencies lies with the UNCITRAL Model Law on Cross-Border Insolvency,[181] which takes a procedural approach to the many substantive problems in multi-state insolvencies.[182] As such, it does not address the range of private international law issues in a multi-state problem – that of choice of forum; recognition and enforcement and choice of law. Instead, it provides for judicial cooperation between states as well as rights of access for foreign insolvency administrators and recognition of foreign insolvency proceedings by participating states.

According to its Preamble, the Model Law mechanisms are to promote certain listed objectives, which include greater legal certainty for trade and investment; and fair and efficient administration of cross-border insolvencies that protects the interests of all interested persons. As such, it contains features essential to the regulation of multi-state insolvency.

---

178 See Hanisch, H., 'Universality' versus Secondary Bankruptcy: A European Debate' (1993) 2 *International Insolvency Review* 151 at 157; Anderson, above note 172 at 693.

179 See Londot, J.K., 'Handling Priority Rules Conflicts in International Bankruptcy: Assessing the International Bar Association's Concordat' (1996) 13 *Bankruptcy Developments Journal* 163 at 173.

180 LoPucki, above note 104 at 734–736.

181 The Model Law is published in Official Records of the General Assembly, Fifty-second Session, Supplement No 17 (A/52/17, annex I) (UNCITRAL Yearbook, Volume XXVIII: 1997, Part Three).

182 See Cronin, M.T., 'UNCITRAL Model Law on Cross-Border Insolvency: Procedural Approach to a Substantive Problem' (1999) *Journal of Corporation Law* 709 (Spring); Pottow, J., 'Procedural Incrementalism: A Model for International Bankruptcy' (2005) 45(4) *Virginia Journal of International Law* 935, available at: <ssrn.com/abstract=646962> (last viewed 31 May 2007).

The United Nations adopted the UNCITRAL Model Law on Cross Border Insolvency in 1997 and recommended that member states adopt it as part of domestic legislation.[183] Since then, the Model Law has been adopted[184] in the British Virgin Islands, Eritrea, Great Britain,[185] Japan, Mexico, New Zealand,[186] Poland, Romania, Serbia and Montenegro, South Africa[187] and the United States of America.[188] Canada has adopted elements of the Model Law although they have not yet been proclaimed into force.[189] Australia has indicated that it will adopt the Model Law as part of its current insolvency law reform activity.[190]

One of the Model Law's most significant contributions is its facilitation for local recognition and enforcement of foreign insolvency administrations. As such, although it is adopted as municipal law, it resembles a multilateral convention. Such conventions have been variously categorized as simple or indirect conventions and double or direct conventions.[191]

A simple or indirect convention is one where states have agreed on recognition and enforcement of judgments resulting from the exercise of

---

183 In addition to the 36 States that are members of UNCITRAL, representatives of 40 observer States and 13 international organizations participated in the deliberations of the Commission and the Working Group. (Guide to the Enactment of the UNCITRAL Model Law on Cross-Border Insolvency, Annex 1 of the Report of the 30th session of UNCITRAL (A/52/17) ['Guide'], paragraph 8).

184 For a useful publication on the domestic legislation adopted in the following jurisdictions, British Virgin Islands; Canada; England; Japan; Mexico; Poland; Romania; Serbia and Montenegro; South Africa and the United States, see Ho, L.C. (ed.), *Cross-Border Insolvency: A Commentary on the UNCITRAL Model Law* (2006, Globe Law and Business, London).

185 Cross-Border Insolvency Regulations 2006 (SI 2006/1030).

186 Insolvency (Cross-Border) Act 2006 (NZ).

187 Cross-Border Insolvency Act (42 of 2000) (SA).

188 Bankruptcy Code, Chapter 15.

189 Statutes of Canada 2005 Chapter 47 amends the Bankruptcy and Insolvency Act 1992 and the Companies' Creditors Arrangement Act 1985. However the amended cross-border insolvency provisions have not yet been proclaimed into force, pending a review of the legislation (and possible amendment) by the Senate Standing Committee: Golick, S. and Wasserman, M.S., 'Canada' in Ho, above note 184 at 37–8.

190 Australian Government Treasury, Corporate Insolvency Reform (2005), available at: <www.treasury.gov.au/documents/1022/PDF/Corporate_Insolvancy_Reform_attachm ent.pdf> (last viewed 31 May 2007).

191 A third kind of convention is the Hague Convention on Choice of Court Agreements of 30 June 2005, prepared by the Hague Conference's Special Commission on Private International Law. It is a mixed convention applicable to civil or commercial matters (excluding, inter alia, 'insolvency, composition and analogous matters') that specifies some agreed grounds of jurisdiction and some prohibited grounds of jurisdiction, but otherwise leaves the question to the law of each member state. See note at: <www.hcch.net/index_en.php?act=conventions.text&cid=98> (last viewed 31 May 2007).

jurisdiction on certain approved grounds. Essentially the rules of jurisdiction provide the conditions governing the recognition and enforcement of foreign judgments and, more specifically, the conditions governing supervision of the jurisdiction of foreign courts.[192] An example in the insolvency context is the European Convention on Certain International Aspects of Bankruptcy (1990) developed by the Council of Europe.[193]

A double or direct convention occurs where the states have agreed on the allocation of jurisdiction in specific matters where a foreign element is involved. Resulting judgments are then recognized and enforced by the other states with minimal grounds[194] for review or challenge.[195] The mandatory rules of jurisdiction and potential automatic recognition and enforcement of any subsequent judgment promote 'clarity, predictability and simplicity' for parties.[196] The EC Regulation on Insolvency Proceedings[197] allocates within contracting states the jurisdiction to open insolvency proceedings that are within its ambit and limits the opening of secondary proceedings to territorial proceedings in those contracting states in which the debtor has assets. As such, the identification of the 'centre of main interests' carries far greater significance under the EC Regulation than it does under the Model Law.

The UNCITRAL Model Law resembles a simple convention in that it determines the foreign insolvency proceedings which will be recognized, based on the exercise of jurisdiction in 'acceptable' circumstances.[198] The effects and relief available following such recognition depend upon whether the foreign proceeding

---

192 See Jenard, P., 'Report on the Convention' in Dashwood, A. et al. (eds), *A Guide to the Civil Jurisdiction and Judgments Convention* (1978, Kluwer, Deventer) at 335.

193 European Convention on Certain International Aspects of Bankruptcy of 5 June 1990 (Istanbul Convention) (1990) ETS No. 136, Appendix III in Fletcher, I.F., *Insolvency in Private International Law* (2nd ed) (2005, Oxford University Press, Oxford).

194 That is subject to the exercise of the doctrine of *forum non conveniens* by the addressed court.

195 Convention on Jurisdiction and the Enforcement of Judgments in Civil and Commercial Matters of 27 September 1968 (Brussels Convention) (1990) 29 *International Legal Materials* 1413. This type was chosen because it was felt that 'within the EEC a convention based on rules of direct jurisdiction as a result of the adoption of common rules of jurisdiction would allow increased harmonization of laws, provide greater certainty, avoid discrimination and facilitate the 'free movement' of judgments ... the ultimate objective'. Jenard, above note 192 at 335.

196 von Mehren, A.T., 'Recognition and Enforcement of Foreign Judgments: A New Approach for the Hague Conference' (1994) 57 *Law and Contemporary Problems* 271 at 283.

197 European Union: Council Regulation (EC) No. 1346/2000 of 29 May 2000 on Insolvency Proceedings, Appendix II in Fletcher, above note 193.

198 As with conventions, there is provision for the exclusion of entities which, for public policy reasons, have specific insolvency procedures such as banks or insurance companies: Model Law, Article 1(2).

is categorized as either (a) a foreign main proceeding or (b) a foreign non-main proceeding.

Insolvency proceedings opened in the state in which the debtor has its 'centre of main interests' are acknowledged as main proceedings.[199] In the absence of proof to the contrary, the centre of a debtor's main interests is presumed to be in the state containing an individual debtor's habitual residence and a corporate debtor's registered office.[200] Insolvency proceedings opened in a state where the debtor has an 'establishment', which has the same definition as in the EC Regulation,[201] are recognized as a foreign non-main proceeding.

Foreign insolvency proceedings opened in a state which does not contain the debtor's centre of main interests or an establishment, are not recognized. The Guide to Enactment specifically acknowledges that there would be no recognition of an insolvency proceeding commenced in a foreign state in which the debtor has assets but no 'establishment'.[202]

The provisions on recognition of a foreign proceeding provide a simple expeditious procedure for local recognition.[203] To halt the 'potential race of the swiftest' to take advantage of local assets, the foreign representative may request the court to grant immediate provisional relief[204] upon the filing of the application, if relief is urgently needed to protect the debtor's assets or the creditors' interests.[205] Recognition of a foreign insolvency proceeding does not import the consequences of the foreign insolvency law into the local system.

It does, however, introduce an immediate and automatic moratorium.[206] The stay does not affect the right to request the commencement of a local insolvency

---

199   Ibid., Article 17(2).

200   Ibid., Article 16(3).

201   Ibid., Article 2(b): 'any place of operations where the debtor carries out a non-transitory economic activity with human means and goods or services'.

202   Guide paragraph 128.

203   Model Law, Article 19. Recognition as a foreign main proceeding is significant in that it provides a rebuttable presumption that the debtor is insolvent for the purposes of commencing local insolvency proceedings.

204   Ibid., Article 19(2). Such interim relief may include: staying local execution proceedings; entrusting the foreign representative (or another person designated by the court) to administer or realise all or part of the debtor's local assets. Unless extended when the recognition is granted, this relief terminates when the application is finally decided upon.

205   Ibid., Article 19: The court may refuse to grant this interim relief if it would interfere with the administration of a foreign main proceeding. This is to foster coordination of proceedings, as does the requirement that the foreign representative advise the court of all foreign proceedings known to him or her.

206   That is a stay on the commencement or continuation of individual actions or individual proceedings concerning the debtor's assets, rights, obligations or liabilities (except to the extent necessary to preserve a claim against the debtor); stay of execution against the debtor's assets; and suspension of the right to transfer, encumber or otherwise dispose of the debtor's assets: ibid., Article 20(3).

proceeding or to file claims in such a proceeding.[207] There may also be exceptions, limitations, modifications or termination in respect of the stay or suspension, in light of local insolvency laws.[208]

Once a foreign proceeding is recognized, either as a main or non-main proceeding, the court may grant relief where necessary to protect the debtor's assets or the creditors' interests. Relief in respect of a foreign non-main proceeding (taking place where a debtor has an establishment) is limited to assets that, according to local laws, should be administered in that proceeding or concerns information required in that proceeding.

When granting or denying relief or in modifying or terminating it, the court is required to satisfy itself that the interests of creditors and other interested persons, including debtors, are adequately protected. Thus local creditor concerns about the 'turnover of assets' to the foreign representative or other designated person may be addressed to the court.

Another important aspect of recognition and enforcement addressed by the Model Law is the facilitation of cooperation between local and foreign courts and representatives. It not only authorises cooperation and direct communication between a local court and foreign courts or foreign representatives[209] but also mandates it.[210] It also expressly permits cooperation and direct communication between identified categories of local representatives and foreign courts or foreign representatives. Thus concurrent proceedings are possible. However, where a foreign main proceeding has been recognized, local insolvency proceedings may only be commenced if the debtor has assets within the jurisdiction.[211]

If local proceedings have already commenced, this does not prevent or terminate the recognition of foreign proceedings. Where there are concurrent foreign and local proceedings for the same debtor, the local court is required to seek cooperation and coordination in accordance with the Model Law.

Nevertheless local proceedings maintain pre-eminence over foreign proceedings.[212] Any relief to be granted to the foreign proceeding must be consistent with the local proceeding. If the foreign proceeding is a main proceeding, the automatic effects pursuant to the Model Law[213] are to be modified and terminated if inconsistent with the local proceeding. Where a local proceeding is pending at the time a foreign proceeding is recognized as a main proceeding, the foreign proceeding does not enjoy the usual automatic effects.

---

207   Ibid., Article 20(4).
208   Ibid., Article 20(2).
209   The insolvency officeholders act under the overall supervision of the relevant courts.
210   Model Law, Article 25: 'the court shall cooperate to the maximum extent possible'.
211   Ibid., Article 28.
212   Guideline to Enactment of the UNCITRAL Model Law on Cross Border Insolvency, paragraph 190. See Model Law, Article 29.
213   Ibid., Article 20.

In summary then, the Model Law addresses jurisdiction only indirectly and the identification of the 'centre of main interests' is significant for the purposes of recognition and enforcement. The main private international law issue that remains unanswered under the Model Law is that of choice of law. This is another significant difference to the EC Regulation that contains 'a miniature code of uniform conflicts rules which are to form an integral part of the Regulation's operations'.[214]

Despite the different approaches to allocating jurisdiction in the EC Regulation;[215] and the UNCITRAL Model Law,[216] they have all used the term 'centre of main interests' to allocate a 'main' administration and have endorsed the concept of secondary insolvency in a multi-state insolvency.

Conclusion

When Thomas Jefferson wrote in 1814 about merchants' lack of attachment to a country, it is unlikely that he could have foreseen the complexities of twenty-first century trade and commerce. Nor could he have foreseen the impact of globalisation and worldwide conglomerates on the ability of a country to regulate merchants with whom they have some contact – especially where such merchants are in fact facing insolvency rather than drawing gains.

Nevertheless, for centuries, the legal systems of trading countries such as England have been adapting their domestic insolvency laws to address defaulting merchants who had connections with more than one state, in case law[217] or statute.[218] However, legal systems have typically done so on an *ad hoc* basis without consideration for a comprehensive integrated approach to multi-state issues.

The branch of municipal law that deals with the resolution of conflicts that arise because of interaction between different legal systems[219] is known as private

---

214 Fletcher, above note 193 at 396.
215 EC Regulation, Article 3(1). It is also significant that the Recital No. 13 states that the 'centre of main interests' should correspond to the place where the debtor conducts the administration of his interests on a regular basis and is therefore ascertainable by third parties. Thus courts have emphasized the importance of creditors' understanding of the debtor's centre of main interests prior to the insolvency proceedings.
216 Model Law, Article 16(3).
217 *Phillips v Hunter* (1795) 2 HBl 402; 126 ER 618.
218 The first English statute on bankruptcy was passed in 1542 (34 and 35 Henry VIII c 4). Specific mention was made of absconding debtors who withdrew into 'a foreign Realm or Country, with the intent to abide and remain there in defraud of creditors'. If the person did not return as commanded, then the debtor was outlawed and the entire debtor's estate ordered to be distributed equally among creditors.
219 Nygh and Davies, above note 74 at 4.

international law.[220] The fundamental questions addressed by private international law provide a useful construct for resolving the issues raised by insolvent merchants who cross borders. However in answering these questions, it is important to consider the essential features of insolvency administrations and their regulation, especially as municipal insolvency laws seek to apply their domestic policy objectives to a multi-state context.

So for example, issues that are highlighted at the cross-roads of private international law and insolvency law include the importance of predictability and transparency of regulation in order to minimise and resolve disputes with the least possible delay and expense. The complex and integrated nature of collective insolvency administrations have practical and legal ramifications where they cross borders. This interconnectedness features not only in the principles within insolvency law that apply to an administration but also to the way in which insolvency law itself is shaped both other laws in their implementation.

The interests to be balanced in an insolvency include those of the debtor, the creditors and the community at large. In a multi-state insolvency, the debtor has connections across borders and yet the creditors themselves may include foreign as well as local entities (and where local creditors themselves are worldwide conglomerates, they perhaps should not qualify for particular protection under domestic insolvency policies). Also the notion of the 'community at large' and its interests loses clarity where a number of legal systems interact – emphasized by the fact that insolvency law is so intimately linked to the commercial, financial and social fabric of a state. Another layer of complexity applicable to balancing these interests is that they may differ depending upon whether the administration is a liquidation or a reorganization (and even during the one proceeding, where they transition from one to the other).

Finally, the interests that might be identifiable before an administration commences may well differ to those once it is underway. For example, the interests of some creditors (such as those of suppliers) may well change between the pre-insolvency stage when the debtor is a going concern to the stage when the debtor is in the process of liquidation of assets. Thus while the 'centre of main interests' of the debtor pre-insolvency may arguably be ascertainable in the majority of cases, the 'centre of main interests' of a global insolvency administration may well be in another state.

This chapter has introduced some of the essential features of insolvency administrations and their regulation before elaborating on the issues that arise where the insolvent debtor has multi-state connections. It also explored the intersection of private international law principles and insolvency law principles in terms of various multi-state insolvency law theories being discussed in the legal literature and a concrete and current example was provided through a brief outline of the UNCITRAL Model Law on Cross-Border Insolvency.

---

220   Also known as conflict of laws.

While private international law has been described as 'a dismal swamp, filled with quaking quagmires',[221] in fact its approach to issues of jurisdiction linked with recognition and enforcement as well as to choice of law provide some useful tools for navigating the complexities of multi-state insolvency. Some useful pointers for future directions in approaching multi-state insolvency regulation can be identified where the private international law questions intersect with insolvency law principles and multi-state insolvency theories.

---

221 See Prosser, D., 'Interstate Publication' (1953) 51 *Michigan Law Review* 959 at 971: 'The realm of the conflict of laws is a dismal swamp, filled with quaking quagmire, and inhabited by learned but eccentric professors who theorise about mysterious matter in a strange and incomprehensible jargon'.

Chapter 3

The Law and Economics of Corporate Insolvency – Some Thoughts

Armin J. Kammel*

Introduction

Corporate insolvency has the inherent problem of large costs of financial distress. As this chapter shows, the reason for the accumulation of these costs can be found in game theoretical actions of creditors who act rational from their individual perspective. However, such rational individual behaviour does not mean that it is to the benefit for the group of creditors as a whole. Therefore, the respective insolvency procedure is crucial on the one hand for debtors to get out of their unfavourable situation as well as on the other hand for creditors who want to be compensated for their loss caused by the debtor's insolvency. The application of the prisoner's dilemma shows that in case of a so-called common pool problem it is difficult to find solutions avoiding such situation. Therefore it is suggested to focus on pro-active measures such as restructuring laws, which might be a way to at least diminish the costs of financial distress.

Any credit or credit extension bears the potential risk that the debtor is not able to repay its debt in due course or that the person or business entity ends up in a financial condition where the assets no longer exceed the liabilities. Therefore, the term 'insolvency' stands for the inability to pay creditors, which itself covers various forms of this inability to pay, such as balance sheet insolvency, cash-flow insolvency (or financial distress), economic failure (or economic distress), liquidation, reorganization or bankruptcy.

However, insolvency *per se* is not necessarily negative, since economic growth in general requires certain non-profitable activities to be phased out in order to spare up room for new ones and therefore, failing projects and the replacement of non-profitable firms has to be seen as a fundamental element of economic growth.[1] This '*constructive destruction*' can be seen as a reallocation of

*   This chapter's findings, interpretations and conclusions are entirely those of the author and do not necessarily represent the views of Austrian Association of Investment Fund Management Companies (VOEIG).

1   The famous economist Joseph Alois Schumpeter stressed in this regard the term 'constructive destruction'. For further information about Schumpeter on innovations and profit, see Kurz, H.D., 'Schumpeter on Innovation and Profits – The Classical Heritage'

investments that can have various peculiarities.[2] In modern economies a significant number of firms are financed by debt and therefore it is not surprising that insolvencies play an inevitable role in the restructuring process of any economy.[3] In this light, insolvency leads to formal bankruptcy when legal procedures are employed to liquidate the insolvent firm's assets in order to pay stakeholders fully or partially according to a priority established in law or contracts.[4]

However, insolvency law generally enables creditors the power to have the assets of a defaulting debtor seized and sold to cover an unpaid debt. Such remedies are fundamental to nowadays market economy[5] and without such powers for creditors, any lending possibility become irrational, since no bank or other creditors would grant a credit to any legal or private person in such a case. When focussing on corporate insolvency law, Mokal argues that it can be seen as dealing with a peculiar set of social, commercial, and legal circumstances which arise when a company becomes insolvent.[6] In this regard, it is claimed that core principles underlying corporate insolvency law are consistent.[7] However, any discussion about insolvency has to a certain extent deal with the issues of

---

(2006) University of Graz, available at: <www.uni-graz.at/vwlwww/wiwise/Kz-Schumpeter6.pdf> (last viewed 31 May 2007).

2   Reallocation of investments can occur within conglomerates, within various sectors of an economy, on a national as well as international level and basically means that one firm disinvests while another one invests in new projects.

3   In this regard, reference may be made to Krueger, A.O., *A New Approach to Sovereign Debt Restructuring* (2002, International Monetary Fund, Washington DC), who tries to develop a new approach to sovereign debt restructuring.

4   See Buttwill, K. and Wihlborg, C., The Efficiency of the Bankruptcy Process: An International Comparison (2004) Ratio Working Paper No 65 at 2. In this context it has to be mentioned that this terminology is predominant in literature but as Buttwill and Wihlborg stress, bankruptcy law is sometimes used as a term for insolvency law including restructuring law. Moreover, some jurisdictions provide legal procedures for restructuring as well as liquidation, whereas other countries handle the restructuring of an insolvent firm in the form of informal negotiation. However, the ultimate purpose of any insolvency regime is to redistribute the assets of uncompetitive or inefficient entities.

5   Therefore the main tasks of insolvency law, according to Finch, V., *Corporate Insolvency Law – Perspectives and Principles* (2002, Cambridge University Press, Cambridge) at 23, are (i) to lay down rules governing the distribution of the assets of an insolvent company, including rules protecting the pool of assets available to creditors; (ii) to provide for management of companies in times of crisis; (iii) to facilitate the recovery of companies in times of financial crisis and to stimulate the rehabilitation of insolvent companies and businesses as going concerns; (iv) to balance the interests of differing groupings and to protect the interests of the public and of employees in the face of financial failures or management malpractices; (v) to encourage good management of companies by sanctioning directors who are responsible for financial collapses where there has been malpractices and by providing for the investigation of the cause of corporate failure and (vi) to dissolve companies when necessary.

6   See Mokal, R.J., *Corporate Insolvency Law – Theory and Application* (2005, Oxford University Press) at 2.

7   Ibid., at 10–16.

efficiency and justice. The two economic concepts of Pareto efficiency[8] and Kaldor-Hicks efficiency[9] are at the centre of this discussion and as the science of Law and Economics points out, efficiency is one of the dominating principles a law should aim at. This view is useful and convincing and should be followed, although it has to be pointed out that the efficiency of the law is not the ultimate normative fulfilment.[10] Nevertheless, as the visions of corporate insolvency law stressed by Finch show, the issue of efficiency will remain the key issue in the future.

Insolvency law scholarship has long been under the influence of the so-called Creditors' Bargain Model (CBM) and Thomas Jackson was the dominant figure and progenitor of this model. Although one can share some of the criticism made about the CBM and Jackson's work,[11] Jackson correctly points out that single creditors realize that a multiple default by the debtor would lead to a multi-party Prisoner's Dilemma if all of them would keep enjoying unrestricted freedom of action. The resulting race to collect the assets of the debtor in case of financial distress is understandable since not all creditors will be paid. In order to cushion negative results of financial distress for the creditors and to minimize the costs of creditors to supervise the debtor, insolvency law has to come of with procedures that ensure that a sound and proper mechanism is in place in case a debtor fails to meet its obligations.

In any case, if a corporate debtor defaults on multiple debts simultaneously, he runs the danger of becoming financially distressed since debt also causes costs *ex post*, in particular after enforcement occurs. Such costs also include so-called direct costs of financial distress like fees of professionals (e.g. lawyers or

---

8   Pareto efficiency states that a distribution of resources is Pareto efficient if any further change would not make one person better off and would make at least one person worse off. See e.g. Posner, R.A., *Economic Analysis of Law* (6th ed) (2003, Aspen Publishers, New York NY) at 12–13.

9   The Kaldor-Hicks efficiency can be seen as the Pareto superiority in the sense that the winners could compensate the losers, whether or not they actually do so. See, among others, Posner, above note 8 at 13.

10 In this regard, it is worth referring to Finch, above note 5 at 28–43, who elaborates on the visions of corporate insolvency law. Finch points out the issues of creditor wealth maximisation, broader contractarianism, community interests, the creation of a forum within which all interests affected by business failure can be voiced, moral concerns in insolvency law or the notion that insolvency law serves a series of values that cannot be organized into neat priorities. No matter which of these issues will dominate the academic discussion in the future, *Finch* is able to name them and provide a helpful framework for it.

11 Mokal, above note 6 at 32–60 heavily criticizes the CBM and Jackson's work. However, although Mokal is too excessive in his remarks, his elaborations give a good overview of the existing literature on the CBM. However, Mokal offers with the so-called Authentic Consent Model (ACM) an alternative to the CBM. Since the CBM represents the 'mutual advantage theory' and the ACM 'justice as reciprocity', both models show certain shortcomings. A further development of the CBM extended with some inputs of the ACM might solve some of the lacks of these theories. However, this remains a challenging task for insolvency law scholarship in the future.

accountants) or indirect costs such as the likely losses resulting from inefficient deployment of a firm's assets *ex post*. This shows that from an *ex post* perspective, a significant seizure of costs occurs.[12] In any case it is important to clarify the situation that leads to such costs in terms of *financial distress*.

However, basically one has to distinguish between the terms financial distress and economic distress. *Financial distress* means that the present value of the expected cash flows generated by the assets of a firm is positive but that the firm's debts exceed the present value of these cash flows. Therefore, the firm is insolvent whereas its assets produce a positive value from a social point of view. In such a case it might be efficient to reduce debt and do some fundamental restructuring in order to get the firm out of troubles. Additionally, a firm might be financially distressed when facing liquidity constraints despite its present value of cash flows from assets exceeds its debts. In such a case, liquidity infusion or the rescheduling of debt might be a solution. Contrary to this, *economic distress* means that the net present value of the firm's assets is negative and a firm then will normally be shut down.[13] In any case, the exercise of the power to have the assets of a defaulting debtor seized and sold to cover an unpaid debt often results in the dismemberment of the debtor's business. The general risk of dismemberment is one of the costs in the context of *financial distress*.

In the following sections, the ground for the further discussion will be laid by giving a general overview of various insolvency procedures[14] before focussing on the discussion of minimizing the costs of financial distress, in particular the costs of financial distress *ex post* since taking them in consideration is essential when designing corporate insolvency procedures. However, since as the following elaborations show, it is difficult to design the 'optimal' corporate insolvency procedure in this regard, it might be useful to strengthen pro-active measures. Moreover, one has to keep in mind that insolvency procedures can be the cause of crises if economically distressed firms are not shut down but rather accumulate losses over time until the banking system and the government are not able to bear the costs of support anymore.[15]

Various Types of Insolvency Procedures

A common classification of insolvency procedures is the distinction between rather creditor-oriented and debtor-oriented ones. Therefore, as this terminology shows,

---

12 *Ex ante* costs such as financial agency costs are likely to occur in this regard.
13 Here reference may be made to the useful elaboration by Kahl, M., 'Economic Distress, Financial Distress, and Dynamic Liquidation' (2002) 57(1) *The Journal of Finance* 135 as well as to Buttwill and Wihlborg, above note 4 at 7.
14 It has to be pointed out that the following discussion is not limited to or exclusively focused on the United Kingdom.
15 Regarding the business cycle implications of financial distress in the context of bankruptcy law, see Suarez, J. and Sussman, O., 'Financial Distress, Bankruptcy Law and the Business Cycle' (2004) OFRC Working Paper Series 2004fe07.

the main indicator is whether an insolvency procedure tends to favour creditors and debtors regarding the claims on the distressed firm's assets as well as in terms of control over these assets. As Buttwill and Wihlborg stress, the existence of an easily accessible restructuring law generally implies a certain degree of debtor orientation because a constraint on the range of contractual solutions to distress situations is implied in this regard. The following table should give an indication in terms of a ranking of various countries insolvency laws stressing the respective creditor-debtor orientation. Although the table is based on some older work done by Wood, it provides a rough idea of how insolvency laws from various countries regarding their respective creditor-debtor orientation could be categorized.[16] According to the table, it seems to be clear that British law is most creditor-oriented, whereas to the contrary, French law is most debtor-oriented. However, in particular British law underwent a certain transformation with the Enterprise Act 2002. The fundamental changes of this Act lead to a different treatment of responsible businesses that either go bankrupt or those where negligence and recklessness has led to bankruptcy. The new dogma under the Enterprise Act 2002 is that bankrupts who are not reckless get a second chance for a fresh start. In addition to this, where they co-operate with the Official Receiver, they will even be discharged from their debts and released from any restrictions after a maximum of twelve months. Contrary to this, reckless bankrupts face much tougher penalties. This implies that in particular the ranking of England shifts towards being more debtor-oriented under certain circumstances.

Nevertheless, the usefulness of Table 3.1 is underscored by the fact that it indicates that developing countries and former colonies predominantly base their insolvency laws on the law of the former colonial power.

What are the main determinants of a high degree of creditor orientation? According to Wood, a high degree of creditor orientation is determined by:

(i) a wide scope and efficiency on bankruptcy of security and title financing;
(ii) weak corporate rehabilitation statutes;
(iii) the fact that insolvency set-off enables a reciprocal unsecured creditor to be paid ahead of other unsecured creditors;
(iv) the recognition of ownership of assets in the possession of the debtor; and
(v) a veil of incorporation and protection of directors against personal liability.

---

16 For Wood, P.R., *Principles of International Insolvency* (1995, Sweet & Maxwell, London), a creditor-oriented law recognizes the claims of creditors to the greatest extent in insolvency, whereas a debtor-oriented law grants debtors to retain a stake and/or control in insolvency – at least to a certain extent.

Table 3.1   Corporate Insolvency Laws and their Creditor-Debtor Orientation

Ranking 1= very pro-creditor-oriented; 10= very pro-debtor-oriented	Countries
1	Former British colonies (with the exception of South Africa and Zimbabwe)
2	Australia, *England*, Ireland
3	Germany, Indonesia, Netherlands, Poland, Sweden, Switzerland
4	Japan, Korea, New Zealand, Norway, Scotland
5	Canada (except Quebec), United States
6	Austria, Czech Republic, Denmark, Slovakia, Botswana, South Africa, Zimbabwe (due to the Dutch influence)
7	Italy
8	Greece, Portugal, Spain and most countries in Latin America (except Paraguay)
9	Belgium, Egypt, former French colonies, Zaire
10	France

Source: *Wood* (1995) with own adaptations.

However, it has to be noted that a rehabilitation statute or a restructuring law generally weakens the position of a creditor since it enables debtors to seek protection against some or all creditors as well as provides the possibility of a court-led solution keeping the debtor in control of the firm. Nevertheless, the more attractive side of restructuring laws from a creditor's point of view is that debtors have a stronger incentive to maximize the value of their assets. Like the table above, the main determinants by Wood just create a certain framework with indicators for differentiation since the distinction of laws being rather creditor-oriented and rather debtor-oriented is not a panacea *per se*.

Other differentiations in this regard are the classifications in terms of the degree to which a law enables firms and creditors to negotiate *ex ante* contracts that will be recognized in formal bankruptcy and restructuring proceedings or in terms of the distinction between contractual and statutory approaches to insolvency law. In this context it is worth mentioning that the contractual approach implies that insolvency law provides the possibility for firms and stakeholders to reach a voluntary contractual agreement[17] that remains valid in case of bankruptcy, whereas the statutory approach leads to an abrogation of such contractual agreements since special statutes apply then in case of bankruptcy.[18]

From an *ex post* point of view, insolvency procedures can be categorized in ones rather allowing excessive survivals or excessive shut-downs of firms. Here it has to be stressed that even in case of liquidation the survival of a firm is possible since the assets of the insolvent firm can be sold as 'going concern'. Moreover, it is possible that creditors agree on an informal work-out prior to bankruptcy with conditions for the owners of the firm.

However, the given overview of the various types of insolvency procedures and the different designs of insolvency procedures in various countries should constitute just the framework in which particular inefficiencies of corporate law procedures should in the following be indicated and discussed.

The Costs of Financial Distress

When dealing with insolvency procedures, it generally has to be kept in mind that insolvency law basically regulates the interactions between debtors and creditors in particular if the later default and the parties are not able to work out their differences outside the respective court system.

In this regard, two main types of conflicts are tackled:

- conflicts between a debtor and its creditors, and
- conflicts among creditors.

In the literature, contributions focussing on *ex post* conflicts, in particular on conflicts among various creditors, prevail. Such conflicts are often discussed in the light of conflicts of interests. Berglöf et al. stress that conflicts among creditors constitutes a major source of complexity, especially when discussed from an *ex post* perspective. However, when being transferred into an *ex ante* framework, the paradox – as they term it – becomes clearer because they ask what sense it makes that a firm contracts with several creditors if insolvency procedures with multiple creditors are so complex and hard to handle. In other words, if these conflicts of interest have to be resolved *ex post* anyway and the resolution of the conflicts is costly, why not trying to find solution *ex ante*? This view can only be supported and therefore the intention of this paper is to simply underscore this statement because it seems that pro-active actions in particular in corporate insolvency law

---

17 The broad-based contractarian approach mentioned by Finch, above note 5 at 33 might be a promising vision for the future to strengthen contractual interaction and cooperation between firms and stakeholders in case of bankruptcy.

18 In England, five main statutory procedures provided by the Insolvency Act 1986 and the Companies Act 2006 have to be mentioned in this regard: (i) administrative receivership, (ii) administration, (iii) winding up, (iv) liquidation and (v) formal arrangements with creditors.

are often neglected. As Berglöf et al. try to resolve this paradox with an optimal contracting approach to corporate debt and bankruptcy,[19] this chapter wants to make aware that legal actions – in particular business restructuring laws – might be a proper solution as well because as one of the tasks of corporate insolvency law states, the recovery of companies in times of financial crisis and the stimulation of the rehabilitation of insolvent companies and businesses as going concerns should be achieved. Therefore, pro-active measures that can be used when stepping in before a serious financial crisis of the company[20] emerges and that accelerates the rehabilitation of companies facing potential insolvencies are necessary. However, one has to keep in mind that the law might only be able to provide little assistance in particular when external factors drive companies out of business. Although the law is not the only measurement to prevent companies from becoming insolvent, the nature of insolvency law can impinge on corporate failure and success in various ways. In order to illustrate the necessity and the positive impacts of *ex ante* legal measures, the inefficiencies of a situation without such measures should be examined.

The Inefficiency of the 'Race to Collect'

The following thoughts are not focussing on the paradox stressed by Berglöf *et al.* but rather target one of its roots, namely the costs of financial distress from an *ex post* perspective. In this regard, it is interesting to scrutinize why *ex post* conflicts, in particular conflicts among various creditors are so costly. A good way to explain the complex issue of costs of financial distress is by making use of some principles of game theory.

---

19 See Berglöf, E. et al., An Incomplete-Contracts Approach to Corporate Bankruptcy (2000) Université de Lausanne Ecole des HEC, DEEP in its series *Cahiers de Recherches Economiques du Département d'Econométrie et d'Economie politique* (DEEP) with number 00.12 at 24, who conclude that if the cash flow is not verifiable and only the collateral value of the firm is verifiable, the debt capacity of the firm is limited to the value of its collateral when the firm borrows from a single creditor and has all bargaining power. The idea behind this assumption is that the creditor cannot expect to receive more than a collateral value in case of liquidation and/or in renegotiation. However, in case a firm borrows from more than one creditor, it is able to increase its debt capacity by pledging its collateral value to more than one creditor by giving each the right to foreclose on its verifiable assets. Consequently, this creates a commitment for the firm to pay out more in good states in order to prevent the exercise of individual foreclosure rights, which furthermore helps raising the firm's debt capacity. In case of multiple creditors, the reduction of negative effects of contractual incompleteness is eased. Therefore, insolvency rules are necessary in order to make individual claims consistent in case of default and to prevent value reducing runs for the assets in such a case.

20 Regarding an extensive discussion of corporate failure, who defines insolvency and in particular the reasons why companies fail, see Finch, above note 5 at 120–140.

However, costs of financial distress are commonly considered as a concomitant feature of debt finance.[21] As Schwartz puts it, the function of insolvency law is basically to minimise the costs of debt finance.[22] Creditors enjoy the legal power to have a debtor's assets seized and liquidated in order to cover debt and existence of this power already gives an *ex ante* incentive to repay. Moreover, the use of such debt causes costs *ex post*, in particular in form of fees of professionals such as lawyers or accountants. Additionally, losses resulting from inefficient deployment of the firm's assets cause costs *ex post* even on a larger scale. However, Finch mentions that the cost issue is just one aspect of the general importance of insolvency law in terms of the broad interaction between corporate insolvency law and corporate failures.[23]

When considering the various legal responses to these costs of *financial distress*, it is in particular worth mentioning Jackson,[24] who underlined that insolvency law exists as a response to a common pool problem[25] faced by creditors and that it is therefore essential that a state supplied insolvency code becomes necessary to mandate a co-operative solution. In Jackson's model,[26] the creditor is

---

21 Regarding a cost and benefit analysis of financial distress based on a sample of 28 firms in Sweden, see Bergström C. and Sundgren, S., 'Restructuring Activities and Changes in Performance Following Financial Distress' (2002) SNS Occasional Paper No. 88.

22 See Schwartz, A., 'A Contract Theory Approach to Bankruptcy' (1998) 107 *Yale Law Journal* 1807.

23 For a more detailed discussion, see Finch, above note 5 at 140–144.

24 See Jackson, T.H., 'Bankruptcy, Non-Bankruptcy Entitlements, and the Creditor's Bargain' (1982) 91 *Yale Law Journal* 857. Although Jackson's work has – partly fundamentally – been criticized among others by Mokal, his work still remains from a Law and Economics point of view, a centrepiece in literature. This view should not preclude consideration of other existing literature but should rather underscore the importance of this work.

25 The so-called common pool problem is well known in the literature of law and economics as well as in environmental economics. See Hardin, G., 'The Tragedy of the Commons' (1968) *Science* 1243, who demonstrates with his famous parable that free access and unrestricted demand for a finite resource ultimately leads to the consumption of the resource through over-exploitation. The consumption results from the benefits of exploitation by the individuals, of whom each wants to maximize its own use of the resource. Moreover, the costs of exploitation are distributed between all the individuals to whom the resource is available. As Hardin points out, the utility to each individual of adding a single animal to its own herd is the value of this animal whereas the cost to the individual is the consumption of the resources of the respective animal divided by the number of communal owners of the common. Consequently, the benefit to an individual of annexing a resource outweighs the cost where communal resources are concerned. When acting rational, all individuals of the community will add as many animals as quickly as they can to their own herds, resulting in the fact that the finite resources of the communal land will quickly become exhausted. For more details on the common pool problems, see Hardin's work.

26 Regarding the elaborations on Jackson's model, reference may be made to Armour, J., 'The Law and Economics of Corporate Insolvency: A Review' (2001) ESRC Centre for Business Research Working Paper No. 197.

characterized by not having the ability to invoke a state-supplied insolvency code. Nevertheless, they are able to make use of court-sanctioned individual debt-collection procedures, whose legal structure is simple and archaic. However, in this model, a creditor first obtains a court judgement against the debtor, certifying that the latter has failed to pay in due debt. On this basis, a state enforcement official is mandated to seize the assets of the debtor to the value of the outstanding debt. If now the debtor does not pay immediately, his original assets are sold and the proceeds passed to the creditor. In case the debtor has more unpaid creditors, the creditors' claims to these proceeds are ranked in the order that writs are delivered to the state enforcement official. As Jackson's model clearly shows, the basic problem of insolvency law is that the system of individual creditor remedies may be bad for creditors as a group when there are not enough assets. Due to the conflicting rights of the creditors, they show a tendency in their efforts for debt-collection, which in the end make the already bad situation even worse. In other words, this behaviour can also be described as a 'first come, first served' approach leading to an inefficient 'race to collect'. This means that the creditor first staking a claim to particular assets of the debtor is generally entitled to be paid first out of these assets. It is like buying tickets for an interesting football game because the people first in line get the most preferred seats, whereas those at the end of the line may eventually be without tickets at all. Analogously to Jackson's model, there are various ways one can stake a place in line because one way is that the debtor simply pays its creditor off or gives the creditor a security interest in certain assets. In other ways the creditor can – according to court decisions – get a so-called execution lien[27] or a garnishment[28] of the debtor's assets. Moreover, a place in line might also be given to a specific claimant by governmental fiat in the form of a so-called statutory lien or similar devices. In any case, creditors are usually paid according to their respective place in line for particular assets. This respective place in line is determined by the time the person acquires an interest in the assets and then takes the appropriate steps to publicize it. If the debtor is solvent, the respective place in line does not really matter, whereas in case the debtor becomes insolvent, the ranking in form of the respective place in line determines the likelihood of a creditor becoming satisfied regarding his claims. This at the first sight logical structure becomes more complex when going into details. The usage of some game theoretical methods, in particular a multiparty game type in form of the so-called prisoner's dilemma[29] will additionally reveal the inefficiency of this structure:

---

27 In the United States context, a so-called execution lien refers to a lien that arises at or around the time the sheriff – based on a judgement and the issuance of a writ of execution – seizes property.

28 The term garnishment is used in the case of intangible personal property, such as an employer's obligation to pay wages to a debtor, for the applicable lien in this regard, arising upon the serving of a writ of garnishment on the employer.

29 In game theory, the prisoner's dilemma is a so-called non-zero-sum game which was first discussed by A.W. Tucker in the 1940s. The game is characterized by two players who try get e.g. rewards from a banker by cooperating with or betraying the respective

Let's assume that a corporate debtor A has two creditors B and C. A owes B and C 90. Furthermore, let's assume that the assets of A are broken up and, if they are sold in bits and pieces, 100 could be realized.

Anyhow, if B and C would make use of their legal power to have a debtor's assets seized and liquidated in order to cover the debt, the vital assets of A for continuing running the business would be sold resulting in a piecemeal sale.

If B and C would cooperate in the sense that they would not make use of their enforcement right, they would be able to agree to a collective decision about the debtor's future. In this case, two approaches can be distinguished: (i) B and C want to sell A's business as going concern rather than as a separate and more complicated collection of single assets or (ii) B and C could try to resolve A's problems by a collective debt renegotiation package in which case certain loans are rescheduled or converted to equity. No matter what approach will be used, if the total payoff to B and C is higher than the sale in bits and pieces, it could be considered efficient to follow the approach in a collective manner.

Moreover, it should be assumed that only one of these versions generates a total return to creditor B and C of 150 and that unilateral co-operation is not successful.

If under these circumstances B enforces, but C not, or vice versa, only the enforcing creditor (either B or C) will be fully repaid, whereas the other one faces a loss. Therefore, the unilateral enforcing creditor's payoff exceeds the payoff that either B or C can expect from cooperation. This has the consequence that both, B and C will seek for opportunities to enforce their respective rights if they believe that the respective other creditor will cooperate. Contrary to this, if unilateral cooperation causes a worse payoff than collective enforcement, B and C will also try to enforce, if they believe that the respective other creditor will do so as well. Therefore, cooperation is strictly dominated by enforcement which has the effect that creditor B or C is always better off enforcing, no matter what the other creditor will decide to do. The payoff system is the same for B and C and due to the same preferences of the two, both creditors will decide to enforce. This result is

---

other player. As in all variants of this game, it is basically assumed that the primary concern of each individual player (in the classical prisoner's dilemma the 'prisoner') is to maximize the own advantage with less concern for the well-being of others. This means that in the prisoner's dilemma, cooperating is strictly dominated by defecting, so that the only equilibrium for the game is for all players to defect. Furthermore, since in any situation playing defect is more beneficial than cooperating, all rational players will play defect. Therefore, the individual players are not able to get together and make a collective decision since their selfishness prevails. Anyhow, the outcome reached by individual action is clearly worse than any cooperative solution. This means in economic terms that the unique reachable equilibrium for the game does not lead to a Pareto-optimal solution, meaning that when two rational players play defect even though the total reward (as the sum of the reward received by both players together) would be greater if both players would cooperate. However, in this context, reference may be made to Cooter, R. and Ulen, T., *Law & Economics* (4th ed) (2004, Addison-Wesley, Reading MA) at 39–42 and in particular Axelrod, R., *The Evolution of Cooperation* (1984, Basic Books, New York NY).

inefficient from an economic point of view because the creditors can only realize 100 instead of the maximum of 150.

This can be summarized as follows:

Table 3.2   The Payoff System

	Enforcement by B	Cooperation by B
Enforcement by C	50, 50	90, 10
Cooperation by C	10, 90	75, 75

Source: Own Creation.

The Difficulty of Decision-Making in General

According to the prisoner's dilemma, collective rights – in this case the rights of the creditors – need collective decision-making. However Jackson showed that a mandatory insolvency procedure would make it possible to avoid the prisoner's dilemma for creditors. When assuming that the legal procedure is able to ensure the correct deployment decision is taken without additional costs, then the payoff to B and C would be (75, 75), in case this procedure is applied. Therefore, a collective *modus operandi* would significantly contribute to reduce the costs of creditor's decision-making by avoiding the likely '*race to collect*'.

Anyhow, such a collective *modus operandi* can only be realized if there is a collective decision. This implies that the process to reach the collective decision is the crucial factor for the efficiency of the procedure. In this context, the following aspects have to be taken into consideration:

> (i) the faster the decisions are made, the lower the direct costs of financial distress;
> (ii) the accuracy of the decisions achieved improves the efficiency of the allocation of the firm's assets *ex post*, and
> (iii) the scope of the strategic behaviour largely depends on the procedure being adopted.[30]

Although these aspects seem to be reasonable, certain incentives and circumstances may lead to a kind of counterproductive action of the creditors.[31] Nevertheless, these stressed incentives and circumstances can significantly be reduced by the specification of a so-called valuation mechanism in advance. Furthermore, their influence can be reduced by trying to homogenize the claims of creditors against the respective firm.

---

30 Armour, above note 26 at 20.
31 In this context, asymmetric information between creditors as well as diverging priorities among creditors should be mentioned.

The Difficulty of Decision-Making in Detail

When going into details of the difficulties of the collective decision-making process, it becomes clear that time is crucial because the quicker the decisions can be taken, the lower the costs of financial distress. Additionally, quick decision-making also lowers the costs of uncertainty of financial distress. Moreover, the accuracy of decisions achieved improves the allocation of the firm's assets *ex post* as well as the scope for strategic behaviour primarily depends on the adopted mechanism.

Besides the necessity for a proper mechanism, it has to be taken into consideration that several factors inhibit collective decision-making by creditors such as:

> (i) individual rights causing a strategic 'hold-up' behaviour;
> (ii) asymmetric information likely leading to disputes over the best means of deploying the assets of the firm; or
> (iii) heterogeneous priorities among creditors,[32]

thus giving parties incentives resulting in the largest payoffs to them. Therefore, a mechanism enabling proper collective decision-making is needed to reduce these unfavourable incentives.

As Baird argues, the best option to determine the value of the debtor's firm is an auction because in such a case, bidders reflect their true incentives to value the firm properly. It is worth mentioning that, for example, with the administrative receivership procedure[33] in the United Kingdom or the auction under Chapter 7 proceedings in the United States, some insolvency laws proposing auctions in such cases exist. However, the solution of an auction is applied in many countries without explicit restructuring law whereas in countries with explicit restructuring laws an independent body with enforcement powers, for example a court, is required in order to come to a conclusion with respect to the value of the firm, and to determine the value-maximizing course of action.[34] As a consequence, a procedure leading to an auction of the respective firm due to the maximization of the debtor's firm's value seems to be useful for solving complex problems of creditor's decision-making. However, there are two strong arguments against the efficiency of auctions in this regard.

The first one is rather a practical matter because if the firm is to be auctioned as a going concern, someone has to guarantee the running of the firm during the auction period, a fact that is often aggravated by the insolvency procedure itself. Additionally, it is often a problem who should oversee the auction process because whilst the residual claimant normally acts as the party with the

---

32 See Baird, D.G., 'The Uneasy Case for Corporate Reorganizations' (1986) 15 *Journal of Legal Studies* 127.

33 Insolvency Act 1986, section 29(2). The availability of administrative receivership has been considerably restricted following the enactment of the Enterprise Act 2002.

34 Buttwill and Wihlborg, above note 4 at 11.

appropriate incentives to determine the optimal amount of time spent soliciting bids, creditor heterogeneity causes the perverse situation that it is often unclear, who the residual claimant is.[35] The administrative receivership in particular reflects this weird situation because the decision about how to sell the firm is placed ultimately in the hands of a secured creditor. However, if the value of the firm exceeds the outstanding secured loan, they are not the residual claimant and may therefore simply have an incentive to have the firm sold in the least risky manner, even if this is for a lower expected value. When opting for a court official to be in charge of the conduct of the sale, it has to be considered that, as Baird or Aghion *et al.* argue,[36] they are not the best choice to perform this task, in particular due to his lack of expertise compared to market participants.

The second one refers to market failures concerning the assets of distressed firms. In case there is no functioning and liquid market for these kinds of assets, an effective reallocation of the resources is not possible. Moreover, it is worth considering that at times when firms are suffering from financial distress, other firms in the same industry, who would actually be the natural buyers of its assets, are likely to be suffering liquidity problems because financial distress is often linked to industry-wide downturns. Hence, assets will be sold at a severe undervalue.[37] Additionally an adverse selection problem could exist because potential buyers are rather avoiding the market because they fear that creditors tend to sell only low-quality firms. In order to solve this liquidity problem, non-cash bids in the sense that shares or securities are exchanged instead of cash could be allowed, which nevertheless itself tends to increase the problem of an auction, since non-cash bids are inherently more difficult to evaluate than cash.

Apart from this, the homogenisation of creditors' claims offers an alternative regarding the reduction of costs of collective decision-making. This is basically logical since the conversion of all claims into equity leads to a collective decision-making which can be conducted with common interest. In order to avoid redistribution tendencies, Aghion *et al.* argue that the usage of options might be an efficient tool. The procedure making use of such a mechanism would mandate the automatic allocation to claimants of options to purchase a fixed number of shares of the distressed firm's equity whereby the number of shares would be equal to the face value of an equal proportion of all senior claims. This procedure would ensure that no creditor ever receives less than the priority entitlement because the creditor either gets bought out at par or he gets an option of a *pro rata* share of the firm's equity. Although theoretically, the usage of options sounds target-oriented, the immanent problem of valuing the firm still exists. This paradox situation causes

---

35 Armour, above note 26 at 22.
36 Baird, above note 32; Aghion, P. et al., 'The Economics of Bankruptcy Reform' (1992) 8 *Journal of Economics and Organization* 523.
37 See Shleifer, A. and Vishny, R.W., 'Liquidation Value and Debt Capacity: A Market Equilibrium Approach' (1992) 47 *Journal of Finance* 4. However, if the current owner is able to bid higher than others, the situation might change since the present owner values his firm higher than other due to the investments he already made.

possibilities for free-riders as well as the existence of 'rational ignorance'[38] meaning that the total investment in valuation is inappropriate.

Since neither the auction nor option mechanisms seem to be the panacea, one has – from a pragmatic point of view – to agree with Aghion et al. that the combination of 'auction' and 'options' seems to be very useful because this would have the following positive implications:

> (i) the solicitation of bids for the firm for a fixed period by a court official;
> (ii) the exercise of options; and
> (iii) finally, the selection of the desired bid by the residual claimants after the options have been exercised.

This significantly diminishes the auctioneer's incentive problem because the decision which bid has to be accepted is made by the parties who consider themselves as residual claimants. Moreover, the information problem faced by claimants in deciding whether or not to exercise their options is reduced, even additionally causing the advantage of having presented the valuations placed on the firm by a number of potential purchasers.

How to Deal with the Limits of this Common Pool Problem?

Despite this pragmatic view regarding the combination of 'auction' and 'option', the proposed solution is not optimal because the auctioneer's incentive problem is diminished but not solved and the information problem faced by claimants in deciding whether or not to exercise their options is reduced but not solved as well. This is the reason why it is extremely difficult to find a satisfactory solution. As the prisoner's dilemma shows, cooperation is strictly dominated by enforcement having the effect that each creditor is always better off by enforcing, no matter what the other creditor will decided to do.

Therefore, it is fundamental for insolvency law to transform the rights of creditors from an individual to a collective basis associated with collective governance mechanisms which is necessary since, as Armour otherwise notes, the destructive effect of allowing creditors, when their power to take control becomes exercisable to apportion control rights on a 'first come, first served' basis. This implies that in the case of enforcement, debt shifts from being an *ex ante* incentive mechanism to the locus of *ex post* control, meaning that it is essential for the respective structure of creditors' rights to be transformed in order to be appropriate for the exercise of control in an efficient manner. However, it has to be kept in

---

38 Rational ignorance is basically considered as the option of an agent not to acquire or process information about some realm. This means that rational ignorance is ordinarily used to describe a citizen's choice not to pay attention to political issues or information, because paying attention has costs in time and effort, and the effect a citizen would have by voting *per se* is usually zero.

mind that the law of secured credit[39] constitutes an exception to this collectivisation because before the commencement of insolvency proceedings, a secured creditor is basically free in case of a defaulting creditor to exercise its rights to seize and sell the charged assets. The difference to an unsecured creditor is that in case of an insolvent debtor, a secured creditor allowed to retain his right to control the charged assets likely leads to inefficient dismemberment of the debtor's business.[40]

Although the common pool problem is able to explain certain facts of corporate insolvency law, it has significant limitations, being:

> (i) the possibility of solving the prisoner's dilemma through ex ante contracting;
> (ii) the role of non-legal mechanisms for solving common pool problems; and
> (iii) the possibility of renegotiation as a substitute for legal insolvency proceedings.[41]

Regarding the limitation in terms of contracting for an insolvency procedure it has to be noted that the common pool problem starts at a stage where the financial distress has already commenced. This implies that at this stage, creditors with just individual enforcement rights face the typical problems and therefore well-known results of the prisoner's dilemma as stressed above. In order to solve these problems related to the prisoner's dilemma, various ideas have been developed but it does not seem that any of these *ex ante* contracting options substantially diminish or even solve the problems.[42]

In terms of non-legal solutions to the common pool problem it has to be stressed that it is usually assumed that insolvency procedure that solves the common pool problem is supplied by law itself. Nevertheless, some non-legal mechanisms can be substitutes for legal solutions, such as the option that the debtor borrows from one significant creditor. In any case, these non-legal solutions do not seem to be a promising alternative.

The third limitation of the common pool problem is the neglect of renegotiation during an insolvency procedure. This means that if the insolvency procedure is inefficient, creditors might be better off by trying to find a solution of the debtor's financial distress without initiating formal proceedings. From an economic point of view it depends on the transaction costs of such a bargaining situation compared to the costs of formal proceedings which solution will be

---

39 Regarding the law of secured credit, reference may be made to McCormack, G., *Secured Credit Under English and American Law* (2004, Cambridge University Press, Cambridge).

40 It is worth noting that the case where the charge covers the total value of the business can be seen as a kind of exception to this distinction.

41 Regarding this and the further elaborations mentioned, reference may be made to Armour, above note 26 at 31–37.

42 Majority voting provisions being included in an issue of bonds have to be named in this context. For further information, reference may be made to Adler, B.E., 'Financial and Political Theories of American Corporate Bankruptcy' (1993) 45 *Stanford Law Review* 311.

chosen. As Armour nicely points out, the option of finding a solution without initiating formal proceedings results in the fact that it is not irrational to cooperate unlike in the traditional prisoner's dilemma. This means in game theoretical terms that the option of both players cooperating becomes the dominant strategy equilibrium. If this would represent the real situation, formal insolvencies would basically not exist. However, reality tells us a different story.

Pro-Activity as the Better Option?

Anyhow, it is interesting to think about an option that at least indirectly but proactively tries to tackle the results of the prisoner's dilemma at its roots. In order to achieve this, insolvency law has to provide options to minimize costs of financial distress. A promising option in this regard is restructuring potentially distressed firms. This means that in case it is foreseeable that a firm will face serious financial problems in the (near) future, measures in the sense of restructuring the business can be applied. Such pro-active action might avoid but at least diminish huge future costs of financial distress. Additionally, such special business restructuring legislation has to provide an effective early warning system, so that the restructuring measures can be applied early enough.

In Austria, special insolvency legislation was issued to install such warning lights in order to prevent insolvency: Therefore, the so-called Business Restructuring Act 1997 (*Unternehmensreorganisationsgesetz*) ('URG')[43] was issued with the intention to avoid business insolvencies by containing provisions for the restructuring of non-insolvent debtor's business. The URG is – despite its name – not an insolvency statute *strictu sensu*, as it does not apply to insolvent undertakings.[44]

The purpose of a proceeding under the URG is to enable businesses that are only in temporary financial difficulties, but that are basically fit to stay in business, to continue to carry out their activities after having undergone a reorganization procedure. The rescue of the company primarily depends on the so-called 'continuation forecast', which constitutes an evaluation of the capitalized value of the anticipated yield of the company. Therefore, it has to be examined whether the economic strength of the firm is sufficient to overcome the current crisis. If this is the case, no insolvency proceedings will be initiated, even though the firm is over-indebted.

---

43 See Austrian Federal Gazette (*Bundesgesetzblatt*) I 1997/114.
44 The URG applies to all kinds of businesses except banks, pension funds, insurance companies and investment firms. For general commentary on its terms, see Klauser, A., Bankruptcy and a fresh start: stigma on failure and legal consequences of bankruptcy – Austria' (2002), available at:
<europa.eu.int/.../entrepreneurship/support_measures/failure_bankruptcy/stigma_study/r eport_aust.pdf> (last viewed 31 May 2007) or Fremuth, A., 'Das Unternehmensreorganisationsgesetz – Gesetzestext und Materialien' (1997) *RdW* 497.

The special characteristic of the URG proceedings is that only the still solvent debtor itself is entitled to apply for the opening of such a business reorganization procedure. Upon application to the insolvency court, which has to include sufficient proof of the need for the business's reorganization and then may include a reorganization plan for the debtor's business, the court initiates the business reorganization proceedings by appointing a temporary reorganization auditor. The significant difference to the regular insolvency proceedings under the Bankruptcy Act 1914 (*Konkursordnung*) or the Settlement and Recomposition of Debts Act 1914 (*Ausgleichsordnung*) is that this court resolution will not be publicly announced.[45]

Anyhow, when the business reorganization proceedings are opened, contractual provisions are ineffective. Furthermore, in case of subsequent bankruptcy, the receiver's right to void a contract concluded between the debtor and a creditor in the course of the business reorganization is subject to stringent limitations, in particular since creditors are not able to challenge the validity of a loan made by a shareholder of a company based on certain principles of corporate requiring that the loan is assimilated into the equity and is therefore subordinated to claims of other creditors. Moreover, while the reorganization plan is in force, the debtor has to report – normally every six months – to the involved creditors about the status of the business as well as the measures taken under the reorganization plan.

The reorganization proceedings will be terminated by the court when:

(i)   the debtor becomes insolvent;
(ii)   the debtor is late in submitting the reorganization plan;
(iii)   the debtor fails to deposit an advance for the temporary reorganization auditor's fees;
(iv)   the debtor violates its duty to co-operate under the plan; or
(v)   the temporary reorganization auditor is of the opinion that the suggested reorganization plan fails to serve its purpose and lacks prospects for success.[46]

As this short introduction to the Business Restructuring Act 1997 shows, it is possible to proactively reduce costs of financial distress at the pre-stage of insolvency if the formally still solvent debtor is willing to apply for a restructuring procedure. This is a two edged flexibility because it is decisive for the avoiding insolvency. On the one side, creditors still depend on the willingness of the debtor to apply for the procedure on the other side the debtor has the chance to avert further damage by making use of this possibility. Despite such legal framework as provided by the Business Restructuring Act 1997 is not able to solve the unsatisfactory situation illustrated by the prisoner's dilemma, it offers at least an option to proactively avoid costs of financial distress.

---

45 See Feuchtinger, G. and Lesigang, M., *Praxisleitfaden Insolvenzrecht* (2005, Linde Verlag, Wien) at 226.
46 See Huber, W., Chapter XXIII in Heller, K., Bahn, G., Huber, W. and Horvath, G. (eds), *Austrian Business Law*, Supplement 8, (2000, Manz, Vienna) at 1–3.

Conclusions

As these thoughts on corporate insolvency in general and the costs of *financial distress* in particular showed, the insolvency procedure and thereby the design of insolvency legislation in general is crucial for debtors to get out of their unfavourable situation. This is in particular the case for creditors who want to be compensated for their loss caused by the debtor's insolvency. However, as the prisoner's dilemma showed, creditors are in the unlucky situation that they rather tend to enforce than cooperate. This action is primarily caused by the respective legal setting and the insolvency procedures being applied. Moreover, it seems that the common pool problem with all its limitations is hardly to avoid.

Although various suggestions from outstanding scholars on how to tackle this problem exist, one way to resolve the problem of *financial distress* and the resulting costs is to focus already at an even earlier stage by implementing business restructuring laws. Such laws necessarily have to create an early warning system indicating that there is a potential danger of future distress. After indicating the existence of a potential danger of future distress, the early warning system then has to activate the necessary restructuring measures so that if not insolvency at all but at least enormous costs of financial distress can be avoided.

However, in order to make pro-active restructuring measures more effective, it is necessary to find ways in order to create more incentives for creditors already at the pre-stage of insolvency to urge the debtor to apply for such a restructuring procedure. This would have the positive side-effect that the creditor's payoff at this stage is significantly higher than by risking the opening of an insolvency procedure with the illustrated prisoner's dilemma. However, Law and Economics literature provided the groundwork in this regard, now it is the task for insolvency law scholarship to move on in order to find efficient and consistent ways to create a legal framework which – in interaction with other measures such as corporate governance or company law provisions – tries to strengthen the pro-active actions in order to better try to avoid corporate insolvency and in particular to limit the costs of financial distress. This paper should be understood as another push in this regard.

PART II
THE RESCUE AND FRESH START CONCEPTS

Chapter 4

The Commencement
of the Company Rescue:
How and When Does it Start?

Colin Anderson and David Morrison

Introduction

The spread of the so called 'rescue culture' in insolvency has been a recognisable trend across jurisdictions in recent times. Company rescue has been established in the United States for a longer period than in other jurisdictions such as Australia. Nonetheless it is difficult to find a developed economy where there has not been at least some consideration given to implementing a specific updated rescue regime aimed at salvaging the corporate structure in certain circumstances of insolvency.

The momentum of company rescue procedures has occurred in the context of each jurisdiction's particular insolvency regime. This makes comparisons between jurisdictions more complex as the underlying institutions and background sentiment need to be considered. However it is possible to identify and examine the common themes that emerge. For example, by way of general observation, corporate rescue provisions are collective in nature in seeking to take into account the interests of the various stakeholders affected by the approach of corporate insolvency and use a regulatory scheme of general applicability of varying degrees to facilitate the process.

Commencement Impact

One fundamental consideration for company rescue provisions is to determine exactly *when* that collective process starts. Practically the date of commencement will impact upon (and in some cases determine) the amount that a stakeholder will receive from the collective procedure. Therefore stakeholders have an incentive to behave in order to preserve or maximise their return from a company rescue.[1]

---

1   See Baird, D.G. and Bernstein, D.S., 'Absolute Priority, Valuation Uncertainty, and the Reorganization Bargain' (September 2005), University of Chicago Law & Economics, Olin Working Paper No. 259, available at SSRN: <ssrn.com/abstract=813085> (last viewed 31 May 2007). Although the authors

Connected with this is the need to determine whether an interest in the entity may be recognized at the particular stage that the process commences such that those that have an interest in the entity at the relevant time that the process commences will potentially have a claim within the process. Hence the timing factor can be critical as to how the available funds are distributed. We suggest however that there are broader policy issues that need to be considered in determining when the procedure ought to commence.

Inevitably there are a range of factors that influence the timing of the commencement of any insolvency procedure and this applies also in the case with corporate rescue regimes. It seems that the key theoretical issue in determining timing is that the collective insolvency process, even if leading to rescue, be commenced at the time that is seen to be 'correct' in the sense that it fits within the aims of the procedure. Jackson explains that '[e]nsuring that bankruptcy cases are initiated only when they are needed, and neither too early nor too late, is a difficult task'.[2] How such an aim translates into practice has not yet been definitively determined.

It seems that from the oft stated goals of rescue procedures, that one basis of establishing the correct time is that the procedure ought to commence when it is not too late to rescue the entity (on the one hand), but also that it is not entered into too quickly by those who might seek to abuse the process. Therefore the process ought to be restricted to those entities that are genuinely in need of it and consequently it is appropriate to review the way that different jurisdictions deal with this issue.

The commencement processes are often overlooked in the analysis of the procedures as the important focus in practical terms will be on the decision making process and who wins or loses control in that context. However it must be recognised that if the commencement procedure operates in a manner consistent with the aims of the procedure it should provide a platform upon which the rest of the elements may effectively and efficiently proceed.

This article provides a study of the Australian, English and United States jurisdictions to determine the requirements for commencement of a corporate rescue. In looking at the procedure for corporate rescue the article specifically examines the administration procedure in the United Kingdom, the voluntary administration process in Australia and the Chapter 11 filing in the United States. It must be noted that the administration process in the United Kingdom and the voluntary administration procedures do not of themselves effect the rescue and it is the procedures that may follow that will provide that. In contrast, in Chapter 11 the rescue plan is an essential part of the process. However, in the case of the

---

postulate that when the priorities set down in a United States Chapter 11 arrangement are not followed, the reason for the departure may sit around uncertainties in the process.

2   See Jackson, T.H., *The Logic and Limits of Bankruptcy Law* (1986, Beard Books, Washington DC) at 193.

Australian procedure, a deed of company arrangement[3] is only able to be entered into from a voluntary administration.[4] In the United Kingdom, a Company Voluntary Arrangement (CVA) may be entered into without administration except in the case of certain minor exceptions the benefit of a moratorium cannot be obtained in those circumstances.[5] In this sense as Goode has described them these Anglo Australian procedures are 'gateways' to the corporate rescue process.[6] This article focuses on how this gate is opened in each of the relevant jurisdictions and does not cover what happens once inside.

The argument proceeds on an analytical conceptual level rather than as a detailed description of each jurisdiction's process. Prior to examining particular aspects of each jurisdiction there is an initial examination of what rescue provisions might ideally provide for in principle insofar as how they commence the process. Following this a fundamental issue of whether insolvency is required for commencement is considered, then a more detailed discussion of procedural requirements in each jurisdiction to commence the relevant process. Finally some conclusions are drawn.

Principles of Commencement

It is possible to argue that there is little justification in breaking up the process of corporate rescue into its various stages. The stages are all the part of the one process. The argument made here however is that entry into the procedure provides a gateway through which the procedure is undertaken. In so doing it needs to operate consistently with the overall principles of the process. This then enables a consideration of what should the process enable with respect to commencement?

We suggest that the commencement process of any successful rescue regime needs to facilitate at least two matters. First, it ought to provide the opportunity for companies that might obtain a better return in reorganization than on a liquidation, to be selected for reorganization. Secondly, it will allow for minimum costs to be incurred with a speedy transition to the external administration. Both of these matters may be viewed as ideals that the rescue regime aims for in terms of reducing the cost of credit.[7]

---

3   The deed of company arrangement gives effect to the rescue and binds dissenting unsecured creditors.

4   Corporations Act 2001 (Cth), section 439C.

5   It is also possible to utilise the scheme of arrangement provisions under the Companies Act 1985, section 425. This procedure is not covered in this chapter.

6   See Goode, R., *Principles of Corporate Insolvency Law* (3rd ed) (2005, Thomson, London) at 328. It is acknowledged that the author is referring to the United Kingdom provision, but the same applies to the Australian voluntary administration process: see Anderson, C., 'Commencement of the Part 5.3A Procedure: Some Considerations from an Economics and Law Perspective' (2001) 9 *Insolvency Law Journal* 4 at 16.

7   For a discussion around the positive economic framework of assessing the procedure in the USA, see Kordana, K.A. and Posner, E.A., 'A Positive Theory of Chapter 11' (October 1998), University of Chicago Law & Economics, Olin Working Paper No.

In relation to the first issue, the commencement process assists in distinguishing those firms that require immediate liquidation from those where stakeholders benefit from a corporate rescue regime. However, it is unlikely that this can be done in the commencement process itself. The ability of most stakeholders to evaluate likely future outcomes is limited without further information. Further difficulties arise with respect to information asymmetry as between stakeholders.[8] It is axiomatic that increased openness of critical information about the relevant entity and its operations provides better decision making regarding business viability and longer-term preservation decisions.

It follows then that there is an inevitable time lag between an entity being identified as being in financial difficulty and when relevant parties[9] reach the point where they determine that they have enough information (or pressure) to support the continuity of the entity by way of rescue procedure.

Whilst the process of decision making is not the focus of this chapter, it is clearly linked to the commencement procedure. The authors believe that it is possible to allow entities to enter into a procedure without the need to be sure that they can be 'rescued'. The commencement step itself requires the ability to identify an entity where there is a *potentially* greater return through corporate rescue. However once the procedure commences the focus then changes to be concerned with making decisions about the entity's future. This means that the commencement process itself facilitates the next stage of the rescue process rather than being part of the rescue itself.

If one views the commencement process in this sense, then the initiation provisions are viewed in the context of being a gateway rather than as a filtering mechanism. Where this important distinction is overlooked then criticism of the procedure tends to confuse the entry mechanism with the decision making procedure.

Although the commencement mechanism will usually signal how the decision about the company's future is made, there is no fundamental reason why this should be so. Thus, for example, a system that involves a court decision as regards commencement might leave the fate of any rescue bid in the hands of creditors to vote upon. The process simply facilitates the evaluation that is to take place once it has commenced – but this is not to say that the steps must be effectively the same.

It is important that the process not be allowed to commence if it is to be used as a means of avoiding obligations without providing a satisfactory resolution

---

61, available at SSRN: <ssrn.com/abstract=137897> (last viewed 31 May 2007) or DOI: <10.2139/ssrn.137897> (last viewed 31 May 2007).

8   See Chen, N., 'Chapter 11, Private Workouts and Corporate Debt Pricing under Asymmetric Information' (13 June 2003), EFA 2003 Annual Conference Paper No. 629, available at SSRN: <ssrn.com/abstract=424283> (last viewed 31 May 2007) or DOI: <10.2139/ssrn.424283> (last viewed 31 May 2007).

9   The decision making mechanism for deciding upon rescue may vary with some jurisdictions opting for a more court influenced decision whilst others may leave matters more in the hands of the creditors or other possible stakeholders.

of insolvency issues. So for example, it should not be possible to utilize corporate rescue procedure to attempt to resolve what are essentially disputes between shareholder groups if no insolvency issue is involved.[10] This is a familiar problem in all insolvency procedures and further the issue is not specifically confined to corporate rescue. It is nevertheless important that potential for abuse of the procedure be controlled as much as possible within the process and if it can be controlled earlier (i.e. at commencement) it is likely to be more effective and less costly to the majority of stakeholders.

It is also desirable that the commencement process be available with a minimum of delay and cost. This is a fundamental requirement of any insolvency procedure but it will be critical to the success of any rescue attempt to enhance the prospects.

Is Insolvency a Requirement?

A starting point when considering the commencement procedures for corporate rescue regimes is to consider if an entity must be insolvent prior to commencement. The arguments for and against this requirement raise fundamental issues as regards the regime itself and it is interesting to observe that the three jurisdictions studied here adopt different approaches.

England

In the United Kingdom, the corporate rescue culture has developed since the major reforms of the Cork Report[11] and the resultant Insolvency Act 1986. Several procedures have emerged[12] that may be utilised where corporate rescue is desired.

---

10   For example in the Australian context, see the facts in the case of *Cadwallader v Bajco Pty Ltd & Ors* [2002] NSWCA 328, which involved a family company where disputes had arisen over how the company should be run and the position of directors and ex directors. In the United States (as discussed below in this chapter), there is no specific requirement for insolvency but the court may dismiss a case 'for cause' which is likely to occur if there is no insolvency issue at stake. By referring to some insolvency issue is not to require that the company be insolvent but that there be some question either arising now or with some reasonable likelihood in the future.

11   Department of Trade and Industry (UK), Report of the Review Committee on Insolvency Law and Practice ('Cork Report') [Cmnd. 8558].

12   These include the company voluntary arrangement procedure (CVA) under Insolvency Act 1986, Part I, which does not provide for any moratorium on debt, and the CVA with a moratorium under Insolvency Act 1986, section 1A and Schedule A1 that provides for certain specified types of companies (namely small companies under the Companies Act 1985 (UK)) to enter into arrangements and obtain a moratorium. In addition it is possible to utilize the schemes of arrangement provisions under Companies Act 1985, section 425, although this is a cumbersome procedure for an insolvency context. There are also non-statute based procedures such as workouts. The

The most significant of the procedures though is the Administration procedure that was considerably altered by amendments that took place via the Enterprise Act 2002.

The process of administration is one that enables other procedures to be entered into so that administration is in this sense temporary.[13] Under paragraph 2,[14] in relation to the administration, an administrator may be appointed by the court, by the holder of a qualifying floating charge[15] or by the company or its directors. It is only in relation to appointment by the court[16] and an appointment by the company or its directors[17] that there needs to be a conclusion that 'the company is or is likely to become unable to pay its debts'.[18]

The requirement does not apply where the appointment is by the holder of a qualifying floating charge.[19] A person is a holder of a qualifying charge if she or he holds a debenture of the company that is secured in accordance with one of the means defined in paragraph 14(3).[20] The charge must be over the whole or substantially the whole of the property of the company.

It is a requirement in respect of the floating charge that the power to appoint an administrator has become exercisable under the terms of the charge. This will not necessarily mean that the company is unable to pay all of its debts and is restricted by the events of default that the charge itself sets out. Therefore the requirement of inability to pay debts is not strictly required. In practical terms though, because the charge is over the whole or substantially the whole of the property of the company, it will be impractical to operate the company to pay other debts if the charge is enforced.

Australia

The United Kingdom approach is similar to the Australian legislation in respect of the insolvency requirement. In Australia, the provisions enabling corporate rescue

---

administration procedure is a process that can enable these other processes to take place.

13   In this respect it is the same as the Australian voluntary administration procedure.
14   Insolvency Act 1986, Schedule B1.
15   Ibid., paragraph 14.
16   Ibid., paragraph 11.
17   Ibid., paragraph 27, which requires that a person who intends to appoint under paragraph 22 must provide a statement of intention to appoint to certain other persons (under paragraph 26) and prior to that must file a statutory declaration with the court which contains inter alia a statement that the company is or is likely to become unable to pay its debts.
18   Presumably this encompasses a requirement that the company be unable to pay its debts as they fall due rather than a balance sheet type test of insolvency.
19   Insolvency Act 1986, Schedule B1.
20   Idem. This includes floating charges as well as charges and other forms of security provided that at least one is a qualifying floating charge.

are found in Part 5.3A of the Corporations Act 2001 (Cth).[21] This procedure was recommended by the Report of the Australian Law Reform Commission in Australia's Insolvency Laws (known as the Harmer Report)[22] and has been in operation since 1993. The procedure is known as Voluntary Administration and like the United Kingdom process is a temporary one that will lead to the company either being liquidated or placed under what is a form of arrangement known as a Deed of Company Arrangement. It is also possible that the company will be returned to its pre administration status quo although this rarely occurs.

One major difference between the Australian and United Kingdom procedure in that there is no opportunity for appointment by a court pursuant to the Australian provisions. Under Part 5.3A, the administration commences when an administrator is appointed.[23] The legislation provides for three distinct ways in which the administration can commence. The appointments may be made by a resolution of the board of directors,[24] by a liquidator or provisional liquidator who had already been appointed to the company[25] or by a charge holder having a charge over the whole or substantially the whole of the company's property.[26]

In the case of appointment by the board of directors or by a liquidator or provisional liquidator, there is a requirement that either the board (or the liquidator as the case may be) is of the opinion that the company is insolvent or is likely to become insolvent. In the case of appointment by a charge holder with the requisite security, there is no requirement that the company be insolvent rather like the United Kingdom provision the charge holder must be entitled to enforce the charge at the time of making the appointment.

The meaning of insolvency under the Corporations Act is found in section 95A that establishes insolvency exists where a person is unable to pay all of their debts as and when they become due and payable. Thus the insolvency requirement with respect to appointment is almost identical in both the Australian and British jurisdictions despite other differences in the manner of appointment.[27] Therefore apart from the situation of the secured creditor appointment, insolvency is fundamental to the use of the procedure in both jurisdictions. This may be contrasted with the position in the United States.

---

21   There is no separate insolvency statute for corporate insolvency in Australia, with the provisions being contained in Chapter 5 of the general statute dealing with nearly all aspects of company regulation. Recent moves to suggest a change in this approach have not been adopted by the Government – see Parliamentary Joint Committee on Corporations and Financial Services Corporate Insolvency Laws: a Stocktake, Senate Printing Unit Parliament House, Canberra (2004) at paragraphs [12.73] to [12.84].

22   Australian Law Reform Commission Report No. 45, General Insolvency Inquiry ('Harmer Report') (1988, AGPS, Canberra).

23   Corporations Act 2001 (Cth), section 435C(1).

24   Ibid., section 436A.

25   Ibid., section 436B.

26   Ibid., section 436C.

27   There are similarities as well but the differences are discussed further below.

The United States

In the Bankruptcy Code 1978, Chapter 11 allows for reorganization of a debtor. The provisions of that chapter may be initiated by the debtor themselves although it is also possible for an involuntary proceeding to commence. However the basis for commencement is a court filing. The commencement of any case (including Chapter 11) requires either a voluntary or involuntary filing.[28]

There is a different approach where there is voluntary or involuntary filing in relation to bankruptcy under the Code. One aspect of this is that where there is an involuntary filing the court may order relief where the debtor is generally not paying debts as they become due unless there is a *bona fide* dispute.[29] However section 101 of the Code defines insolvency in terms where liabilities on a discounted basis exceed assets. Thus the concept of insolvency differs. However it is more significant in the case of Chapter 11 filings to look to voluntary cases[30] and section 301 requires only that the applicant be a debtor under the relevant chapter. The term debtor is defined in section 109 which apart from some minor exceptions[31] allows any debtor allowed to file under Chapter 7 to also file under Chapter 11.[32]

The lack of an insolvency requirement in relation to a filing under Chapter 11 should however also be seen in the context of the nature of the process under the Bankruptcy Code. The process involves a court filing as the trigger for all of the consequences that the procedure will involve. Hence unlike the Anglo–Australian approach, in the United States there is a direct opportunity for the court to dismiss a case 'for cause'[33] although this is strictly not a condition of filing. This does not mean though that the court will impose a de facto insolvency test as 'a requirement that a Chapter 11 petition be filed in good faith appears nowhere in Chapter 11 of the Bankruptcy Code'.[34] Thus to the extent that the good faith requirement in relation to Chapter 11 filing is implied by the courts, it appears to deal not so much with the solvency of the debtor as with the question of the debtor

---

28   Bankruptcy Code 1978, sections 301 and 303.
29   It may also make orders where a secured creditor has acted within a 120-day period prior to filing.
30   See Block-Lieb, S., 'Why Creditors File So Few Involuntary Petitions and Why the Number is Not Too Small' (1991) 57 *Brooklyn Law Review* 803.
31   These being stockbrokers and commodity brokers as well as certain banks and like bodies.
32   There are some minor exceptions in relation filing under Chapter 7 such as railroads, certain foreign insurance companies etc. note also that the term person in section 109 will include a corporation by virtue of section 101.
33   Section 1112(b) and note also that the case may be converted to a Chapter 7 – a liquidation. It must also be recognised that there is opportunity to apply to the court under the Anglo–Australian models as well where there appears to be abuse of the process.
34   See Mojdehi, A. and Gertz J., 'The Implicit 'Good Faith' Requirement in Chapter 11 Liquidations: A Rule in Search of a Rationale? (2006) 14(1) *American Bankruptcy Institute Law Review* 143 at 144.

being solvent *and continuing to deal with his or her assets* rather than handing them over.[35]

The Comparative Aspect of the Insolvency Requirement

Nevertheless, the lack of a direct requirement for insolvency is a point of difference in approach in the three countries studied. The United States position has been justified on the basis that 'insolvency may not be easy to measure at the outset of a case'.[36] Such a justification seems weak as whilst not every case may be clear cut, there is reason to believe that in many instances it will be clear or at least apparent enough. Where there is some doubt it may be covered by the phrase 'likely to become insolvent'. The use of such a requirement will at least force those attempting to use the procedure to consider the use in that context rather than in the context of a strategic advantage.

The lack of a requirement for insolvency is also justified on the basis that creditors may pre-empt a bankruptcy test because they may be aware that the debtor stands a chance of becoming bankrupt. Hence creditors may grab assets that in a bankruptcy will distributed in an orderly and rateable fashion. The ability of the debtor to go to a bankruptcy procedure before insolvency occurs is justified on this ground. This however may be overcome by the use of the phrase 'likely to become insolvent'. Further the ability to claim back antecedent transactions in the bankruptcy should provide a disincentive for creditors to do so.

As Jackson has pointed out,[37] the use of insolvency test to establish the right to an insolvency procedure may not always be sufficient but that does not mean that using a case by case approach to establish those commencements undertaken in bad faith is a better method of proceeding. That is because the case by case analysis is likely to be expensive and given the different decisions that may be made in individual circumstances, inconsistent.[38] It will be more effective to provide for the test within the requirements to utilise the procedure and allow a case by case analysis of those situations where the requirement has not been met. This suggests that the Anglo–Australian test of insolvency or likely to become insolvent provides, at least in theory, more likelihood of procedures being commenced only where they are likely to be beneficial generally rather than be

---

35   Ibid., at 158.

36   See Baird, D.G., *The Elements of Bankruptcy* (2001, Foundation Press, New York NY) at 8.

37   See Jackson, above note 2 at 199.

38   Although it has been suggested that relative priorities are preferable to absolute priority in order to preserve creditors rights where the firm cannot be quickly auctioned: Baird, D.G. and Rasmussen, R.K., 'Control Rights, Priority Rights, and the Conceptual Foundations of Corporate Reorganizations' (2001) 87 *Virginia Law Review* 921, available at SSRN: <ssrn.com/abstract=278841> (last viewed 31 May 2007).

utilised for example by an interest group to gain a strategic advantage of some kind.

The approach of not requiring any insolvency by debtors filing to commence a bankruptcy procedure but requiring creditors to do so, also suggests an inconsistency in approach. The debtor is in fact the most likely party to be aware of the company's correct financial position and to seek strategic advantage in relation to corporate rescue or reorganization processes and that appears to support the view that it is for the debtor to establish the insolvency as a basis for using the procedure.

One argument that can be presented in favour of the United States approach is that an insolvency requirement may be seen to unduly inhibit attempts at reconstruction and recovery because it enables commencement at a stage that is too late. It is also suggested that the use of insolvency tests are likely to delay attempts at solving an enterprise's financial difficulties. This argument has some merit and again calls into consideration the need to balance encouraging early action on the one hand and providing too much opportunity for strategic behaviour on the other.

The argument was recently considered in the Australian context by the Corporations and Markets Advisory Committee.[39] That Committee recommended against easing the requirement of insolvency or likely insolvency as the trigger for voluntary administration.[40] Their rejection of easing the insolvency requirement was based on the grounds that the current wording provided enough scope for situations where appointments were appropriate[41] and that any alternative would leave the prospect of appointment as 'too open ended'. The Committee also pointed out that because shareholders as well as creditors have their rights frozen under the voluntary administration procedure it means that there is a real risk of the procedure being abused in situations where a dispute arises between the board and the shareholders or groups of shareholders.

The above analysis suggests that as the financial situation of corporations will at any time sit on a continuum between firms that are financially sound and those that are insolvent the Anglo-Australian approach in this area sets the threshold for using the relevant procedure more closely to the point of insolvency whereas there may be more of a chance that the United States approach will allow for a commencement further away from the point of insolvency.

---

39   Generally referred to as CAMAC. This is a government funded advisory group which advises on corporate and related law issues.

40   Of interest is the Corporations and Markets Advisory Committee Rehabilitating large and complex enterprises in financial difficulties Report 2004, CAMAC, Sydney (October 2004) at 20–25, available online at: <www.camac.gov.au> (last viewed 31 May 2007).

41   Reference was made to *Crimmins v Glenview Home Units Pty Ltd* [2001] NSWSC 699 at [51] where Palmer J stated that '... the scope for forming an opinion of likely insolvency is very broad ... a director may legitimately form the view that insolvency is likely ten years hence ...'. If such a broad interpretation is available it makes it easy to justify an appointment.

The generous interpretation of the terms used in the Anglo-Australian legislation may reduce these perceived differences somewhat practically but the United States approach seems to lead to a more strategic use of the process whereas the Anglo-Australian approach may prevent earlier efforts to deal with the insolvency. The use of the criteria cannot be entirely separated from the process itself however and the existence of the specialist bankruptcy court at the centre of the United States system probably enables the more liberal standard to work effectively in that jurisdiction. This is in contrast with the approach in the Anglo-Australian procedures that would necessarily involve greater expense were the case by case approach adopted as well as requiring a court determination in circumstances where minimal court involvement is part of the aim of the Anglo-Australian procedure.

Procedural Requirements

The different approaches taken regarding commencement are reflected in the procedure that is adopted in each of the jurisdictions. Whilst there is much similarity between the Australian and the United Kingdom approaches there are important differences. The approach in the United States reflects a very different regime with specialist courts having the central role.

As outlined above, the administration procedure in the United Kingdom can be commenced in one of three ways.[42] The Australian voluntary administration procedure may also be commenced in one of three ways[43] however as between the United Kingdom and the Australian procedure there are only two parties that are the same in each jurisdiction.[44] In the United States, the procedure is commenced only by a filing in the Bankruptcy Court although this may be done by either voluntarily by a debtor[45] or by an involuntary process by creditors[46]. As noted above it is regarded as relatively rare for the creditors to initiate proceedings particularly in Chapter 11.

---

42 Namely by a Court order, by a holder of a qualifying charge, or by the company or its directors.

43 Under the Australian provisions it is by the directors or a liquidator (or provisional liquidator) or a holder of a charge over the whole or substantially the whole of the assets.

44 Namely the board and a qualifying charge holder. The tests for qualification for the charge holder are essentially the same in each jurisdiction. The only difference in qualification is that the United Kingdom provisions refer to a floating charge only whereas in Australia there is no such limitation.

45 Bankruptcy Code 1978, section 301.

46 Ibid., section 303. It should be noted that this section requires at least three creditors and there may be other restrictions depending upon the circumstances.

Who May Commence?

Since the process may be commenced by the debtor in the United States and by the directors in both the United Kingdom and Australia, there is a clear consensus across the jurisdictions that attempts to rescue a company or at least its business should be able to be initiated by those stakeholders that are in control of the company. This has a fundamental logic attached to it in that the controllers of the business will be seeking to ensure that the company survives because it is their reputation as well as their investment[47] that will be at stake. In addition it is this group that is generally best informed about the position of the business financially and from a theoretical perspective may have incentives to otherwise hold out from entering into formal insolvency procedures in the belief that a turnaround in fortunes is just ahead.

It is important that the legislation provide the appropriate incentives for directors or management to enter into the procedure at a stage when there is a chance of success. It appears to be the case that most of the procedures examined will be commenced in this way in all three jurisdictions.[48] Therefore what follows in terms of discussion about the differences may raise possible difficulties that have less practical significance. However if the other forms of commencement are of little use this discussion is useful because it can then be asked 'why do such differences need to exist at all?'.

Impact of other Insolvency Procedures

Another similarity is that each jurisdiction allows commencement when another procedure has already begun. Australia is unique in providing for the direct appointment by a liquidator or provisional liquidator where the company is insolvent.[49] In Australia, neither the directors nor a qualifying charge holder can appoint an administrator once the company is being wound up.[50]

---

47   This could be a financial investment but it will almost certainly be the investment of time and energy as well, for which see Blair, M. and Stout, L., 'A Team Production Theory of Corporate Law' (1999) 85 *Virginia Law Review* 247.

48   In the United States, see Block-Lieb, above note 30, and also Warren, E., and Westbrook, J., *The Law of Debtors and Creditors* (4th ed) (2001, Aspen Law and Business, New York NY) at 500 where it is stated that 'In principle, a business will always file in Chapter 11, rather than Chapter 7, unless there is absolutely no hope of financial survival. In the United Kingdom, there appears to be no statistics and it must be recognized that holders of qualifying charges have a power to withhold consent from such appointments but Goode comments that 'out of court administration is likely to be the norm': see Goode, above note 6 at 345. In Australia again there are no statistics kept on whether the appointments are made by the directors, liquidators or qualifying charge holders but it is generally accepted that by far the majority of appointments are made by the board of directors: see Anderson, C., 'The Australian Corporate Rescue Regime: Bold Experiment or Sensible Policy?' (2001) 10 *International Insolvency Review* 81 at 85.

49   Or likely to become insolvent: Corporations Act 2001 (Cth), section 436B. The only

In the United Kingdom, a somewhat similar prohibition applies so that appointments may not be made when there is either a voluntary winding up or a winding up order by the court.[51] However, this is subject to two exceptions in the case of a court ordered winding up and one exception in the case of a voluntary winding up. Under both forms of winding up, the liquidator may make an application to the court for an administration order[52] whereas under a court ordered winding up it is also possible for a qualifying charge holder to apply to the court[53] for an administration order.

In the United States, the court is already involved in the procedure so that a change in the regime must go through that venue – as it must in the United Kingdom. There is the ability to convert from either Chapter 7 liquidation to a Chapter 11 case and vice versa through the court application.[54] The conversion may be asked for by any party of interest. There are some limits in this however in that a conversion from a Chapter 7 to a Chapter 11 case cannot occur if the application is by a debtor and the court had already converted it to a Chapter 7.[55]

The ability to appoint an administrator directly from liquidation[56] without court involvement provides an interesting feature of a voluntary administration in Australia and shows determination in the framing of the procedure to avoid court costs. There are only two constraints on the liquidator's action here. First it is always subject to the general duties that exist in relation to liquidators.[57] Second the appointment requires approval by the court if the liquidator seeks to have themselves appointed as the administrator.[58]

The provision for appointment by a liquidator in Australia was suggested in the Harmer Report and states to be aimed at 'operating as a mechanism for converting a members' voluntary winding up to the administration procedure'[59] where there was an opportunity to promote a deed of arrangement. The ultimate wording used in the provision does not; however limit the appointment to the

---

court involvement is if the liquidator or provisional liquidator wishes to appoint himself or herself as the administrator then leave of the court must be obtained: section 436B(2). It is likely though that this will usually be the case in such appointments given the liquidator's existing knowledge of the company.

50 Corporations Act 2001 (Cth), section 436A(2).

51 Insolvency Act 1986, Schedule B1, paragraph 8.

52 Ibid., paragraph 38.

53 Ibid., paragraph 37.

54 Bankruptcy Code 1978, sections 706 and 1112.

55 Ibid., section 706(a).

56 It should also be noted that there is no distinction drawn between court ordered and voluntary winding up in section 436B – however see the discussion below about how it originated.

57 Discussed generally in Keay, A., *McPherson's: The Law of Company Liquidation* (4th ed) (LBC, Sydney, 1999) at 357ff. Thus, for example, it would seem possible to attack a decision to appoint an administrator by a liquidator on the basis that it represents a breach of the duty to realise assets within a reasonable time.

58 Corporations Act 2001 (Cth), section 436B(2).

59 Harmer Report at paragraph [63].

situation of a voluntary winding up. Thus the power was envisaged to exist in the context of a range of amendments where creditors' voluntary liquidations were to be abolished.[60] If there were no creditors' voluntary winding up, the suggestion was that the liquidator in a members' voluntary winding up, where he or she discovers the company is insolvent, would move to a voluntary administration. Ultimately, though there was no abolition of the creditors' voluntary winding up provisions,[61] which suggests that the legislature may have inserted the provisions without fully understanding the significance of them. Further the ability of a liquidator to appoint an administrator is not restricted to voluntary windings up. Under the Australian provisions therefore the liquidator has a wide power and the exercise does not of itself require approval from the court or the creditors.[62]

One of the strange consequences of the wording of the Australian provisions and the ability of the liquidator to appoint without a court order is that it is possible for liquidations and voluntary administrations to operate concurrently.[63] This is because there is no specific provision that terminates the liquidation where an appointment of an administrator is made by a liquidator. Unlike the United Kingdom provisions that require a court order for the appointment of an administrator once the company is in liquidation, there is not necessarily any such hearing in Australia. Even where there is an application for leave to appoint himself or herself by the liquidator, there is no requirement that any winding up order be discharged – again unlike the United Kingdom.[64] In Australia, it is left to the applicant administrator (or liquidator) to seek an order of the court to terminate the winding up.[65] The result is additional costs in the form of court applications that the procedure is designed to avoid.

---

60   Ibid., at paragraph [57].
61   Corporations Act 2001 (Cth), section 496(1) and section 497. The continued existence of creditors' voluntary winding up has been criticized in the CASAC Report, which has recommended its abolition: Legal Committee of the Companies and Securities Advisory Committee Corporate Voluntary Administration Final Report (June 1998) at paragraph 8.70. The government has refused to accept this though and has preferred to propose changes to the voluntary winding procedure: Corporations Amendment (Insolvency) Bill 2007 (Cth) Items 89–90, available at: <www.treasury.gov.au/ contentitem.asp?NavId=&ContentID=1186> (last viewed 31 May 2007).
62   The court's approval must be sought only if the liquidator seeks to appoint himself or herself as administrator so in these circumstances there is a review of the liquidator's decision: In relation to the case law on this see, for example, *Re Depsun Pty Ltd* (1994) 13 ACSR 644, *DCT v Foodcorp Pty Ltd* (1994) 113 ACSR 796, *Beatty v Brashs Pty Ltd* (1998) 26 ACSR 685, *Re Cobar Mines Pty Ltd* (1998) 30 ACSR 125 and *Re Intag International Limited and the Corporations Law* [1999] NSWSC 571 (unreported Young J, 9 June 1999).
63   It has been held that the powers of the liquidator cease but are revived once the administration ends in the same way that the director's powers would do so. The liquidation thus also revives: see *Re Nardell Coal Corporation Pty Limited* [2004] NSWSC 281.
64   Insolvency Act 1986, Schedule B1, paragraph 38.
65   Corporations Act 2001 (Cth), section 482.

The existence of provisions in all jurisdictions allowing the conversion from liquidation type procedure to a corporate rescue process – either directly or through a court application – does suggest a need to link the administration/rescue process to liquidation. Whilst it is recognised that a legitimate outcome of an administration both in Australia and in the United Kingdom is liquidation,[66] it must also be noted that a corporate rescue regime will have at least part of its focus upon the continued existence of the company. Once a company is in liquidation however, the focus has always been on winding up the company's affairs.[67] It may be argued that the liquidation process ought to continue to its conclusion without the possibility of changing to another administration part way through.

Powers Given

In addition to these considerations, there are broad powers given to liquidators in both Australia[68] and the United Kingdom,[69] the powers given to a liquidator are now quite extensive. Thus it is reasonable to consider whether any justification exists to grant the liquidator a power to change or ask the court to change the type of administration in progress.

It seems that the answer lies in the ability to choose an effective regime that can maximize the benefits for particular stakeholders. An ability to move with minimum cost between the various regimes to the one best suited to a particular commercial outcome, seems desirable.

In the context of rescue procedures, it seems reasonable and apposite that if an administration/rescue procedure appears to be the most effective legal mechanism for the facilitation of the re-organization of a business (or even to maximize the value by sale as a going concern in a situation of insolvency), then the mechanism needs to be available even in circumstances where a liquidation was the procedure originally entered into. Therefore although the powers exist for a liquidator to do this, the circumstances where the powers are exercised are not always conducive to a commercially satisfactory result.[70] We believe that there will be a saving in terms of net costs in a corporate rescue as opposed to liquidation.[71]

---

66 In Australia the courts have recognized that voluntary administration may be used even though there is no prospect of saving the company: see *Dallinger v Halcha Holdings Pty Ltd (admr apptd)* (1995) 18 ACSR 835 at 842 per Sundberg J who said 'Section 435A does not in my view require Pt 5.3A to be limited to the case where at the date of the administrator's appointment, there is some prospect of saving the company from liquidation'.

67 Keay, above note 57 at 357.

68 Corporations Act 2001 (Cth), section 477.

69 Insolvency Act 1986, Schedule 4.

70 For an Australian example, see *Re Cobar Mines Pty Ltd* (1998) 30 ACSR 125 where the company moved from administration to liquidation and then back again in order to achieve funding for the payment of debts owing to creditors.

71 This is not to suggest that the position can be stated with any certainty as to whether the costs of attempting to save a particular company or its business are less than any benefits that might accrue. It is just that the benefits may exist and should be used to

Movement between Procedures

Thus there is a common thread in the jurisdictions that provides opportunity for increasing returns to creditors by moving from one procedure to another. The ability to move between the various procedures with fewer costs will, all other things being equal, create a stronger insolvency regime that accurately responds to the particular situation which the company faces as the insolvency develops. By reducing the barriers to such movement, the costs of the insolvency regime are reduced and that will benefit creditors in the longer term. The extent that this can occur expeditiously raises the need to evaluate efficiency of both liquidation and the administration/rescue procedures. It also emphasises the need to consider all forms of insolvency administrations when considering matters of policy.

However if this much appears to be common then what are the differences in the procedure? Despite the common heritage and the approach in Australia to follow closely the English law in many aspects of corporate law and insolvency more generally, there is a difference in the ability of creditors to seek commencement of a voluntary administration.

The Australian provisions are unique in that a court is unable to commence the voluntary administration process; it may only be done in an out of court procedure in contrast with the United States system that places the court at the centre of the bankruptcy process generally. The United Kingdom provisions sit in between the two ends of the spectrum in this matter, and allow *inter alia* for an application to be made to the court for an order by 'one or more of the creditors'[72] as well as certain other stakeholders.[73] There are of course conditions[74] in terms of inability to pay debts and that the order is reasonably likely to achieve its purposes.[75]

The inability of a court on application by a creditor to make an order for the commencement of a voluntary administration has been the source of criticism of the Australian regime[76] but recent proposed amendments do not make any

---

match against the costs of any rescue. As to this issue generally, see Warren, E., 'Bankruptcy Policy' (1987) 54 *University of Chicago Law Review* 775 at 787.

72   Insolvency Act 1986, Schedule B1, paragraph 12. It may also be noted that unlike in the United States, the creditor here may be a contingent and a prospective creditor.

73   Ibid., paragraphs 37 and 38, including, as discussed above, a qualifying charge holder and a liquidator.

74   Ibid., paragraph 11.

75   Ibid., paragraph 3, setting out the purposes. Essentially these involve rescuing the company as a going concern or achieving a better result for the creditors than winding up or realising property for secured or preferential creditors.

76   Companies and Securities Advisory Committee (CASAC) Legal Committee Corporate Voluntary Administration Final Report (June 1998) at paragraphs 7.8–7.9. The Report recommended that creditors be given a general right to apply to the court for an order to place the company in voluntary administration as an alternative to asking for a winding up based on the view that creditors should not be restricted to asking for a winding up when the directors are not acting to deal with the insolvency of the company.

suggestion for change.[77] In Australia, a qualifying charge-holder (and no other creditor) has the right to appoint an administrator[78] resulting in an inequity between creditors in effecting appointment. The United Kingdom system that enables the court to make an appointment – even if it is not widely used – is conceptually more sound in encouraging so far as is possible the rescue of the company or its business. The Australian provisions in this area are likely to result in liquidation of the company where the directors refuse to act to deal with the insolvency.[79]

There is no means whereby the 'court application approach' of the United States can be evaluated as being better or worse than the 'avoid the court application approach' in Australia.[80] The United Kingdom approach provides a hybrid model being somewhere in between the two jurisdictions with appointment being possible either out of court or by court appointment. It seems however that the United Kingdom corporate rescue regime is closer to the Australian approach overall.

There are many institutional and social factors[81] that make comparative evaluations of the means of commencement an imprecise judgement. The best that can be done is to track movements in legislation towards one approach or the other. The changes to the United Kingdom provisions as a result of the Enterprise Act 2002[82] may be viewed, in broad terms at least, as a movement towards the Australian approach. On the other hand, there was a concerted push in Australia to adopt a United States-style Chapter 11 for larger companies in 2002 when the Government referred the question of how best to rehabilitate large and complex enterprises in financial difficulties to the advisory CAMAC panel.[83] Ultimately that suggestion was rejected by CAMAC[84] and then by the Government[85] but it does

---

77   Corporations Amendment (Insolvency) Bill 2007 (Cth), available at <www.treasury.gov.au/contentitem.asp?NavId=&ContentID=1186> (last viewed 31 May 2007).

78   Either secured or unsecured.

79   It may be noted though that a liquidator may subsequently appoint an administrator under Corporations Act 2001 (Cth), section 436B, however in practical terms this is not likely to happen except in very limited circumstances as the liquidator is generally focused on closing the business rather than having it survive.

80   Or the United Kingdom hybrid approach for that matter.

81   For example Australia relies heavily on the registration of liquidators to ensure that standards of independence and public interests are maintained in any voluntary administration. It does not have a specialist court with any detailed expertise in 'running' a corporate rescue. On the other hand there appears to be extensive expertise within the legal profession in the United States with its specialist court that can take account of these factors.

82   Goode describes these changes as having 'revolutionized the law governing administrative receivership and administration' Goode, above note 6 at 318.

83   CAMAC being the Corporations and Markets Advisory Committee: See Corporations and Markets Advisory Committee Rehabilitating large and complex enterprises in financial difficulties Discussion Paper 2003, CAMAC, Sydney (September 2003).

84   Corporations and Markets Advisory Committee Rehabilitating large and complex enterprises in financial difficulties Report 2004, CAMAC, Sydney (October 2004) in Chapter 2: available online at: <www.camac.gov.au> (last viewed 31 May 2007).

show that there are elements of dissatisfaction with both approaches and that no one way of dealing with corporate rescue will provide a panacea for difficulties that will arise with such a regulatory system from time to time.

View of Creditors

The commencement processes between the jurisdictions also differ in their approach to secured creditors. It is a feature of the Anglo-Australian approach that the holders of a qualifying charge are given controlling positions in relation to appointment. No such power exists in the United States system. The United States provides a much more even handed approach between creditors insofar as the commencement processes are concerned[86] whereas the Anglo-Australian approach, based on a long history of powers of private appointment of receivers by secured creditors, allows a preferred position within the administration process.

Westbrook[87] has described this issue in terms of a struggle for control in bankruptcy.[88] It is argued by Westbrook that there is in the bankruptcy reorganization process 'bankruptcy control' over the assets of value by way of the either debtor in possession in the United States (or an administrator in the United Kingdom and Australia) taking control away from secured creditors. This does not happen in liquidation where generally the secured creditor is able to deal with the charged assets. It is possible therefore that the controlling position of secured creditors in terms of appointment that exists in the United Kingdom and Australian provisions represents an attempt to maintain some rights in the hands of at least the largest of the secured creditors even though the right of appointment[89] may be of limited value given the duty of the administrator once appointed to act in accordance with the legislation and the interests of all creditors generally rather than focus on the secured creditor's interest.

The role of secured credit in insolvency has produced much debate and there seems to be a clear difference between the United States approach and the Anglo-Australian view that perhaps reflects the stronger regulatory position of the

---

85   The Government released a draft Bill of proposed changes in November 2006 and these are aimed at strengthening the voluntary administration procedure without making fundamental changes: Corporations Amendment (Insolvency) Bill 2007 (Cth), available at: <www.treasury.gov.au/contentitem.asp?NavId=&ContentID=1186> (last viewed 31 May 2007).

86   This may also apply to the overall procedure as well although this is a much broader issue than that which is being raised here.

87   See Westbrook, J., 'The Control of Wealth in Bankruptcy' (2004) 82 *Texas Law Review* 795.

88   Ibid., at 804–805, where Westbrook makes the point that there is no issue with respect to priority for the secured creditor in that priority is generally maintained in the relevant procedure but that there is conflict over control of the process between the general creditors and the secured creditor.

89   And in the case of the United Kingdom the right to refuse consent to appointment by the directors or the company: Insolvency Act 1986, Schedule B1, paragraph 26.

financial institutions in both the United Kingdom and Australia as compared with the more competitive environment of banking in the United States.

In Australia, appointment of an administrator may be made by a person who has a charge[90] over the requisite level of the company's property provided the charge is enforceable.[91] This applies only where the company is not already in liquidation.[92] Whilst this on its face appears similar to the United Kingdom provision, it is important to realise that there is an important difference. This is that in Australia the relevant charge-holder in this situation has the power to appoint a receiver to the company as an alternative to appointing an administrator.

The requisite level of property over which the charge must exist to be able to appoint an administrator is the whole, or substantially the whole, of the company's property. No definition is given in the Corporations Act as to what the 'whole or substantially the whole' of the property means.[93]

The origin of the right to appoint an administrator in Australia is the Harmer Report[94] that appears to base the right of a qualifying charge holder to appoint the administrator on two broad grounds, namely that:

- default under a charge is likely to indicate an inability to pay debts, and therefore the availability of the procedure is triggered;
- the creation of the right and the use of it by a secured creditor results in better protection for unsecured creditors as compared with the appointment of a receiver.

Neither of these justifications is particularly compelling. However, whilst the initial point (the default point) may be true in many situations, O'Donovan points out that 'mortgage debentures usually provide a wide variety of grounds on which the charge created by the debenture becomes enforceable'.[95] Accordingly, the power to appoint in this case is quite wide. Default will not therefore necessarily mean that the company is insolvent in accordance with section 95A and there is no general right held by creditors to have an administrator appointed in the case of insolvency under the Australian regime. The need to have insolvent companies put under external administration is probably more important to unsecured creditors simply because they have no security to rely upon. If this

---

90   'Charge' is defined in Corporations Act 2001 (Cth), section 9. It means a charge created in any way and includes a mortgage and an agreement to give or execute a charge or mortgage.

91   Section 436C. As to the meaning of 'enforceable', no definition is given in the Corporations Act in this context, but section 9 does define 'enforce' where the company is 'under administration'. These situations are likely to apply in this context as well.

92   Section 436C(2).

93   See, however, the discussion and reference to the United Kingdom provisions and interpretation in O'Donovan, J., *Company Receivers and Managers* (2nd ed) (LBC Information Services, Sydney) (loose-leaf service) at paragraph [30.30].

94   Harmer Report at paragraph [66].

95   O'Donovan, above note 93 at paragraph [30.30].

argument is valid, an unsecured creditor should perhaps also have a right to seek appointment.[96]

The second (better protection) justification implies some altruism on the part of the charge holder. The appointment is only likely to be made where some benefit accrues to the qualifying charge holder and in the case of Australia, this does not come from the appointment of a receiver.

In the United Kingdom, there is a power to appoint an administrator by a qualifying charge holder. As Goode explains,[97] there are three requirements[98] that need to be satisfied for this type of appointment:

- the charge is a qualifying floating charge;
- the chargee is the holder of such a charge; and
- the power to appoint has become exercisable under the charge.

A qualifying charge has to be a floating charge and it must either specifically state that paragraph 14 of Schedule B1 of the Insolvency Act applies to the charge or it purports to empower the holder of the floating charge to appoint an administrator or an administrative receiver.[99] In order to be the holder of such a charge the person must have a debenture secured by a qualifying charge that relates to the whole or substantially the whole of the company's property. Alternatively where there is more than one charge (or other forms of security), then the total amount must comprise the whole or substantially the whole of the property of the company and at least one of the charges must be a qualifying charge.[100] The final requirement is that the charge must be enforceable.

Although rights to appoint an administrative receiver remain for charges created before 15 September 2003 and some other minor exceptions,[101] the difference between the Australian and the United Kingdom position is now that the right to appoint an administrative receiver[102] no longer exists in the United Kingdom.[103] In this context, it is interesting to note that the right to appoint a receiver is not something that appears to be controversial in Australia and the

---

96   As discussed above.
97   Goode, above note 6 at 20.
98   In addition, permission must be obtained from a prior qualifying charge holder if one exists after giving written notice of at least two business days notice: Insolvency Act 1986, Schedule B1, paragraph 15.
99   Administrative receivership was abolished with the adoption of the new provisions relating to administration as a result of the Enterprise Act 2002 (UK). Special provisions relate to Scotland.
100   Insolvency Act 1986, Schedule B1, paragraph 14(3).
101   Ibid., section 72A.
102   In Australia, the term administrative receivership is not used but the characteristics of the Australian receivership is in the important respects the same particularly in relation to the appointee being agent of the company and the receiver's rights to act primarily in the interest of the appointor provided it is done in good faith.
103   Rights to appoint a receiver remain but the receiver's powers are very limited in comparison to the usual position in Australia.

recent reviews of the legislation have not raised it as an issue. This may be because the secured creditors have, to a large extent, supported the voluntary administration processes and have not sought to exploit their rights at the expense of the more general procedure.

In the United Kingdom, the qualifying charge holder also has the right to prevent an appointment by the directors or the company although it would be possible for those parties to seek an appointment by the court. In addition in the event of a court ordered winding up, it is possible for the qualifying charge holder to apply to the court for an order appointing an administrator, ending the liquidation.[104]

Conclusion

This chapter has examined the commencement of the corporate rescue/ reorganisation provisions in three jurisdictions (United Kingdom, United States and Australia). It proceeds on the basis that these types of provisions are significant if not central to the operation of the insolvency laws in all three jurisdictions. The detailed analysis is therefore necessary to determine if these commencement provisions operate effectively or ideally, given the similar commercial environments as between jurisdictions.

The chapter determines that whilst there is some common ground between each of the regimes considered, there are also differences and these differences are significant.

Whilst the analysis here is restricted to commencement procedures, the authors do not deny other equally important aspects of corporate rescue. It is the view of this paper however that the commencement procedures clearly establish the most fundamental issues with respect to the advantages that may be taken by corporate participants in the process and identifying those that are able to initiate that advantage.

The analysis reveals that the primary driver in all jurisdictions is the debtors themselves through the directors of the relevant company. This cross-border consistency suggests that the provisions recognize that rescue or reorganization is a management issue faced by the company in financial difficulty since they are most likely to have the greatest day to day knowledge of the company's operations. Accordingly it may be appropriate to also recognize that a failure to act with respect to financial difficulty represents behaviour that is to be discouraged.

The analysis also shows the different approaches in relation to the role of the court in the processes examined ranging from virtually no involvement (in Australia) to the central role played in the United States. This issue appears to therefore depend upon the institutions that exist in each jurisdiction for ensuring a check on the process. As there is significant regulation surrounding the registration of insolvency practitioners in Australia the limited role of the court may be

---

104   Insolvency Act 1986, Schedule B1, paragraphs 8(1)(b) and 37.

appropriate however the existence of specialist bankruptcy courts in the United States enables a more independent supervision of the commencement procedure, In the United States, however, this independent supervision is coupled with the lack of a requirement of insolvency to file and the ability of the debtor to remain in possession after commencement. Because of these institutional factors it is not possible to suggest that one approach is better or worse than another but that does not mean that recognition of other jurisdictions may not provide insights that may assist in improving a particular system.

The absence of an insolvency requirement in the United States legislation has been criticized though the impact is lessened because of the institutional structure of the process there. Nevertheless it is possible to recognize that absent those structures in Australia and the United Kingdom, the insolvency requirement is fundamental as means of determining the appropriate boundaries of the procedure in an effective manner that reduces costly court battles. The jurisdictions also differ in relation to the role of secured creditors and whether they may play a role in the commencement of the procedure as an alternative way of enforcing their rights. This aspect might be usefully examined in further study particularly as to how issues of control of the process and priority with respect to payment may be dealt with in a rescue scenario.

Chapter 5

A Comparative Analysis of Administration Regimes in Australia and the United Kingdom

Andrew Keay

Introduction

It is trite to say that in the past 20 years corporate rescue has gradually increased in importance and emphasis around the world. Corporate rescue has been defined as 'a major intervention necessary to avert the eventual failure of the company'[1] and 'the revival of companies on the brink of economic collapse and the salvage of economically viable units to restore production capacity, employment and the continued rewarding of capital and investment'.[2] Often a critical aspect of any potential rescue is for the debtor company to enter some form of shelter regime which will enable the company to avail itself of a moratorium in relation to claims against it, and permit an arrangement of some sort that will facilitate rescue being agreed and put in place. If the rescue of an insolvent or near-insolvent company is to occur, generally the company's directors require time to consider what options are available and to confer with creditors while the company is safe from attack by impatient and/or disgruntled creditors, so it is often imperative that the company is able to embrace some kind of shelter. If rescue is going to be considered by the creditors they will often want to ensure that the property and business of the company is preserved, if practicable and possible, during the period when directors are seeking advice and contemplating rescue, and while they are themselves possibly assessing the company. The classic shelter regime is probably perceived to be that provided by Chapter 11 of the United States' Bankruptcy Reform Act 1978. Shelter regimes have been introduced in two other developed countries, the United Kingdom and Australia in the past 20 years, with the former's being known simply as 'administration' and the latter's 'voluntary administration'. While the forms of administration in both countries are long-standing, they have both been the subject of significant scrutiny in recent years. The United Kingdom's regime was subject to substantial overhaul with the passing of the Enterprise Act 2002.

---

1 See Belcher, A., *Corporate Rescue* (1997, Sweet and Maxwell, London) at 8.
2 See Omar, P., 'Thoughts on the Purpose of Corporate Rescue' [1997] 4 *Journal of International Banking Law* 127.

The Australian regime was the subject of close examination in 2003 and 2004 by a parliamentary Joint Committee on Corporations and Financial Services, and by the Corporations and Markets Advisory Committee, and there are indications from the Federal Government in Australia that there will be some reform of the voluntary administration process in the near future, although it is referred to merely as 'fine-tuning'.[3]

The chapter, after providing a detailed background to the procedures under view and a consideration of the purposes of these procedures, provides an analytical comparison of the United Kingdom and Australian regimes, with particular emphasis on appointment of administrators, creditors' meetings, the role of courts, the end of and exit from the regimes and what can be done concerning pre-administration transactions and irresponsible trading. This analysis will point up aspects of good practice and problem areas that might both be considered by United Kingdom and Australian law-makers and practitioners, as well as those persons interested in insolvency law and practice in other jurisdictions that are contemplating introducing or reforming a shelter regime. Comparing the legislation in the two jurisdictions is helpful and instructive as the United Kingdom and Australia are both common law jurisdictions with similar corporate law and insolvency law regimes, and this enables us to focus on the differences in the respective laws without the impediment of having to take into account differences in the structure of the respective legal systems. Also, the jurisdictions maintain a very similar ethos to the regulation of insolvency, and employ similar terms and approaches.

It should be pointed out at the outset that neither administration nor voluntary administration is a rescue procedure *per se*. They certainly are shelter regimes, and they can be viewed as preliminary regimes to possible rescue, but a rescue process might not follow from administration or voluntary administration, and if one does follow, it will be totally separate from these regimes.

Finally, it is not intended to explain, other than briefly, the process that is involved with either of the regimes under examination as that has been ably done in each jurisdiction already.[4] My main aim is to focus on those aspects of both

---

3   Parliamentary Secretary to the Treasurer, the Hon. Chris Pearce MP, 12 October 2005, and available at: <www.treasury.gov.au/documents/1022/PDF/Corporate_Insolvancy_Reform_attachment.pdf> (last viewed 31 May 2007). The proposals are now contained in the Corporations Amendment (Insolvency) Bill 2007.

4   For instance, for the United Kingdom, see Bailey, E., Groves, H. and Smith, C., *Corporate Insolvency Law and Practice* (2nd ed) (2001, Butterworths, London); Finch, V., *Corporate Insolvency Law: Perspectives and Principles* (2002, Cambridge University Press, Cambridge); Fletcher, I.F., *The Law of Insolvency* (3rd ed) (2002, Sweet and Maxwell, London); Goode, R., *Principles of Company Insolvency Law* (3rd ed) (2005, Sweet and Maxwell, London,); Keay, A. and Walton, P., *Insolvency Law: Corporate and Personal* (2003, Pearson, Harlow); Davies, S. (ed.), *Insolvency and the Enterprise Act 2002* (2003, Jordans, Bristol); Doyle, L. and Keay, A., *Insolvency Legislation: Annotations and Commentary* (2nd ed) (2006, Jordans, Bristol) at 619–734. For Australia, see Murray, M., *Keay's Insolvency: Personal and Corporate Law and Practice* (5th ed) (2005, Law Book Co, Sydney); Anderson, C. and Morrison, D.,

regimes that enable us to draw some interesting comparisons, although of course to make the discussion understandable it will be necessary to outline some aspects of the respective procedures. I should add by way of disclaimer that the chapter does not purport to be exhaustive. There are many issues that I have not been able to broach, given the limits of space, and some of the issues that I have broached, I have not done so comprehensively. The United Kingdom's regime will be referred to as 'administration' while the Australian regime will be referred to as 'voluntary administration'.[5]

Background

The starting-point for a consideration of the issue under study is the enactment of the Insolvency Act 1986 in the United Kingdom. This legislation unified both personal and corporate aspects of insolvency law for the first time in the United Kingdom. It was a response to the recommendations of the well-known Cork Report, a report flowing from a comprehensive and lengthy investigation into, and consideration of, United Kingdom insolvency law.[6] The Cork Committee[7] recognised that companies could sometimes be rescued by the appointment of an administrative receiver (a receiver appointed by a secured creditor holding a floating charge over the whole, or substantially the whole, of a company's property[8] (referred to in this chapter, for ease of exposition, as 'a substantial chargeholder'), but that unsecured creditors or chargeholders who were not substantial chargeholders could not initiate such a regime. So, the Cork Report recommended the introduction of administration in order to fill a void. However, initially administration was infrequently employed, something that is quite understandable with new methods and processes, but as can be seen from the table below, numbers stayed about the same and did not increase on a sustained basis until after 1999. By then, as we will see, the Government was committed to introducing some wide-ranging changes. It should be noted that at this time administration could only be commenced by court order on the application, primarily of the company itself or a creditor.[9]

Crutchfield's Annotated Corporate Voluntary Administration Law (3rd ed) (2002, Law Book Co, Sydney); O'Donovan, J., *Company Receivers and Administrators* (Law Book Co, Sydney, loose-leaf).

5   This term is technically a misnomer as a company can go into administration involuntarily at the behest of a chargeholder, but generally it is the company who decides that administration is appropriate for it.

6   The Report of the Insolvency Law Review Committee, Insolvency Law and Practice, Cmnd 858 (1982, HMSO, London).

7   Taking its name from the chairman of the committee, Sir Kenneth Cork.

8   Insolvency Act 1986, section 29(2).

9   Ibid., section 9(1). This provision has now been repealed by Enterprise Act 2002, section 248. Courts still retain the power to make administration orders: Insolvency Act 1986, paragraphs 10–12 of Schedule B1.

Table 5.1   Administration Procedures

1987	1988	1989	1990	1991	1992	1993	1994
131	198	135	211	206	179	112	159
1995	**1996**	**1997**	**1998**	**1999**	**2000**	**2001**	**2002**
163	210	196	338	440	438	698	643

Source: Insolvency Service Statistics.

Moving to the other end of the earth, voluntary administration was introduced as a result of the recommendations of Australia's equivalent to the Cork Committee, the Australian Law Reform Commission's General Insolvency Inquiry[10] (commonly known as 'the Harmer Committee'[11]). The Harmer Committee was concerned that there was insufficient flexibility in determining the fate of insolvent companies.[12] Too often the liquidation of an insolvent company was viewed as the only viable option. The two regimes which could be invoked by companies that were insolvent or near-insolvent, without the need for liquidation, official management (a procedure borrowed from South Africa) and schemes of arrangement (under what is now section 411 of the Corporations Act 2001 (a provision that is generally akin to section 425 of the British Companies Act 1985)), were not frequently used; where schemes of arrangement were used it was only generally for large companies because of the significant costs involved. There was clearly a need for a fresh form of regime and the Harmer Committee saw voluntary administration as the answer to that need. The Committee noted that in 1988 there was:

> very little emphasis upon or encouragement of a constructive approach to corporate insolvency by, for example, focussing on the possibility of saving a business (as distinct from the company itself) and preserving employment prospects.[13]

The Committee wanted a process that was capable of swift implementation, uncomplicated and inexpensive, and flexible, providing alternative forms of dealing with the financial affairs of the company.[14]

It is helpful to note that unlike the United Kingdom, the Australian authorities determined not to unify personal and corporate insolvency provisions.[15] As a result, while the Insolvency Act 1986 is the central piece of United Kingdom legislation with which we need to be concerned, the central piece of Australian

---

10   Report 45, 1988, Canberra.
11   Taking its name from its chairman, Ron Harmer.
12   Above note 10 at paragraph 53.
13   Ibid., at paragraph 52.
14   Ibid., at paragraph 54.
15   See Keay, A., 'The Unity of Insolvency Legislation: Time for a Re-think?' (1999) 7 *Insolvency Law Journal* 4.

legislation is the Corporations Act 2001 (formerly known as the 'Corporations Law') and Part 5.3A in particular.

The Harmer reforms were encapsulated in the Corporate Law Reform Act 1992 which became law in June 1993. While a number of important changes were introduced by this legislation, voluntary administration was very much the centrepiece of the reforms. In contrast to the United Kingdom's innovation, the new Australian regime was used widely from its genesis[16] and this continues to be the case.[17] The Australian legislation gave power to the directors, the company's liquidator (with leave of the court) or a substantial chargeholder to appoint an administrator.[18]

Returning to the United Kingdom, changes to the United Kingdom administration process can be traced back to 1999 when the Government began to focus on the need for more corporate rescue in the United Kingdom. In 1999, the then Secretary of State for Trade and Industry and the Chancellor of the Exchequer established a government review of corporate rescue and business reconstruction mechanisms and in September of that year a consultation document was produced by a review group.[19] As time went on there were indications that the Government wished to provide the right legal *milieu* for the fostering of a rescue culture. This culminated in the introduction to the House of Commons, in March 2002, of the Enterprise Bill, Chapter 10 of which focused on insolvency reform. After several debates, and the accommodation of some suggested amendments by the House of Lords, the Enterprise Act was passed and received the royal assent on 7 November 2002. The parts of the Act that dealt with corporate insolvency reforms became operative from 15 September 2003 and these provisions have, *prima facie* at least, revolutionised the amount of use of administration. To foster a better environment for corporate rescue, the Government sought to make the administration process more efficient and less costly. A major development is that administration can commence without the need for an order from a court. An administrator may be appointed extra-judicially by the company itself, the directors,[20] or a substantial chargeholder.[21] A substantial chargeholder is able to appoint, if either on its own or together with other securities, it holds what is known as a 'qualifying charge'. A qualifying charge is one that relates to the whole or substantially the whole of the company's undertaking and the debenture

---

16   Statement by Australian Society of Certified Practising Accountants, 18 January 1994; Lawson 'VAs proving useful in saving firms, insolvency experts say' (Australian Financial Review, 15 February 1994) at 34.

17   During the 2003 year, 40.3 per cent of all companies entering formal insolvency regimes went into voluntary administration. See Australian Parliament's Joint Committee on Corporations and Financial Services, Corporate Insolvency Laws: A Stocktake (30 June 2004) at paragraph 2.28, available at: <www.aph.gov.au/senate/committee/corporations_ctte/completed_inquiries/2002-04/ail/report/ail.pdf>   (last viewed 31 May 2007).

18   Corporations Act 2001, sections 436A, 436B and 436C.

19   'A Review of Company Rescue and Business Reconstruction Mechanisms'.

20   Insolvency Act 1986, Schedule B1, paragraph 22.

21   Ibid., paragraph 14.

creating the charge provides for the charge to be enforceable. A creditor who is not a substantial chargeholder can still petition the court for an administration order, as can the directors or a substantial chargeholder,[22] but this would be done in rare cases. Absent where it is appropriate for purposes of exposition or critical comparison, we will not concern ourselves with applications for administration orders from the courts. Like the Australian regime, administration seeks to provide one that can be implemented quickly and inexpensively, and is flexible in that it might lead to other regimes or arrangements, depending on the financial position of the company. The number of administrations has increased significantly since the commencement of the operation of the Enterprise Act, as indicated by the following table.[23]

Table 5.2   Post-Enterprise Act Administration Procedures

2003 (last quarter)	2004	2005	2006
247	1,601	2,257	3560[24]

Source: Insolvency Service Statistics.

While the United Kingdom was reviewing its rescue procedures and deciding how administration could be better utilised, Australia was putting in train a process for the comprehensive assessment of, inter alia, voluntary administration. In September 2002, the Australian government asked the Corporations and Markets Advisory Committee ('CAMAC') to evaluate the voluntary administration procedure as far as large and complex companies were concerned. Following this, the Australian Parliament's Joint Committee on Corporations and Financial Services ('the Joint Committee'), was given a broader brief, namely to perform an evaluation of the operation of Australia's corporate insolvency laws.[25] The Joint Committee, during its consideration of corporate insolvency issues, took a substantial amount of evidence and accepted many submissions from interested parties and bodies, particularly in relation to voluntary administration. Overall, in its report, delivered on 30 June 2004, the Joint Committee's conclusion was that the voluntary administration process is a useful and valuable process for companies that are facing collapse[26] and should be retained as a central feature of Australian corporate insolvency law.[27] When CAMAC reported in October 2004, it found that the voluntary administration process was workable and sound as far as large and

---

22   Ibid., paragraph 12(1).
23   Based on Insolvency Service statistics and available at: <www.insolvency. gov.uk/otherinformation/statistics/200702/table3.htm> (last viewed 31 May 2007). These statistics only cover England and Wales.
24   At the time of writing, this figure was provisional only.
25   Above note 17 at paragraph 1.1.
26   Ibid., at paragraph 5.3.
27   Ibid., at paragraph 5.41.

complex companies were concerned, but that the law could be changed to benefit all administrations, whether involving large or small entities.[28] One of the reasons for the wide-ranging use of the procedure was probably that there was no need to involve the courts. Also, it was helpful that the banks seemed to accept and use the procedure from the start, even though, unlike the United Kingdom which has effectively ended the use of administrative receivership (simply known as 'receivership' in Australia and other jurisdictions),[29] with a few exceptions, in relation to charges created after 15 September 2003, the equivalent of administrative receivership could still be used.

As the Australian regime has been operating longer than the United Kingdom regime, certainly in the latter's new form, there is much a more developed jurisprudence. I should point out that unless the contrary is indicated, any references to paragraphs in the chapter are to paragraphs in Schedule B1 of the Insolvency Act 1986 and any references to sections will be to sections in Part 5.3A of the Australian Corporations Act 2001.

Purposes of the Regimes

The first thing to note is the purposes of the respective regimes. Unsurprisingly, the two regimes have similar purposes. The stated purpose of voluntary administration is to provide for the business, property and affairs of an insolvent company to be administered in a way that maximises the chances of the company, or as much as possible of its business, continuing in existence or, if this is not possible, results in a better return than would be the case if there was an immediate winding up of the company.[30]

Paragraph 3 provides that the administrator of a company must perform his functions with the objective of:

(a)   rescuing the company as a going concern, or
(b)   achieving a better result for the company's creditors as a whole than would be likely if the company were wound up (without first being in administration), or
(c)   realising property in order to make a distribution to one or more secured or preferential creditors.

---

28   See page 6 of the Report. The report can be accessed at: <www.camac. gov.au/camac/camac.nsf/byHeadline/PDFFinal+Reports+2004/$file/Large_Enterprises_report_Oct04.pdf> (last viewed 31 May 2007).

29   Administrative receivership involves the appointment of a receiver by a secured creditor who holds a charge of the whole, or substantially the whole, of the property of a company (Insolvency Act 1986, section 29(2)).

30   Corporations Act 2001, section 435A.

Rescuing the company as a going concern in fact means 'the company and as much of its business as possible'.[31] Consequently, priority is given to the saving of the business of the company.

With both regimes the rescue of the company is paramount, but they are realistic and provide that if this is not possible, then the aim is to get a better result for creditors than they would get if the company entered liquidation.

General

Both the United Kingdom and Australian authorities explored the possibility of invoking a similar regime to the American Chapter 11 bankruptcy procedure, but eventually they rejected the process. Chapter 11 embraces a debtor-in-possession concept, for the most part. This means that unless there has been fraud or other misconduct committed by the directors, the company's management stays intact and runs the company, under the general auspices of the bankruptcy court. A critical aspect of both regimes under review is that they favour placing the property and affairs of the company in the hands of an independent person, a qualified insolvency practitioner, with the existing management of the company losing control. After saying that, there will often be significant dependence on information and even advice from the directors. But the administrator in both jurisdictions has the power to remove a director, as well as appointing a director.[32] The administrator acts as the agent of the company.[33]

It is notable that the United Kingdom legislation is far longer and seeks to cover more eventualities than its Australian counterpart. The Australian legislature has seen fit to endow the courts with a broad discretion (more of this later under the heading 'Court Involvement'), to fill in gaps in the application of the law governing the regime. The United Kingdom Parliament has constructed a more detailed and prescribed regulatory system, and while the judges may have to make a number of decisions in relation to administrations, they do not have the broad discretion that the Australian courts have. Perhaps the fact that there have been many cases heard under the Australian provisions is indicative of the fact that the provisions do not specify enough details. Having said that, there is already quite a sizeable corpus of cases in the United Kingdom dealing with the new regime, and this is being added to daily.

As one would expect with regimes which include shelter characteristics, both the United Kingdom legislation in paragraph 43 and the Australian in section 440D provide for a moratorium on civil actions against the company[34] and court proceedings in relation to company property or against the company cannot

---

31   Explanatory Notes to the Enterprise Act 2002, paragraph 647.
32   Paragraph 61; section 442A.
33   Paragraph 69; section 437B.
34   Even where in the United Kingdom an application has been made for an administration order, an interim moratorium applies between the time of the application being made and the order (paragraph 44).

proceed or be commenced unless the administrator gives written consent, or the leave of the court is secured.[35] But, while the moratorium applies immediately once an administrator is appointed in Australia, in the United Kingdom it only applies once notice has been filed at court. But an interim moratorium does operate once a substantial chargeholder, appointing under paragraph 14, or the company or directors, appointing under paragraph 22, files with the court a notice of intention to appoint.[36]

In both jurisdictions, the administrator is required to carry out his or her functions in the interests of the company's creditors as a whole.[37] This, therefore, rules out giving preference to any group of creditors, save when it comes to distributions or any other action and sanctioned by legislation. However, given the fact that in both jurisdictions insolvency practitioners rely heavily on obtaining assignments of work from the banks, they might be thought to be susceptible to some pressure from banks.[38] The courts must be vigilant in this regard, if an application to review the actions of administrators comes before them but, of course, frequently it is likely that no review of the discharge of the functions of administrators will occur because of lack of information, inclination and money on the part of the creditors.

Again unlike the Chapter 11 regime in the United States, both the United Kingdom and Australia require the company to be insolvent or likely to become insolvent before administration can be embraced, although there is an exception where a substantial chargeholder appoints out-of-court in the United Kingdom. The dispensation for chargeholders might be an attempt to encourage secured creditors to see administration as a substitute for administrative receivership.

The United Kingdom regime lasts for 12 months unless there are permitted extensions.[39] Conversely, the Australian regime does not set a specific time period (save where there is no creditors' meeting before the elapse of five days after the close of what is known as 'the convening period', a period of 21 days from the commencement of administration), but provides that a number of events will see the termination of the administration.[40] The United Kingdom legislation provides that an administrator's term of office may be extended (once) by a period of up to six months if the creditors' consent.[41] Alternatively, an administrator's term might be extended by the court, on the application of the administrator.[42] There is no limit on the time that the court can set, and a court is empowered to make more

---

35 *Re Atlantic Computer Systems plc* [1992] Ch 505; *Foxcraft v The Ink Group Pty Ltd* (1994) 15 ACSR 203.

36 Paragraph 44(2)–(4).

37 Paragraph 3(2); section 437A. See *Lam Soon Australia Pty Ltd v Molit (No 55) Pty Ltd* (1996) 14 ACLC 1737.

38 See Finch, V., 'Control and co-ordination in corporate rescue' (2005) 25 *Legal Studies* 374 at 389.

39 Paragraph 76. The administration may come to an end in other circumstances. See paragraphs 79(1), 80(3), 81(1), 82(3)(a), 83(6)(a) and 84(4).

40 These are numerous and are discussed at text accompanying notes 148–153.

41 Paragraph 76(2)(b).

42 Paragraph 76(2)(a).

than one extension, but is not able to extend the term where a time limit has expired.[43] In contrast, the Australian courts have made orders *ex post facto* under the broadly interpreted section 447A.[44]

While the Australian legislation specifically states that a director's liability under a guarantee cannot be triggered by administration, and it is assumed that this is done so as not to deter directors from putting their company into administration, there is no such provision in the United Kingdom.

Now it is intended to move on to examine the most important elements of both regimes.

Appointment

Voluntary administration may only commence by way of out-of-court appointments, by the company,[45] a substantial chargeholder[46] or the liquidator of the company (with leave of the court[47]). The vast majority of voluntary administrations have been initiated by the company itself.[48] Besides permitting the directors (under paragraph 22) or a substantial chargeholder (under paragraph 14) appointing an administrator out of court in the United Kingdom, these persons are also permitted to go to court and seek an administration order.[49] This might be done by the latter where a company wishes:

> to avoid the potentially adverse impression conveyed by an out-of-court appointment with the attendant lack of publicity. Administration orders made in respect of Football League clubs post 15 September 2003 provide good examples of such court appointments.[50]

Also, the company must seek an administration order, rather than appointing an administrator itself, if it has been in administration in the previous 12 months.[51] If an appointment is made out of court, the United Kingdom process is more complicated than the Australian in that while no judicial order has to be made,

---

43   Paragraph 77.
44   For example, see *Re Ricon Constructions Pty Ltd* (1998) 16 ACLC 76; (1998) 26 ACSR 655; *Re Vouris* (2004) 22 ACLC 822.
45   Section 436A.
46   Section 436C.
47   Section 436B(1)-(2).
48   For an example of an appointment by a chargeholder, see *Re James Developments Pty Ltd* (1999) 17 ACLC 291 and for an appointment by a liquidator, see *Re Origin Internet Solutions Pty Ltd* [2004] FCA 382.
49   Paragraph 12(1)(a)-(c). If a substantial chargeholder applies, there is no need to establish that the company is or likely to become unable to pay its debts (paragraph 35).
50   Doyle and Keay, above note 4 at 630. There are a host of British football clubs who have entered administration in recent years.
51   Paragraph 23.

certain documents have to be filed at court. Where a substantial chargeholder exists (as will usually be the case), the company or the directors must file a notice of intention to appoint with the court and, once an appointment has been made another document, a notice of appointment must also be filed at the court[52] and this can only be done once five business days has elapsed after the chargeholder has been advised of the intended appointment.[53] An appointment may not be made under paragraph 22 after the elapse of a period of ten business days beginning with the date on which the notice of intention to appoint is filed under paragraph 27(1).[54] Administration actually only commences once a notice of appointment has been filed.[55] Where there is no substantial chargeholder, the company or the directors do not have to file a notice of intention to appoint.[56] Why filing in the court is required is not clear. It could possibly be to ensure publicity, although this could be better achieved by filing at Companies House (the place where certain formal documents of companies are required by legislation to be filed), and something that occurs in Australia (filing of notice of appointment is with the Australian Securities and Investments Commission which, like Companies House in the United Kingdom is a repository for certain company documents). The more likely primary reason is to ensure that administrators appointed out of court can be recognised as officers of the court and, therefore, they are covered by the European Union Regulation on Insolvency Proceedings 2000,[57] which is having a marked effect on insolvency law and practice in the United Kingdom. Unless a court is involved in some way, a procedure cannot be covered by the EU Regulation.

In Australia, once the board of directors resolves that the company is insolvent, or likely to become insolvent at some future time, and that an administrator be appointed, they can appoint a qualified person, namely a registered insolvency practitioner. As with the United Kingdom regime, substantial chargeholders must be given notice of the action that the company is taking, namely the administrator must give notice of appointment, by the end of the next business day, to the chargeholder.[58] Clearly there is a difference between the United Kingdom and Australian regimes in that with the former a substantial chargeholder must be notified before the appointment takes effect, while in the latter jurisdiction the chargeholder is notified after the appointment. Notwithstanding the different order, the same result follows, essentially, in that under the Australian scheme a holder of a qualifying charge can trump the appointment of the administrator by appointing a receiver and manager to take

---

52 Companies are also obliged to send notice of this to any substantial chargeholder, and this must be done five days before the intention to appoint is lodge (paragraph 26).
53 Paragraph 26.
54 Paragraph 28(2).
55 Paragraphs 19 and 31.
56 Paragraph 30.
57 Council Regulation 1346/2000. This regulation seeks to incorporate the European Union regulations designed to harmonise insolvency proceedings across the European Community.
58 Section 450A.

charge of company assets (assuming the deed of charge so permits). Under the United Kingdom regime, the chargeholder merely pre-empts the company appointment in that it can decide, after receiving notice from the company about an appointment, to appoint a person of its own choice to be administrator.[59] It will be noted that unlike in the United Kingdom, Australia has not sought to abolish administrative receivership, although its use has waned significantly because the banks have tended to be relatively happy with voluntary administration. In the United Kingdom, receivers can now only be appointed, except in a few specialised cases, in relation to charges that were created before 15 September 2003.

Both systems require the company, if it is going to appoint, to give notice to a substantial chargeholder, and it is obviously designed to protect such chargeholders, something that has been the focus of both jurisdictions for many years. While both jurisdictions favour substantial chargeholders, the United Kingdom regime does so more than the Australian, notwithstanding the fact that the United Kingdom has effectively abolished the use of administrative receivership for post-15 September 2003 charges. Paragraph 36 provides that where an administration application is made to the court and it is by a person who is not a substantial chargeholder, if a substantial chargeholder applies to the court to have a specified person appointed as administrator, the court is to grant the latter application unless it thinks it right to refuse the application because of the particular circumstances of the case.[60] Also, where a substantial chargeholder is prevented from appointing out-of-court under paragraph 14 by virtue of the company being in compulsory liquidation, paragraph 37 allows the chargeholder to make an administration application.

A possible advantage of the United Kingdom approach is that, while it occurs rarely, unsecured creditors (including prospective and contingent[61])are entitled to apply for an administration order,[62] whereas in Australia such creditors are left to presenting winding-up petitions against the company. While CAMAC in a 1998 Report[63] advocated individual creditors being able to initiate administration in Australia, its latest Report, in 2004, is against that idea,[64] for reasons which we do not have sufficient space to consider here. Initiating administration rather than winding up might be, on limited occasions, more advantageous to creditors.[65]

Something that the United Kingdom Government might consider is to emulate the Australian provisions as far as they allow a liquidator to appoint an

---

59   With charges created before 15 September 2003, the chargeholder may appoint an administrative receiver if the charged deed so permits.
60   Paragraph 36(1)(b).
61   Paragraph 12(4).
62   Paragraph 12(1)(c).
63   Legal Committee of the Companies and Securities Advisory Committee, *Corporate Voluntary Administration*, June 1998. The report is available at: <www.camac.gov.au/camac/camac.nsf/byHeadline/PDFFinal+Reports+1998/$file/Cor porate_Voluntary_Administration_Final_Report,_June_1998.pdf> (last viewed 31 May 2007).
64   Above note 28 at page 27.
65   For instance, in *Re Logitext.uk Ltd* [2004] EWHC 2899; [2005] 1 BCLC 326.

administrator, without court order (providing it is not the liquidator himself or herself), for presently in the United Kingdom a liquidator must apply for an administration order,[66] taking time and costing money.

Creditors and Creditors' Meetings

Getting creditors involved in the process of administration is important and it is the creditors who have to sanction any rescue process that might follow administration. As United Kingdom administrators have to formulate proposals within eight weeks of appointment,[67] it has been asserted that they 'will have to be in possession of detailed information on nearly all aspects of the company and its business before they agree to act'.[68] With respect, this will depend very much on the type, size and state of the company's business. In Australia, where the time-frame has been tighter administrators have been able to put proposals together quite quickly. Here the administrator has to convene and conduct two meetings of creditors during the life of the administration. The first meeting is to be held within five business days of the commencement of the administration.[69] The second meeting of creditors, which the administrator must convene, is far more substantive. It must be held within five business days after the end of the convening period. The 'convening period' is, ordinarily, 21 days from the day when the administration commences. The period can be extended, and often is, by the courts provided an application is made for extension within the original convening period.[70] The courts have shown their willingness, in many cases, to accommodate administrators by granting them generous extensions. Furthermore, courts have granted extensions, pursuant to their general discretionary power in section 447A (a power to which I will return later) to make such orders as they think fit about how Part 5.3A of the Corporations Act should operate, even where the application is made after the end of the convening period.[71] All of this is in line with the apparent desire of the courts to assist in making the voluntary administration process work.[72]

Besides extending the time for the holding of the second meeting, the Australian legislation allows for the meeting to be adjourned from time to time, and up to 60 days from the date when the meeting was first held.[73] It has been held

---

66   Paragraph 38.
67   Proposals must be presented to creditors within eight weeks of appointment (paragraph 49(5)(b)).
68   Above note 38 at 383.
69   Section 436E(2).
70   Section 439A(6).
71   For example, see *Re Greg Sewell Forgings Pty Ltd* (1995) 13 ACLC 1172.
72   This is demonstrated in such cases as *Cawthorn v Keira Constructions Pty Ltd* (1994) 13 ACSR 337; *Australasian Memory Pty Ltd v Brien* (2000) 200 CLR 270; (2000) 34 ACSR 250.
73   Section 439B(2).

that even where the 60 day period has elapsed, courts can extend the life of the administration by using their wide discretionary power under section 447A.[74] Rather than opting for a short period of time in which the creditors' meeting is to be held, the United Kingdom legislation provides that the meeting must be held within 10 weeks.[75] While this seems lengthy, it is not as lengthy as that operating in relation to Chapter 11 bankruptcies, where 120 days is permitted for the proposal of a reorganisation plan.

At the second meeting under the Australian scheme, creditors may resolve to accept one of the following:

- that the company execute a deed of company arrangement;
- that the administration should end; or
- that the company be wound up.[76]

The hoped-for result of the meeting is that there will be a resolution that a deed of company arrangement be executed. These deeds, which can be as innovative as the creators wish them to be, are equivalent, in many ways, to company voluntary arrangements in the United Kingdom insolvency scheme.

The issue of speed is important. It is critical that a company's fate is decided quickly so that creditors are not kept waiting for a long period for their money or an idea when they might receive some payment, remembering that their right to take proceedings is stayed. It is also critical for employees, whose future is in jeopardy in many cases. As Vanessa Finch has said, 'Tight scheduling is desirable in so far as it protects against indecision and tardiness on the part of the administrator'.[77] But a process that does not give time for investigation and proper planning can be counter-productive, and thus there has to be a balance.

One of the aspects of the voluntary administration process which has caused problems in Australia is the fact that the first meeting is to be held within five business days of the commencement of the administration.[78] The purpose of the meeting is to allow the creditors to determine whether to appoint a committee of creditors.[79] It has been suggested that the time frame for the meeting is too tight and that the administrator cannot be expected to do much in the limited time available; this is so especially given the fact that usually he or she will be coming fresh to the company. The time constraints are such that pressure is placed not only on the administrator, but on the creditors as well; at best creditors will have only two or three business days notice of the meeting. Voluntary administration was designed originally for small – medium sized companies, but many large companies have wanted to avail themselves of the procedure, and this is where the time constraints really cause problems. The tight time frame has been

---

74   *Cawthorn v Keira Constructions Pty Ltd* (1994) 13 ACSR 337.
75   Paragraph 51(2).
76   Section 439C.
77   Above note 38 at 386.
78   Section 436E(2).
79   Section 436E(10).

acknowledged in a number of Australian reports, and most recently it has been recommended by the Joint Committee,[80] and CAMAC,[81] that the time for the first meeting should be extended to eight business days and the time for the second meeting should be extended to 25 business days, with the convening period limited to 20 days.[82] Under the recommendations an application for an extension of the convening period would still be permitted, so a lengthening of the period is not being traded for loss of the right to seek extensions in appropriate cases. The United Kingdom's Schedule B1 does not lay down a mandatory tight frame, because while paragraph 51(2)(a) provides that an initial creditors' meeting should be held as soon as reasonably practicable after the commencement of administration,[83] the administration has got 10 weeks in which to hold the meeting[84] (subject, perhaps, to creditor complaint).[85] This provision has both positive and negative effects. First, on the positive side of things administrators are able, in the main, to undertake investigations, prior to the first meeting, of the company's affairs, and do this far more thoroughly than their Australian counterparts and, hence, are able to provide creditors with a better view of the company and its future (if any), as well as ensuring that any important aspects of the company's affairs are dealt with. On the negative side though, if a meeting is not held for some time after the commencement of the administration it means that creditors might receive little or no information concerning the company until the meeting, and by the time of the meeting the administrator might have done so much work that the creditors might be reluctant to seek his or her removal and replacement if they are unhappy with the performance. One advantage of the Australian scheme is that the creditors can vote to remove the administrator at the first meeting, although creditors have little to go on in deciding whether the person appointed should remain in post, whereas under the United Kingdom regime a creditor will have either to requisition a creditors' meeting to consider a resolution to remove the administrator, or to apply to the court for the removal of the administrator, assuming that a substantial chargeholder has not trumped the company's appointment.

A second problem with the first meeting in Australia is that the meeting can only deal with any resolution to change administrators and a resolution to form a creditors' committee. Now for those who cannot abide meetings, this might seem to be attractive, but anecdotal evidence from insolvency practitioners in Australia suggests that some administrators are rather embarrassed by the lack of business

---

80   Above note 17, Recommendation 15.
81   Above note 28, Recommendation 7 (at 114).
82   Above note 17, Recommendation 16.
83   Although the holding of the creditors' meeting is generally mandatory, an administrator may dispense with an initial creditors' meeting where he or she intends to apply to the court or file a notice under paragraph 80(2) for the administration to cease at a time before a statement of proposals to creditors has been sent out.
84   Paragraph 51(2)(b).
85   Paragraphs 107 and 108 allow for the extension of the ten-week period by the court or creditors, subject to certain limitations.

undertaken at the meeting. Sometimes the meeting is effectively over in a few minutes. A longer period before the initial meeting is held would be better as the creditors would be given an opportunity to see if the administrator is up to the task or whether he or she is a tame administrator ready to do the bidding of the directors. The United Kingdom scheme overcomes these deficiencies because, as mentioned above, the initial meeting can be held up to 10 weeks after the commencement of administration, and creditors can replace the administrator at a meeting (as can a substantial chargeholder who appointed the administrator),[86] if there is no substantial chargeholder and the administrator was appointed by the company or the directors.[87] An application to court for an order of removal would be needed where these circumstances did not exist.[88] I should add that if creditors want to replace the administrator, they must have 10 per cent of the total debt of the company so that they can requisition a creditors' meeting (either an initial meeting under paragraph 52(2), or a meeting after the initial meeting).[89]

I have already mentioned some of the recommendations that have been made in Australia concerning the timing of meetings. The Government has recently announced that it is going to introduce reforms that will introduce greater flexibility in relation to the timing of creditors' meetings and clarify certain requirements. Specifically:[90]

- the court will be granted an express power to extend the convening period on an application made after the convening period has ended;[91]
- the law will be clarified to confirm the power of administrators to adjourn a meeting for up to 60 days, or to a date which is notified within the 60 day period;
- the convening period will be calculated from the day after the administration begins; and
- the law will be clarified to state that creditors may only remove an administrator and appoint a replacement administrator at the first meeting through a single resolution.

The Australian regime appears to be predicated on the assumption that there will be, in effect, only one substantive creditors' meeting – this is the second meeting (that is the one that must be held at the end of the convening period) – that can be adjourned from time to time, but there is no reference to a further meeting.

---

86   Paragraph 92. The company or the directors of the company may replace an administrator where the company or the directors appointed the administrator (paragraphs 93(1), 94(1)).

87   Paragraph 97.

88   Paragraph 88(1).

89   Paragraph 56(1).

90   Above note 3.

91   This means that reliance on the broad discretionary power in section 447A will no longer be required.

But in the United Kingdom, while one meeting is probably going to be the norm in practice:

> it is submitted that there is no good reason why in appropriate circumstances a meeting should not be summoned if requested or directed under para[graph] 56(1) (despite that provision being headed 'Further creditors' meetings') or by the administrator himself under para[graph] 62 prior to the initial creditors' meeting. This might conceivably arise in a case of urgency or one in which the weighing up of creditors' views at an early stage and on a formal basis is deemed necessary by the administrator to assess the viability of the administration.[92]

While the Australian provisions do not allow explicitly for the same approach, it is suggested that a court could, pursuant to section 447A, permit a further meeting if required for some reason.

Unlike Australia, where there must be a creditors' meeting to decide the fate of the company,[93] in the United Kingdom, the administrator is in fact permitted to decide not to call a meeting where he or she thinks:

(a) that the company has sufficient property to enable each creditor of the company to be paid in full;

(b) that the company has insufficient property to enable a distribution to be made to unsecured creditors other than by virtue of section 176A(2)(a); or

(c) that neither of the objectives specified in paragraph 3(1)(a) and (b) can be achieved.[94]

But, as indicated earlier, the administrator must summon a creditors' meeting if it is requested by creditors of the company whose debts amount to at least 10 per cent of the total debts of the company.[95]

Interestingly, paragraph 58(1) allows anything which is required or permitted by or under Schedule B1 to be done at a creditors' meeting, to be done by correspondence between the administrator and creditors. This takes note of the problems that often exist in getting creditors to a meeting and also it may take into account changes in technology. I would submit that e-mail messages could be regarded as correspondence. The Australian legislation does not provide for this more informal way of getting creditor wishes, perhaps because it is now 14 years old. However, the Joint Committee recommended that the Government consider technology and electronic commerce options to enhance communications and

---

92   Doyle and Keay, above note 4 at 678.
93   See section 439C.
94   Paragraph 52(1).
95   Paragraph 52(2).

reduce costs in insolvency regimes in general.[96] CAMAC has also recommended something similar.[97]

While the rights of secured creditors are protected in both regimes, neither, unlike the position in other jurisdictions, provides for any super-priority to anyone who extends credit to the company, therefore there might be difficulty in obtaining such credit. In appropriate cases the existing creditors might be willing to provide some level of credit. Of course, they would have to be convinced that they were not 'throwing good money after bad'.

Court Involvement

Unlike with many rescue regimes around the world, voluntary administration in Australia was designed so that there would be little or no court involvement, and in this regard it was quite revolutionary. If courts were to be involved, it was to be in a supervisory role, acting as facilitators and reviewers with respect to the procedures and issues which might arise under the scheme. The vision was to have a non-interventionist judiciary. This was a vision which was far different from what presently operates in the United States, where the courts often are involved heavily both in the review of the plan which is to be implemented and the protection of creditors.[98]

While there are differences when it comes to court involvement in the United Kingdom, the two regimes are similar now in that if the company or a substantial chargeholder appoints the administrator then it is very possible that the United Kingdom courts will not be called upon, save for being used as a repository for the notice of intention to appoint and the notice of appointment. However, it must be emphasised that an application can still be made in the United Kingdom for an administration order from a court. Absent exceptional circumstances, such as where a winding-up petition has been presented against the company,[99] it is likely that the only applicant for an order will be a creditor who is not a substantial chargeholder.[100]

While the Australian system was predicated on the concept of ensuring minimal court involvement, it has been acknowledged that there have been many

---

96   Above note 17, Recommendation 20.
97   Above note 28, paragraph 2.5, Recommendation 6.
98   This, and other factors, has precipitated criticism in the United States. See, for example, Bradley, M. and Rosenzwig, M., 'The Untenable Case for Chapter 11' (1992) 101 *Yale Law Journal* 1043 at 1085. For a discussion of voluntary administrations in light of Chapter 11, see Griggs, L., 'Voluntary Administration and Chapter 11 of the Bankruptcy Code (US)' (1994) 2 *Insolvency Law Journal* 93.
99   In such a case the company would have to apply for an administration order. For example, see *Re AMCD (Property Holdings) Ltd* (High Court for England and Wales, 15 June 2004) (unreported).
100   For example, see *Re Simoco Digital UK Ltd* [2004] EWHC 209; [2004] 1 BCLC 541; *Re Logitext.uk Ltd* [2004] EWHC 2899; [2005] 1 BCLC 326.

cases involving voluntary administration, and the courts have certainly played an important role in the development of the regime,[101] particularly in a supervisory sense. The supervisory role of the courts is well illustrated by section 447E. This enables a court, where it is satisfied that the administrator of a company under voluntary administration has managed, or is managing, the affairs of the company in a manner which is prejudicial to the interests of some or all of the company's creditors or members or has acted, is intending to act or has failed to act and prejudiced interests of creditors or members, to make an order as it thinks just. This is not a unique kind of provision and it is broadly equivalent to the United Kingdom's paragraph 74. Having said that the latter provision talks about unfairly harming the interests of creditors rather than simply prejudicing creditors.[102] Importantly, under the United Kingdom provision there must be unfairness as well as harm, and that duplicates the approach taken in section 459 of the United Kingdom Companies Act 1985 in protecting shareholders.

The important role that courts play, even in the Australian system can be seen from the fact that they might be involved in:[103]

- giving an extension of the time which is prescribed under the legislation for the convening of the second creditors' meeting (held pursuant to section 439A);[104]
- ordering a chargee or a receiver who entered into possession or assumed control of company property or entered into an agreement to sell such property in order to enforce a charge before the commencement of the administration, not to perform certain functions;[105]
- granting leave to a chargee to enforce a charge during the currency of the administration;[106]
- ordering a receiver or other person enforcing a right over property held by the company, and who was appointed after the commencement of the administration, not to perform certain functions;[107]
- granting leave to a liquidator or provisional liquidator to appoint himself or herself as the administrator of a company;[108]
- appointing a fresh administrator where an administrator has ceased to act;[109]

---

101 The Honourable David Malcolm (Chief Justice of the Western Australian Supreme Court), Opening Address, National Conference of the Insolvency Practitioners' Association of Australia, 28 October 2004, Perth, Australia.

102 Doyle and Keay, above note 4 at 698–699, assume that harm is equivalent to prejudice.

103 The following points are not intended to be exhaustive.

104 Section 439A(6). Such orders are quite frequently sought.

105 Section 441D(2).

106 Section 440B.

107 Section 441H(2).

108 Section 436B(2). This is discussed by Young J in *Re Depsun Pty Ltd* (1994) 12 ACLC 482 where his Honour specifically noted the lack of guidance in the sub-section.

- removing an administrator, on the application of the Australian Securities and Investments Commission or a creditor;[110]
- giving directions, on the application of the administrator, about a matter arising in connection with the performance or exercise of any of the functions and powers of the administrator;[111]
- declaring whether or not a purported appointment of an administrator is valid;[112]
- giving leave to the administrator to dispose of property that is subject to a charge.[113]

The United Kingdom courts are also given similar kinds of powers, such as:

- removing[114] or replacing the administrator;[115]
- terminating the administration on the application of the administrator;[116]
- examining the conduct of an administrator;[117]
- empowering the administrator to dispose of property subject to security;[118]
- having the power to make a number of orders if the administrator reports that the creditors' meeting has not accepted the administrator's proposals.[119]

The powers that are granted to the Australian courts are broad, general discretionary powers, with little attempt by the legislature in the legislation to provide any guidelines for the courts in their exercise of the powers. A prime example of a lack of direction in relation to the powers granted to the courts is found in section 447A.[120] The section empowers a court, in its discretion, to make orders as it thinks appropriate about how the voluntary administration scheme is to operate in relation to the company which is the subject of any application brought before it. The provision has been referred to in the courts as 'unusual'.[121] The reason for this description is that the section, according to one decision, proceeds

---

109   Section 449C(6).
110   Section 449B.
111   Section 447D(1).
112   Section 447C(2).
113   Section 442C(1).
114   Paragraph 88.
115   Paragraph 95
116   Paragraph 79.
117   Paragraph 75.
118   Paragraph 71. The security must not consist of a floating charge.
119   Paragraph 55.
120   For a recent case invoking the section, see *Re Centaur Mining & Exploration Ltd (in Liq) (Receivers and Managers Appointed)* [2005] VSC 367, relying on the High Court case of *Australasian Memory Pty Ltd v Brien* (2000) CLR 270; (2000) 34 ACSR 250.
121   *Brash Holdings Ltd v Katile Pty Ltd* (1994) 13 ACSR 505.

on the basis that Part 5.3A is inadequate in the provision which it makes for the voluntary administration process, and as a result the court is required to fill in the gaps by exercising wide powers.[122] Through the use of section 447A in particular, courts have played a crucial role in the development of voluntary administration. The courts have concluded that section 447A is an integral aspect of Part 5.3A and should be given wide operation.[123] The fact of the matter is that the provision has been able to be employed so as to circumvent some of the factors that might stultify the effective operation of voluntary administration, but it has been criticised for, *inter alia*, being able to lead voluntary administration in any direction that the courts wish,[124] and fails to provide certainty for all concerned.[125] It may be that the courts can be said to be able, almost, to re-write the legislation in some cases. This appears to be the view of one Victorian Supreme Court judge (when giving an extra-judicial address), Dodds-Streeton J, when she said that the provision was: '[T]antamount to legislative power on the court to remake Part 5.3A according to the needs of a particular case'.[126]

But while the United Kingdom does not imitate section 447A, its courts are not without an increase in discretion under the new scheme. For instance, there is scope for the use of judicial power and discretion in relation to consideration of the powers of administrators as they seek to fulfil the objectives of administration (contained in paragraph 3). That said, the United Kingdom legislation does tend to be more prescriptive. For example, any decision taken by a creditors' meeting in relation to the proposals of an administrator in the United Kingdom has to be reported to the court,[127] and it is an offence if it is not done.[128] In Australia, such action is not required, and this does not appear to have caused any problems. It causes one to inquire whether the need to report to the court is an unnecessary exercise.

Returning to section 447A, while there is no provision in the United Kingdom legislation that provides such breadth, administrators in the United Kingdom do have the right under paragraph 63 to seek directions from the court, as do Australian administrators,[129] so that where a situation is not covered by the Act or Rules, courts can assist administrators. Paragraph 63 states that the administrator

---

122 Ibid., at 507.
123 *Australasian Memory Pty Ltd v Brien* (2000) 200 CLR 270; (2000) 34 ACSR 250.
124 See Bennetts, K., 'Voluntary Administration: Shaping the Process Through the Exercise of Judicial Discretion' (1995) 3 *Insolvency Law Journal* 135.
125 See Keay, A., 'Court Involvement in Voluntary Administrations and Deeds of Company Arrangement: Powers, Problems and Prognoses' (1995) 13 *Company and Securities Law Journal* 157.
126 The Honourable Julie Dodds-Streeton, 'Voluntary Administrations – the Ansett Group', a paper delivered at the Third Annual Insolvency Practice Symposium on 26-27 February 2003 and referred to in Moore, K., 'Is the voluntary administration process in Australia flexible enough?' (2004) 19 *Insolvency Law & Practice* 171 at note 6.
127 Paragraph 53(1)(a).
128 Paragraph 53(3).
129 Section 447D.

may 'apply to the court for directions in connection with his functions'. This represents a step forward for judicial discretion as it is less specific than the former section 14(3) of the Insolvency Act. The power in paragraph 63 has to be read in conjunction with paragraph 68(2) under which the court may give directions in connection with any aspect of the management of the company's affairs, business or property. Yet even here there is a limitation on court discretion as the directions can only be given in any of the four circumstances identified in paragraph 68(3). Nevertheless, 'the scope of the words "in connection with his functions" is extremely broad and, in practice, will catch an almost endless range of circumstances'.[130]

Courts in both the United Kingdom and Australia are given powers to ensure that they prevent any abuses by administrators, but after saying that the courts in both jurisdictions are very reluctant to query the commercial judgments of administrators, just as they have been in relation to the work of liquidators. In this regard, courts in both jurisdictions have made it plain that an administrator, like a liquidator, should not employ an application for directions as a means of avoiding what amounts in substance to a matter of commercial judgment by seeking to place the burden of such a decision on the court.[131] The Australian courts have said that their power to supervise administrators is not to be used to make or re-make commercial decisions of administrators.[132]

Undoubtedly the judges in both jurisdictions have been innovative in ensuring that the process of administration works. There are many instances of innovation in Australia. One example is the case of *Deputy Commission of Taxation v Portinex (No1)*,[133] where the judge used section 447A to validate the appointment of an administrator despite the fact that the appointment at the relevant board meeting was invalid as there was not the required quorum. But even in the United Kingdom there are examples, such as *Re ML Design Group Ltd*,[134] where administrators applied to the court under paragraph 55 for an order that their appointment should cease. Due to the fact that there are no rules of procedure applicable to paragraph 55, the judge applied rule 2.114(1)(3) of the Insolvency Rules 1986 that operated in relation to analogous provisions under paragraph 79. Another example is found in *Re TT Industries Ltd*[135] where the administrator applied to the court, under paragraph 76(2)(a), for the extension of the administration, after having obtained an earlier extension from the creditors. In this case the administrator made his application before the end of the administration period, but the application was not heard by the court until after the close of that period. According to paragraph 77(1)(b), any extension had to be made before the

---

130   Doyle and Keay, above note 4 at 686.
131   For instance, see *Re NS Distribution Ltd* [1990] BCLC 169 at 171; *Re T & D Industries plc* [2000] All ER 333 at 344.
132   *Re Pan Pharmaceuticals Ltd* [2003] FCA 855.
133   [2000] NSWSC 99; (2000) 156 FLR 453.
134   17 January 2006, Chancery Div, Richard Sheldon QC sitting as a Deputy High Court Judge in Chancery. See [2006] All ER (D) 75 (Jan).
135   [2006] BCC 372.

expiration of the administrator's term of office. Nevertheless, the court granted the application and said that, on its correct construction, paragraph 77(1)(b) did not deprive the court of jurisdiction to hear the application and make the necessary order in the situation where the application was made before the expiration of the term of office and there was a real possibility that the manner in which the application was dealt with by the court played a part in the fact that no order was made before expiration of the administration.

Transactional Avoidance and Illicit Trading

While an administrator in the United Kingdom is entitled to take proceedings pursuant to the provisions of the Insolvency Act 1986 which are designed to allow for the adjustment of pre-administration (or pre-liquidation) transactions,[136] such as preferential transfers,[137] the same cannot be said of an administrator in Australia.[138] The fact that Australian administrators cannot take action can lead to the kind of situation that occurred in *St Leonards Property Pty Ltd v Ambridge Investments Pty Ltd*,[139] where the directors were seeking to use the administration process to protect pre-administration transactions that benefited them. Notwithstanding this kind of abuse, the 2004 CAMAC Report specifically rejected the idea of giving administrators the power to challenge pre-administration transactions.[140]

In neither jurisdiction are administrators entitled to initiate proceedings against directors for illicit trading, known as wrongful trading in the United Kingdom[141] and insolvent trading in Australia.[142] These provisions, in general terms, enable a court to order directors of insolvent companies to make contributions to the company, but proceedings can only, for the most part, be commenced by liquidators.[143] The upshot of this is that where an administrator is of the view that the directors have been guilty of illicit trading, he or she must take action to have the administration converted into a liquidation, which can take time and will incur costs. It should be noted that it is thought that voluntary administration has been used as a safe haven in Australia by directors who are

---

136   Sections 238–245.

137   Section 239.

138   But regulation 5.3A.02 of the Corporations Regulations 2001 does provide that an administrator must, in setting out his or her opinions in a statement mentioned in section 439A(4)(b), specify whether there are any transactions that appear to the administrator to be voidable transactions in respect of which money, property or other benefits may be recoverable by a liquidator.

139   (2004) 210 ALR 265.

140   Above note 28, Recommendation 20, paragraph 3.6, at 53–54.

141   Insolvency Act 1986, section 214.

142   Corporations Act 2001, section 588G.

143   For a discussion of the respective provisions in an analytical comparative context, see Keay, A. and Murray, M., 'Making Company Directors Liable: A Comparative Analysis of Wrongful Trading in the United Kingdom and Insolvent Trading in Australia' (2005) 14 *International Insolvency Review* 27.

concerned that they are close to committing insolvent trading[144] and it is likely that United Kingdom directors will embrace the same action in relation to wrongful trading, now that administration is far easier for companies to initiate. Even under the old procedure it seems that the directors in *Re Chancery plc*[145] sought, *inter alia*, to use the administration order process to protect them from wrongful trading.

There is a greater tie up between voluntary administration and Australia's illicit trading provision (insolvent trading – section 588G) compared with the United Kingdom. In fact in Australia section 588H(6)(a) provides that the steps taken to appoint an administrator is a matter that can be taken into account by a court in determining whether a defence under section 588H(5) that the director took all reasonable steps to prevent the company from incurring further debts (on becoming aware of insolvency) has been made out. There is no indication in any United Kingdom policy documents or legislation that administration could be a way out for directors who are concerned about the fact that they might be committing wrongful trading. However, one would think that advisers will suggest administration as a course of action where there is danger of wrongful trading, in those cases where directors do in fact consult practitioners.

Ending and Exiting the Regimes

Under the Australian legislation, it is hoped that the administration process will lead to the company, with the approval of the creditors, entering into a deed of company arrangement. This deed will form the basis of the rescue process. Similarly, in the United Kingdom, administration might be followed by the company entering into a company voluntary arrangement. But a deed of company arrangement might not eventuate and in Australia the voluntary administration will end if: the creditors resolve that it should end[146] or the company should be wound up;[147] the court orders termination;[148] the convening period elapses without a creditors' meeting having taken place;[149] the second meeting of creditors ends without a resolution being passed pursuant to section 439C;[150] the court orders winding up.[151]

In the United Kingdom, an administration will end if the administrator believes that the purpose has been achieved; in such a case the administrator must file a notice with the courts.[152] The courts may order the end of administration if:

---

144   See Herzberg, A., 'Why are there so Few Insolvent Trading Cases?' (1998) 6 *Insolvency Law Journal* 177.
145   [1991] BCC 171 at 172.
146   Section 435C(2)(b).
147   Section 435C(2)(c).
148   Section 435C(3)(a).
149   Section 435C(3)(b).
150   Section 435C(3)(e).
151   Section 435C(3)(g).
152   Paragraph 80.

administrators make an application where they think the purpose of administration cannot be achieved in relation to the company, they think the company should not have entered administration, or a creditors' meeting required the making of the application;[153] a creditor applies to the court and can demonstrate an improper motive on the part of the person appointing the administrator;[154] the creditors challenge the conduct of the administrator;[155] the creditors cannot agree to the revised proposals of the administrator;[156] and the public interest so dictates.[157]

Where a deed of company arrangement is not entered into in Australia, the company usually enters liquidation. The creditors can decide at the second meeting that the company should be wound up[158] and the administrator becomes the liquidator.[159] A similar situation exists in the United Kingdom, where a movement from administration to creditors' voluntary liquidation can occur, but this may happen without the need for meetings of creditors.[160] All that the administrator must do, to take the company into creditors' voluntary liquidation, is, if he or she thinks that the total amount which each secured creditor is likely to receive has been paid or set aside for such creditors and that a distribution will be made to unsecured creditors,[161] to inform the Registrar of Companies by notice and to file a copy with the court and every creditor of which the administrator is aware.[162] The liquidation does not commence until the Registrar of Companies registers the documents.[163] While at one time it was thought that this avenue was not open where a company had been placed in administration by the court (the company had to enter compulsory liquidation), unless the administrator obtained a court order to terminate his or her appointment, it is now clear that all companies in administration can take advantage of this avenue[164] and this is likely to keep down costs (such as the cost of returning to court).

---

153   Paragraph 79.
154   Paragraph 81. It has been submitted that the proper approach to considering this issue involves a two-stage process. 'First, that the court should be concerned in establishing, as a matter of fact, the motive on the part of the applicant for an administration order or the appointor in an out-of-court appointment; secondly, it falls to the court to consider whether, in the particular circumstances of a case, that motive is improper'. (Doyle and Keay, above note 4 at 708).
155   Paragraph 74(4)(d).
156   Paragraph 55(2).
157   Paragraph 82.
158   Section 439C(c).
159   Section 446A(1)-(4).
160   Paragraph 83.
161   Paragraph 83(1).
162   Paragraph 83(3)-(5). In Australia, the administrator is obliged to file a notice with ASIC that the company is moving from administration into liquidation, as well as advertising this fact in a relevant newspaper (section 446A(5)).
163   See Todd, G., 'Administration Post-Enterprise Act – What are the Options for Exit?' (2006) 19 *Insolvency Intelligence* 17 at 18.
164   *Re Ballast plc* [2004] EWHC 2356 (Ch); [2005] 1 WLR 1928; [2005] BCLC 446; [2005] BCC 96.

Another avenue that might be taken in the United Kingdom, and which is mandatory if the administrator thinks that the company has no property which might permit a distribution to its creditors, is that the administrator is to put in motion the necessary process to have the company dissolved.[165] This required course of action can be disapplied by order of the court,[166] perhaps where the administrator feels that there is a need for further investigations into the affairs of the company. What has caused some uncertainty in the United Kingdom is whether a transition from administration to dissolution is to be followed where the company did have property that was realised at some point in the administration (and distributions were made to creditors), or is it only required action where the company never had property during its time in administration? While in a dictum in *Re Ballast plc*[167] Blackburne J took the view that the latter was the correct approach to take, the former view appears to be the stronger, certainly given the decision of Rimer J in *Re GHE Realisations Ltd*.[168]

Taking Over From Liquidation?

There are some indications, more from Australia than the United Kingdom at the moment, that administration is gradually usurping liquidation's position as the most prevalent end for an insolvent company, and this is the case even with companies that have little chance of being rescued.

Australia's Harmer Committee made it patently clear that it felt that there should be a reduction in the number of liquidations as a considerable number of companies were entering liquidation, when they should be the subject of a rescue process. Undoubtedly the United Kingdom authorities were of the same view. Hence, one expects to see a diminution of the liquidation figures for both jurisdictions, and this has in fact occurred as far as creditors' voluntary liquidations are concerned.

In Australia, directors are able to initiate voluntary administration in circumstances where they would once have initiated a creditors' voluntary winding up, and an interesting point is that evidence given to the Joint Committee suggests that the voluntary administration procedure is being used as a means to enable directors to avoid subsequent investigations into their conduct.[169] While the Australian courts have indicated that they will not tolerate inadequate

---

165   Paragraph 84. Companies that are subject to an administration order may also take this route without being concerned about seeking a court order: *Re Ballast plc* [2005] 1 WLR 1928; [2005] BCLC 446; [2005] BCC 96; *Re Preston & Duckworth* [2006] BCC 133.
166   Paragraph 84(2).
167   [2004] EWHC 2356 (Ch); [2005] 1 WLR 1928; [2005] BCLC 446; [2005] BCC 96 at paragraph 20.
168   [2005] EWHC 2400 (Ch); [2006] BCC 139. Also, see *Re Preston & Duckworth* [2006] BCC 133.
169   Above note 17 at paragraphs 5.23–5.24.

investigations by administrators,[170] they will not expect an administrator to carry out as exhaustive investigations as a liquidator, because, *inter alia*, of the time constraints prevailing in an administration.[171] The United Kingdom has not had the new scheme long enough for us to say with conviction that the approach is the same. The time constraints in the United Kingdom are not as demanding as they are in Australia, but having said that, how often will the scope of the investigations undertaken by administrators come under judicial scrutiny? The answer probably is: not often.

Administrators in Australia are required to report to the regulator,[172] the Australian Securities and Investments Commission ('ASIC'), any incidents of misconduct with respect to any type of company. But the ASIC has received few reports from administrators[173] and this is somewhat of a concern. It fuels speculation that some directors are using administrations to avoid a close examination of their activities. This was suggested in research conducted by the ASIC, where it was found that the aim behind embracing administration in 20 per cent of the companies studied was to achieve liquidation.[174] Interestingly, apart from noting the fact that administrations are used in the way just described, the Joint Committee, reporting in 2004, refrained from making any recommendations on the point. Perhaps this is implicit acceptance that administration might be used to limit the investigation of companies, but that this is a reasonable price to pay for the overall success of the voluntary administration regime. So, perhaps we will see in the United Kingdom directors of companies that do not have viable businesses commencing administration as an alternative exit route to liquidation because it might constitute a way of reducing the chances of wide-ranging investigations of company affairs and the reasons for the demise of the company, and subsequent questioning of those who managed the company.[175] This strategy might also be encouraged by the fact that in the United Kingdom a company can go straight from administration to dissolution.[176]

It is interesting to note that in Australia the courts have stated that it is not necessarily an abuse of the voluntary administration process to put a company into administration when it is clear that it cannot be saved from liquidation.[177] However, if this is the case then the directors must have formed a reasonable

---

170 *Re Bartlett Researched Securities Pty Ltd* (1994) 12 ACSR 707 at 710; *Deputy Commissioner of Taxation v Pddam Pty Ltd* (1996) 19 ACSR 498.

171 *Hagenvale Pty Ltd v Depela Pty Ltd* (1995) 17 ACSR 139 at 145.

172 Section 438D.

173 See Proctor, A., 'Current Developments in the ASC's Enforcement Programs' (1996) 8 *Australian Insolvency Bulletin* 11 at 14. The ASC was the former name of the ASIC.

174 'A Study of Voluntary Administrations in New South Wales' (ASC Research Paper 98/01, Sydney, 1998).

175 A point also made by Larkin, B. and Smith, A., 'Pre-Packaged Business Sales Following the Introduction of the Enterprise Act 2002' (2004) 1 *International Corporate Rescue* 78 at 83.

176 See Keay, A., 'What Future for Liquidation in Light of the Enterprise Act Reforms?' [2005] *Journal of Business Law* 143.

177 *Dallinger v Halcha Holdings Pty Ltd* (1996) 14 ACLC 263.

opinion that administration would lead to a better return for creditors or would improve the position of the company.

Notwithstanding some questions about whether creditors' voluntary liquidation should be abolished, the Australian Joint Committee recommended retaining it, but recommending that the procedure for initiating it be made easier.[178]

The number of creditors' voluntary liquidations in the United Kingdom since 1997 are as follows:[179]

Table 5.3   Creditors' Voluntary Liquidation Procedures

1997	1998	1999	2000	2001
7875	7987	9071	9392	10297
2002	**2003**	**2004**	**2005**	**2006**
10075	8950	7608	7660	7719

Source: Insolvency Service Statistics.

At first, the table suggests that the number of creditors' voluntary liquidations have fallen in the two full years that the new administration regime has been available, and this is the case when compared with the figures in 1999–2003. But on closer examination one can see that the numbers are approximately the same as those in 1997 and 1998. In fact when one adds the liquidations and the administrations together in 2004 and 2005, the suggestion is that the number of insolvencies is increasing. But analysis of that fact is something that has to be left to another day.

Conclusion

The fact that the Australian voluntary administration has been given a clean bill of health by the recent report of the Joint Committee, together with its apparent success, might will encourage the United Kingdom Government and also those still somewhat sceptical about the new scheme for administration and corporate rescue.

Clearly, as demonstrated in the above discussion, there are now great similarities between the two regimes examined here. Perhaps one of the major differences between the two regimes is that while the United Kingdom has a heavily prescribed framework, the Australian is rather a light touch system, with the courts given a very broad discretion. While the make-it-work approach of the Australian judiciary might well be emulated indirectly in the United Kingdom, it is probable that the absence of a broad discretion akin to section 447A might hamper,

---

178   Above note 17, Recommendation 54 (at paragraph 12.23).
179   Based on Insolvency Service statistics available at: <www.insolvency.gov.uk/ otherinformation/statistics/general/corp-e-w-s.htm> (up to 2004), <www.dtistats.net/ sd/insolv/> (up to 2005) and <www.insolvency.gov.uk/otherinformation/ statistics/200702/index.htm> (up to 2006) (all pages last viewed 31 May 2007).

to some extent, the development of administration in the United Kingdom, perhaps as far as large companies are concerned, although it must be said that this does not appear to be happening at the moment. It seems that the discretionary power in section 447A has played an important part in not only facilitating the process in individual cases, but it has also smoothed the way generally for voluntary administration, and particularly in complex administrations. Section 447A has been used, *inter alia*, to cure defects and remedy technical faults, but it has also been used more widely in making voluntary administration work.[180] Having said that, the United Kingdom legislation does permit a court, on the application of an administrator, to vary time periods[181] and this will undoubtedly be used, and is likely to assist the smooth operation of many administrations. It remains to be seen whether it is sufficient to permit the scheme to work as well as it appears to have done in Australia.

The fact that the United Kingdom system does not give the courts the same degree of discretion as in Australia and the legislative framework is more complex might lead to the conclusion that it is not as user-friendly as the Australian voluntary administration procedure. Undoubtedly, whatever the growth rate of administrations, it is likely that at some stage there will have to some fine-tuning, but the regime is clearly being well-used.

While undoubtedly there are similarities in the regimes of both jurisdictions, and it is hard to think that the United Kingdom amendments in 2002 were not inspired somewhat by the Australian regime, and its apparent success in a very similar legal system, there are some critical differences. Statistics in Australia indicate that voluntary administration has clearly surpassed liquidation in terms of number of regimes initiated. This has not occurred in the United Kingdom, but the trend appears to be that creditors' voluntary liquidations are decreasing, certainly when considered in relation to recent years. Nevertheless, on the statistics that we have at the moment, it could be some time before administrations exceed liquidations, especially when one factors in compulsory liquidations.

Both regimes undoubtedly have benefited from the fact that courts do not, necessarily, have to be involved at any stage in the process, and where they are involved the cases that have been decided seem to suggest that the courts are endeavouring to make the procedures work. While we have some empirical evidence in Australia that voluntary administration is making corporate rescue conducive, we do not have that yet in the United Kingdom, something that will be needed in the short-medium term to permit the Government to assess whether administration, since the Enterprise Act changes, has indeed been a successful innovation.

---

180   See *Deputy Commissioner of Taxation v Portinex Pty Ltd* (2000) 34 ACSR 391 at 398.
181   Above note 17 at paragraph 107.

Chapter 6

Consuming Passions: Benchmarking Consumer Bankruptcy Law Systems

Donna McKenzie Skene and Adrian Walters

Introduction

Insolvency law is an important component of business law. It informs the terms on which credit is advanced to the corporate sector and provides formal mechanisms to deal with multiple default. Given the global economic significance of business and business default, it is small wonder that international institutions such as the International Monetary Fund, the World Bank and the United Nations Commission on International Trade Law have all developed their own benchmarks against which domestic insolvency systems may be judged.[1] These benchmarks have helped to influence the transition in a number of jurisdictions towards more rescue-oriented systems by emphasizing the need for domestic laws to provide a formal company rescue/reorganization procedure alongside, and as an alternative to, a cessation of business/liquidation procedure.

The importance of this recalibration of corporate insolvency laws – designed to preserve rather than destroy value in distressed corporate enterprises where possible – cannot be underestimated. However, insolvency laws must accommodate natural persons as well. There is nothing new in this notion. Indeed, what we in Britain[2] call bankruptcy or personal insolvency law – meaning that part of our insolvency laws which governs the insolvency of natural persons and unincorporated associations – predates corporate insolvency law by centuries, even millennia.[3] As originally conceived, bankruptcy law was designed to provide

---

1 See, for example, The UNCITRAL Legislative Guide on Insolvency Law, available at: <www.uncitral.org/uncitral/en/uncitral_texts/insolvency/2004Guide.html> (last viewed 31 May 2007).

2 That is, England and Wales and Scotland.

3 'The first dawn of bankrupt-law in Scotland is perceptible in a very remote age; for the *cessio bonorum* of the Roman law was adopted by us even so early as the date of Regiam Majestatem [fourteenth century]. By this benevolent institution, a remedy was provided against the perpetual imprisonment of insolvent debtors, when honest, and willing to convey everything to their creditors': Bell, *Commentaries on the Law of Scotland* (2nd ed) at x. For the development of Anglo-American bankruptcy law, see Fletcher, I.F., *The Law of Insolvency* (3rd ed) (2003, Sweet and Maxwell, London) in

creditors with a means of collective execution on the assets of merchant debtors.[4] It was not until the mid-nineteenth century that non-trader debtors became eligible for bankruptcy relief in British and American law. After the advent of modern legal forms such as the joint-stock corporation in the Victorian era, corporate insolvency laws were invariably adapted from bankruptcy laws. Thus, the entire corpus of corporate and personal insolvency law in Scotland, England and Wales and cognate jurisdictions was fashioned originally as a creditor-oriented response to business failure and default.

Despite their origins, personal insolvency systems in Britain, as elsewhere, no longer *function* primarily as systems for the adjustment of business indebtedness. The last quarter century has witnessed a rapid expansion of consumer credit, manifested most notably through the proliferation of credit card lending. This expansion has led to what social scientists term the 'democratisation' of consumer credit,[5] a process in which credit is extended to social groups to whom it was not traditionally available. Western economies have become dependent on high levels of spending financed by rising house prices and credit: a state of affairs in which consumers are encouraged to take risks. These factors have led to increasing household debt burdens,[6] increasing over-indebtedness and, in Britain, a significant rise in the numbers of debtors seeking relief through formal insolvency proceedings. The demography of personal insolvency has been transformed. In 2005, consumer debtors comprised around 70 per cent of the total debtors who sought formal debt relief (either through bankruptcy or an individual voluntary arrangement) in England and Wales. In Scotland, on the same measure (consumer debtors as a proportion of debtors entering sequestration or a protected trust deed), the figure was nearer 90 per cent.

Chapters 1 and 2; Graham, D., 'Shakespeare in Debt? English and International Insolvency in Tudor England' (2000) 13(5) *Insolvency Intelligence* 36 and 13(6) *Insolvency Intelligence* 44, 'A Dark and Neglected Subject: Landmarks in the Reform of English Insolvency Law' (2002) *International Insolvency Review* 97; Graham, D. and Tribe, J., 'Bankruptcy in Crisis – A Regency Saga' (2004) 17(6) *Insolvency Intelligence* 85 and 17(10) *Insolvency Intelligence* 134; Skeel, D., *Debt's Dominion* (2001, Princeton University Press, Princeton); Tabb, C.J., 'The Historical Evolution of the Bankruptcy Discharge' (1991) 65 *American Bankruptcy Law Journal* 325. For a Scottish account, see McKenzie Skene, D.W., 'Morally Bankrupt? Apportioning Blame in Bankruptcy' [2004] *Journal of Business Law* 171.

4   Idem. See also Weisberg, R., 'Commercial Morality, the Merchant Character, and the History of the Voidable Preference' (1986) 39 *Stanford Law Review* 3.

5   See Niemi-Kiesiläinen, J., Ramsay, I. and Whitford, W.C. (eds), *Consumer Bankruptcy in Global Perspective* (2003, Hart Publishing, Oxford) at 2–4.

6   The Bank of England's Statistical Release (December 2005) records aggregate personal debt in the United Kingdom at GBP 1,157.5 billion of which GBP 962.5 billion was secured on a dwelling and GBP 192.3 billion was unsecured: see <www.bankofengland.co.uk/statistics/li/2005/dec/lendind.pdf> (last viewed 31 May 2007). Aggregate household debt grew from 40 per cent of aggregate annual household income in 1980 to 140 per cent of aggregate annual household income in 2005.

The phenomenon of rising consumer over-indebtedness has prompted several jurisdictions to adjust their insolvency laws.[7] In Britain there has been growing recognition that insolvency law needs to be updated to reflect the transformation described above.[8] This derives from a concern that systems well equipped for dealing with business debtors are not appropriate for dealing with consumer debtors, many of whom have few or no non-exempt assets. Accordingly, British policymakers are developing more consumer-oriented approaches.

Consumer over-indebtedness raises wider socio-economic concerns. Firstly, there are concerns of the 'ticking time bomb' variety. Highly leveraged consumers are vulnerable to sudden drops in income caused by changes in their personal circumstances, such as job loss, illness or family breakdown, or changes in the general economic outlook. Over-indebtedness may therefore act as a brake on spending and consumption which, over time, will affect growth in economies, like ours, that depend on sustained consumer spending. Secondly, there are concerns about the social impact of over-indebtedness on families and communities. Yet, despite these concerns hardly any attention has been paid at the international level to the potential global socio-economic impact of consumer over-indebtedness.[9] This contrasts with the global interest in business insolvency and rescue. One exception is INSOL International's *Consumer Debt Report*[10] which sets out a series of high-level principles and recommendations that provide a template for the enactment or reform of domestic consumer insolvency laws. The aim of this chapter is to review the INSOL principles using the emerging consumer bankruptcy systems in Scotland, England and Wales[11] to illustrate how these principles may be used to benchmark consumer bankruptcy systems.[12]

---

7   See Kilborn, J., 'The Innovative German Approach to Consumer Debt Relief: Revolutionary Changes in German Law, and Surprising Lessons for the United States' (2004) 24 *Northwestern Journal of International Law and Business* 257, 'La Responsabilisation de l'Economie: What the United States Can Learn From the New French Law on Consumer Overindebtedness' (2005) 26 *Michigan Journal of International Law* 619, 'Continuity, Change and Innovation in Emerging Consumer Bankruptcy Systems: Belgium and Luxembourg' (2006) 14 *American Bankruptcy Institute Law Review* 69; Niemi-Kiesiläinen et al. (eds), above note 5.

8   See Insolvency Law and Practice, Report of the Insolvency Law Review Committee, Cmnd 8558 (1982) in Chapters 1 and 6; Productivity and Enterprise: Insolvency – A Second Chance, Cm 5234 (2001) at paragraphs 1.45–1.48; Personal Bankruptcy Reform in Scotland: A Modern Approach (2003, Scottish Executive) at paragraphs 1.6–1.8.

9   There is passing reference to consumers in the UNCITRAL Legislative Guide on Insolvency Law, above note 1 at 1 but its focus is on debtors engaged in economic activity and consumer insolvency issues are not addressed.

10   INSOL International, Consumer Debt Report – Report of Findings and Recommendations (May 2001), available at: <www.insol.org/pdf/consdebt.pdf> (last viewed 31 May 2007) ('the INSOL Report' or 'the Report').

11   In England and Wales, some reform has already happened as a result of the Enterprise Act 2002 ('EA 2002'). A number of further reforms have been consulted on and which will implement some of these is progressing through Parliament in the form of the Draft Tribunals, Courts and Enforcement Bill, Cm 6885 (July 2006). In Scotland, the

The INSOL Report

The genesis of the INSOL Report was a meeting on consumer debt problems at the 1997 INSOL World Congress in New Orleans.[13] Following further meetings in 1999 at the INSOL Pacific Conference in Auckland, New Zealand and the INSOL Conference of the Americas in Bermuda, the INSOL Consumer Debt Committee ('the Committee') was established.[14] The Report is the first (and so far only) report of the Committee's findings.

The preface to the Report notes that the Committee grew out of an enthusiasm to tackle a problem recognized as being of increasing worldwide significance. The Committee's long-term aim is to provide a resource for countries developing or reforming laws and systems designed to deal with the problems of consumer debtors and, as noted above, the Report sets out the underlying principles on which consumer insolvency laws might be based. [15] It also makes recommendations for the reduction, if not avoidance, of consumer debtor insolvencies and the amelioration of their social and psychological consequences.

The Report commences with a discussion on solving consumer debt problems.[16] Against that background, it sets out four principles underlying the resolution of such problems and ten recommendations for achieving these.

Bankruptcy and Diligence etc (Scotland) Act 2007 ('BD(S)A 2007') received Royal Assent on 15 January 2007 but the majority of its provisions are not yet in force; further reforms for which it paves the way have also been consulted on.

12   For some previous suggestions for reform of personal insolvency law in England and Wales formulated in the light of the INSOL Report, some of which are now in fact in prospect, see Milman, D., *Personal Insolvency Law, Regulation and Policy* (2005, Ashgate, Aldershot) at 154–155.

13   Preface to the INSOL Report.

14   Idem.

15   Idem.

16   INSOL Report at 4. The Report recognizes that solving consumer debt problems is complex, particularly as these are often caused by or related to the kinds of socio-psychological factors already mentioned above, such as divorce, redundancy, job loss, disability etc. On such factors as causes of consumer debt problems in Britain see, for example, Citizen's Advice, 'In Too Deep' (2001); Kempson, E., 'Over-indebtedness in Britain: A Report to the Department of Trade and Industry' (2002, DTI); Kempson, E. and Dominy, N., 'Mapping the Can't Pay/Won't Pay Divide' (2003, Department for Constitutional Affairs); Consumer Credit Counselling Service, Deconstructing Debt (2003); Kempson, E., McKay, S. and Willits, M., 'Characteristics of families in debt and the nature of indebtedness' (2004, Department for Work and Pensions); OXERA, Are UK Households over-indebted? (2004, Report prepared for the Association for Payment Clearing Service, British Bankers Association, Consumer Credit Association and Finance and Leasing Association; Citizens Advice Scotland, On the Cards – the debt crisis facing Scottish Citizens Advice Bureaux Clients (2004); Over-indebtedness in Britain: A DTI Report on the MORI Financial Services Survey 2004 (2005, DTI); Griffiths Commission on Personal Debt, 'What price credit?' (2005); Report of the Working Group on Debt Relief (2005, Scottish Executive). For the United States, see in particular the Consumer Bankruptcy Project I of 1981, the Consumer Bankruptcy

The first principle is a fair and equitable allocation of consumer credit risks. The recommendations for achieving this are that legislators:

(i)   should enact laws which provide for a fair and equitable, efficient and cost-effective, accessible and transparent settlement and discharge of consumer and small business debts;

(ii)   may consider providing for separate proceedings, depending on the circumstances of the consumer debtor;

(iii)   should consider providing for separate or alternative proceedings for consumer debtors and small businesses; and

(iv)   should ensure that consumer insolvency laws are mutually recognized in other jurisdictions and aim at standardization and uniformity.

The second principle is the provision of some form of discharge of indebtedness, rehabilitation or 'fresh start' for the debtor. The recommendation for achieving this is simply:

(v)   that legislators should offer consumer debtors a discharge of indebtedness as a tailpiece of a liquidation or rehabilitation procedure.

The third principle is extra-judicial rather than judicial proceedings where there are equally effective options available. The recommendations for achieving this are that:

(vi)   legislators should encourage extra-judicial or out-of-court proceedings for solving consumer and small business debt problems; and

(vii)   governments, quasi-governmental or private organizations should ensure the availability of sufficient competent and independent debt counselling.

The fourth principle is prevention to reduce the need for intervention. The recommendations for achieving this are that:

(viii) governments, quasi-governmental or private organizations should set up educational programmes and improve information and advice on the risks attached to consumer credit;

(ix)   lenders should observe the way in which credit is made available to consumers and small businesses, information is presented and the way those credits are collected; and

---

Project II of 1991 and the Consumer Bankruptcy Project III of 2001, the results of which are discussed respectively in Sullivan, T.A., Warren, E. and Westbrook, J.L., *As We Forgive Our Debtors; Bankruptcy and Consumer Credit in America* (1989, Oxford University Press, Oxford); *The Fragile Middle Class; Americans in Debt* (2000, Yale University Press, New Haven); and Warren, E. and Tyagi, A.W., 'The Two Income Trap: Why Middle Class Mothers and Fathers are Going Broke' (2004) 10(3) *Feminist Economics* 123. For the United Kingdom government's strategy for tackling over-indebtedness among consumers, see: <www.dti.gov.uk/consumers/consumer-finance/over-indebtedness/index.html> (last viewed 31 May 2007).

(x)   organizations of lenders and consumers should set up joint programmes to monitor consumer loan delinquencies.

This chapter concentrates on the first three principles and the recommendations for implementing them as those most relevant to the ongoing reform of consumer bankruptcy laws in Scotland, England and Wales. There are other ongoing reforms in both jurisdictions, for example reform of consumer credit legislation, [17] which address at least some of the issues raised by the fourth principle and the recommendations relating thereto. However, these are distinct in nature from the other principles and recommendations, which are focused on the relevant consumer bankruptcy laws themselves, and for reasons of space will not be considered.

Structural Issues

The Report accords considerable importance to the way in which consumer bankruptcy systems are structured. Thus, the key recommendations for achieving the first principle (a fair and equitable allocation of consumer credit risks) are that legislators may consider providing for separate proceedings depending on the circumstances of the consumer debtor and should consider providing alternatives for consumer debtors and small businesses. The Report notes that different routes to a discharge may be provided depending on the debtor's particular situation and the nature of his debts[18] and suggests that a debtor with no redemption capacity,[19] survival debts and no prospects of improvement in his financial situation within a reasonable time requires a different approach to a debtor with accommodation debts only.[20] It also suggests that where the insolvency is only likely to be temporary provided the debtor is given breathing space, he should be allowed an opportunity to restructure his earnings and spending.[21] In addition, one of the recommendations for achieving the third principle (extra-judicial rather than

---

17   See, for example, the Consumer Credit Act 2006.
18   INSOL Report at 18. The Report distinguishes between different types of consumer debts, which it categorizes as survival debts (an accumulation of recurrent debts for the basic necessities of life which occurs when the debtor's household has to live at a social minimum for any length of time); over-consumption debts (caused through over-consumption by a debtor who originally has a budget surplus but finances an extravagant lifestyle with borrowed money); compensation debts (resulting from over-consumption by a debtor typically suffering from deprivation or social exclusion); relational debts (acquired through connection with others, e.g., marriage, death); accommodation debts (caused by the inability to adapt to either an adverse change in circumstances or a failure of anticipated prosperity) and fraudulent debts (where a debtor wilfully over-commits himself financially): INSOL Report at 4–6.
19   The amount available to creditors after taking into account the debtor's reasonable needs: Ibid., at 8–9.
20   Ibid., at 18.
21   Idem.

judicial proceedings where there are equally effective options available) is that legislators should encourage extra-judicial proceedings for solving consumer and small business debt problems since extra-judicial procedures have clear advantages for both debtors and creditors.[22]

The current systems in Scotland, England and Wales rate well when benchmarked against these recommendations and will rate better still if and when the ongoing reforms are implemented. Both jurisdictions have a judicial procedure for the liquidation of assets of individual debtors (whether business or consumer debtors) through which they may obtain a discharge in return for the surrender of non-exempt assets and surplus income: in England and Wales, bankruptcy under Part IX of the Insolvency Act 1986 ('IA 1986'); in Scotland, sequestration under the Bankruptcy (Scotland) Act 1985 ('B(S)A 1985'). Both jurisdictions also have a variety of alternative procedures available to consumer debtors depending on their circumstances.

In England and Wales, the main alternative to bankruptcy is an individual voluntary arrangement ('IVA') under Part VIII of IA 1986. An IVA is a composition or scheme of arrangement[23] which arises from a proposal made by an individual debtor (whether a business or consumer debtor) to his creditors. It is essentially an extra-judicial procedure as the court has only a limited supervisory role.[24] The proposal, which may encompass the debtor's assets or income or both, is formulated by the debtor in conjunction with an insolvency practitioner ('the nominee').[25] The creditors vote on the proposal and, if it is approved, the nominee becomes the supervisor of the IVA and oversees its implementation. The key feature of an IVA, and a critical requirement of an extra-judicial procedure according to the Report,[26] is that it binds dissenting creditors:[27] if the proposal is approved by the requisite majority,[28] all creditors who were entitled to vote are bound regardless of whether or how they voted. IVAs provide debt relief and are

---

22   Ibid., at 25.
23   IA 1986, section 253(1).
24   Ibid., sections 256A(3), 259, 262, 263(3)-(5). The court's involvement is greater if the debtor applies for a stay under section 253 pending the holding of the creditors' meeting to vote on the proposal. However, a debtor is no longer obliged to apply for a stay following the amendment of Part VIII of IA 1986 by the Insolvency Act 2000. An approved IVA is subject to a limited right of challenge by dissentient creditors under section 262.
25   Ibid., section 256(1)(a).
26   INSOL Report at 25.
27   IA 1986, section 260.
28   For the proposal to become binding, it must be approved by a majority of creditors in excess of three-quarters by value: IA 1986, sections 257–258; Insolvency Rules 1986 (SI 1986/1925), rule 5.23. This threshold will be reduced to a simple majority in cases where the debtor's unsecured debts do not exceed GBP 75,000 if reforms proposed by the government with the aim of increasing consumer access to the IVA are implemented: 'Improving Individual Voluntary Arrangements' (Insolvency Service, 2005). See further McKenzie Skene, D.W. and Walters, A., 'Consumer Bankruptcy Law Reform in Great Britain' (2007) 81 *American Bankruptcy Law Journal* 477.

usually proposed as a means of avoiding bankruptcy, although an undischarged bankrupt may also propose an IVA with a view to having the bankruptcy annulled.[29]

In Scotland, the main alternative to sequestration and broadly comparable to an IVA in England and Wales is a protected trust deed ('PTD'). A debtor (whether a business or consumer debtor) may grant a trust deed for creditors conveying specified assets and/or income to a named trustee to be administered for the benefit of creditors. At common law, creditors who do not accede to a trust deed are not bound by it, but a trust deed which satisfies certain conditions may, and in practice generally will, be converted into a PTD which binds all creditors.[30] PTDs operate as an extra-judicial form of sequestration that provides debtors with a discharge.

In addition, debtors with a reasonably stable and consistent income can choose from a variety of formal and informal debt management options, all designed to extend payments over time and so enable the debtor to repay in full but over a longer period. These mechanisms may be particularly appropriate for those debtors mentioned in the Report who have got into temporary difficulty and just need some breathing space to sort out their affairs.

In England and Wales, the relevant options are a county court administration order ('CCAO') under Part VI of the County Courts Act 1984 ('CCA 1984') or a debt management arrangement ('DMA'). CCAOs provide a means of dealing with debt problems outside the bankruptcy system for a limited class of debtors (whether business or consumer debtors).[31] Although in principle

---

29   IA 1986, section 261. EA 2002 also introduced a fast-track IVA procedure ('FTVA') administered exclusively by an official receiver, a state official who administers bankruptcies and investigates the debtor's affairs in the public interest, which provides a streamlined procedure accessible only by undischarged bankrupts: IA 1986, sections 263A-G. For a recent review of the IVA process, see Green, M., 'Individual Voluntary Arrangements, Over-indebtedness and the Insolvency Regime' (November 2002), Short Form Report, available at: <www.insolvency.gov.uk/insolvency professionandlegislation/policychange/ivapolicyresearch/shortformreport.doc>   (last viewed 31 May 2007). For earlier accounts of the operation of IVAs in practice, see Pond, K., 'The Individual Voluntary Arrangement Experience' [1995] *Journal of Business Law* 118 and 'An Insolvent Decade: The Changing Nature of the IVA 1987–1997', SSRN Working Paper Series, available at: <papers.ssrn.com/sol3/papers.cfm?abstract_id=139556> (last viewed 31 May 2007).

30   The trust deed must convey to the trustee the debtor's estate excluding property that would not vest in a trustee in sequestration under B(S)A 1985, section 33(1) and the trustee must follow the procedure set out in B(S)A 1985, Schedule 5. Where a defined percentage of creditors does not object, all creditors are bound by the PTD and there are limited rights of challenge to it. Creditors who objected to the trust deed or did not receive the relevant notice have no higher right to recover their debts than acceding creditors (B(S)A 1985, Schedule 5, paragraph 6) although they may apply for the debtor's sequestration in certain limited circumstances: B(S)A 1985, Schedule 5, paragraph 7.

31   Total indebtedness must not exceed the current county court limit of GBP 5,000 and must include at least one judgment debt, although a CCAO will not automatically be

they can be used to provide debt relief,[32] they are essentially court-based debt management plans which offer the debtor respite from enforcement and rescheduling of debts, repayments being consolidated into a single monthly payment into court. DMAs are informal arrangements entered into between debtors and their creditors. Commonly arising after the debtor has sought debt advice from the voluntary sector or a private sector debt management company, DMAs typically provide for repayment in full over time or repayment on the terms of the DMA until such time as the debtor has sufficient resources to meet the repayments as originally contracted. Where a provider is involved, repayments are made to the provider in a consolidated form and then distributed among creditors. However, DMAs are not legally binding, do not give rise to a stay on individual collection efforts and are currently unregulated.

In Scotland, the relevant options are the statutory debt arrangement scheme ('DAS') under Part I of the Debt Arrangement and Attachment (Scotland) Act 2002 ('DAA(S)A 2002') and a voluntary arrangement with creditors at common law. The DAS allows individual debtors (whether business or consumer debtors) with multiple debts to enter into a debt payment programme for payment of their debts from surplus income while protected from enforcement action.[33] It can bind dissenting creditors.[34] The debtor does not receive a discharge, although it is open to individual creditors to agree to waive interest on or compound their debts. Voluntary arrangements with creditors are similar to DMAs in England and Wales. They typically provide for rescheduling of debts requiring repayment in full over time rather than debt relief and cannot bind dissenting creditors.

Both jurisdictions therefore offer a menu of options which, on paper, caters for debtors in a variety of circumstances: a formal asset liquidation procedure leading to discharge; an alternative procedure leading to discharge; and procedures for debt management which are more appropriate for debtors in temporary difficulties who need breathing space to re-order their affairs. There are proposals to introduce yet further options in England and Wales exclusively for consumer debtors: a simplified IVA ('SIVA'); a debt relief procedure for 'no income, no

---

invalidated should it turn out that the indebtedness exceeds GBP 5,000: CCA 1984, section 112(5).

32   CCA 1984, sections 112(6), 117; Kempson, E. and Collard, S., 'Managing Multiple Debts: Experience of County Court Administration Orders among debtors, creditors and advisors' (2004, Department for Constitutional Affairs).

33   For a detailed description of the history and operation of the DAS, see McKenzie Skene, D.W., 'Dealing with Multiple Debt – An Examination of the Proposed Debt Arrangement Scheme in Scotland' (2002) 6 *Insolvency Lawyer* 212; 'The Debt Arrangement Scheme' 2003 *Scots Law Times* 289 and 'The Debt Arrangement Scheme Goes Live' 2004 *Scots Law Times* 237.

34   In principle, all creditors whose debts are included in a debt payment programme must consent to it: Debt Arrangement Scheme (Scotland) Regulations 2004 (SSI 2004/468) as amended, regulation 22(1). However, the DAS administrator may dispense with the consent of non-consenting creditors within certain limits and, in those circumstances, approve the application if it is fair and reasonable, notwithstanding that all creditors have not consented to it: ibid., regulation 26(1).

asset' debtors ('NINAs') to be known as a debt relief order ('DRO') and a regulated form of DMA. An additional procedure specifically for NINAs was rejected in Scotland, but the BDS(A) contains new provisions meant to provide access to existing procedures for such debtors who may currently be denied this. These developments, together with the related issue of debtor choice, are considered below.

British law diverges from the recommendations insofar as they mandate provision of separate proceedings specifically for consumer debtors. The current procedures are open to all individual debtors, whether business or consumer debtors. Both jurisdictions have recently considered and rejected the idea of separate bankruptcy/sequestration proceedings for consumer debtors [35] and, in Scotland, a proposal to restrict the DAS to consumers and small traders only[36] was abandoned. It is difficult to see how completely separate regimes for consumer and business debtors would work in Britain, where the primary distinction in insolvency law is between individual (business or consumer) debtors and other debtors rather than between consumer debtors and (any form of) business debtors. Although the Report is correct in noting that individual business debtors may raise different issues from non-traders, it suggested that the British system works quite well.[37] It should be noted, however, that the proposed new alternative procedures of SIVAs, DROs and regulated DMAs in England and Wales will be available to consumer debtors only.

---

35   In England and Wales, the issue of whether the reforms in EA 2002 should be extended to consumer debtors proved controversial and during the parliamentary debates on the legislation repeated attempts (ultimately unsuccessful) were made to amend it to distinguish between business and consumer debtors, in particular in relation to the discharge period. In Scotland, see Personal Bankruptcy Reform in Scotland, above note 8, paragraph 4. The extension of the EA 2002 reforms to consumer debtors prompts the concern that the increased risk-taking which they were designed to encourage in entrepreneurs was undesirable in consumers. One response is: why leave consumer debtors who have no means to pay in the bankruptcy system when you will never get anything out of them and quick, routinized processing is administratively less of a headache?

36   Enforcement of Civil Obligations in Scotland (April 2002, Scottish Executive Consultation Paper) paragraph 4.153 and Q.4D.4.

37   The distinction between individual and other forms of debtor is imperfect in Scotland because insolvent non-company debtors (with the exception of limited liability partnerships) are generally subject to sequestration in the same way as individuals whereas in England and Wales, partnerships are subject to a modified version of the insolvency regimes applicable to companies and thus there is a more perfect division between individual and other kinds of debtors. The Scottish system might usefully consider whether this is a more appropriate way of dealing with debtors other than individuals, but it is suggested that this does not detract from the basic premise that all individuals, whether consumer or business debtors, can properly be accommodated within a regime designed specifically for individual as distinct from other kinds of debtors.

A 'Fresh Start' for Consumer Debtors

The second principle identified in the Report is the provision of 'some form of discharge of indebtedness, rehabilitation or 'fresh start' for the debtor' and, to reiterate, the recommendation for achieving this is that legislators should offer consumer debtors a discharge of indebtedness as a tailpiece of a liquidation or rehabilitation procedure. While discharge, debtor rehabilitation and 'fresh start' are separately enunciated, the INSOL Report does not at first sight appear to regard them as separate concepts with different content. The implication is that the debtor's 'fresh start' is confined to the debt forgiveness that discharge provides:

> In whatever form a discharge ultimately takes, debtors should have an opportunity to obtain relief from pre-existing indebtedness and to have a fresh start, free from their past financial obligations.[38]

However, the Report's overall emphasis is on the provision of processes that not only resolve the debtor's immediate financial problems (through discharge) but also deal with the underlying causes of over-indebtedness so as to prevent the debtor from getting into unmanageable debt again.[39] This suggests a wider concept of debtor rehabilitation and economic reintegration in which discharge is a crucial first step.[40] The text accompanying the second principle and the supplementary recommendation should be read in this light.

In crafting the discharge, the INSOL Report urges legislators to consider the following issues of detail:

(i)   the extent to which debtors should be required to contribute to the estate from ongoing income;

(ii) what debts should be excluded from the scope of the discharge;

(iii) whether debtors should be allowed to discharge their debts more than once and, if so, whether they should be required to wait for a minimum period before qualifying to receive a further discharge;

(iv) whether legal restrictions should be imposed on debtors – such as restrictions on obtaining new credit – either during the proceeding or as a condition of discharge; and

(v)   the extent to which debtors should be able to reaffirm debts discharged by legal process.

While the drafters of the Report have sought to be sensitive to cultural differences, there is a clear sense that they regard the 'fresh start' as a universal principle which should be presumptively broad in scope. The implication is that income capture, the categories of non-dischargeable debt, legal restrictions on

---

38   INSOL Report at 22.

39   Ibid., at 6.

40   See, generally, Gross, K., *Failure and Forgiveness* (1997, Yale University Press, New Haven CT). In this respect, the Report has a decidedly Anglo-Saxon bias which reflects the composition of the Committee.

debtors and the scope for revival of debts through reaffirmation should not be so broad as to undermine the 'fresh start'.

The current systems in Scotland, England and Wales rate highly when benchmarked against this principle. Debtors have 'an opportunity to obtain relief from pre-existing indebtedness and to have a fresh start, free from their past financial obligations'[41] through a variety of means.

Firstly, debtors may obtain a discharge through bankruptcy/sequestration. In England and Wales, debtors receive an automatic discharge of all bankruptcy debts,[42] broadly defined to include 'any liability under an enactment, any liability for breach of trust, any liability in contract, tort or bailment and any liability arising out of an obligation to make restitution'.[43] The categories of non-dischargeable debt are limited,[44] but there is a 'ride-through' provision preserving the right of secured creditors to enforce against their collateral notwithstanding the discharge of the underlying debt.[45] The court has no power to deny discharge outright although it can suspend discharge where debtors fail to comply with their statutory obligations to co-operate with the official receiver ('OR') and/or their trustee in bankruptcy.[46] In Scotland, a debtor obtains an automatic discharge of 'all debts and obligations contracted by him, or for which he was liable, at the date of sequestration'.[47] The categories of non-dischargeable debt are limited,[48] but again

---

41   INSOL Report at 22.
42   Defined as 'any debt or liability to which [they are] subject at the commencement of bankruptcy': IA 1986, sections 281, 382(1)(a).
43   Ibid., section 382(4).
44   They are: debts arising from fraud or fraudulent breach of trust; fines imposed in respect of a criminal offence; and student loans. Liability to pay damages in respect of personal injuries and debts arising under an order made in family proceedings are also presumptively non-dischargeable but can be released by the court.
45   IA 1986, section 281(2).
46   Ibid., section 279(3)-(4). The trustee in bankruptcy may be the OR or an insolvency practitioner from the private sector. Insolvency practitioners are usually only appointed in cases where there are assets to be realized. In practice the OR acts as trustee in most cases: see Insolvency Service, Characteristics of a Bankrupt (2006), available at: <www.insolvency.gov.uk/insolvencyprofessionandlegislation/ policychange/cob.pdf> (last viewed 31 May 2007).
47   B(S)A 1985, sections 54–55. A debtor may also obtain a discharge at any time after the date of sequestration if an offer of composition is accepted following the procedure set out in B(S)A 1985, section 56 and Schedule 4. However, this occurs rarely in practice. The debtor must promise to pay at least 25p in the pound and the procedure is cumbersome, although it will be streamlined by the BD(S)A 2007.
48   Ibid., section 55(2). They are: fines or other penalties payable to the Crown; fines imposed in a district court; certain compensation orders; bail; liability for fraud or breach of trust; aliment (the Scottish term for the obligation of support due to a spouse or child) or periodical allowance (the Scottish term for income payments which may be ordered to be made to an ex-spouse following divorce) which could not be claimed in the sequestration; and child support maintenance prior to the date of sequestration. Liability for all student loans will be added to this list by the BD(S)A 2007, thus aligning the position with that in England and Wales.

there is a 'ride-through' provision preserving the right of secured creditors to enforce against their collateral notwithstanding the discharge of the underlying debt.[49] The court has no power to deny discharge outright, although it may defer it on cause shown.[50] The discharge in both jurisdictions is therefore generous in scope, notwithstanding some minor differences in the categories of non-dischargeable debt. Indeed, the British discharge is more generous than the discharge in Chapter 7 of the United States Bankruptcy Code, which is qualified by a much wider range of non-dischargeable debts[51] and can be denied completely on specified conduct grounds.[52]

In England and Wales, reforms introduced by the EA 2002 with effect from 1 April 2004 liberalized the bankruptcy discharge further. The discharge now takes effect after the expiry of one year from the commencement of bankruptcy,[53] a reduction from the previous period of three years, and can be obtained earlier where the OR considers that investigation of the debtor's conduct and affairs is unnecessary or concluded and files a notice with the court to that effect. The EA 2002 also triggered the abolition of numerous statutory restrictions applicable to undischarged bankrupts that were regarded as outdated and stigmatic.[54] This deregulatory policy was balanced by the introduction of a new system of post-bankruptcy restrictions targeted at culpable debtors. However, these do not detract from the principle that debtors are entitled to a swift and broad discharge regardless of their pre-bankruptcy conduct. Furthermore, debtors are not prevented from obtaining more than one discharge and do not have to wait for a specified minimum period before becoming eligible for another discharge.[55] Again, this contrasts with the position in the United States where a debtor who receives a discharge in Chapter 7 must wait eight years before qualifying for another discharge through a Chapter 7 filing.[56] These reforms currently apply only in England and Wales, but similar reforms will be introduced in Scotland by the BD(S)A 2007.[57] However, the Scottish reforms will not permit automatic discharge

---

49   Ibid., section 55(3).

50   Ibid., section 54(3).

51   11 USC §523; Ziegel, J.S., *Comparative Consumer Insolvency Regimes – A Canadian Perspective* (2003, Hart Publishing, Oxford) at 42–4.

52   11 USC §727.

53   IA 1986, section 279.

54   EA 2002, sections 265–8. Some restrictions have been retained, most notably the ban on undischarged bankrupts acting as insolvency practitioners or, in the absence of permission from the court, as company directors: see Company Directors' Disqualification Act 1986, section 11; Walters, A. and Davis-White, M., *Directors' Disqualification and Bankruptcy Restrictions* (2005, Sweet and Maxwell, London) in Chapter 11.

55   Before EA 2002, automatic discharge was not available to debtors who had been undischarged bankrupts in the 15 years prior to the commencement of their latest bankruptcy.

56   11 USC §727(8).

57   See the BD(S)A 2007.

before the expiry of one year[58] and the current restrictions on a debtor re-applying for sequestration within five years of a previous sequestration have been retained.[59]

The rationale of the EA 2002 reforms is to reduce the stigma of bankruptcy for business debtors and encourage honest but failed entrepreneurs to re-engage in commercial risk-taking.[60] Since in practice, bankruptcy and sequestration function primarily as mechanisms for forgiving consumer debt, the business orientation of this policy seems rather incongruous. However, the reforms in England and Wales did nothing to affect the eligibility of consumer debtors who qualify on the same terms as their business counterparts for the benefits of discharge. The Scottish version of the reforms will also apply to both business and consumer debtors.

Secondly, debtors may obtain a discharge through an alternative procedure. Debtors who enter into an IVA and comply with its terms can expect to receive a generous discharge. Since in legal theory an IVA is a contract capable of being imposed on non-assenting parties by means of statutory machinery, the scope of the discharge depends on the terms of the IVA approved by the creditors. However, it is standard practice to provide that the debtor will be released from all the debts within the compass of the IVA if he complies fully or substantially with his IVA obligations, compliance being certified by the supervisor.[61] Thus, discharge through an IVA depends on the debtor's ability to honour the IVA terms.[62] In practice, those terms will depend on what the creditors are prepared to accept and there is currently scope for them to demand modifications to the proposal before approving it.[63] As noted above, debtors can agree to contribute assets or surplus income or a combination of both towards payment of their debts. The pattern in the market place is for IVAs to take the form of five-year income

---

58   As at present, however, the debtor will still be able to obtain an earlier discharge via the composition procedure referred to above.

59   B(S)A 1985, section 5(2B). This restriction does not apply where the debtor is applying for his own sequestration with the consent of a qualified creditor, but this is rare. The requirements for sequestration are discussed in more detail below.

60   'Bankruptcy: A Fresh Start – A Consultation on Possible Reform to the Law Relating to Personal Insolvency in England and Wales' (2000, Insolvency Service); 'Productivity and Enterprise: Insolvency – A Second Chance', Cm 5234 (2001). See also Milman, D., above note 12; Ramsay, I., 'Bankruptcy in Transition: The Case of England and Wales', in Niemi-Kiesiläinen et al. (eds), above note 5; Walters, A., 'Personal Insolvency Law After the Enterprise Act: An Appraisal' (2005) 5 *Journal of Corporate Law Studies* 65. In Scotland, an additional reason is the need to keep a level playing field between the two jurisdictions: Personal Bankruptcy Reform in Scotland, above note 8; 'Modernizing Bankruptcy and Diligence in Scotland: Draft Bill and Consultation' (2004, Scottish Executive).

61   See Association of Business Recovery Professionals (R3), Standard Conditions for Individual Voluntary Arrangements, clauses 9–10.

62   In default, the supervisor or a bound creditor may petition for bankruptcy: IA 1986, sections 264(1)(c), 276.

63   Ibid., sections 258(2)-(5). Creditor modifications would not be permitted in SIVAs: Improving IVAs, above note 28.

payment plans proposed by salaried debtors with few assets.[64] It follows that, in the majority of IVAs, discharge is conditional on the debtor maintaining payments over time that will produce a better dividend for creditors than bankruptcy.

Debtors entering a PTD in Scotland can also expect to receive a generous discharge. The scope of the discharge also depends on the terms of the PTD, but in practice, it will usually provide for discharge of all debts and liabilities for which the debtor was liable when the trust deed was granted after a specified period. This will normally be three years – the same period (currently) as sequestration – although it is not unknown for PTDs to last longer to allow the debtor to make sufficient contributions to ensure creditors get a better return than in sequestration. In practice, most PTDs rely on income payments over the lifetime of the PTD to achieve this, since although a PTD captures broadly the same non-exempt assets as would be captured in sequestration,[65] most debtors have few such assets. So long as the terms of the PTD are complied with, however, the debtor will be discharged irrespective of how much, if any, of the debts are actually paid, although recent proposals for the introduction of a minimum dividend as well as a maximum period of three years for a PTD would change this if enacted in their current form. However, these proposals are currently being reconsidered.

Thirdly, an additional route to discharge will become available in England and Wales if proposals for the introduction of DROs, targeted at NINA debtors,[66] are implemented, while in Scotland a limited element of debt relief in the form of cancellation of interest and charges accruing during the debt payment plan following its successful completion has now been introduced into the DAS.[67]

The discharge in bankruptcy and sequestration is automatic and, once the Scottish version of the EA 2002 reforms is in force, will be available throughout Britain no later than one year from the commencement of the proceedings. The limits on the scope of the discharge are within the boundaries contemplated by the Report. There are no grounds on which the court can deny discharge outright.

---

64 PricewaterhouseCoopers, 'Living on Tick: The 21st Century Debtor' (2006), available at: <www.pwc.com/uk/eng/about/svcs/brs/PwC-IVAReport.pdf> (last viewed 31 May 2007). The five-year payment plan is the default model for the proposed consumer IVA: Improving IVAs, above note 28.

65 As it is a condition of a trust deed becoming a PTD that it conveys to the trustee the debtor's estate excluding property that would not vest in a trustee in sequestration, the assets to be included in a PTD are not identical to those which would be included in a sequestration because certain assets are excluded from sequestration by provisions other than B(S)A 1985, section 33(1). Nevertheless, there is a broad equivalence.

66 'A Choice of Paths – Better options to manage over-indebtedness and multiple debt', CP 23/04 (2004, Department of Constitutional Affairs); 'Relief for the Indebted – An Alternative to Bankruptcy?' (2005, Insolvency Service); Draft Tribunals, Courts and Enforcement Bill, Cm 6885 (July 2006); Tribunals, Courts and Enforcement Bill (currently before Parliament). The NINA proposals are considered below. See also the literature on over-indebtedness above note 16 and McKenzie Skene and Walters, above note 28.

67 The Debt Arrangement Scheme (Scotland) Amendment Regulations 2007 (SSI 2007/262).

Those debtors who wish to avoid the greater restrictions, publicity and scrutiny associated with bankruptcy and sequestration can pursue alternative routes to discharge by entering an IVA or PTD which, in practice, will usually involve sustaining payments from surplus income for a sufficiently long period to satisfy the dividend expectations of creditors. There are also provisions for income payments for up to three years and, given the one-year discharge period in bankruptcy and (prospectively) sequestration, future income accruing after discharge can be captured. The Report indicates that provision for income capture beyond 'the termination of proceedings' is not ideal.[68] However, under the OR's current operational guidelines in England and Wales, non-compliance with an income payments order or agreement[69] is unlikely of itself to lead to an application for suspension of discharge with the result that, in practice, discharge is not conditional upon contributions from income.[70] In Scotland, the AIB's Notes for Guidance for Trustees suggest that unreasonable delay in agreeing a voluntary income contribution or failure to comply with an income contribution order may be a ground for deferral of discharge, but in practice, any such failure on the debtor's part is unlikely in isolation to lead to an application to deferral.

Finally, debtors in Britain can agree to reaffirm discharged debts. In England and Wales, on ordinary principles of contract law, a creditor would have to provide fresh consideration (such as further credit) for a promise to repay a discharged debt,[71] whereas, in Scotland, a gratuitous promise is binding and no such consideration would be required. It is not known to what extent reaffirmation agreements are relied on by British creditors to reverse the effects of discharge, though they are not thought to be prevalent. Overall, there is little to detract from the view that British law provides opportunities for discharge within what the drafters of the Report would regard as tolerable limits.

Balancing the Interests of Debtors and Creditors

The first principle in the INSOL Report is that there should be a fair and equitable allocation of consumer credit risks within domestic consumer bankruptcy systems. Two of the recommendations for achieving this have already been discussed earlier in relation to structural issues; the other two are, firstly, that legislators should enact laws to provide for a fair and equitable, efficient and cost-effective, accessible and transparent settlement and discharge of consumer and small business debts and, secondly, that legislators should ensure that consumer insolvency laws are mutually recognized in other jurisdictions and should aim at standardization and uniformity. For reasons of space, the second of these will be

---

68   INSOL Report, 23.
69   IA 1986, sections 310–310A.
70   Insolvency Service Technical Manual, Chapter 31.7 and Case Help Manual, available at: <www.insolvency.gov.uk/freedomofinformation/index.htm> (last viewed 31 May 2007).
71   This follows from *Heather & Son v Webb* (1876–1877) LR 2 CPD 1.

dealt with only briefly here by stating that there are no less than four different sets of domestic provisions for mutual recognition and assistance in operation in Britain all of which apply to consumer insolvency proceedings: section 426 of the IA 1986 (which applies to certain designated, mostly former Commonwealth, countries); the EC Regulation on Insolvency Proceedings [72] (which applies between the members of the European Union with the exception of Denmark); the Cross-Border Insolvency Regulations 2006 [73] (which enact a modified version of the UNCITRAL Model Law on Cross-Border Insolvency and apply to any country); and the common law (which also applies to any country). [74] The current systems in Britain therefore rate highly when benchmarked against this recommendation. The first recommendation will now be discussed in greater detail.

Fair and Equitable Balance

The Report recognizes that consumer bankruptcy systems must strike a balance between the interests of debtors and creditors. As a recent report from a leading accountancy firm put it, 'insolvency should not be an encouragement to default, neither should it reduce a debtor to permanent penury'. [75] In terms of balance, the imposition of an automatic stay is seen as important, not only to protect the debtor from undue harassment, but also as an intra-creditor device designed to prevent creditors gaining advantages over each other by pursuing unilateral collection efforts. This is reflected in British law by the collective nature of insolvency proceedings. In bankruptcy and sequestration, a stay arises by operation of law [76] whereas in an IVA or PTD a stay will be provided as a standard term. [77] In addition to a stay, the principal debtor-creditor balancing mechanisms alluded to in the Report concern the composition of the debtor's estate and the notion of 'good faith' debtors. These are considered in turn.

---

72   Council Regulation (EC) No 1346/2000 of 29 May 2000 on insolvency proceedings.

73   SI 2006/1030.

74   For an excellent discussion of all four, see Fletcher, I.F., *Insolvency in Private International Law* (2nd ed) (2005, Oxford University Press, Oxford) and *Supplement to Second Edition* (2007, Oxford University Press, Oxford). See also Marshall, J. (ed.), *European Cross Border Insolvency* (2004, Sweet and Maxwell, London); Moss, G., Fletcher, I.F. and Isaacs, S. (eds), *The EC Regulation on Insolvency Proceedings: A Commentary and Annotated Guide* (2002, Oxford University Press, Oxford); Omar, P., *European Insolvency Law* (2004, Ashgate, Aldershot); Silkenat, J.R. and Schmerler, C.D. (eds), *The Law of International Insolvencies and Debt Restructurings* (2006, Oceana Publications, New York NY); Wessels, B., *Current Topics of International Insolvency Law* (2004, Kluwer, Deventer).

75   'Living on Tick', above note 64. See also Keay, A., 'Balancing Interests in Bankruptcy Law' (2001) 30 *Common Law World Review* 206 and Milman, above note 12 in Chapter 6.

76   IA 1986, section 285(3); B(S)A 1985, section 37, which provides that enforcement procedures carried out by creditors after the date of sequestration will be of no effect.

77   Standard Conditions, above note 61, clause 4(3).

The Estate The issues here are two-fold. Firstly, what assets should the debtor be allowed to keep beyond the reach of his creditors? Secondly, given that consumer debtors will often have few assets, but ongoing earnings, to what extent should they be required to contribute to the estate from future income? The INSOL Report makes the following statements about these issues:

> The system should not be abusive to debtors and not necessarily designed just to protect and maximize value for creditors. It should contain a balanced approach to give the debtor the possibility of a second chance. Apart from the excluded property that will remain with the debtor, the entire estate should be available for creditors. The law should therefore provide the trustee or administrator with sufficient powers to nullify avoidable actions.

> The law will determine which assets of the debtor will be available for distribution among the creditors and consequently which assets will be excluded. The debtor should be able to maintain a reasonable standard of living. Where the law provides for a redemption capacity, the excluded income of the debtor is set according to a standard that the necessary living expenses ... of the debtor and his dependants can be met.

While pitched at a high level of generality, these statements recognize that some level of asset exemption is required as a necessary part of the 'fresh start' and that debtors who have redemption capacity can be expected to contribute from future income within reasonable limits. The Report looks with disfavour on jurisdictions that require redemption capacity to be surrendered for periods as long as seven or eight years as a pre-condition of discharge. This is consistent with its Anglo-Saxon bias towards a market-based conception of the 'fresh start' in which the priority is the speedy reintegration of the debtor into the market and credit economy. As we will see, British law is very much in tune with the Report's approach to these issues.

In England and Wales, the estate of a debtor who files for bankruptcy vests by operation of law in his trustee in bankruptcy.[78] Assets acquired after the commencement of bankruptcy, but before discharge, can also be reached.[79] The estate can be augmented further by recourse to trustee avoiding powers which *inter alia* enable assets disposed of during defined periods before the bankruptcy to be clawed back.[80] Exempt assets are limited to tools used in the debtor's employment, business or vocation, items necessary for satisfying the basic needs of the debtor and his family[81] and future pension rights.[82] Similarly in Scotland, the estate of a

---

78   IA 1986, sections 283(1), 306.
79   Ibid., section 307.
80   Ibid., sections 284, 339–344.
81   Ibid., section 283(2), though see also section 308 which enables the trustee to claim exempt property for the estate where its realizable value appears to exceed the cost of a reasonable replacement.

debtor who is sequestrated vests by operation of law in the trustee in sequestration;[83] assets acquired after the date of sequestration but before the date of discharge also vest in the trustee;[84] and the estate can be augmented by recourse to avoiding powers enabling claw-back of assets disposed of during defined periods before sequestration.[85] Exempt assets are also similar: tools of trade (including a car) up to a prescribed limit, currently GBP 1,000, and items reasonably required to meet the basic domestic needs of the debtor and his family[86] as well as, in most cases, pension rights.[87] The policy in both jurisdictions is to prevent creditors from realizing assets crucial to the debtor's basic survival and ongoing productive capacity which if taken away could reduce the debtor to poverty and possible long term dependence on the welfare system. Although neither jurisdiction has a homestead exemption,[88] in England and Wales, the debtor's interest in a dwelling house ceases to be comprised in the estate at the end of three years from the commencement of bankruptcy.[89] This provision – another product of the EA 2002 reforms – seeks to prevent trustees from keeping estates open indefinitely with the aim of realizing the debtor's interest, possibly years after discharge, at the top of a rising market.[90] The BD(S)A 2007 will introduce a similar provision in Scotland for the same reasons.[91]

In contrast to bankruptcy and sequestration, the parameters of the estate in an IVA are not defined by law. Indeed, there is no estate as such as there is no mechanism for the automatic vesting of the debtor's property in the supervisor. The contributions required from the debtor, whether from income, assets or some combination of the two, are a matter for bargaining between the parties. The approval process, mediated by the nominee, is the forum in which debtor and creditor interests are balanced. The creditors may wish to extract their pound of

---

82   Welfare Reform and Pensions Act 1999, section 11 reversing *Re Landau* [1998] Ch 223. For a detailed description of the bankrupt's estate see, e.g. Milman, above note 12 in Chapter 3.

83   B(S)A 1985, section 31(1).

84   Ibid., section 32(6).

85   Ibid., sections 34, 35, 36, 36A-F and 61. There are also common law provisions. The Scottish provisions differ in a number of respects from the avoidance provisions in England and Wales, but have the same rationale of recovering property regarded as having been wrongly disposed of within specified periods before sequestration.

86   Ibid., section 33(1)(a) and (aa) which import certain exemptions from diligence (execution) contained in DAA(S)A 2002.

87   Welfare Reform and Pensions Act 1999, sections 11 and 12 (as applied to Scotland by section 13); the Occupational and Personal Pension Schemes (Bankruptcy) (No 2) Regulations 2002 (SI 2002/836). See further McKenzie Skene, D.W., 'Whose Estate Is It Anyway? The Debtor's Estate On Sequestration' 2005 *Juridical Review* 311.

88   The issue of homelessness as a possible consequence of sequestration was raised by the ECC in its Stage 1 Report with a recommendation that the Scottish Executive ensure consistency with its policies on tackling homelessness.

89   IA 1986, section 283A.

90   For criticism of this practice, see *Re Byford (deceased)* [2003] BPIR 1089 at [15].

91   BD(S)A 2007, section 19(2).

flesh but will need to adjust their demands to ensure that the terms imposed on the debtor are realistic and achievable.[92] Debtors who are salaried homeowners will usually be expected to release at least some of any equity as well as making income contributions under a payment plan.[93]

The position in relation to PTDs is slightly different: as noted above, one of the conditions for a trust deed becoming protected is that the debtor must convey to the trustee broadly the same estate as would vest in a trustee in sequestration, although as in an IVA, there is no automatic vesting by law in the trustee.[94] Subject to this, however, the debtor may decide what to include in the trust deed and, since most debtors have few non-exempt assets, they rely on income payments. There is no bargaining process as such, but if creditors are unhappy with the projected return, they may object to the trust deed in an attempt to prevent it becoming protected. The debtor will therefore try to ensure that the projected return will be acceptable to creditors. As in an IVA, debtors who are homeowners will usually be expected to release at least some of any equity.

As regards contributions from future income, we saw earlier that there is scope for debtors in bankruptcy or sequestration to be required to make income payments to their estates.[95] IVAs and PTDs also function predominantly as mechanisms that offer a discharge in return for full or substantial completion of a payment plan. Underpinning these legal techniques is the principle that debtors with redemption capacity should be required to make at least some contribution towards payment of their debts as the price of debt forgiveness. This 'can pay, should pay' principle is central to the way that British law balances the interests of debtors and creditors. Consistent with the tenor of the Report, debtors cannot be required to contribute more than three years' worth of surplus income in bankruptcy and sequestration.[96] In England and Wales, income is broadly defined[97]

---

92   'The bargaining process should be done in good faith on both sides if it is to succeed: the debtor cannot expect to carry on as before, but neither should he be reduced to a bare existence as it gives no incentive to maintain a challenging payment plan over five years. Bankruptcy may then seem a better alternative' ('Living on Tick', above note 64).

93   Improving IVAs, above note 28, paragraphs 60–64.

94   He may, however, take title to the assets if required.

95   IA 1986, sections 310-310A; B(S)A 1985, section 32(2).

96   The issue of income payments continuing beyond discharge was discussed earlier. Some concern was expressed about the proposed differential periods for discharge and income contributions in Scotland and the issue of synchronizing the two periods was considered. However, altering part of the overall 'package' in this way this would have had significant implications for the balance between debtors and creditors as well as introducing differences between the reforms north and south of the border. The ECC, while taking the view that synchronization would have obvious benefits, recognized that it would have implications for creditors and so took the view that it would not be correct to make such a change.

97   IA 1986, section 310(7)-(9): '… the income of the bankrupt comprises every payment in the nature of income which is from time to time made to him or to which he from time to time becomes entitled, including any payment in respect of the carrying on of

but income payments can only be demanded if they do not reduce the income of the bankrupt below what appears to be necessary for meeting the reasonable domestic needs of the bankrupt and his family.[98] In practice, it falls to the OR and, in the event of disagreement, the court to determine what expenses are allowable in calculating surplus income under the 'reasonable domestic needs' test. It is understood that the OR will not seek income payments from debtors whose only source of income is state benefits or whose surplus income is nominal. In cases where the debtor has surplus income, the OR's guidelines suggest that only 50–70 per cent of this redemption capacity should be sought by way of contribution to the estate.[99] Similarly, in Scotland, statute provides that income contributions can be demanded only where there is income in excess of that which the court considers suitable for the debtor's own aliment and any 'relevant obligations'.[100] It is specifically provided that that amount must not be less than the total of any income received by the debtor by way of guaranteed minimum pension in respect of the debtor's protected rights as a member of a pension scheme[101] and that in deciding the amount to allow for any 'relevant obligation', the court is not bound by any prior court order or agreement fixing the amount of any aliment or periodical allowance,[102] but beyond these limited provisions, there is no further statutory guidance as to how a suitable amount to allow the debtor is to be calculated. The AIB's Guidance Notes for Trustees suggest that contributions should not be expected if the debtor is unemployed and in receipt of social security benefits, but contributions should normally be considered where the debtor is employed. They also encourage trustees to reach agreement with the debtor on the amount of any contribution to avoid an application to the court and, in practice, this is generally what happens.

Thus, in bankruptcy and sequestration, debtors are classified as 'can pays' or 'can't pays' through the application of statutory tests that seek to balance the interests of debtors and creditors in the manner contemplated by the Report. Moreover, these tests are sufficiently open-textured to accommodate shifting social perceptions of what amounts to a minimum standard of living.[103]

---

any business or in respect of any office or employment and … any payment under a pension scheme …'. Payments by way of guaranteed minimum pension or payments giving effect to the bankrupt's protected rights as a member of a pension scheme are excluded.

98   Ibid., section 310(2).

99   For further information on how the income payments regime is administered in practice see the 'Insolvency Service Technical Manual', Chapter 31.7 and 'Case Help Manual', available at: <www.insolvency.gov.uk/freedomofinformation/index.htm> (last viewed 31 May 2007).

100 'Relevant obligations' are aliment, periodical allowance and child support: B(S)A 1985, section 32(2).

101 Ibid., section 32(2A).

102 Ibid., section 32(3).

103 So, for example, under the OR's guidelines referred to above, items such as a TV licence, reasonable mobile phone costs and car tax will usually be treated as part of the debtor's domestic needs.

We have seen that debtors with surplus income can opt to avoid bankruptcy or sequestration by entering into an IVA or PTD. In an IVA the balance is struck through the bargaining process as described above. The creditors' perceptions of what is or is not a 'reasonable domestic need' will therefore carry considerable weight in determining the quantum of the debtor's redemption capacity. It follows that this more private process may produce outcomes that differ from those produced by the state administered income payments process in bankruptcy and sequestration. However, creditors would be unwise to pitch their demands too high for the reasons suggested earlier. While in a PTD there is no bargaining process as such, creditors who are dissatisfied with the projected return can object to the trust deed and thus try to prevent it becoming protected. The debtor will therefore seek to fix his contributions at a level likely to be acceptable to creditors. In practice, PTDs will aim to offer a better return to creditors than sequestration and debtors will often make greater contributions than would be demanded in sequestration in order to persuade creditors to accept a PTD. Thus, an appropriate balance can also be struck between debtors and creditors via a PTD.

Deserving Debtors The text accompanying the first principle in the INSOL Report contains the following statement:

> The object of the law is to provide for a discharge or fresh start for the consumer debtor that cannot reasonably repay its creditors, provided that the debtor acted in good faith both as to the way the debts arose and as to the reason the debts cannot be repaid.

This gives scope for legislatures to ration the 'fresh start' according to desert and recalls the well known pronouncement of the United States Supreme Court in *Local Loan Co v Hunt* that the primary objective of bankruptcy law is to give 'the honest but unfortunate debtor ... a new opportunity in life and a clear field for future effort, unhampered by the pressure and discouragement of pre-existing debt'.[104] Distinguishing between 'deserving' and 'undeserving' debtors involves striking a balance not only between the interests of debtors and creditors but also between the interests of debtors and society. Put crudely, it may be thought that debtors who infringe their obligations to society cannot expect to be recipients of society's largesse. This, of course, masks a wide spectrum of possible judgments that could be made about the nature of social obligations and values in any given society.

In both jurisdictions, the pursuit of the public interest is a core objective of the bankruptcy system. In England and Wales, as well as surrendering his assets and contributing to his estate from surplus income, a bankrupt must submit to an initial investigation carried out by the OR who is under a statutory obligation to investigate the conduct and affairs of each bankrupt.[105] In practice, all bankrupts

---

104   292 US 234 at 244 (1934).
105   IA 1986, section 289(1). The OR may choose not to investigate if it is thought that an investigation is unnecessary: section 289(2).

are subjected to the OR's standard vetting procedures the purpose of which is to identify and protect any assets and to establish whether or not the debtor's conduct should be investigated further. However, as noted earlier, debtor misconduct is not a ground for denial of discharge. Misconduct is dealt with instead through the post-discharge bankruptcy restrictions regime introduced by EA 2002, or in severe cases, through the criminal justice system. The post-bankruptcy restrictions regime mirrors the United Kingdom's company directors' disqualification regime.[106] Its purpose is to protect the public from bankrupts who have acted recklessly, irresponsibly or dishonestly through the imposition of legal restrictions and disabilities.[107] The theory is that, while such bankrupts may be released from their debts, they should be subjected to continuing restrictions beyond discharge in order to protect the public from any repetition of their misconduct. A debtor subject to post-bankruptcy restrictions is prohibited from acting in various capacities (such as company director or insolvency practitioner) and from obtaining credit above a prescribed amount (currently GBP 500) without disclosing that he is subject to restrictions. Bankruptcy restrictions can be imposed by means of court order, or by the debtor giving an undertaking to the Secretary of State for Trade and Industry, in either case for between two and 15 years depending on the severity of the misconduct.[108] As conceived, bankruptcy restrictions orders and undertakings are intended to limit the debtor's ability to re-enter the credit economy, thus confining the scope of the 'fresh start' to discharge of old debts. The restrictions are a matter of public record of which the credit reference agencies are expected to take note. The system is therefore designed to increase the information available to the credit markets and enable lenders to differentiate between culpable and non-culpable debtors when making lending decisions.[109] In Scotland, the debtor's affairs are also

---

106 Company Directors' Disqualification Act 1986. See generally Walters and Davis-White, above note 54.

107 McKenzie Skene, above note 3; Walters, above note 60.

108 For the statutory provisions see IA 1986, section 281A and Schedule 4A. The main kinds of conduct which the court (or Secretary of State) are directed to take into account are: failing to keep records accounting for a loss of property occurring within two years of the bankruptcy application; failing to produce such records; entering into specified transactions avoidable on bankruptcy; failing to supply goods or services wholly or partly paid for; pre-bankruptcy trading when the debtor knew or ought to have known that he would be unable to pay his debts; incurring debts pre-bankruptcy which the debtor had no reasonable expectation of being able to pay; failing to account satisfactorily for a loss of property/insufficiency of property to meet bankruptcy debts; gambling, rash and hazardous speculation or unreasonable extravagance materially contributing to or increasing the extent of the bankruptcy; neglect of business affairs materially contributing to or increasing the extent of the bankruptcy; fraud or fraudulent breach of trust; and failing to co-operate with the OR or trustee. The court is also directed to consider whether the bankrupt was an undischarged bankrupt within the six years preceding the bankruptcy. The kinds of conduct listed are clearly relevant to both business and consumer debtors.

109 Walters, above note 60; 'Insolvency Service, Evaluation of Bankruptcy Restrictions Orders – Second Interim Evaluation Report' (March 2006), available at:

subject to compulsory investigation[110] and he is under a statutory obligation to co-operate fully in the sequestration even after discharge.[111] Potentially criminal conduct is reported to the relevant authorities for possible prosecution and a bankruptcy restrictions regime virtually identical to that in England and Wales will be introduced by the BD(S)A 2007.[112] As already noted, debtor misconduct is not a ground for denial of discharge although it is currently a ground for deferring discharge.[113] The future interaction of the provisions for deferral of discharge and the bankruptcy restrictions regime so far as it relates to conduct has not been expressly articulated by policymakers, but it is anticipated that debtor misconduct will be dealt with through bankruptcy restrictions rather than deferral of discharge.

Debtors who enter into IVAs or PTDs are not subject to the same level of scrutiny as debtors who enter bankruptcy/sequestration and, in particular, are not subject to the (in Scotland, forthcoming) bankruptcy restrictions regime. However, nominees will be expected to bar debtors from accessing SIVAs where their conduct, were they to become bankrupt, would be likely to attract bankruptcy restrictions.[114] Similarly, proposed reforms to PTDs, which contemplate some alterations to the process by which a trust deed becomes protected, include as a matter for consideration in that process whether it is likely that a bankruptcy restriction order would be granted in sequestration. As indicated, however, these proposals are currently under review.

The attempt made in British personal insolvency law to differentiate between culpable and non-culpable debtors is within the parameters that the Report gives to legislators to restrict a full 'fresh start' to 'good faith' debtors.

<www.insolvency.gov.uk/insolvencyprofessionandlegislation/legislation/reform.htm> (last viewed 31 May 2007).

110 Currently, this is begun by the interim trustee and carried on by the permanent trustee, who have statutory obligations in this respect: B(S)A 1985, sections 2(4), 3(1). In summary administration cases under B(S)A 1985, Schedule 2A the permanent trustee is directed to comply with this obligation only insofar as, in his view, it would be of financial benefit to the estate and in the interests of the creditors to do so, which gives him a discretion in the matter where investigation appears to be unnecessary. This provision will be extended to all cases by the BD(S)A 2007.

111 Various specific duties are imposed on the debtor by B(S)A 1985 and section 64(1) sets out a general obligation to co-operate with the permanent trustee which is specifically exempted from the discharge by B(S)A 1985, section 55(2)(e). There is no corresponding obligation to co-operate with the interim trustee, but B(S)A 1985, section 18 makes it an offence for the debtor to fail without reasonable excuse to comply with certain directions or requirements of the interim trustee or to obstruct the interim trustee in carrying out certain functions.

112 BD(S)A 2007, section 2.

113 *Nicol's Tr v Nicol* 1996 GWD-10-531.

114 Improving IVAs, above note 28 at paragraphs 32, 34.

Efficiency, Cost-Effectiveness and Transparency

Recognizing that consumer debtors rarely have large estates, the Report places a premium on efficiency and cost-effectiveness. Three points are highlighted: (i) the need for estates to be administered by skilled trustees or administrators; (ii) the need to avoid complex and time-consuming procedures; and (iii) the allocation of costs. On the first point, the affairs of individual insolvents in Britain are handled by a combination of dedicated state apparatus (the OR in England and Wales; the AIB in Scotland) and the insolvency practitioner profession. Any efficiencies to be gained from specialization are therefore likely to be captured. On the third point, the Report's steer is towards a fair allocation of costs among all stakeholders, the implication being that, as bankruptcy systems serve the interests of debtors, creditors and society, the costs should be spread accordingly. In England and Wales, the principal burden falls on the creditors, although, in voluntary bankruptcy, the OR's initial screening costs are met by the debtor from the deposit which must be paid when the petition is filed. In keeping with the Treasury's principles of public administration, the system is therefore self-financing and only the public interest aspects (i.e. the bankruptcy restrictions regime) are funded from the public purse.[115] In Scotland, the principal burden also falls on the creditors as the costs of administration are met from the debtor's estate. However, in sequestrations where there are insufficient funds in the estate to meet the costs of administration and the AIB is acting as trustee, the costs of administration fall on the public purse. The costs of administering the bankruptcy restrictions regime will also fall on the public purse.

On the second point, considerable attempts are being made in Britain to simplify and streamline insolvency proceedings. In England and Wales, the bankruptcy process is increasingly seen as an administrative process in which the role of the courts – the main function of which is to provide a forum for the resolution of disputes – should be reduced. This is borne out in recent years by the introduction of income payments agreements, which bind debtors without the need for a court order,[116] and the abolition of the requirement for debtors to apply for an interim order before proposing an IVA.[117] Further simplifications are in the pipeline. The granting of bankruptcy orders is likely to become a routinized process administered by the OR outside the court system with the debtor able to obtain and file the relevant documents online. As noted above, a streamlined procedure, the SIVA, designed to increase accessibility of IVAs to consumer

---

115   The government's desire to persist with levying a contribution from debtors towards the administrative costs of their bankruptcy through mandatory imposition of the OR's deposit is a key driver behind the proposed introduction of DROs for NINA debtors: see further below.

116   IA 1986, section 310A (introduced by EA 2002).

117   Insolvency Act 2000, section 3 and Schedule 3 (amending Part VIII of IA 1986). Debtors may still choose to apply for an interim order (giving rise to a moratorium) if they wish: compare IA 1986, sections 252 and 256A. In the majority of IVAs, the debtor proceeds without incurring the extra cost of an interim order application.

debtors, is also proposed.[118] The idea is to reduce the fixed costs associated with setting up an IVA through procedural simplification and standardization in order to create a cost-effective model capable of balancing the interests of debtors and creditors, while providing sufficient incentives to insolvency practitioners to operate it. SIVAs would be restricted to consumer debtors whose unsecured debts do not exceed GBP 75,000 (though non-eligible debtors could still propose IVAs under existing law). The procedure would be greatly simplified to drive down set-up costs. The approval threshold would be reduced from its current level (in excess of 75 per cent of creditors by value) to a simple majority by value,[119] there would be no creditors' meeting and creditors would not be permitted to propose modifications. Creditors would vote in favour or against the proposal in writing within a prescribed period on a 'take it or leave it' basis.[120] The onus would be on the nominee to ensure that the best deal is proposed using a standardized approach to the assessment of allowable expenses and disposable income.[121] The mandatory regulatory requirement for the nominee to have a face-to-face meeting with the debtor would be lifted to trim costs and to facilitate further the routinized processing of consumer debtors.[122] A default period of five years' duration would be written into law to reflect existing market practice. It is hoped that cost savings from procedural streamlining and standardization will improve access for consumer debtors who have relatively low debt burdens. The insolvency practitioner's fees would also be spread over the life of the arrangement to provide a better balance for creditors, increasing the likelihood that creditor approval would be forthcoming.[123]

In Scotland, similar emphasis has been placed on streamlining procedures, at least in sequestration. Thus, under the BD(S)A 2007, debtor applications for sequestration will be dealt with by the AIB rather than the court; all other bankruptcy proceedings, with limited exceptions, will be consolidated in the sheriff court;[124] the roles of interim and permanent trustee will be combined;[125] and the

---

118   Improving IVAs, above note 28.

119   Ibid., paragraphs 34, 89–93. This is designed to reduce the influence of creditors who choose not to support the process or who have unrealistic dividend demands. A more radical non-voting model for qualifying debtors whose debts do not exceed GBP 30,000 was also proposed but met with an unfavourable response from the credit industry during the consultation process: see 'Insolvency Service, Improving Individual Voluntary Arrangements – Summary of Responses and Government Reply' (2006).

120   Improving IVAs, above note 28 at paragraphs 35, 73–7, 84–8.

121   Ibid., at paragraphs 34, 78–83.

122   Ibid., at paragraphs 33–5, 51–4.

123   Ibid., at paragraphs 106–124. This meets creditor concerns about the fact that practitioners can currently draw all of their fees from realizations achieved in the early years of an IVA. Where the IVA subsequently fails, creditors may receive little or nothing because realizations have already been absorbed in costs.

124   The sheriff court is the principal inferior court in Scotland. At present, some applications for sequestration and certain other bankruptcy proceedings are dealt with by the Court of Session, the supreme civil court in Scotland.

procedure for obtaining a discharge by composition, referred to above, will be simplified. The proposed reforms to PTDs arguably have the opposite effect, making the procedure more complex and increasing the regulatory burden associated with this procedure. Thus, for example, the proposals would add an extra layer of approval by the AIB before a trust deed can become protected and increase the administrative burdens on the trustee before, during and at the end of the PTD. However, following consultation, many of these proposals are under review and it is anticipated that many of the proposals which would result in additional complexity/administration will be abandoned.

Finally, with regard to transparency, the Report states that debtors and creditors must be able to monitor the process and have the opportunity to be heard, receive notices and exercise their rights. In Scotland, England and Wales the various statutory regimes make detailed provision in these respects for both debtors and creditors and other relevant parties.

Accessibility and Debtor Choice

The Report stresses that access to debt relief for those who need it should not be restricted by cost barriers and/or excessive and complex procedural formalities. As noted earlier, it also encourages legislators to offer a choice between a 'bankruptcy' or 'rehabilitation' procedure, each tailored to the needs of particular groups of debtors. The issues of accessibility and debtor choice are linked because if the debtor's access to the regime that is most suitable for his circumstances is restricted, he may be left with no real choice.

In terms of tailoring the range of options to the circumstances of particular groups of debtors, as we have seen, the Report distinguishes between debtors who have no redemption capacity and no immediate prospects of improving their financial situation and debtors who only have accommodation debts and whose financial difficulties may therefore be temporary. As regards the former, bankruptcy leading to a swift discharge is regarded as appropriate on the basis that 'there is no benefit extending insolvency procedures for a longer period, thus extending the agony of a hopeless situation'. [126] As regards the latter, a 'rehabilitation' procedure, possibly involving a composition or scheme of arrangement is seen as more appropriate.

British law conforms closely to this pattern. In England and Wales, notwithstanding the business-oriented rhetoric which accompanied the EA 2002 reforms, bankruptcy functions as a routinized debt relief process for consumer debtors with no means of contributing (either from assets or income) towards payment of their debts. Debtors with means, particularly salaried debtors, may opt to avoid the greater publicity and scrutiny associated with bankruptcy, by signing up to an IVA (or a SIVA once it is introduced). Debtors with redemption capacity

---

125 At present, all sequestrations are administered initially by an interim trustee appointed by the court; the interim trustee is subsequently replaced by a permanent trustee elected by the creditors or appointed by the court.

126 INSOL Report at 25.

who file for bankruptcy rather than opting for an IVA can still be required to contribute to their estates through the income payments regime. In Scotland, the pattern is similar. The vast majority of sequestrations involve consumer debtors, most of whom have no income and no assets. Debtors with means, particularly salaried debtors, can opt for a PTD or the DAS instead of sequestration, but if they choose sequestration, they will still be required to contribute their non-exempt assets and surplus income for the relevant period to the estate.

In keeping with the second principle, the Report's steer is towards the provision of different routes to discharge. Although it talks of debtors whose difficulties may only be temporary being given 'breathing space ... [in which] to restructure [their] earnings and spending', it does not explicitly recognize that this objective might be achieved via mechanisms that provide for a stay coupled with restructured payments over a longer period. As mentioned earlier, debtors in Britain can opt for debt management rather than debt relief through the formal and informal mechanisms described earlier. Indeed, the trend is increasingly towards formal mechanisms with the advent of the DAS in Scotland and the inclusion of enabling powers in the Tribunals, Courts and Enforcement Bill allowing for the establishment of approved debt management schemes that would effectively put DMAs on a statutory footing and lead to their greater regulation.[127]

While on this issue Britain is fully INSOL-compliant, it may be argued that British debtors, particularly debtors in England and Wales, have too much choice. At the level of crude incentives, it is not obvious why debtors would choose long term debt management rather than debt relief.[128] Similarly, it is not clear why salaried debtors with no non-exempt assets would choose to pay for five years under an IVA or SIVA in England and Wales when income payments in bankruptcy are limited to three years. It is true that bankrupts are subjected to greater scrutiny and publicity than is the case with IVA debtors. It is also true that debtors risk the imposition of post-discharge restrictions in bankruptcy, although in practice the risk is less than 10 per cent because of limits on the capacity of the Insolvency Service to investigate and process cases. Yet, the available evidence suggests that the credit industry does not treat IVAs any more favourably than bankruptcy for the purposes of lending decisions: the market simply classifies entry into any formal insolvency procedure as 'default'. So the choice for this type of debtor comes down to a five-year payment plan in an IVA or a three-year payment plan in bankruptcy, albeit that the latter is more widely publicized and carries greater risks as regards legal restrictions. Once the risk of failure to complete the IVA is factored in, bankruptcy may appear more attractive in pure economic terms, although of course, a range of other variables such as the

---

127 These regulated DMAs would be legally binding on creditors and give rise to a moratorium. As currently envisaged, it would also be open to scheme operators to provide for some element of debt write-off as an incentive for the debtor to maintain the scheduled repayments.

128 Nor is it immediately obvious why the government has committed in the Tribunals, Courts and Enforcement Bill to retaining CCAOs whilst also making provision for an out-of-court debt management equivalent in the form of regulated DMAs.

perceived stigma of bankruptcy,[129] the debtor's own moral values and the role of intermediaries may affect the choice. In Scotland, this issue does not arise so starkly in relation to the choice between sequestration and PTDs, because a PTD normally lasts for three years, the same period as income contributions in sequestration, although it will often be more expensive for a debtor who will generally have to offer creditors greater returns than they might expect on sequestration to persuade them to accept a PTD.

It is suggested that, more often than not, a critical factor will be the process by which debtor choice is mediated. If the debtor's point of entry into the system is a debt management provider, the debtor may be influenced to opt for a DMA. Similarly, if the debtor's point of entry is an insolvency practitioner, the debtor may be influenced to opt for an IVA or PTD. Virtually all bankruptcies and sequestrations are processed by the state agencies unless the debtor has sufficient assets/income to make it worthwhile for an insolvency practitioner to act as trustee. Private operators who specialize in IVAs/PTDs or DMAs therefore have no particular stake in encouraging debtors to file for bankruptcy or sequestration. The complexity of the choices on offer in legal and economic terms gives rise to critical questions concerning the means by which debtors are channelled towards particular options and how such processes should be co-ordinated and regulated.[130] The provision of sufficient competent and independent debt counselling forms the subject of a separate recommendation in the Report to which we return below.

In terms of accessibility, as we saw earlier, considerable attempts have been, and continue to be made, towards procedural simplification of the various debt relief options. Two issues have given cause for concern both of which relate to the plight of NINAs. These are: (i) in England and Wales, the high cost of filing for bankruptcy which acts as a barrier to NINAs and (ii) in Scotland, the legal requirements for sequestration which act as a barrier to sequestration generally.

In England and Wales, debtors are required to pay a deposit to defray the OR's initial costs as well as the court fee when filing a bankruptcy petition. The deposit and court fee are currently GBP 325 and GBP 150 respectively: a total of GBP 475. Payment of the deposit is not means-tested and, because of the way that the OR is financed, the government insists that it cannot be waived even for those who cannot afford it. It has been held that the levying of the deposit does not infringe the due process rights of a debtor who does not have the means to pay it on the analysis that bankruptcy relief is a 'paid for' service or benefit rather than a

---

129 See Tribe, J., 'Bankruptcy Courts Survey 2005 – A Pilot Study' (2006); 'Insolvency Service, Attitudes to Bankruptcy' (2006), available at: <www.insolvency.gov.uk> (last viewed 31 May 2007). Both of these surveys find that bankruptcy is still seen as stigmatic.

130 McKenzie Skene and Walters, above note 28. See also Ramsay, I., 'Models of Consumer Bankruptcy: Implications for Research and Policy' (1997) 20 *Journal of Consumer Policy* 269 at 277. The trend towards increasing juridification of the role of intermediaries seen in the context of the DAS, DROs and regulated DMAs may, in part, be a response to these concerns.

fundamental human right.[131] However, policymakers have recognized that the deposit requirement may have the effect of barring NINAs from access to bankruptcy. NINAs do not have the means to propose an IVA or enter into a debt management plan. The risk is that the poorest debtors in our society – many of whom are long-term sick or unemployed – are simply left at the mercy of their creditors if they cannot access bankruptcy. Many debtors in the NINA category will not have had access to mainstream credit. Their creditors are often drawn from the sub-prime market. Faced with saturation and increasing competition in the mainstream market, sub-prime lenders have turned to borrowers who, in the past, would not have been able to get credit because of lack of repayment capacity or damaged credit histories. These lenders charge higher interest rates than mainstream lenders to reflect the additional risk and employ more intensive collection techniques. Vulnerable debtors who cannot access bankruptcy on cost grounds are left exposed to 'door knocking' even where there is no realistic prospect of repayment.

Rather than offer means-tested waiver or reduction of the deposit, the government is committed to establishing the DRO system alluded to earlier for NINAs barred access to bankruptcy by the prohibitive filing cost.[132] The scheme will be administered by the OR. A court-based scheme was considered inappropriate because debt relief falls outside the dispute resolution and enforcement functions of the courts and, it is thought, would be better and more cost-effectively delivered by the Insolvency Service.[133] DROs are targeted at NINAs who have no realistic prospect of being able to pay even some of their debts. To be eligible for a DRO, the debtor's total debts (secured and unsecured), the value of his property (if any) and his monthly surplus income (after deduction of his and his family's reasonable domestic needs) must not exceed prescribed levels. These are yet to be set out in draft regulations but, at the consultation stage, the upper limits suggested for total indebtedness, value of property and surplus income were GBP 15,000, GBP 300 and GBP 50 per month respectively. The inclusion of secured debts in calculating total indebtedness will effectively exclude homeowners with mortgage debts. Once granted, a DRO will trigger a moratorium on creditor collection efforts. Debts listed in the order will usually be discharged after one year. DRO applications will be made online through an approved intermediary drawn from the money advice sector who will effectively act as

---

131 *R v Lord Chancellor, ex parte Lightfoot* [2000] QB 597. The government's position is that the deposit is necessary in order to meet the costs of administering bankruptcies. Waiver of the deposit would mean that the cross-subsidizing of cases in which debtors have no non-exempt assets by cases in which there are assets would have to increase significantly to enable the system to remain self-financing, i.e. creditors of debtors with sufficient non-exempt assets to pay a dividend would pick up the tab.

132 For background, see Choice of Paths and Relief for the Indebted, above note 66. The process of implementing these proposals has begun with the publication of the Tribunals, Courts and Enforcement Bill, currently before Parliament.

133 The scheme is modelled on a similar 'no asset' procedure shortly to be adopted in New Zealand. See Telfer, T., 'New Zealand Bankruptcy Law Reform' in Niemi-Kiesiläinen et al. (eds), above note 5.

gatekeeper. A fee of around GBP 100 will be charged to cover costs. This represents a significant discount on the costs of filing for bankruptcy. Given reduced scope for scrutiny, a range of anti-abuse provisions are contemplated including: publicity requirements; a right for creditors to object on prescribed grounds; a power in the OR to revoke DROs in prescribed circumstances; similar restrictions to those applicable to undischarged bankrupts (e.g. on obtaining credit); mechanisms for dealing with changes in the debtor's financial circumstances; criminal sanctions for wilful non-disclosure of information; and an extension of the post-discharge bankruptcy restrictions regime to DROs.

In Scotland, it is not the cost of applying for sequestration which is the issue for debtors,[134] but the legal requirements. In contrast to the minimal eligibility requirements in England and Wales, in Scotland a debtor may currently apply for his own sequestration only where he (i) has the concurrence of a qualified creditor [135] or (ii) satisfies a number of other requirements, [136] including a requirement that he is *either* apparently insolvent[137] *or* has granted a trust deed for creditors which has failed to become protected. In practice, obtaining the concurrence of a qualified creditor is rare and most debtors wishing to apply for sequestration seek to meet the alternative requirements. Many debtors cannot do so, however, because they cannot establish apparent insolvency and have not granted a trust deed which has failed to become protected. This is a problem for NINA debtors because they do not have the means to enter a PTD or the DAS and, if they cannot access sequestration, they effectively have no access to an appropriate procedure.

---

134 The current fee for a sequestration petition is GBP 63.
135 B(S)A 1985, section 5(2).
136 Ibid., section 5(2)-(2B).
137 This concept was introduced by B(S)A 1985, section 7 which sets out the following ways, reminiscent of the now generally outmoded concept of 'acts of bankruptcy', in which a debtor may become apparently insolvent: sequestration in Scotland or bankruptcy elsewhere in the United Kingdom; giving of written notice of inability to pay debts in the ordinary course of business; signing a trust deed for creditors (whether it becomes a protected trust deed or not); service of a charge for payment and expiry of the days of charge with no payment being made; attachment, attempt to attach or other seizure of moveable property under a summary warrant and no payment being made; making of a decree of adjudication for payment or in security; sale of effects under a sequestration for rent; making of a receiving order in England and Wales; revocation of a debt payment programme made under Part 1 of DAA(S)A 2002 where any debt being paid under the programme is constituted by a decree or document of debt as defined by that Act; service of a statutory demand for a liquid debt of not less than GBP 750 to which no response is given; and the debtor being subject to 'main' insolvency proceedings in another European Union state. However, debtors seeking to petition for their own sequestration cannot satisfy the apparent insolvency requirement by their own actions alone, e.g. by giving written notice of inability to pay debts in the ordinary course of business or by signing a trust deed for creditors.

The problem of apparent insolvency as a barrier to sequestration has long been recognized [138] and some changes to the definition designed to ease the problem had already been made prior to the BD(S)A 2007. The BD(S)A 2007 will make one further technical change concerning the enforcement of summary warrants which should result in more debtors being able to establish apparent insolvency in future, thus indirectly extending debtor access to sequestration, but it was recognized that this was not a complete solution. [139]

The Scottish Executive established a Working Group on Debt Relief to consider NINA debtors. The Working Group, which reported in June 2005, [140] revisited the issue of debtor access to sequestration in the context of debtor access to debt relief generally and for NINAs in particular. It considered but rejected a separate NINA procedure for Scotland on the basis that it would add further complexity to an already complex area of law and favoured widening debtor access to sequestration as the solution to the NINA problem. It identified two categories of NINAs: 'true' NINAs, i.e. NINAs with no reasonable prospect of paying off their debts within a reasonable time, for whom immediate access to sequestration was appropriate; and 'temporary' NINAs, i.e. NINAs whose status had resulted from a change of circumstances but whose finances might subsequently improve with the result that they might then be able to pay off their debts within a reasonable time, for whom access to sequestration should be delayed to see whether that further change of circumstances did occur. Having considered various ways of extending access to sequestration for 'true' NINAs, it ultimately recommended the introduction of a 'single gateway' procedure designed to give true NINAs immediate access to sequestration and temporary NINAs a breathing space. [141] This approach is consistent with the approach to different types of debtors advocated in the Report.

---

138   Personal Bankruptcy Reform in Scotland, above note 8 at paragraph 6.3 referring to an earlier consultation The Bankruptcy (Scotland) Act 1985, 'A Consultation Follow-Up: Protected Trust Deeds and Other Issues' (Scottish Office, July 1998). As its name suggests, that consultation followed an earlier consultation 'Apparent Insolvency, A Consultation Paper on Amending the Bankruptcy' (Scotland) Act 1985 (Scottish Office, July 1997). Apparent insolvency is the most significant but not the only barrier to debtor access to sequestration. Before a debtor can petition for sequestration without the concurrence of a qualifying creditor, he must also establish that there has been no award of sequestration in the preceding five years and that he has the qualifying level of debt, currently GBP 1,500. This will be increased to GBP 3,000 by the BD(S)A 2007.

139   In light of information received from the advice sector, the Scottish Executive has indicated that this change may allow around 20–25 per cent of those persons who currently cannot access sequestration as a result of inability to establish apparent insolvency to do so, but that still left 75–80 per cent of these debtors unable to do so.

140   Available at: <www.scotland.gov.uk/Topics/Justice/Civil/17868/rwgdr> (last viewed 31 May 2007).

141   The proposed procedure envisaged the making of an application for debt relief by an approved money adviser on behalf of the debtor where an independent assessment of the debtor's financial position showed that there was no suitable alternative procedure

The Scottish Executive has accepted that widening access to sequestration was the appropriate solution for NINAs, but adopted a different route from that proposed by the Working Group. Thus, the BD(S)A 2007 will alter the requirements for a debtor application for sequestration to allow a debtor who satisfies certain conditions to establish that he is 'unable to pay his debts' as an alternative to establishing apparent insolvency or the grant of a trust deed which has failed to become protected. The proposed conditions which the debtor will have to satisfy in such cases, which would be subject to change by regulation, are that his weekly income does not exceed GBP 100, he does not own any land and the total value of his assets does not exceed GBP 1,000. Debtors who do not satisfy these conditions will, however, still have to satisfy the existing conditions for a debtor application. Although this solution does go some way to addressing the NINA problem, it may be seen as more mechanistic and less rounded than that proposed by the Working Group.

Debt Counselling

One of the recommendations for achieving the third principle (extra-judicial rather than judicial proceedings where there are equally effective options available) is that governments, quasi-governmental or private organizations should ensure the availability of sufficient competent and independent debt counselling. The accompanying text notes that the often complex problems of both a legal and socio-psychological nature faced by consumer debtors require the input of professional independent debt counsellors specialized in negotiating arrangements with creditors and knowledgeable about the specific problems of consumer debtors who have expertise in the legal, financial and social aspects of consumer debt problems and the ability to give relevant information and advice. [142] This is particularly important in the British context because of the complex choices on offer.

On the face of it, Britain rates highly with regard to the provision of debt counselling and advice. Debtors in Britain have several potential sources of free, independent money advice. The main sources are nationwide networks such as Citizens Advice, Money Advice Trust (which operates National Debtline, a telephone advice service), Advice UK and a range of other not-for-profit providers

---

(e.g. the DAS or a PTD). That application would result in an immediate award of sequestration for a true NINA or a moratorium of up to 12 months, with provision for re-assessment at appropriate intervals, for a temporary NINA. In the latter case, the moratorium would either be terminated as and when the debtor ceased to be a NINA (which the Working Group envisaged would happen where the debtor's circumstances changed to the extent that either he could be expected to pay off his debts in full or he became able to access an alternative to sequestration, such as the DAS or a PTD) or an award of sequestration would follow where the debtor remained a NINA at the end of the moratorium.

142   INSOL Report at 27.

such as the Consumer Credit Counselling Service (which operates a separate Scottish Debtline). These providers are financed by a mixture of state, credit industry and charitable funding with local authorities taking a lead role in supporting the voluntary advice sector.[143] Many areas also have a variety of other local advice agencies, including Law Centres, which either specialize in or can provide specialist advice on debt problems. The government is investing GBP 45 million over two years to increase provision of face-to-face debt advice[144] and the Scottish Executive has committed an additional GBP 3 million per annum to the provision of money advice services. The Scottish Executive has also produced information packs detailing sources of free, independent advice available in Scotland.[145] Other initiatives, such as a pilot in-court advice scheme based on an earlier successful pilot in Edinburgh Sheriff Court, are also ongoing.[146] Some money advisers who have undergone specialized training are certified as approved money advisers for the purpose of the DAS, which can only be accessed through such an adviser. Debtors may, of course, obtain advice directly from a lawyer or insolvency practitioner and there are also a variety of 'for profit' fee-charging agencies. Despite this wealth of provision, there are concerns about the capacity of the system to deliver appropriate advice, whether the various agencies involved in the provision of debt advice and debt solutions are sufficiently joined up[147] and whether key players such as the voluntary sector are adequately resourced to meet demand.[148]

While many debtors do make use of the money advice services on offer when they encounter debt problems, money advice is not a pre-requisite for accessing any of the debt relief or debt management procedures currently available with the exception of the DAS in Scotland which, as noted above, can only be accessed through an approved money adviser. There is nothing else comparable to the compulsory debtor counselling and education requirements which may be found in the bankruptcy laws of some other jurisdictions, notably the United States and Canada. The possibility of introducing such provisions has been floated in Britain – most recently by the Working Group on Debt Relief in Scotland, which

---

143   In Scotland, local authorities also provide free, independent money advice direct.

144   See DTI, Tackling Over-indebtedness, Annual Reports for 2005 and 2006, available at: <www.dti.gov.uk/consumers/consumer-finance/over-indebtedness/index.html> (last viewed 31 May 2007).

145   These are available in paper format and online.

146   The in-court advice project is funded by the Scottish Executive and managed by Citizen Advice Scotland. The participating courts are in Aberdeen, Airdrie, Hamilton and Kilmarnock. If successful, the scheme could be adopted throughout Scotland.

147   In England and Wales, a debt advice 'gateway' involving a number of voluntary sector advice providers has been piloted through which debtors can be referred to a specialist debt solution provider (such as an insolvency practitioner) drawn from a panel. Membership of the panel, and therefore eligibility for referrals, is established through an open tender process against agreed criteria. This kind of infrastructure has the potential to channel debtors via telephone money advice into SIVA/IVA.

148   So, for example, despite the Scottish Executive's additional funding for money advice, there is currently a shortage of approved DAS advisers across Scotland.

recommended compulsory referral to independent money advice for all debtors seeking sequestration – but there is a strong tendency for government to rely on the third sector and the market to work matters out rather than to mandate. Instead, there is a much greater emphasis on improving financial awareness and budgeting skills within the general population as an *ex ante* measure falling within the statutory remit of the principal financial regulator, the Financial Services Authority. This *ex ante* approach is itself consistent with one of the Report's recommendations for achieving the fourth principle (prevention to reduce the need for intervention) to the effect that governments, quasi-governmental or private organizations should set up educational programmes and improve information and advice on the risks attached to consumer credit. Nevertheless, as we have seen, there is also a growing emphasis on schemes involving approved intermediaries (e.g. DAS and DROs) who may perform *de facto* educative functions. This, in turn, may lead to the increasing juridification of the role of the voluntary sector in the provision of debt advice.

Conclusion

At a macro level, it can be seen that in almost all respects, the emerging British consumer debt systems conform closely to the principles set out in the Report. This is, perhaps, no surprise given that they represent a broadly Anglo-Saxon vision. Is such a vision appropriate, however, or do international benchmarks need to be settled on by more widely representative constituencies? Or, assuming increasing credit card penetration in hitherto more cautious jurisdictions, are we converging towards an Anglo-Saxon approach to consumer bankruptcy, albeit one in which there are still considerable debates about the precise implementation of the 'can pay, should pay' principle? On the face of it, this might be suggested by the recent reforms in the United States, but scholars have been cautious about the degree of any such convergence.[149] It is suggested that this issue would repay further consideration.

At a micro level, the results of our benchmarking exercise suggest that the Report needs to 'drill down' more in relation to the key issue of debtor choice. The importance of the principle that consumer debtors should have a choice of alternative procedures suitable to their circumstances is not disputed, but the complexity of the choices in Britain (particularly England and Wales), highlights the point that the process by which choices are mediated in a functional sense is equally as important, if not more so. The same issues have arisen in relation to other systems, in particular in the debates on the choice between Chapter 7 and

---

149 See Ramsay, I., 'Functionalism and Political Economy in the Comparative Study of Consumer Insolvency: An Unfinished Story from England and Wales' (2006) 7 *Theoretical Inquiries in Law* 625; Tabb, C.J., 'Lessons from the Globalisation of Consumer Bankruptcy' (2005) 30 *Law and Social Inquiry* 763; Ziegel, J.S., 'Facts on the Ground and Reconciliation of Divergent Consumer Insolvency Philosophies' (2006) 7 *Theoretical Inquiries in Law* 299.

Chapter 13 in the United States, where some commentators have called for simplification in the form of a single chapter.[150] The regulatory challenges that are the flipside of debtor choice may also impact on our conception of bankruptcy law for consumer debtors. The Report can be seen as suggesting that bankruptcy law is (or should become) a species of consumer protection law.[151] This issue too would repay further consideration.

---

150 See Braucher, J., 'A Fresh Start for Personal Bankruptcy Reform: The Need for Simplification and a Single Portal' Arizona Legal Studies Discussion Paper 06–22 (June 2006), available at: <ssrn.com/abstract=912561> (last viewed 31 May 2007) and on experience in Canada, Ramsay, I., 'Market Imperatives, Professional Discretion and the Role of Intermediaries in Consumer Bankruptcy' (2000) 74 *American Bankruptcy Law Journal* 399. The possibility of the creation of a single gateway has also been raised, though not acted on, in Britain (most recently by the Working Group on Debt Relief) as has the possibility of other networking mechanisms of the kind referred to above note 147.

151 The Report specifically suggests that when a debtor's situation becomes so severe that there is no prospect of satisfaction of the debts and the effective social functioning of the debtor is impaired or prevented, there is a clear task for the legislator and that the consumer debtor should not be penalized, but offered some form of protection: INSOL Report at 6 (emphasis supplied).

PART III
INTERNATIONAL INSOLVENCY INITIATIVES

Chapter 7

Coming to Terms with the COMI Concept in the European Insolvency Regulation

Paul Torremans

Introduction

The European Insolvency Regulation[1] has now been operational for a couple of years already and it is therefore interesting to have a look at the case law that has resulted from it. The problems with the implementation of the Insolvency Regulation seem to focus on its Article 3(1) and the concept of the centre of a debtor's main interests ('COMI') as a ground for opening main insolvency proceedings, if the sample of cases highlighted below is a fair representation of the numerous reported and unreported applications of the Insolvency Regulation. It is therefore proposed to look in a bit more detail at the interpretation and analysis of Article 3(1). In a second stage, we will then look at the way in which the courts in a number of member states have applied it in some of the first cases to reach the courts under the new regime.[2]

---

1   Council Regulation (EC) 1346/2000 on Insolvency Proceedings of 29 May 2000 [2000] OJ L160/1 (in force 31 May 2002) ('Insolvency Regulation').
2   Tribunal de Commerce de Charleroi (Commercial Court Charleroi, Belgium), judgment of 16 July 2002, *Me Hertsens v. SARL Bati-France* [2004] *Tijdschrift voor Belgisch Handelsrecht* 811; Rechtbank van Koophandel Tongeren (Commercial Court Tongeren, Belgium), judgment of 20th February 2003, *Voorlopige bewindvoerders van de SPRL C v. SPRL C* [2004] *Tijdschrift voor Belgisch Handelsrecht* 70; *Re ISA Daisytek SAS et alia*, High Court of Justice, Chancery Division, Leeds District Registry, judgment of 16 May 2003 [2004] *Tijdschrift voor Belgisch Handelsrecht* 813; Cour d'Appel de Versailles (Court of Appeal of Versailles, France), judgment of 4 September 2003, *ISA Daisytek SAS et alia v. Me Valdman et alia* [2004] *Tijdschrift voor Belgisch Handelsrecht* 820; *In the Matter of Eurofood IFSC Ltd and in the Matter of the Companies Acts 1963 to 2001*, Irish Supreme Court, judgment of 27 July 2004.

Article 3(1): An Analysis

The best way to achieve harmonisation in the area of cross border insolvencies is to give insolvency proceedings to a single court for each cross-border insolvency case. This would also fit in with the unity principle. The Insolvency Regulation's basic rule in Article 3(1) does just that. The connecting factor used to determine which court will have jurisdiction is 'the centre of a debtor's main interests'. This flexible criterion is thought to provide a link to the place where the debtor was economically active and where one is likely to find assets. The Insolvency Regulation gives the courts of the member state on the territory of which this centre of the debtor's main interests in situated jurisdiction to open insolvency proceedings. We are concerned here with the main or primary proceedings that will have effect in the Community as a whole. These proceedings are deemed to be universal in scope, they encompass all the debtor's assets on a worldwide basis and they affect all creditors wherever they are located. Some courts accept, albeit with regret, that there will be a single court with main insolvency proceedings jurisdiction on the basis of the identification of the centre of the debtor's main interests.[3] This is no doubt a positive development.

But how is the key concept of the 'centre of main interests' defined? Recital 13 to the Insolvency Regulation retains the principle that was originally set out in the Virgos-Schmit Report to the 1995 Convention and according to which the concept corresponds to the place where the debtor conducts the administration of his interests on a regular basis and which place is therefore ascertainable by third parties. A first key point to make is that this concept can only work in conjunction with the unity and universality principle with which it is supposed to work if it points to a single place. The aim is to have one court that is competent to open a single set of insolvency proceedings, leading to a single worldwide insolvency case. If the centre of main interests concept is used to identify this court, it should lead to a single place. The use of the word 'main' helps in this respect, as it leaves on one side all places where the debtor has a centre of his ancillary interests and all temporary places where the debtor establishes the centre of his main interests are also ruled out as Recital 13 refers to the place where the administration of the debtor's interests is conducted on 'a regular basis'. Every debtor is therefore supposed to have only a single 'centre of main interests'[4] and the application of the Insolvency Regulation should steer clear of the trap in which the French courts seem to have fallen in a similar context. Decree no. 85-1388 of 27 December 1985 refers to the concept of the debtor's 'principal établissement' and gives insolvency jurisdiction to the court in the territory of which this 'principal établissement' is

---

3   See, for example, Tribunal de Commerce de Charleroi, judgment of 16 July 2002, *Me Hertsens v. SARL Bati-France* [2004] *Tijdschrift voor Belgisch Handelsrecht* 811 for a correct approach and Rechtbank van Koophandel Tongeren, judgment of 20 February 2003, *Voorlopige bewindvoerders van de SPRL C v. SPRL C* [2004] *Tijdschrift voor Belgisch Handelsrecht* 70 for an incorrect approach.

4   See Bogdan, M., 'The EU Bankruptcy Convention' (1997) 6 *International Insolvency Review* 114 at 119.

located for those cases where there is no seat of the (company of the) debtor in France. The French courts have almost always interpreted this to mean that they can have jurisdiction if the debtor has a 'principal établissement' in France, rather than only if the company's single 'principal établissement' is located in France.[5] As a result debtors that operate at a truly international level could have more than one 'principal établissement' and the French courts will have bankruptcy jurisdiction if at least one of them is located in France. This type of approach is clearly not acceptable under the Insolvency Regulation. The court will have to identify the debtor's single centre of main interests in the world and will only be able to take cross-border insolvency jurisdiction if that single centre of main interests is located in the territory of the court.

The Insolvency Regulation's concept of the centre of the debtor's main interests is nevertheless very flexible in nature. The Insolvency Regulation tries to enhance legal certainty further though through the introduction of a rebuttable presumption that the centre of main interests of a company or a legal person is the place of its registered office.[6] Although the Insolvency Regulation is silent on this point, it is presumably up to the party that does not want the presumption to apply to discharge the burden of proof. Such proof to the contrary will have to show that this is not the place where the debtor conducts the administration of its interests on a regular basis and presumably also that there is another identifiable centre of main interests where the debtor conducts the administration of its interests on a regular basis.[7] It is indeed not conceivable that a debtor will have no centre of main interests.[8] The court will always be able to choose the main interests of the debtor among its interests as no specific requirements need to be met and these interests will always be administered from somewhere. Article 3(1) clearly envisages that there will always be a centre of main interests and allocates insolvency jurisdiction to a single court as long as that centre is located in the Community.[9]

Even though Article 3(1) does not provide a presumption to determine the centre of main interests of natural persons, it seems logical to assume that a distinction can be drawn between traders or natural persons engaging in a professional activity and natural persons that fall outside this category. A trading or other professional activity is indeed bound to give rise to the very strong likelihood

---

5   See Péricard, A., 'La faillite de la BCCI: quelques enseignements tirés des conflits judiciaires issus d'une faillite bancaire internationale' [1996] *Banque et Droit* (special issue, April 1996) 21.

6   This corresponds to a principle already in use in most member states. See, in relation to the EU Insolvency Proceedings Convention 1995, Idot, L., 'La 'faillite' dans la Communauté: Enfin une convention internationale?' (1995) 21 *Droit des Procédures Collectives Internationales* (Issue 1) 34 at 47.

7   See Verougstraete, I., *Manuel de la faillite et du concordat* (1998, Kluwer Editions Juridique Belgique, Waterloo) at 627.

8   Compare Fletcher, I., *Insolvency in Private International Law: National and International Approaches* (Oxford Monographs in Private International Law) (1999, Clarendon Press, Oxford) at 261, who considers a negative conflict to be a 'somewhat unlikely' possibility.

9   See also Insolvency Regulation, Recital 14.

that the centre of the main interests of such natural persons will be located in the place where they carry out this trading or professional activity.[10] This seems to be the place where they conduct the administration of their interests on a regular basis. For other natural persons this is bound to be the place of their habitual residence.[11] Any non-professional interest is bound to circle around the place of residence of the debtor, especially as the term 'habitual' refers to the place where the debtor usually or mainly resides and this corresponds to the idea that the debtor conducts the administration of his interests there 'on a regular basis'. In relation to natural persons there is clearly a change here when compared to the former rigid reference under Belgian law to the place where the natural person was registered. One may easily be registered in one place and conduct the administration of his interests in a different place. The place of registration may nevertheless remain a valuable tool or factor to determine the centre of main interests of a debtor, especially when it comes to natural persons that do not engage in any form of trading or professional activity.[12] In many cases it will still provide an important indication, but it can no longer be the determinative factor.[13]

All this leads to the point that the Insolvency Regulation introduces a flexible tool. The place from where the administration of the interests is conducted seems to be preferred above the place where the assets are located. The same tendency is also clear from the presumption. The place of the registered office, or the statutory seat for the civil law countries,[14] is preferred to the place where the offices or production facilities are located in case they are located in different places. This approach also has the additional advantage that there will only be one registered office or one statutory seat, which facilitates the identification of a single centre of main interests, whereas there may be for example more than one place where production facilities are located. The management of the administration aspect clearly takes centre stage. On the other hand, there is also a reference in Recital 13 to the fact that the centre of interests corresponds to the place where the debtor conducts the administration of his interests on a regular basis and

---

10 See Paragraph 75 of the Virgos-Schmit Report. Insolvency Regulation, Article 3(1) was copied without change from the 1995 Convention.

11 Idem. It should be kept in mind though that the Insolvency Regulation does not decide whether or not such a person can be subject to insolvency proceedings, but leaves this to the substantive laws of the member state concerned.

12 See Claeys, M., 'De bevoegdheidsregels voor de internationale faillietverklaring naar huidig en toekomstig recht' (1997) 30 *Tijdschrift voor Belgisch Handelsrecht* 501 at 509.

13 See De Wulf, H. and Wautelet, P., 'Aspecten van international privaatrecht' in Braeckmans, H., Dirix, E. and Wymeersch, E. (eds), *Faillissement en Gerechtelijk Akkoord: Het Nieuwe Recht*, (1998, Kluwer Editions Juridique Belgique, Waterloo) 132 at 151–152.

14 The French language version of the Insolvency Regulation refers to the 'siege statutaire' and the Dutch language version refers to the 'statutaire zetel'. Registration of a company is an alien concept to the company laws of most member states and is replaced the statutes of the company determining a statutory seat that replaces the place of incorporation in the common law tradition.

specifically that this place is therefore ascertainable by third parties. The logic behind the requirement that the place must be ascertainable by third parties is a simple one.[15] Creditors and other interested parties need to be able to determine the debtor's centre of main interests if Article 3(1) of the Insolvency Regulation is supposed to work and if they are to be able to bring insolvency proceedings in the court that has jurisdiction. In this sense the creditors are able to calculate in advance the legal risk they are taking in case of an insolvency in dealing with the debtor.[16] For natural persons at least this ascertainable place where the debtor administers his interests seems to refer back to the place of the assets. This illustrates the flexibility of the concept of the centre of main interests rather than a paradox or a contradiction. For companies and legal persons preference is given to a formal criterion, i.e. the place of the registered office, making it easy to determine a single place where the centre of the debtor's main interests is located. That place is also easily ascertainable by any interested third party. The fact that this is based on a rebuttable presumption means that in appropriate cases, such as when the debtor has nothing more than a letterbox in the place where it is registered, the formal criterion can be set aside in favour of an entirely flexible determination of the centre of the debtor's main interests on the basis of the facts of the case. For natural persons the Insolvency Regulation does not bother with formal criteria as there is not necessarily an obviously suitable criterion that fits all possible scenarios. Here a purely factual criterion is used and applied to the facts of each case. That criterion is the question where they conduct the administration of their interests on a regular basis.

Overall, Article 3(1) of the Insolvency Regulation seems to provide the right balance between legal certainty on the one hand and flexibility on the other hand. There remains a risk though that several courts will take insolvency jurisdiction in a particular case on the basis of slightly different interpretations of Article 3(1),[17] but this seems to be the inevitable price one has to pay for any form of flexibility in this area. One important problem has not been addressed though. The Insolvency Regulation does not provide any specific tool to deal with the insolvency of groups of affiliated companies. Article 3(1) as it stands needs to be applied separately to each of the affiliated companies in as far as they have a separate legal personality.[18] Article 3(1) may therefore give primary insolvency jurisdiction to the courts of different member states for each of the affiliated companies. It is easy however to imagine a scenario where it would be desirable to

---

15 See also Fletcher, I., 'A New Age of International Insolvency – The Countdown Has Begun' [2000] 13(8) *Insolvency Intelligence* 57 at 59.

16 See Paragraph 75 of the Virgos-Schmit Report. Article 3(1) was worded identically in the 1995 Convention.

17 For example if one court accepts that on the facts of the case the presumption has been rebutted (in favour of a real centre of interests based on assets and commercial activities in its area), whilst the second court decides that the presumption applies in the same case (on the basis of a registered office that is not entirely fictive in its area).

18 See Paragraph 76 of the Virgos-Schmit Report. Article 3(1) was worded identically in the 1995 Convention.

let one court deal with the whole set of cases of insolvency of closely related affiliated companies. The Insolvency Regulation fails to provide an adequate solution for such a scenario.[19]

Finally, Article 3(1) of the Insolvency Regulation only establishes the insolvency jurisdiction of the court of a member state. It does not deal with the issue which court in that member state will have jurisdiction. 'Territorial jurisdiction within [each member state] must be established by the national law of the [member state] concerned'.[20] And Article 3(1) can only apply if such a centre of main interests is found within the Community. If the centre of main interests is located outside the territory of the European Union, the Insolvency Regulation does not apply, no court will have jurisdiction on the basis of it and the matter is left to the laws of the member states.[21]

The main advantage of Article 3(1) is that it allows for a quick and rather straightforward determination of a single court that has jurisdiction to deal with the entire insolvency. That court can then take urgent action to preserve the assets for the creditors. Recital 16 to the Insolvency Regulation emphasises this point when it states that this court 'should be enabled to order provisional and protective measures from the time of the request to open proceedings'. It is indeed the case that preservation measures both prior to and after the commencement of insolvency proceedings are of primary importance to guarantee the effectiveness of these proceedings and especially to stop any fraudulent disposal of assets. Having a single court in charge for the whole case in the Community is a clear advantage in this respect. The court can order provisional protective measures covering assets not only in the court's own territory, but in the whole of the Community.[22]

The Case Law

The flexibility of the concept of the debtor's centre of main interest does in practice not only appear to be one of the stronger points of the Insolvency Regulation, it also appears as a criterion that is prone to very divergent interpretations.

Two views are becoming apparent. There are first of all those courts that place the emphasis squarely on Article 3(1) of the Insolvency Regulation. They therefore work with the presumption contained in this article and assume that the debtor's centre of main interest corresponds to the statutory seat of the company or its place of incorporation. They accept that that presumption can be overturned but they are reluctant to do so. This approach is very clearly taken by the Tribunal de

---

19 See Balz, M., 'The European Union Convention on Insolvency Proceedings' (1996) 70 *American Bankruptcy Law Journal* 485 at 503–504.
20 Insolvency Regulation, Recital 15 *in fine*.
21 Ibid., Recital 14 and Fletcher, above note 8 at 260, commenting on Article 3(1) in the context of the 1995 Convention.
22 Ibid., Recital 16 and Omar, P., 'New Initiatives on Cross-Border Insolvency in Europe' [2000] *Insolvency Lawyer* 211 at 214.

Commerce in Charleroi (the Commercial Court of Charleroi, Belgium). The court accepts that the presence of an effective statutory seat in France means that the company Bati-France has the centre of its main interests in France, even though the court is confronted with evidence demonstrating that the company Bati-France was effectively to a large extent run from its Belgian establishment by its Belgian managing director. One can derive from this the conclusion that the court would only be prepared to overturn the presumption contained in Article 3(1) of the Insolvency Regulation if the evidence would have shown the statutory seat to be wholly fictitious. That approach is also apparent in the decision of the Rechtbank van Koophandel Tongeren (the Commercial Court of Tongeren, Belgium). In the view of the court the company involved was effectively based in Belgium and it was by all means being run from there. The statutory seat in Luxembourg was entirely fictitious. One can of course criticise the court for taking jurisdiction on this basis at a time when it is clear that the court in Luxembourg has already taken jurisdiction, rather than to accept and recognise that decision of the Luxembourg court as the Insolvency Regulation proposes, but that is another mater which need not be addressed in this context. Perhaps the clearest example of this view is found in the Eurofood IFSC Ltd decision of the Irish Supreme Court. The court asked the European Court of Justice for a preliminary ruling,[23] but at the same time its own views are very clearly expressed in the judgment. Eurofood was part of the Parmalat empire and had been established in Dublin as a financial vehicle under advantageous Irish tax laws. There is hard evidence in the case that over a 15 year period only three major transactions took place and that Parmalat had appointed Bank of America to run the company on a day to day basis. Two of the four directors were Italians. The Irish Supreme Court sees nevertheless very little reason to depart from the presumption in Article 3(1) of the Insolvency Regulation. The company has been established correctly in Ireland, its board met regularly in Ireland and all the regular company law obligations have been met. The court therefore comes to the conclusion that we are not dealing with a fictitious seat or place of incorporation and that its suggestion almost to the European Court of Justice is that this means that the presumption should not be rebutted and that Eurofood had its centre of main interests in Ireland.

At the other end of the spectrum we find the opposite view which is evident in cases such as Daisytek in the United Kingdom. Here the starting point is not Article 3(1) of the Insolvency Regulation, but Recital 13 to the Insolvency Regulation. That recital hints at the fact that the centre of main interest shall correspond to the place where the debtor conducts the administration of his interests on a regular basis and is therefore ascertainable by third parties. There is therefore a much greater willingness to overturn the presumption, as soon as the criterion in Recital 13 does not point squarely in the direction of the statutory seat or the place of incorporation. The Daisytek court clearly goes down this path when

---

23 Case C-341/04. Advocate General Jacobs delivered his opinion on 27 September 2005. He suggested to the Court that the approach taken by the Irish Supreme Court is the correct approach in this matter. As we will see later on the Court eventually followed its Advocate General on this point. *Eurofood IFSC Ltd* (Case C-341/04) [2006] BCC 397.

deciding whether or not it has main insolvency jurisdiction not just over the holding company in the UK, but also over the various trading companies in the group some of which had statutory seats in France or Germany. For the French company, the court focuses on the amount of supervision and direction exercised by the holding company. Factoring agreement were organised for the trading companies by the holding company, the CEO of the holding company spends 40 per cent of his time on the management of the French trading company, it gets financial support from the holding company and the majority of the goods are supplied to it by the holding company. In the view of the court the key point is that:

> the identification of 'the debtor's main interests' requires the court to consider both the scale of the interests administered at a particular place and their importance and then consider the scale and importance of its interests administered at any other place which may be regarded as its centre of main interests, whether as a result of the presumption in Article 3(1) or otherwise.[24]

A lot of emphasis is also placed on the fact that the place from where the interests are administered needs to be ascertainable by third parties. In the view of the court these third parties are the creditors. In conclusion the court easily overturns the presumption and takes main insolvency jurisdiction over the trading companies.[25]

The existence of these two divergent approaches is clearly not desirable. We are after all dealing with a single community instrument that is supposed to work in the same was across the borders of the member states. The English approach looks particularly problematic, mainly because it creates massive amounts of uncertainty. But there is more. The third parties that need to be able to ascertain the place from where the debtor administers its interests cannot only be the creditors. The Insolvency Regulation carefully uses the term third parties as a generic term, where in other places it specifically uses the term creditors. It is therefore for a much wider group of third parties that as a result of the administration of the interests the place must be identifiable as a centre of main interests. These are not cumulative requirements for the Insolvency Regulation, but one flows from the other. In the absence of a fictitious seat or place of incorporation such a wider audience will find it much harder to disregard the seat or place of incorporation, which is used by the (trading) company in its relations with the outside world. On the positive side, the test that is proposed to check whether the presumption is to be rebutted is very helpful indeed, but it will result in far fewer cases in which the presumption is

---

24   *In Re ISA Daisytek SAS et alia*, High Court of Justice, Chancery Division, Leeds District Registry, judgment of 16 May 2003 [2004] *Tijdschrift voor Belgisch Handelsrecht* 813, per McGonigal J.

25   This conclusion was almost grudgingly accepted by the French courts, see Cour d'Appel de Versailles, judgment of 4 September 2003, *ISA Daisytek SAS et alia v. Me Valdman et alia*, [2004] *Tijdschrift voor Belgisch Handelsrecht* 820. The judgment of the Court of Appeal was in the post Eurofood era confirmed by the Supreme Court, Cour de Cassation, Chambre commerciale, case 03-19863, judgment dated 27 June 2006.

effectively overturned when the arguments put forward above are taken into account when applying it.

One could of course also come to an even more disturbing conclusion. Indeed on the basis of Article 3(1) of the Insolvency Regulation almost all courts seem to be able to grab main insolvency jurisdiction. That is clearly not what the Insolvency Regulation had in mind. Be that as it may, the Insolvency Regulation also does not contain specific rules for groups of companies. The existence of separate legal personality is respected strictly by the Insolvency Regulation and a separate set of insolvency proceedings for each company is envisaged. The Daisytek court was clearly unhappy about this and placed a lot of emphasis on the coordination of activities within the group in order to effectively overturn the presumption and deal as a single court with the insolvency of the whole group. It is submitted that this is a dangerous road to go down. In the first place does it require an erroneous interpretation of the Insolvency Regulation which violates its terms and secondly one should not be blinded by the practical result achieved in this case. Here the holding company was located in a member state, but the reality is that the vast majority of holding companies that has trading companies and subsidiaries across the European Union are not necessarily located in the European Union themselves. Surely the aim of European Union insolvency harmonisation cannot have been to hand over the vast majority of cases concerning companies established in the European Union to foreign courts over which one has no control and that are not part of the harmonised system. At best, this means that the Insolvency Regulation would not apply and that we go back to national rules. But these national rules have proven to be vastly ineffective on many occasions. This can therefore not be the way forward, as the decision of the Irish Supreme Court, in which the holding group's arguments are squarely rejected, demonstrates correctly. One should nevertheless keep in mind that we are solely concerned here with the interpretation of the Insolvency Regulation. That Insolvency Regulation has no specific rules for holding companies and multinational corporate groups. Bending the general rules to overcome this lacuna would be a dangerous step. Instead one should look towards adopting specific legal rules at European level to deal with the issue.[26]

The Court of Justice has now rendered its eagerly awaited judgment in the Eurofood case. Its decision clearly states that the concept of the centre of main interests needs to receive an autonomous interpretation, i.e. its needs to have a uniform meaning in all member states, without reference to pre-existing national concepts. The autonomous interpretation set out by the Court in its judgment goes in the direction of the first alternative highlighted above. This becomes clear when the Court starts by putting the emphasis on the ascertainability of that place for third parties. The Court does so with a reference to Recital 13, but clearly with a different emphasis than the Daisytek Court:

---

26 See on this topic Ronen-Mevorach, I., 'Centralising Insolvencies of Pan-European Corporate Groups: A Creditor's Dream or Nightmare' [2006] *Journal of Business Law* 468.

> the 'centre of main interests' should correspond to the place where the debtor conducts the administration of his interests on a regular basis and is therefore ascertainable by third parties.[27]

Indeed, the Court derives from this starting point that the centre of main interests must be identified on the basis of criteria that are both objective and ascertainable by third parties. Only such criteria guarantee legal certainty and forseeability, which are vital components of the framework set up by the Insolvency Regulation, especially as the latter in its Article 4(1) links the applicable law too to determination of the court with jurisdiction in relation to the main insolvency proceedings.[28]

The presumption in Article 3 therefore becomes an essential tool and one that should not easily put aside. Or, as the Court puts it:

> It follows that, in determining the centre of the main interests of a debtor company, the simple presumption laid down by the Community legislature in favour of the registered office of that company can be rebutted only if factors which are both objective and ascertainable by third parties enable it to be established that an actual situation exists which is different from that which locating it at that registered office is deemed to reflect.[29]

Even in order to rebut the presumption, the emphasis is on ascertainable and objective factors, albeit ones that point away from the presumption.[30] The example given by the Court is striking in this respect. A mere letterbox company that does not carry out any business in the territory of the Member State in which its registered office is situated, but that does carry out activities in another country where also all is assets are located has indeed no links apart from the letterbox registration with the country indicated by the presumption, but has instead business activities and assets as objective and ascertainable factors pointing to another country. But the mere fact that a company's economic choices are or can be controlled by a parent company in another Member State is not enough to rebut the presumption laid down by the Insolvency Regulation if a company carries on its business in the territory of the Member State where its registered office is situated.

The presumption in Article 3 set the rule and is hard to rebut. The facts of the Eurofood case clearly did not allow for the presumption to be rebutted. Eurofood carried on its business from its registered office in Ireland and regular

---

27 Case C-341/04 *Eurofood IFSC Ltd* [2006] BCC 397, at paragraph 32 of the judgment.

28 See Lechner, R., 'Waking from the Jurisdictional Nightmare of Multinational Default: The European Council Regulation on Insolvency Proceedings' [2002] *Arizona Journal of International and Comparative Law* 975 at 1017, see also Torremans P., *Cross Border Insolvencies in EU, English and Belgian Law* (2002, Kluwer Law International, The Hague).

29 Case C-341/04 *Eurofood IFSC Ltd* [2006] BCC 397, at paragraph 34 of the judgment.

30 The emphasis on ascertainability is also emphasised by Ronen-Mevorach, above note 26 at 478.

boards meeting to for example place there. In the words of the Court the position could be summarised as follows:

> [W]here a debtor is a subsidiary company whose registered office and that of its parent company are situated in two different Member States, the presumption laid down in the second sentence of Article 3(1) of the Regulation, whereby the centre of main interests of that subsidiary is situated in the Member State where its registered office is situated, can be rebutted only if factors which are both objective and ascertainable by third parties enable it to be established that an actual situation exists which is different from that which locating it at that registered office is deemed to reflect. That could be so in particular in the case of a company not carrying out any business in the territory of the Member State in which its registered office is situated. By contrast, where a company carries on its business in the territory of the Member State where its registered office is situated, the mere fact that its economic choices are or can be controlled by a parent company in another Member State is not enough to rebut the presumption laid down by the Regulation.[31]

Conclusion

It is submitted that in applying Article 3(1) of the Insolvency Regulation courts should for the reasons set out above be extremely reluctant to overturn the presumption which relies on the statutory seat or the place of incorporation. The test set out in the Daisytek case, when implemented as set out above, can be a good tool to determine when the presumption should be overturned and which factors should be taken into account in such a balancing act. Clearly the strength of the arguments in favour of the place of incorporation and the statutory seat is such that clear evidence of a fictitious seat or place of incorporation must be available before the presumption can be effectively so overturned. The decision of the Irish Supreme Court in the Eurofood case sets out the arguments clearly in this respect.

Arguments that boil down to existence and effective operation of a group structure have no place in this context as the Insolvency Regulation does not take them into account. It is up to the legislator to amend the Insolvency Regulation in case this would result in too may separate proceedings, but the courts should no try to fix this potential problem by means of an unduly wide interpretation of the terms of the Insolvency Regulation.

When the Irish Supreme Court referred its preliminary questions on these issues surrounding Article 3 of the Insolvency Regulation to the Court of Justice one hoped that this would lead to early clarification of the matter. In a certain sense the Court's decision in Eurofood has indeed provided such clarification. The presumption stands strong and the emphasis is on the need for objective and ascertainable factors to rebut it. Such rebuttal will therefore succeed only rarely. This is also the approach which we traced and supported throughout this

---

31 Case C-341/04 *Eurofood IFSC Ltd* [2006] BCC 397, at paragraph 37 of the judgment.

contribution. Needless to say though that this optimistic feeling should not hide the fact that the judgment, in line with the Insolvency Regulation, does very little to address the specific needs of the insolvencies of holding companies and multinational corporate groups.

Chapter 8

The Dominance of Main Insolvency Proceedings under the European Insolvency Regulation

Margreet B. de Boer and Bob Wessels

Introduction

> Main insolvency proceedings and secondary proceedings can ... contribute to the effective realisation of the total assets only if all the concurrent proceedings pending are coordinated. The main condition here is that the various liquidators must cooperate closely, in particular by exchanging a sufficient amount of information. *In order to ensure the dominant role of the main insolvency proceedings* (italics supplied), the liquidator in such proceedings should be given several possibilities for intervening in secondary insolvency proceedings which are pending at the same time. For example, he should be able to propose a restructuring plan or composition or apply for realisation of the assets in the secondary insolvency proceedings to be suspended ...

thus states Recital no. 20 preceding the text of the European Union Insolvency Regulation.

In this chapter, we will focus our attention on the provisions in Chapter III ('Secondary Insolvency Proceedings') of the Insolvency Regulation, which vouch for the coordination of main insolvency proceedings and secondary insolvency proceedings, as well as for the dominant role of the main insolvency proceedings. After a short comment as to the concept of secondary proceedings in relation to the Insolvency Regulation, an outline of what we will call the 'community' powers and the domestic powers of the liquidator in the main proceedings is made. Thereafter, attention will be paid to Articles 31(1) and (2) which reflect a fundamental element of the Insolvency Regulation, i.e. the coordination of main insolvency proceedings and secondary insolvency proceedings: the liquidator in the main proceedings and the liquidators in the secondary proceedings shall be duty bound to communicate information to each other and to cooperate with each other. On the other hand, Article 31(3) is a reflection of the dominant role of the main proceedings: the liquidator in the secondary proceedings shall give the liquidator in the main proceedings an early opportunity of submitting proposals on the liquidation or use of the assets in the secondary proceedings. Other reflections of the dominant role of the main proceedings are found in Articles 33 and 34. Article 33 provides for a stay of the process of liquidation in secondary proceedings, while Article 34 provides for measures ending secondary insolvency proceedings by a rescue plan, a composition or a comparable measure. As is principally the case in Article 33, it is the main liquidator on which Article 34 hinges.

The Function of Secondary Proceedings

Prior to a detailed examination of the mutual relationship between main proceedings in one member state and one or more secondary proceedings in other member states, some comments follow concerning the concept of secondary proceedings in relation to the Insolvency Regulation system. This concept within the European Union can be traced back to the European Convention on Certain Aspects of Bankruptcy, signed in Istanbul on 5 June 1990.[1] Its introduction then is based on the utility of secondary proceedings from the perspective of local creditors.[2] The first significant point to note therefore is that main insolvency proceedings, opened in one member state do not deprive the courts in other member states of the authority to open secondary proceedings, for which see Article 16(2) of the Insolvency Regulation. The universal effect of the main proceedings throughout the European Community does not apply to the secondary proceedings, opened in another member state, whilst the effects of the secondary proceedings may not be challenged in other member states as Article 17 states. Because the procedural and substantive effects of the secondary proceedings are determined by the *lex concursus*, through rules contained in Articles 4 and 28, the focus of the secondary proceedings is the protection of local interests.[3]

There are however other aspects of this primary function of secondary proceedings, which allows us to view the secondary proceedings as being a national proceeding, with quite a European context:

> (i)   despite secondary proceedings being opened in another member state (in which the debtor has an establishment, see Article 3(2) and Article 2(h)), the secondary proceedings are concerned with the same (insolvent) debtor as the main insolvency proceedings;

---

1   For a list of signatories and ratifications, see the Council of Europe website at: <conventions.coe.int/Treaty/EN/CadreListeTraites.htm> (last viewed 31 May 2007). Article 44(k) of the Insolvency Regulation has replaced the Istanbul Convention, which was signed by seven states and ratified by only one state (Cyprus).

2   See Balz, M., 'The European Convention on Insolvency Proceedings' (1996) 70 *American Bankruptcy Law Journal* 485.

3   See Kolmann, S., *Kooperationsmodelle im Internationalen Insolvenzrecht. Empfielt sich für das Deutsche internationale Insolvenzrecht eine Neuorientierung?* Schriften zum Deutschen und Europäischen Zivil-, Handels- und Prozessrecht (2001, Verlag Ernst und Werner Gieseking, Bielefeld) characterizes this focus understandably as a 'protective function' (*Schutzfunction*).

(ii)   despite the secondary proceedings only being permitted to be proceedings as listed in Annex B, and therefore winding-up proceedings with territorial effect (Article 3(2) and Article 27), Chapter III of the Insolvency Regulation provides the liquidator appointed in the main insolvency proceedings with several powers to change the character of the secondary proceedings and to align the proceedings in accordance with developments in the main proceedings;

(iii)   despite 'local' creditors being able to lodge claims in secondary proceedings, they are also allowed to lodge claims in the main proceedings or in other secondary proceedings (Article 32).

The Spanish professors Miguel Virgós and Francisco Garcimartín refer to secondary proceedings having an auxiliary function and therefore should be considered in the context of the main proceedings.[4] The Insolvency Regulation does not aim to ring-fence secondary proceedings; these proceedings have their formal character and comprise assets, located in its territory, but the regulations' concept of the universality of the main proceedings 'is allowed to become fragmented, but is not finally renounced'.[5] The mutual connection between both proceedings is founded on the maxim that, ultimately, the administration concerns one debtor with one estate and one group of creditors. See Recital no. 3, indicating that the Regulation stems from the need for 'coordination of the measures to be taken regarding an insolvent debtor's assets'. This may be referred to as the principle of unity of estate.

Community Powers of the Liquidator in Main Proceedings

The concept of one debtor with one estate to satisfy all creditors is reflected – though less systematically – by the powers assigned to the liquidator in the main insolvency proceedings by the Insolvency Regulation. The following illustrates these rights and powers:

---

4   See Virgós, M. and Garcimartín, F., *The EC Regulation on Insolvency Proceedings: A Practical Commentary* (2004, Kluwer Law International, The Hague) at paragraph 287. For a discussion of the supportive function of secondary proceedings, see e.g. Duursma-Kepplinger, H., Duursma, D. and Chalupsky, E., *Europäische Insolvenzverordnung Kommentar* (2002, Springer, Wien) Art. 27, nr. 11ff; Staak, K., *Der deutsche Insolvenzverwalter im europäischen Insolvenzrecht. Eine Analyse der EG-Verordnung Nr. 1346/2000 des Rates vom 29. Mai 2000 über Insolvenzverfahren unter besonderer Berücksichtigung der Person des deutschen Insolvenzverwalters,* Europäischen Hochschulschriften, Reihe II, Rechtswissenschaft, Vol. 3889 (2004, Peter Lang, Frankfurt am Main) at 483; Ehricke, U., 'Das Verhältnis des Hauptinsolvenzverwalters zum Sekundärinsolvenzverwalter bei grenzüberschreitenden Insolvenzen nach der EuInsVo' *ZIP* 25-26/2005, 1106.

5   See Fletcher, I., *Insolvency in Private International Law: National and International Approaches* (Oxford Private International Law Series) (2nd ed) (2005, Oxford University Press, Oxford) at paragraph 7.136.

(i)   he has the power to apply for secondary proceedings in other member states (Article 29);

(ii)   he can ask liquidators in the secondary proceedings for information (Article 31(1)); and

(iii)   he can demand that they cooperate with him (Article 31(2));

(iv)   he can exercise the power to put forward certain proposals in the context of the secondary proceedings (pursuant to Article 31(3));

(v)   he may request a stay of the process of liquidation in these secondary proceedings (Article 33(1));

(vi)   he may request the termination of a stay (Article 33(2));

(vii)   he may propose a rescue plan in the secondary proceedings (see Article 34(1)), also during the stay of the process of liquidation (Article 34(3));

(viii) he shall lodge in other proceedings claims which have already been lodged in the main proceedings (Article 32(2));

(ix)   he has the power to participate in the other proceedings on the same basis as the creditors (Article 32(3));

(x)   he has the right to request the return to the main proceedings of anything already obtained by creditors as they have satisfied their claims by any means on the assets of the debtor situated in the other member state (Article 20); and

(xi)   he has the power to collect any remaining assets from the secondary proceedings if all claims in these proceedings have been met (Article 35).

These powers have their origin in the Insolvency Regulation and therefore may be regarded as the 'community' powers of the main liquidator. In addition, he may use in the whole of the European Union (except for Denmark) his domestic powers, for which see Article 18. The recitals devote only a few words to the guiding notion of unity of the estate. Recital no. 3 states that 'The activities of undertakings have more and more cross-border effects and are therefore increasingly being regulated by Community law. While the insolvency of such undertakings also affects the proper functioning of the internal market, there is a need for a Community act requiring *coordination of the measures to be taken regarding an insolvent debtor's assets*'. See also Recital no. 12, explaining the characteristics of main proceedings and secondary proceedings, adding that '*Mandatory rules of coordination* with the main proceedings satisfy the *need for unity* in the Community'. Furthermore, Recital no. 20 states that 'Main insolvency proceedings and secondary proceedings can, however, contribute to the *effective realisation of the total assets* only if all the concurrent proceedings pending are coordinated. The *main condition here is that the various liquidators must cooperate closely*, in particular by exchanging a sufficient amount of information', while Recital no. 21 sets out the principle that '*Every creditor*, who has his habitual residence, domicile or registered office in the Community, *should have the right to lodge his claims in each of the insolvency proceedings pending in the Community relating to the debtor's assets* ... (italics supplied).

Domestic Powers of the Liquidator in Main Proceedings

Article 18 acknowledges the general authority of the main liquidator to exercise his powers in other member states. Article 19 comprises a rule relating to the proof of his appointment. In principle the liquidator, appointed by a court which has jurisdiction pursuant to Article 3(1), has the authority to exercise all the powers conferred on him by the *lex concursus* in other member states. Recognition of main proceedings under Article 16 includes recognition of the liquidator appointed in such proceedings. His powers shall be recognised 'automatically' in all member states. In these states the liquidator may exercise the powers conferred to him by the *lex concursus*.[6] The liquidator can exercise his power abroad in principle without any prior or further formality, especially without having to obtain an exequatur, without having to propose a form of bail and, furthermore, without the need to ensure publication of his appointment in one or more other member states.[7]

The number of powers that a liquidator may have, the nature of such powers and their legal effects are all determined by the *lex concursus*. Furthermore, the *lex concursus* is decisive with regard to the liquidator's legal tasks, duties, the scope of his power and the grounds and procedure for his removal. Therefore, in Dutch main proceedings the appointed liquidator will also be subject to supervision by the supervisory judge (*'rechter-commissaris'*) when taking steps in other member states. Virgós and Garcimartín submit that the *lex concursus* will also be decisive in determining the liquidator's liability for failure or weakness of performance, including the standard of care required.[8] The possibility cannot be excluded however that certain (third) parties could start liability proceedings before the courts of the state within the territory of which certain acts of the liquidator have caused damages, when to such claims the law of the latter member state will be applicable.

Article 18(1), second sentence, explicitly provides for the main liquidator's power to remove the debtor's assets from the territory of the member state in which they are situated, subject to Articles 5 and 7. The provision creates a substantive rule, as this power may also be exercised when the *lex concursus* does not include a power of this nature. It is therefore a pure community power. One may submit that the power to remove assets already flows from Article 18(1), first sentence, and Article 4(2)(c). The express stipulation follows however from the need to remove any doubt.[9]

---

6   We agree with the proposition of Berends A.J., *Grensoverschrijdende insolventie* (1999, Nederlands Instituut voor het Bank- en Effectenbedrijf, Amsterdam) at 152, that Article 18(1) is, in this regard, helpful as a practical repetition of Insolvency Regulation, Article 4(2)(c), but is unnecessary.

7   See also De Boer, M.B., 'Schuldsanering met grensoverschrijdende gevolgen' *SchuldSanering* 2001/6, 13.

8   Virgós and Garcimartín, above note 4 at paragraph 364.

9   See Virgós-Schmit Report (1996) at paragraph 161, in which it is stipulated that when removing assets the liquidator must respect Articles 5 and 7, as the main proceedings

The liquidator in the main insolvency proceedings only has authority to exercise his powers in the other member states within the limits of the Insolvency Regulation, for which see Article 18(1), first sentence, and therefore only 'as long as no other insolvency proceedings have been opened there nor any preservation measure to the contrary has been taken there further to a request for the opening of insolvency proceedings in that state'. This limitation relates to the possibility of opening secondary insolvency proceedings pursuant to Article 3(2). The Virgós-Schmit Report refers to this limitation as a logical restriction, since the assets cannot be subject to the powers of two different liquidators: 'Once territorial proceedings have been opened, the direct powers of the liquidator in the main proceedings no longer apply to assets situated in the state of the opening of the territorial proceedings. The liquidator in the territorial proceedings has exclusive powers over those assets. This does not imply that the main liquidator loses all influence over the debtor's estate situated in the other ... state, but that that influence must be exercised through the powers conferred on that liquidator by [the Regulation] to coordinate the territorial proceedings and the main proceedings'.[10] As indicated, the limitation in Article 18(1), first sentence, also concerns situations in which provisional protective measures are incompatible with the exercise of the powers of the main liquidator where these have already been adopted as a consequence of the request to open secondary proceedings. Examples of measures of this type in the Netherlands include the placing under seal of the estate, provided in Article 7 of the Faillissementswet, as well as measures to protect the interests of creditors pursuant to Articles 225 and 290 of the Faillissementswet.

Compliance with the Law of the Member State Approached

In addition to the limitations on the liquidator's powers, Article 18(3) contains the provision that the liquidator in the main proceedings shall, in exercising his powers, comply with the law of the member state within the territory of which he intends to take action, in particular with regard to procedures for the realisation of assets. Such powers may not include coercive measures or the right to rule on legal proceedings or disputes.[11] The Virgós-Schmit Report[12] explains how compliance with a member state's law takes shape. The following points can be noted: the general principle of prohibition of the exercise of coercive powers in another state

---

cannot affect rights in rem of creditors or third parties over assets situated, at the time of the opening, in a member state other than the state of the opening of proceedings.

10 Virgós-Schmit Report, at paragraph 163.

11 Article 18(2) relates to the liquidator appointed in secondary proceedings and therefore by a court which has jurisdiction pursuant to Article 3(2). He may in any other member state claim, through the courts or out of court, that moveable property which was removed from the territory of the state of the opening of proceedings to the territory of that other member state after the opening of the insolvency proceedings. Furthermore, he may bring any action, in the interests of the creditors, to set aside. On these additional powers of the secondary liquidator, see Wessels, B., *International Insolvency Law* (2006, Kluwer, Deventer) at paragraph 107062.

12 Virgós-Schmit Report, at paragraph 164ff.

applies to a foreign main liquidator, thus he may only take action in other states if he complies with this principle.[13] For this reason, Article 18(1) expressly prohibits direct recourse to coercive measures. In fact, according to the Virgós-Schmit Report: 'Any use of force or coercive action is excluded'. In any given case where the persons affected by a liquidator's act do not voluntarily agree to their performance and coercive measures are required with regard to assets or persons, the liquidator must apply to the authorities of the state where the assets or persons are located to have them adopted and implemented. Moss and Smith correctly submit that local courts should have a 'big-hearted' attitude: 'Also, as a matter of principle, local law and courts should as far as possible make available to liquidators in main proceedings all the remedies available to local liquidators, so as to avoid discrimination against an European Union citizen. This may sometimes necessitate the opening of secondary proceedings'.[14] The English text ('shall comply') appears to be stricter than various other texts, see the Netherlands: '*eerbiedigen*' (which is the equivalent of 'to respect'), France: '*doit respecter*', Spanish: '*deberá respectar*'. The rational is that the main liquidator 'must take the constraints of the outside world as a given'.[15] The liquidator shall exercise his powers without infringing the laws of the state in which he takes action. Although the liquidator may transfer assets belonging to the estate to another member state, this power may be subject to rules limiting the free movement of goods. An asset, for instance, may be part of the historical and cultural heritage of a member state and may be subject to an export ban protected under Article 36 of the EC Treaty.

Where local law provides for certain formal procedures for the realisation of assets, the liquidator shall comply with the law of the state in which the assets are located. The *lex concursus* of the main proceedings establishes the extent of the powers of the liquidator and the manner in which such powers may be exercised. Only the *lex concursus* of the main proceedings is decisive with regard to, for example, whether the sale of immoveable property can be a private market transaction or if a sale by public auction is necessary. Once the *lex concursus* has determined the form of sale, the procedures by which the assets are realised must be in accordance with the provisions of the national law of the approached member state. If the latter *lex fori concursus* requires a sale by public auction, the procedure for carrying out this sale in the state where the immoveable property is situated shall therefore be determined by the law of that latter state. On the other hand if

---

13 The Insolvency Regulation, quite rightly, is built on the principle that a person may not act as judge in his own case. Such a situation would be in direct conflict with the English law 'principle of natural justice *nemo judex in sua causa*', see *Ex parte Pinochet* [2000] AC 119 (HL), mentioned in: Moss, G., Fletcher, I. and Isaacs, S. (eds), *The EC Regulation on Insolvency Proceedings – A Commentary and Annotated Guide* (2002, Oxford University Press, Oxford) at paragraph 8.165. See also Staak, op. cit., at 144.

14 Moss, G. and Smith, T., Chapter 8 in Moss et al., above note 13 at paragraph 8.165.

15 See further Virgós and Garcimartín, above note 4 at paragraph 369, and Staak, above note 4 at 143, who correctly submits that the principle of the *lex concursus* of the main insolvency proceedings stays intact, with due respect to the *lex fori* of the other member state.

Dutch insolvency law prescribes the approval of the court when a liquidator intends, for example, to start civil law proceedings, the foreign main liquidator does not need this approval, as Article 18(3) does not function as a conflict of law rule.[16]

Objection to the Exercise of Powers

The Insolvency Regulation does not provide for any form of objection to the main liquidator's performance. Due to the lack of provisions regarding objections to the exercise of powers by the liquidator and the lack of provisions requiring the liquidator to act or prevent the liquidator from acting, the Virgós-Schmit Report submits that the authorities of the member states within which the powers are intended to be exercised shall have jurisdiction to decide if the grounds for opposition lie in the non-recognition of the proceedings opened in another member state or of the judgment appointing the liquidator.[17] The examples given relate to a situation in which the grounds for opposition are a breach by the liquidator of the provisions of the Regulation which govern the exercise of his powers in other states, such as Article 18(1) or Article 3(3). Alternatively: 'If the opposition concerns the substance of the exercise of those powers, i.e. the justification for a measure which the liquidator intends to take, jurisdiction lies with the judicial authorities of the state of the opening of the proceedings'.[18] It should be noted that a Dutch main liquidator in main insolvency proceedings being bankruptcy liquidation will be subject to Article 69 of the Faillissementswet:

> 1. Each of the creditors, the appointed creditors committee and also the bankrupt, may file a petition with the supervisory judge to object against any act of the liquidator or to procure that the supervisory judge orders the liquidator to perform or refrain from performing any intended act. 2. Within three days the supervisory judge must issue his decision having heard the liquidator.

Duty to Communicate

Within the framework of the Insolvency Regulation, the main insolvency proceedings and the secondary proceedings are interdependent proceedings which concern one debtor having 'several centres of activity and assets' spread over several territories.[19] It is therefore logical that Article 31(1) states that, subject to the rules restricting the communication of information, the liquidator in the main proceedings and the liquidators in the secondary proceedings shall be duty bound

---

16 See Berends, A.J., *Insolventie in het internationaal privaatrecht*, Doct. Thesis Vrije Universiteit (2005, Amsterdam) at 342.

17 Virgós-Schmit Report, at paragraph 166.

18 See also Bogdan, M., additional comments in Moss and Smith, above note 14 at paragraph 8.166.

19 Virgós-Schmit Report, at paragraph 229.

to communicate information to each other. The mutual duty to communicate and to cooperate, for which see Article 31(2), is a fundamental element of the Insolvency Regulation and therefore liquidators in both main and secondary proceedings must be seen as principle agents for realizing the goals of the Insolvency Regulation, as stated in Recitals nos. 2 and 3: 'The proper functioning of the internal market requires that cross-border insolvency proceedings should operate efficiently and effectively' and where insolvency of businesses 'also affects the proper functioning of the internal market', the need for coordination of the measures to be taken regarding an insolvent debtor's assets is in the hands of the liquidators.

The Netherlands Royal Committee on Private International Law submits that it is generally desirable to be aware of the main liquidator's point of view once secondary proceedings have been opened. The Committee is of the opinion that, other than under participation as referred to in Article 34, the interests of a main liquidator would be sufficiently protected if the liquidator in the secondary proceedings opened in the Netherlands is duty bound by Article 31(1) to communicate 'any information which may be relevant to the other proceedings' and to cooperate under Article 31(2). The Committee proposed that the foreign liquidator should be informed by the liquidator of secondary proceedings about 'all important sessions and decisions in the Dutch proceedings, whereupon the foreign liquidator independently can intervene in the Dutch proceedings'.[20] It should be emphasised that the duties of communication (and cooperation) are mutual, thus the main liquidator will also be obliged to inform the liquidator in secondary proceedings and to cooperate with him.

It follows from the quotation that the Netherlands Royal Committee on Private International Law seems to be of the opinion that the duty to communicate is limited to procedural insolvency topics. However, this is not compatible with the text of Article 31(1), which states that the duty to communicate relates to 'any information which may be relevant to the other proceedings, in particular the progress made in lodging and verifying claims and all measures aimed at terminating the proceedings'. The opinion of the Committee is also incompatible with the Virgós-Schmit Report, which lists the topics covered by the mutual duties to communicate as:

(i)   the assets;
(ii)   the actions planned or underway in order to recover assets: actions to obtain payment or actions to set aside;
(iii)   possibilities for liquidating assets;
(iv)   claims lodged;
(v)   verification of claims and disputes concerning them;
(vi)   the ranking of creditors;
(vii) planned reorganization measures;
(viii) proposed compositions;

---

20 See Netherlands Royal Committee on Private International Law: Advice concerning the EC Insolvency Regulation (13 March 2002) at paragraph 6.1, available in Dutch through the Justice Ministry website at: <www.justitie.nl> (last viewed 31 May 2007).

(ix)   plans for the allocation of dividends; and
(x)   the progress of operations in the proceedings.[21]

The above demonstrates that the duty to communicate includes several topics of a non-procedural nature. On the other hand, it also demonstrates that there is a limit to the extent of the details which must be shared with liquidators in other proceedings.[22]

The duty to communicate may be limited, the scope of the duty can be surmised from the first words of Article 31(1): 'Subject to the rules restricting the communication of information'. The duty to communicate information may be limited by national legislation on data exchange, e.g. legislation relating to the protection of computerised personal data. Both liquidators shall 'immediately' communicate any information which may be relevant to the other proceedings. The time period will be totally dependent on the circumstances.[23]

Duty to Cooperate

In addition to the mutual duty to communicate, Article 31(2) establishes, 'subject to the rules applicable to each of the proceedings', a mutual duty to cooperate. The liquidator in the main proceedings and the liquidators in the secondary proceedings shall be duty bound to cooperate with each other. The liquidators have a duty 'to act in concert with a view to the development of proceedings and their coordination, and to facilitate their respective work', thus the Virgós-Schmit Report.[24] The Virgós-Schmit Report is less clear with regard to a second systematic principle of the Regulation, i.e. that the creditors may participate in several proceedings as noted in Article 32(1). Therefore, to ensure the smooth course of operations in the various proceedings and the alignment of distributions, sharing of information and cooperation between the liquidators is necessary.

The structure of the cooperation required can be identified in Recital no. 20, cited above:

(i)   aim: main insolvency proceedings and secondary proceedings can only 'contribute to the effective realisation of the total assets' if all the concurrent proceedings pending are coordinated;
(ii)   nature: the main condition being that the various liquidators 'must cooperate closely, in particular by exchanging a sufficient amount of information'.

The practical implications of cooperation (and communication) have been pointed out in several legal commentaries; such implications include:

---

21 Virgós-Schmit Report, at paragraph 230.
22 See also Berends, above note 6 at 179, who submits that liquidators do not have to mutually communicate all trivial information.
23 Staak, above note 4 at 166, suggests a maximum period of 14 days.
24 Virgós-Schmit Report, at paragraph 232.

(i)   the necessity of understanding the powers of the foreign liquidator and of having (general) knowledge of the insolvency law system of the other member state;

(ii) the use of a common language (English is most commonly suggested in this respect);

(iii) the use of technology (special servers; chatrooms);

(iv) translations and their costs.[25]

Proposals on the Liquidation or the Use of Assets

Article 31(3) reflects the dominance of the main proceedings. It provides that the liquidator in the secondary proceedings shall give the liquidator in the main proceedings an early opportunity of submitting proposals on the liquidation or use of the assets in the secondary proceedings. Under the system of the Insolvency Regulation it follows that the secondary liquidator informs, in a timely manner and under his own initiative, the main liquidator in order that the main liquidator will not be confronted with a fait accompli. As a consequence of this obligation the main liquidator may be able, for example, to prevent the sale of assets involved in the secondary proceedings, the preservation of which may be deemed desirable in respect of the reorganisation of the business at the centre of main interests. Another consequence could be that he will request for a stay of the process of liquidation under Article 33, for which see below. The 'dominance' of the main proceedings has been recognized by the Düsseldorf Court on 9 July 2004, which stated that Article 31 contains extensive mutual duties of cooperation and exchange of information between liquidators under which the secondary proceedings are regularly subordinated to the needs of the main proceedings; the court refers to Article 31(3).[26]

The obligation laid down in Article 31(3) concerns important assets or decisions, such as the continuation or cessation of the activities of the establishment in the secondary proceedings. It should not be interpreted so widely that, in practice, it paralyses the work of the liquidator in the secondary proceedings.[27] The provision itself leaves open questions. It does not, for example, contain a rule concerning the secondary liquidator taking notice of the proposals of the main liquidator. Furthermore, the provision lacks a rule concerning how conflicts between the main and the secondary liquidator are to be decided. Moss and Smith submit that Article 31(3) does not contain any suggestion that the secondary liquidator should follow the proposals of the main liquidator. [28] These authors are of the view that the main liquidator may appeal against any action taken by the secondary liquidator. We submit that the main liquidator also has

---

25 Practical guidelines to assist liquidators in their efforts of cross-border communication and cooperation in insolvency practice may be expected in 2007, see Wessels, B., 'It's Time To Cooperate' (2005) 2(6) *International Corporate Rescue* 291.

26 Düsseldorf Court judgment of 9 July 2004, ZIP 2004, 1514; NZI 2004, 628, comments by Pannen, K. and Riedemann, S., EWiR 2005, 177 (*ISA Deutschland GmbH*).

27 Virgós-Schmit Report, at paragraph 234.

28 Moss and Smith, above note 14 at paragraph 8.231.

locus standi under the applicability of the secondary proceedings. In practice, it seems to follow that under Articles 33 and 34 the main liquidator will submit proposals of a nature that are sufficiently favourable to the secondary liquidator for such a liquidator to follow.[29]

Stay of Liquidation in Secondary Proceedings

One of the possibilities for intervening the liquidator in main proceedings is given in order to ensure the dominant role of the main insolvency proceedings, is to apply for realisation of assets in the secondary proceedings to be suspended, either in whole or in part.[30] For this important power of the liquidator to request to stay the process of liquidation Article 33(1) provides its basis. Article 33 also deals with the grounds to reject such a stay and the period of the stay of the process of liquidation. Article 33(2) also provides for the anticipated termination of the stay of liquidation. Though by this provision 'the primacy of the main proceedings' is established, the interests of the creditors in the secondary proceedings are equally taken into account,[31] as appears from Article 33(1), first sentence, second passage and Article 33(2) second dash, *in fine*.

It should be noted at the outset that an order given by the court to stay the process of liquidation in secondary proceedings does not have as a consequence that the winding-up proceedings will be ended. The law applicable to the secondary proceedings (*lex fori concursus secundi*) will remain applicable and determines in this way the legal consequences of the secondary proceedings. The stay of the process of liquidation does also not have as a consequence – as Bogdan remarks[32] – that the liquidator in the main proceedings is empowered to use the assets which are hit by the stay. He also is not authorised to realise these assets himself.

As the liquidation activities within the secondary proceedings (wholly or partially) are suspended, the effect of a stay conform Article 33 is that for the time being certain actions will be stopped in a preparatory phase or in its first phase of execution.[33] Article 33 only can be effective if the 'process of liquidation' has been entered into. See for an illustration the Austrian Court's decision in *Collins & Aikman Products GmbH*,[34] which held that a stay of the process of liquidation should not be considered when liquidation has not been entered into in the secondary proceedings and the liquidator of the main proceedings has not issued a proposal for the liquidation. It is submitted though that the latter requirement is not

---

29 See Kolmann, above note 3 at 350.
30 Cf. Insolvency Regulation, Recital no. 20.
31 Virgós-Schmit Report, at paragraph 241.
32 See Bogdan, M., additional comments in Moss and Smith, above note 14 at paragraph 8.249.
33 Cf. Virgós-Schmit Report, at paragraph 246.
34 Leoben Court judgment of 31 August 2005, NZI 2005, 646 (*Collins & Aikman Products GmbH*), comments by Paulus, C., NZI 2005, 647.

included in Article 33(1). According to the court, the purpose of the stay of the liquidation process and of the duty of liquidators to cooperate is to prevent a split liquidation of the assets which belong to the estate of the secondary proceedings. A stay of execution of course does not affect the execution of rights *in rem* as referred to in Article 5.[35]

The rule on the stay of liquidation does apply in the secondary proceedings as well as in the independent territorial proceedings according to Berends, who notes that Article 33 contributes to the system of the Insolvency Regulation, i.e. that there is only one main proceeding in one member state and one or more secondary proceedings in other member states.[36] Article 34(3) provides that during the stay of the process of liquidation the liquidator in the main proceedings may propose in the secondary proceedings measures as e.g. a rescue plan or a composition.

Request from the Liquidator to stay the Process of Liquidation

According to Article 33(1), first sentence, the court, which opened the secondary proceedings, shall stay the process of liquidation in whole or in part on receipt of a request from the liquidator in the main proceedings, provided that in that event it may require the liquidator in the main proceedings to take any suitable measure to guarantee the interests of the creditors in the secondary proceedings and of individual classes of creditors.

The Insolvency Regulation does not provide for procedural rules, apart from the assignment of the competent court.[37] The law of the state in which the secondary proceedings were opened is applicable. Thus this law determines the form and the specific content of the request, the possibility of a hearing of the liquidator in the secondary proceedings as well as the possibility of filing an appeal in the case the request has been denied or awarded. In the Netherlands a request for a stay of the liquidation proceedings shall according to Article 5(3) of the Faillissementswet be filed by a solicitor (*procureur*) with the court (civil section of the court in first instance; *rechtbank*), which has opened the secondary proceedings.[38] Against the decision on the request by the court general available appeal to the Court of Appeal is excluded; appeal (*cassatie*) can only be lodged to the Netherlands Supreme Court.[39]

The court has to consider the request for a stay in relation to the interests of the creditors in the main proceedings. In the view of the Virgós-Schmit Report, the grounds for a request of a stay may be appraised only in relation of the interests of

---

35 Wessels, above note 11 at paragraph 10870.
36 Berends, above note 6 at 182.
37 We assume that in any case the court in first instance is competent, also when only in appeal secondary proceedings were opened.
38 Faillissementswet, Article 361(2) dictates the application by analogy of Faillissementswet, Article 5(3) in Dutch proceedings for the discharge from debt of natural persons, the other winding-up proceedings in the Netherlands (see Annex B).
39 Netherlands Code of Procedural Law, Article 426.

those creditors; the court may not refuse the stay except if it is manifestly not in the interests of the creditors in the main proceedings.[40] The interests of the creditors in the main proceedings in the stay of the process of liquidation to be taken into consideration by the court, will have – according to the Virgós-Schmit Report – different aspects:

> For example, the preservation of the estate situated in the state of the secondary proceedings may be useful with a view to selling the main business of the secondary establishment to a purchaser or with a view to a composition. The safeguarding of some of the elements of the assets, useful within a reorganisation, or with a view to a sale 'en masse' together with some of the assets involved in the main proceedings may justify a partial stay on the liquidation.[41]

It is up to the liquidator in the main proceedings to inform the court in this aspect: the liquidator has to ground that a stay of the proceedings is in the interests of the creditors of the main proceedings. It should be noted that the Insolvency Regulation lacks rules with regard to cross-border information of courts in proceedings in different member states.

In the Netherlands, when bankruptcy liquidations as main proceedings are opened, the creditors may benefit from a stay of the process of liquidation in foreign secondary proceedings when it appears – through the communicated information of the secondary liquidator – that a creditor in the secondary proceedings or a third party abroad is interested in acquiring the 'establishment' (in the foreign country) and the assets, which may be located in the Netherlands where the main proceedings were opened.[42] Contrary to what seems to be the point of view of Kayser,[43] a stay of the process of liquidation does not have as its sole aim to enable the liquidator in the main proceedings to propose a 'global liquidation plan'. In the member state where the main proceedings are opened, Article 33 may bring relief when in that country as main proceedings reorganization-proceedings have been opened, the success of which will be endangered by one or more secondary proceedings (being winding-up proceedings) elsewhere. The power to request a stay may be exercised too with the aim 'to permit the sale of an entire business as a going concern or to permit a unified transnational reorganization', according to the views of Bufford and others.[44] This all does not mean that the interests of all the creditors in the secondary proceedings as well as those of certain groups of creditors are not taken into account by the court. The court may require the liquidator in the main proceedings to take any suitable measure to guarantee the

---

40 Virgós-Schmit Report, at paragraph 242.
41 Virgós-Schmit Report, at paragraph 243.
42 Wessels, above note 11 at paragraph 10869.
43 See Kayser, N., A Study of the European Convention on Insolvency Proceedings (1998) 7 *International Insolvency Review* 117.
44 See Bufford, S., Adler, L., Brooks, S. and Krieger, M., *International Insolvency* (2001, Federal Judicial Center, Washington DC) at 82. Also of this view, see Balz, above note 2 at 525; Kolmann, above note 3 at 337.

interests of the creditors in the secondary proceedings and of individual classes of creditors according to Article 33(1), first sentence, second passage. Thus the court may impose on the liquidator in the main proceedings a guarantee which it determines as appropriate, before ordering the stay.[45]

Finally some remarks may be made about multiple cross-filing of claims and the granting of a request for a stay of liquidation. Any creditor may lodge his claim in the main proceedings and in any secondary proceedings, for which see Article 32(1). Multiple cross-filing relates to the concept, laid down in Article 32(2), that the liquidators in the main and any secondary proceedings shall lodge in other proceedings claims which have already been lodged in the proceedings for which they were appointed, provided that the interests of creditors in the latter proceedings are served thereby, subject to the right of creditors to oppose that or to withdraw the lodgement of their claims where the law applicable so provides.[46] When the court is considering a stay, the text of the Insolvency Regulation nor the Virgós-Schmit Report take in account the possibility that one creditor, several creditors or all the creditors in the main proceedings has/have lodged his/their claim(s) in the secondary proceedings or, reversely, one creditor, several creditors or all the creditors in the secondary proceedings has/have lodged his/their claim(s) in the main proceedings. In the view of Berends, when appraising the request of a stay of liquidation the interests of the creditors in the secondary proceedings should not be considered by the court.[47] Though in this case discernment of the 'creditor's interests' will not always be easy, we agree with Berends. We are of the opinion that this discernment regards all persons involved in the main proceedings, who have become creditors in the secondary proceedings by lodging their claims.[48]

Grounds to Refuse the Stay

From the text of Article 33(1), second sentence, is becomes clear that a request filed by the liquidator to stay the process of liquidation may be rejected only if it is manifestly of no interest to the creditors in the main proceedings. The interpretation of the word 'manifestly' in this rule raises difficulties, as its meaning is not clear. In Article 26, dealing with public policy, 'manifestly' means that only in exceptional circumstances the rule of Article 26 may be applied.[49] It seems that in Article 33(1), the word 'manifestly' is equally used in a similar sense (Dutch: '*kennelijk*'; German: '*offensichtlich*'; French: '*manifestement*'). It is therefore submitted that the possibility of a rejection of a request to stay has to be interpreted strictly and may be applied only in exceptional circumstances; in this way too

---

45 Virgós-Schmit Report, at paragraph 244.
46 For critical comments on this burdensome administrative duty, see Wessels, above note 11 at paragraph 10863ff.
47 Berends, above note 6 at 183.
48 As previously expressed in Wessels, above note 11 at paragraph 10876.
49 Cf. Virgós-Schmit Report, at paragraph 204.

Moss and Smith.[50] See in this light, the decision of the Austrian Court, referred to earlier, which held that a stay of liquidation proceedings may only be rejected if the 'liquidation' is manifestly of no interest to the creditors in the main proceedings. This latter argument appears to be incompatible with Article 33(1), second sentence, as the criterion laid down is that 'the request for staying the liquidation' is manifestly of no interest to the creditors in the main proceedings. Berends seems to be less strict, as he attaches to 'manifestly' the interpretation that when the court 'is not sure about the fact whether the stay is in the interests of the creditors of the main proceedings, he has to grant the request'.[51]

It is remarkable that the court in secondary proceedings may order a measure upon a request to stay the process of liquidation or – according to the text of Article 33(1), second sentence – may reject this request by assessing interests of creditors in the main proceedings only. How will the court – apart from the grounds brought forward by the main liquidator – have any knowledge of these interests? The Insolvency Regulation does not provide for rules as to cross-border information of courts in proceedings in different member states. Moreover, there is no duty of the main liquidator to provide information in this regard, which information will lead to scrutinising the request which the main liquidator thinks is in the best interest of the estate. Most probably, the interests here overlap, in that the main liquidator will ground that a stay of liquidation is in the interest of the creditors of the main proceedings.

Period of the Stay of Liquidation

Pursuant to Article 33(1), last two sentences, a stay of the process of liquidation may be ordered for up to three months and may be continued or renewed for similar periods. In case of a continuation or a renewal, the Insolvency Regulation again does not provide – apart from vesting the international competence of the court – for any procedural rules. The stay is therefore limited to a maximum period of three months and may be continued for a similar period of three months maximum each time, the number of successive extensions not being limited. After the extinction of a stay with a restart of the liquidation process, a new order to stay the liquidation may be given and this order may be renewed, the number of successive extensions not being limited as well.[52] Attention should be paid to Article 33(1) and the submission that a requested stay of liquidation may only be rejected if it is manifestly of no interest to the creditors in the main proceedings. This rule will apply as well – although the text is silent – when a continuation of the stay or a renewal of a stay of liquidation is requested by the liquidator in the main proceedings, a view with which Berends concurs.[53] The provision with regard to a continuation or a renewal of a stay presumes that the court in the secondary

---

50 Moss and Smith, above note 14 and commentary under Article 33; similarly, see Wessels, above note 11 at paragraph 10653.
51 Berends, above note 6 at 184.
52 Virgós-Schmit Report, at paragraph 245.
53 Berends, above note 6 at 184.

proceedings is allowed to include rules for providing appropriate information, to be given to the court, in his order to stay the process of liquidation, for which see also the views of Moss and Smith.[54]

Anticipated Termination of a Stay of Liquidation

A stay of the process of liquidation may be terminated at any time by the court, which opened the secondary proceedings. The court decides – as Article 33(2) defines – (i) at the request of the liquidator in the main proceedings, or (ii) of its own motion, at the request of a creditor or at the request of the liquidator in the secondary proceedings if that measure no longer appears justified, in particular, by the interests of creditors in the main proceedings or in the secondary proceedings. We would submit that the text is confusing here, as it seems that the latter ground only relates to the reasons to be given by those persons who may invite the court to take a decision of its own motion. The Virgós-Schmit Report[55] supports the view that this article should be read as follows and that the decision of the court to terminate the stay shall be given:

(i)   at the request of the liquidator in the main proceedings;
(ii)   of its own motion;
(iii) at the request of a creditor; or
(iv)   at the request of the liquidator in the secondary proceedings,

while for all requests the same appraisal has to be applied by the court, i.e. that the measure of a stay of liquidation no longer appears justified, in particular, by the interests of creditors in the main proceedings or in the secondary proceedings.

Here again, the Insolvency Regulation does not – apart from the assignment of the international competence of the court in Article 33(2), in other words the court referred to in paragraph 1 is the court which opened the secondary proceedings[56] – provide for procedural rules. The law of the state in which the secondary proceedings were opened is applicable: thus this law determines the form and the specific content of the request, a hearing of parties interested, for example when the request was filed by a creditor the liquidator in the main proceedings who initially requested the stay and/or the liquidator in the secondary proceedings, as well as the possibility of filing an appeal in the case the request has been denied or awarded. In the Netherlands, the rules applicable to filing a request for a stay of liquidation apply equally to a request to terminate a stay.

When a stay of liquidation no longer appears to be justified the courts terminates it. Reason for an anticipated termination of a stay may be found in the interests of the creditors in the secondary proceedings or in the interests of the

---

54 Moss and Smith, above note 14 and comments under Article 33.
55 Virgós-Schmit Report, at paragraph 247.
56 We assume that is meant the competence of the court in first instance in any case, also when only in appeal secondary proceedings were opened.

creditors in the main proceedings.[57] The grounds for termination may be appraised at a wider context than is the case when granting a requested stay of liquidation, as the interests of the creditors in the secondary proceedings can be taken into consideration as well. As noted in the Virgós-Schmit Report: 'Consideration of the interests of the creditors in the secondary proceedings may lead by themselves to an end of the stay'.[58] The word 'appears' in Article 33(2) seems to indicate that a marginal test would be allowed only and not a full test. The latter view is supported as this will align systematically with the granting of a stay, in that a request for a stay has to be granted unless it is 'manifestly' not in the interests of the creditors in the main proceedings. Thus the grounds for anticipated termination of a stay of the process of liquidation are more general than those taken into account when granting a request for a stay, while also the group of persons which may request for an anticipated termination is wider as a stay of the process of liquidation may only be ordered at the request of the liquidator in the main proceedings.

It is submitted that the court will verify that measures required and established when granting a stay of the process of liquidation (see Article 33(1), first sentence, second passage: the court 'may require the liquidator in the main proceedings to take any suitable measure to guarantee the interests of the creditors in the secondary proceedings and of individual classes of creditors') will be terminated at the same time.

Measures Ending Secondary Insolvency Proceedings

Another possibility the liquidator of the main insolvency proceedings is given for intervening in the secondary proceedings in order to ensure the dominant role of the main insolvency proceedings is provided in Article 34.[59] Where the law applicable to secondary proceedings allows for such proceedings to be closed without liquidation by measures as for instance a rescue plan or a composition, the liquidator in the main proceedings may propose such a measure, in addition to those stipulated by that law,[60] for which see Article 34(1), first sentence. Closing of the secondary proceedings though shall in principle not become final without the consent of the liquidator in the main proceedings, for which see Article 34(1), second sentence. Pursuant to Article 34(2), any restriction of the creditor's rights arising from such a measure may not have effect in respect of the debtor's assets not covered by those proceedings without the consent of all the creditors having an interest. Finally, Article 34(3) provides that during a stay of the process of liquidation only the main liquidator is – besides the debtor, with the consent of the main liquidator – empowered to propose in secondary proceedings measures as e.g. a rescue plan or a composition.

---

57 Cf. Virgós-Schmit Report, at paragraph 247.
58 Ibid., at paragraph 247.
59 Cf. Insolvency Regulation, Recital no. 20.
60 Virgós-Schmit Report, at paragraph 248.

Proposal to Close the Secondary Proceedings without Liquidation

In Article 34(1), first sentence, an autonomous power has been conferred upon the liquidator in the main proceedings: the main liquidator may file a proposal for a rescue plan, a composition or a comparable measure. Whether a formal request has to be filed by the liquidator in the main proceedings, what specific information has to be provided, whether the liquidator in the secondary proceedings will be heard and whether the granting or rejection of the request can be appealed is not provided for by the Insolvency Regulation. These items are subject to the law applicable to the secondary proceedings assuming that the applicable law allows for such proceedings to be closed without liquidation by such a measure. For a practical application in the United Kingdom, see the order in the MG Rover case for a stipulation that in the United Kingdom the time limit for administrators to circulate proposals to creditors and to convene a meeting may be extended in each case by seven days from the day that the order was issued.[61]

In the Netherlands, a specific provision, relating to this situation, has been introduced. In Dutch insolvency proceedings the possibility of proposing a scheme for a composition is given to the debtor himself.[62] Article 172a of the Faillissementswet provides that the articles of Chapter Six, Scheme for a Composition[63] are applicable by analogy in case a scheme for a composition is proposed by the liquidator in the main proceedings as meant in Article 34(1), first sentence. Equally the articles relating to a scheme for a composition in the proceedings of postponement of payment and the debt discharge of natural persons, as they have been declared applicable by analogy.[64] In all cases the liquidator may propose such a measure himself, a solicitor (*procureur*) not being required.

Consent of the Liquidator in Main Proceedings

In the context of a rescue plan or a composition, creditors in the secondary proceedings may agree with the closure of the proceedings without winding-up liquidations taking place. In that context the creditors may accept a rescheduling of debts or waive some of their rights while at the same time the debtor may undertake to meet certain conditions.[65] As a consequence, the contents of such a measure may influence the interests, to be considered in the main proceedings. Therefore Article 34(1), second sentence, provides that 'to become final, such a measure must obtain the consent of the liquidator in the main proceedings'. According to the Virgós-Schmit Report,[66] the liquidator, in adopting his decision, may take into consideration all the interests of the creditors in the main

---

61 Order of the High Court of Justice (Chancery Division Birmingham), 13 June 2005 (*Order in MG Rover Nederland BV*).
62 Faillissementswet, Articles 138, 252 and 329.
63 Ibid., Articles 138–172.
64 Ibid., Articles 281(2) and 333a (respectively).
65 Virgós-Schmit Report, at paragraph 249.
66 Ibid., at paragraph 249.

proceedings, the interests in reorganizing and continuing the main business included. Berends has pointed at the discrepancy between the wording of Article 34(1), second sentence ('Closure of the secondary proceedings by a measure ... shall not become final without the consent of the liquidator in the main proceedings ...') and the passage in question in the Virgós-Schmit Report[67] ('... to become final, such a measure must obtain the consent of the liquidator in the main proceedings').[68] In Dutch insolvency legislation, this has led to a specific provision in case the main liquidator does not refuse explicitly and does not agree explicitly either.

In case the liquidator in the main proceedings does not agree with a rescue plan or a composition, Article 34(1), second sentence, second passage, provides that – although the agreement of the liquidator in the main proceedings is lacking – the measure 'may become final if the financial interests of the creditors in the main proceedings are not affected by the measure proposed'. The Insolvency Regulation does not provide with a standard to apply in interpreting these 'financial interests'. The Virgós-Schmit Report submits that the concept of financial interests is more restrictive than that of the interests of the creditors in the main proceedings, which may justify a stay of secondary proceedings: 'The financial interests are estimated by evaluating the effects which the rescue plan or the composition has on the dividend to be paid to the creditors in the main proceedings. If those creditors could not reasonably have expected to receive more, after the transfer of any surplus of the assets remaining in the secondary proceedings (ex Article 35), in the absence of a rescue plan or a composition, their financial interests are not thereby affected'.[69] See in this light also, the views expressed by, *inter alia*, Berends and Kolmann.[70] A further view, this time by Kemper, advocates the interpretation of the norm 'financial interests' in a narrow manner.[71] In the same vein, see the submission that 'financial interests' is a narrower concept than that of the 'interests' of the creditors in the main proceedings, used in other provisions.[72]

As is the case with a request for a stay of the process of liquidation, the closure by a measure as a rescue plan or a composition is considered by the court in weighing the ('financial') interests of the creditors in the main proceedings. Here as well the question is in which way the court will be informed with regard to these interests as the Insolvency Regulation does not provide for cross-border communication between courts in different member states. Article 34(1), second sentence, second passage, presumes the consent of the main liquidator is missing ('failing his agreement'). Therefore the information before the court will result from the request to approve the proposed measure on the one side and on the other side from the main liquidator disagreeing to the proposed measure; the court will

---

67 Virgós-Schmit Report, at paragraph 249.
68 Berends, above note 6 at 187.
69 Virgós-Schmit Report, at paragraph 249.
70 Berends, above note 6 at 187; Kolmann, above note 3 at 353.
71 See Kemper, J., 'Die Verordnung (EG) Nr. 1346/2000 über Insolvenzverfahren' *Zeitschrift für Wirtschaftsrecht (ZIP)* 2001, 1619.
72 Virgós and Garcimartin, above note 4 at paragraph 453.

be informed *ex parte* in case the main liquidator does not agree or does not disagree to the proposed measure. Thus the court's information will flow from the secondary liquidator's duty to inform the court – if and so far this duty exists – and whose information will contain also the data the secondary liquidator has learned in the context of his duty concerning cross-border communication and cooperation. Where the court is allowed to terminate of its own motion the stay of the process of liquidation, it is perhaps not too bold to suggest that the court should question the liquidator in the secondary proceedings.[73]

Supposing that the law applicable to the secondary insolvency proceedings allows for such proceedings to be closed without liquidation by a rescue plan or a composition etc., it is left to this law to provide for procedural rules in the context of Article 34(1). In this respect the Insolvency Regulation does not provide for any procedural rules.

The situation where the agreement of the main liquidator is lacking with respect to a composition is covered in the Netherlands by Article 153(2)(4°) of the Faillissementswet. It states that the court will withhold its approval to a proposed scheme of arrangement (*akkoord*), when the liquidator in proceedings as meant in Article 6(1), third sentence, of the Faillissementswet (i.e. the liquidator in main proceedings opened outside the Netherlands) withholds his agreement to this scheme, unless the court judges that the scheme of arrangement does not affect the financial interests of the creditors in the main proceedings. It should be noted that in this specific provision the Dutch word '*onthouden*' (withhold) has been used to cover the situation that the foreign main liquidator, after having had an opportunity to express his point of view, refrains form agreeing with the proposed scheme but did not communicate an explicit refusal. A similar rule has been inserted for proceedings concerning debt discharge of natural persons in Article 338(2), second sentence, of the Faillissementswet, and erroneously for the postponement of payments proceedings in Article 272(2)(5°) of the Faillissementswet, as these last proceedings are not characterised as winding-up proceedings.[74]

Restriction of Creditors' Rights

Secondary proceedings are characterised by their territoriality. The effects of those proceedings shall be restricted to the assets of the debtor situated in the territory of the member state in which they are opened. A rescue plan or another measure referred to in Article 34(1), which restricts creditor's rights, may therefore – as follows from Article 34(2) – apply to the assets covered by the secondary proceedings only and not to the debtor's assets situated outside the territorial reach of the secondary proceedings:

> A composition confined in its effects to the assets involved in the proceedings shall be arrived at under the conditions laid down by the applicable law and, where appropriate, by a majority decision of the

---

73 See also Wessels, above note 11 at paragraph 10886.
74 *Surseance van betaling* has correctly not been listed in Annex B of the Regulation.

creditors. The rights of all the creditors, including the minority creditors who disagree with the measure, would be affected as regards the assets relevant to those proceedings. A composition restricting creditor's rights may be reached in the secondary proceedings with effects on assets not covered by those proceedings, provided that it is agreed to by every creditor concerned by that measure, i.e. having an interest affected by the measure. (As stated by the Virgós-Schmit Report.)[75]

According to Berends,[76] creditors having voted against a specific measure will not be restricted in their rights with regard to assets located abroad and not covered by the secondary proceedings, as they are with regard to these assets not bound by the specific measure.

An extraterritorial effect of a measure as a rescue plan is allowed only with the consent of all the creditors having an interest, for which see Article 34(2), *in fine*. By the words 'all the creditors having an interest' is meant all creditors whose interests are affected by the proposed measure. Moss and Smith include in this group also creditors with a right in rem or holding a retention of title as well as those who have an interest 'in a prospective dividend as an unsecured creditor'.[77] Kortmann and Veder submit that an extraterritorial effect of a measure as a rescue plan etc. may include assets located in another member state as well, if and as far the creditors have consented.[78] In our opinion, this approach may rest on the interpretation of the words 'having an interest'.[79]

Proposal to Close during a Stay of the Liquidation Process

A stay of the process of liquidation as meant in Article 33 postpones the process of liquidation and can be requested by the liquidator in the main proceedings. During this period, the course of the main proceedings does not have to be disrupted by measures not agreed to by the main liquidator.[80] In Article 34(3), it is provided that during a stay of the process of liquidation which is ordered pursuant to Article 33, only the liquidator in the main proceedings or the debtor, with the former's consent, may propose measures as a rescue plan or a composition etc.; no other proposal for such a measure shall be put to the vote or approved. The reason therefore is given in the Virgós-Schmit Report:

> Efforts to bring about the reorganisation of the main business may have led to a stay. Article 34(3), prohibiting for the duration of the stay any composition not proposed by the liquidator in the main proceedings or by

---

75 Virgós-Schmit Report, at paragraph 250.
76 Berends, above note 6 at 188.
77 Moss and Smith, above note 14 and comments under Article 34.
78 See Kortmann, S. and Veder, M., 'De Europese Insolventieverordening' *Weekblad voor Privaatrecht, Notariaat en Registratie (WPNR)* 6421 (2000), 769.
79 As already stated in Wessels, above note 11 at paragraph 10668.
80 Virgós-Schmit Report, at paragraph 251.

the debtor with his agreement, enables the interests of the creditors, who brought about the stay to be taken into consideration.[81]

Conclusion

The Insolvency Regulation's concept of the European Union-wide universality of main proceedings is that, ultimately, the administration concerns one debtor with one estate and one group of creditors: the principle of unity of estate. This maxim dominates the mutual relationship between the main insolvency proceedings opened in one member state and one or more secondary proceedings opened in another member state in order to protect the local interests. In line with this maxim the Insolvency Regulation assigns the liquidator in the main insolvency proceedings with powers, for example those in Articles 31, 33 and 34, which powers may therefore be regarded as community powers. In addition, the liquidator in the main proceedings has in principle the authority to exercise all the powers conferred upon him by the *lex concursus* in other member states. These so-called domestic powers may be exercised within the limits of the Insolvency Regulation, i.e. 'as long as no other insolvency proceedings have been opened ...', for which see Article 18(1), which relates to the possibility of opening secondary insolvency proceedings pursuant to Article 3(2).

Once secondary proceedings have been opened in another member state, the liquidator in the secondary proceedings is attributed exclusive (domestic) power over the assets situated in that member state depriving the main liquidator of his domestic powers in this respect. This does not involve that the secondary proceedings are completely separated from the main proceedings and that the main liquidator has become broken-winged. On the contrary, as the main insolvency proceedings and the secondary proceedings are interdependent proceedings, the liquidator in the secondary proceedings has to fulfil his task under the dominance of the main liquidator. Coordination of the secondary proceedings and the main proceedings is essential for the effective realisation of the total assets. So Article 31(1) and (2) provides for the mutual duty to communicate any information which may be relevant to the other proceedings – within limits as to the extent of the details or national legislation – and to cooperate. Equally essential in this respect is that the main liquidator may intervene in secondary proceedings. In summary:

(i) The main liquidator shall be given by the liquidator in the secondary proceedings an early opportunity of submitting proposals on the liquidation or use of the assets in the secondary proceedings, for which see Article 31(3). This obligation regards important assets or decisions only. A rule is lacking how conflicts between the main liquidator and the secondary liquidator are to be decided; we submit that the main liquidator has *locus standi* under the applicability of the secondary proceedings;

(ii) The main liquidator may apply for realisation of assets in secondary proceedings to be suspended for a certain period: a stay of the process of

---

81 Idem.

liquidation on a request of the main liquidator, to be considered by the court in relation to the interests of the creditors in the main proceedings, for which see Article 33(1); an anticipated termination of a stay being provided by Article 33(2). As the Insolvency Regulation does not provide explicitly for cross-border information of courts in proceedings in different member states, it is up to the main liquidator to ground that a stay of the proceedings is in the interests of the creditors of the main proceedings;

(iii) The main liquidator may file himself a proposal for a rescue plan, a composition or a comparable measure in the secondary proceedings in case this is allowed under the law applicable to secondary proceedings, for which see Article 34, first sentence. When such a measure was proposed by others than the main liquidator, it needs, in order to become final, the consent of the liquidator in the main proceedings; failing his agreement, such a measure may become final if the financial interests of the creditors in the main proceedings are not affected by the measure proposed, as foreseen in Article 34(1), second sentence. Here again the court has eventually to consider the proposed measure in weighing the financial interests of the creditors in the main proceedings, while the Insolvency Regulation does not provide for cross-border communication between courts in different member states.[82] During a stay of the process of liquidation, only the main liquidator or the debtor with the former's consent may propose a rescue plan etc.[83]

The main proceedings being more or less fragmented by the opening of one or more secondary insolvency proceedings in other member states, the liquidator in the main proceedings is empowered to leave his mark upon the general course of the total insolvency-unwinding. Considering the community powers conferred upon the liquidator in the main proceedings, assigning him as a dominant player, he may well be labelled as the liquidator 'en-chef'. In this way, the Insolvency Regulation's concept of European Union-universality – the principle of unity of estate – is respected without injuring the justified protection of local interests.

---

82 It is beyond the scope of this article to further elaborate that the Insolvency Regulation also does not forbid cross-border communication between courts, see e.g. Paulus, above note 34 and comments under Article 31, at paragraph 5ff.

83 Cf. Insolvency Regulation, Article 34(3).

PART IV
FINANCE AND SECURITY ISSUES

Chapter 9

Bank Insolvency and the Problem of Non-Performing Loans

Andrew Campbell[1]

Introduction

Bank insolvency has been a significant problem in many parts of the world in the last 30 years. There have been waves of bank failures in developed, developing, and countries with transitional economies.[2] Between 1997 and 2002 banks had to be closed in more than 50 countries.[3] This chapter focuses on one particularly important aspect of the cause of bank insolvency: the relationship between non-performing loans ('NPLs') and bank failure.[4] It will consider both the prevention and control of NPLs and in so doing will examine regulatory and supervisory issues as well as initiatives for dealing with impaired assets. The need for an effective bank insolvency law is a crucial factor which is also addressed. The main aim of the chapter is to provide some guidance on a framework for developing and transitional economies, many of which are still suffering severe problems with NPLs.

The Background

The final quarter of the twentieth century witnessed a huge amount of instability in the banking markets throughout the globe with more than 160 countries

1   I would like to thank Peter Cartwright and Andrew Keay for their helpful comments on an earlier draft. I would also like to thank the anonymous referee for the extremely helpful comments and suggestions.
2   For reading on these, see FDIC, Lindgren, C-J., Garcia, G. and Seal, M., Bank Soundness and Macroeconomic Policy (1996, International Monetary Fund, Washington DC).
3   Supervisory Guidance on Dealing with Weak Banks (2002, Basel Committee on Banking Supervision, Bank for International Settlements, Basel) at 2.
4   The scale of the NPL problem in some countries has led to banking crises of such severity that large parts of the entire banking system of the country have been affected. See Lindgren, C-J., Balino, T., Enoch, C., Gulde, A-M., Quintyn, M. and Teo, L., 'Financial Sector Crisis and Restructuring Lessons from Asia', Occasional Paper No. 188 (2000, International Monetary Fund, Washington DC).

experiencing banking crises so severe as to have systemic implications.[5] These problems have not been limited to specific geographical areas nor to any particular type of economy. Developed economies, such as the United States, Sweden and Japan and developing countries, including much of Latin America and South East Asia, and transitional economies, have had significant crises relating to NPLs.[6] China, an example of an economy which has been in transition, may currently be experiencing the biggest problem of them all.[7]

To date most of what has been written on NPLs has been by bankers and economists and the literature has tended to concentrate on the problems of developing an effective method for the disposal of these bad debts rather than the provision of a regulatory and legal framework for their prevention and control.

Banks – The Public Perception versus the Reality

The public perception of banks in most developed countries tends to be that they are a safe place to deposit savings.[8] Banks are expected to be conservative in their approach to doing business, and there is the public misconception that the bank is actually looking after the money of its depositors, like a quasi-trustee. The legal reality is that the relationship of banker and depositor is that of debtor and creditor and this was held to be the English common law position by the House of Lords in *Foley v Hill*,[9] a position confirmed by Atkin LJ in *Joachimson v Swiss Bank Corporation*,[10] where he stated that 'the bank undertakes to receive money and to collect bills for its customer's account. The proceeds so received are not to be held in trust for the customer, but the bank borrows the proceeds and undertakes to repay them'. The legal position is therefore that this contractual relationship gives the bank the freedom to do what it wishes with the money on deposit, subject, of course, to the bank exercising its duty of care[11] and complying with regulatory minimum capital ratio requirements.[12] This means that with the exception of a

---

5   'Statistics from International Monetary Fund' (2004, International Monetary Fund, Washington DC). For detailed statistics relating to systemic banking crises, see Dell'Ariccia, G., Detragiache, E., and Rajan, R., 'The Real Effect of Banking Crises', Working Paper WP/05/63 (2005, International Monetary Fund, Washington DC).

6   Ibid.

7   'China's Bad Loans Outstrip Reserves' (*Financial Times*, 3 May 2006).

8   Except in those countries where bank failure and loss of savings is relatively common, as in the United States for example. All banks that are members of the Federal Deposit Insurance Corporation's deposit insurance scheme will display the fact in all their branches as customers are generally unwilling to make deposits with uninsured banks.

9   (1848) 2 HL Cas 28.

10   [1921] 3 KB 110 at 127.

11   In English law this is a common law duty. For an account of the extent of the duty, see Hapgood, M., *Paget's Law of Banking* (12th ed) (2003, Butterworths, London) at 119.

12   In each jurisdiction, banks will be required to comply with certain minimum capital requirements. While there are no internationally agreed levels, most countries now aim to comply with the capital ratios suggested by the Basel Committee on Banking

small percentage which has to be kept in cash, or in very safe form such as government securities, the bank will seek to use the deposits to maximise its profits. In the traditional model of a commercial bank this means that most of it will be used to lend to a variety of types of borrowers.

Banking is therefore a business which constantly has to face risks and deal with them. There are many potential sources of risk including liquidity risks, interest rate risk, market risk, foreign exchange risk, political risks.[13] Because of the subject matter of this chapter the discussion restricts itself to a consideration of credit risk.

Credit risk is the risk that a loan that has been granted by a bank will not be repaid, either partially or in full, when due. In some situations full payment may not be made when it is due, but will eventually be made. In some cases the bank will have to accept that its borrower will not be in a position to repay the amount due. In the worst case scenario the borrower will be bankrupt and be unable to pay any of the amount owed.

In many banking systems, sophisticated techniques are used to manage credit risk and keep it at an acceptable level. Heffernan[14] suggests that there are essentially four factors involved in the analysis of credit risk.[15] The first is in relation to pricing the loan. The classic approach is to charge a higher rate of interest where the borrower is considered to have a higher risk profile. Lower risk borrowers will generally be charged a lower rate of interest. There are two potential problems with this strategy; a higher rate of interest may put the borrower under additional financial strain and make default more likely; where the loan market is buoyant the bank may not be able to charge the rate of interest it feels would be appropriate to deal with the risk factors.[16] The second factor is to impose specific credit limits so that no single borrower[17] will be able to borrow more than a specified amount. The third factor is the use of security[18] to reduce risk. The

---

Supervision in the Basel Capital Accord. At the time of writing, this is undergoing a revision and a new Accord, generally referred to as Basel II, will come into force in the near future.

13   For an excellent discussion of the risks banks face, see Heffernan, S., *Modern Banking in Theory and Practice* (2005, Wiley, Chichester) in Chapter 5 'Management of Risks in Banking'.

14   Ibid.

15   These are also factors which could be described as being involved in the management of risk.

16   Of course, regardless of what interest rate is being applied, it cannot have the effect of protecting the bank if the borrower becomes insolvent and has to be liquidated. A higher interest rate will not have provided much extra by way of compensation should the borrower get into financial difficulties not long after the loan has been granted.

17   Care has to be taken to ensure that borrowers who are connected will not be able to circumvent these limits.

18   The term 'collateral' is used in many jurisdictions. The legal framework for the granting of security varies greatly between jurisdictions. Guarantees tend to be widely used, but in many jurisdictions in Asia, the laws on enforcement of guarantees are weak and they tend to be ineffective.

effectiveness of this as a risk reduction factor depends on the quality of security which can be provided and also on how the laws in the jurisdiction allow enforcement and whether any security survives the relevant insolvency regime.[19] The final factor for the reduction of credit risk is diversification. This is where banks should ensure that their loan portfolios are spread widely, particularly in relation to such matters as geographic spread and types of borrower. Concentrated lending has often been a problem in banking crises.[20]

Credit risk analysis can be undertaken in a variety of ways with both qualitative and quantitative factors being used and effective management of credit risk can have the effect of minimising risk but it can never totally eradicate it. Accordingly what is required is a legal framework which can ensure that credit risk factors are minimised, and this, to work well, will have to be supported by an effective system of regulation and supervision. This subject is discussed at various places throughout this chapter.

Defining a Non-Performing Loan

One of the issues which need to be addressed is to reach agreement about what is a non-performing loan. As yet there is no international agreement on this term but the Asian Development Bank is of the view that 'the accepted international standard for classification of loans as non-performing is 90 days or more overdue'.[21] This approach is also supported by the Bank of Thailand which states 'a non performing loan is a loan of which the principal and or interest has not been paid over three months from the due date specified in the contract'.[22]

In some jurisdictions a quantitative approach is taken and this would include the number of days overdue while in others the approach may be based on qualitative factors such as available information on the borrower.

The lack of a definition presents problems and it would be helpful if a common approach could be found. To use the Asian Development Bank's approach of 90 days for those countries where NPLs are still problematic may be a worthwhile starting point but attention needs to be paid to loans which are in the process of becoming impaired.

A different approach is taken in the International Financial Reporting Standards which provide that:

---

19   There is considerable divergence in approaches internationally, see, for example, the different approaches to set-off in Johnston, W. and Werlin, T. (eds), *Set-Off Law and Practice: An International Handbook* (2006, Oxford University Press, Oxford).

20   The savings and loans crisis in the United States, for example. For a detailed account of this, see Olson, G.N., *Banks in Distress: Lessons from the American Experience of the 1980s* (2000, Kluwer Law International, London).

21   Information from Asian Development Bank website at: <www.adb.org> (last viewed 31 May 2007).

22   From Bank of Thailand's website at: <www.bot.gov> (last viewed 31 May 2007).

a financial asset ... is impaired and impairment losses are incurred if, and only if, there is objective evidence of impairment as a result of one or more events that occurred after the initial recognition of the asset (a 'loss event') and that loss event (or events) has an impact on the estimated future cash flows of the financial asset ... that can be reliably estimated.[23]

This highlights the nature of the problem. Having a 90-day limit is a useful tool but an approach is needed which ensures that developing problems are being continuously monitored. This is a topic which will be returned to later in this chapter.

The Connection between Non-Performing Loans and Bank Failure

Studies into the causes of bank failure indicate that poor asset quality is the major contributing factor in many cases. In particular, problems with the banks' loan portfolios have been very significant in all the banking crises in recent years.[24] Problems with bank lending can range from excessive specialisation (the concentration of loans to one sector of the economy, a geographical region or to a certain concentrated group of borrowers) to poor risk selection. A major study by the Bank of England found that in a study of 22 failed banks poor lending was a significant contributing factor in 16 of the cases.[25] An examination of some well known recent bank failures provides significant evidence that poor lending can quickly lead to major problems. In the United States the collapse of Continental Illinois in 1984[26] provides an illustration of the problems of NPLs. Despite appearing to be a well capitalised bank which was in compliance with regulatory requirements it collapsed quite suddenly when the full extent of its bad loans became known. It had also failed to make sufficient provision against bad debts. Its NPLs had reached 7.7 per cent of its total loan portfolio.[27] In the United Kingdom in the same year Johnson Matthey Bankers was found to have a total amount of

---

23 International Accounting Standard 39 'Financial Instruments: recognition and measurement'. The International Accounting Standards Committee and the International Organisation of Securities Commissions agreed on the need for the production of a set of international accounting standards which would become the minimum standards of international best practice. These were published in 1998 and the Basel Committee on Banking Supervision, at the request of the G7 undertook a review of the standards insofar as they apply to banks. The Report to the G7 Finance Ministers and Central Bank Governors on International Accounting Standards was published in April 2000 and is available at: <www.bis.org/publ/bcbc70.htm> (last viewed 31 May 2007). See particularly the comments on IAS 39.

24 Olson, above note 20; Lou, J., *China's Troubled Bank Loans: Workout and Prevention* (2001, Kluwer Law International, London).

25 See Jackson, P., *Deposit Protection and Bank Failures in the United Kingdom* (1996, Bank of England, London).

26 At the time of its collapse, it was the seventh largest bank in the United States.

27 See the case study in Heffernan, above note 13 at 273.

NPLs which exceeded the entire capital base of the bank.[28] In fact its bad loans amounted to approximately 50 per cent of its total loan portfolio.

Other examples in the recent past include Canadian Commercial Bank in Canada, Banco Español de Credito in Spain and Crédit Lyonnais in France (on more than one occasion). Since these examples banking crises involving impaired loans have occurred internationally, most recently in Turkey and the Philippines.

A study by Beattie et al. concluded that 'bad debts are by far the most common cause of bank failures'.[29] These two studies highlight clearly the relationship between insolvent banks and a failure both to recognise developing loan portfolio problems and to make adequate provision for potential bad debts.

In some jurisdictions, the United States in the 1980s being a notable example,[30] the problems associated with non-performing loans in the 1980s were the result of mismanagement in relation to lending policies which led to an excessively high risk profile developing. This was also the case with Johnson Matthey Bankers, Canadian Commercial Bank, Banco Español de Credito and Crédit Lyonnais. There has been no suggestion of adverse political interference in the United States but this has certainly not been the case in many of the countries that have experienced severe problems in the banking systems because of non-performing loans. Political interference has been especially present in relation to lending to state owned enterprises in some transitional economies.

Addressing the Problem

To address the problem three distinct aspects will be considered. First, how can NPLs be prevented, or at least kept to manageable levels? Second, where there are existing NPLs how can these be dealt with? Third, how should we treat banks that are insolvent as a result of NPLs?

According to the Financial Stability Institute, addressing the problems of non-performing loans NPLs is a continuing challenge. Andrew Crockett argues:

> Initially NPLs may not seem to have serious negative effects. Banks remain liquid, and depositors retain their confidence in the system. Over time, however, the size of the problem grows, especially if banks are allowed to accrue interest on their NPLs. Eventually, the efficiency of the banking system is comprehensively undermined as the task of making new loans to productive enterprise takes second place to juggling a portfolio of bad loans whose collectability is very low. The fiscal cost of

---

28   Ibid.
29   See Beattie, V., Casson, P., Dale, R., McKenzie, G., Sutcliffe, C. and Turner, M., *Banks and Bad Debts: Accounting for Losses in International Banking* (1995, Wiley, Chichester) at 1; Lou, above note 24.
30   'History of the Eighties: Lessons for the Future Vols I and II' (1997, Federal Deposit Insurance Corporation, Washington DC) provides a detailed account and examination of the crisis in the United States.

cleaning up the banking system can become so large as to be itself an obstacle to needed action.[31]

Crockett's observation that at first the problem does not necessarily appear very serious because the banks may still appear to be liquid and profitable has often been a crucial factor. Where NPLs are not being recognised as such and interest is continuing to accrue as normal, all parties may feel that all is well. However, if a borrower has been unable to meet loan payments as and when due and if the loan payments are in arrears for 90 days or more there are clear warning signs that both the capital value of the loan and any accrued interest may not be recoverable.

In some countries banks have been allowed to roll up interest on some loans for many years, thereby giving the impression that these loans are profitable, when, in fact, they are just a growing problem. The accruing interest has the effect of magnifying the problem. It may seem surprising that such a situation would be allowed to develop. However there may, in the absence of an effective regulatory framework, be incentives for the management of weak banks to 'turn a blind eye' to a growing NPL problem. According to Tanaka and Hoggarth, in situations where there is no regulatory intervention the management may take a gamble on the small chance that these loans may be recoverable. This practice is known as a 'gamble for resurrection'.[32] The incentive to hide NPLs, coupled with the opportunity to be able to do so because of weak regulation, creates a dangerous situation where losses can increase to an unacceptable level without actually being recognised as such. In many of the countries which been severely affected this has been a major problem.

Stage One – Prevention and Control

Stage one of the safety net is about prevention and control. Even the best run bank in a well supervised jurisdiction will experience occasional problems with NPLs, so it has to be recognised that the aim of the supervisor is to ensure that adequate policies are in place at banks to minimise risks as far as possible, and to ensure that troubled borrowers are subject to appropriate scrutiny and action.

Banking regulation is a subject about which much has been written and in this section the focus is only on highlighting some of the significant issues which this chapter is addressing.[33] Banks, wherever located, will be subject to a regime of

---

31   'Strengthening the Banking System in China: Issues and Experience', Bank for International Settlements Policy Paper No. 7 (1999, Bank for International Settlements, Basel) at 337. At the time, Crockett was General Manager of the Bank for International Settlements.

32   See Tanaka, M. and Hoggarth, G., 'Resolving Banking Crises – An Analysis of Policy Options', Bank of England Working Paper 293 (2006, Bank of England, London) at 4.

33   For further reading, see Asser, T., 'Legal Aspects of Regulatory Treatment of Banks in Distress' (2001, International Monetary Fund, Washington DC); Cranston, R.,

regulation and supervision. The motivation for the introduction of banking supervision in the United States was the international banking crisis of the 1930s and, as noted by Hupkes,[34] the areas of responsibility of bank supervisors have been expanding ever since, but often as a reaction to crises rather than as planned actions taken beforehand. This is perhaps inevitable, at least to some extent, but the work of the Basel Committee on Banking Supervision has been extremely influential in strengthening banking supervision in many countries. Indeed many jurisdictions have in the recent past introduced new laws for the regulation of banks based on the minimum standards of international best practice as developed by the Basel Committee. The Committee's work is examined below in the section on international efforts.

Banking supervisors, to be effective, must have adequate legal powers to undertake their task. Such powers will include a licensing system, and the supervisor will require a range of tools for corrective action including the ultimate weapon, the power to withdraw the banking licence and close down banks. Ideally corrective action should be taken as soon as problems have been identified to ensure that matters can be corrected and brought under control. In relation to NPLs, the supervisor must have power to require that internal control systems are in place and are being adhered to and this will include the right to be provided with such information as is required, plus ideally the power to conduct on-site examinations.

In addition to having a system of prudential regulation and supervision, there is a need for a provider of emergency liquidity financing[35] to banks that are experiencing liquidity problems. This will normally be done by the central bank provided that the requesting bank can meet certain conditions. Such lending by the central bank should, at least in theory, be made only to banks which are illiquid but solvent and that its use should be discretionary to prevent an increase in moral hazard[36] in the financial system. The central bank should charge a penalty rate of

---

Principles of Banking Law (2nd ed) (2005, Oxford University Press, Oxford); Campbell, A. and Cartwright, P., *Banks in Crisis: the Legal Response* (2002, Ashgate, Aldershot).

34 See Hupkes, E., 'Insolvency: Why a Special Regime for Banks?', in *Current Developments in Monetary and Financial Law* (Volume 3) (2005, International Monetary Fund, Washington DC) at 471–472.

35 Often referred to as the 'lender of last resort'.

36 Moral hazard is a term which originated in the insurance markets. It relates to the effect of insurance on the behaviour of the insured. To ensure there is no increase in moral hazard where a central bank is the lender of last resort there is a need for constructive ambiguity, that is, there must be some doubt as to whether assistance will be provided by the central bank. Moral hazard may increase and market discipline decrease if there is a guarantee in advance that any bank which finds itself in financial difficulties would automatically receive financial assistance from the central bank. According to the G-10, 'any precommitment to a particular course of action in support of a financial institution should be avoided by the authorities, who should retain discretion as to whether, when and under what conditions support would be provided. In addition, when making such a decision, it is important to analyse rigorously

interest and expect to be provided with collateral. In practice the use of emergency liquidity financing greatly assists the banking sector to keep functioning but where a bank is experiencing serious NPL problems the use of a temporary source of financing is unlikely to be enough to deal with its problems.[37]

Stage Two – Managing Impaired Assets

The management of impaired assets is both a complicated and important aspect of the bank insolvency process, especially where the problem is systemic. Effective management of these assets may create far greater value over the longer term than would be achieved by an immediate sell off, but of course, poor management could have the opposite effect. Indeed in many systemic banking crises in recent years it is not an exaggeration to say that the amount and scale of impaired assets, and especially NPLs, has meant that liquidators have been unable to deal with them effectively.[38]

Because of the nature of NPLs, the normal liquidation approach under the corporate insolvency laws of the country concerned will often be insufficient to provide an effective collection and disposal mechanism. This is because it will usually be a complex, time consuming and resource intensive process, to collect what is owed from these borrowers and the immediate disposal of impaired loans will often not be possible due to a lack of potential purchasers.

In relation to some loans, the liquidator will be able to determine that they are irrecoverable and that they should immediately be written off. Where there is no realistic chance that a loan will be recoverable, or if the potential amount recoverable would not justify the expense and effort involved in its collection, the best course of action to take is to write it off and show it as having a zero value. In many cases, however, the problem that will be faced by the liquidator is how to deal with those loans which, although impaired, do still have some value, either current or potential.

---

whether there is a systemic threat and, if so, what options there may be for dealing with systemic contagion effects in ways that limit the adverse impact on market discipline' (from 'Real-Time Gross Settlement Systems' (1997, Bank for International Settlements, Basel)).

37   In practice the classical or theoretical approach, is frequently not followed. For further reading on this topic see, for example, Campbell, A., 'Emergency Liquidity Financing for Banks in Distress: a Legal Framework for Developing Countries' [2006] *Lloyd's Maritime and Commercial Law Quarterly* 96; Delston, R. and Campbell, A., 'Emergency Liquidity Financing by Central Banks: Systemic Protection or Bank Bailout?', in *Current Developments in Monetary and Financial Law* (Volume 3) (2005, International Monetary Fund, Washington DC) and Lastra, R., 'Lender of Last Resort: an International Perspective' (1999) 48 *International and Comparative Law Quarterly* 340.

38   For an indication of the scale of the problem, see the figures provided by PricewaterhouseCoopers in NPL Asia (2006) Issue 7 (2006, PricewaterhouseCoopers, London).

To attempt an immediate sell-off of loans will generally be problematic for the following reasons. First, it may be very difficult to accurately assess their value and second there may not be a market for the purchase of distressed debt. Indeed, in most developing or transitional economies such a market is not likely to exist.

So where it is not possible for a liquidator to sell the NPLs, a way has to be found to transfer these 'bad' assets so that the balance sheet of the insolvent bank is healthier and therefore making the bank a more likely target for a prospective purchaser.[39] The removal of such 'bad' assets will give greater transparency to the process and any buyer can see exactly what they are taking on.[40]

Depending on the overall strength of the economy and the availability or otherwise of a market for the sale of impaired loans, an immediate attempt to sell the NPLs may not, in any event, be the most productive approach to take. Where there has been a systemic crisis and the banking system has been weakened, there is likely to be shortage of liquidity within the system which will inevitably manifest itself in a shortage of potential purchasers. Also, where the lending problems are the result of an adverse economic shock,[41] it is likely that those borrowers who are in default may recover sufficiently to be in a position to repay some or all of their outstanding commitments at a future date. While this will generally take some time to achieve it will result in a better financial solution.

If there is not to be an immediate sell-off, thought must be given as to how to manage the impaired assets of the bank before they can eventually be disposed of. Where the insolvent organisation is a bank there will inevitably be a large loan portfolio which needs to be managed unless it is possible for the liquidator to find another bank that would be willing to buy all the loans. This, in most cases, is highly unlikely.

The major method for dealing with NPLs that has developed in the last twenty years is for the public authorities to create an institution, or institutions, to be responsible for dealing with the NPLs of all of the insolvent banks. These are generally referred to as asset management companies ('AMCs') and these have been described as:

> A special purpose company set up by a government, a bank, or by private investors to acquire loans and other assets, a majority of which are usually impaired, for subsequent management (including restructuring) and in many cases, sale to investors.[42]

---

39   This is discussed further below in the section on restructuring.
40   The term 'good bank – bad bank' was used to illustrate that what was being done was the transfer of the bad assets from a troubled bank leaving behind a 'good bank' with clean assets only – this is discussed further in the section on bank insolvency laws and procedures. When used in the United States in the 1980s and in the Nordic countries the purpose was generally to make these banks more attractive to potential bidders.
41   This may be caused, for example, by the failure of a particular industry or a harvest failure in an agricultural economy.
42   'Supervisory Guidance on Dealing with Weak Banks' (2002, Bank for International Settlements, Basel) at 53.

In most cases the AMC will be a state owned organisation, which will need to have the legal powers necessary to be able to manage the NPLs and eventually to dispose of them.

The establishment of an AMC to buy the NPLs from the individual banks is the approach which has become the most widely used and accepted method internationally and it has now been used in many countries where there has been a systemic banking crisis involving a significant section of the banking sector. A systemic banking crisis would justify the costs involved in establishing one or more AMCs whereas isolated problems at individual banks would generally not.[43]

A question that is often asked is whether the use of AMCs to deal with the problem of NPLs is actually an efficient solution to the problem. What follows here is a consideration of the benefits and drawbacks.

An initial benefit of this approach is the possibility of being able to offer a 'clean' bank for sale and this is considered further in the section on bank insolvency. The increase in transparency coupled with less risk should, as mentioned above, make the bank more marketable to potential buyers. Second, an AMC will be a specialised vehicle which exists solely for the maintenance and disposal of the loan portfolio. It should therefore be in a position to develop specialist expertise in doing this.[44] A liquidator would not be expected to have such expertise either. As the sole purpose of the AMC is to look after NPLs it should not be distracted from its purpose. In theory at least the staff of the AMC should develop expertise and efficiency and have an increased chance of maximising value.

Third, as Lou points out,[45] by removing NPLs, the bank, if it still operating, can concentrate on its sound business without the diversions caused by looking after a portfolio of NPLs.

On the negative side, the use of AMCs in many jurisdictions has often been ineffective. They have often been poorly resourced, overly bureaucratic and lacking in the necessary legal powers to effectively pursue loan defaulters. Where the lack of an effective set of legal enforcement powers exists, this can provide an incentive to borrowers to continue to avoid making repayments in the knowledge that there is little likelihood that enforcement action will be taken against them. A further criticism is that they may be faced with political interference, especially when the defaulting borrowers are state owned enterprises. A final point is that it will often be the case that the AMC is staffed with public officials rather than loan enforcement experts and there may be a lack of incentive to maximise recoveries.

AMCs have proved to be very costly to maintain and this has had negative effects on total value recovered even where the AMC has been otherwise effective. Dong He has conducted a study of the South Korean AMC, which is referred to as

---

43   The failure of a single large bank may, however, justify establishing an AMC.
44   It may be the case that a bank which has had to have its NPLs transferred to an AMC has demonstrated that it did not possess such expertise.
45   Lou, above note 24 at 100–110.

KAMCO,[46] in which he makes a number of very relevant observations. In particular he argues that the development of a market for distressed debts was a critical factor in the successful disposal of NPLs by KAMCO and also that it was able to develop and adapt a number of techniques for loan disposals, which will assist in providing direction to AMCs in other jurisdictions. The difficulties in deciding between a quick recovery via an early disposal and the possible maximisation of value by managing and waiting are also highlighted and it is only with experience that this can be judged. Despite the relative success of KAMCO in disposing of NPLs the paper concludes that its operations were expensive.

The country which is currently giving most cause for concern in relation to its huge NPL problem is China. As a result of this growing problem the Chinese authorities established four AMCs in 1999 which are State owned, non-banking financial institutions. Each AMC is given responsibility for a group of individual banks in contrast to the approach taken generally where an AMC will have responsibility for all distressed loans in the banking system.[47] The Chinese approach has been subject to much criticism both for providing a public subsidy for state owned commercial banks[48] and for being 'vulnerable to state interference'.[49] At this stage it is far too early to attempt to analyse the level of effectiveness of China's AMC policy.[50]

Stage Three – The Treatment of Insolvent Banks

It is generally the case that banks are considered to have certain special features which justify the use of a bank insolvency framework that will in a number of respects be different to that which applies to non-bank corporations under general corporate insolvency law[51]. Most developing countries and those in transition have, in recent years, been introducing bank insolvency laws, either on their own or as part of their general banking laws.[52]

---

46   See He, D., 'The Role of KAMCO in Resolving Non-Performing Loans in the Republic of Korea', International Monetary Fund Working Paper WP/04/172 (2004, International Monetary Fund, Washington DC).

47   In the United States (the Resolution Trust Company), South Korea and Malaysia, the AMCs were for the entire banking system.

48   See Hsu, B., Arner, D., Wan, Q. and Wang, W., 'Banking Liberalization and Restructuring in Post-WTO China' (2005) 20(1) *Banking and Finance Law Review* 55.

49   Lou, above note 24 at 99.

50   Figures from PricewaterhouseCoopers (above note 38) show that out of USD 170 billion acquired by the AMCs in 1999 approximately USD 105 billion had been sold for USD 22 billion.

51   The United Kingdom is an example of a country with no special insolvency laws for banks; Campbell and Cartwright, above note 33.

52   This is often done as a result of technical assistance programmes provided by the World Bank, International Monetary Fund, Asian Development Bank and the European Bank for Reconstruction and Development.

Why are banks considered in need of special treatment when it comes to insolvency? There are several reasons which are thought to justify this different treatment. First, the health of the banking system is invariably of vital importance to the economy of the country and, in particular, to the payments system. Another significant factor is that financial problems at one bank may lead to problems at other banks and precipitate a systemic banking crisis with runs by depositors spreading from bank to bank. In the last 25 years there have been many examples of systemic banking crises and one significant factor is the speed with which they can develop and spread. This leads to many otherwise healthy banks being caught up in the crisis. How is it that a crisis can spread in this way? This has to do with the basic nature of the business of banking. As was seen earlier in the typical banking model, a bank borrows money, primarily from its depositors, and then lends most of this to a variety of borrowers. The bank will keep a relatively small percentage of its assets in cash or near cash assets.

Borrowing and lending in this way leads to the inevitable problem of maturity transformation,[53] as depositors will normally be legally entitled to repayment of their deposits on demand.[54] For many banks deposits will form the largest class of liabilities on the balance sheet and as they can be subject to immediate claims for repayment they are extremely liquid. The contrast with the asset position is quite significant as the major asset class of most commercial and savings banks will be their loan portfolios. Loans, from the legal perspective, may be either repayable on demand[55] or repayable at a fixed future date with interest, and perhaps, capital repayments being made throughout the lifetime of the loan. In the case of banks which lend on commercial or residential property this may be for a very long period. Residential mortgages in most countries are now often made for a period of 25 years or more.

The loan portfolios of banks tend to be relatively illiquid even when economic conditions are strong and lending policies are robust. In those situations where the bank has a legal entitlement to make a demand for immediate payment, it would be unusual for a borrower to be in a position to repay the entire amount of the loan, both capital and interest, with immediate effect. Accordingly, even a well managed bank with a strong balance sheet can find itself subject to liquidity problems should demands from depositors exceed normal expectations over a period of time. As a result of this, most developed banking systems have in place a liquidity funding mechanism to assist in the normal day-to-day operations of the interbank market and, as has already been seen, in most countries the central bank will also be able to provide emergency liquidity financing in appropriate

---

53   This term is used to describe the mismatch between borrowers and depositors. The phrase 'borrow short and lend long' is often used to describe this position.

54   In some cases this may be subject to a period of notice which has been contractually agreed at the outset.

55   This is typically the case in many jurisdictions unless there is a specific agreement to the contrary. See *Rouse v Bradford Banking Co* [1894] AC 586 and *Cripps & Son v Wickenden* [1973] 1 WLR 944.

situations.[56] If the bank's problem is simply one of liquidity rather than insolvency, the bank can usually be restored to regulatory compliance in a short time. However, a liquidity problem may, and often does, indicate more serious problems which should be investigated immediately by the bank supervisor.[57] The situation, where there is some doubt as to the quality of some of the bank's loan portfolio, will be a matter which has to be taken into consideration when deciding what action is to be taken by the supervisor.

In relation to an insolvent bank, another feature which distinguishes its insolvency from other types of corporations is that the banking supervisor and the central bank will inevitably be involved from the beginning of the process, either to quickly close down the bank or, alternatively, to assist in seeking to attempt to promote an outcome which is least damaging in the circumstances.[58] Where a bank is discovered to be insolvent,[59] the banking supervisor will have to assess very quickly what action should be taken and in doing so certain matters will have to be taken into account. These include the systemic importance of the bank, the impact on depositors and the deposit insurance fund and whether it would be possible to minimise the impact of the insolvency by using techniques which may allow for the sale of all or at least part of the bank.

On a discovery of insolvency, rather than illiquidity, the banking supervisor should have power to immediately appoint a conservator to take control of the bank while the various possibilities are considered.[60] In some countries this can be done as an administrative act whereas in others it will require a judicial decision.[61]

---

56   Above note 37.

57   This will often not be done however, usually because of limited resources available to the supervisor.

58   In most jurisdictions the bank regulator will be given legal power to commence insolvency proceedings and will also have power to withdraw the banking licence.

59   There are two tests for insolvency; the balance sheet test and the cash-flow test. For banks there is a third one. This is what is referred to as 'regulatory insolvency'. This refers to the situation where a bank has insufficient capital to meet its capital requirements but is still solvent on a balance sheet and cash-flow basis. In this type of situation, a supervisor may exercise forbearance and keep the bank under close scrutiny as it attempts to nurse itself back to full compliance.

60   In some countries, the United States for example, the relevant regulator has the right to do this on an out of court basis. In some countries this can only be done by court order. The term conservator is being used here but internationally there is a lack of consistency and various terms are used e.g. receiver, administrator or official manager.

61   There has been considerable debate as to whether it is better to use an administrative or a judicial procedure. As yet there is no consensus on the subject. Switzerland has recently introduced an administrative procedure and Singapore is, at the time of writing, having a consultation process on a banking bill which contains an administratively based bank insolvency law. In the view of this writer what is important is that the law allows for an expedient resolution procedure rather than whether it is administrative or judicial in nature. An administrative procedure has the advantage of speed which may not be available in some jurisdictions where a court based procedure must be used and where the judiciary may not be terribly cooperative. However, court based procedures can be effective as was shown in the Barings Bank

This will lead to either an immediate liquidation of the bank or some form of restructuring. Regardless of which process is used one of the factors which the conservator and bank regulator will want to consider is the need for the matter to be resolved without delay to ensure that any disruption to the rest of the financial system is limited.

Since the massive banking failures in the United States in the 1930s a number of resolution techniques have been developed by the Federal Deposit Insurance Corporation ('FDIC'),[62] which, although responsible for paying compensation to insured depositors, also acts as receiver on virtually all bank insolvencies in the United States.[63] Since then the FDIC has been responsible for the creation of a number of strategies for dealing with insolvent banks. Two resolution techniques in particular have been developed which are likely to be of use for an insolvent bank with a problematic loan portfolio and these will be focused on here. Of course, where it proves impossible to successfully restructure the insolvent bank, or where there remains a part of the bank which is hopelessly insolvent, there will have to be a liquidation.

Assuming that the management of the insolvent bank is unable to put together a restructuring plan on its own,[64] it will become necessary for the bank supervisor, in conjunction with the conservator, to consider either the possibility of promoting an attempt at a merger or acquisition or, alternatively, a purchase and assumption transaction. These alternatives to liquidation will only be available where the law actually permits such creative techniques to be used and it remains the case that in many jurisdictions, and especially in developing countries, no alternatives to a liquidation procedure will exist. Where the law does not provide for any alternatives, this may often lead to an unnecessary liquidation with the result that the entire process is economically inefficient.[65] It is also possible that, where there are no alternatives to liquidation, the banking supervisor may resist closing the bank for as long as possible in the hope that the bank, maybe with an

---

crisis in London where Vice-Chancellor Scott was willing to hear the petition for an administration order during a weekend to ensure that the matter could be resolved before the markets opened on the Monday morning. For an account of this, see 'The Administration of Barings: Future History' (1995, Ernst & Young, London).

62   For a detailed account of the FDIC and the strategies referred to above see Pesak, F.K., 'Federal Deposit Insurance Corporation: the First Fifty Years' (1984, FDIC, Washington DC) and the FDIC's 'History of the Eighties: Lessons for the Future' (Volumes 1 and 2) (1997, FDIC, Washington DC).

63   A notable feature of bank insolvency in the United States is that it is a purely administrative process with no initial court involvement and with the deposit insurance agency acting as the receiver. The deposit insurer will, in addition to being the receiver, also inevitably be a major creditor and this produces a situation which would not be acceptable in many jurisdictions.

64   In some cases, it may be possible for the insolvent bank to organise a restructuring but in practice this is quite rare. As the banking supervisor will have removed control from the bank's management it is more likely that outside parties will be involved.

65   The liquidation procedures will often be conducted in a lengthy and inefficient manner.

injection of public funds, will be able to return to a position of compliance. It is arguably much better to have a bank insolvency law which allows for possible alternatives to outright liquidation of non-compliant banks.

The possibility that a healthy bank would consider merging with or acquiring an insolvent bank is one which is worth exploring,[66] although where the insolvent bank has a significant amount of unquantifiable NPLs it will probably be very difficult to find another bank which would be willing to take on such a commitment.[67]

One significant advantage of a merger or acquisition, where this is a possibility, is that it will be a private sector transaction without the need for an injection of public money. Too often in bank insolvencies in many jurisdictions there has been an immediate and automatic call for an injection of public funds and often this has been made available without giving thought to the effect of this on market discipline.[68] There is arguably a need for a change of attitudes in many countries to promote private sector solutions as far as possible with public funds being used only in the most exceptional of circumstances, such as where there is an unacceptable level of systemic risk in the banking system.

In many developing countries the acquiring body will often have to be a foreign bank as there will be no domestic banks with sufficient financial strength to be able to consider a merger or acquisition. The opportunity to be able to move into a new market will often be the feature which makes the transaction attractive to the potential acquirer but the entry of foreign banks raises both policy and regulatory issues.[69]

A major advantage of using this approach is that, from the legal perspective on a merger or acquisition, the insolvent bank ceases to exist as a legal entity and there is therefore no need for a liquidation process. This saves both time and money. Other significant advantages include that depositors will be fully protected,[70] there will be no drain on the deposit insurance fund and depositor confidence will be maintained.

As all of the insolvent bank will have been transferred to the acquirer, the NPL problem will not need any form of public resolution. It is, of course, vitally important that the banking supervisor has assessed the financial position of the acquiring bank to ensure that it will still be solvent and fully compliant after the transaction has been completed. It may be necessary for the supervisor to show a

---

66   The ING acquisition of Barings in 1995 is an example of this.

67   Although in some cases, as in Barings Bank, the name and reputation were thought to be worth acquiring. It may also give a bank an opportunity to move into a new market. It may also be the case that a foreign bank could use this as a method of gaining entry to a new market.

68   In some jurisdictions, particularly in parts of Asia and transitional economies, the automatic response to an insolvent bank is still to use public funds to nationalise it.

69   This raises supervisory and licensing issues but these are not being considered here.

70   Depositors will have their deposits transferred to the acquiring bank and while this may cause a degree of inconvenience in some cases it is far less disruptive than where each individual depositor has to submit a claim to a deposit insurance agency.

degree of forbearance in this situation but great care will have to be taken to monitor the position. The final advantage of a merger or acquisition is that it minimises market disruption and where it can be achieved it is generally thought to provide the optimum outcome.

However, more often than not, it will not be possible to find a willing party for a merger or acquisition. As a result of this, a technique has been developed which has become widely used in banking crises. It was originally developed by the FDIC in the United States but variations on the theme have also been designed elsewhere. This is what has become known as a 'purchase and assumption' transaction. It has often been possible to structure a purchase and assumption transaction where an attempt at a merger or acquisition has already failed. In a purchase and assumption transaction the financially healthy bank will buy some of the assets and some, or all,[71] of the liabilities of the insolvent bank subject normally to the impaired assets being excluded from the sale.[72] As Hupkes notes,[73] it is the assumption of all the potential liabilities of the bank that is often a major deterrent to a potential acquirer and the major reason to avoid a merger and acquisition. From the legal perspective, a purchase and assumption transaction differs from a merger and acquisition in that in the former what is being transferred are assets and liabilities while in the latter the corporate body and licence are being acquired.

A purchase and assumption transaction which involves an assumption of the entire business, including all of the liabilities, is a possibility but generally it would be preferable for an acquirer to opt for ownership of the bank rather than its business which will, of course, be insolvent. The development of the purchase and assumption transaction was an attempt to remove this potential barrier. The purchase and assumption transaction is particularly relevant where the insolvent bank has a problem with non-performing loans. An acquirer may be willing to purchase the healthy parts of the business but will not wish to take on a large amount of impaired assets, especially where the extent of the problem may not be possible to assess with any accuracy in the time available.

Because it is recognised that keeping the good parts of the business going will be more economically efficient than a straightforward liquidation of the insolvent bank, there will normally be an attempt by the regulator to encourage another bank, or banks, to consider acquiring an insolvent bank on a purchase and assumption basis. Of course, the regulator will have no power to force other banks to do this and such an attempt will often be unsuccessful.

To encourage another bank to acquire the insolvent bank, it will be necessary, and will have to be allowable under the law of the country, to take whatever action is needed to make the transaction attractive to the acquirer. As

---

71   But this would be unusual. See later discussion.

72   In some cases the impaired assets are purchased subject to some sort of guarantee as to the maximum liability.

73   See Hupkes, E., *The Legal Aspects of Bank Insolvency: A Comparative Analysis of Western Europe, the United States and Canada* (2000, Kluwer Law International, London) at 89.

noted above, the central bank or regulator will not normally be empowered to force one bank to acquire another so the law needs to provide the power to separate the bad assets from the good. Where the bad assets are removed, this is generally referred to as a 'clean bank' purchase and assumption transaction. This approach has proved to be particularly useful where the insolvent bank has a portfolio of NPLs. It will be a time consuming task to accurately assess the exact state of the loan portfolio and, as time will inevitably be of the essence, it may be simpler and more effective for the entire loan portfolio to be left behind for subsequent transfer to an AMC. It is particularly important that all aspects of the purchase and assumption transaction are dealt with quickly to minimise disruption of business which will, amongst other things, assist in the maintenance of the value of the business.

Another possibility is to structure a purchase and assumption transaction in a way which allows the acquirer to take on bad assets on the basis that there is a guaranteed maximum cap on the amount of liabilities that are being acquired.[74] One advantage of this approach is that it does not leave impaired assets which have to be managed by a receiver or transferred to an AMC.

In the purchase and assumption transaction scenario, what is left of the insolvent bank will be liquidated with the effect that in virtually all cases the shareholders of the insolvent bank will receive nothing. In addition, the management no longer have a bank to manage, although in some situations the acquiring bank may decide to retain the services of some of the senior executives, but this would be subject to any restrictions that may be placed on them by the banking regulator.[75]

It is only where it is not possible to find a suitable acquirer that an immediate liquidation process will be used. In most respects the liquidation of a bank is undertaken in exactly the same way as the liquidation of any other corporate entity. However, the situation may be different where there exists a deposit insurance scheme or, alternatively, where some degree of legal priority is given to bank depositors.[76] Deposit insurance is becoming more common internationally and in the recent past a number of countries have introduced schemes.[77]

In those countries where depositors are provided with a guaranteed degree of protection by way of a deposit insurance scheme, the deposit insurer will be

---

74   This is what happened in the Barings Bank failure in the United Kingdom.

75   For example, do they still meet the 'fit and proper' and other requirements?

76   The United States and Switzerland are examples of jurisdictions where depositors are given priority in an insolvency and where in either country the deposit insurance fund makes payments to depositors their claims are subrogated to the deposit insurer. According to the International Association of Deposit Insurers there are now approximately 95 countries with formal explicit deposit insurance schemes including all the Member States of the European Union. Figures from the International association of Deposit Insurers, Basel.

77   The United States introduced deposit insurance in the Banking Act 1933. All members of the European Union have introduced deposit insurance as a result of Directive 94/19/EC of 30 May 1994. Many other jurisdictions have also introduced schemes.

legally obliged to compensate the depositors in accordance with the scheme. It will then have a subrogated claim in the liquidation proceedings. Where the amount of coverage provides 100 per cent cover up to a generous level, this will have the effect of removing 1000s of potentially relatively small claims from the liquidation process and can therefore speed up the proceedings thereby keeping costs to a lower level than would have been the case if each claim had to be dealt with individually.[78]

In some jurisdictions, depositors are given priority on the liquidation of the bank so that even where there is no deposit insurance scheme depositors will at least be able to jump the queue in some respect. In the United States, the deposit insurer, the Federal Deposit Insurance Corporation, also enjoys the same level of priority in respect of any subrogated claim that it has.[79] However, in most countries depositors are not given any special priority on the liquidation of a bank and are simply treated as unsecured creditors. Without deposit insurance they will suffer losses which may be as much as the total of their deposits.

International Efforts

The most significant work to promote international best practice for the regulation and supervision of banks has been undertaken by the Basel Committee on Banking Supervision,[80] which in 1997 produced the Core Principles for Effective Banking Supervision.[81] The Basel Core Principles provide a framework for setting minimum standards for effective supervision and although voluntary have developed into what is generally regarded as international best practice. The Core Principles have been described as 'soft law par excellence' by Cranston.[82] They provide a minimum set of standards and do not prescribe any particular legal

---

78   In the United States depositors at each insured bank are fully protected up to $100,000. Anyone with more than this amount will normally have accounts at more than one bank to ensure full coverage. This means that on a bank failure in the United States the depositors will be largely removed from the insolvency proceedings.

79   Federal Deposit Insurance Act 1950 (12 USC 1821(d)(11)(ii)) provides that depositors, including subrogated claims, will rank after the administrative expenses of the receiver and ahead of all other creditors.

80   This was established by the Central Banks of the G10 countries in 1975. At present it comprises senior representatives of central banks and banking regulators from Belgium, Canada, France, Germany, Italy, Japan, Luxembourg, the Netherlands, Spain, Sweden, Switzerland, the United Kingdom and the United States. The committee is based in Basel in Switzerland at the Headquarters of the Bank for International Settlements. Its website address is: www.bis.org/bcbs> (last viewed 31 May 2007).

81   Generally referred to as the Basel Core Principles. At the time of writing the Basel Committee had issued a consultative document reviewing the Core Principles. It is likely that any changes which result from the consultation process will aim to strengthen the risk reduction function.

82   See Cranston, above note 33 at 64.

framework. Accordingly countries are free to choose to implement the provisions of the Core Principles to suit their own circumstances.

In this part of the chapter, two issues relating to NPLs are addressed. First, how can the framework for regulation and supervision of the banking system, and individual banks within the system, provide a framework for their prevention and control? Second, is there a need for individual banks to be subject to a legal framework for effective internal control systems? In many of the recent banking crises referred to earlier, either or both of these ingredients were missing.

Here, the focus is on those aspects of the international efforts which have a direct effect on the NPLs. However, it is worth emphasising that the lack of a strong regulatory and supervisory culture is likely to have adverse effects on the entire banking system and can raise systemic risk and increase moral hazard.[83]

One of the reasons for the growth in importance of the work of the Basel Committee is the use by the World Bank and the International Monetary Fund of the Core Principles[84] as a benchmark for aspects of the Financial Sector Assessment Programme ('FSAP')[85] undertaken in individual member countries by the International Monetary Fund and the World Bank. According to Gianviti,[86] the FSAP:

> is a joint program of the World Bank and the International Monetary Fund designed to strengthen the assessment and monitoring of member countries' financial systems, so as to develop strategies and policies the strengthening of systems, as needed.

Although the FSAP is a voluntary programme its importance as a financial sector diagnostic tool has been growing.[87]

In relation to bank lending, the Core Principles recognise the need for effective regulation and supervision of bank lending. Principle 8 provides, *inter alia*, that:

> supervisors must be satisfied that banks have a credit risk management process ... with prudent policies and processes to identify, measure, monitor and control credit risk ... This would include the granting of loans and making of investments, the evaluation of the quality of such loans and

---

83   For further reading on this, see Hupkes, above note 73; Asser, above note 34 and Campbell and Cartwright, above note 33.

84   And other Basel initiatives.

85   The FSAP was introduced in 1999.

86   See Gianviti, F., 'Legal Aspects of the Financial Sector Assessment Program', in Current Developments in Monetary and Financial Law (2005, International Monetary Fund, Washington DC) at 219. This paper is an excellent guide to the FSAP programme.

87   See the Report on the Evaluation of the Financial Sector Assessment Program (2006, International Monetary Fund, Washington DC).

investments, and the ongoing management of the loan and investment portfolios.[88]

The Core Principles also provide guidance on a range of matters related to lending and risk reduction policies and these cover having in place adequate policies, practices and procedures for the evaluation of loans and the adequacy of provisions for bad loans;[89] limits on large exposures especially to connected borrowers;[90] country risk and international lending;[91] comprehensive risk management process;[92] and adequate internal controls.[93]

The Core Principles provide a broad framework and are now widely followed internationally but the Basel Committee has also produced more detailed guidance for credit risk assessment and management. In fact the Basel Committee has, from its inception in the mid-1970s, been actively concerned with internal control systems in banks and in 1998 it produced a Framework for Internal Control Systems in Banking Organisations,[94] which was aimed at strengthening the ways banks would be expected to conduct their internal control systems. The Basel Committee, and indeed most bank supervisors, has identified the need for more effective internal control systems for banks as a priority. According to the Basel Committee, 'a system of effective internal controls is a critical component of bank management and a foundation for the safe and sound operation of banking operations'.[95] It was recognised that the lack of effective internal control systems had been a major factor in the problems faced by many banks in many countries[96] and that there was a real and urgent need for an international initiative to strengthen the position.

The original Framework contained five internal control elements which covered 13 Principles. The control elements were split into the following categories: management oversight and the control culture; risk recognition and assessment; control activities and segregation of duties; information and communication; monitoring activities and correcting deficiencies.[97]

This was followed in July 1999 by the publication by the Basel Committee of Sound Practices for Loan Accounting and Disclosure,[98] but this has recently been superseded by new guidance on the subject which was published in June

---

88   Principle 8, the Core Principles for Effective Banking Supervision (2006, Basel Committee on Banking Supervision, Basel). A revised version of the Core Principles came into effect in October 2006, replacing the 1997 version.

89   Ibid., Principle 9.

90   Ibid., Principles 10 and 11.

91   Ibid., Principle 12.

92   Ibid., Principles 13 to 16.

93   Ibid., Principle 17.

94   1998, Bank for International Settlements, Basel.

95   Ibid., at 1.

96   Ibid.

97   Ibid., at 2–5.

98   'Sound Practices for Loan Accounting and Disclosure' (1999, Basel Committee on Banking Supervision, Bank for International Settlements, Basel).

2006. This new guidance is entitled Sound Credit Risk Assessment and Evaluation for Loans[99] and it aims to address the issues of how common data and processes related to loans can be used to assess credit risk, accounting for loan impairment and the determination of regulatory capital requirements.

The new guidance uses 10 principles which fall into two broad categories. These are 'Supervisory Expectations Concerning Sound Credit Risk Assessment' and Valuation for Loans' and 'Supervisory Evaluation of Credit Risk Assessment for Loans, Controls and Capital Adequacy'. According to the Basel Committee, the guidance 'is intended to provide banks and supervisors guidance on sound credit risk assessment and valuation policies and practices and loans regardless of the accounting framework applied.[100] It is worth pointing out that this guidance is aimed at being consistent with the International Financial Reporting Standards which apply to the impairment of loans,[101] and it is extremely important that this approach has been taken.

The focus of the guidance is on policies and practices that are aimed at promoting a better environment for the improvement of the assessment and control of credit risk. In addition to focusing on the risks involved, the guidance also considers governance issues and this includes the responsibilities of the Board of Directors and senior management of banks for ensuring that appropriate risk assessment and internal controls processes are in place and that adequate provision has been made for bad loans.

Clearly, from what has been seen in many of the banking crises in the last 25 years, the publication of this new guidance is much needed. From the perspective of a well-developed and modern banking system, much of what is contained within the guidance would be expected to be part of the normal practice of banks. However, many developing and transitional economies have not had the resources, expertise or experience to promote such systems. Of course, it should not be forgotten that many of those countries which suffered severe problems with NPLs were neither developing or transitional, the United States, Sweden and Japan for example. So it is arguably just as relevant and necessary for developed countries.

As compliance with this guidance will be one of the factors that the FSAP will take into account, there is an opportunity for a much improved framework for a more effective system for credit risk assessment as well as a system for a realistic valuation of loans. It has to be recognised that, while this guidance is a major step forward, it would be wrong to expect it to be easily implemented in many developing and transitional countries without receiving technical assistance from the relevant international bodies to ensure that staff are fully trained.[102]

99　'Sound Credit Risk Assessment and Valuation of Loans' (2006, Basel Committee on Banking Supervision, Bank for International Settlements, Basel).

100　Ibid., at 2.

101　See the International Accounting Standards, especially Accounting Standard 39. Discussed above note 23.

102　This includes such bodies as the World Bank, International Monetary Fund, European Bank for Reconstruction and Development and the Asian Development Bank.

Conclusions

It is always better to attempt to prevent a crisis than to have to deal with its aftermath but the complete avoidance of bad debts and bank failure would be impossible in practice so there will always be a need for a strategy to deal with bad debts, even in the best run banking system, as long as banks are involved in the risky business of lending money.

There is a need to put in place a framework to minimise the number of NPLs. This is arguably the most important aspect of the issue and an effective system of banking supervision and regulation is fundamental to this. The work of the Basel Committee has contributed much and its latest guidance for promoting internal controls has the potential to assist in improving the situation in many countries. Lenders need to adhere to the principles of good lending and have in place workable risk-management systems using internationally accepted accounting practices in order to minimise problems and to ensure that developing problems are recognised early.

The establishment of internal control systems in accordance with Basel should be essential to ensure the minimisation of the problem of NPLs, but this can be achieved only after an effective system of prudential regulation and supervision has been put in place. This goes beyond simply having in place a regulatory framework. The supervisor must be provided with adequate enforcement powers and be sufficiently well resourced (and this includes trained and experienced staff) to undertake the task effectively. Also of particular importance is that for the supervisor and central bank to be effective they must be free from political interference as far as possible. This has certainly not been the case in a number of countries with NPL problems.

A framework for dealing expeditiously and effectively with insolvent banks needs to be established and this should provide for restructuring where this might be possible and an effective liquidation process where it is not. The lack of an effective legal framework for bank insolvency has been a significant factor in many of the countries which have experienced regular banking crises and high levels of NPLs.

Much work has already been done at the international policy level and the work of the Basel Committee has been the most significant factor.[103] The use of the FSAP programme has also been a major factor in encouraging countries to deal with the problems of having adequate regulation for their financial sectors but progress on bank insolvency regimes has been slower and much remains to be done in this area.

The results to date have been mixed with some significant improvements in some countries but with severe problems remaining in some others. In some jurisdictions the problems do not seem to have been addressed at all.

---

103 But see also the work undertaken by the International Monetary Fund, the World Bank, Asian Development Bank, European Bank for Reconstruction and Development and the Financial Stability Institute.

In many ways the use of AMCs continues to be a controversial topic which has been the subject of much criticism. The experience of the use of AMCs has been mixed. In some countries, South Korea and Japan for example, they are thought to have been relatively successful but, as noted above, they have proved expensive to operate.

One of the major issues which it raises is that, where it is believed that the central bank (or Ministry of Finance) will ensure that NPLs are purchased, there is little incentive for management to improve its credit risk management control to ensure that the amount of new NPLs is greatly reduced. To date, this has been problematic.

Once the NPLs have been transferred to the AMC, it is necessary to ensure that the AMC has sufficient legal powers, and adequate resources, to undertake its task effectively. Legal power will have to be given to enable the management of the AMC to effectively carry out its mandate. There is as yet no agreement as to what the mandate of an AMC should be. The primary purpose, however, must be to maximise the value of the NPLs and to dispose of them as expeditiously as possible, as this will assist in minimising the costs to the public.

It would also be good practice to ensure that there is adequate transparency in the process as the scope for unfair advantage and corruption is considerable. This clearly suggests that AMCs should be subject to regulation and supervision by the bank regulator.[104]

The AMC should, ideally, be given a degree of discretion in relation to such matters as debt forgiveness or forbearance but in many jurisdictions this has not been done. Ideally, an AMC should be able to use a number of techniques such as swaps, including equity for debt, and securitisation as well as loan sales. It has to be recognised that it will often be very difficult to dispose of the loans at, or soon after, the time of the crisis so the difficult issue of when to sell becomes important. Also, the fact that one of the major tasks for an effective AMC will be its ability to manage the NPLs while awaiting a more appropriate time for arranging the sale. Assessments will have to be made of the prevailing economic situation. Criticisms will inevitably be made if it appears that the timing of disposals was ill judged.

As noted by Dong He,[105] the development of a market for the sale of NPLs is a vital component and for most countries this means that the market should be opened up to non-domestic operators as well as domestic. By doing this the opportunity to sell distressed loans increases greatly.

A second criticism is that AMCs by their very nature assist in the disposal of a problem but do nothing to prevent the occurrence, or reoccurrence, of the same problem. A third criticism is that invariably public funds are used and may provide a subsidy to the bank concerned. Unless this is done in an appropriate manner, this can be seen as rewarding poor performance instead of penalising it. A fourth criticism is the possibility that the use of AMCs lead to an increase in moral hazard in the financial system. This could certainly be true if there is am assumption that an AMC will be responsible for cleaning up by taking NPLs from distressed banks.

---

104   Or another suitable body such as the Ministry of Finance.
105   Above note 46.

It is likely that moral hazard has been increased in many jurisdictions because of the introduction of hastily introduced and poorly designed schemes which were seen as an automatic place for NPLs to go. As with emergency liquidity financing, great care has to be taken to ensure that constructive ambiguity exists and that there is no guarantee in advance for banks.

AMCs have been a useful tool to use in the aftermath of a systemic banking crisis but have worked better in some countries than in others. Where a market for the disposal of NPLs was either already in existence or was subsequently developed, there was a much better chance of AMCs having a degree of success.

One of the worrying factors in the use of AMCs in a number of jurisdictions is that there can arise an automatic assumption that bad loans will be purchased by the AMC even though there is very little value and, where the bank involved has very little franchise value, even after the removal of the NPLs. In such a case the more correct approach to take would be to consider alternative courses of action such as, but not restricted to, liquidation. There is a real danger that an AMC may be viewed as a place that will as a matter of course agree to purchase NPLs. Where this happens, there is no incentive for management to improve internal controls which obviously, in some situations, could lead to complacency.

But is the use of an Asset Management Corporation the best solution? This is something about which there is still considerable disagreement but it is worth noting that while they may be a necessary, or at least unavoidable, vehicle to use where NPLs are a significant problem they do nothing to deal with the causes of the problem and are therefore of very limited use in the prevention of NPLs.

The use of AMCs must not be thought of as a solution to the problem of NPLs. They are a necessary tool where there has been a significant amount of NPLs in a banking system and as yet no better system has been found for the management of these impaired assets in developing countries. However, in many jurisdictions it appears to have been forgotten that transferring NPLs to an AMC means that the problem has only been moved to another place. It has not been resolved.

Chapter 10

In Re: Spectrum Plus – Less of a Bang than a Whimper?

Sandra Frisby[1]

Introduction: Spectrum and Its Issues

From the academic lawyer's perspective, the decision of the House of Lords in *In Re Spectrum Plus*[2] offered a wealth of opportunity for analysis, critique and debate. Ostensibly, at least, the *Spectrum* litigation was of considerable commercial significance in that it seemed directed towards settling the question of whether, as a matter of law, it was possible for banks and other lending institutions to acquire an enforceable fixed charge over the book debts of their corporate borrowers. Should the Law Lords collective judgments rule that possibility out, the ramifications on the provision of corporate finance, particularly to small and medium sized companies[3], appeared potentially ominous.[4] In contrast, the dividend prospects for unsecured creditors of an insolvent company might seem to be improved.[5]

Thus, the *Spectrum* decision assumed a certain gravitas which, it is suggested, may be overstated. Whilst this chapter does not in any way refute its doctrinal value, it attempts to demonstrate that, in practice, its significance may be limited to a fairly narrow set of circumstances. Equally, its application to the central question of the effectiveness of fixed charges over *book debts*[6] may be of almost academic importance.

The basis of this assertion is empirical: this chapter draws upon a database of 2063 companies which entered either administrative receivership or administration between September 2001 and September 2004. The database was compiled by extracting information from reports filed by insolvency practitioners at Companies House in relation to these companies and was then analysed in an

---

1   Thanks are due to the Insolvency Service for its sponsorship of a programme of empirical research which informs a substantial part of this chapter. The author would also like to thank Professor Howard Bennett, Professor Michael Bridge, Professor Adrian Walters, John Armour and Michael Jones for their incisive contributions to numerous discussions on the question of fixed charges over book debts.
2   [2005] UKHL 41 (hereinafter *Spectrum*).
3   Hereinafter 'SMEs'.
4   See below.
5   Ibid.
6   As opposed to other asset groups.

attempt to evaluate the impact of the Enterprise Act 2002 on insolvency outcomes.[7] The same reports may assist in demonstrating the central thesis of this Chapter, that the *Spectrum* outcome had been very likely anticipated long before the case itself reached first instance, and that those potentially affected were in a position to take steps to neutralise any prejudice threatened by it. The real questions raised by *Spectrum*, therefore, are to what extent it will accelerate a trend in corporate finance which had already gained substantial momentum and whether or not this is a desirable development.

Spectrum in The House of Lords: Overview

It is not proposed to here rehearse the entirety of the *Spectrum* litigation.[8] Essentially, the decision concerned the characterisation of a charge, described in the debenture granting it as 'specific', over the book debts of Spectrum Plus, a company in liquidation. The company was prohibited from dealing with the uncollected debts[9] and was required to pay collected debts into an account with the chargee bank. The terms of the charge were very similar to those employed in the debenture in *Siebe Gorman & Co Ltd v Barclays Bank*,[10] where the charge was held to be fixed. The chargee sought a declaration that the documentation created a fixed charge over the debts, undoubtedly prompted to test the water following the decision of the Privy Council in *Agnew v Commissioner of the Inland Revenue*.[11] In his judgment in that case, Lord Millett had hinted, in barely veiled terms, that *Siebe Gorman* may have been incorrectly decided *on its facts*.[12]

The outcome in *Spectrum* was perhaps not unexpected. Their Lordships adopted Lord Millett's two-stage test, from *Agnew*,[13] to determine the nature of a charge. The first stage is one of construction of the charging documentation to determine what rights and obligations the parties intend to confer upon one another as regards the charged property. The second stage is one of characterisation: do the rights and obligations conferred, *objectively considered*, render the charge fixed or floating? The touchstone here is *control*: which party, the chargor or chargee, has control of the deployment of the charged asset? In the context of the proceeds of book debts, the Law Lords in *Spectrum*, mirroring Lord Millett's analysis in

---

7	For the report on the findings and a description of the methodology, see Frisby, S., Report on Insolvency Outcomes (2006), available through the Insolvency Service Website at: <www.insolvency.gov.uk/insolvencyprofessionandlegislation/research/corpdocs/InsolvencyOutcomes.pdf> (last viewed 31 May 2007).

8	For a detailed exposition, see Berg, A., 'The Cuckoo in the Nest of Corporate Insolvency: Some Aspects of the Spectrum Case' [2006] *Journal of Business Law* 22.

9	By selling, assigning, factoring, discounting or charging them without the chargee's consent.

10	[1979] 2 Lloyd's Rep 142.

11	[2001] UKPC 28, [2001] 2 AC 710.

12	Ibid., at paragraphs 38, 48.

13	Ibid., at paragraph 32.

Agnew,[14] considered that where the chargor company was able to freely access the value represented by book debt realisations then the charge was inevitably floating:

> In my opinion, the essential characteristic of a floating charge, the characteristic that distinguishes it from a fixed charge, is that the asset subject to the charge is not finally appropriated as a security for the payment of the debt until the occurrence of some future event. In the meantime the chargor is left free to use the charged asset and to remove it from the security. On this point I am in respectful agreement with Lord Millett.[15]

On the facts, the company was indeed 'free to use the charged asset'[16] and so the charge was properly characterised as a floating charge.

Spectrum: Why it Might Matter

The amount 'at stake' in *Spectrum* was GBP 16,136, this being the sum owed to the company's preferential creditors.[17] By statute, preferential debts are payable out of the proceeds of floating charge assets in priority to the claims of the floating chargeholder,[18] whereas the proceeds of *fixed charge* assets are not. Thus, if the charge in *Spectrum* was fixed the charge holder could lay claim to the GBP 16,136, if it was floating that sum was payable to the preferential creditors.

The critical disadvantage of the floating charge is that it is vulnerable to what Armour has astutely described as a form of statutory 'taxation'.[19] Given the omnipresence of the floating charge, and its propensity to allocate the entirety of the corporate estate to its holder, a series of legislative developments sought to restore some financial content to the claims of other (unsecured) creditors. Thus a category of debts were denominated as preferential in the Preferential Payments in Bankruptcy Act 1888 with the result that certain claims for parochial rates and taxes and for unpaid wages and salaries[20] were elevated above those of the charge holder. This statutory redistribution mechanism[21] has remained a feature of insolvency legislation ever since, although the categories of preferential creditors have changed over time.[22]

---

14 Ibid., at paragraph 47.
15 [2005] UKHL 41 at paragraphs 111, 112, 117, per Lord Scott of Foscote. See also Lord Hope of Craighead at paragraph 62 and Lord Walker of Gestingthorpe at paragraph 151.
16 By drawing on its account with the chargee.
17 Which, at that time, included the Crown in respect of collected taxes. The Crown's preferential status was prospectively abolished by Enterprise Act 2002, section 251, which came into force on 15 September 2003.
18 Insolvency Act 1986, sections 175 and 45 and Schedule B1, paragraph 65(2).
19 See Armour, J., 'Should we Redistribute in Insolvency?', Chapter 9 in Getzler, J. and Payne, J. (eds), *Company Charges: Spectrum Plus and Beyond* (2006, OUP, Oxford) at 190.
20 See Preferential Payments in Bankruptcy Act 1888, section 1.
21 Armour, above note 19.
22 Most notably with the abolition of the Crown's preferential status (above note 17).

A further, more recent innovation to similar effect is to be found in section 176A of the Insolvency Act 1986, which requires liquidators, administrators and administrative receivers to set aside a 'prescribed part' of floating charge realisations for the benefit of unsecured creditors.[23] Moreover, administration expenses, which include the administrator's remuneration, take priority over the claims of floating charge holders[24] and, whilst liquidation expenses are not currently so prioritised,[25] legislative reform is expected to restore that precedence and so further eat into the pool of assets available to chargees.[26]

Finally, a further provision that has a potentially erosive effect on the value of the floating charge as a security device may be found in paragraph 70 of Schedule B1 to the Insolvency Act 1986. This allows an administrator to dispose of or take action in relation to property which is subject to a floating charge, although the charge holder enjoys the same priority in relation to 'acquired' property.[27] In the context of book debts, therefore, an administrator who finds himself without 'free' assets with which to mount a potentially beneficial trading strategy, might avail himself of book debt realisations. The hierarchy of objectives in administration requires that an administrator perform his functions with a view to rescuing the company as a going concern *or* to achieving a better result for creditors generally than would be the case in a winding up.[28] The realisation of property in order to make a distribution to secured or preferential creditors[29] is plainly the objective of last resort, and it is at least arguable that where an administrator considers that a trading strategy which makes use of book debt realisations has the potential to benefit the general body of creditors then he is duty-bound to adopt it. This in itself may not lead to a loss of value to the charge holder, but in circumstances where book debt realisations are consumed in a fruitless attempt at rescue or realisation maximisations, and no 'substitute' is available, such loss is certainly a possibility.[30]

The above demonstrates the fragility inherent in the floating charge: its financial content is rendered vulnerable by statutory provisions designed to enhance the position of creditors other than its holder. To the extent that the claims of such creditors are substantial the floating charge is effectively valueless, and this

---

23 The amount of the prescribed part is 50 per cent of the first GBP 10,000 of realisations and 20 per cent of any amount above that, with a ceiling of GBP 600,000.

24 Insolvency Act 1986, Schedule B1, paragraph 99(3).

25 Following the decision of the House of Lords in *Buchler v Talbot* [2004] UKHL 9.

26 See Companies Act 2006, section 1282. At the time of writing this provision is expected to enter into force in October 2007.

27 Property which directly or indirectly represents the property disposed of: paragraph 70(3).

28 Insolvency Act 1986, Schedule B1, paragraph 3(1)(a)-(b).

29 Ibid., paragraph 3(1)(c).

30 Whether or not the charge holder in such circumstance would be able to recover any deficit from the administrator personally is debatable. A cause of action might be found in paragraph 74(1)(a), but it is not immediately obvious, absent extreme carelessness, that a claim would succeed.

may not be an unusual state of affairs. The database referred to above[31] recorded, *inter alia*, the amount of preferential debt owed at the commencement of the insolvency procedure in question. Prior to the abolition of the Crown preference some very sizeable sums were to be found owing, which is perhaps not surprising given that collected taxes are payable over in arrears and would no doubt represent a convenient 'emergency fund' for financially troubled companies. Whilst the Crown no longer enjoys preferential status, thus swelling the floating charge content, the prescribed part ostensibly represents a concomitant drain on it.[32] Further, the increasing emphasis on corporate rescue and the enfranchisement of all creditors as espoused by the Enterprise Act 2002 may see an overall increase in procedural costs and expenses in administration, which are of course borne by the floating charge.

On the other hand, the floating charge entitles its holder to appoint an administrative receiver[33] or an administrator,[34] thus conferring a hefty bargaining chip should it become necessary to bring the borrower into line, and also allowing a degree of control, arguably varying depending upon whether the appointment is of a receiver or an administrator, in any insolvency. This entitlement is not one to be taken lightly and, indeed, lends support to an assertion that the floating charge is as much about debtor control as it is about priority.[35] However, it is indisputable that control *ex ante* is no compensation for loss of value *ex post*, and this is doubly so when the control has been enjoyed all along: the Enterprise Act entitlement to make an administration appointment conferred on qualifying floating charge holders is a clear concession to the prospective prohibition on appointing an administrative receiver.

Moreover, to the extent that *Spectrum* qualifies the capacity of lenders to take fixed charges over book debts it should be acknowledged that an asset of proportionately substantial value will be shunted from the fixed to the floating charge pool and so become subject to the statutory 'taxation' identified above. The orthodox genre of floating charge assets would, pre-*Spectrum*, have comprised such assets as raw materials, work-in progress, stock and other items that might be expected to 'revolve' as a matter of routine. Whilst a sizeable value might be attributed to these in the company's books they become subject to what might be described as 'insolvency-related depreciation' once formal insolvency proceedings are commenced. Raw materials, for example, may be subject to enforceable retention of title clauses. The insolvency value of stock and work-in-progress will largely depend upon whether these can be sold as part of a going concern sale of

---

31 Above note 7.
32 Although this is not an immediate *quid pro quo*: the section 176A obligation applies only to charges created after 15 September 2003, leaving holders of charges granted prior to that date to reap the benefits of section 251.
33 Provided that the charge pre-dates 15 September 2003: Insolvency Act 1986, section 72A(4).
34 Ibid., Schedule B1, paragraph 14.
35 For a thorough and incisive treatment of this idea see Mokal, R.J., *Corporate Insolvency Law: Theory and Application* (2005, OUP, Oxford) in Chapter 5.

the company's business, in which case they will tend to realise more, or whether they are sold piecemeal on a break-up basis, in which case their value may be nugatory.

This is not to say that book debts are not subject to a similar depreciatory pressure. In some cases insolvency set-off[36] might operate so as to render some portion of a debt uncollectable, and it is not inconceivable that opportunistic debtors of an insolvent company might attempt to avoid full payment of their obligations by asserting a right to set off in less than meritorious circumstances. Nevertheless, the true value of a debtor ledger, even should insolvency occur, is almost certainly more precisely predictable than that of other forms of revolving asset and, in any event, an experienced insolvency practitioner may well be able to counter debtor misbehaviour so as to minimise depreciation. It remains the case, therefore, that the loss of book debts from the fixed charge portion of the security might be expected to come as a severe financial blow to lending institutions, and one which they would wish to sidestep. The next section considers whether it might be possible to do so.

Tax Avoidance

The Control Test: Blocking the Account?

> If the legislature subjects particular types of voluntary transaction to statutory 'taxation' (as through the prospect of redistribution in insolvency), then sophisticated parties may be expected to structure their affairs differently so as to avoid the ambit of the legislation.[37]

The decision in *Spectrum* relates specifically to an agreement that allowed the borrowing company access to the value represented by collected book debts. The company was financed in what might be termed the 'traditional' manner: it was granted an overdraft facility by its bank, and in return granted the bank a package of fixed and floating charges over its assets and undertaking. This is a reasonably common arrangement for the financing of SMEs in the United Kingdom and the charging formula as regards book debts was no doubt equally common following the successful outcome, from the lenders' perspective, of *Siebe Gorman*.[38] It is that formula that the House of Lords' decision renders ineffective, on the basis that the effective control of the deployment of the charged asset lay with the chargor. This was so notwithstanding the chargee's contractual entitlement to remove 'drawing' rights on the account.[39] The state of the law is neatly encapsulated by Anderson, who puts the matter thus:

---

36 See Insolvency Rules 1986 (SI 1986/1925), rule 4.90.
37 Armour, above note 19 at 190.
38 Above note 10.
39 C.f. Lord Phillips' judgment in the Court of Appeal: [2004] EWCA Civ 670.

It is submitted that this House of Lords' decision will put an end to the days of banks allowing proceeds of book debts to be paid into current accounts held by those banks and from which the borrower is permitted to carry on its business.[40]

The question examined here is whether or not institutional lenders[41] who wish to continue lending on the traditional lines described above[42] will be able in future to structure their loans, and specifically their charges over book debts, so as to satisfy the control test as pronounced in *Spectrum*. Notably, their Lordships did not attempt to catalogue the methods by which adequate control of debts, or, indeed, other forms of revolving asset, could be demonstrated, focusing entirely on the construction and characterisation of charge in hand. This approach is perfectly justifiable for, as Berg remarks:

> ... whether the chargee has control of the charged assets is a question of commercial reality, not legal technicalities.[43]

It does, however, offer chargees some room for manoeuvre in structuring their charges over book debts with a view to securing the necessary control.

One obvious method would be to prohibit pre-collection dealings with the debts, whether by assignment, charge or otherwise, entirely, and to further call for payment of the proceeds into a blocked account to which the chargor has no access whatsoever unless with the consent of the chargee. This would appear to correspond to a *Re Keenan Bros Ltd*[44] type charge, which was cited in *Agnew* as an example of an effective fixed charge over book debts. Berg questions the correctness of this assertion, referring to the fact that the 'blocked account' was not in fact opened or operated until five months after the execution of the charge, and that in the interim the company had paid its debts into its current account with the bank and had drawn on that account routinely and without restriction.[45] In other words, just as Slade J. had misapprehended the facts in *Siebe Gorman*, so too had Lord Millett in relation to *Re Keenan Bros*. Notwithstanding any misunderstanding, though, it appears that a blocked account of the *Keenan* variety, as understood by Lord Millett, would satisfy the control test on the authority of *Agnew*, from which that test originated.

It would obviously be commercially unworkable for the proceeds of a blocked account to be wholly unavailable to the chargor, as this would deprive the company of the cash flow necessary to conduct its business. What is required is a method by which funds can be released from the blocked account for that purpose, and it appears from *Spectrum* that such a method would necessarily require the

---

40 See Anderson, K., 'The Spectrum Plus Case' (2005) 16 *International Company and Commercial Law Review* 405 at 409.
41 For all intents and purposes, the major clearing banks.
42 This assumption is tested below.
43 Berg, above note 8 at 32.
44 [1986] BCLC 242.
45 Berg, above note 8 at 45–46.

chargee's active consent to a release. Berg[46], in this regard, draws attention to the observations of Lord Walker in *Spectrum* that the archetypal distinction between a fixed and a floating charge is as follows:

> So long as the [fixed] charge remains unredeemed, the assets can be released from the charge *only with the active concurrence of the chargee* ... Under a floating charge, by contrast, the chargee does not have the same power to control the security for its own benefit ... and unless and until the chargee intervenes (on crystallisation of the charge) it is for the trader, and not the bank, to decide how to run its business.[47]

How is this to be read? On the one hand, Lord Walker's words could be taken to suggest that a request for a release of assets (i.e., funds from the blocked account and into a current account) must be made by the chargor and met with an affirmative decision from the chargee. There are certain logistical difficulties if this is the case, not least that it would incur transaction costs for both parties if what is necessary is a request and a decision *each time* such a release is required to furnish cash-flow requirements. Such costs could be minimised, on the other hand, if the parties could agree *ab initio* that a certain amount, or a certain proportion of the funds in the blocked account, were to be released into a current account on a regular basis at the discretion of the chargee.[48]

This method was proposed by Oditah as capable of constituting a valid fixed charge prior to the decision of the House of Lords in *Spectrum*[49] and it is submitted that *prima facie* it remains a realistic proposition. It is the chargee who retains dominion over the blocked account and the funds therein and the chargee who has control over the 'drip' process by which the charged assets are released from the charge and into the hands of the chargor. However, with customary acuity, Oditah then raises what is probably the critical question:

> ... but how long is a piece of string? What if the blocked account were emptied daily into the chargor's general (unblocked) account, pursuant to a contractual arrangement between the parties, so that the blocked account was no more than an intermediate or conduit account, a resting place before the proceeds reached their intended destination, namely the chargor's general account?[50]

This observation was directed towards the particular facts of *Re Keenan*, but is arguably a question that could be asked of an arrangement such as that described above. Even if control of the 'drip' process notionally remains with the chargee, to

---

46 Ibid., at 32.

47 [2005] UKHL 41 at paragraphs 138–9 (italics added).

48 Say once a month. Anyone who has ever requested a direct debit from a current account into an ISA account will appreciate the relative ease with which this kind of arrangement can be set up and operated.

49 See Oditah, F., 'Fixed Charges and Recycling Proceeds of Receivables' [2004] *Law Quarterly Review* 533 at 539.

50 Ibid., at 540.

the extent that it takes place automatically and without any genuine decision-making process on the part of the chargee,[51] there is at least an argument that the substance of the arrangement allows the chargor access to the charged asset in a qualitatively similar manner to that enjoyed by the chargor in *Siebe Gorman*. In both cases the chargee's *de facto* control might realistically be described as hypothetical. In relation to *Siebe Gorman*, Lord Phillips, in the Court of Appeal in *Spectrum*, laid emphasis on the chargee's contractual entitlement to prohibit drawings on the account. This reasoning was controverted in the House of Lords, and one might properly ask whether an entitlement to *allow* access, as opposed to prohibit it, is substantially any different.

The enquiry is rendered even more intricate by virtue of the definition of floating charge provided by section 251 and Paragraph 111 of Schedule B1 of the Insolvency Act 1986. The 'taxing' provisions of that Act allocate assets subject to a floating charge to other claimants in priority to the chargee. However, the definitions refer to a charge 'which as created was a floating charge'. As Berg points out, there is therefore an argument that as long as the charging agreement allocates genuine control to the chargee *at the time of the execution of the charge*, then that charge is fixed and not within the ambit of the 'taxing' provisions.[52] And then there is the further awkward issue of whether post-contractual conduct can properly be taken into account at either the construction or characterisation stages of Lord Millett's test from *Agnew*.[53]

The Control Test: Policy Considerations?

The above discussion raises more question than it answers. The difficulty is in predicting the future application of the control test to particular forms of debenture which attempt to submit book debts to valid fixed charges, given the understandable lack of prescription by the Law Lords in *Spectrum*. More specifically, the question is whether institutional lenders will be amenable to test out drafting initiatives that attempt to satisfy the control test when there is a possibility, and not necessarily a remote one, that these, while technically pristine, will be picked apart in the name of policy by future courts.

To take an example, consider Berg's argument above to the effect that a genuinely blocked account which is later unblocked will nevertheless avoid taxing provisions by virtue of the fact that the charge, *as created*, was a fixed and not a floating charge. There is an inexorable logic to this contention but it is submitted that it is not invulnerable. The definition of a floating charge in section 251 was

---

51 An interesting evidential point!

52 Berg, above note 8 at 42. But see Atherton, S. and Mokal, R.J., 'Charges Over Chattels: Issues in the Fixed/Floating Jurisprudence' (2005) 26 *Company Lawyer* 10 at 16–17, where an argument is made that post-contractual variation of an agreement may create a new floating charge, which will be void for want of registration under Companies Act 1985, section 395.

53 Both Berg, above note 8, and Atherton and Mokal, above note 52 consider the post-contractual conduct arguments at some length.

introduced to avoid a particular mischief, that of automatic crystallisation clauses which diverted floating charge assets from their intended beneficiaries under the statutory scheme.[54] It might be thought ironic that a provision intended to *avoid* that mischief should be prayed in aid to *achieve* a remarkably similar result. One might go further and tentatively predict some very strong judicial resistance to such a conclusion, so strong that recourse to some broad notion of legislative policy might prove overwhelmingly tempting.

It is patently obvious that the jurisprudence on the fixed/floating charge dichotomy is driven by the legislative policy impetus towards redistribution, and that the division would be of no practical significance were it not for that policy.[55] Both Lord Scott and Lord Walker in *Spectrum* made explicit reference to Parliamentary strategy in their judgments. Lord Scott had this to say:

> But the judicial process over the years whereby the concept of a 'floating charge' has been developed must, in my opinion, keep in mind the mischief that these statutory provisions were intended to meet and, in particular, that on a winding up or receivership preferential creditors were to have their debts paid out of the circulating assets, sometimes referred to as ambulatory assets, of the debtor company in priority to a debenture holder with a charge over those assets.[56]

This reference to 'circulating' or 'ambulatory' assets is pivotal in defining the scope of the redistributive policy, and is of considerable vintage. But here one encounters a certain obscurity. It is absolutely correct to state that Parliament's intention is that floating charge assets should be available to meet the claims of preferential creditors and those entitled to share in the prescribed part: however, Parliament has studiously avoided any attempt to stipulate *which* assets should be considered 'floating charge' assets, the test for which has been left entirely to the common law.

It is worth noting that the justification for submitting only *ambulatory* (i.e., floating charge) assets to statutory taxation has not been meaningfully debated in Parliament since 1897. Armour notes that the debates preceding the enactment of the Preferential Payments in Bankruptcy (Amendment) Act 1897 fastened upon what he describes as a 'labour theory of value': floating charge assets would be produced as a result of the efforts of the workforce, therefore the unpaid workforce should be able to lay claim to them in the event of their employer's insolvency.[57] Presumably the same could not be said for non-revolving assets (i.e., fixed charge assets), and this rationale was echoed in the first case to consider whether or not such assets were vulnerable to other claimants. In *Re Lewis Merthyr Consolidated*

---

54 See *Re Griffin Hotel Co Ltd* [1941] Ch 129, *Re Woodroffes (Musical Instruments) Ltd* [1986] Ch 366, *Re Brightlife Ltd* [1987] Ch 200.

55 For an excellent discussion of this matter, see Calnan, R.J., 'Floating Charges: A Proposal for Reform' (2004) 9 *Butterworths Journal of International Banking and Financial Law* 341.

56 [2005] UKHL 41 at paragraph 98. See also Lord Walker at paragraph 141.

57 Armour, above note 19 at 195–6.

Collieries Ltd,[58] the question was whether section 107(1) of the Companies (Consolidation) Act 1908 required preferential debts to be paid out of fixed, as well as floating charge assets. The wording of the section stated quite baldly that such debts were to be met 'out of any assets coming to the hands of the receiver ... in priority to any claim for principal or interest in respect of the debentures'. Tomlin J rejected a literal reading of the section and held that the words 'any claim for principal or interest' were qualified by the earlier reference to a debenture holder taking possession under a *floating charge.*[59] He continued:

> I quite understand that in regard to a floating charge there may be a reason for giving the priority, because until the receiver is appointed or possession is taken, the charge does not crystallise, and it may well be said that this particular class of debts, which may perhaps have contributed to produce the very assets upon which the floating charge will crystallise, are proper to be paid out of those assets before the debenture holder takes his principal and interest out of them. That seems to me to be a perfectly intelligible reason for the legislation, and is in accord with the view which I take of the section.[60]

This value-added validation works very well in relation to the claims of employees. Of course, the categories of preferential debts have both expanded and contracted since they were first introduced in 1888, and it is debatable as to whether the Crown's earlier preferential status as regards collected taxes might fit as comfortably within this justification as do employee claims. Further, it is not only preferential creditors who now lay claim to floating charge assets but also unsecured creditors entitled to share in the prescribed part. To the extent that unsecured creditors include amongst their ranks *trade* creditors who have supplied goods or services on credit terms, again the value-added reasoning has some resonance. Those goods or services will have been employed in the business to generate further goods or services, and, critically, to generate debts owed *to* the business. Might this be available for judicial use as a policy justification for scrutinising any purported fixed charge over book debts with particular rigour?

Once again it is extraordinarily difficult to predict whether a pioneering judge would be disposed to probe deeply into the question of legislative intention when it comes to the question of whether seemingly ambulatory assets like book debts *ought* to be the subject of a valid fixed charge. As noted above, there has been no unequivocal legislative statement on this point, and the opportunity to make one in the Enterprise Act 2002 was eschewed, for whatever reason. Nevertheless, those charged with drafting debentures containing fixed charges over book debts must surely wonder whether even the most technically immaculate arrangement might yet be vulnerable to attack on policy grounds.

---

58   [1929] 1 Ch 498.
59   Affirmed by Lord Hanworth in the Court of Appeal: [1929] 1 Ch 498 at 512.
60   Ibid., at 507–508.

Satisfying the Control Test: Is it Worth the Candle?

The previous sections have attempted to demonstrate the possible financial consequences of *Spectrum* to institutional lenders and the potential for avoiding those consequences by modifying standard form charging documents. It is submitted that the predominant impediment to such attempts is that there will remain an element of uncertainty as to the likely success or otherwise of any modification, however carefully structured. Pure control over the proceeds of book debts can only incontrovertibly be achieved by locking them up in a blocked account and this is logistically disagreeable. Releasing those proceeds might be done on a 'request and consent' basis, but, as Armour points out, this might prove overly expensive and, further, banks might be deterred from such a course by the spectre of shadow directorship.[61] Arrangements for proceeds to be dripped out of a blocked account and into a current account may prove problematic on technical or policy grounds.

However much financial institutions might wish to retain the priority that a fixed charge over book debts affords them, it is submitted that there is no immediately obvious method of so doing where the advance is made on an overdraft or fixed term loan basis. This, however, is only half the story. The remainder of this chapter examines whether the above arguments are not, in any event, academic.

Pre-Empting Spectrum

The Move to Asset-based and Receivables Financing

> Following Spectrum Plus there will undoubtedly be a change in conventional secured overdraft lending as banks and other lenders accept that their security may rank behind other creditors. Plainly, this may make such lending more expensive. There will, however, be opportunities for the specialist lending market (and, in particular, invoice discounters and factors) to develop products and systems which allow borrowers to realise the value of their book debt as efficiently as possible.[62]

The move towards receivables financing is very well documented by Armour, who demonstrates the increasing use of invoice discounting along a time line beginning with the outset of the *Agnew* litigation at first instance in New Zealand.[63] Regard to empirical data such as this is to be welcomed, as it may assist in shedding light upon the historical responses of lending institutions to particular litigation and, therefore, suggest what future responses might be expected. The author's own

---

61 Armour, above note 19 at 203.
62 See Flood, R., 'Spectrum Plus: Legal and Practical Implications' (2006) 17 *International Company and Commercial Law Review* 78 at 78.
63 Armour, above note 19 at 203 et seq.

empirical research into insolvency outcomes[64] may also be of some service in this regard. It will be recalled that it comprises a database of 2063 companies, and information relating to them gleaned from reports filed at Companies House. For the purposes of this Chapter the reports have been revisited and new information gathered, as detailed below. Further, and as part of the original research, a number of interviews with insolvency practitioners and bankers were conducted and, where their remarks are relevant to the current enquiry, these too will be included.

It is first necessary to briefly describe the practice of receivables financing. Essentially it involves a company 'selling'[65] its debtor ledger and receiving in return a cash advance and possibly one or more services, which might include sales ledger administration, protection against bad debts and debt collection services. Receivables financing can be divided into two basic genres, factoring and invoice discounting,[66] and the precise terms of the agreements within these two categories vary according to the requirements of the company. The main distinction between the two is that invoice discounting involves the company collecting the assigned debts as agent for the financier, whereas factoring generally involves the financier taking over the collection exercise.

Notwithstanding that receivables financing transactions are structured as an assignment of the debtor ledger, or a proportion of it, their resemblance to a loan agreement is palpable. Indeed, receivables financiers, both factors and invoice discounters, routinely take packages of charges over the assets of their 'borrowers'. This, and the prevalence of receivables financing agreements generally, can be demonstrated by examining administrative receivership appointment trends in recent years. The database referred to above contained information on 953 companies that entered into administrative receivership between September 2001 and September 2004. This information included the identity of the administrative receiver's appointor. The profile of appointors over the entire three year period breaks down as follows:

It will be noted from Figure 10.1 that 22 per cent of receivership appointments over the period were made by receivables financiers. The vast majority of these were made by independent operators, i.e., by firms not allied to one of the major clearing banks. These banks have, for the most part, established receivables financing arms, which may do business as an arm of the main bank or through a distinct corporate entity.

A number of observations can be made at this stage. Firstly, given that over one fifth of all appointments in the period were made by receivables financiers it is clear that this form of financing is an established feature of the SME market. Year on year charts demonstrate no significant variance in the proportion of appointments made by receivables financiers.[67] Secondly, it is worth noting that receivables financiers, as well as taking an outright assignment of book debts, are

---

64 Above note 7.
65 Or, more accurately, assigning.
66 Armour, above note 19 at 204–205.
67 Above note 7 in Appendix.

Figure 10.1   Profile of Appointors

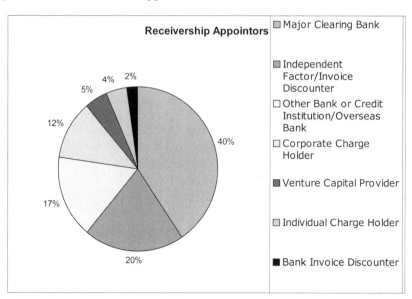

Source: Own Database.

also taking packages of charges over corporate assets.[68] Thirdly, and perhaps critically, the combination of outright assignment and charge (which acts as a sweeping up device, as well as an enforcement mechanism) is a supremely effective method of avoiding the statutory taxation described earlier. Even were the assignment to be considered to be one by way charge,[69] the charge (as long as it is registered, and the above suggests that this will inevitably be the case) will pass the control test in *Spectrum* with flying colours. Therein lies the beauty of receivables financing in this regard: whether the company collects the debts as agent of the financier and is under a duty to account, or whether the financier collects the debts, in both cases the company has no access to the proceeds. The cash flow problem associated with blocking an account into which debts are paid simply does not arise, as the revolving nature of the agreement means that new advances are provided by the financier on a periodic basis.

Receivables financing therefore represents a far more pragmatic solution to any prospective difficulties raised by *Spectrum* than engaging in potentially expensive and uncertain attempts to draft fixed charges over debts to satisfy the control test. It would, of course, be startling if sophisticated financial institutions

---

68 Which will inevitably include a floating charge, so as to entitle the holder to make the appointment of an administrative receiver in the first place: Insolvency Act 1986, section 29(2).

69 See, for example, *Orion Finance Ltd v Crown Financial Management Ltd* [1996] 2 BCLC 78 at 84–5.

had not recognised this for themselves, and, further, had not attempted to exploit the possibilities on offer. The fact that only 2 per cent of receivership appointments in the given period were made by bank-associated receivables financiers does not necessarily mean that this exploitation is not taking place. It can be explained, in part at least, by the fact that in many cases companies will raise funds on both overdraft terms and through receivables financing, and in many cases the same bank will provide both. In such cases, should a receivership appointment be necessary it may well be that the traditional banking arm, and not the receivables financing arm, makes the appointment. Equally, there may be a trend towards the major clearing banks steering their more problematic borrowers towards independent receivables financiers. Interviewees, when questioned on this point, confirmed that this was the case, a typical comment being the following:

> The factoring route, historically, was always perceived as finance of the last resort and there's been a drive, over many years, to change that image, and when the clearers started to do it that helped. Then *Brumark* [*Agnew*] and *Spectrum* came along, and it was just so much easier for the banks to move their lending into invoice discounting or factoring to solve that problem. It's become more and more the practice, off-balance sheet funding in some form has always been there but it is becoming more common.

It is also notable that whilst this 'trend' may have been accelerated by *Agnew*, which must have been perceived as something of a shot across the bows of lenders, it did not *begin* with *Agnew*. There has been an increasing move away from traditional overdraft or fixed-term lending, with the finance being provided by a single lender, towards a fragmentation of security or quasi-security interests being taken by a number of separate lenders which, between them, encompass the borrower's entire asset base. This has emerged as the banks themselves have taken stock and come to appreciate the benefits of such a scheme, in contrast to the limitations of the overdraft. One banker interviewee put the matter thus:

> If you talked to a banker ten years ago, he would tell you that the trouble with the overdraft was that it was just so clumsy and inflexible, and that what was needed was something much more specific, targeted lending against different assets. So [asset based lending] does allow the banks themselves to minimise their risk and make more money, and, to a certain extent, there's fragmentation in the sense that you'll get asset financing but a lot of that will come from the big banks as well … It allows them to lend more money against the assets, so it's a win-win situation for the lender, you get better focused security and you know exactly what you're lending against, you've got the security of collecting from that position and you focus on the risks associated with a particular asset. You can then go to 80%–85% of the asset value as opposed to the typical 55%–60% overdraft level.

To attempt to glean how far this movement was advanced, the author returned to the original database and randomly sampled 200 companies which went into either administration or receivership between January and September 2004. Statements of affairs for each were recovered, and these demonstrated the extent to which asset-based lending was used to finance the business in question. 'Asset-based lending' here includes not only receivables financing but also the acquisition of tangible assets on hire purchase or chattel lease terms, an area occupied by a number of high-profile firms including the clearing banks. For each company, the profile of financing arrangements was recorded to determine whether it was financed purely by bank loan or overdraft, by receivables financing or from some other source,[70] and whether it was in possession of assets[71] under a leasing or hire purchase transaction. Combinations of these possibilities were also recorded, and the results are detailed in the charts below.

Figure 10.2   Profile of Financing Arrangements in Administrative Receivership

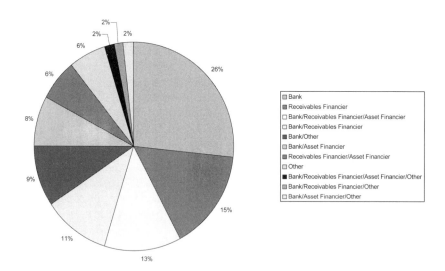

Source: Own Database.

As can be seen, 53 per cent of the 64 companies in administrative receivership in this sample were financed by a combination of methods. The lone financier, whether a bank lending on overdraft terms, a non-bank secured lender or a receivables financier accounts for 47 per cent of the sample.

---

70 The category of 'Other' includes secured loans from shareholders or directors, as well as finance advanced by non-bank corporate charge holders.
71 Excluding real property.

Figure 10.3   Profile of Financing Arrangements in Administration

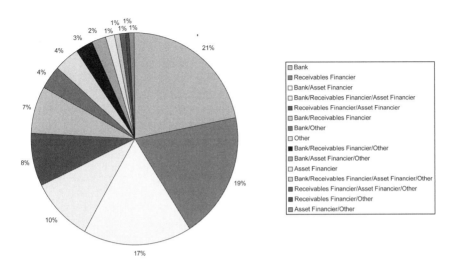

Administration 2004

Legend:
- Bank
- Receivables Financier
- Bank/Asset Financier
- Bank/Receivables Financier/Asset Financier
- Receivables Financier/Asset Financier
- Bank/Receivables Financier
- Bank/Other
- Other
- Bank/Receivables Financier/Other
- Bank/Asset Financier/Other
- Asset Financier
- Bank/Receivables Financier/Asset Financier/Other
- Receivables Financier/Asset Financier/Other
- Receivables Financier/Other
- Asset Financier/Other

Source: Own Database.

Figure 10.3 provides the same information for 136 companies in administration. The picture here is slightly more complicated in that there appears to be a greater number of 'combinations' of financing methods, but this can be explained by the fact that, unlike receivership, administration can be effected where no floating charge holder exists. Overall, however, there does not appear to be any notable variance from the receivership position, with 52 per cent of the sample of 136 companies financed by a lone operator. These charts are intended to demonstrate the key point that companies are, as often as not, seeking methods of financing their businesses from a number of diverse sources, rather than through the traditional secured loan or overdraft route.

A further enquiry was as to the relative effectiveness, from the lender's perspective, of lending against receivables as opposed to an overdraft facility or loan globally secured by a package of fixed and floating charges. This was answered by recording the amount outstanding to *all* secured creditors (for the purpose of this enquiry, chargees and receivables financiers) and comparing it to the return to those same creditors during the procedure itself. The same process was then carried out, but this time recording only the amount owed and the return to the *receivables financier*. The results make interesting reading.

Figure 10.4　Returns to 'Secured Creditors' in Receivership

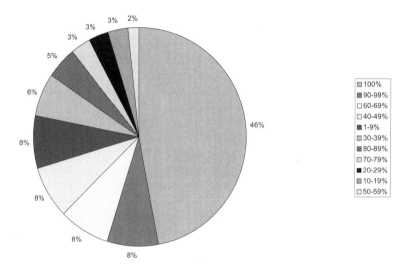

Returns to 'Secured Creditors': Receivership

☐	100%
■	90-99%
☐	60-69%
☐	40-49%
■	1-9%
☒	30-39%
■	80-89%
☐	70-79%
■	20-29%
▨	10-19%
☐	50-59%

Source: Own Database.

Figure 10.4 demonstrates the proportion of returns to *all* creditors lending to the companies in the sample either through loan/overdraft facilities secured by charges or through receivables financing. As can be seen, in less than half the cases in the sample the security cover proved adequate to discharge the entire amount owed. Further, in 28 per cent of cases secured creditors as a genus received less than half the amount owed to them.

The position is not dissimilar in administration, with 50 per cent of secured creditors receiving a 100 per cent return on the advances, and 29 per cent receiving less than half of what was owed. If nothing else, these two charts suggest that security, of itself, is no cast-iron guarantee of full recoveries against an insolvent corporation. However, when the 'lending' is made through receivables financing, the picture changes quite radically, as Figures 10.6 and 10.7 demonstrate.

Figure 10.5   Returns to 'Secured Creditors' in Administration

Returns to 'Secured Creditors': Administration

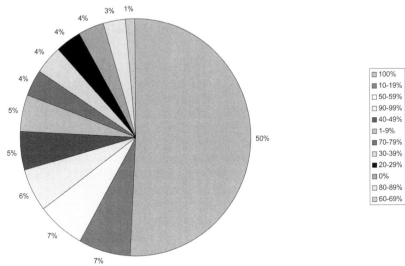

Source: Own Database.

Figure 10.6   Returns to Receivables Financiers in Receivership

Returns to Receivables Financiers: Receivership

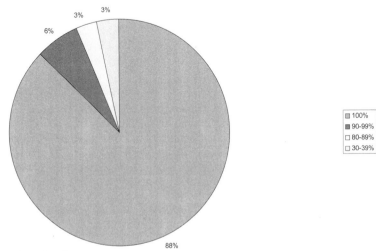

Source: Own Database.

For all cases in receivership where money had been advanced through receivables financing, the financier received a 100 per cent return in 88 per cent of cases and in only 3 per cent of cases was less than 50 per cent recovered. When one turns to the same enquiry for cases of administration the same general trend towards much higher recoveries is revealed.

Figure 10.7   Returns to Receivables Financiers in Administration

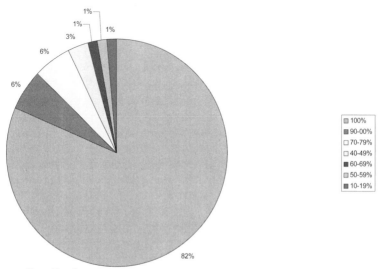

Returns to Receivables Financiers: Administration

Source: Own Database.

Once again, 100 per cent returns to receivables financiers are far more common than to secured creditors generally. Equally, low rates of recovery (50 per cent or less) are far less prevalent. This tendency is even more pronounced when one recalls that the figures for *all secured creditors* included a proportion of cases where a receivables financier recovered in full.

The above experiment in comparison should perhaps be treated with some caution, using as it does a relatively small number of companies in a limited timeframe. No statistical significance is claimed in relation to it, but it is submitted that it does appear to demonstrate some substantial advantages in terms of the level of returns to receivables financiers in insolvency. It was noted above that one of the benefits of the use of receivables financing is that it avoids the effects of statutory taxation by ring-fencing the proceeds of book debts from demands made on floating charge realisations. It should be acknowledged that it is not entirely clear to what extent this advantage explains the much higher level of recoveries to receivables financiers. To begin with, the chargees in the sample would all have benefited from the abolition of the Crown's preferential status as far as the floating charge portion of their security was concerned, as all entered into the procedure in question after the coming into force of the Enterprise Act 2002. Therefore, preferential creditors would be considerably less of a drain than would have been the case in a sample from, say, September 2002 to September 2003. However, this assumes, almost certainly wrongly, that where the chargee was a bank lending 'traditionally' its charge over book debts would have been treated as floating and so vulnerable to preferential claims. It should also be noted that none of the cases in the sample would have been subject to the demands of the prescribed part in section 176A of the Insolvency Act 1986, as the charges in question were all granted prior to 15 September 2003, but again this 'taxation' would only apply were the charge over book debts to be treated as floating.

There are two further explanations for the enhanced performance of receivables financing in the returns stake. The first would apply where the company was financed by both overdraft and receivables financing and the latter enjoyed priority over the former. Some interesting, and probably academic questions arise here on the application of the rule in *Dearle v Hall*[72] that where competing assignments are concerned priority goes to the first assignee to give notice to the account debtor, but it is far more likely that priority will be granted to the receivables financier consensually. This is not an unusual arrangement where the company is in need of further funding which its bank is unwilling to provide. The second explanation has been touched upon above, and that is that receivables financing, as a form of asset-based lending, is inherently more certain in terms of risk assessment. As Armour points out, asset-based lending can focus on the expected value of an asset in insolvency, whereas more traditional bank lending, which he terms 'relationship lending' focuses more on the value of the enterprise as a whole, and in this sense the former has something of an advantage:

> ... a ... financier, specialising in lending against receivables, may be expected to have a comparative advantage in performing such assessments over banks lending on an overdraft basis, which specialise in making general assessments about debtors' business prospects.[73]

A very similar point could be made about financing arrangements for tangible assets which, as Figures 10.2 and 10.3[74] demonstrate, feature in 31 per cent of the receivership sample and 41 per cent of the administration sample. Hire purchase and chattel leasing agreements are structured so as to provide what in substance amounts to a security-type interest to the lessor should the lessee default, and this is done primarily by reference to the value of the asset, a far more certain yardstick than the prospects of the lessee's business and the likelihood of default.

It is dangerous to make sweeping predictions, but nevertheless it is submitted that the trend towards asset-based financing will continue into the long-term, especially amongst the SME market. This will be attributable at least in part to the *Spectrum* decision, but also because of asset-based lending, both against

---

72 (1828) 3 Russ 1.
73 Armour, above note 19 at 204.
74 Above at 253–254.

receivables and tangible assets, is simply a far more effective method of protecting against insolvency by reducing the risk of over-exposure. This does not necessarily spell the end of relationship banking, however, as the major clearing banks, having already established a practice of lending against receivables through their invoice discounting arms whilst providing further finance on the basis of other assets and the prospects of the business, will probably continue along this path. The final dimension of the investigation, therefore, is as to whether or not the net result of these developments is generally positive.

The Fragmentation of Security: Possible Ramifications

Armour makes a highly cogent argument that attempts to redistribute in insolvency via statutory taxation are likely to be counter-productive as the tax-bearing parties, usually institutional lenders, are sophisticated enough to restructure their lending methods so as to avoid the tax.[75] The move towards receivables financing and other asset-based lending methods demonstrates how this may be done reasonably effectively, and the process appears already advanced. At the risk of stating the obvious, one should not overlook the fact that this can be seen as a desirable development from the perspective of *borrowers* as well as of lenders. Asset-based financing, and particularly borrowing against the security of receivables, may allow companies to borrow more and, in the words of one insolvency practitioner, 'to make their assets work twice as hard for them'. In times of growth, which will be reflected in the size of the debtor ledger, this may mean easier and quicker access to necessary funding, particularly for SMEs. There is certainly a question as to whether this kind of finance is more expensive for companies than borrowing on overdraft terms. Confines of space do not allow for an examination of this matter here, except to mention the general view that competition to lend money is reasonably healthy at present, and that this may be working to the advantage of borrowers. Two observations from interviewees, one a banker and the other an insolvency practitioner, may be salient here:

> Broadly speaking I would say that the factoring/invoice discounting industry proportionately attracts more troubled businesses than the banks. Of course, it's cheaper lending if you go to a bank, so why would you go to a factor? Now there are reasons you might in that credit is flexible and as you expand they'll give you more money, so you might be a successful business but expanding, so you'd go with invoice discounting.

> The market works well, and particularly for the SME company, where the world and his wife will be wanting to lend money to them. So assuming the company raises its money when it's looking okay, they will probably have played off two or three debt financiers against each other, and there are two main parameters I guess, one is the percentage advance that you can get, which can be anything from 60% to maybe 90%.

---

75 Armour, above note 19 at 190.

The critical point to note here is that any adverse effects of a large-scale migration from relationship to asset-based lending will be experienced by both the borrower and its *unsecured* creditors *only* should financial difficulties arise. Whilstever the corporation remains profitable it can enjoy the flexibility offered by the fragmentation of its secured borrowing base and no external effects should tarnish this method of financing. In times of marginal solvency, and on formal insolvency, however, a different state of affairs emerges.

The most obvious outcome of the trend towards asset-based lending is that statutory taxation schemes will simply be avoided and the redistributive policy of the legislature thwarted. As only floating charge assets are diverted from the charge holder, assets subject to fixed charges or owned outright by a 'funder', whether it be a receivables financier taking an outright assignment of book debts or a financier using leasing or hire purchase arrangements, will be invulnerable. This, however, does not represent any change from the position prior to *Spectrum* or even *Agnew*, except perhaps in terms of extent. Hire purchase and leasing transactions worked in exactly the same way, and charges over book debts along the lines of the *Siebe Gorman* formula were effective to safeguard the proceeds of debts from other claimants. Thus, as one insolvency practitioner interviewee put it:

> ... we are finding it rarer and rarer to go into a small/medium sized basic business, a metal bashing business or whatever, and finding that there are any unencumbered assets. We typically find a sale and lease back of property, the book debts have been factored, the plant and machinery has finance on it and the bank will have an overdraft and a charge on any goodwill. When you then come to realise the assets you can find that there's nothing covered by a floating charge, it's arguably all fixed charge, and that means that there's even less coming through to unsecured creditors because of the way the funding market is changing.

One possible development post-*Spectrum* that might be predicted is an acceleration of attempts to subject such items as stock and raw materials to fixed, as opposed to floating charges. In certain types of businesses, where large amounts of stock or materials are routinely held, it might be possible to satisfy the control test from *Spectrum* by an insistence on the part of the chargee that these assets may not be disposed of or utilised without express permission. In the same way that lenders might attempt to block accounts into which the proceeds of debts might be paid and periodically agree to releases, so too might they adopt a similar tactic in relation to valuable items of stock or materials. Several interviewees mentioned that they had encountered such arrangements, which would suggest that the cost of 'micro-managing' tactics such as this might, in appropriate circumstances, be considered worthwhile.

There would be potential pitfalls associated with such a tactic of course. The inevitable competition with retention of title claimants would occur, as might the question of whether purported fixed charges over revolving *tangible* assets might attract rigorous judicial scrutiny on the kind of policy grounds mentioned above in relation to fixed charges over book debts.[76] Equally, the more a lender exercises *de facto* control over the destination of stock and raw materials the more problematic it might become to avoid an allegation of shadow directorship in the event of insolvency, especially where attempts to control the use of the proceeds of book debts were also in place. At some point it is not inconceivable that an attempt to protect a security interest might nevertheless be viewed as dominion over the course of the business sufficient to attract liability. It will therefore be a matter of fine judgment as to whether it would be worthwhile to attempt routinely to draw revolving tangible assets into the fixed charge portion of the security. Nevertheless, now that *Spectrum* offers House of Lords authority that the control test applies it remains a possibility that lenders will attempt to test its parameters. Success in this regard would drain the floating charge pool even further.

A more worrisome consequence of an increasingly fragmented security base within companies might be predicted, and that is that it may have some impact on the incidence of either corporate or business rescue.[77] This much was noted by Armour, who draws a distinction between the ability of relationship lenders and asset based lenders to make informed decisions about the fate of troubled borrowers and to act upon those decisions in a manner that may benefit parties other than themselves.[78] This distinction may be manifested at different stages along the path or corporate decline. To amplify, the 'concentrated' relationship lender, with its focus on the performance of the *business* of the company, is incentivised to monitor that performance and to intervene at a reasonably early stage should warning bells sound. This intervention typically takes the form of submitting the borrower to the attention of a specialist department within the lender's operations in an attempt to reverse the decline. Such a strategy is reasonably well documented and was investigated by Franks and Sussmann, who noted that the majority of firms entering 'intensive care' exited without resort to formal insolvency proceedings.[79] Interview data from the author's own research into insolvency outcomes also suggests that this interventionist technique is used wherever possible and can be highly successful. One insolvency practitioner commented:

> It's a wide church now, number one, the banks are more alert, I personally think the banks have done a very good job, I think they should be congratulated on the way they've invested in their own turnaround teams. About 10 years ago those turnaround around teams were pretty naff, but now I think they've got a lot of experience and expertise and they are now, generally, pretty good teams.

76　See above at 245–7.

77　The distinction being between a 'rescue' of the corporate entity, which will restore it to its original owners, and a 'rescue' of the business of that entity, usually through a going concern sale of that business to an independent or connected party.

78　Armour, above note 19 at 219.

79　See Franks, J., and Sussman, O., 'Financial Distress and Bank Restructuring of Small to Medium Size UK Companies' (2005) 9 *Review of Finance* 65.

A banking interviewee explained the procedure as follows:

> If you use the dreadful medical analogies that are always used in this field of human endeavour, they come to us when they've got a mild cold rather than pneumonia. The vast majority of companies which come to us get returned into the 'good bank', and that's our mission in life, to try and restore them to strength. So we employ teams of people located around the country, around the world now in fact, who are a mixture of bankers, accountants, lawyers, venture capitalists, people have come from strategy/consultancy businesses, that sort of thing. When something comes to us it will still be very much trading, but it will be an anticipation that it may be about to breach its covenants.

One important factor in the ability of lenders to exercise these strategies is their control over the borrower, and where lending is concentrated this is readily available. However, where there exist fragmented security interests a proportion of this control may be lost: influence over the borrower may be diluted, and other secured creditors may themselves be in a position to stymie one lender's 'rescue' strategy in pursuit of their own interests. Three interviewees remarked that this was already happening in larger corporate insolvencies:

> Now you have situations where the bank is out-manoeuvred, if you like, by other stakeholders who don't have the company's interests as much at heart. We found this with a case last year, quite a big case, where there was a clearing bank who are probably at the forefront of restructuring and trying to work things through, even to the point of putting more money in to sort the problem out. That bank was basically blown out by an asset based lender who said, 'No, we just want the money out now', and who wasn't interested in a restructure at all. You have situations now where those competing stakeholders, there may be an asset-based lender, a clearing bank, some other stakeholder, an equity house for example, don't all have the same interest in supporting the business. In the old days you would be dealing with the bank's relationship manager and the owner of the business trying to sort it out, but not now. The result of that is that you can find you're spending a lot of time in a game of poker with various stakeholders negotiating for a better outcome under their own agendas as opposed to an overall result for the business in dealing with its problems.[80]

It should be acknowledged that those banks who actively intercede do so as much out of enlightened self-interest as philanthropy: if their efforts are successful they will be able to maintain a more profitable and hence less troublesome customer which will hopefully be better able to service the outstanding obligation going forward. One further, and very important point is that in a typical relationship-lending scenario, withdrawal from the relationship can be expensive

---

80 The other two interviewees made similar observations, and also commented upon the emergence of a 'distressed debt' market and the possibly negative influence of bondholders on large-scale rescue attempts.

and difficult. Calling in an overdraft is all very well and good, but that move will almost inevitably have to be accompanied by the appointment of an administrator (or administrative receiver if circumstances allow), which in turn engenders a further layer of costs (which the lender may have to meet) and a general depreciation of asset value which, again, will be borne by the lender to the extent its security cover is plunged into deficit.[81]

This can be compared with the relative ease with which an asset-based lender can exit. In the case of receivables financing, it may be simply a matter of either refusing to make further advances and collecting out on the assigned ledger. This would be a route open to factoring firms, and they have the specialist expertise necessary to carry out the task effectively. For invoice discounters, the 'fallback' charge would allow the appointment of an insolvency practitioner, but without falling prey to the statutory taxation that that route would prompt. The appointment of an insolvency practitioner may, in any event, be appropriate because of the office-holder's extensive management powers, which would allow for a period of trading in an attempt to avoid a depreciation of the value of the debtor ledger, as explained by one interviewee:

> Sometimes you'll find that it's all right saying that they're your debts and you can collect them, but sometimes the strategy is wider than that, you need there to be a slow run-down of the business so as to preserve the debtors. If you just walk away from the business there might be a load of half-finished contracts and people will say, 'Well you haven't finished my contract, I've suffered a loss, don't expect me to pay for the earlier contract you did complete', they'll just exercise set-off. So, for a smooth run-down, or a sale of the business, it's better to have an insolvency practitioner in place. The reason for having a charge is one, it gives you more assets and two, it gives you more control.

As far as hire purchase and chattel lease creditors are concerned, the same applies. Notwithstanding the ability of administrators to temporarily 'block' enforcement proceedings[82] or to dispose of assets held under such transactions,[83] the owner or lessee of the asset is guaranteed compensation in either event, and can, therefore, simply await its payment over.[84] It is possible, therefore, that the greater opportunity for withdrawal open to an asset-based financier may, if exercised, operate to the detriment of the borrower. This may be felt at two stages: firstly, at the point where some form of rescue attempt is being contemplated by a bank creditor through its specialised department, and, secondly, once an insolvency proceeding is in force. In the first instance, asset-based lenders may simply refuse to co-operate in refraining from 'enforcement' tactics, and in the second, particularly with receivables financiers, they may refuse to make the further advances necessary to fund an attempt to sell the business as a going concern.

---

81   See, on insolvency depreciation, above at 241.
82   Insolvency Act 1986, Schedule B1, paragraphs 43, 111.
83   Ibid., paragraph 72(1).
84   Ibid., paragraph 72(3).

Starved of cash, an insolvency practitioner in such circumstances will have little option but to liquidate any available assets, make employees redundant and leave what might be a viable business to founder.

The above is perhaps a somewhat simplistic analysis in certain respects. It does not take into account the possibility of a 'pre-packaged' sale of the business through administration or receivership,[85] which would avoid periods of trading for which funding would be necessary. Equally, simply because opportunities for a reasonably easy exit strategy exist does not necessarily mean that they are routinely taken advantage of, although, for the most part, interviewees suggested that they were encountering a rather different approach to troubled customers from asset-based lenders than they would expect from relationship lenders.[86] The overall picture is no doubt far more complex than this and will certainly be worth monitoring for the future developments, but it is nevertheless submitted that the real danger of the fragmentation of security lies here. It may operate to suppress 'rescue' initiatives in relation to both the corporate entity and its business and so will lead to a more general loss of value to *all stakeholders* in the insolvent company, except those in a position to lend on the basis of assets and to exit swiftly and cheaply.

Conclusion

The above discussion does no more than present a thumbnail sketch of the *Spectrum* decision itself, the possible responses to it and the possible consequences of those responses. It is far too early in the day to attempt to make confident forecasts of whether the decision will accelerate a trend towards asset-based lending already reasonably advanced, or, indeed, quite what effect such an acceleration will have on insolvency outcomes such as returns to preferential creditors, distributions under the prescribed part, and the incidence of corporate and business rescue. Too many as yet unknown variables exist to make anything other than a few tentative observations on the possible ramifications of *Spectrum*.

However, it is submitted that the decision itself comes towards the end of a protracted story rather than at its beginning. *Spectrum* may prompt further litigation, as institutional lenders consider variations of standard form debentures that may satisfy the control test, and in relation to both book debt proceeds and revolving tangible assets. It is, though, equally likely that they will continue along the route to focusing on asset-based lending themselves. To the extent that this development is coupled with a continuing 'relationship' dimension, as where overdraft and asset-based lending are housed under one roof, one might expect rescue attempts to continue to be made. Moreover, if the positive reports of the

---

85 For a fuller exposition on the subject of pre-packs, see above note 7, at 69 et seq. See also Finch, J., 'Pre-packaged administrations: Bargains in the Shadow of Insolvency or Shadowy Bargains' [2006] *Journal of Business Law* 568; Walton, P., 'Pre-packaged administrations – Trick or Treat?' (2006) 19 *Insolvency Intelligence* 113.

86 Above note 7 at 39 et seq.

level of competition in the lending market are accurate, it is conceivable that independent receivables financiers will mimic their banking counterparts and adopt a pro-active approach to their troubled customers. The legacy of *Spectrum*, therefore, has yet to materialise, but its emergence will make fascinating viewing in the interim.

PART V
INNOVATIONS IN INSOLVENCY

Chapter 11

A Plea for the Development of Coherent Labour and Insolvency Principles on a Regional Basis in the SADC Countries

Stefan van Eck and André Boraine

Introduction

The Southern African Development Community's ('SADC')[1] motto in their coat of arms reads 'Towards a Common Future'. Article 5 of the SADC Treaty spells out one of the main objectives of SADC, namely 'to promote sustainable and equitable economic growth and socio-economic development through deeper cooperation and integration'. The aim of this chapter is thus to look into some employment law issues in insolvency in a few selected SADC countries against this backdrop. Some pertinent issues in this regard are to what extent there is a coherent approach and the alignment between the various labour and insolvency laws within the countries included in the discussion.

In August 2003, SADC members' Heads of State and Government signed the Charter of Fundamental Social Rights in SADC. One of the objectives of this charter is to promote the harmonisation of social security schemes of member states.[2] Other goals include the alignment of policies regarding freedom of association and collective bargaining,[3] equal treatment for men and woman,[4] protection of children and young people,[5] protection of elderly persons,[6] protection of people with disabilities,[7] and the promotion of workplace democracy.[8]

---

1   The establishment of SADC occurred through a treaty, signed on 17 August 1992 in Windhoek, Namibia. On 14 August 2001, Heads of State and Government signed an Agreement Amending the SADC Treaty.
2   The Charter of Fundamental Social Rights in SADC of 26 August 2003, Article 10.
3   Ibid., Article 4.
4   Ibid., Article 6.
5   Ibid., Article 7.
6   Ibid., Article 8.
7   Ibid., Article 9.
8   Ibid., Article 13. This article provides that employees must have the right to information and to participate in consultations in connection with technological changes to employers and restructuring of undertakings but it is silent on transfers of

During May 2004, a draft text of the Code on Social Security for SADC was finalised. This Code constitutes an attempt to set into operation key provisions of the Charter of Fundamental Social Rights by creating a framework for benchmarking social security provisioning.[9] This is a momentous initiative towards taking steps in realising one of the goals of SADC namely, the harmonisation of policies in the Southern African region.[10]

Should one consider aspects like unemployment, poverty levels and infrastructure, Western Europe and the Southern African region are worlds apart. However, it is submitted that there are similarities between the present day situation in SADC and the position in Western Europe before the establishment of the European Union. Over a period spanning decades rather than years, lobbyists who were in favour of the introduction of harmonised social security, labour and insolvency policies,[11] were responsible for the implementation of numerous European instruments, approximating laws of European countries in respect of amongst others the following areas:

- Laws regarding equal pay for men and women;[12]
- Laws regulating the implementation of the principle of equal access to employment, vocational training and promotion and working conditions for men and women;[13]
- Laws making provision for prohibiting discrimination especially against women;[14]
- Laws directing employers to inform employees of the conditions applicable to the contract or employment relationship.[15]
- Laws regarding collective redundancies;[16]

---

businesses as going concerns and assistance to employees when employers become insolvent.

9   Draft Code on Social Security (2004) at 1.
10   However, it can be argued that there is still along way to go. The draft Code on Social Security for SADC has been sent to all SADC National Committees for comment. Once comments have been received on this document from all SADC member countries, the draft code will be sent to SADC's Integrated Committee of Ministers before the code will be implemented. Although the cut-off date for comments was set for November 2004, only three member countries have responded during the middle of 2005. As far as can be ascertained, the only other instrument that has been published is the Code on HIV and Employment 1997.
11   See Woolfrey, D., 'Harmonisation of Southern Africa's Laws in the Context of Regional Integration' (1991) *Industrial Law Journal* 703 at 707. In this evolutionary process of developing aligned policies, there was initially a debate on whether only the economic and financial fields had to be covered or whether it also had to include social and labour standards.
12   Directive 75/117/EC of 10 February 1975.
13   Directive 76/207/EC of 9 February 1976.
14   Directive 2000/78/EC of 27 November 2000.
15   Directive 91/533/EC of 14 October 1991.
16   Directive 98/59/EC of 20 July 1998.

- Laws regulating transfers of businesses or undertakings (or parts thereof) as going concerns;[17] and
- The approximation of laws of member countries relating to employees in the event of the insolvency of their employer.[18]

One of the significant lessons that can be learnt from the European Union experience is that the development of international instruments promoting unified principles for member states does not occur over night. It is an evolutionary process. To illustrate, the European Directive on Equal Pay for Men and Women was signed during 1975 and the amended Directive regulating the Transfer of Businesses as Going Concerns was implemented during 2001.

This chapter will argue in favour of harmonisation of not only social security regimes, but also ultimately, to approximate labour and insolvency laws of members of the SADC region. Apart from the positive vision of one day establishing a vibrant Southern African economic hub that would enhance job creation and work towards the eradication of poverty, closer economic cooperation also has an ugly face to it, namely that of unfair competition and social dumping. This has to be avoided at all costs.

During this age of globalisation, sticky policy issues relating to 'protection of employee rights', as opposed to 'market flexibility', has become central to the debate about the development of our future world society. Foreign investors who are in business to optimise profits and dividends for their shareholders are no longer restricted to national boundaries.[19] Dissimilar labour and insolvency laws in neighbouring countries create uneven markets. Progressive labour laws generally guarantee minimum wages and make provision for compulsory contributions to social security funds. This has a definite impact on production costs. Countries with highly regulated labour relations regimes, protect their employees from exploitation, but they are at a disadvantage in respect of their neighbours who have adopted more flexible and permissive labour laws. Woolfrey points out that in a region where capital is mobile, 'business may be attracted to those areas where labour standards are low or non-existent'.[20] In order to remain competitive, countries could opt for deregulatory policies which could lead to 'social dumping'. It is submitted that one way of creating a relatively even playing field and to avoid

---

17　Directive 77/187/EC of 14 February 1977 (as amended in 1998). See also the more recent Directive 2001/23/EC of 12 March 2001 and the discussion thereof in Todd, C., Du Toit, D. and Bosch, D., *Business Transfers and Employment Rights* (2004, LexisNexis Butterworths, Durban) at 13.

18　Directive 2002/74/EC of 23 September 2002, amending Directive 80/987/EC of 20 October 1980.

19　Unfortunately, investors do not take economic risks by investing in foreign countries for the sake of uplifting employees and creating wealth for the host country.

20　Woolfrey, above note 11 at 709, referring to the comments by Hepple, B., 'The Crisis in EEC Labour Law' (1987) *Industrial Law Journal* 77, to wit that in the European context, this could lead to 'social dumping', namely, 'countries with high levels of social protection are reducing this to meet competition from countries with low labour costs'.

a race to the bottom is to introduce common standards for all members of the particular region.

The focus of this chapter thus falls on a particular area of labour relations regulation, namely: How trouble-free (or problematic) would it be for a prospective investor to buy an undertaking as going concern in one of the countries in the SADC region, and what rights do workers (and creditors) have when a particular business becomes bankrupt? It is unfortunate that the SADC Charter of Fundamental Social Rights does not contain any goals, as one would find in some of the countries in the region, in respect of the harmonisation of principles relating to transfers of businesses as going concerns and insolvency matters.[21] A carefully balanced framework that will see to it that the region as a whole is not capable of being classified as one that is either being over-regulated – or one that exploits workers solely for the benefit of the foreign investor should be supported.[22]

This contribution further purports to illustrate, by means of a standardised case study, how far apart African countries in the same region are in respect of the topic under discussion. The discussion focuses on a comparison between three SADC counties regarding: what protection do workers have when a business is transferred as going concern, especially when it is faced with bankruptcy?

The Case Study

The chapter will be dealt with against the backdrop of the following case study:

> A successful European textile import and export company (Euro Textiles Inc) wishes to expand its operations by buying a textile manufacturing plant in one of the SADC countries. South African based textile company (SA Textiles Inc.) operates clothing factories in South Africa, Namibia and Botswana. The Namibian and Botswana branches have been formally incorporated as foreign companies in accordance with the laws of Namibia and Botswana respectively and are referred to as SA Textiles Inc, Namibian Textiles Inc and Botswana Textiles Inc. Each of the three entities owns land and a factory in their respective jurisdictions, each employs more or less 100 workers (comprised roughly of 70 per cent local employees and 30 per cent migrant workers) from neighbouring countries.
>
> SA Textiles provides raw materials to Namibian Textiles Inc and Botswana Textiles Inc. Due to internal managerial problems at SA Textiles Inc, the particular factory has run on a loss since 2006 and is declared bankrupt after one of its major creditors, the Bank of South Africa, has initiated bankruptcy proceedings. This leads to financial

---

21 The Charter of Fundamental Social Rights, Article 13, does, however, make provision that member countries shall create an enabling environment so that employees have the right to information and the right to consultation and participation in the process when the decision is taken to restructure operations.

22 Southern Africa is in need of the creation of 'good jobs'. This often entails permanent positions which offer relatively high salaries. Such employees contribute towards the payment of taxes and generally make contributions towards social security funds.

problems for Namibian Textiles Inc and Botswana Textiles Inc at the beginning of 2007. For purposes of standardisation of our example, each of the three entities:

- owes various creditors the equivalent of ZAR 3 million;
- owns assets amounting to ZAR 1 million;
- has encumbered assets (covered by securities and mortgages) amounting to ZAR 500,000;
- has unencumbered assets valued at ZAR 500,000;
- has not paid the employees for the last three months of services rendered.

SA Textiles Inc owns a small office block equipped with furniture and computers in Europe since it imports some of its base materials from Europe. There is no mortgage bond registered over this property but SA Textiles employs 5 people at this foreign office, namely a South African as its foreign representative and 4 assistants who are citizens of member states of the European Union.

Euro Textiles Inc has EUR 1,000,000 at its disposal for investment and it wants to buy one of three textile factories mentioned above. It is submitted that one of the determining factors for Euro Textiles Inc, in deciding which undertaking to buy, would be the scope and content of the respective labour laws that apply in the different countries that regulate the transfer of the businesses as going concerns and the position of workers of insolvent employers. In other words, how flexible or regulated are different jurisdictions' labour and insolvency regimes?

Supranational Instruments

In evaluating the position of SADC countries, it is worthwhile considering the benchmark that has been set on the supranational level, most notably by the International Labour Organisation ('ILO') and the European Union, in respect of the transfers of businesses as going concerns and claims of workers against their bankrupt employers. South Africa, Namibia and Botswana are all members of the ILO. Whereas ILO conventions are silent on principles regarding transfers of businesses as going concerns, the European Union has introduced Directives in this regard that bind member states to which we will return later in the discussion.

The ILO Protection of Workers' Claims (Employer's Insolvency) Convention ('ILO Insolvency Convention')[23] gives ratifying countries the option of either accepting Part II or Part III of the ILO Insolvency Convention. Part II of the ILO Insolvency Convention makes provision that members who accept the obligations of this part should provide protection to employees for claims against their bankrupt employers by means of a privilege, so that they are paid out of the assets of the insolvent employer before non-privileged creditors can be paid their share.[24] Article 6 provides that the privilege shall cover at least:

---

23   Convention 173 of 1992.
24   Ibid., Article 5.

(a) the workers' claims for wages relating to a prescribed period, which shall not be less than three months, prior to the insolvency or prior to the termination of the employment;

(b) the workers' claims for holiday pay due as a result of work performed during the year in which the insolvency or the termination of the employment occurred, and in the preceding year;

(c) the workers' claims for amounts due in respect of other types of paid absence relating to a prescribed period, which shall not be less than three months, prior to the insolvency or prior to the termination of the employment;

(d) severance pay due to workers upon termination of their employment.[25]

Part III of the ILO Insolvency Convention makes provision for signatories to this part to create independent guarantee institutions that would stand in for worker's claims against their insolvent employer's.[26] The independent fund, with assets separate from the assets of the employer, would pay out these claims.[27] Article 12 of the ILO Insolvency Convention provides that the workers' claims protected pursuant to this Part of the Convention shall include at least:

(a) the workers' claims for wages relating to a prescribed period, which shall not be less than eight weeks, prior to the insolvency or prior to the termination of the employment;

(b) the workers' claims for holiday pay due as a result of work performed during a prescribed period, which shall not be less than six months, prior to the insolvency or prior to the termination of the employment;

(c) the workers' claims for amounts due in respect of other types of paid absence relating to a prescribed period, which shall not be less than eight weeks, prior to the insolvency or prior to the termination of employment;

(d) severance pay due to workers upon termination of their employment.

Returning to the transfers of businesses as going concerns, the EC Acquired Rights Directive of 1977[28] was repealed and replaced by Directive 2001/23/EC of 12 March 2001. In essence, this directive provides three levels of protection.

---

25 Ibid., Article 7, which provides that: 1. National laws or regulations may limit the protection by privilege of workers' claims to a prescribed amount, which shall not be below a socially acceptable level. 2. Where the privilege afforded to workers' claims is so limited, the prescribed amount shall be adjusted as necessary so as to maintain its value. Article 8 regulates that: 1. National laws or regulations shall give workers' claims a higher rank of privilege than most other privileged claims, and in particular those of the State and the social security system. 2. However, where workers' claims are protected by a guarantee institution in accordance with Part III of this Convention, the claims so protected may be given a lower rank of privilege than those of the State and the social security system.

26 Ibid., Article 9.

27 Directive 2002/74/EC of 23 September 2002, amending Directive 80/987/EC of 20 October 1980, makes provision that European Union members subscribe to Part III of the ILO Insolvency Convention.

28 As amended in 1998.

Firstly, it provides for the transfer of all contracts of employment (with all of its rights and obligations) from the old to the new employer;[29] secondly, it protects employees against dismissal by the old or new employer due to the transfer but this does not stand in the way of the dismissal of employees on ground of 'economic, technical or organisational reasons';[30] and thirdly, it requires the old and new employers to inform and consult the representatives of the employees affected by the transfer.[31] It is interesting that in the context of this discussion, this directive provides that unless member countries provide otherwise, the first two categories of protection mentioned above, do not apply to any transfer if the old employer is subject to bankruptcy proceedings, and if a country should decide to comply under insolvency proceedings under insolvent circumstances, it may be permissible to alter such employees terms and conditions of employment to safeguard opportunities by ensuring the survival of the undertaking.[32]

In the discussion that follows, it will become apparent that some countries in the SADC region have been strongly influenced by either the one or the other of the ILO Insolvency Convention and the European Directive, but that there is a strong sense that there are great disparities between the SADC member countries regarding transfers and protection of employees claims during insolvency.

South Africa

Transfer of an Undertaking as a Going Concern

Shortly after South Africa's first democratic elections during 1994, we saw the introduction of a new and modern Labour Relations Act ('LRA').[33] Amongst other things, it regulates collective bargaining, the right to strike, unfair dismissal law and transfers of undertakings as going concerns. Although not a European Union member, South African policy makers were strongly influenced by the European Directive which protects employees with the transfer of an undertaking as a going concern when the corresponding transfer provisions for the LRA were drafted. The principles of the LRA comply with all three layers of protection provided for in the European Directive. Firstly, section 197(2) of the LRA provides for the automatic transfer of all contracts of employment (with all rights and obligations) from the old employer to the new employer in the event of the transfer; secondly, section 187(1)(g) makes it an 'automatically unfair dismissal' if an employee is dismissed if the reason for the dismissal is 'a transfer, or a reason related to a transfer'; and thirdly, section 197(6) provides that any agreement regulating the transfer must be

---

29   Directive 2001/23/EC of 12 March 2001, Article 3.
30   Ibid., Article 4.
31   Ibid., Article 7.
32   Ibid., Articles 5(1) and (2)(b).
33   Act 66 of 1995.

concluded with the employees' representatives after disclosure of all relevant information during the negotiation of such an agreement.[34]

In the South African context, once it is ascertained that a 'business' is being 'transferred' in solvent circumstances,[35] the consequences that find application in terms of section 197(2)[36] are that: the new employer is automatically placed in the position of the old employer in respect of all contracts of employment in existence directly before the transfer; all rights and obligations in existence between the workers and their old employer directly before the transfer, remain in force between the workers and the new employer after the transfer; anything done before the transfer by the old employer, including the unfair dismissal of the employee is considered to have been done by the new employer; and the transfer does not interrupt the employees' continuity of employment and the worker's contract of employment continues with the new employer.

Translated to the hypothetical case study, it would entail the following, should Euro Textiles Inc decide to buy the South African textile plant:

- Euro Textiles Inc may not decide to buy the business and only to take say 70 of the 100 employees;
- If the employees were paid ZAR 5,000 per month, and they were entitled to contributions to medical aid and pension fund by the old employer before the transfer, the new employer will also have to maintain the same conditions of service;
- If SA Textiles Inc were to unfairly retrench some of the employees based on operational grounds before the transfer, Euro Textiles Inc can be held liable for the unfair dismissal;[37] and

---

34   It is submitted that technically the South African model does not strictly comply with the third level of protection. There is no specific obligation on employers to consult with employees during the transfer situation. However, it could be asked why it is necessary to 'consult' when all contracts are in any event being transferred automatically. Only when changes to conditions of service are being contemplated, a duty to negotiate (that is deemed to be a stronger and more onerous duty on employers than to consult) is imposed on employers.

35   LRA, section 197 defines the terms 'business' and 'transfer' for the purposes of both sections 197 and 197A. A 'business' is defined to 'include the whole or part of any business, trade, undertaking or service'. The word 'service' was included in the 2002 amendments to the LRA. 'Transfer' is defined to 'mean the transfer of a business by one employer ('the old employer') to another employer ('the new employer') as a going concern'.

36   This is unless the parties have agreed otherwise in terms of section 197(6).

37   *SA Municipal Workers Union & Others v Rand Airport Management Co (Pty) Ltd & Others* 2005 26 ILJ 67 (LAC). Included under the prominent cases, apart from the Rand Airport Management case, where employee rights during the transfer of businesses as going concerns have been upheld, are: *Schutte & Others v Powerplus Performance (Pty) Ltd & Another* 1999 20 ILJ 655 (LC); *Foodgrow, a Division of Leisurenet Ltd v Keil* 1999 20 ILJ 2521 (LAC); *Success Panel Beaters & Services Centre CC v NUMSA* 2000 6 BLLR 635 (LAC); *NULW v Barnard NO (Vittmar*

- If the workers had 10 years of service with SA Textiles Inc prior to the transfer, and Euro Textiles Inc decided to retrench the workers on operational grounds 1 year after the transfer, the new employer would have to pay 11 years severance pay to each of the workers in consideration of the dismissal.

In two respects, South Africa seems to have extended the protection in favour employees even further than what is required by the general norm of the European Directive. In the first instance, no provision is made for the fact that it would not amount to unfair dismissal should the genuine reason for the dismissal be the operational requirements of the employer. In the *Rand Airport* case[38] the Labour Appeal Court in South Africa has given an extensive interpretation to the meaning of 'dismissal' based on 'a transfer, or a reason related to a transfer' and has made no distinction between dismissal based on operational requirements and dismissal based on the transfer (as has been done in the European text). It has been argued that this may deter buyers from considering the possibility of buying businesses as going concerns, especially in the case of businesses on the brink of financial ruin.[39] In the second instance, it was decided to extend the coverage of the transfer protection to the situation of the transfer of insolvent businesses to new employers.

Section 197A(1) applies to the transfer of a business if the old employer is *insolvent*, or where a scheme of arrangement or compromise is entered into to avoid the winding-up or sequestration of the employer for reasons of insolvency. Once determined that section 197A(1) is applicable to a particular scenario, the consequences in terms of section 197A(2) will be that '[d]espite the Insolvency Act 1936' and 'unless otherwise agreed in terms of section 197(6)' that 'the new employer is automatically substituted in the place of the old employer in all contracts of employment in existence immediately before the old employers provisional winding-up or sequestration',[40] and further that 'all the rights and obligations between the old employer and the and each employee at the time of the transfer remain rights and obligations between the old employer and each employee'.[41]

This makes it clear that even after sequestration or liquidation, the buyer cannot buy the business and only take over some but not all of the employees, nor would it be entitled to change conditions of service without reaching agreement

---

Industries (Pty) Ltd) 2001 9 BLLR 1002 (LAC); *National Education Health & Allied Workers Union v University of Cape Town & Others* 2003 24 ILJ 95 (CC).

38   *SA Municipal Workers Union & Others v Rand Airport Management Co (Pty) Ltd & Others* 2005 26 ILJ 67 (LAC).

39   See van Eck, B.P.S., 'Transfer of Businesses as Going Concerns: The Over-protection of Employees under Insolvent Circumstances' (2006) 2 *De Jure* 405.

40   LRA, section 197A(2)(a).

41   Ibid., section 197A(2)(c).

with the employees in order to secure the survival of an insolvent business as provided for in the European Directive.[42]

Effect of Insolvency on the Contract of Employment

Before 1 January 2003, section 38 of the Insolvency Act (24 of 1936) ('IA') had the effect that the sequestration of the insolvent employer (or the winding-up of a company or closed corporation) automatically terminated all the contracts of employment between the insolvent employer and his or her employees, subject to the right of the employees to claim compensation from the insolvent estate for any damages sustained in consequence of such termination. Interpretational problems occurred between labour law and insolvency law because if a business is transferred as going concern, there were no contracts to transfer. Upon the insistence of the trade union movement, and our constitutional 'right to fair labour practices' the IA and the LRA were amended towards the end of 2002 and the beginning of 2003.[43]

The new section 38 of the IA provides for the initial suspension of contracts of service between insolvent employers and their employees. This would typically resolve the problem if the business was sold out of the insolvent estate. All contracts of employment could then be transferred to the new employer.[44] After the suspension one of two things could happen: Firstly, the trustee or liquidator could terminate some or all of the contracts of employment after following a retrenchment procedure similar the normal retrenchment procedures prescribed in terms of the LRA[45] or the contracts would terminate automatically after the window period of 45 days after the appointment of the final trustee or liquidator. This could typically be between three and six months after the initial sequestration.

---

42   The question has been raised whether this does not border on over-regulation in the South African context in so far as it could even be to the detriment of the notion of business rescue. See Boraine, A. and van Eck, B.P.S., 'The New Insolvency and Labour Legislative Package: How Successful was the Integration?' (2003) 24 *Industrial Law Journal* 1840 at 1868; van Eck, B.P.S., Boraine, A. and Steyn, L. 'Fair Labour Practices in South African Insolvency Law' (2004) *South African Law Journal* 902 at 925 in this regard.

43   The amendments to the LRA came into effect on 1 August 2002. See the Labour Relations Amendment Act (12 of 2002), GG 23540.

44   After the suspension, employees will not be required to tender their services in terms of their contracts; the trustee or liquidator is not obliged to remunerate them but the Employees are entitled to unemployment benefits in terms of the Unemployment Insurance Act (63 of 2001).

45   Contracts may only be terminated after the final trustee or liquidator has entered into consultations with specified parties, including registered trade union representatives and the employees themselves under IA, section 38(5). The consultations must be 'aimed at reaching consensus' on appropriate measures to save or rescue the whole or part of the business of the insolvent employer. The trustee or liquidator must receive and consider written representations within 21 days of the appointment of the final trustee or final liquidator for a company: IA, section 38(7).

Trustees and liquidators who are unwilling to take risks in relation to the dismissal of employees will in all probability let the 45 days run out and contracts will terminate automatically. Where a business is transferred as a going concern in the circumstances envisaged in section 197A(1)(a)-(b), section 197A(2)(a) will prevail 'notwithstanding anything to the contrary contained in the IA'.

Hence, notwithstanding the fact that section 38(9) of the IA provides that 'all suspended contracts of service shall terminate 45 days' after the appointment of the final trustee or liquidator (and other instances) as discussed above, once a transfer of the insolvent's business takes place, such contracts will 'revive' and be transferred to the new employer in terms of section 197A. From this it is clear that the problem that existed with the old section 38 of the IA is still there and that the only effect is that the old problems have been postponed to a later date unless the trustee or liquidator has in fact secured a transfer of the business to a new employer.[46]

It is clear that section 38 of the IA promotes the idea that consultations should take place with the view of reaching consensus on 'measures to save or rescue the whole or part of the business'. However, section 187(1)(g) of the LRA specifically stipulates that dismissal is automatically unfair if the 'reason for dismissal is ... a transfer, or a reason related to a transfer, contemplated in section 197 or 197A'. Should a trustee, liquidator or new employer buy the business of an insolvent employer and terminate any of the contracts of employment pursuant thereto, they will run the risk of an automatic unfair dismissal dispute should any retrenchment take place.[47] An old employer will also be responsible for the consequences of an automatic unfair dismissal if a retrenchment were to be affected in order to make a floundering business more attractive for a potential buyer.

Claims against the Insolvent Estate and Social Security Benefits

South Africa has not adopted any part of the ILO Insolvency Convention. South African insolvency law does not provide for a guarantee fund that will pay salaries and other benefits in arrears at the time of bankruptcy as provided for in Part II of

---

46   The new section 38 appears to give the trustee or liquidator the power to terminate contracts of employment in order to make it more attractive for prospective buyers. Contracts are also terminated after the 45-day period. However, the LRA, section 197A(2)(a) provides that whenever a business is being sold as a going concern all contracts are transferred.

47   Council Directive 2001/23/EC, Article 4 provides as follows: 'The transfer of the undertaking, business or part of the undertaking shall not in itself constitute grounds for dismissal by the transferor or transferee. This provision shall not stand in the way of dismissals that may take place for economic, technical or organisational reasons entailing changes in the workforce'. The corresponding provisions in the LRA do not contain similar qualifications. In the recently reported *SA Municipal Workers Union & Others v Rand Airport Management Co (Pty) Ltd & Others* 2005 26 ILJ 67 (LAC), it became apparent that employers are at risk when discussing the possibility of a transfer during retrenchment proceedings.

the ILO Convention. However provision is made for certain preferences for employee claims in the event of the insolvency of the employer.[48]

The South African IA makes provision that acknowledged secured creditors would, in principle, obtain payment from the proceeds of their securities. The proceeds of unencumbered assets as well as surplus income derived from an encumbered asset will form the free residue fund, being the surplus income derived from an asset serving as real security and the income from unsecured assets, is used to pay the creditors with (statutory preferential claims, and then to pay the concurrent creditors. The order of preference provided for in the IA is as follows:[49]

(1) In the case of natural person debtors, funeral costs of the insolvent, his wife or children up to a maximum of ZAR 300. Anything above ZAR 300 is a concurrent claim.

(2) In the case of natural person debtors, death-bed expenses up to a maximum of ZAR 300.

(3) Sequestration and administration costs.

(4) Certain sheriff's charges incurred for legal proceedings before sequestration.

(5) *Salary and wages of employees and related claims in arrears.*[50] The benefits included under this heading are:

- wages in arrears for a period not exceeding three months (the maximum amount allowed under this provision being ZAR 12,000);[51]

- payment in respect of any period of leave or holiday due to the employee which has accrued as a result of his or her employment by the insolvent in the year of insolvency or the previous year (the maximum amount allowable under this provision being ZAR 4,000);

- any payment due in respect of any other form of paid absence for a period not exceeding three months prior to the date of liquidation (the maximum amount allowed under this provision being ZAR 4,000);

- any severance or retrenchment pay due to the employee in terms of any law, agreement, contract, wage-regulating measure *or as a result of termination in terms of section 38* (the maximum amount allowed under this provision being ZAR 12,000);[52] and

---

48 It is submitted that if such a fund is introduced, that it must be done in all SADC counties, otherwise it may lead to unfair competition and social dumping. In South Africa, no such obligation has been set for employers to join insurance companies to guarantee the payment of employee claims upon insolvency.

49 IA, sections 96–103.

50 Since 1 September 2000, this claim has moved up a notch in the priority list in terms of the Judicial Matters Second Amendment Act (122 of 1998). The ex-employees' preference was previously governed by the Insolvency Act, section 100(1) which ranked those preferential claims directly after the statutory claims listed in paragraph 6 below.

51 It is submitted that the limitation of this amount would fall foul of the ILO Insolvency Convention.

52 In terms of the IA, section 38(11), read with the amended section 98A(1)(a)(iv), employees whose contracts of service have terminated are entitled to this preference. The claim must be calculated in terms of the Basic Conditions of Employment Act (75

- a maximum amount of ZAR 12,000 payable thereafter in respect of any contributions payable by an insolvent, including contributions payable in respect of his employees, to any pension or provident fund, medical aid or unemployment fund or any similar scheme or fund.[53]

(6) Some statutory claims like the following rank *pari passu* and abate in equal proportion if necessary in terms of section 99 of the IA, for instance: compensation in terms of the Occupational Injuries and Diseases Act (130 of 1993); amounts owing to the South African Revenue Services in terms of the Income Tax Act (58 of 1962) (e.g. income tax deducted from an employee's salary); amounts owing by the insolvent as an employer in terms of the Occupational Diseases in Mines and Works Act (78 of 1973); or unemployment insurance contributions due to the Unemployment Insurance Fund in terms of the Unemployment Insurance Contributions Act (4 of 2002).

(7) Income tax due by the insolvent.

(8) Claims secured by a *general* bond and certain special notarial bonds registered before 7 May 1993 outside the province of Natal as provided for in sections 1(2) and 1(4) of the Security by Means of Movable Property Act (57 of 1993).

(9) If any balance remains, it is used to pay the concurrent creditors in proportion to their claims. Thereafter interest on such claims, if such claims are settled in full, from the date of sequestration to the date of payment in proportion to the amount of each such claim.

In terms of the recent statutory improvements of the position of employees in insolvency, employees will become entitled to unemployment benefits during the period of suspension of the contracts of employment.[54] In addition, an employee whose contract of employment has been suspended or terminated will now become entitled to claim compensation from the insolvent estate of his or her former employer for loss suffered by reason of the suspension or termination of a contract of service prior to its expiration.[55] This claim will be the employee's weekly or monthly salary minus benefits received from the Unemployment Insurance Fund. It could also

---

of 1997) ('BCEA'), section 41 which section now provides for the payment of severance pay equal to at least one week's remuneration for each completed year of continuous service with that employer, calculated in accordance with the BCEA, section 35 in instances where an employee is dismissed for reasons based on the employer's operational requirements, or whose contract of employment terminates or is terminated in terms of the IA, section 38.

53   The claim for salary or wages enjoys preference above the claims for leave, other paid absence and severance or retrenchment pay, which rank equally and abate in equal proportions if necessary. These preferential claims, within their respective order of preference introduced by the new IA, section 98A, rank equally and abate in equal proportions if necessary. The balance of any claims not covered by section 98A will be claimed concurrently with that owed to the general unsecured or concurrent creditors.

54   IA, section 38(3); see also the discussion above.

55   Ibid., section 38(10).

include damages suffered as a result of the termination of a contract of service prior to its expiration in terms of the original terms of the contract.[56]

Any balance still due and payable to an employee after the preferential portion of his or her claims has been paid under (5) above, will be treated as a concurrent claim. It must however be noted that where the free residue is insufficient to pay the costs of sequestration or winding-up and administration that ranks third in the order of payment, all concurrent creditors must in principle make contributions towards settling the short-fall in this regard.[57]

From the above, it seems clear that the provisions of the IA could very well be in compliance with the standard set in terms of Part II of the ILO Convention. Although the IA makes provision for statutory caps, article 7 of the Convention states that: 'national laws or regulations may limit the protection by privilege of workers' claims to a prescribed amount, which shall not be below a socially acceptable level'. When this is done, the privilege afforded to workers' claims must 'be adjusted as necessary so as to maintain its value'. This has recently been done in the South African context when the amount was amended from ZAR 5,000 to ZAR 12,000 for wages in arrears.

Application to Case Study

The secured creditors will in principle be paid out of the net income derived from the sale of the encumbered assets. After the payment of costs of winding-up and administration ranking in position three, the free residue will be utilised to pay the respective preferential claims that might exist in the estate ranking between positions four to eight. Of particular importance will be the preferential payments to employees in position number five on the list.

The concurrent creditors, including employees that have claimed over and above their respective preferential portions will also be treated as concurrent creditors for such claims. It is to be noted that payments of claims against the free residue will only continue for as long as there is money available in the fund. If the funds are depleted before the costs of administration have been paid, nobody else down the list, including the employees will receive any payment.

Apart from the fact that employees will enjoy unemployment benefits during the period of suspension of their contracts of employment following the

---

56   Previously it was generally accepted that employees whose services terminated as a result of insolvency were not entitled to the statutory severance benefits provided for in the BCEA, section 41. The amended BCEA, section 41(2), read together with the new IA, section 38(11), now effectively provides that, for the purposes of severance benefits, these employees will be treated as employees who have been dismissed because of the employer's operational requirements. It is, however, submitted that any contract of service that terminated in terms of the former section 38 would also give rise to a preferential claim for severance pay in view of the amended BCEA, section 41(2), read with the former IA, section 98A(1)(a)(iv).

57   IA, section 106. Thus, where an employee has proved a concurrent claim over and above his preferential claims/he may also be saddled with a claim by the liquidator in this regard.

bankruptcy of their employer, South African law does not provide for a guarantee fund that will pay salaries and other benefits in arrears at the time of bankruptcy. For such claims, the employees must claim against the insolvent estate of the employer as explained above.

Namibia

Introduction

With Namibia's independence from South Africa, it retained significant portions of South African Law. During 2004, Namibia published a new Labour Act ('NLA'),[58] replacing the pre-existing Labour Act (6 of 1992). For the purposes of this chapter, the focus will fall on the recently implemented NLA. Namibia's insolvency and company legislation is still basically the same as the South African versions of these pieces of legislation. The Preamble of the new NLA includes the sentiment of giving effect, if possible, to the conventions and recommendations of the International Labour Organisation.[59]

In this part of the chapter, the rights of workers working for Namibian Textiles Inc will be discussed against the background of the possibility that Euro Textiles Inc desires to buy its textile undertaking that is faced with bankruptcy.

The NLA covers most labour related issues, such as fundamental rights and protection (including a prohibition against child labour and forced labour),[60] basic conditions of employment,[61] termination of employment,[62] health and safety matters,[63] and collective labour law issues[64] under one act.

---

58   15 of 2004. See Government Gazette No. 3339 of 2004 dated 8 December 2004. the Act was passed on 14 October 2004.

59   A number of other sentiments include the goal to further a policy of labour relations conducive to economic growth, stability and productivity by *inter alia*: promoting an orderly system of free collective bargaining; improving wages and conditions of employment; advancing individuals who have been disadvantaged by past discriminatory laws and practices; promoting sound labour relations and fair employment practices; setting minimum basic conditions of service for all employees.

60   Included under NLA, Chapter 2 are issues like prohibition against child and forced labour.

61   Included under NLA, Chapter 3 are issues like hours of work, leave and termination.

62   Included under NLA, Chapter 4 are issues rights and duties of employers and employees and the appointment of safety representatives and committees.

63   Included under NLA, Chapter 5 are issues like unfair disciplinary action and unfair actions against employees (and trade unions) and employers (and employer's organisations).

64   Included under NLA, Chapters 6-7 are issues like registration of trade unions, organisational rights of registered trade unions and strikes and lockouts.

Transfer of the Business as a Going Concern

The NLA does not expressly protect workers' rights during the process of the transfer of a business as going concern. In the drafting of this modern labour act, policy makers decided not to introduce protection as contained in the European Union Directive or as introduced into the South African LRA.[65] Consequently, Namibian labour legislation does not specifically prescribe that all contracts of employment must be transferred from the old employer to the new employer if a business is sold as going concern. The NLA does also not list dismissal because of a transfer as an impermissible reason for dismissal.

The NLA does, however, regulate 'Dismissal arising from redundancies'.[66] It makes provision that, should any employer intend to reduce the workforce 'arising from the reorganisation or transfer of the business … for economic or technological reasons' an employer must notify the Labour Commissioner and any recognised trade union of the intended dismissal four weeks before the dismissal.[67] There also rests a positive duty on the employer to negotiate with the trade union (or with the workers) in an attempt to reach consensus on amongst others alternatives to dismissal, criteria for selecting the employees for dismissal and conditions for the dismissal.[68] If after the negotiations there is no agreement between the parties, either party may refer the dispute to the Labour Commissioner who may refuse to approve the dismissal or who may approve the dismissal subject to any conditions set by the Commissioner.[69] If an employer fails to adhere to the redundancy provisions of the NLA, the employer could be liable on conviction to be imprisoned for a period not exceeding 12 months or a fine not exceeding NAD 10,000.[70]

Where does this leave the international investor? From the above it is clear that the Labour Commissioner would be entitled to refuse any dismissals that may take place on grounds of redundancies prior to, or after a transfer as going concern. Based on the fact that there is no general duty that all contracts must be transferred and the fact that dismissals associated with transfers of businesses are not prohibited, it is doubtful that the Labour Commissioner would introduce such a blanket prohibition on any dismissals in accordance with standards implemented in the European Union and South Africa. It does however leave any potential buyer with a measure of uncertainty as to how the Labour Commissioner would implement his or her discretion.

---

65   See the discussion above.
66   NLA, section 33.
67   Ibid., section 33(1)(a).
68   Ibid., section 33(1)(d).
69   Ibid., section 33(4). The decision of the Labour Commissioner may be referred to the Labour Court on review.
70   Ibid., section 33(6).

Effect of Bankruptcy on the Contract of Employment

Section 38 of the Namibian Insolvency Act reads as follows:[71]

> The sequestration of the estate of an employer shall terminate the contract of service between him and his employees, but any employee whose contract of service has been so terminated shall be entitled to claim compensation from the insolvent estate of his former employer for any loss which he may have suffered by reason of the termination of his contract of service prior to its expiration.

It is clear from this section that the sequestration of an insolvent estate of an employer terminates all contracts of service (employment) between the insolvent employer and his/her employees subject to the right of the employees to claim compensation for any damages sustained in consequence of such termination.[72]

The termination will take effect as from the day the sequestration order is granted (in the case of compulsory sequestration the effective date will be the date of the provisional order).[73] In the case of a company, winding-up commences on the date when the application is lodged at the registrar in case of a winding-up by way of a court order.[74] In case of voluntary winding-up, only voluntary winding-up by creditors is relevant for the purposes of this discussion since this procedure deals with a company that is unable to pay its debts and section 38 will therefore apply.

It is clear that section 38 applies to individual contracts of employment. What is not so clear is if the section will also terminate collective agreements, such as recognition agreements or bargaining council agreements, on the same basis between the employer and his employees.[75]

---

71 61 of 1936. This Act is basically similar to the South African IA, although the latter has been amended and contains some new provisions, especially regarding the position of employees on insolvency of their employer, differing from the Namibian Act.

72 Although only the estate of a 'debtor' as defined in the Namibian Insolvency Act, section 2, can be sequestrated, section 38 will, nonetheless, also operate in the case of a company wound-up due to its inability to pay its debts due to the operation of the Companies Act (61 of 1973), section 339.

73 See the definition of 'sequestration order' in the Namibian Insolvency Act, section 2.

74 See the Companies Act, section 348, and in the case of voluntary surrender on date of registration of the special resolution to wind-up the company – see Companies Act, section 352(1).

75 See Olivier, M.P. and Potgieter, O., 'The Legal Regulation of Employment Claims in Insolvency and Rescue Proceedings: A Comparative Enquiry' (1995) 16 *Industrial Law Journal* 1295 at 1321. The basis for the application of rights and obligations flowing from a collective agreement in a particular business hinges on the existence of the individual contract of employment. It is submitted that these rights and obligations will only terminate in so far as they apply between the insolvent employer and his employees but that the collective agreement as such is not affected by section 38.

In spite of this provision in the Namibian Insolvency Act, the NLA provides, amongst other situations, that a contract of employment terminates automatically one month after the sequestration of an employer who is an individual or one month after the winding up of an employer in case of a juristic person like a company.[76] However, the NLA allows the trustee or liquidator to give notice to terminate such a contract during the period of suspension.[77] Such a termination must accord with Part F of the NLA which regulates termination or a collective agreement.

Although it may have been more logical to address this issue in the IA, the section 31(3) of the NLA provides that if the employment agreement is terminated by liquidation, sequestration or death of the employer, the employee becomes a preferential creditor in respect of any remuneration due or monies payable to the employee in terms of the NLA.[78]

It seems that section 31(1) of the NLA, which terminates contracts one month after sequestration, is difficult to reconcile with section 38 of the Insolvency Act since there are no apparent cross-references between these two provisions. It is also not clarified if contracts are suspended and what the rights and duties of employees and employers are during this one month period.

One possible explanation for section 31(1) of the NLA, is that the termination for the contracts of employment are postponed until one month after bankruptcy in order to make it possible for a trustee or liquidator to be appointed and to enable him/her to assist with the sale and transfer of the business out of the bankrupt estate. If this was the intention a one-month period will definitely not be sufficient to meet this aspiration.[79]

In the absence of precedents in this regard, a Namibian labour relations practitioner[80] has offered a second possibility for the termination of contracts of employment one month after sequestration that goes as follows: The preceding section 30, deals with payment instead of notice of termination. Section 31(1) would secure an employee one-month additional wages should the contract be terminated on grounds of the sequestration or death of the employer while the executor, or liquidator may terminate the employment during the last month by notice, which implies that a fair hearing must be conducted and if so, the employee might have a claim for compensation based on termination by notice.

It is also important to note that the section provides that an employer must not, whether notice is given or not, dismiss an employee without a valid and fair

---

76   NLA, section 31(1)(a).
77   Ibid., section 31(2).
78   Ibid., section 31(1) provides that a contract of employment terminates automatically one month after the death or sequestration of the employer or one month after the employer is wound up or after a partnership is dissolved.
79   Generally negotiations about the buying of businesses take longer than 30 days to conclude and insolvency proceedings take much longer to finalise than 30 days.
80   This possibility was raised by Advocate Pieter de Beer, Associate Director, Human Capital Consulting Ernst & Young (Namibia) during a consultation between the authors and himself.

reason and without following the relevant procedures set out in the NLA. However, neither the NLA nor the Insolvency Act prescribes what procedures the curator or liquidator must follow before terminating the contracts of the employees.

Claims against the Insolvent Estate and Social Security Benefits

Similar to the position in South Africa, there is no central guarantee fund or independent agencies that would guarantee the payments of employees' claims for the eight weeks of employment as suggested by Part III of the ILO Insolvency Convention.[81] In this regard, both these jurisdictions have not followed the example set by the European Union. The question remains whether it complies with Part II of the ILO Insolvency Convention that creates a preference of at least three months wages.

In terms of the Namibian Insolvency Act, employees acquire a statutory preferential claim for a certain portion of salary, wages and bonuses in arrear.[82] The balance of the last mentioned claims will be concurrent claims. They also acquire a statutory right to claim compensation for the premature termination of their contracts of employment in terms of section 38 of the Insolvency Act. They then have unliquidated concurrent claims against the estate for damages for breach of contract.

Section 31(3) of the NLA, however, also refers to a preferential right of employees whose contracts have terminated, by specifically referring to *any* remuneration due or monies payable in terms of the NLA. Since these preferences override any other law, it seems that they prevail over the preferences created under the Insolvency Act. It this is correct, they would for instance, rank first in the order of preferences above funeral, death-bed and sequestration costs.[83] Section 31(3) clearly states that:

> Despite the provisions of any law to the contrary, an employee whose contract is terminated in the circumstances referred to in subsection (1) is a preferential creditor in respect of any remuneration due or monies payable to the employee in terms of this Act.[84]

Apart from section 11(1) that sanctions every employee's right to monetary wages to which he or she is entitled, section 34 of the NLA grants a statutory right to severance pay to employees under certain conditions.

As a general rule, a creditor who wishes to share in the proceeds of the assets in an insolvent estate must formally prove his claim at a meeting of creditors but special rules apply in the case of claims for salary or wages in arrears when

---

81   See the discussion above.
82   Namibian Insolvency Act, section 100.
83   Ibid.
84   Section 1 defines 'remuneration' the total value of all payments in money or in kind made or owing to an employee arising from the employment of that employee, whilst NLA, Part B deals with the calculation of various wage rates.

employees prove such claims.[85] In particular an employee is entitled to the preferential portion for salary, wages and bonuses in arrear in terms of section 100(1) and (2) of the Insolvency Act even though he has not proved his claim in terms of section 44 of the Insolvency Act.[86] The trustee may, however, require such employee to submit an affidavit in support of his claim. Employees claiming from the insolvent estate should thus ensure not to lodge a claim where it is not required to do so in order to evade a possible liability to contribute towards the costs of sequestration and administration where the free residue is insufficient to meet these expenses. A creditor who proves a formal claim against an insolvent becomes liable in principle to make a contribution towards costs of sequestration and administration, if the free residue is insufficient to pay such costs in terms of section 106. For claims over and above the preferential portion, they will have no choice but to prove a formal claim if they want to pursue any such claims by running the risk to become burdened with a contribution liability.

How will section 31(3) of the Labour Act affect this? Employees have preferential claims up to a maximum of NAD 5,000 for salary or wages in arrears but not exceeding two month's salary or wages due and owing prior to date of sequestration.[87] They also have preferential claims for bonuses due in respect of leave or holiday not exceeding 21 days provided that not more than NAD 2,500 shall be paid out.[88] Claims exceeding these limits are of a concurrent nature. The claims referred to in section 100(1) and (2) rank *pari passu* and abate in equal proportion, if there are not sufficient funds in the free residue to pay them in full.[89] It is uncertain how the preferential payments referred to in section 31(3) of the NLA will rank if they include other amounts as those provided for in section 100 of the Insolvency Act.

The free residue is used to pay the creditors with preferential claims, and then to pay the concurrent creditors. Preferential claims are those which are preferred by operation of law and which are paid first in accordance with the prescribed order of preferences. At present the preferential portion of the claims in favour of employees of an insolvent employer will in accordance with the Insolvency Act rank the sixth place in the order of preferences.[90] The unsecured creditors are paid out of the free residue within a prescribed order of payment. Certain claims of employees against the estate of the insolvent employer-debtor rank as a statutory preferential claim to a limited extent. Should the claim of a particular employee exceed the preferential amount he or she will have the right to claim the balance of his or her claim as a concurrent creditor at the end of the queue. In the last instance, the employee will increase his or her risk to become liable to make a contribution as to the general cost of administration.

---

85   Namibian Insolvency Act, sections 44(1) and 100(3).
86   Ibid., section 100(3).
87   Ibid., section 100.
88   Ibid., section 100(2).
89   Ibid., section 100(4).
90   Ibid., sections 96–102.

At present the order of payment in terms of the Namibian Insolvency Act, which resembles the earlier position in South African IA, is as follows:

(1)   Funeral costs of the insolvent (when a natural person), his wife or children up to a maximum of NAD 300. Any claim over and above NAD 300 is a concurrent claim.[91]

(2)   Deathbed expenses(in case of a natural person insolvent) – maximum NAD 300.[92]

(3)   Sequestration and administration costs.[93]

(4)   Certain sheriff charges incurred for legal proceedings before sequestration.[94]

(5)   A number of statutory claims like compensation for occupational injuries and diseases and certain tax claims rank *pari passu* and abate in equal proportion if necessary.[95]

(6)   Salaries/ wages etc in arrears as explained above.[96]

(7)   Income tax due by the insolvent.[97]

(8)   Claims secured by a general bond over movable property in terms of section 102 of the Insolvency Act.

(9)   If any balance remains, it is used to pay the concurrent creditors in proportion to their claims. (Thereafter interest on such claims, if such claims are settled in full, from the date of sequestration to the date of payment in proportion to the amount of each such claim.)[98]

Paragraphs (1)-(8) list the claims that enjoy preference by creating an order of preference i.e. (1) must be paid before (2) etc – until the free residue is depleted. Paragraph (3) provides for the general cost of administration. After these preferences have been paid out and if any funds are still left in the free residue, the concurrent claims mentioned in paragraph (9) will be paid. As stated above it is not clear how section 31(3) of the NLA will impact on paragraph (6) of the current ladder of payments in Namibia.

The above caps on compensation have not been amended for a number of years. The question may be asked if this will comply with the requirement set in Article 7 which suggests that signatories to the ILO Insolvency Convention should reconsider the amount and amend it from time to time.

Application to Case Study

---

91   Ibid., section 96(1).

92   Ibid., section 96(2).

93   Ibid., section 97(2)-(3).

94   Ibid., section 98(1)-(2).

95   Ibid., section 99(1)(a)-(e).

96   Ibid., section 100, which contains a partial preferential claim for salaries and bonuses in arrears at this point, as explained above. It is, however, unclear how the general preference created in terms of the NLA, section 31(3) will impact on this insolvency preference.

97   Ibid., section 103.

98   Idem.

In terms of the Insolvency Act, the position regarding the payment of creditors will be, apart for the claims of employees, exactly the same as is in South Africa.[99] Namibian employees will rank in position number six on the ladder of payments and their preferential portions of their respective claims will be much smaller than is the case in South Africa. There is no provision that the employees will have a right to claim unemployment benefits during the period of suspension of their contracts of employment following the bankruptcy of the insolvent employer.

It is uncertain if the drafters of the NLA have consulted the insolvency fraternity in the drafting of the new NLA. However, as outsiders to the Namibian legal system, it seems that the NLA and the Namibian Insolvency Act have not been satisfactorily aligned. It seems highly unlikely that employee claims have intentionally been promoted, by the NLA, above significantly important claims such as funeral, death-bed and sequestration costs as prescribed buy the Namibian Insolvency Act.

Should this in fact be the position, namely that all employee claims are given preferential status above all other claims of creditors, Namibian Labour Laws would definitely comply with Part II of the ILO Insolvency Convention that requires a preference of at least three month's wages in the event of the insolvency of the employer.

Botswana

Introduction

Of the countries investigated in this chapter, the Botswana Employment Act ('BEA') of 1982 is the longest serving labour act on the statute books.[100] Despite this, the BEA has been amended relatively recently in order to comply with Part II of the ILO Insolvency Convention.[101] More will be said about the reforms that took place under the section dealing with worker's claims against the bankrupt estate of the employer.

Transfer of the Business as a Going Concern

Under the heading 'Change of Employer' in section 28 of the BEA, it is stated that:

> (1)   If a trade, undertaking, business or enterprise (whether or not it be established by or under any written law) is transferred from one person to another and an employee in the trade, undertaking, business or enterprise continues to be employed therein, the period of

---

99   See above.

100   29 of 1982.

101   Convention 173 of 1992. Botswana only accepted Part II of the ILO Insolvency Convention. The Employment (Amendment) Act (14 of 2003) was brought into force on 22 August 2003.

continuous employment immediately proceeding the transfer shall be deemed, for the purposes of this Act, to be part of the employee's continuous employment with the transferee immediately following the transfer.

(2)   If, by or under any written law, a contract of employment between a body corporate and an employee is modified by the substitution or some other body corporate as the employer, the period of continuous employment immediately preceding the substitution shall be deemed, for the purposes of this Act, to be part of the employee's continuous employment with such other body corporate immediately following the substitution.

(3)   If, on the death of an employer, an employee continues to be employed by the legal personal representatives or trustees of the deceased, in their capacity as such, the period of continuous employment immediately preceding the death shall be deemed, for the purposes of this Act, to be part of the employee's continuous employment with the legal personal representatives or trustees immediately following the death.

(4)   If there is any change in the partners, legal personal representatives or trustees who employ any person, that person shall be deemed, for the purposes of this Act, to remain in employment with the same employer and such change shall be deemed, for the purposes of this Act, not to interrupt such employment'.

From the above provisions, it seems clear that there is no explicit duty on any new employer to take over all contracts of employment from the old employer when a 'change of employer' would occur. It also seems that there is no clear prohibition against the dismissal of employees (by either the old or new employer) because of the dismissal. This state of affairs, in our view, constitutes a less stringent and more flexible situation compared to what the labour relations position in South Africa and the European Union would entail. Translated to our case study, the BEA would therefore not place a positive duty on Euro Textiles Inc to take over all contracts of employment should it decide to buy Botswana Textiles Inc. and it would not be precluded from terminating some or all of the contracts of employment after the transfer, subject to compliance with the redundancy provisions of the BEA.

It seems that the focus of the protection provided by the BEA in the transfer situation is in respect of the transfer of years of service. Years of service will not be interrupted and if the new employer were to dismiss employees on grounds of redundancy, the new employer would have to pay severance pay to the dismissed employees for years of service with the old employer.[102] If Euro Textiles Inc were to step into the shoes of the old employer, the old contracts would remain in place, and it seems that it would not be necessary to obtain consensus from the employees to transfer the contracts of service. However, there is no express provision that states that the employer must take over all contracts of employment, nor is there a

---

102   BEA, section 27.

provision that prohibits the new employer to dismiss employees on grounds of redundancy after such a transfer.

Effect of Insolvency on the Contract of Employment

Insolvency as such is regulated by the Insolvency Act 1929. Section 85 deals with the claims of employees against the insolvent estate as well as the termination of their contracts of employment in insolvency.[103] Section 85(3) provides that where a servant (employee) claims a preferential amount for wages for the month or week current with the sequestration,[104] he or she shall be obliged to continue in the service of the estate during the remainder of such month or week and at the end thereof the contract of employment shall be determined. The legal representative (liquidator) of the estate may request the employee to remain longer in the service of the estate. The right to claim damages in spite of the previous position is nevertheless preserved in terms of section 85(4). It is thus clear that bankruptcy of the employer will usually cause the contracts of employment to terminate although the liquidator may extend the contract with the view of finalising the business of the estate.

Although Part III of the BEA contains general guidelines for the termination of a contract of employment, most notably on grounds of operational requirements, there is no indication in the BEA that it would apply to insolvent employers.[105]

Claims against the Insolvent Estate and Social Security Benefits

As mentioned above, Part II of the ILO Insolvency Convention makes provision that employees should enjoy a privilege in respect of claims against the insolvent estate of the employer and Part III makes provision for the institution of an independent guarantee fund.

---

103   See Insolvency Act 1929, section 38 with regard to the termination of contracts of apprenticeship, which reads as follows: (1) The sequestration of an estate shall be a complete discharge of the indenture of apprenticeship or articles of agreement of any person then apprenticed or articled to the insolvent if that person gives notice in writing to the trustee to that effect. (2) Upon application made by that person the trustee may consent to his proving a concurrent claim against the estate for such of any money paid by him or for him to the insolvent as a fee as the trustee, subject to an appeal to the court, thinks reasonable, regard being had to the amount of the fee, the unexpired term of the indenture or articles, and the other circumstances of the case.

104   See the order of preference below.

105   Of general importance to redundancies under solvent circumstances are sections 25, 28 and 29. Section 25 provides for termination in case of redundancy where the main principle to be applied is the first-in-last-out principle. Section 28 provides for severance benefits on termination of a contract of employment. In terms of section 29 some rights of employees are protected when the business is transferred to a new employer, like continuous employment in spite of the transfer as explained above. Although specific reference is not made to the duties on the liquidator, it is submitted that the same procedures will have to be followed.

Section 91 of the BEA, under the heading 'Priority of Wages', provides as follows:

> Notwithstanding the provisions of any other law, whenever any attachment has been issued against the property of an employer in execution of any judgment against him, the proceeds realized in pursuance of such execution shall not be paid by any court to the judgment creditor until any judgment obtained against the employer in respect of an employee's wages has been satisfied to the extent of a sum not exceeding 3 months' wages to the employee:
>
> > Provided that nothing in this section shall prevent an employee from recovering any balance due on such judgment by ordinary process of law'.

The Botswana Government has amended the BEA to bring it in line with the above provision of Part II of the ILO Insolvency Convention in order to grant better protection to employees' claims when the employer becomes insolvent.[106] The relatively new statutory preference covers three month's wages, leave pay and severance benefits resulting from work performed within a period of 24 months prior to insolvency or employment termination. However, this provision seems to contradict the preference in favour of employees in terms of section 85 of the Insolvency Act 1929.[107] From this it seems that the one hand did not take note of the other when labour laws were reformed without making cross-reference to the insolvency situation. This undoubtedly leaves room for interpretational and alignment problem between labour and insolvency legislation.

Apart from specific provisions regulating the payment of secured claims out of the proceeds of secured property, sections 82 to 88 of the Insolvency Act 1929 makes provision for the payment of the following unsecured claims and within the following order:

(1)   Funeral and deathbed expenses.[108]
(2)   Costs of sequestration.[109]
(3)   Costs of execution.[110]
(4)   Servants' wages. Section 85 provides a preference against the free residue in this regard. The amount is restricted to BWP 100 for wages in arrear for one month as well as wages for the month current with the sequestration of the employer where the employer is employed on a monthly basis and a similar provision is provided for where the employer is employed as such but on a weekly basis. The wages must be paid out of available assets and no formal claim needs to be lodged for this part of the claim.[111] The claim for the

---

106   See Botswana Daily News Report dated 26 March 2003.
107   Idem.
108   Insolvency Act 1929, section 82.
109   Ibid., section 83.
110   Ibid., section 84.
111   Ibid., section 85(1)-(2).

wages during the month or week of sequestration is subject to the employer still making his services available to the liquidator as provided for in section 85(3).[112] Section 85(4) also preserves the right to claim damages against the estate over and above these preferential claims. This would presumably be of a concurrent nature.

(5) Preference in regard to taxes on income.[113]

(6) Landlord's hypothec.[114]

(7) General bond and general clauses.[115]

Application to Case Study

When applied to the case study, it appears that the contracts of employment entered with Botswana Textiles Inc will terminate in terms of section 85 of the Insolvency Act. Employees will enjoy a limited preferential claim as well as a concurrent claim for damages against the estate in terms of this section but the case might well be that section 91 of the BEA does afford them better protection in this regard. It is however unclear to the authors how these provisions relate to each other. The employees will not have the benefit of any other form of social security under these circumstances.

Conclusion

The three jurisdictions compared in this chapter share the same legal roots to some extent. In spite of this fact, it is clear that there are significant dissimilarities between these systems. It is submitted that the differences between the rest of the countries in the SADC region might even be greater.

In South Africa, there would be an obligation on Euro Textiles Inc to take over all contracts of employment under solvent and insolvent circumstances. Contracts of employment are not terminated automatically upon sequestration but they will terminate after a window period of 45 days after the appointment of the final liquidator.

In Namibia, there is no such obligation, but there is the possibility that the Labour Commissioner may not sanction the dismissal of redundant employees. Contracts terminate one month after sequestration of the employer in terms of the NLA, but they terminate immediately upon sequestration in terms of the Insolvency Act.

In Botswana, provision is made for the protection of employees during the transfer of a business as going concern. However, the protection is limited. Employees are only protected in so far as their years of service with the old employer will be transferred to the new employer 'if' the new employer decides to

---

112 See the section above dealing with Claims against the Insolvent Estate and Social Security Benefits.

113 Insolvency Act 1929, section 82.

114 Ibid., section 87.

115 Ibid., section 88.

take over all employees. There is no positive duty on the employer to take over all contracts of employment. Apart from this protection, employees seem to have a preferential claim for the last three months of the salary above all other claims in terms of the BEA.

The disparities show that there is a need for harmonisation. If this does not happen, a country like South Africa could for instance lose out on the possibility of Euro Textiles Inc investing in South Africa. It could even lead to allegations of unfair competition and the remote possibility of social dumping where South Africa could decide to deregulate. However, taking account of the strong political position of South African trade unions, backed by the constitutional right to fair labour practices, it is doubtful that employee rights will be diminished or tempered in the near future. In general the harmonisation of the labour and commercial laws like insolvency of SADC countries in general might prove to be beneficial to the whole region in the long run since it will enhance uniformity and mobility within the region.

Chapter 12

Widening the Insolvency Lens:
The Treatment of Employee Claims

Janis Sarra

Introduction[1]

Corporate insolvency affects multiple parties with interests and investments in the firm. Its impact on employees, however, is particularly significant. Employees are both an asset of the corporation in terms of their labour inputs and the informational capital that they contribute, and they are creditors when the firm is financially distressed as they frequently have wage and other claims that have not been satisfied. Employees usually have undiversified investments in a corporation such that the relative impact of the firm's dissolution is much more severe than the impact on other creditors. Unlike many commercial creditors, employee loss of employment during insolvency can create significant financial hardship, can result in significant psychological and other health effects from the stress of no income, and can create ripple effects in the economy and the local community in which the insolvent corporation was located.

Different countries have different normative conceptions of both the value of contributions by employees to commercial activity and the generation of firm wealth and of the rights and obligations that should flow from such contributions. This chapter explores the contours of this issue by examining models for the treatment of employee claims, and how they might be better conceptualized and effected in a modern insolvency regime.

There have been a number of major corporate insolvencies internationally, affecting 1000s of workers. The few examples here are illustrative only. Enron's collapse resulted in more than 4,500 employees losing employment. In addition to lost jobs, most employees had much of their life savings invested in the corporation and lost those retirement savings.[2] The insolvency of Canadian Airlines placed 4,000 thousand jobs at risk. The bankruptcy of Ansett Airlines in Australia affected 16,000 employees, who had claims of more than AUD 670 million.[3] Other cross-

---

1   My thanks to Anjali Coyle, UBC Law III, for her research assistance.
2   See McNulty, S., 'Skilling is jailed for 24 years over Enron' (*Financial Times*, 24 October 2006).
3   Department of the Parliamentary Library, Australia, 'Corporate Insolvencies and Workers' Entitlements' (E-Brief) (15 September 2004), available at:

border or global insolvencies, such as Calpine, WorldCom and Parmalat resulted in thousands of jobs at risk or lost. Almost 60,000 people lost part or all of their pension benefits in the United Kingdom as a result of recent pension terminations in that country.[4] Recently, entire sectors such as automobile manufacturers, steel and airlines have experienced financial distress.

The risks to employees of corporate insolvency are multi-fold. There is a risk of loss or actual loss of employment; risk of loss of wage and other compensation claims; risk of loss of pension savings, or in the case of pensioners, risk of loss of the pension itself. In some jurisdictions, such as the United States, employees have been encouraged to invest in the firm's stock as their retirement programme, and hence they incur these investment losses as well.

While there is broad acknowledgement of the risks and harms to employees from firm failure, there is not consensus on the appropriate measures that should be undertaken to try to mitigate these losses. Various nation states have adopted different strategies, from employee priority systems, to insurance or guarantee funds. Other states have failed to address employee losses, other than ranking them as unsecured claimants, resulting in serious consequences for the workers employed in insolvent corporations in these jurisdictions. The range of public policy choices and decisions made in respect of such priorities or programmes may affect the availability and cost of credit in domestic or international markets.

Hence, the challenge is to discern the strategies appropriate for particular economic systems. On the one hand, it is unlikely that any one approach to the treatment of employees is appropriate for all countries; on the other, with the global nature of many corporate activities, there is increasingly a need for global or cross-border solutions to a corporation's or corporate group's financial distress.

There are numerous issues raised when considering options for protection of employees during insolvency. What is the nature of wage protection during insolvency, and can one draw any conclusions as to what kind of system of wage preference, super-priority or guaranteed insurance is the most appropriate means of reducing hardship for employees during insolvency and bankruptcy? How does one address the issue of outstanding contributions to pension funds owing at the time of firm insolvency? Is there liability of corporate officers for employee claims, and finally, what is the role of employees in a restructuring process?

Treatment of employee claims in an insolvency law regime must provide protection to employees; at the same time, the system must recognize the need for certainty in capital markets so that senior lenders can make prudent lending choices before, during and after insolvency. This balance is particularly significant where workout capital is needed to assist debtor companies to restructure when they are

---

<www.aph.gov.au/library/intguide/econ/insolvencies.htm> (last viewed 31 May 2007). AUD 670 million is approximately EUR 408 million.

4   See Sprayregen, J.H.M. and Mazza, J.J., 'Weaving the Safety Net for an Aging World: Lessons Learned from the Pension and Insolvency Systems of the US, UK and Germany' (28 April 2006, Report for the OECD) at 5, citing Hewitt Associates (October 2004) and 'UK Pension Rules' (Part I), available at: <www.oecd.org> (last viewed 31 May 2007).

potentially viable in the longer term. Policy choices in respect of employee and pensioner claims must be balanced with the interests of other lenders during insolvency. Lenders wish certainty in their credit decisions and hence any policy change to support workers in a particular jurisdiction must be undertaken within the context of encouraging further credit and creating a system in which enforcement of creditors' claims is transparent and predictable. Absent such a system, the cost of credit can become unduly high and its availability uncertain.

This chapter assesses the nature of the risk to employees, the principles that have been developed to consider their interests and the kinds of initiatives that are currently undertaken in different jurisdictions. Understanding the historical and social underpinnings of nations' insolvency regimes is important for consideration of employee protection. The chapter is not intended to be a comprehensive study of multiple countries, but rather, uses the different approaches as illustration that there are a variety of public policy choices that should be considered. It concludes that a multifaceted approach to employee protection offers the most promise for reducing risk to employees and that such programmes, if properly designed, can continue to encourage capital investment in financially distressed firms.

Snapshot: The Nature of the Risks to Employees from Corporate Insolvency

Employees' interests in the financially distressed firm run along a continuum of interests.[5] Employees' contributions to productivity, innovation and firm synergies frequently enhance firm value. They have often contributed their labour and loyalty over an extended period, conferring value on the corporation on the basis of implicit or explicit promises of job security. The promise gives rise to contributions to the firm in the form of time, energy and creativity over and above the current wage/labour exchange. On insolvency, the employees' investments in this respect are not adequately protected by employment contracts or statutory minimum protections as these provisions are aimed solely at fixed capital claims.[6]

Most employees are employed full time for a single firm; hence the investment of their labour is undiversified, as is their risk if the firm fails. The nature of employees' investment in the firm means that job loss and the diminution or loss of their compensation claims can have a devastating effect on both individuals and the local economies that their wages support. Even where workers are underemployed or contingently employed, there can be serious losses on firm failure. Most jurisdictions operate on the deferred compensation system, specifically, workers deliver their labour today in return for the promise of job security or a pension at the end of the employment relationship. At the point of a firm's insolvency, workers have often already delivered their part of the employment contract, and yet there are not sufficient assets for the debtor corporation to meet its obligations. The rise of pension fund deficits is the most

---

5   See Sarra, J.P., *Creditor Rights and the Public Interest, Restructuring Insolvent Corporations* (2003, University of Toronto Press, Toronto) at 70.

6   Idem.

serious example of this. Fiona Stewart observes that the majority of employees are unlikely to have portfolios of sufficient size or the investment expertise necessary to hedge the risk to their pension assets because for many workers, occupational pension benefits constitute a large proportion of total retirement savings; at the same time, employees generally want low risk exposure when it comes to the security of their pension income.[7]

Absent catastrophic events or rapid market changes, most firms gradually become insolvent, with their financial and governance problems exacerbated over time. Often, at the point of insolvency, employees have already made concessions in their employment contracts, concessions made to help prevent the firm from sliding into insolvency. If the workplace is unionized, employees have frequently agreed to concessions in collective bargaining agreements that govern the employer-employee relationship. These concessions often have been made as a means to help the firm remain competitive in global capital markets. Competition from corporations 'forum or country shopping' where their activities are movable has also created some downward pressure on wages and other compensation, leaving workers in developed nations particularly vulnerable to pressure for early concessions that may preserve the corporation in the jurisdiction and hence preserve their ongoing investments in the jobs. However, where these corporations subsequently become insolvent, the concessions already made are not fixed recoverable claims in insolvency proceedings. Moreover, employees must accept a further discounted value on their claims arising out of their labour investments. One example is General Motors, which recently reduced its labour and pension liabilities by USD 15 million through renegotiating its contracts.[8]

While corporations increasingly have cross-border operations, employees are domestically employed, subject to domestic labour and insolvency laws. While there is a move towards increased comity and international cooperation in respect of insolvency proceedings, cross-border issues can bump up against domestic laws that protect workers' claims at the point of firm financial distress. In turn, this may affect strategies by both debtor corporations and creditors in terms of the preferred forum of insolvency proceeding, where they hope to shift the priority of employee claims. Since employees suffer from information asymmetries and unequal bargaining power, they are often not involved in the court cases that determine questions of jurisdiction and may consequently suffer some prejudice in the choice of regime.

In some cases, employee stock ownership plans may unnecessarily increase the undiversified risks to employees, and several jurisdictions have undertaken regulatory responses to address this risk. In cases such as Enron, employee investments were further at risk because their own pension plans had not been

---

7   See Stewart, F., 'Benefit Security Pension Fund Guarantee Systems' (2007, OECD Working Papers on Insurance and Private Pensions No. 5) at 5–6, available through OECD Publishing at: <doi:10.1787/260604113335>.

8   See Johnson, G., 'Insolvency and Social Protection: Employee Entitlements in the Event of Employer Insolvency' (28 April 2006, OECD Report) at 2, available at: <www.oecd/daf/corporate-affairs> (last viewed 31 May 2007).

prudently diversified; the pension plan had about 60 per cent of its investments in Enron stock. That meant employees lost their jobs, their equity investments in the firm, and their pensions.

While many developed nations have social support programmes in place to mitigate the scope of loss to workers on firm failure, in a number of emerging nations, there are few, if any, such programmes available to employees. Thus the social supports in place for employees that lose their employment due to insolvency vary considerably from nation to nation. Where an economy is suffering, such as during the Asian financial crisis or the current economic struggles of emerging African nations, employees of bankrupt firms often cannot find replacement jobs and there are few social safety nets. In turn, this situation leads to increased poverty and a downward cycle of economic and social harm.

In numerous developed countries, so-called legacy industries have been at risk, such as the steel industry in the 1990s; the airline industry and the automobile industry in the 2000s. They are referred to as legacy industries because corporations in these sectors have made longstanding pension and other commitments to employees that have been under-funded over numerous years, and now face balloon or other payments due to these 'legacy' costs. Debtors that seek to shed such legacy costs through insolvency often fail to acknowledge that employees have already paid for such benefits through the deferred compensation system and hence their investments are at particular risk. While some fault lies with pension law systems, in terms of financial authorities failing to adequately monitor and enforce pension laws, the ease with which insolvency is used to cure this financial liability for some of the corporation's most vulnerable creditors is problematic. Similarly, the fault may lie in part with corporate directors, who have failed in their oversight obligations to ensure that pension and other commitments have been properly funded. While some jurisdictions place personal responsibility on directors and officers for such failures, these provisions are frequently not enforced. The failure of pension regulatory officials to address these issues when the firm is financially healthy leads to employees suffering disproportionate harms at the point of insolvency.

In summary, employees' undiversified investments in the employer in the form of human capital, productivity exchanged for job security and unmet retirement savings promises, amplify the economic, social and psychological damage flowing from an employer's insolvency. Where the assets of the retirement savings plans or other forms of deferred compensation are comprised of significant investments in the employer's securities, then the impact is exacerbated. The absence of protection for such investments in insolvency proceedings that allow a business enterprise to shed such costs represents a significant policy challenge for insolvency law and for those other legal regimes whose provisions might address a more effective protection of the employees' investments while the employer is financially healthy.

International Principles in Respect of Employees and Insolvency

International organizations have acknowledged the hardship faced by employees at the point of firm insolvency. The extent of their concern differs; however, what they have in common is recognition that some special protection may be justified.

The World Bank in its Principles and Guidelines for Effective Insolvency and Creditor Rights Systems called for special recognition and treatment of labour claims on the basis that 'workers are a vital part of an enterprise and careful consideration should be given to balancing the rights of employees with those of other creditors'.[9] At the same time, the Principles call for *pari passu* distribution to unsecured creditors unless there are compelling reasons to justify priority status.[10] In respect of treatment of contractual obligations, the World Bank Principles specify that exceptions to the general rule of contract treatment in insolvency proceedings should be limited, clearly defined and allowed only for compelling commercial, public or social interests, such as in establishing special rules for treating employment contracts and collective bargaining agreements.[11]

At the same time, the World Bank has observed that the protection of employees must be balanced with the need for commercial certainty and healthy capital markets. The World Bank's Principles state that insolvency systems, through commercial laws, should both preserve the legitimate expectations of creditors and encourage greater predictability in commercial relationships by upholding, to the maximum extent possible, the relative priorities of creditors established prior to insolvency.[12] Hence, while recognizing that protective

---

9   The World Bank, 'Principles and Guidelines for Effective Insolvency and Creditor Rights Systems' (April 2001). Principle C.12.4 (2005 Revision) in 'Effective World Bank Principles for Effective Insolvency Systems and Creditor Rights Systems: A Review of the ROSC Experience and Next Steps' (June 2005) at 19, available at: <www-wds.worldbank.org/external/default/WDSContentServer/WDSP/IB/2005/07/ 01/000012009_20050701152900/Rendered/PDF/328530rev.pdf> (last viewed 31 May 2007). Its guidelines were established after consultations with 75 different jurisdictions.

10   Ibid., Principle C12.3, which specifies: 'Following distributions to secured creditors from their collateral and payment of claims related to costs and expenses of administration, proceeds available for distribution should be distributed pari passu to the remaining general unsecured creditors, unless there are compelling reasons to justify giving priority status to a particular class of claims. Public interests generally should not be given precedence over private rights. The number of priority classes should be kept to a minimum'.

11   Ibid., Principle C10.4.

12   Ibid., Principle C12.1, which specifies: 'The rights of creditors and priorities of claims established prior to insolvency proceedings under commercial or other applicable laws should be upheld in an insolvency proceeding to preserve the legitimate expectations of creditors and encourage greater predictability in commercial relationships. Deviations from this general rule should occur only where necessary to promote other compelling policies, such as the policy supporting reorganization or to maximize the insolvency estate's value'.

measures may be appropriate, the World Bank's focus is on how this can be accomplished such that priorities are consistent in and outside of insolvency.

In assessing its Principles, a 2005 World Bank study found that no country assessed was fully in compliance with all of the principles. It found that the most significant deficiencies among countries assessed to date have been ineffectual implementation of laws due to weak or lax institutional and regulatory frameworks; and that countries with stronger and more effective institutional and regulatory frameworks generally have more effective and efficient insolvency systems, even when the laws have not been modernized. The most common institutional problems were the result of inadequate training of judges and administrators; inefficient case administration procedures; lack of transparency and inconsistency in decision-making; and ineffective regulation to redress problems of corruption and the risk that interested parties may unduly influence the courts and other decision makers. The World Bank also concluded that creditor rights systems in developing countries reflect a wide range of practices based on legal heritage, often not updated to take account of modern lending and collateral practices and needs.[13] These findings are significant for employee claims as employees are generally less able to protect themselves from inefficiencies in the enforcement system and less able to protect themselves from insolvency risk through private contracts.

The UNCITRAL Legislative Guide on Insolvency Law also discusses the importance of special treatment of employees during insolvency:

> 72. In a majority of States, workers' claims (including claims for wages, leave or holiday pay, allowances for other paid absence and severance pay) constitute a class of priority claims in insolvency. In a number of cases those claims rank higher than most other priority claims, specifically tax and social security claims, and in a few cases, as noted above, above secured claims (see paras. 63 and 64). The approach of providing priority for workers' claims is generally consistent with the special protection that is afforded to employees in other areas of insolvency law (see chap. II, para. 145), as well as with the approach of international treaties on protection of workers. In some insolvency laws, the importance of maintaining continuity of employment in priority to other objectives of insolvency proceedings, such as maximization of value of the estate for the benefit of all creditors, is evidenced by a focus on sale of the business as a going concern (with the transfer of existing employment obligations), as opposed to liquidation or reorganization where these obligations may be altered or terminated.

> 73. In some States, employee claims are afforded priority, but will rank equally with taxes and social security claims in a single class of priority claims and may be satisfied proportionately in the event of insufficient funds. In others, no priority is provided for employee claims and they are ranked as ordinary unsecured claims, although in some cases payment of certain obligations accrued over specified periods of time (e.g. wages and

---

13   Ibid., at 10–11.

remuneration arising within three months before commencement of insolvency proceedings) may be guaranteed by the State through a wage guarantee fund or insurance scheme providing a separate source of funds to ensure the settlement of employees' claims. The fund guaranteeing the payment of such claims may itself have a claim against the estate and may or may not have the same priority provided that the ranking of claims is determined by the law of the State of the opening of the proceedings (whether main or secondary)'.[14]

The International Labour Organization ('ILO') Protection of Wages Convention specifies that in the event of bankruptcy or liquidation of a company, workers should be treated as privileged creditors in respect of wages owing for service rendered during the period prior to the bankruptcy or liquidation, or paid their wages owing up to a prescribed amount as may be determined by national laws or regulation.[15] Hence it advocates a priority of payment either for a specified period or a capped amount as a method to reduce the risks associated with bankruptcy for employees.

The ILO Termination of Employment Convention specifies that employees should be given reasonable notice of termination and that workers should have direct participation rights in employment termination when job loss is due to insolvency and restructuring or downsizing.[16] The ILO recommended a baseline amount for which employees should be protected, including: a severance allowance or separation benefits based on length of service and amount of wages, to be paid by the employer directly or by an employer contribution fund; unemployment insurance or social security; priority for workers' claims for wages for a period of three months or more prior to the insolvency or termination of employment; vacation pay claims for work performed up to two years prior; claims for amounts due for other types of paid absences dating three months or more before the insolvency; and severance pay due to workers on the termination of their employment.[17] The ILO Conventions, while proposing a comprehensive approach to worker protection, are not, however, binding.

On a regional basis, there are also principles or best practices being promulgated. EU directives are a combination of public policy principles and a direction to member states in their approach to specific issues. The EU Employee Protection Directive 80/987/EEC specifies that guarantee institutions should secure

---

14 'UNCITRAL Legislative Guide on Insolvency Law' (2005) at 287–8, available at: <www.uncitral.org> (last viewed 31 May 2007).

15 International Labour Organization, C95 Protection of Wages Convention (1949), Article 11.

16 International Labour Organization, C158 Termination of Employment Convention (1982), Article 11.

17 International Labour Organization, C173 Protection of Workers Claims (Employer's Insolvency) Convention (1992), Articles 6 and 12. Australian Workplace, 'General Employee Entitlements and Redundancy Scheme' (GEERS), available at: <www.workplace.gov.au/Workplace/WPDisplay/0,1251,a3%253D3649%2526a0%25 3D0%2526a1%253D517%2526a2%253D623,00.html> (last viewed 31 May 2007).

employees' outstanding claims relating to their employment.[18] It requires member states to ensure that outstanding claims from 18 months prior to insolvency are paid; however, member states can set limits on liability for employees' outstanding compensation claims as long as the member states notify the Commission of the methods they utilized to reach those limits.[19] European Council Directive 98/59/EC requires that any employer considering collective dismissals consult with workers' representatives first, with a goal of reaching an agreement, where possible, that may curtail the need for the dismissals.[20]

The European Union amended the 1980 Directive in 2002 to enhance protections for employees on insolvency.[21] There are extensive definitions in the directive as to what constitutes an employee, with the term employee defined liberally. 'Employee' means a person who has entered into or worked under a contract with an employer, whether the contract is for manual labour, clerical work or any other work, is expressed or implied, oral or in writing, and whether it is a contract of service or apprenticeship or other type of contract. 'Employee' and any reference to employment includes: self-employed workers without staff, who are economically dependent on just one customer or principal; workers with a contract of training; home workers; and those equated under national law with paid workers.[22] The Directive allows member states to make their own decisions regarding employee protection, but sets some best practice provisions, particularly for wage protection funds and the obligation to disclose national practice.[23]

---

18   Council Directive 80/987/EEC on the approximation of the laws of the member states relating to the protection of employees in the event of the insolvency of their employer, amended by Council Directive 2002/74/EC of 23 September 2002. See 'Social Policy: European Parliament Backs New Insolvency Directive', European Report (15 May 2002).

19   Ibid., Section II, Articles 4(2)-4(3).

20   Ibid.

21   For the purposes of this Directive, an employer shall be deemed to be in a state of insolvency where a request has been made for the opening of collective proceedings, as provided for under the laws, regulations and administrative provisions of a member state, based on insolvency of the employer and involving the partial or total divestment of the employer's assets and the appointment of a liquidator or other persons empowered by the public authority, and the competent authority has established that the employer's undertaking or business has been definitively closed down and that the available assets are insufficient to warrant the opening of the proceedings; and, in general, that the available assets are insufficient to meet the debts incurred by the business.

22   Ibid.

23   Ibid. Outstanding pay claims shall include any elements of remuneration specified by the member states (in accordance with national law and/or national collective agreements) such as the basic salary and overtime, shift work, dangerous work, holiday and end-of-year allowances and holiday and Christmas bonuses during the preceding half-year. It shall also include indemnities or compensation owed for terminating the contract of employment. Article 3(2) specifies that: 'The claims taken over by the guarantee institution shall be the outstanding pay claims relating to a period prior to and/or, as applicable, after a given date determined by the member

member states are directed to take the necessary measures to ensure that guarantee funds or other institutions guarantee payment of employees' outstanding claims resulting from contracts of employment or employment relationships or severance pay due to workers on termination.[24] However, it specifies that member states may continue to exclude such programmes from the scope of the Directive, if it is already customary to do so under national law.

The Directive requires member states to specify the length of period for which outstanding claims are to be met by the guarantee institution; however, this may not be shorter than a period covering the last six months for which pay or other claims stemming from the termination of employment are still outstanding. Member states may set a ceiling on payments to be made by the guarantee institution.[25]

These international statements of principle or best practice reflect the fact that there is recognition of the special hardship faced by employees at the point of financial distress. Yet most stop short of suggesting that special protection for employees is a necessary or essential element of a fair and efficient insolvency regime. The issue of priority of claims, wage and pension guarantee funds and the treatment of collective agreements are all issues that require policy discussion and in some instances, difficult public policy choices.

Focusing the Lens: Approaches to Protection of Employees during Insolvency

While the discourse on insolvency law theory places secured creditors at the top of the hierarchy of claims when a firm is insolvent, the reality in many jurisdictions is that this supposedly inviolate principle is qualified or tempered by legislation that provides employees with a limited priority for wage claims. Internationally, different systems have chosen different priorities. The normative debate that arises is where and to what extent on the hierarchy of claims should employees receive priorities or other special treatment, given the undiversified nature of their claims and their risk at the point of firm insolvency. The contours of the debate include the need to give recognition to the vulnerability of employees at the time of firm financial distress, at the same time as recognizing that creditors require certainty in their credit risk.

---

states. The claims taken over by the guarantee institution shall be the outstanding claims for pay and the corresponding social security contributions relating to a period prior to and/or, as applicable, after a given date determined by the member states.

24   This is subject to Article 4. Article 5 specifies that member states shall lay down detailed rules for the organization, financing and operation of the guarantee institutions, complying with the following principles in particular: (a) the assets of the institutions shall be independent of the employers' operating capital and be inaccessible to insolvency proceedings; (b) the employers and the public authorities shall ensure the funding of the institutions; (c) the institutions' liabilities shall not depend on whether or not obligations to contribute to financing have been fulfilled.

25   Article 4(3). When they exercise this option, they are to inform the Commission of the methods used to set the ceiling.

Many jurisdictions provide some wage protection during insolvency. The civil law jurisdictions, which traditionally have given greater recognition to employee rights and social claims in general, frequently have had more comprehensive protection of workers' claims. Hence the protection of wage and other compensation claims in bankruptcy is grounded in broader historical, political and social reasons for the development of recognition of workers as important stakeholders in a conception of the corporation that is broader than shareholder interest.

The principal strategies for treatment of employee compensation claims are: a priority or preference claim made directly to the debtor corporation or to the administrator or trustee of the bankrupt estate; a guarantee fund or insurance fund that pays out the claims to employees; or some combination of these approaches. There is a need for transparency in respect of treatment of employee claims, as well as predictability, so that creditors can make informed lending choices after assessing insolvency risk.

The definition of compensation to which employees are entitled also varies jurisdiction to jurisdiction. In some jurisdictions, the types of entitlements that employees can claim are limited, serving as a cost control device. There are often caps on amounts of claims on a preferred basis, such as in Canada, and/or limits on the period retroactive to the insolvency or bankruptcy for which claims can be made. Moreover, while wages and vacation pay may be covered, severance and termination costs sometimes are not covered by any preference or priority, given that severance and termination pay can be substantially greater than outstanding wage amounts. Other amounts, such as expenses, commissions, maternity leaves, vary in their treatment. Wage and pension guarantee funds have been utilized in various jurisdictions, with different models creating different priorities of payment and timing of payment. These legislative strategies are set out in some detail below.

Priority or Preference Systems

One approach is to impose a special priority or preference for employee claims. All insolvency systems set a hierarchy of claims, often with secured claims having first call on the assets of a bankrupt corporation. A preferred claim or priority claim, is one that is placed above other creditors in the hierarchy. While the hierarchy of claims is most significant when the assets of the corporation are being liquidated in order to satisfy creditors' claims, the hierarchy can also be significant for restructuring proceedings. If the debtor corporation fails to garner the requisite creditor support for a restructuring plan, the corporation will be liquidated under either insolvency or bankruptcy proceedings. Hence, those with secured claims, and in some cases preferred claims, have the greatest bargaining power in a workout proceeding. Hence granting employees a priority claim in liquidation also enhances their potential ability to have a voice in any negotiations for a going forward strategy in a corporate restructuring.

There are countries in which a preference or priority for employee compensation claims is the sole protective device for employees. The actual placement of the priority in the hierarchy of claims also varies from jurisdiction to jurisdiction. Employee claims can be positioned before or after secured claims; before or after taxing authorities or other government claims; and before or after other specified claims that have been recognized as a public policy priority in a particular country. In a few cases, employees are given a super-priority over all claims.

Yet even where there is a limited super-priority for employee compensation claims, amounts owing are not fully covered by the priority. As a cost saving device, and to provide certainty to senior lenders as to the scope of any priority claim, the priorities for employee claims are usually capped at a particular amount and usually limited in terms of a specified period prior to the firm filing insolvency or bankruptcy proceedings. In many countries, the residual amount of workers' claims after the preference or priority claims have been satisfied are unsecured claims, for which employees are entitled to share on a *pro rata* basis with other unsecured creditors.

Wang Huaiyu has set out a typology of preferences and priorities that can be granted to employees' claims, observing that in order to establish and perfect an efficient labour market and to defend principles of fairness and equitable treatment, most countries give labour creditors certain priority rights:[26]

a) Give the employees absolute priority protection, *i.e.* employee rights come prior to secured creditors' rights. Countries with such regulations are Brazil (this section is being modified in a new law), Chile, Columbia, Indonesia (specified in the New Labour Law in 2003), and Mexico.

b) Provide absolute priority to employee creditors with certain restrictions. For example, employee creditors meeting certain requirements have priority over secured creditors within a certain period. Countries using this approach are the Czech Republic (Secured creditor's can only can be repaid preferentially from 70 per cent of the value of the security, the remaining 30 per cent is to be added to the bankrupt's assets. Employees are paid preferentially with 30 per cent of the bankrupt's assets. Unpaid employees and secured creditors are repaid as common creditors from the remaining 70 per cent), Russia (employee creditors come prior to fixed security after it expires), Spain (within the last 30 days).

c) Secured creditors come prior to employee creditors while employee creditors come prior to floating security creditors. Examples are Australia; Bermuda; England; Hong Kong, China; Israel; Romania; Scotland; Singapore; Slovakia; and Wales.

d) All secured creditors' rights are prior to employee creditors' rights while employee creditor rights are prior to common creditors' rights. See Austria, Canada, Hungary, Japan, Malaysia, Norway, South Africa, Sweden, Switzerland, Thailand, Venezuela, Viet Nam, the US, and so on. Among the above, generally speaking, there are certain restrictions on employee creditors' rights in items c) and d), including restrictions on time and amount.

---

26   See Wang, H.Y., 'An International Comparison of Insolvency Law' (28 April 2006, OECD Report) at 4, available at: <www.oecd.org> (last viewed 31 May 2007).

e)   Employee creditors do not enjoy any priority. They are repaid together with common creditors. Estonia, Germany and other countries have such regulations.[27]

Brazil offers an example of a jurisdiction with a priority approach to employee compensation claims. Brazil grants a super-priority for employee compensation claims. Previously without a cap on the claims, Brazil's new federal bankruptcy and restructuring law, which came into effect in 2006, now places a cap on the amount of this priority claim.[28] The new restructuring regime, *recuperação da empresa*, is aimed at trying to prevent premature liquidation and to encourage business plans that preserve, where possible, the going concern value of an insolvent firm.[29] Employee claims rank ahead of secured creditors in bankruptcy and liquidation proceedings, including salary, vacation pay and bonus and other entitlements.[30] Work related injury compensation takes priority over all employee claims, followed by labour and social security, including salaries, vacation pay, bonuses and severance pay. The cap on the amount of employee claims is 150 minimum monthly wages, signalling the amount of liability that creditors or potential investors face where employee compensation is outstanding for the insolvent corporation.[31] The new insolvency law has affirmed Brazil's commitment to employees of financially distressed firms while trying to foster a healthier debt market through greater certainty in lending and liability terms.[32] There is no guarantee fund under the Brazilian system and thus the super-priority is the sole protective measure to protect employees' interests.

India is another example of a system that uses a preference system to address employee compensation claims during insolvency. In India, the ranking of

---

27   Ibid., at 3.
28   Federal Law No. 11.101 came into effect in 2006. Liquidation procedures, called *falência*, have been streamlined and modernized.
29   *Recuperação da empresa* allows for both pre-packaged out-of-court restructuring of insolvent companies and a court-supervised restructuring called *recuperação extra-judicial*.
30   Secured creditors' claims have risen in priority over tax claims, which historically have been very large, often placing secured claims under water; hence, this is an important and timely change to the scheme of priorities under the legislation. See The Hon. Sidnei Beneti, Brazil Court of Appeals, 'Successful Restructuring of Parmalat Brazil Concludes' (November 2006, NCBJ) and 'Bankruptcy Reform in Brazil' (2006, NCBJ); Valente de Paiva, L.F. and Jarvinen C., 'The New Bankruptcy and Restructuring Law in Brazil', 28th Annual Current Developments in Bankruptcy & Reorganization (2006).
31   Approximately USD 13,000 or EUR 9,500.
32   The statutory reforms are also aimed at increasing the level of transparency in such workouts, so that unsecured creditors can better appreciate where they are situated in the hierarchy of claims during the process and make meaningful decisions about the resolution of the insolvency. It is also aimed at encouraging a greater degree of involvement in restructuring proceedings by both secured and unsecured creditors. The new Brazilian Bankruptcy Law adopts many of the principles of the UNCITRAL Legislative Guide on Insolvency Law and the World Bank principles.

wage claims is divided into two groups, workers and white collar employees. Workers rank equally with the secured creditors on a *pari passu* basis, while white collar employees rank equally with government tax and fiscal claims and they rank below the secured creditors' and workers' claims.[33] The government and employee claims are labelled as preferential payments, as they rank ahead of unsecured claims. The priority amount includes wages or salaries not exceeding four months in the year prior to bankruptcy and includes accrued holiday pay, amounts owed under the Employees' State Insurance Act 1948, workers' compensation legislation and pension fund benefits. There is no insurance scheme or wage guarantee fund. However, India is considering moving to a combined system of preferred claims and a guarantee fund, by creating a new compensation fund to enhance employee insolvency protection measures in addition to its current preference system. Proposed amendments to India's Companies Act 2002, enacted but not yet in force, provide for a Rehabilitation Fund to be established, which will provide interim payments of workers' claims pending rehabilitation.[34]

Canada offers a very limited preference system. In Canada, employee claims rank fourth in priority after secured creditors, administrative and other specified charges for a limited amount of CAD 2,000 per employee for salaries, wages, commissions and vacation pay during the six month period prior to bankruptcy.[35] This places a fixed amount of wage claims above unsecured claims. For any amounts owed to employees above the cap, the claims are unsecured claims and rank on a *pari passu* basis with other unsecured creditors. Generally, the limited wage claim preference in Canada is viewed as inadequate because often there are not enough assets remaining in the corporation to meet the preferred claims. Canada, in its comprehensive amendments to the Bankruptcy and Insolvency Act 1992 ('BIA'), enacted in November 2005, but not yet proclaimed in force, will create a further priority in wage claims.[36] Canada does not currently

---

33   Professor Vaneeta Patnaik, personal correspondence (1 November 2006).
34   Companies (Second Amendment) Act 2002 (enacted but not yet in force); pursuant to Companies Act 2002, section 529.
35   CAD 2,000 is approximately EUR 1,323. There is an additional CAD 1,000 available to travelling sales people for disbursements in the period prior to bankruptcy. CAD 1,000 is approximately EUR 661.
36   On 25 November 2005, Canada enacted Chapter 47 of the Statutes of Canada (not yet in force as of 15 June 2007), undertaking comprehensive reforms of the Bankruptcy and Insolvency Act 1992 and the Companies' Creditors Arrangement Act 1985, as well as creating a national wage earner protection fund for the first time. However, the legislation still has not been proclaimed in force. On 8 December 2006, the Canadian Government signalled that it would introduce further amendments early in 2007, tabling a 'Ways and Means' motion with more than 80 pages of technical and administrative amendments, largely responding to concerns expressed by insolvency professionals in respect of the need for consistency between the statutes, the need to provide clarity on some issues such as treatment of eligible financial contracts, and the need for greater protection of insolvency professionals from successor employer liabilities where they continue to operate the business pending resolution of the insolvency proceeding: Notice of Ways and Means Motion to introduce an Act to

have a guarantee wage fund, but it has proposed implementing a wage earner protection programme, as discussed below.

Proposed amendments to Canadian insolvency legislation would create a 'limited super-priority' in the BIA that would cover bankruptcies and receiverships.[37] The limited super-priority will allow unpaid wage claims, up to CAD 2,000, to be paid out of the proceeds of current assets, including inventory, accounts receivable and cash on hand, ahead of secured creditors. The existing preferred status will remain for any amounts owing, under the CAD 2,000 cap, that were not satisfied through the current assets, if there are any fixed assets left after the claims of secured creditors and the claims of preferred creditors that take priority over unpaid wage claims are satisfied.[38] With the new limited super-priority, combined with the existing preferred creditor status of unpaid wage claims, it is estimated that the Government will be able to recover up to half of unpaid wage claims. The super-priority, in addition to protecting employee claims, is aimed at deterring strategic behaviour on the part of employers, i.e. the moral hazard of those debtors that may forego paying wages in the period leading to bankruptcy on the understanding that payment would be forthcoming from the proposed wage earner protection fund discussed below. The deterrent is provided through allowing the federal government to assume the rights of unpaid employees against the directors of insolvent companies under existing provisions in labour and corporate statutes.[39] The threat of a legal action from the federal government to recover unpaid wages will provide a strong incentive for corporate directors to take steps to ensure that the business does not default on its obligation to pay wages as they become due. The limited super priority should provide an incentive for employers to meet their payroll obligations, which will prevent abuse of the proposed wage guarantee fund. The limited super-priority will give unpaid wage claims up to CAD 2,000 priority ahead of secured creditors on current assets. Arguably, secured lenders will increase monitoring of debtors to ensure that they meet their payroll obligations, as any amounts for unpaid wages that accumulate will reduce the amount that those creditors can realize from the current assets.

Similarly, the United States Bankruptcy Code grants employees unsecured, priority claims against the debtor to a maximum of USD 10,000 for unpaid wages and benefits.[40] Pre-petition unpaid wages have preference over general unsecured claims. The claims must arise from the period of 90 days prior to bankruptcy filing employee. Benefit plan contributions must be within 180 days from bankruptcy or

---

amend the Bankruptcy and Insolvency Act, the Companies' Creditors Arrangement Act, the Wage Earners Protection [Program] Act and Chapter 47 of the Statutes of Canada, 2005 (8 December 2006, Library of Parliament). On 13 June 2007, the Canadian Government introduced Bill C-62 incorporating the Ways and Means Motion and, on 15 June 2007 gave the Bill its 2nd and 3rd reading and sent it to the Standing Senate Committee on Banking, Trade and Commerce for final deliberation.

37   Sections 81.3 and 81.4.
38   Set out under section 136(1)(d).
39   Sections 36(1)(b) and 36(2).
40   11 USC §507(a)(4). USD 10,000 is approximately EUR 7,300.

termination of business. Preferred claims include earned wages, salaries, commissions, vacation pay, sick leave pay, severance pay, and contributions to employee benefit plans. If the debtor corporation is liquidated, employees may not receive the amount of the preferred claims as the claims rank after secured claims and other priority creditors.

In Mexico, specified worker entitlements have a first priority for payment of three months salary in lieu of severance pay.[41] However, there are frequently not sufficient assets to cover the claims and workers are not covered fully. There has been considerable pressure by secured creditors to change the regime as it subordinates their interests, in turn, arguably increasing the cost and availability of credit.[42] In Mexico, the risk to employees is exacerbated by the fact that its social safety nets are generally underdeveloped and under-funded. There is also an issue of deferred liquidation, where directors and officers may delay insolvency filings, which can be prejudicial to employee claims.[43]

In Argentina, there is also a special priority in liquidation for certain employee claims. A general priority is provided for employees by granting a lien on general assets of the debtor where special priority claims are not paid. There is no priority over secured claims on immovable assets. The priority includes wage arrears up to six months prior to filing and redundancy claims up to three months salary. The special priority covers wage arrears, redundancy claims, last month payment, payment in lieu of notice, unfair discriminatory dismissal, worker injury, holiday pay and specified other compensations. There is no guarantee fund in Argentina.

In South Africa, there is a limited preference against unencumbered assets of the estate, but no preference over secured creditors. Employee wage claims are first, wages up to 3 months or ZAR 12,000.[44] Next ranked and paid on a *pari passu* basis, are holiday pay up to ZAR 4,000, paid leave up to ZAR 4,000, and severance up to ZAR 12,000.[45] There is no guarantee fund other than the general benefits of Unemployment Insurance Act (63 of 2001).

The granting of super-priority, whether over all secured claims or only inventory or movable assets, clearly offers the most protection to employee claims, assuming that a system is in place for fair, efficient and timely payment of claims. While senior secured lenders sometimes have protested the granting of super-priority of claims, there appears to be no empirical studies that suggest that where

---

41   See Oscos Coria, D.U. and Oscos Abogados, 'The New Mexican Law on Commercial Insolvency' (2001) at 4, available at: <www.iiiglobal.org/country/mexico/mex_insolv.pdf> (last viewed 31 May 2007).

42   See Herrera, I. et al., (Excelsior (Mex.), 11 December 1999), available at: <www.excelsior.mx/9912/991211/nac13.html> (last viewed 31 May 2007).

43   See Rowat, M., 'The World Bank Group, Reforming Insolvency Systems in Latin America', *Public Policy for the Private Sector*, Note No. 187 (June 1999), available at: <www.worldbank.org/html/fpd/notes/187/187summary.html> (last viewed 31 May 2007). See also Posthuma, R.A. et al., 'Labor and Employment Laws in Mexico and the United States: An International Comparison' (2000) 51 *Labor Law Journal* 95.

44   ZAR 12,000 is approximately EUR 1,249.

45   ZAR 4,000 is approximately EUR 416.

claims are capped and thus certain, that the cost and availability of credit has been negatively affected.

Li Guoqiang observes that banks and other financial institutions can play a role in preventing enterprises from defaulting on wages and social security premiums, and that they may strengthen loan risk controls if employee claims have a priority claim.[46] Li observes that, currently, banks do not evaluate the enterprises' risk of wage default and social security premiums when lending, and in China, only a few banks prohibit lending to debtors that have defaulted on more than a certain amount of wages. Implementing a priority for employees may create the appropriate incentives for secured lenders to monitor treatment of employees prior to firms filing for insolvency or bankruptcy. Since banks and other senior lenders have the bargaining power to extract information from debtor companies and the resources to monitor the debtor's activities in respect of meeting employee claims, arguably it is more efficient to structure a priority scheme that maximizes protection to workers and places the monitoring costs where they can be most effectively borne.

Guarantee Funds and Insurance Systems

While the priority approach does offer some financial relief to employees, protection of employees solely through wage priority systems is often not sufficient to fully protect workers' claims. Where the claims rank behind secured creditors, there are frequently few, if any, funds to satisfy these preferred claims. As a result, some jurisdictions have adopted wage protection or guarantee funds as a mechanism to ensure that some or all of employee compensation claims are met during insolvency. Where wage and compensation guarantee funds have been utilized, there are different models creating different priorities for payment and timing of payment. The underlying policy objective of such funds is to provide timely financial relief to employees. While employees have frequently lost their going forward income, they are guaranteed compensation for some of the outstanding wages and benefits owing.

There are three key aspects of an insurance scheme or guarantee fund: the source of funding, the level of benefits payable, and the timeliness of payments. In terms of funding sources, one option is a sector funded or employer funded guarantee system, with funds raised by premiums levered on debtor corporations operating within the country. Another funding mechanism is through the general tax base, as is proposed for the new Canadian Wage Earner Protection Fund, which has not yet been proclaimed in force. Another option is an employee contribution based system, although arguably, employees are the least well positioned to make contributions towards such a fund, particularly in those jurisdictions in which employees are barely earning a living wage.

The second aspect of a guarantee fund is the level of benefits provided. Some funds cap the level of benefits to a fixed amount or a percentage of total

---

46   See Li, G.Q., 'The Establishment of Limited Priority of Workers' Claims in the Enterprise Bankruptcy Law of China' (28 April 2006, OECD Report) at 6.

income. Some limit the period for which wages can be claimed, although this can be problematic as jurisdictions vary considerably in the normal hold-back of wages and other compensation. In Canada and the United States for example, wages are frequently paid on a bi-monthly basis, hence wage arrears are typically in fixed amounts. For systems in many emerging nations, where employees are paid less frequently, such as monthly, or in industries where wages are held back and paid semi-annually, fixed time frames for payment of entitlements can significantly prejudice employees. Moreover, if the time frame is too short, there are incentives on debtor corporations to stop payments for a time period, both to divert funds from employees to other creditors with the expectation that a guarantee fund will cover the rest of payments and to disentitle employees for the amount owing in the period outside of the specified time frame.

Another cost control device under a guarantee fund system is to limit the type of entitlements that employees can claim for, such limiting claims to wages and vacation, but excluding the more costly termination and severance entitlements. While such a strategy controls costs, it arguably excludes payments that employees particularly require when faced with sudden job loss. In some jurisdictions, such as Australia and Brazil, there is a further prioritizing of employees in that injured workers are given a preference in compensation owing, on the theory that they are the least able to find new employment as an economic cushion to their financial distress.

The third issue is how timely payments to employees are under the guarantee fund or insurance system. The most effective guarantee fund model allows for payment of employees up-front, rather than requiring the employees first to seek to recover from the employer. This is optimal because there is often a large time lag between the debtor's insolvency and the payout of proceeds from the estate, particularly when secured creditors must be satisfied prior to employee claims. Moreover, employees often do not have the resources or energy to pursue the claims, particularly as they are also seeking employment at the same time. It is at the point of job loss that employees' economic vulnerability is the greatest and hence the point at which funds should be placed in their hands. If payments are made immediately to employees from the guarantee fund, the guarantee fund then can be subrogated to the employees' claims and the fund expends the time and energy to realize some or all of the claims through the insolvency or bankruptcy process. In Belgium, if a debtor corporation is unable to pay entitlements within fifteen days of the close of the business, a wage protection fund called the Fund for Compensation in Case of Closures of Laid Off Workers immediately commences payment on its behalf.[47] Workers must first have pursued the claim with the employer, but are eligible for fund payments if the employer has not paid within 15 days of the actual closure of the business. The Fund is run by the National

---

47   EMIRE, Belgium Notice, available at: <www.eurofound.ie/emire/BELGIUM/ NOTICE-BE.html> (last viewed 31 May 2007). Workers can access the fund for wages and other remuneration, leave bonus and salary in lieu of notice to a maximum of BEF 900,000 per employer (now approximately EUR 24,000).

government, funded through social security. Employers make extra social security contributions based on the size of business and total salary costs.[48]

In Ireland, under the Protection of Employees (Employers' Insolvency) Act 1984, employee entitlements are paid out of the Social Insurance Fund when an employer becomes insolvent and is unable to pay employee claims. The fund will pay for wages, up to a capped amount per week for a total of eight weeks; holiday pay up to eight weeks; sick pay up to eight weeks; deductions such as union dues and private health and life insurance that were deducted from wages and not turned over, up to eight weeks; minimum notice of termination; damages at common law for wrongful dismissal awarded by a court up to 104 weeks of wages; and amounts awarded under the Anti-Discrimination Pay Act 1974 and the Employment Equity Act 1977.[49]

Arguably, a guarantee or insurance fund enhances certainty, because it does not interfere with the pre-insolvency hierarchy of claims. However, equally, it can transfer the costs of insolvency to the state, and absent sectoral funding, can shift the burden of payment inappropriately. There is also the issue of incentive effects, in terms of whether the existence of a guarantee fund encourages insolvent firms to let payment of amounts owing to employees slide in the period prior to filing an insolvency proceeding, as they know that the guarantee fund will cover the amount.

Regimes that use a single protection type of insolvency protection, as have been reviewed here, are helpful but limited in their scope. However, it is possible to combine types of protection for employee claims, allow the protections to enhance one another, while still creating certainty in the credit system.

Bifocals: Systems that have Combined Both a Priority System and a Guarantee Fund or Insurance System

The problems associated with limited priority systems as inadequate to protect employees' compensation claims and guarantee funds as potentially creating inappropriate incentives, can be addressed by implementing a combined wage priority and guarantee fund system. The guarantee fund can be designed to pay employee claims immediately, when the resources are most needed. The claim is then subrogated and a statutory priority to recover the amount of the claim means that the fund's costs are partially covered by the insolvent firm that caused the pay-out cost.

A number of jurisdictions have approached the treatment of employee claims with a dual focus lens, by granting both a priority/preference for employee compensation claims during insolvency and creating a wage or pension guarantee fund or insurance scheme that serves as a social safety net in meeting outstanding wage and benefits claims. This combined protection system appears to be a function of a mature economic system and developed insolvency law regime. A combined employee protection system is aimed at having the debtor corporation or

---

48   Ibid.
49   Protection of Employees (Employers' Insolvency) Act 1984, section 6.

bankrupt estate pay the claims where the assets are sufficient, but providing a social safety net for a portion of the claims where the assets are insufficient. A number of jurisdictions allow for employee claims to be paid at the outset of insolvency, with the state taking subrogation of the claims and seeking to realize on the claims from the bankrupt estate.

Arguably, a combined employee protection system also creates the appropriate incentives. The difficulty with a system that offers solely a guarantee fund is that debtor corporations have an incentive to avoid payments to employees in the period leading up to insolvency if they can rely without impunity on a public fund to meet those claims. Even if debtors do not wish to engage in such conduct, they may be placed under pressure by senior creditors to do so where there is a guarantee fund available in order that more money is directed to those creditors. The combined system ensures that the debtor corporation considers employee claims as one of the priorities in an insolvency proceeding, while still offering guaranteed protection to employees where assets are inadequate.

The United Kingdom is an example of a combined system. Employees have a preferential claim under the Insolvency Act 1986. Employee wage and leave claims are given preference over debts secured by a floating charge, but rank below debts secured by a fixed charge and administration costs. The preference includes employee remuneration in the four months immediately prior, up to a maximum amount, and all accrued annual leave due upon termination of employment.[50] There is a National Insurance Fund that protects United Kingdom employees on insolvency, provided by the Employment Rights Act 1996. It provides for the payment of outstanding employee entitlements up to an indexed amount, including payment for wages up to eight weeks, statutory payments for time off work including suspension on medical or ante natal grounds, any protective award, annual leave up to six weeks, compensation awards for unfair dismissal and redundancy payments, and pay in lieu of notice.

Where an employee in the United Kingdom has been unsuccessful in having her or his claim paid by the debtor corporation, the employee can apply to the Fund for payment. The Secretary of State then assumes the employee's right as a preferential creditor, up to the amount paid out of the fund, in order to recover the payment. In 1998–1999, GBP 143 million of payments were made to employees under 80,000 claims for payment and the Fund recovered GBP 21 million.[51] In 1997–1998, 85 per cent of all claims were paid within ten weeks. The estimated administrative cost for the Redundancy Payments Service to process the claims was GBP 9 million in 1998–1999. The National Insurance Fund is funded primarily by employers and employees through national insurance contributions.[52]

Hence, the United Kingdom combined employee protection system adopts a two stage approach, requiring first that employees seek to recover from the debtor

---

50   Hon. P. Reith, Minister for Employment, Workplace Relations and Small Business (Australia), 'The Protection of Employee Entitlements in the Event of Employer Insolvency, The Overseas Experience' (1999). GBP 800 is approximately EUR 1,171.

51   Ibid.

52   Ibid.

corporation; and then, where employees are unable to recover, the guarantee fund pays out the amount and then tries to recover from the estate. While less than 20 percent of the costs are recovered from the insolvent corporation, millions of pounds are recovered, ensuring that debtor corporations do not simply by-pass their payment obligations under insolvency law. The difficulty with the United Kingdom system is that it places an onus on employees first to try to recover their wage claims from the debtor, requiring them to expend time and energy in the pursuit of their claims at a time when they are most financially at risk and searching for new employment. Although the goal of payment within ten weeks of application is laudable, it may be inadequate when added to the period that the employee has sought to recover the claim from the debtor.

Japan grants preferred status for employees' unpaid wage claims, ranking after secured creditors and tax claims, for up to six months prior to bankruptcy. The Japan Labour Health and Welfare Organization under a guarantee scheme allows recovery up to 80 per cent of unpaid wages and retirement allowance for employees that left a firm six months prior to and not greater than two years prior to the firm's insolvency.[53]

Another example of a combined employee protection system is Australia. In Australia, the current priority for payment during insolvency is set out in the Corporations Act 2001, with secured creditors ranking ahead of employees. Certain employee entitlements are preference claims ranking ahead of unsecured creditors.[54] This includes wages, superannuation contributions, payments in lieu of notice, annual leave, long service leave, workers' compensation payments and redundancy. There is no monetary or time limit given to wages and other entitlements.[55] The Australian government considered adopting a super-priority (called maximum-priority in Australia) for employee claims, conducting a major public consultation process in 2004. The super-priority being considered would have ranked ahead of secured creditors on insolvency.[56] After strong opposition from the finance sector, the super-priority has not been implemented and appears not to be a legislative priority.[57]

In addition to the limited current priority over unsecured claims, the Australia insolvency system has a wage protection fund. The General Employee Entitlements and Redundancy Scheme (GEERS) was implemented by administrative order,[58] providing a relatively high degree of protection for

53   Johnson, above note 8 at 20.

54   Corporations Act 2001, section 556 (Australia).

55   See Symes, C., 'A New Statutory Directors' Duty for Australia – A 'Duty' to be Concerned about Employee Entitlements in the Insolvent Corporation' (2003) 12 *International Insolvency Review* 133.

56   Although the government said that it would provide an exemption for small business from this proposal to eliminate any impact on small business lending.

57   Symes, above note 55; confirmed by personal correspondence (5 March 2005).

58   The original Australian wage protection fund was called the Employee Entitlements Support Scheme (EESS), a scheme for basic payments of employee entitlements funded by the national government, which was replaced by GEERS in 2001.

employees during insolvency. Employees that lose their job and entitlements due to their employer becoming insolvent or bankrupt are eligible for assistance under the GEERS.[59] Where the employee has a legal entitlement derived from legislation, an award, a statutory agreement or a written contract of employment, at the date of the debtor corporation's insolvency, employees are eligible to receive payments. The payments cover all unpaid wages, all accrued annual leave, all accrued long service leave, all accrued pay in lieu of notice and up to eight weeks redundancy entitlements.[60] Payments made under the GEERS are subject to annual income cap of AUD 98,200 for 2006-2007.[61] Eligible claimants who earn more than the scheme's cap will be paid as if they earned a rate equivalent to the scheme's income cap. Employees are not eligible where they are a shareholding director or a relative of a shareholding director; are a defined relative of the former employer; or an independent contractor of the debtor.[62]

Under the Australian system, insolvency practitioners have a role in processing and expediting payments to employees. Employees submit a GEERS claim form to the insolvency practitioner managing the winding-up of the business, not later than 12 months after losing their job. The insolvency practitioner verifies outstanding employee entitlements based on the employment records and then provides the government with the claim and verification of entitlement. The GEERS funds are advanced to the insolvency practitioner after the entitlement data is confirmed and the insolvency practitioner deducts tax and makes the GEERS payments to employees. The objective of the system is to try to have the funds to the employees within four weeks of the insolvency practitioner providing verified entitlement data.[63]

In the event of liquidation, the Australian Government is a priority creditor under section 560 of the Corporations Act 2001 to the extent of the amount that it has advanced under the GEERS. If a Deed of Company Arrangement is proposed and the creditors vote for a deed rather than for the company to be wound up, the deed would include the priorities of section 556(1) in relation to the entitlements to be paid to employees. Further, in relation to its advances for payments of employee

---

59   The firm must be insolvent or bankrupt on or after 12 September 2001.

60   Australian Chamber of Commerce and Industry, 'Government should abandon changes to ranking creditors on insolvency' (February 2004), available at: <www.acci.asn.au> (last viewed 31 May 2007); GEERS 2005, available at: <www.workplace.gov.au/Workplace/WPDisplay/0,1280,a3%253D3649%2526a0%25 3D0%2526a1%253D517%2526a2%253D623,00.html> (last viewed 31 May 2007); Corporations Law Amendment (Employee Entitlements) Act 2000 and Corporations Act 2001 (Australia).

61   The cap was AUD 75,200 for 2001–2002, AUD 81,500 for 2002-2003, AUD 85,400 for 2003-2004 and AUD 90,400 for 2004–2005. AUD 98,200 is approximately EUR 61,710.

62   Employees are also ineligible where they lodge their claim 12 months after employment was terminated or where they resigned from employment (in most cases) or had their employment terminated before 12 September 2001 (although they might be eligible under the Employee Entitlements Support Scheme).

63   GEERS 2005.

entitlements, the Government would require that any deed that is presented to the creditors for their consideration provide for the same priority as the Government would receive under section 560 of the Corporations Act 2001 in relation to such an advance under a winding up. If at the end of the administration, the company is restored to the directors other than pursuant to a Deed of Company Arrangement and it continues to trade, the loan that the Government has advanced is repaid within four weeks of the end of the administration.[64] The Australian system offers greater protection of employee claims than some other guarantee systems as it places a generous cap on the amount of claims that can be recovered under the guarantee system and because it combines the limited priority claim and the GEERS as protective strategies.

France also has a combined employee protection system. There is super-preference for wages not paid in the previous 60 days; and a general preference over personal property and real estate for unpaid wages for six months prior to adjudication. Employee claims have priority over secured claims, but not those with retention of title. Priority claims include wages, paid leave, improper termination and certain dismissal allowances. There is also a compulsory insurance fund called the *Association pour la gestion du régime d'assurance des créances des salariés* ('AGS'). Employees may recover from the AGS when the debtor has insufficient assets or recovery is expected to be protracted. Employees may collect even if employer did not contribute. By Law no. 2004-391 of 4 May 2004, compensation agreements concluded 18 months prior to filing are not covered by the AGS.

Paul Omar observes that, in France, workers enjoy a number of privileges in insolvency, owing to very favourable conditions in France's social legislation for employees and those on apprenticeship contracts.[65] In the case of continuation plans, the law provides that sums owed to employees will be paid in priority to all other debts, without any delays or postponements.[66] In insolvency proceedings, the employees benefit from a right to payment of two months salary plus any holiday entitlement falling due, fixed by reference to the previous month's wages sheets, which the debtor or administrator, if one is appointed, is required to pay within ten days of the opening judgment being pronounced. The administrator is authorised to pay the equivalent of a month's salary before the ascertainment of debts is carried out.[67] If funds do not exist, the administrator may postpone any payment until the first receipts are made resulting from sales prior to the opening of proceedings or from the continuation of business.[68] If this does not occur within a very short period, what normally happens is that the administrator will ask the AGS to

---

64   Idem.

65   See Sorensen, A. and Omar, P., *Corporate Rescue Procedures in France* (1996, Kluwer, The Hague) in Chapter 17, the position being maintained through later reforms.

66   Commercial Code (as amended by Law no. 2005-845 of 26 July 2005), Article L. 625-8, available at: <www.legifrance.gouv.fr> (last viewed 31 May 2005).

67   Ibid.

68   Ibid.

advance the necessary funds.[69] The AGS is then subrogated to employees' rights for the purpose of any dividends in the case of a sales plan or liquidation. In liquidation, French employees receive any balance due after calculating the total amount due to them, less any advances from the AGS.[70] Any entitlements that employees have enjoy first ranking for the purposes of payments. The AGS will also enjoy subrogation to this position, except in liquidation, when any advances made during insolvency proceedings are postponed till after the payment of legal fees.[71]

In Finland, wages and salaries have a statutory preference that ranks behind secured creditors with a fixed charge and administration costs.[72] Secured creditors holding a floating charge enjoy only partial priority, with the priority limited to 60 per cent of the floating charge.[73] The other 40 per cent of the value of the collateral subject to the floating charge is made available to unsecured claims, including employee wages that have priority over all general unsecured credit and tax claims. Finland established a Wage Guarantee Fund in 1993, funded by all employers collectively, with employers contributing 0.05 per cent of employee wages.[74] Employees can claim wages earned in the three months prior to their application to the wage guarantee fund.[75]

Bergstrom et al. studied the effects of Finland's reduction in priority for secured floating claims on distributions and administrative costs in liquidating bankruptcy cases. They found that there were distributive effects; specifically, payments to unsecured creditors were significantly higher after reform than prior, with mean payments to unsecured increasing from 0.9 per cent to 4 per cent. They also found that the priority reform did not significantly affect total payments to creditors, concluding that this was because Finnish banks, which hold almost all of the floating charges, became much more diligent in monitoring and in restricting credit earlier. The study notes that Finnish floating charges are weaker instruments than floating charges in the United States, in that they apply only to inventory, accounts receivable and other assets that turn over.[76] Their study offers one of the few empirical studies of the effects of changes in priority of claims.

---

69   Omar, above note 65.
70   Employment Code, Articles L. 143-10 and 143-11-4; Commercial Code, Articles L. 625-9 and L. 626-20.
71   Omar, above note 65.
72   Prior to 1993, creditors holding a floating charge had priority for 100 per cent of their collateral. The claims are equal in priority to unpaid alimony (effective 1993).
73   See Bergstrom, C. et al., 'On the Design of Efficient Priority Rules for Secured Creditors: Empirical Evidence from a Change in Law' (2004) 18 *European Journal of Law and Economics* 273 at 274.
74   The Wage Guarantee Fund Act no. 53/1993 (Finland).
75   The amount of payments to each employee from the fund is capped at FIM 90,000 (CAD 24,620).
76   Ibid., at 275.

Italy is another example of a combined employee protection system. In Italy, an employee can recover up to 80 percent of entitlements owing.[77] Claims have a general priority over movable property. The priority claims include wages, severance pay, retirement/indemnity, sickness compensation, payment in lieu of notice, holiday pay, redundancy and unfair dismissal claims. There is no priority over claims secured by fixed or immovable assets. A special public fund, the *Cassa Integrazione Guadagni* ('CIG'), is used to protect employees' income, financed by companies and the state and administered by the National Institute of Social Insurance. The CIG protects the income of employees affected by lay-offs or suspension by paying up to 80 per cent of their lost wages. In industry, the CIG operates through two forms of intervention (ordinary and special), governed by a series of laws.[78] CIG allows recovery for maximum 12 months or 36 months in a five-year period, depending on a number of factors. A trade union disclosure and consultation procedure is a prior condition for the admissibility of a debtor's request for the CIG's intervention, and often leads to negotiations.[79] Devised originally as a means of temporary income protection for employees, the fund was extended to insolvency cases where there is no prospect of a return to the normal production and work pattern, with special provisions for firms with greater than 50 employees, for artisanal enterprises whose main customers are enterprises experiencing serious economic difficulties, for agricultural and stock-rearing co-operatives and specified firms in the catering, restaurant, construction and agricultural sectors.[80]

---

77   EMIRE, Italy: Wages Guarantee Fund (CIG), European Foundation for the Improvement of Living and Working Conditions, available at: <www.eurofound.eu.int/emire/ITALY/WAGESGUARANTEEFUNDCIG-IT.html> (position as at 12 December 2006, last viewed 31 May 2007).

78   Ibid. The main laws are Law no. 1115 of 5 November 1968, Law no. 164 of 20 May 1975, Law no. 675 of 12 August 1977 and Law no. 223 of 23 July 1991, which greatly reduced the distinction between the two forms. The European Foundation for the Improvement of Living and Working Conditions reports that: 'Payments under ordinary intervention are granted by the National Institute of Social Insurance to workers who have been laid off or put on short-time working because of immediate circumstances which cannot be blamed either on the employer or on the employees, or because of temporary market situations; payments under special intervention are granted by the Ministry of Labour and Social Insurance, on the advice of the Interministerial Industrial Policy Committee (CIPI), to both blue-collar and white-collar workers who have been laid off (and to blue-collar workers put on short-time working) because of company reorganization, restructuring or conversion, or a company's economic difficulties that are of particular social importance as regards local employment'.

79   Ibid.

80   Ibid. The European Foundation observes that Law no. 223 of 23 July 1991 did, however, seek to restore the Fund to its original function of providing assistance during purely temporary labour surpluses. It imposed a rigid time-limit on eligibility for making up lost pay, and recourse to special availability-for-employment and workforce-reduction procedures in cases where the surplus is structural or there is no prospect of re-employing the surplus employees. This objective has only partially been

Germany offers a different model of a combined system. In Germany, employees rank with unsecured creditors on a *pari passu* basis. There is a national insolvency fund that provides funds where the assets are not sufficient to pay employee claims.[81] There is, however, the possibility of using a social welfare plan for employees that face severe disadvantages due to a firm's insolvency, whereby employees are awarded first priority in insolvency, with a limitation to one third of all assets. Under German law, the purchaser has to reach a settlement with the liquidator and the labour organization with regard to a social plan for those employees it does not want to take over.[82] The Federal Institute for Employment guarantees outstanding wages for three months prior to bankruptcy, funded in part by employer contributions.[83] The three month period is with regard to the period before the insolvency procedure; in the period after the start of the insolvency procedure, the employees only receive payment if the bankrupt's estate has sufficient assets.[84] Hence while the system is for the most part reliant on the guarantee fund to protect workers' claims, there are exceptional circumstances in which employees receive a priority charge.

Under China's new Enterprise Bankruptcy Law, secured claims have first priority with respect to the security, followed by employee claims, including wages and labour insurance premiums, unemployment insurance and minimum living security, followed by taxes and then unsecured claims.[85] In China, there is an unemployment insurance regime, funded by employer and employee contributions, that covers compensation for entitlements owed on a priority basis during insolvency, as well as additional compensation up to 80 per cent of the national minimum wage for up to two years.[86] The scope of coverage is broad, including

---

achieved, because as a result of the serious economic crisis suffered by Italy from 1992 onwards the legislators have intervened to modify the legal rules governing the Fund's operation, both extending the time-limit on eligibility for special intervention to make up pay and extending such eligibility to areas where it was formerly excluded.

81   *Insolvenzordnung* 1999 (InsO), available at: <http://www.bmj.bund.de/images/11317.pdf> (last viewed 31 May 2007).

82   See Jung, L., 'National Labour Law Profile: Federal Republic of Germany' (April 2001), available at: <www.ilo.org/public/english/dialogue/ifpdial/info/national/ger.htm> (last viewed 31 May 2007).

83   Reith, above note 50.

84   Jung, above note 82.

85   Enterprise Bankruptcy Law, Articles 32 and 37; see Wang, W.G., 'The Order of Payment of Workers' Claims and Security Interests under China's New Bankruptcy Law', OECD Report (28 April 2007) at 2, available at: <www.oecd.org> (last viewed 31 May 2007). Article 32 specifies: 'With respect to claims secured with property that are established before bankruptcy is declared, the creditors enjoy the right to receive repayment with priority with respect to such security. With respect to claims that are secured with property whose amount exceeds the value of the security collateral, the part that is not repaid constitutes a bankruptcy claim, and will be repaid in accordance with the bankruptcy proceedings'.

86   See Lee, V., Research and Library Services Division, Legislative Council Secretariat, Unemployment Insurance and Assistance Systems in Mainland China 5 (2000),

wages, medical expenses, support for the disabled, basic pension and medical insurance premiums in arrears and compensation payable to employees according to the law, making its coverage one of the most expansive, although not all employees receive coverage under the system.[87] China's new bankruptcy legislation is aimed at addressing the deferred liquidation tendencies of the system, whereby state-run or owned enterprises delay filing insolvency proceedings due to custom in respect of reluctance to acknowledge financial distress and loss of job security in a culture where life-long employment has been considered important.[88] Uneven enforcement of laws means has meant uncertainty for insolvent debtors and all their creditors, including workers. The Chinese system engages in systematic retraining and job referral services as an aid to workers recovering from job loss due to insolvency.

The World Bank observes that amounts paid in China are based on a formula that applies a multiplier to an employee's current salary and takes into account length of service, observing that while this recognizes their investments in the firm, the actual amounts paid to employees within a firm can be inequitable.[89] The Chinese system is an illustration of an emerging nation that is struggling to find the appropriate mechanism to protect workers in its revamping of bankruptcy law. In addition to the challenges of finding the appropriate political balance, it must try to provide certainty to new capital investing in the country. It also illustrates the need for transparency and certainty, whatever the choice of model is, and the need to ensure employees are treated fairly and equitably within the system of employee protection created.

While Canada is currently a preference claims only regime, with one very limited pension guarantee fund in one of its provinces, as discussed below, it has proposed moving to a combined employee protection system. Recent reforms to Canadian insolvency and bankruptcy legislation, enacted but not proclaimed in force as of 15 June 2007, propose a new Wage Earner Protection Program ('WEPP'), established to make payments to individuals in respect of wages owed to them by employers who are bankrupt or subject to a receivership. The fund will be available to all employees that have worked with the employer for at least three months.[90] The amount that may be paid to an eligible individual is the amount of

---

available at: <www.legco.gov.hk/yr99-00/english/sec/library/e18.pdf> (last viewed 31 May 2007).

87   Li, above note 46 at 6.

88   Ibid.

89   The World Bank, East Asia and Pacific Region Private Sector Development Unit, *Bankruptcy of State Enterprises in China – A Case and Agenda for Reforming the Insolvency System*, i and ii (20 September 2000).

90   WEPP, section 6(2) specifies that an individual is ineligible to receive a payment in respect of any wages earned during a period in which the individual was an officer or a director of the former employer; had a controlling interest, within the meaning of the regulations, in the business of the former employer; or occupied a managerial position. Hence it attempts to prevent abuse of the WEPP by excluding individuals from receiving WEPP payments who would have had privileged information on the financial situation of the company and who may forego payments for themselves

wages owing to the individual to a maximum of CAD 3,000 that were earned in the six months immediately before the date of bankruptcy or the first day on which a receiver was appointed, less any deductions applicable to the payment under a federal or provincial law, or an amount equal to four times the maximum weekly insurable earnings under the Employment Insurance Act.[91] The six-month period will allow employees who work irregular hours for the business and who may not have worked in the period immediately preceding the bankruptcy or receivership, to be eligible for payment, if they have unpaid wage claims that significantly predate the insolvency of the employer. It will also provide a balance between the need to ensure that unpaid wage earners, who may go through long periods of working without receiving wages, are protected, without providing an incentive for unpaid wage earners to continue to work without receiving wages for an indefinite period of time.

Under the proposed Canadian WEPP, debtors could arguably hire workers in the period leading up to their insolvency without intending to pay those workers, on the understanding that the WEPP would not cover them, given that an employee must have worked for the debtor for at least three months in order to be eligible to receive a WEPP payment. However, the statute grants authority to make regulations to exempt certain workers in special circumstances, particularly workers with limited tenure, such as seasonal workers, temporary workers or students, from the three month restriction. If these types of workers were expressly protected, it would strike a balance between the need to deter abuse of the programme and the need for flexibility to meet the needs of workers in a variety of situations. Directors or officers will be ineligible to receive WEPP payments because it would be inappropriate to compensate individuals who bear some responsibility for the insolvency of the business and who may be responsible for incurring liabilities for unpaid wages.[92]

The Canadian government estimates that 97 per cent of unpaid wage claims in cases of receivership and bankruptcy are less than CAD 3,000 and hence that the WEPP will assist employees in recovering most of their claims.[93] Though information on the identity of WEPP claimants and the amounts of their claims will be produced by insolvency professionals, ultimate responsibility for determining the amount of each entitlement to the WEPP will lie with the Minister

---

knowing they would receive payment from the WEPP; and/or bear responsibility for the insolvency of the business.

91   Ibid., section 7(1). The limit on the amount of wages covered is set according to the amount of maximum insurable earnings under the Employment Insurance Act 1996 (EI) for a four week period (maximum insurable earnings for one week is CAD 750; for a four week period, the maximum is currently CAD 3,000, approximately EUR 1,985).

92   This constitutes a violation of labour or employment standards legislation in all jurisdictions.

93   The maximum amount of payment from the WEPP corresponds with the maximum insurable earnings under the EI programme as this amount closely approximates the average (mean) industrial wages of a full-time worker in 2004, which, according to the Labour Force Survey, was CAD 777.73.

or its designate.[94] Under the proposed WEPP, every trustee and receiver will be required to identify each individual who is owed wages by a bankrupt or insolvent employer, earned during the six month period immediately before the date of the bankruptcy or receivership; determine the amount of wages owing to each individual in respect of that six month period; inform each individual of the existence of the programme and the conditions under which payments may be made; provide the Minister and each individual with prescribed information in relation to the individual and the amount of wages owing in respect of the six-month period.[95] The WEPP will subrogate the unpaid wage earner's claim as a creditor to the bankrupt or insolvent employer, in order to allow the Canadian Government to recover from the assets of the bankrupt estate where possible, in place of the wage earner.[96]

Canada's proposed WEPP received broad political support during the Parliamentary process. The delay in proclaiming the law in force is largely due to political disagreements regarding proposed changes to pension claim priorities, which are discussed below, at a time when there is a minority government. However, these differences appear to have been resolved and as this book goes to press, an amending Bill C-62 received third reading on 15 June 2007 and is now scheduled for debate before the Canadian Senate Committee; it brings the WEPP a substantial step closer to enactment.

Treatment of Pension Claims

Pensions have become a critically important issue in insolvency. Enron's employees had defined-contribution retirement savings accounts, called 401(k)s after the paragraph of the United States Tax Code that brought them into being in the early 1980s.[97] Enron's employees were strongly encouraged to invest in the company's stock. Enron employees were allowed to invest up to 15 per cent of their salary in the pension plan and Enron would match 50 per cent of that amount with its stock as its contribution to the 401(k). Enron's plan offered employees 18 investment options, including a range of mutual funds and its own stock, but by the end of 2000, 60 per cent of the plan was invested in Enron shares, i.e. not prudently diversified prior to the firm's collapse.[98] Of that 60 per cent, 82 per cent was Enron

---

94   WEPP, section 21. This will ensure accountability as the Minister will be responsible for the administration of the programme.
95   Ibid., section 21(1). The information will be prescribed in Regulations to be promulgated.
96   Ibid., section 21(1)(e).
97   See Hill, A., Wine, E. and McNulty, S., 'A poor retirement: The bankruptcy of Enron has brought into uncomfortably sharp focus broader doubts about the way that US employees invest for their old age' (Financial Times, 12 December 2001).
98   Ibid. They report that the allocation to Enron rose that high at least partly because Enron matched employee contributions to their own retirement accounts with company stock rather than cash.

stock chosen by employees from the 'options'. The losses were exacerbated when Enron 'locked down' its 401(k) plan in the months just before the firm's collapse, not allowing employees to sell Enron shares out of their plan.[99]

Hill et al. have observed that Enron was not alone in offering to match employee contributions with stock instead of cash, reporting that about 2,000 United States companies do so.[100] That represents only 0.5 per cent of 401(k) plans, but the practice affects a greater proportion of workers because the companies are among the biggest and oldest in the United States, with many of the Fortune 500 companies running their plans in this manner. Among 140 of the largest companies, the average allocation to company stock in the 401(k) plan is about 35 per cent.[101] At General Electric, for example, 75 per cent of the defined-contribution plan consists of GE stock and about 78 per cent of Coca Cola's plan is invested in the company's shares.[102]

When debtor corporations control the pension plan, they may stop contributing as the firm becomes increasingly financially distressed and divert funds to other more pressing creditor payments. A firm may also invest the assets of the pension primarily or solely in the corporation's own stock, contrary to prudent pension and trust rules, and when it becomes financially distressed, employees lose both their employment and their pensions. Guarantee funds can provide confidence to workers that at least some of their pension promises will be met even where they are concerned about their employers' future ability to pay.[103]

Stewart makes the following observation about the lack of diversification of pension risk:

> 7. The problem of diversification becomes even more key when pensions are funded via a book reserve system. In such cases, pension benefits are not secured by an external pool of diversified assets, as pension assets form part of the plan sponsor's balance sheet. As a consequence a book reserve system can be likened to a funded system in which all of the pension plan assets are invested in a single security – i.e. the debt of the sponsoring firm. If the plan sponsor were to go bankrupt the accrued pensions of both active and retired workers would clearly be at risk. In theory pension fund trustees could overcome this concentrated exposure, for example by shorting the sponsoring company's stock. However restrictions will usually be in place to prevent this and, where the pension fund is particularly large compared with the market capitalization of the sponsoring firm, such action could have an extremely adverse effect on the share price. Hence benefit guarantee schemes are often compulsory for firms operating internal forms of funding (as is the case in Germany and Sweden).[104]

---

99   Ibid.. The share value went from USD 80 per share the year prior to being worthless.
100 Ibid.
101 According to the Committee on the Investment of Employee Benefit Assets, a group of corporate pension plan sponsors.
102 Ibid.
103 Stewart, above note 7.
104 Ibid., at 6.

Pension guarantee funds, as exist in Sweden, Germany, Ontario Canada and the United States, offer a means for pensioners to have relief from the effects of a debtor company's insolvency. Such funds offer pensions to those members of defined benefit pension plans where the debtor has under-funded the pension plan and then subsequently become insolvent. Defined benefit plans are plans in which an employer promises that employees will receive a specified income based on a formula, usually calculated by length of service and salary levels. Legislation requires that the employer pre-fund this promise by contributing an amount to a pension fund each year, which, if it earns the assumed ratio of return when invested, should be sufficient to fund the promised benefit when the employee retires.

Guarantee funds hedge against the risk that particular debtors will not adequately fund their pension promises. There is an issue, however, of the cost of such guarantee funds, given the growing number of under-funded pension plans. Even where they are funded through industry contributions, there is a tendency to under-estimate the amounts required and it may be that higher premiums are required, or that premium should be geared to those sectors with a higher risk of firm failure. It can also lead to prudently invested pension funds subsidizing those with imprudent management through higher premiums.

Stewart has advocated principles for the successful operation of a pension benefit guarantee system:

- *Limited benefit coverage:* in order to limit moral hazard, certain benefits should be excluded from coverage, including improvements granted prior to insolvency and placing a ceiling on benefit coverage.
- *Risk based market pricing of premiums:* based on the expected claim levels for the insured, reflecting the likelihood of the plan sponsor becoming insolvent (via proxy measures such as credit rating and swap levels), the likely size of the claim, the extent of the pension plan's under-funding, and the risk inherent in any asset liability mismatch.[105]
- *Accurate, consistent and transparent funding rules:* pension benefits should as far as possible be fully funded, and plan sponsors should be required to act swiftly in order to limit losses and guarantee flow.
- *Prudent asset liability management:* pension funds should be encouraged to follow prudent asset allocation strategies, which avoid large swings in funding levels, again limiting potential claims and making the guarantee scheme more affordable.
- *Adequate powers:* a pension guarantee scheme needs to have adequate powers to avoid moral hazard, and prevent plan sponsors using their guarantee as a 'put' for their pension liabilities. For example, extra premiums or collateral must be requested (and paid) as a scheme becomes more under-funded or the risk of insolvency at the plan sponsor rises.[106]

---

105 Ibid., at 12, where she suggests that: 'Over the long term the aggregate level of premiums (+investment returns) should reflect aggregate claim levels (and maybe a surplus should also be built), with flexibility need to adjust premium levels as reality veers from estimates'.

106 Ibid., at 12–13.

The United States has recognized the special nature of pensions as a form of social safety net and hence has accorded lost pensions a special status through the Pension Benefit Guarantee Corporation, which covers single and multi-employer defined contribution pension plans, covering 34.2 million American workers.[107] Maximum benefits, depending on years of service and age, are USD 47,659 under a single employer plan and USD 12,870 under a multi-employer pension scheme.[108] Early retirement and unvested benefits are not covered.[109]

The United States pension guarantee fund contrasts with treatment of wages and other compensation in the United States, which are given a limited preferred status, but no safety net in the form of a wage guarantee fund. James Sprayregen and James Mazza observe that a number of factors in recent years, including a decline in the United States stock market, lowering interest rates, and an increase in the ratio of retirees to active workers have left United States employers with massively under-funded defined benefit pension plans.[110] Where a debtor corporation has under-funded or failed to take prudent actuarial investment advice, there may not be sufficient funds generated to cover the amount that is owing to pensioners at a date in the future. This problem has been exacerbated by both market fluctuations and by failure of government pension regulatory authorities to enforce adequate funding of debtors when they are financially healthy. In some instances, companies, through under-funding, have diverted assets that were necessary to be directed towards adequate investment in order that defined pension obligations would be met. Yet, when the firm becomes financially distressed, absent pension claims as a preferred claim, workers' claims for under-funded pensions are unsecured claims. In 2005, the unfunded pension liabilities in the United States were estimated to be USD 146 billion.[111]

Defined contribution pension plans, while not facing the same kind of insolvency risks, can create risks for employees where they over-invest their contributions in their employer's stock. The shift in North America from defined benefits pension plans to defined contribution pension plans has shifted the risk of adequate pension income from the debtor to employees, although, as noted above, the risks are increasing considerably for employees in defined benefits plans as well.

Sprayregen and Mazza report that United States debtors utilize Chapter 11 of the United States Bankruptcy Code to shed onerous pension liabilities by terminating plans. Under the Employee Retirement Income Security Act 1974 ('ERISA'), a pension plan sponsor may terminate its defined benefit pension plan if a bankruptcy court finds that termination of the plan is necessary for the sponsor to operate outside of bankruptcy.[112] The Pension Benefit Guaranty Corporation, a

---

107   Ibid., at 19.
108   Ibid., at 14. USD 47,659 is approximately EUR 34,893; USD 12,870 is approximately EUR 9423.
109   Idem.
110   Sprayregen and Mazza, above note 4 at 2.
111   Ibid.
112   Ibid., referred to as 'voluntary' or sponsor-initiated termination.

state created agency that insures and oversees the defined benefit pension system in the United States, may approve 'distress termination' of a pension plan if certain termination criteria are met, but not if it would violate the terms and conditions of an existing collective bargaining agreement.[113] The debtor must seek relief from its collective bargaining obligations under Section 1113 of the Bankruptcy Code, which sets out a process that accords special protection to these contracts and requires the debtor to bargain with the union.[114] However, debtors can also by-pass their unions by seeking a settlement with the Pension Benefit Guaranty Corporation in which it can authorize termination of a pension plan.[115] When a debtor's defined benefit pension plan is terminated through the Chapter 11 bankruptcy process, the Pension Benefit Guaranty Corporation takes over the plan and administers it going forward, paying pension benefits up to a guaranteed amount to plan participants.

Ontario is the only province of 13 provinces and territories in Canada that has a Pension Benefit Guarantee Fund ('PBGF'), covering over 1 million beneficiaries.[116] When a company with an under-funded pension plan covered by the PBGF fails, a plan administrator is appointed and makes a 'PBGF declaration', valuing the guarantee promised by the organization. The PBGF then makes an allocation to the pension fund, with the cash used by the fund to cover its liabilities through such strategies as buying annuities.[117] Employees are guaranteed pension benefits up to a maximum of CAD 12,000 and multi-employer schemes are excluded, making this only a modest programme at best.[118] The Ontario fund does not provide for any indexing of benefits.

One difficulty with guarantee funds for pension plans is that they have a strong risk of being under-funded themselves, raising questions about their long-

---

113   Ibid., citing 29 USC §1341 (ERISA §4041).

114   Ibid. They also report that under 29 USC §1342 (ERISA §4042), the PBGC has the right to seek an 'involuntary' termination of a pension plan if it determines that, among other things, the plan has not been properly funded, or the PBGC's possible long-run loss with respect to the plan may reasonably be expected to increase unreasonably if the plan is not terminated.

115   Ibid. The PBGC may terminate a pension plan under 29 USC §1342 (ERISA §4042) notwithstanding any alleged limitations that may exist in collective bargaining agreements with unions, 29 USC §1342(a) (ERISA §4042a). For example, in the United Air Lines, Inc. Chapter 11 case, the PBGC agreed to let the company to terminate the company's defined benefit pension plans by invoking its involuntary termination power, hence abrogating the need for the company to seek Section 1113 relief. The PBGC accepted a package of consideration from United, including stock and some notes that were contingent on the reorganised company satisfying certain performance metrics, in exchange for settling all pension issues with the company. Although a number of United's unions challenged PBGC's power to do this, the courts have upheld the debtor's settlement agreement with the PBGC, for which see *In re UAL Corp.* 428 F 3d 677 (7th Cir 2005).

116   Available at: <www.fsco.gov.on.ca/english/pensions/pbgf-20050331.pdf> (last viewed 31 May 2007).

117   Stewart, above note 4 at 19.

118   Ibid. CAD 12,000 is approximately EUR 7,938.

term sustainability. In the United States, it is estimated that the Pension Benefit Guarantee Corporation is running a deficit of approximately USD 24 billion as a result of the volume of terminated unfunded benefit plans, expected to rise to USD 86.7 billion by 2015.[119] In Ontario, the PBGF currently has a deficit of CAD 237 million and the Ontario government has made an interest free loan of CAD 330 million to the fund to assist with its financial difficulties.[120]

Sprayregen and Mazza observe that while ERISA in the United States provides the Pension Benefit Guaranty Corporation with certain statutory lien rights to protect itself when certain events occur in connection with an under-funded pension plan, such as the debtor ceasing to make minimum funding contributions, after a Chapter 11 filing is commenced, the Bankruptcy Code's automatic stay generally prevents the guaranty corporation from attaining secured or priority status in a bankruptcy case; and its lobbying efforts to change this status or to strengthen ERISA's minimum funding rules to help prevent plans from becoming too under-funded have not received any political support.[121]

In the United Kingdom, the government has enacted the Pensions Act 2004, effective April 2005, which created the Pension Protection Fund ('PPF') to pay compensation to members of defined benefit pension plans when an employer becomes insolvent or its pension plan is under-funded.[122] The Fund covers 10–15 million pension fund members.[123] The United Kingdom Pension Protection Fund is funded by compulsory premiums charged to employers with pension plans covered by the PPF's programme. Benefits are capped at approximately GBP 25,000 per year.[124] Unlike the Ontario Fund, the British Fund will be indexed.

The Pension Protection Fund has been given broad powers to address under-funding, such as the ability to impose a risk-based premium where it finds under-funding, as a means of creating an incentive to fund properly pension plans and to cure any under-funding relatively early. Moreover, the British Pensions Act 2004 grants the Pensions Regulator powers to intervene in specified events, such as takeover or sale of assets, to ensure that appropriate pension funding is occurring. The Pensions Regulator can seek to secure extra financial support for the pension scheme by issuing a Financial Support Direction or Contribution Notice against the principal employer or a group company that directly or indirectly holds more than 30 per cent of the principal employer's share capital.[125] A Financial Support Direction can only be issued to a corporation where the principal employer is a service delivering company or the value of the assets of the principal employer and its associates is less than 50 per cent of the scheme when valued on a buyout basis,

---

119 Ibid. at 4, citing US Congressional Budget Office estimates.
120 Stewart, above note 7 at 20, citing financial statements of the Pension Benefit Guarantee Corporation.
121 Ibid., at 4.
122 Sprayregen and Mazza, above note 4 at 5, citing Anon., 'Risk Based Levy Update Published by Pension Protection Fund' (2006) 27(1) *Company Lawyer* 22.
123 Stewart, above note 7 at 21.
124 GBP 25,000 is approximately EUR 36,605.
125 Sprayregen and Mazza, above note 4 at 6.

and it must be issued within one year of the event.[126] A Contribution Notice may only be issued where the employer has acted with the purpose of avoiding pension liabilities, and can be issued against a natural or legal person up to six years after an event.[127]

A fraud compensation levy will also be paid by both defined benefit and defined contribution schemes if and when a separate fraud compensation fund created under the legislation is required to pay out substantial sums after a case of fraud occurs.[128] From 2006/2007, the initial levy system will be replaced by a Pension Protection levy, made up by a scheme-based element relating to the level of a pension scheme's liabilities, such as number of members and the amount of pensionable earnings in respect of active members and a risk-based levy that will take account of the level of the scheme under-funding and the likelihood of sponsoring employer insolvency.[129]

Germany has a three-tier system of pensions; the state-run mandatory pension system (*Rentenversicherung*), which covers all employees and certain other beneficiaries; second, company-sponsored occupational pension schemes (*Betriebliche Altersvorsorge*); and third, private pension planning.[130] There is no requirement to offer pensions, but if offered, there are mandatory requirements under the *Gesetz zur Verbesserung der Betrieblichen Altersversorgung* that prescribes how pensions fare in a restructuring or an insolvency of the company.[131] If a debtor corporation commences a formal insolvency proceeding, a collective insurance scheme, called the *Pensions-Sicherungs-Verein Versicherungsverein auf Gegenseitigkeit* ('PSVaG') takes over, funded through contributions of those companies that have non-funded pension plans.[132] The PSVaG is an independent

---

126 Ibid., at 6. A buyout basis is the cost of purchasing annuities to provide all the benefits that the scheme promises.

127 Idem. Any liability is calculated on a buyout basis. For either notice to be issued, the pension scheme must be under-funded on an FRS17 basis, specifically, the pension valuation accounting standard used by United Kingdom companies and an event must have occurred.

128 Stewart, above note 7 at 21.

129 Ibid.

130 Sprayregen and Mazza, above note 4 at 6, citing *Schaub ArbR-Hdb.* §80 et seq. Sprayregen and Mazza observe that in contrast to the United States, the second tier company sponsored pension plans usually do not need to be 'funded' as they are backed by the general assets of a company as opposed to a specific asset pool set aside for the beneficiaries.

131 Ibid., citing *Gesetz zur Verbesserung der Betrieblichen Altersversorgung* (BetrAVG) vom 19.12.1974, BGBl. I, S. 3610, §7-15. They report that the liabilities are recorded as general unsecured liabilities of a company and hence there are no 'underfunded' pension plans as long as the corporation is solvent, the pension obligation is deemed to be covered.

132 Ibid., citing BetrAVG, §10. Companies can opt out of the PSVaG or significantly lower their contributions to the PSV by converting to 'funded' models or by transferring their pension liabilities to a third party such as a pension insurance fund or life insurance company. Alternatively, companies can opt to segregate an asset pool (Pensionsfonds) and back pension obligations with external investments as is the case

body by law, operating as a mutual insurance association, founded by the *Bundesvereinigung der Deutschen Arbeitgeberverbände e.V.*, the *Bundesverband der Deutschen Industrie e.V., and the Verband der Lebensversicherungs-Unternehmen e.V.*, and the PSVaG is subject to supervision from the Federal Financial Supervisory Authority (BaFin).[133] The PSVaG protects current and future beneficiaries in the event of employer insolvency, covering 60,000 companies and 8.7 million beneficiaries, with insured benefits of EUR 251 billion, with around 440,000 individuals currently receiving EUR 55.2 million in monthly payments.[134] The PSVaG assumes the pension liabilities and is subrogated as a general unsecured creditor to the claims of the beneficiaries; however, given the low recovery to unsecured creditors in German insolvencies, the PSV shoulders the pension costs of most insolvencies. An increasing trend by distressed investors in Germany is to use strategically insolvency proceedings to shed burdensome pension liabilities.[135]

Sprayregen and Mazza make an important observation about pension funding protection in developing countries that are implementing occupational pension plans to attract and retain talented employees. They note that while developed countries attained their economic prosperity before their populations became too old, developing countries are getting old before they ultimately get rich and hence there is a need to devise systems that support those aging populations before these economies attain their economic potential.[136]

Arguably, there is a moral hazard in respect of pension schemes. If a debtor as plan sponsor knows that upon bankruptcy its pension fund liabilities will be covered, even if sufficient assets are not available to back these promises, Stewart suggests that they may be incentivised to indulge in irresponsible behaviour, leaving others to cover the costs of the pension promises they have made. She observes that moral hazard can be avoided in part by not covering increases in benefits awarded in a period leading up to bankruptcy, as is the case with the PSVaG in Germany and similar measures to address the moral hazards.[137] An OECD report specifies that the German government plans to change financing of the PSVaG system to a fully funded status, driven by the shift away from fully

---

in other countries such as the US, ibid. See 'German Pensions Insolvency Protection Fund Proposes Move to a Full-Funding Model', European Pensions and Investment News, May 2005; Mercer Human Resource Consulting (2005), Pension Funding in Germany, June 2005.

133 Stewart, above note 7 at 26.

134 Ibid. The employers covered by the PSVaG hold around two-thirds of all German occupational pension assets.

135 Ibid., at 7, citing BetrAVG, §7(1)-(2). They report that in certain defined circumstances the PSV can also take over pension obligations in an out-of-court restructuring under BetrAVG, §7(1)-(2). However, this is a rare occurrence as the PSV wants to minimize incentive to companies offloading their pension liabilities in an out-of-court restructuring.

136 Ibid., at 8, citing Trinh, T., (2006), 'China's Pension System: Caught Between Mounting Legacies and Unfavourable Demographics' (Deutsche Bank Research).

137 Stewart, above note 7 at 6.

insured pension schemes to non-insured or partially insured schemes and the rise in bankruptcies. A new fund will be created, into which employers will pay for a period of 15 years, covering the cash value of the current payable and vested benefits.[138]

Japan has yet a different model of pension plan guarantee fund. Most of Japan's long-established pension plans are defined contribution plans, Employee Pension Funds ('EPFs'), which are pension plans with over 500 members for single-employer schemes or over 3000 for multi-employer schemes. For EPFs created after April 2005, over 1000 members are required for single employer schemes and over 5000 members for multi-employers schemes.[139] The Pension Guarantee Program set up by the Pension Fund Association (PFA) provides termination insurance for EPF plans.[140] The essential characteristics of the programme are that it is a mutual aid system of EPFs, which aims at securing minimum preserved benefits, within certain limits, in the case of dissolution due to bankruptcy or business deterioration of sponsoring companies. All EPF funds must make contributions to this scheme.[141] If an EPF is wound up, the PFA takes over the Substitution Component in exchange for collecting the amount equal to the minimum funding required for this component (known as the 'Minimum Technical Provision of the Substitution Portion' or MTPSP).[142] Any remaining assets are distributed to all plan participants, who can choose to take the portion of these residual assets due either as a lump sum or an annuity. The guarantee scheme covers only those participants who choose the annuity option.[143] The maximum guaranteed benefit is 0.3x the Substitution Component and half of the benefits exceeding this amount.[144] The benefits that the programme pays is in principle the amount of unfunded liability; however, a ceiling of JPY 7 billion is imposed on the amount of the unfunded liability. The government also allows another type of protection for the Substitution Component via a system called *daiko henjo*.[145] Stewart reports that, since April 2002, EPF schemes have been allowed to hand back this Substitution Portion to the government, a measure recognized as part of the de-regulation of the operation of corporate defined benefit pension plans. Any EPF scheme that carries out a *daiko henjo* operation will be converted to a 'New

---

138 Ibid., at 27.
139 Ibid., at 31.
140 Ibid., under the Employees Pension Insurance Law 1942 (EPIL).
141 Ibid., at 33, where Stewart reports that premiums are determined by three components: *per capita* premiums according to the number of participants; premiums in proportion to the total benefit amount guaranteed; and premiums in proportion to the amount of unfunded liabilities; and that the maximum of the sum of first two components is set at JPY 8.82 million and the maximum of the third component at JPY 0.861 million. The ceiling means that larger companies pay lower guarantee premiums.
142 Ibid.
143 Ibid.
144 Ibid. The present value of the maximum guaranteed benefit is referred to as the Ceiling Amount.
145 Ibid.

Defined Benefit Pension Plan'.[146] The Pension Guarantee fund in Japan can refuse a claim if funding levels are too low; however, to date, it has run with excess contingency reserves.[147]

Sweden has a pension scheme covering public sector workers, and two main occupational pension schemes, known as the ITP for private-sector white collar workers and SAF-LO for blue collar workers.[148] The pension schemes must insure the risk of insufficient assets in the case of insolvency with a guarantee fund managed by the Pension Guarantee Mutual Insurance Company ('FPG'), which transacts insurance only for the safeguarding of pension rights.[149] Swedish pensions are provided on a contractual basis, with 90 per cent of the workforce being covered by collective agreements between unions and employers.[150] In the case of a debtor company's insolvency, the FPG buys out benefits with the insurance company Alecta.[151] The Swedish system assesses the risk of a corporation to insolvency and covers its exposure by running an in-house rating agency, analysing corporate accounts, historical performance, profitability, industry factors, leverage and where applicable external ratings.[152] Insurance is available based on the risk assessment, available to higher risk companies only with a security bond or backup credit guarantees. Stewart observes that unique among guarantee schemes, the full benefits are covered with no restrictions.[153] The system is funded on employer contributions.[154] In 2005, premiums of SEK 248 million (EUR 26 million) were collected; and insurance exposure amounted to

---

146 Ibid., at 31–33, where Stewart reports that, as of September 2004, a total of 784 new DB funds had been set up, 546 via *daikyo henjo* operations.

147 Ibid.

148 Ibid.

149 Ibid., at 29, where Stewart reports that another entity, the PRI (Pension Registration Institute), records the pension promises made by each employer, calculates the value of these obligations on a standard basis and serves as an intermediary that receives the employer contributions and eventually makes the payments to retirees. FPG reinsures its liabilities to protect itself against extraordinarily high claims in any single year. Stewart gives an excellent summary of the system in this work.

150 Ibid.

151 Ibid., meeting the full cost for securing the benefits in the case that liabilities were book reserved, and the shortfall in cases where liabilities were partially funded.

152 Ibid.

153 Ibid.

154 Ibid. Stewart reports that for employers using the book reserve method, the 2006 yearly contribution was 0.3 per cent applied to total book reserved pension liabilities. The company pays the same premium to the FPG regardless of whether collateral has been pledged or not, or whatever its credit rating, except where the entire pension commitment is covered by a bank guarantee (when a lower premium applies), but this is unusual. Policyholders have an obligation to help the FPG to meet claims should reserves be totally exhausted. In this case additional charges may be made, capped at 2 per cent of pension liability of a company. Members who have been policy holders for 10+ years qualify for a policy holder's bonus if board of FPG decides to grant one.

SEK 120 billion (EUR 12.7 billion), with six claims being made.[155] Stewart reports that the Swedish pension guarantee fund is the most successful currently in existence, because of its rigorous screening procedure on a large scale, its careful funding model and its almost full coverage of employee entitlements.[156]

With the populations of most countries rapidly aging, the issue of pension coverage is becoming increasingly pressing and the above schemes have all, to a greater or lesser degree, attempted to address the issue of firm failure or firm inability to provide pension coverage. It is evident that the issues facing pension claimants are some of the most significant facing employees, as those at or nearing pensionable age are no longer able to recoup some of their insolvency losses with future employment.

Conclusion

A healthy mix of priority/preference claims system and some form of guarantee fund or insurance is the most appropriate mechanism to protect employee claims during insolvency. Those systems that offer only one form of protection tend to under-protect employee claimants in terms of their relative risks associated with firm insolvency. However, the optimal mix of priority and guarantee systems depends a great deal on the economic and social structure of each country, on the composition of the workforce, on the financial stability of the sectors in which corporate activity is most concentrated and on the availability of other social safety nets.

There are also numerous issues beyond the scope of this chapter that impact the treatment of employees' claims during insolvency. First is the interaction of labour relations regimes with insolvency regimes, including respecting collective agreements at various stages of a firm's financial distress, as in Canada. Second, are formal programmes that grant employees participation rights in decisions in respect of business closures, such as under French or Belgian law.[157] Third, job retraining is a necessary part of the social safety net to assist in retooling employees' skills so that they can find new employment in a rapidly changing economy, although the extent of these programmes varies considerably. Finally, there is the question of the duties of directors and officers in respect of employee claims, including personal liability for wages and remitting pension contributions, as in Canada, and prohibitions on entering agreements or conducting transactions with the intention of defeating the recovery of employee entitlements, as in

---

155   Ibid. A bonus of SEK 147 million (EUR 15.5 million) was granted.
156   Ibid.
157   See, for example, French Commercial Code, Article L. 631-17.

Australia.[158] Each of these remedial measures creates a different filter through which employee protections are enhanced or diminished. The public policy issues raised by each are substantial and require further study.[159]

---

158 Corporations Act 2001 (Australia), Part 5.8 and section 596A, which makes it an offence if a person (director or others) enters into an agreement or transaction with the intention of preventing recovery of employee entitlements or significantly reducing their entitlements. 'Agreement' is broadly defined, and includes formal or informal agreements, oral or written, whether or not having legal or equitable force. The objective of this section is to deter, by criminal sanctions, the misuse of company structures to avoid payments to employees that are owed on liquidation. The penalty is up to AUD 110,000 (approximately EUR 67,000) and/or 10 years imprisonment.

159 In 2007–2008, the author, with the support of the International Insolvency Institute, will conduct an empirical study of the treatment of social claims in insolvency, including an assessment of many of these issues across multiple jurisdictions.

Chapter 13

The Claim Against an Insolvent for Environmental Damage

Leonie Stander

Introduction

The purpose of this chapter is to investigate the liability for environmental damage briefly according to the South African law and to expand on the position of the insolvent estate and liability insurance for environmental damage. Attention will be drawn to the polluter pays principle, lender liability, the argument of personal liability of the trustee or liquidator where the responsible person[1] becomes bankrupt as well as risk management. Thereafter, the legal position regarding the situation where the bankrupt[2] effected liability insurance prior to sequestration or liquidation will be addressed. The purpose is to determine whether section 156 of the Insolvency Act (24 of 1936) is also applicable in the case where the 'polluter' affected a general liability policy or a liability policy for environmental damage and, therefore, effectively gives the injured party a preferential claim in the insolvent estate.

---

1   Whether a natural or juristic person or partnership.
2   Whether a natural or juristic person or partnership.

The Polluter Pays Principle

Introduction

Any attempt to implement a 'polluter pays'[3] principle must include some mechanism for redirecting the pollution costs[4] back to the ultimate polluter, either directly or indirectly.[5] It aims at charging polluters the costs of action to combat the pollution they cause, so as to encourage them to reduce pollution and endeavour to find less polluting products or technologies.[6] Hunter[7] renames the principle 'the polluter and user pays principle' and states that 'under this principle States should take those actions necessary to ensure that polluters and users of natural resources bear the full environmental and social costs of their activities'.[8]

Resource economists refer to pollution as an 'externality', referring to the fact that polluters get a free ride by passing on the cost of dealing with pollution on to society at large or on to the environment.[9] The polluter pays principle is

---

3   The perpetrator himself bears the costs of the environmental damage he caused and not the consumer, state or society at large. This is one of the basic principles of environmental management that were set out with the aim of 'guiding the government in achieving the vision of sustainable development': Draft White Paper on Environmental Management Policy for South Africa, Department of Environmental Affairs and Tourism Pretoria, July 1997 at 68; White Paper on a Minerals and Mining Policy for South Africa, Department of Minerals and Energy Pretoria, 1998 at 58. See also Kidd, M., 'The pursuit of environmental justice in South Africa', in Bosselman, K. and Richardson, B.J., *Environmental Justice and Market Mechanisms: Key Challenges for Environmental Law and Policy* (1999, Kluwer Law International, London) at 335. This was also the principle guideline underlying the First Environmental Action Programme of the European Communities in 1973 and has been recognized in numerous international treaties, for which see Costi, A., 'Reconciling environmental justice and development in transition economics', in Bosselman and Richardson, above at 316. In general, see Glazewski, J., *Environmental Law in South Africa* (2004, Butterworths, Durban) at 19.

4   Which include the expense of preventing and controlling pollution, for which see Hunter, D., Salzman, J. and Zealke, D., *International Environmental Law and Policy* (2nd ed) (2002, Foundation Press, New York NY) at 415.

5   See Boyle, A.E., 'Making the Polluter Pay? Alternatives to State Responsibility in the Allocation of Transboundary Environmental Costs' in Francione, F. and Scovazzi, T., *International Responsibility for Environmental Harm* (1991, Graham & Trotman, London) at 363.

6   See Oosthuizen, F., 'The polluter pays principle: Just a buzz word of environmental policy?' (1998) *South African Journal of Environmental Law and Policy* 356; Faure, F. and De Smedt, K., 'Should Europe harmonise environmental liability legislation?' (2001) 9 *Environmental Liability* 220; Hunter, Salzman and Zealke, above note 5 at 413.

7   Hunter, Salzman and Zealke, above note 5 at 412.

8   Bosselman refers to the duties and responsibilities of the perpetrator, independently of the states concerned: Bosselman, K., 'Justice and the environment' in Bosselman and Richardson, above note 3 at 55.

9   Hunter, Salzman and Zealke, above note 5 at 130.

designed to internalize environmental externalities[10] by ensuring that the full environmental and social costs (including costs associated with pollution, resource degradation and environmental harm) are reflected in the ultimate market price[11] for goods or service. Environmentally harmful and unsustainable goods will tend to cost more and consumers will then switch to less polluting substitutes.[12]

The polluter pays principle can be implemented through a variety of methods aimed generally at internalizing environmental costs, including for example the use of taxes or fees, or the elimination of subsidies for pollution control.[13] Nonetheless, Hunter demonstrates that another clear way of applying the polluter pays principle is the imposition of liability on the person who causes environmental damage.[14]

Liability is a certain way of making people realize that they are also responsible for possible consequences of their acts with regard to nature.[15]

This will ensure that greater caution will be applied to avoid occurrence of damage to the environment. Socially responsible behaviour is thus induced by establishing legal liability for environmental damage. The threat of legal action to recover damages is the economic instrument that internalizes the external costs in the first instance.[16] Therefore, the ultimate tool to internalize externalities is legal liability.[17]

Environmental Damage

Environmental damage is of a complex character. The different aspects of damage resulting from accidents which affect the environment make the problem of their compensation particularly difficult to deal with. Maffei explains that some claims have an exclusively economic character. However, the economic element is less evident in claims relating to a 'lost enjoyment' or to a 'lost image'. In claims concerning so-called ecological damage the economic element is lacking.[18] While the term 'environmental damage' is used in certain international conventions, for

---

10   See Kiss, A. and Shelton, D., *International Environmental Law* (3rd ed) (2004, Transnational Publishers, New York NY) at 118.

11   Getting the price right for the environmental resource that is being over-used: Hunter, Salzman and Zealke, above note 5 at 130.

12   Ibid., at 412. In this sense, the polluter pays principle means that the cost of pollution must be internalized by the producer, that is, the cost of clean products must be built into the production process.

13   Ibid., at 414.

14   Ibid., at 140, 414. 'This principle calls for the allocation of the financial consequences of a harmful activity not to the victims, to uninvolved states or individuals, or to the international community as a whole, but to the person who has control over the polluting activity. This is usually also the person who benefits from it economically': Kummer, K., *International Management of Hazardous Wastes* (1995, Oxford University Press, Oxford) at 36.

15   Ibid., at 415.

16   Ibid., at 140. See also Kiss and Shelton, above note 11 at 117.

17   Ibid., at 140.

18   See Maffei, M.C., 'The Compensation for Ecological Damage in the 'Patmos' Case' in Francione and Scovazzi, above note 6 at 381.

example the Civil Liability Convention of 29 November 1969, it is studiously avoided in South African legislation. The Marine Pollution (Control and Civil Liability) Act[19] does not use the term, but specifies what kind of environmental damage may be claimed.[20] The quantum of 'damage' usually, as a point of departure, is the cost of clean-up[21] and/or the difference in market value of, for example a (commercial) tree plantation before the damaging event, or the fishermen's (or even the hotelier's) loss of earnings.[22] But 'environmental damage' as central concept also includes natural resources damage and environmental damage.[23]

Thus, in a much more complex sense 'environmental damage'[24] is very difficult to quantify because the environment has no market value.[25] It is difficult to evaluate ecological damage (that is damage to the environment itself, such as injury to the biomass) apart from any harm suffered by those who exploit its resources.[26] Maffei refers to ecological damage as a kind of damage devoid of an economic value but based on a legal interest of the state in protecting the quality of the public domain.[27] According to Kummer, an increasing number of relevant conventions adopt a fairly comprehensive definition of damage,[28] including not

---

19   8 of 1981.

20   E.g. section 9(2)(b)(ii) which refers to coastal birds.

21   These include financing emergency remedial action, reimbursing early restoration work, paying the cost of cleaning up, costs of material and equipment purchased for the clean-up, costs of using public buildings and providing other goods in substitution for repair.

22   Categories of damages include, for example (and depending on the circumstances), damage to human health or loss of life and property damage. Compensation thus includes individual claims such as loss of income or health complications, lowered property values, lost business, non-compliance to environmental laws and regulations, the costs of coastline and harbour restoration and non-payment of due taxes, fees or charges, et cetera.

23   That is, damage to the environment (nature) or its components (natural resources). Examples here would include damage to the air (say by emission of noxious gases), to tree plantations (say by fire), to soil (say by contamination), to water (say by toxic spills).

24   Hunter, Salzman and Zealke, above note 5 at 415.

25   Some harm may be estimated with a degree of confidence. But how does one measure damage to ecosystems, many of which provide an ecological service (for example a wetland provides a natural filtration plant for polluted water)? See Hunter, Salzman and Zealke, above note 5 at 144 for another example of the complicated nature of estimating the monetary value of this type of damages.

26   For a discussion of this aspect, see Kiss and Shelton, above note 11 at 354–6.

27   Maffei, above note 19 at 381.

28   For a detailed discussion of the different definitions of environmental damage, see Larsson, M-L., *The Law of Environmental Damage* (1999, Kluwer International, Stockholm) at 117 ff. This writer refers to repair and restoration; preventative costs and costs due to damage. She differentiates between 'costs' and 'damage'. She also indicates (at 125) that there is a separation between damage and compensable damage. Environmental damage is defined as all adverse effects on man, his artifacts and the

only quantifiable economic loss, but also damage to the environment. The latter usually covers the costs of measures of reinstatement, sometimes extending to monetary compensation in cases where reinstatement is not possible or practical.[29] It also covers preventative measures taken to prevent further deterioration of the affected ecosystem.[30]

Because of the difficulty in quantifying, measuring or evaluating ecological damage, such damage was, in the past, not compensated. Guidelines for quantifying ecological damage are, therefore, very scarce. In international practice, if it is impossible to restore the prior conditions fully, the parties may agree on compensation. Damages may also be estimated according to accepted case law from other fields,[31] or according to the principles in other domestic legislation or treaties regarding the environment to which the state is a party.[32] Measuring damages for environmental harm, however, remains filled with uncertainties. Also, if it is possible to fix abstract criteria for the assessment of damage, there will always be a certain degree of uncertainty in such evaluation.[33] Compensation requires that there be identifiable victims with standing to bring an action. This may not be the case for all environmental harm, for example that caused on the high seas, in Antarctica, or in outer space, or that for which no economic harm can be shown. Damage in these places or of these types risks escaping protection if no specific norm is adopted.[34]

Maffei[35] illustrates that currently the courts waver between restrictive decisions admitting compensation for easily quantifiable losses – that is economic damages suffered and expenditures incurred for restoration – and wider opinions admitting compensation for damages which are more difficult to evaluate and constitute a middle course between economic and non-economic damage, for example lost enjoyment and lost image and finally also the admittance by courts of compensation for ecological damage independently of the existence of economic damage. However, whatever the outcome, the responsible person will have to make good the harm.[36]

The Responsible Person

Under a civil liability system, the person primarily liable to compensate environmental damages is the person who had actual operational control[37] of the

---

environment. Compensable damage is harm expressed in economic terms (see also at 143).

29   For example, the costs of restoration of the ecosystem or to remedy damage as fully as possible: Kiss and Shelton, above note 11 at 220, 347, 354.
30   Kummer, above note 15 at 241.
31   Kiss and Shelton, above note 11 at 354.
32   Maffei, above note 19 at 382ff.
33   Ibid., at 391.
34   Kiss and Shelton, above note 11 at 375.
35   Maffei, above note 19 at 391.
36   Therefore, formulating a comprehensive definition of environmental damage as well as guidelines for quantifying ecological damage falls outside the ambit of this study. See below.
37   See also Hunter, Salzman and Zealke, above note 5 at 415.

facility, activity or product concerned at the time damage occurred. However, responsibility may also rest with those who contributed to acts which caused environmental damage,[38] or who had power to prevent it.[39] Hence it is necessary to determine not only how widely that group should be defined,[40] but also the basis upon which liability between liable parties should be apportioned.[41]

The position of banks as lenders is of particular interest. To evaluate effectively and accurately the position of banks lending money to industries, developers and businesses for economic development, it is necessary to consider also the position of international financial institutions. International financial institutions (and development agencies) have been entrusted with a broad and universally recognized role in promoting sustainable development.[42] That mandate entails a special responsibility.[43] For these institutions, environmental protection and human resource development objectives nowadays represent core aspects of their expanded development mandates. They must, therefore, be deemed not merely authorized but legally required to pursue these objectives actively in their various lending operations in developing member countries. Such an affirmative obligation is neither absolute nor unlimited. Rather, multilateral development banks will be required to take reasonable steps in support of sustainable development. It is said[44] that multilateral development banks have a clear

---

38   Where the parties have acted together or have each had the capacity to influence each other's conduct.

39   See Winter, G., *European Environmental Law A Comparative Perspective* (1996, Dartmouth, Aldershot) at 232.

40   The list of targets of liability is breathtaking in its scope. A full discussion thereof falls outside the scope of this contribution. Briefly this group may include current landowners, past landowners, exploiters, producers, occupants, contractors, users, officers, employers, directors, shareholders, managers in the performance of their duties and anyone responsible for a dangerous activity with a dangerous substance.

41   Concurrent offenders are jointly and severally liable for damage and injuries that are indivisible and flow from combined activities of connected contingencies, even though such liability was not specifically stated. Defenders may escape such liability where it is possible to prove that the damage is divisible. From the plaintiff's point of view, joint and several liability has the great advantage of allowing a recovery action to be focused on one or two key (and sufficiently solvent) players – the 'deep pocket': Winter, above note 40 at 232–3.

42   Sustainable development can be understood either as economic development consistent with the needs of ecological sustainability or as ecological sustainability consistent with the needs of economic development: Bosselman and Richardson, above note 3 at 4. Another definition of sustainable development is development which meets the need of the present without compromising the ability of future generations to meet their own needs (Kidd, above note 3 at 328).

43   See Handl, G., 'The legal mandate of Multilateral Development Banks as agents for change toward sustainable development', in Bronkhorst, S.A. (ed.), 'Liability for Environmental Damage and the World Bank's Chad-Cameroon Oil and Pipeline Project', Selected Papers of the NC-IUCN Symposium, The Hague (25 February 2000) at 76.

44   Ibid., at 98.

international legal obligation to avoid causing environmental harm in developing member countries and, indeed, to incorporate environmental protection and social development objectives into all of their activities in developing member countries. Multilateral development banks must then exercise sufficient control over a project they finance or co-finance, to prevent its ultimate execution in a manner inconsistent with established multilateral development bank policy, if not public international law.[45] The multilateral development banks thus are obliged to incorporate environmental protection and social development objectives into all of their activities.[46] They should monitor effectively all parties involved. In order to have the project parties act in conformity with the applicable laws and other regulations, they should establish an independent, transparent and external monitoring structure as an integral part of the project's legal framework.[47]

It is the author's view is that the general duty to assess environmental impacts is increasingly considered as extending to all activities, even those which do not create an impact outside the limits of national jurisdiction.[48] Taylor observes that not only multilateral financial development assistance, but also unilateral financial development assistance is under pressure to become contingent upon environmental assessment and monitoring.[49] Given the urgent need for comprehensive environmental protection, financial institutions and banks should be held responsible to make good the damage/harm caused, in the absence of environmental assessment and monitoring measures as well as in the absence of effective unilateral trade measures. It is suggested that their approach in lending money to developers, industries and businesses should be to evaluate how the particular business allows for the optimal use of the country's resources in accordance with the objective of sustainable development. Such a liability on financial institutions may be seen as a market mechanism; as an economic instrument designed to implement and enforce environmental objectives.

The basis for this liability is ecological sustainability. As such, ecological principles need to shape economic and financial decisions. Therefore, law reform should include accountability of lender banks[50] to ecological principles. Law reform should thus incorporate ecological factors in gross domestic product accounting. To strengthen the provisions for environmental liability, those sectors of the economy that play a critical role in shaping access to development capital should be targeted. It is the author's view that lender liability for environmental harm will be a positive step in this direction.[51] However, this liability should not be

---

45   Ibid., at 77.
46   Ibid., at 98.
47   Ibid., at 99.
48   See also Kiss and Shelton, above note 11 at 144, 150–153.
49   See Taylor, P., 'An ecological approach to international trade law' in Bosselman and Richardson, above note 3 at 199.
50   Also other financial institutions and insurance firms.
51   The same can be said for the development of shareholder liability for corporate environmental damage. The manipulation of bankruptcy codes by polluters to escape liability and financial obligations should also be taken into consideration.

unconditional, unjust or unfair. In addressing this matter, Wilkinson refers to two landmark cases in the United States.[52]

In *United States v Maryland Bank & Trust* (1986), a mortgagee, having purchased the mortgaged property outright at a foreclosure sale, was held to be acting to protect its investment, rather than its security. The court refused to place the bank in a better position than any other purchaser: to do so would, it reasoned, provide the bank with a windfall by enabling it to purchase a low-price property which might otherwise be unsaleable. In *United States v Fleet Factors* (1990), a lender having a factoring agreement, whose involvement with management did not, in fact, extend as far as day-to-day involvement with the operations of a facility, was determined to be an 'owner'. The critical point here was that the lender could affect hazardous waste management decisions if it so chose.

Wilkinson demonstrates that the decision in *Maryland Bank* and *Fleet Factors* caused widespread concern amongst American lending institutions, in response to which the Environmental Protection Agency promulgated regulations establishing that they will not seek to defray their costs against a lender which has the mere capacity or ability to influence, or the unexercised right to control facility operations.[53] Wilkinson's view is that environmental protection may be ill served by exposing lenders to liability for pollution costs. He feels that liability risks may act as a disincentive to the financing of redevelopment of so-called 'brownfield' sites. According to him the reuse of industrial land is an important element in preventing urban sprawl and limiting impacts on biodiversity.[54] He also refers to the European and United Kingdom polluter pays regimes which have sought to avoid the United States approach.

The Explanatory Report to the Lugano Convention of 16 September 1988 states that:

> an outside person who has made possible or facilitated a dangerous activity, for example by lending funds for investment in the said activity, may not be considered to be the operator, unless he exercises effective control over the activity in question.[55]

The legal position currently in South Africa is that the lender bank is as such not responsible for environmental damage caused by the borrower. But, in order to protect its security, the lender bank may become involved in the management of the company, for example by insisting upon certain management

---

52   See Wilkinson, D., *Environment and the Law* (2002, Routledge, London) at 127.
53   Ibid., at 127.
54   Ibid., at 127.
55   Ibid., at 127. He points out that the recent European Union White Paper on Environmental Liability advises that 'lenders not exercising operational control should not be held liable'. He refers to Environmental Protection Act 1990 (UK), section 78A, where a 'mortgagee not in possession' is expressly excluded from the definition of 'owner'. He is convinced that this does not entirely resolve the problem, since mortgagees may need to take possession in order to realise their security.

practices. Where this gives the bank capacity to control[56] the company's operations effectively, it confers in the author's view an inference of culpability if environmental damage ensues from the activity of the company. On the other hand, the bank which lent money to the landowner may, for example, have only the conventional security of being able to force a sale of the land. If enforcement of the security involves the bank or his agent taking physical control of the land for the purposes of selling it, there is a prospect of the bank being cast in the role of the owner (even if only for a brief period) and thus it also confers an inference of culpability. This should not be the case. The principle should be that a bank or other financial institution who holds indicia of ownership primarily to protect his security interest in a site, without participating in its management, is not an 'owner' or 'operator'. Only where the lender bank exercises effective control over the operation, business or activity should it be held responsible.

When financing a project, a lender will normally carry out a due diligence investigation into the project. This would necessarily include the review of any environmental impact assessment as well as environmental authorisations and management plans or programmes. The lender would, therefore, be well placed to examine the potential of the project to cause environmental damage. Should a financial institution decide not to review environmental aspects of the project in order to escape the link via control, it could be accused of negligence. This may be sufficient to link the harm caused by the borrower with the actions of the lender.[57]

Companies and office bearers at those companies can incur liability for damage caused to the environment under statute and in terms of the common law. Under the common law delictual liability would depend upon proof of the separate elements of delict.[58]

Once the 'polluter' is identified, the 'pays' principle comes into operation. This entails[59] focusing liability for the (1) repair, restoration and clean-up of the environment; (2) provision of other environmental goods in substitution for repair which cannot be carried out because the damage is irreversible;[60] (3) prevention, reduction and regulation of pollution and environmental damage; and (4) payment of compensation for damages suffered by the environment and humans as a result of the pollution or environmental damage.

---

56 Control may have a very wide definition and would depend on the facts of each case. Participation in management of the borrower's activities or even voting rights or board representation could be examples of control.

57 See De Kock, L. and Gunn, A., 'Lender liability in South Africa for environmental damage', Environmental Practice Group Newsletter January 2006, available at: <www.edwardnathan.com> (last viewed 31 May 2007).

58 Idem.

59 In general, see Glazewski, above note 4.

60 This item remains controversial. See Winter, above note 40 at 234. The writer says that without it, irremediable damage (such as the extinction of a species, or the destruction of fauna) remains outside a liability system, and there is no incentive in civil liability terms for firms whose activities may cause such damage to internalise their external effects.

An Enforceable Principle

If the polluter pays principle is not yet acceptable as a general rule[61] in the case of environmental damage, the time has come to give serious consideration to the development of the South African environmental law in that direction. If society is serious about sustainable development and there is a genuine commitment towards ecological preservation and sustainability, the acceptability of fault based liability should be reconsidered, at least where serious damage to the environment is under discussion.

The polluter pays principle, which is based on the global idea of sustainable development, could become an enforceable principle in South African environmental law through the influence of international environmental law. The cornerstone of environmental law in South Africa is the Constitution of the Republic of South Africa 1996.[62] The Constitution confirms the common law position that customary international law is recognised as law in the Republic, unless it is inconsistent with the Constitution or an Act of Parliament.[63] This induces the question whether the polluter pays principle is a customary international law principle. The polluter pays principle is founded in the Stockholm Declaration.[64] Although the Stockholm Declaration is a 'soft law' declaration,[65] the principle could eventually become customary international law on the strength of the cumulative enunciation thereof by numerous non-binding texts, expressing the opinion juris of the world community.[66] It is, for example, enunciated in the Rio Declaration[67] and is also one of the cornerstones of the European Community Environment Policy.[68] Kummer indicates that the principle has widespread

61   Boyle, above note 6 at 376 says 'although endorsed as a policy by the OECD and the European Union, the 'polluter pays' principle remains insufficiently grounded in State practice to represent a principle of contemporary international law'.
62   Referred to below as the Constitution.
63   Constitution, section 232.
64   Part 1 of the Declaration of the United Nations Conference on Human Environment (Stockholm, 16 June 1973). See also Hunter, Salzman and Zealke, above note 5 at 140.
65   See Glazewski, above note 4 at 33.
66   Hunter, Salzman and Zealke, above note 5 at 356 ff. See for example the Council Recommendations of the Organization for Economic Cooperation and Development (May 26, 1974); Note on the Implementation of the Polluter Pays Principle (Nov 14, 1974); Agenda 21 (A/Conf 151/26 1991).
67   See Principles 13 and 16 of the Rio Declaration on Environment and Development (Rio de Janeiro, 13 June 1992). See also Backes, C., Drupsteen, T.G., Gilhuis, P.C. and Koeman, N.S.J., *Milieurecht* (5th ed) (2001, WEJ Tjeenk Willink, Deventer) at 35.
68   See EC Treaty, Articles 100 and 130 and in successive Programs of Action on the Environment (Kiss and Shelton, above note 11 at 118); Winter, above note 40 at 285. According to Kiss and Shelton, above note 11 at 118, Convention on the Protection of the Marine Environment of the Baltic Sea Area (Helsinki, 9 April 1992), Article 3(4) states the principle as an obligatory norm, while Convention on the Protection and Use of Transboundary Watercourses and International Lakes (Helsinki, 17 March 1992),

support.[69] Kiss and Shelton[70] refer to the International Convention on Oil Pollution Preparedness, Response and Cooperation 1990, which states that the polluter pays principle 'is a general principle of international environmental law'.[71] In the Advisory Opinion on the Legality of the Treaty on Nuclear Weapons,[72] the Vice President of the International Court of Justice, Judge Weeramantry, examined a number of environmental law principles, including the polluter pays principle and the burden on the 'polluter' of making adequate reparation to those affected. He stated that 'these principles of environmental law thus do not depend for their validity on treaty provisions. They are part of customary international law. They are part of the *sine qua non* for human survival'. Larsson[73] declares that the polluter pays principle is increasingly acknowledged as 'a binding principle of law' and has been recognized as 'a general principle of international environmental law'. Kidd calls it 'one of the basic principles of environmental management'.[74]

According to section 233 of the Constitution, the principles and content of international conventions could be, and in some instances should be, referred to and preferred in the interpretation of any legislation. This section substantiates the argument that, when acknowledged as customary international law, these conventions should serve as guidelines for the formulation and incorporation of the polluter pays principle in South African legislation.[75]

It is the author's view that nearly universal adoption of the polluter pays principle indicates the development of customary law, but it is clear that, although the polluter pays principle may be approaching customary status in terms of European Union, OECD and UNECE agreements, it generally still lacks sufficient support internationally.[76]

Nationally, the situation is as follows: An environmental clause has been included in the Bill of Rights chapter of the Constitution. Section 24 states:

> Everyone has the right –
> (a)   to an environment that is not harmful to their health or well-being; and
> (b)   to have the environment protected, for the benefit of present and future generations, through reasonable legislative and other measures that –
>   (i)   prevent pollution and ecological degradation;
>   (ii)   promote conservation; and

Article 2(5) includes it as a guiding principle. For more sources, see Kiss and Shelton, above note 11 at 118ff.

69   Kummer, above note 15 at 36. She voices the opinion that the principle is also supported by a number of international legal instruments addressing civil liability for environmental damage. See at 238–43.

70   Kiss and Shelton, above note 11 at 118.

71   Preamble to the Convention (London, 30 November 1990).

72   (1996) 35 ILM 809.

73   Larsson, above note 29 at 92.

74   Kidd, above note 3 at 335.

75   See also Oosthuizen, above note 7.

76   See above note 52.

> (iii) secure ecologically sustainable development and use of natural resources while promoting justifiable economic and social development.

By including environmental rights as fundamental justiciable human rights, the Constitution by necessary implication requires that environmental consideration be accorded appropriate recognition and respect in the administrative process in South Africa.[77] Commentators are in agreement that the Bill of Rights and, therefore, the environmental right, not only has vertical application[78] but also horizontal effect.[79] The extent of such horizontal application is still debated.[80] A distinction is made between 'direct' and 'indirect' horizontality.[81] In the environmental context direct horizontality would mean that the environmental right is a substantive right that could be invoked directly in private disputes. For example, a private individual could sue a mining company where his or her health and/or well-being are adversely affected by the company's activities.[82] Indirect horizontality would mean that the plaintiff could only invoke the environmental right to supplement an existing legal right against the mining company.[83]

---

77 See *Director: Mineral Development, Gauteng Region and Sasol Mining (Pty) Ltd v Save the Vaal Environment and others* 1999 (2) SA 709 (SCA) 719.

78 This means it is enforceable against the legislature, the executive, the judiciary and all organs of state. The right contained in section 24(a) could be used to stop any state action or decision which threatens or harms the environment so as to affect detrimentally any person's health or well-being.

79 This means it can be invoked in disputes between private parties where the state is not involved at all. See also Havenga, P., 'Liability for environmental damage' (1995) *South African Mercantile Law Journal* 189ff. The Constitution, section 8(2) provides that a provision of the Bill of Rights binds a natural or juristic person if, and to the extent that it is applicable, taking into account the nature of the right and the nature of any duty imposed by the right.

80 See Glazewski, above note 4 at 72 ff. According to Kidd, above note 3 at 330, this provision (section 8(2)) is rather vague and thus any suggestion of its scope is subject to some doubt. However, given the nature of the right and the fact that non-state entities are frequently responsible for actions detrimental to the environment and people's health, he submits that the environmental right would bind private and legal persons as well as the state. Yet even if this were not the case, most private action is carried out under some or other state authorization in any event (for example permits). So private action detrimental to the environment could be targeted indirectly through the authorizing officer.

81 See Cheadle, H. and Davis, D., 'The application of the 1996 Constitution in the private sphere' (1997) *South African Journal of Human Rights* 44; Havenga, above note 80 at 189 (and the authority cited in footnote 16), 190.

82 Glazewski, above note 4 at 74.

83 Idem. See also Havenga, above note 80 at 190, who submits that the practical implication of indirect horizontal application of the Bill of Rights means that legal rules which are formulated to incorporate policy considerations in their application, that is, so-called open-ended standards or principles, will have to be interpreted and applied to reflect the basic values of the Bill of Rights.

In determining whether a right is directly horizontal, regard must be given to the nature of the right.[84] That certain rights find horizontal expression at common law and in statutes gives a clue as to the suitability of the right for horizontal application. Subsection 24(a) of the Constitution closely resembles the common law principle of neighbour law which is based on the Roman law maxim *sic utere tuo* principle. Accordingly, it would be eminently suitable for horizontal application to private persons. According to Glazewski, an environmental right, being one capable and suitable for horizontal application, can, in disputes between private persons, be applied both directly and indirectly.[85]

The inclusion of an environmental clause in the Bill of Rights is a conscious adoption of an environmental or ecological norm. The object of section 24 of the Constitution is to preserve a clean and healthy environment and prevent environmental pollution.[86] Although section 24 does not explicitly refer to the polluter pays principle, it does not contradict its purpose and application.[87]

Because of the fact that until now the issue with regard to environmental damage has rather been how to prevent such damage than to hold polluters liable for damage caused, the requirements for liability are not consistent and vary from act to act. Some acts found liability on fault, some acts expressly provide that fault is not required and some acts do not expressly so provide but fault is not a requirement for liability.[88] It is submitted, based on the discussion below, that the

---

84   See Constitution, section 8(2).

85   Glazewski, above note 4 at 75.

86   The effect of the environmental clause is that general principles of law which incorporate policy considerations in their formulation, will have to be applied in such a manner that the values which underlie the environmental clause are duly reflected.

87   Oosthuizen, above note 7 submits that because section 24 of the Constitution imposes an obligation on the state to adopt 'reasonable legislative and other measures' to, inter alia, protect the environment, adoption of the polluter pays principle may be regarded as one of those 'other measures' that could be taken. The purpose and application of the principle may thus be implied by section 24. Section 24(b) gives the government the responsibility to ensure, within reason, that the environment is protected. There is a positive duty on the government to implement the contents of section 24. By implication this supposes the government to be primarily concerned with the implementation of the polluter pays principle.

88   In *Lascon Properties (Pty) Ltd v Wadesville Investment Company (Pty) Ltd and another* [1997] 3 All SA 433 (W), for example, the Court considered whether a breach of anti-pollution measures prescribed by a statute and regulations made thereunder which caused damage could give rise to a claim for damages independently of the *actio legis Aquiliae* or whether it had to be brought within such action and satisfy the Aquilian action. In the Court's view, the regulation: (a) had been *prima facie* enacted for the benefit of the owners of land which might have been polluted as a result of the actions of a mining company; (b) imposed a duty in absolute terms, and persons who suffered as a result of a failure to comply with such duty should be entitled to compensation therefore; and (c) had clearly been intended to place both the duty to prevent the escape of noxious water arising from mining operations and the risk of damage caused by such water on the persons responsible for and benefiting from the mining operation. The Court concluded that there seemed to be an inference that the

time has come to acknowledge that with regard to environmental harm and damage, the polluter pays principle and with that strict liability is the rule rather than the exception. Firstly, the polluter pays principle has been adopted in a number of policy documents in South Africa,[89] including the White Paper on a Minerals and Mining Policy for South Africa[90] and the White Paper on Environmental Management in South Africa.[91] Of mention also may be section 31A of the Environment Conservation Act (73 of 1989), sections 2(4)(p) and 28 of the National Environmental Management Act (107 of 1998),[92] section 19 of the National Water Act (36 of 1998), section 30 of the National Nuclear Regulator Act (47 of 1999), sections 37–38 of the Mineral and Petroleum Resources Development Act (28 of 2002) and section 7 of the National Environmental Management: Biodiversity Act (10 of 2004).

Section 31A of the Environment Conservation Act[93] states that if the Minister, Premier, government institution or responsible authority is of the view that a person is performing an activity which could seriously damage or detrimentally affect the environment, the competent authority may call upon the offender to stop the activity and/or take steps to reduce the harm. Should the person fail to comply with the notice, the authority may itself take steps and recover the costs it incurred from the party concerned. It is again submitted that this section supports the object in view and applies the polluter pays principle.

Section 19 of the National Water Act explicitly adopts the polluter pays principle.[94] It identifies polluters who would be liable to pay prevention and/or remedial costs for environmental pollution or the adverse effects of pollution. This section thus attempts to give the principle legal content. This accords with the objective to harmonise national environmental liability laws and the objective to provide sound legal basis for establishing liability for environmental protection, pollution and damages.[95]

NEMA determines the environmental management principles.[96] These principles are applicable not only to organs of state, but also to private juristic persons in the same way that the environmental right in the Bill of Rights has horizontal application as argued earlier. These principles are crucial and stipulate internationally emerging environmental norms such as, *inter alia*, the

---

legislature had intended to provide a civil remedy for damage caused by a breach of the regulation extending beyond a mere interdict. The breach of such a statutory duty causing damage gives rise to a claim for damages independently of the *actio legis Aquiliae* and such claim need not satisfy the requirements of aquilian liability.

89   See Glazewski, above note 4 at 19, 480.
90   N 2359/1998 Government Gazette No 19344.
91   N 749/1998 Government Gazette No 18894, Chapter 3.
92   Referred to below as NEMA.
93   73 of 1989.
94   See also Glazewski, above note 4 at 623–4.
95   Oosthuizen, above note 7 at 360.
96   Section 2(4)(p), NEMA.

precautionary principle,[97] the preventative principle[98] and the polluter pays principle.[99]

Although section 28 of NEMA does not explicitly refer to the application of the polluter pays principle, subsections (1), (2), (8) and (11) supply good guidelines for the interpretation of the principle with reference to persons who would possibly be liable, conduct, and the proof of environmental damages.[100] The polluter pays principle is also reflected in the directive that costs of remedying pollution, environmental degradation and consequent adverse health effects must be paid for by those responsible for harming the environment.[101] The same can be said with regard to costs of preventing, controlling or minimising further pollution, environmental damage or adverse health effects. The principle of polluter pays is also reflected in other principles such as the duty of care, environmental justice and life cycle liability.

Most important is that NEMA provides for a general duty of care and remediation of environmental damage. The principle embodies the duty of any person who causes, has caused, or may cause significant pollution or degradation of the environment to take reasonable measures to prevent such pollution or degradation from occurring, continuing or recurring, or, in so far as such harm to the environment is authorised by law or cannot reasonably be avoided or stopped, to minimize and rectify such pollution or degradation of the environment. Through section 28 of NEMA thus creates a statutory duty of care which imposes strict liability.[102] Thus, a person adversely affected as a result of a failure to comply with the duty of care should be entitled to compensation. The breach of such a duty causing damage gives rise to a claim for damages independently of the *actio legis Aquiliae* and such claim need not satisfy the requirements of aquilian liability. This

---

97   Glazewski, above note 4 at 18. The precautionary principle is manifest, e.g. in the principle that a risk-averse and cautious approach is applied, which takes into account the limits of current knowledge about consequence of decisions and actions.

98   Ibid., at 18. The preventative principle is, e.g. reflected in the phrase that disturbance of the ecosystems and loss of biological diversity are to be avoided, or minimized and remedied.

99   Ibid., at 142.

100 Oosthuizen, above note 7 at 359. There is uncertainty as to the fact whether the establishment of fault to constitute liability is a prerequisite. Some writers and academics are of the view that negligence must be proven and others are of the opinion that strict liability is applicable. See Glazewski, above note 4 at 148 ff.

101 Glazewski, above note 4 at 480.

102 This viewpoint is controversial, but see *Bareki NO and Another v Gencor Ltd and Others* 2006 1 SA 432 (T) 440; De Kock and Gunn, above note 58; Glazewski, above note 4 at 152; Feris, L.A., 'The asbestos crisis – the need for strict liability for environmental damage' 1999 *Acta Juridica* 302. Generally strict liability requires no fault or negligence. Different legal systems have adopted different approaches to establish strict liability, ranging from rebuttable presumptions of fault where the burden of proof shifts to the manufacturer, to irrefutable presumptions of fault. See Oosthuizen, above note 7 at 360 for an argument on fault-based liability and also De Villiers, C., 'Micro wave: macro damage' (1996) 4 *Juta's Business Law* 174; Havenga, above note 80 at 193.

accords with the decision in *Lascon Properties (Pty) Ltd v Wadeville Investment Co (Pty) Ltd & Another.*[103]

Section 30 of the National Nuclear Regulator Act explicitly places strict liability on the holder of a nuclear installation licence, whether or not there is intent or negligence on the part of the holder. Such holder is liable for all nuclear damage caused by or resulting from the relevant nuclear installation during the holder's period of responsibility.

Lastly, the same principles enunciated in NEMA apply also in terms of section 37 and 38 of the Mineral and Petroleum Resources Development Act and section 7 of the National Environmental Management: Biodiversity Act.[104]

It is submitted that this direction of development in the South African environmental law accords with, and leads the way to the acceptance of the polluter pays principle as general rule.

The Insolvency Practitioner and Personal Liability

Environmental claims from the period before the bankruptcy are as such not privileged. It is submitted first that a claim against an insolvent debtor for costs of remedying any environmental damage affecting immovable property of the debtor, should be a provable claim against the insolvent estate, whether the damage occurred before or after sequestration/liquidation. This is so because a person's bankruptcy does not exempt the trustee from any duty imposed by any environmental act. It is also general knowledge that there is nothing in the law of insolvency which affects unexecuted contracts in general; the contract is neither terminated nor modified, nor in any other way altered by the insolvency of one of the parties except in one respect, and that is that, because of the supervening concursus, the trustee cannot be compelled by the other party to perform the contract. The trustee steps into the shoes of the insolvent. He can elect whether to abide by the contract or to repudiate it.[105] Nothing in the law excuses the trustee from performing the insolvent's obligations which fall due to be performed between the date of sequestration and the date on which the trustee makes his election.[106]

Secondly, it is submitted that any claim against the sequestrated/liquidated estate for the costs of remedying any environmental damage affecting immovable property of the insolvent estate should be secured by a charge on such property and on any other immovable property of the insolvent estate that is related to any

---

103 [1997] 3 All SA 433 (W). In order to sue for a breach of a statutory duty, a person had to show that (1) the statute was intended to give a right of action; (2) he was one of the persons for whose benefit the duty was imposed; (3) the damage was of the kind contemplated by the statute; (4) the defendant's conduct constituted a breach of the duty; and (5) the breach was caused or materially contributed to the damage.

104 See also National Environmental Management: Air Quality Bill (B62-2003).

105 *Smith & Another v Parton NO* 1980 (3) SA 724 (D).

106 *Porteous v Strydom NO* 1984 (2) SA 489 (D).

activity that caused the environmental damage. The charge should rank above any secured claim against the property, falling in the same category as the claims and charges mentioned in section 89(1), (4) and (5) of the Insolvency Act.[107] This would compel banks and other financiers who so readily lend capital to persons, businesses and industries who are performing activities which could seriously damage or detrimentally affect the environment, to require strict implementation of reasonable measures to prevent environmental harm. They should, in cases like these, exercise more control over the said activities and operations. This viewpoint is motivated by a serious need and genuine aspiration to improve ecological sustainability. It is the writer's view that the basic objective of sustainable development will be furthered by creating such a secured claim for the costs of remedying[108] any environmental damage caused by the use (or other related activity) of the property.

Another subject of great uncertainty concerns the environmental liability of trustees.[109] There is presently no statutory limit on the environmental liability of trustees. In principle a person's bankruptcy[110] does not affect any of the rules on fines, injunctions, clean-up, et cetera or exempt the trustee from any duty imposed by any environmental act. A trustee may thus be affected by legal provisions designed to attach personal liability on those involved in the management of businesses. Because trustees may in certain circumstances take over the day to day running of a business that is bankrupt,[111] they are, under these provisions, particularly at risk.

---

107   Act 24 of 1936.

108   This includes repair, restoration and clean-up.

109   This includes liquidators of companies or close corporations.

110   Or a company's or close corporation's bankruptcy.

111   The trustee in an insolvent estate is required to realise the assets as soon as possible and has no power to carry on the business of the estate without instructions from the creditors. In deciding whether to seek authority to continue the business the trustee should have regard for the prime consideration that ordinarily it is not part of the process of administration of an insolvent estate to speculate with property thereof but that, on the contrary, there should be a speedy realization of such property (*Thorne v The Master* 1964 (3) SA 38 (N); see also Meskin, P.M., *Insolvency Law and its Operation in Winding-up* (2002, Butterworths, Durban) at 5-78-81). If the continuation of the business on a temporary basis would be for the ultimate benefit of the creditors, the trustee would be able to carry on, although he would still require the authorization of the creditors or the Master. But ultimately the trustee must proceed to sell all the property of the estate in accordance with the directions of the creditors. The liquidator of a company is in the same position in this regard. In the case of a voluntary winding-up, the company must forthwith cease to carry on its business, except in so far as this may be required for the beneficial winding-up of the company: Companies Act (61 of 1973), section 353(1). If the business must be carried on, it will be solely with a view to winding-up. The business may not be carried on to make a profit or to increase the value of the shares or for any other purpose. The same applies with regard to the powers of a liquidator in a winding-up by the court: section 386(3)-(4).

Reading the different environmental statutes and the sections referred to above, one sees that they provide that 'any person(s) who commits (or allows or permits)' a specified act will be guilty of an offence. A trustee who participates in running a business could fall within this definition. Provisions may contain a clause imposing personal liability on 'anyone who had the charge (or management or control) of the source of contaminant'; or 'anyone who is, or was, in occupation of the source of contamination'; or 'anyone who has control of the pollutant that is spilled'. Such environmental provisions could attach personal liability to a trustee if, upon the facts, he were adjudged to be 'the person by whose act (or default) the nuisance was caused'. It is also submitted that an insolvency practitioner could be caught by wording such as 'any person who was purporting to act (as director, manager, secretary or other similar officer of the body corporate) in any such capacity'; or 'the person in control of the land' or 'any person who has the right to use the land at the time ...' or 'the owner of the land at the time ...' or 'any person who was responsible for or who directly or indirectly contributed to ...'.

One must consider liability in the following two scenarios: First, where environmental damage occurs during bankruptcy (after the appointment of the trustee) and second, where the damage occurred prior to his appointment.

With respect to pre-appointment damage, the author considers that the provisions of the Insolvency Act[112] do not make the trustee personally liable for the costs of, for example, clean-up, any more than they make a trustee liable for any of the other debts of the estate.[113]

Situations may arise where there is such a heavy burden (to remedy any environmental damage) on property of the insolvent estate that the trustee is not able to sell that property profitably or economically. The writer submits that the trustee should, in these circumstances, be allowed to abandon the property within a reasonable time after his appointment and with authorization from the creditors of the estate. The exercise of this power should be subject to approval by the court and to conditions the court may think necessary because public interest is at stake. Subject to the conditions set by the court, the trustee should immediately inform the Minister of Environmental Affairs so that he can assume the responsibility. The effect of abandonment is that the property becomes *bona vacantia* and as such accrues to the state. Claims for costs of remedying the condition or damage shall thus not rank as costs of administration.[114]

---

112 24 of 1936. The position is the same with regard to a liquidator of a company or close corporation.

113 If this view is incorrect, which is doubtful, the trustee should be able to obtain a court order limiting his liability under the environmental laws, to the value of the assets under administration. In essence what happens then is that the secured creditor's security is being consumed by the trustee's liability for pre-appointment environmental misconduct of the insolvent (debtor).

114 Therefore, the approval of the court is necessary. Abandonment of property is not an unfamiliar idea in insolvency law. The UNCITRAL Draft Legislative Guide on Insolvency Law (30 September 2003) contains the following provision: 'Burdensome, no-value and hard-to-realize assets: 88. It may be consistent with the objective of maximizing value and reducing the costs of the proceedings to allow the insolvency

It is clear that after commencement of insolvency proceedings all administrative action has to be addressed to the trustee and not the debtor. Since all administrative and disposing powers are passed to the trustee, the trustee is the only person entitled to perform any legal action in respect of the estate. He is under a duty to perform the necessary actions on behalf of the estate and its creditors. Costs and damages incurred by the trustee's actions can be reclaimed by the trustee as privileged debts. He could charge it as costs of administration.[115] The trustee must thus perform those statutory obligations that are imposed on the insolvent to protect public health and safety.[116] Therefore, the submission is that the insolvent estate is liable for any environmental damage or harm caused and not the trustee personally.[117]

There is a viewpoint that the trustee should be personally liable under environmental laws where, in running the business of the insolvent, the trustee is the one responsible for the occurrence of environmental damage by failing to adhere to the relevant laws and principles.[118] This author does not agree. The

---

representative to relinquish the estate's interest in certain assets, including land, shares, assets subject to a valid security interest, contracts and other property, where the insolvency representative determines relinquishment to be in the interests of the estate and additionally where a secured creditor obtains relief from the stay. The exercise of that power may be subject to approval by the court and to certain conditions, such as that the relinquishment does not violate any compelling public interest that may exist, for example, where the asset is environmentally dangerous or hazardous to public health and safety. An insolvency law may also need to address who might be entitled to claim the relinquished assets. Situations in which this approach may be appropriate include where assets are of no or an insignificant value to the estate (e.g. the security interest exceeds the value of the encumbered asset); where the asset is burdened in such a way that retention would require excessive expenditure that would exceed the proceeds of realization of the asset or give rise to an onerous obligation or a liability to pay money; or where the asset is unsaleable or not readily saleable by the insolvency representative, such as where the asset is unique or does not have a readily apparent market or market value. Where a secured creditor is given an asset relinquished by an insolvency representative, the insolvency law might provide that the secured creditor's claim is reduced by the value of the relinquished asset. Creditors should be provided with notice of, and given an opportunity to object to, any proposal by the insolvency representative to relinquish assets'.

115   At the moment claims from the period before the bankruptcy are, as said before, not privileged and, therefore, claims will only be privileged if environmental damage occurred during the insolvency process.

116   Nothing in the Insolvency Act exempts a trustee from any duty in this regard, e.g. a duty to report or make disclosure imposed by environmental law and legislation.

117   If the estate cannot afford the costs of taking the necessary precautions, the trustee should abandon the property (subject to approval by the court and to conditions the court may think necessary, within a reasonable time – the property becomes *bona vacantia*) and again, immediately inform the Minister of Environmental Affairs, who must then assume the responsibility.

118   See also Phillips, V., 'Environmental considerations for insolvency practitioners – Part 1: Environmental Law and personal liability' (1992) 8(3) *Insolvency Law & Practice* 86. Questions such as: 'Can administrative orders be treated as privileged debts?' and

general principle in the insolvency law is that the trustee stands in a fiduciary relationship to the insolvent and to the creditors of the insolvent estate. This entails that he should act honestly and with good faith in all his dealings in the course of his administration of the estate. The creditors have a right to institute action against the trustee in cases which involve some irregularity or maladministration of the estate. He owes a duty to the creditors to act diligently and scrupulously, and may be personally liable if he fails to perform this duty. Thus, a trustee has to take normal safety precautions that would be expected from the management of the business,[119] and if he does not, he may be personally liable.[120] As trustee he has a duty to act reasonably and responsibly, especially where environmental harm is a possibility.

In the words of Phillips,[121] insolvency practitioners should thus beware of the ever-expanding scope of environmental legislation and it is advisable that they enquire about a company's environmental record before taking up an appointment.[122]

'Can the trustee discharge his responsibilities for contaminated property by abandonment?' are highly controversial.

119 Or partnership or company.

120 A trustee should, in the writer's opinion, not be personally liable for any environmental condition that arose or any environmental damage that occurred after his appointment. If it is established that the condition arose or the damage occurred as a result of the trustee's negligence or wilful misconduct, he is responsible as against the creditors for maladministration and neglect of his duties (because of the fact that the insolvent estate has to pay compensation for environmental damage, the creditors receive much less than they should).

121 Phillips, above note 119 at 88.

122 In contrast with the South African position, the Bankruptcy and Insolvency Act 1992 (Canada) contains, *inter alia*, the following provisions defining the liability of the trustee in section 14.06: '(2) Notwithstanding anything in any federal or provincial law, a trustee is not personally liable in that position for any environmental condition that arose or environmental damage that occurred (a) before the trustee's appointment; or (b) after the trustee's appointment unless it is established that the condition arose or the damage occurred as a result of the trustee's gross negligence or wilful misconduct. (4) Notwithstanding anything in any federal or provincial law but subject to subsection (2), where an order is made which has the effect of requiring a trustee to remedy any environmental condition or environmental damage affecting property involved in a bankruptcy, proposal or receivership, the trustee is not personally liable for failure to comply with the order, and is not personally liable for any costs that are or would be incurred by any person in carrying out the terms of the order, (a) if, within such time as is specified in the order, within ten days after the order is made if no time is so specified, within ten days after the appointment of the trustee, if the order is in effect when the trustee is appointed, or during the period of the stay referred to in paragraph (b), the trustee (i) complies with the order, or (ii) on notice to the person who issued the order, abandons, disposes of or otherwise releases any interest in any real property affected by the condition or damage; (b) during the period of a stay of the order granted, on application made within the time specified in the order referred to in paragraph (a), within ten days after the order is made or within ten days after the appointment of the trustee, if the order is in effect when the trustee is appointed, by (i)

Risk Management

The duty to take reasonable measures imposes, as mentioned earlier, strict liability.[123]

> I accordingly agree with the submission that [sections] 28(1) and (2) create at least a strict liability. It may be that in some cases they even create an absolute liability ... Furthermore, no statutory defences are created by NEMA in favour of the person who has caused the pollution. Indeed, in terms of the latter part of [section] 28(1), even where significant pollution or degradation of the environment is authorised by law or cannot be reasonably avoided or stopped, the person who causes, has caused or may cause such pollution or degradation must take reasonable measures to minimise and rectify such pollution or degradation of the environment. This may be another example of absolute liability. Conduct which is not unlawful because it is authorised by law nevertheless gives rise to a duty to take reasonable measures.[124]

It is thus possible that a person may have acted without *mens rea* yet still be regarded as having failed to take all reasonable measures or reasonable care.[125] For

---

the court or body having jurisdiction under the law pursuant to which the order was made to enable the trustee to contest the order, or (ii) the court having jurisdiction in bankruptcy for the purposes of assessing the economic viability of complying with the order; or (c) if the trustee had, before the order was made, abandoned or renounced or been divested of any interest in any real property affected by the condition or damage. (7) Any claim by Her Majesty in right of Canada or a province against the debtor in a bankruptcy, proposal or receivership for costs of remedying any environmental condition or environmental damage affecting real property of the debtor is secured by a charge on the real property and on any other real property of the debtor that is contiguous thereto and that is related to the activity that caused the environmental condition or environmental damage, and the charge (a) is enforceable in accordance with the law of the jurisdiction in which the real property is located, in the same way as a mortgage, hypothec or other security on real property; and (b) ranks above any other claim, right or charge against the property, notwithstanding any other provision of this Act or anything in any other federal or provincial law. (8) Notwithstanding subsection 121(1), a claim against a debtor in a bankruptcy or proposal for the costs of remedying any environmental condition or environmental damage affecting real property of the debtor shall be a provable claim, whether the condition arose or the damage occurred before or after the date of the filing of the proposal or the date of the bankruptcy.

123 Glazewski, above note 4 at 152.

124 *Bareki NO and Another v Gencor Ltd and Others* 2006 1 SA 432 (T) 440–441.

125 The steps, measures or care which are 'reasonable' in any case depend on the particular facts. Thus no liability will arise in the case of uncontrollable natural disasters which cannot be averted even after reasonable measures have been taken. The general rule is that the plaintiff shall bear the burden of proof, and the one who causes damage to other people by engaging in abnormally dangerous activities must prove any exemption applicable.

this reason risk management is a very important part of a company's business strategy.

Proper risk management regarding a company's liability in the case of environmental damage can be classified mainly in two categories of minimizing measures. These are (a) risk management *per se* and (b) the transfer of the risk. Risk management entails the taking of certain measures or steps by the company itself, such as regular, timely and uniform reporting from the operating line through senior management to the board of directors; prompt identification and resolution of environmental issues; establishment of preventative programmes and procedures; third party inspections and identification of developing issues or trends.[126] One reason why firms do not invest the time and money in risk management plans is that it may be very difficult for the firm to compute the reduction in probabilities and losses that will occur if they implement such a plan.[127]

Transfer of risk entails the financial and the contractual transfer of risk. In the latter, parties contractually agree upon who will be liable should environmental damage occur. For example, a company concludes a contract with the sub-contractor specifying that the sub-contractor will be liable for any damage resulting from the sub-contractor's acts.

Financial transfer of risk entails self-insurance and outsurance. Some form of underwriting of liabilities is essential if a civil liability system were to work in practice.[128] Self-insurance may be implemented by creating rehabilitation funds. The problem with rehabilitation funds is that in the case of sequestration/liquidation the assets – that is the money in the fund – will form part of the person's/company's insolvent estate. As such it will not be exclusively available for the cost of remedying environmental damage. The fund should be structured in such a manner that the sequestration/liquidation of the creator of the fund will have no effect on the assets in the fund. It is submitted that when a trust, a close corporation or a section 21 [of the Companies Act] company is created specifically for this purpose, there is a real transfer of assets to a distinct entity. The funds in the trust, section 21 company or close corporation will not form part of the insolvent estate. All three options will be suitable to be used as a rehabilitation fund. Yet all three options are not equally efficient. In the case of a

---

126   See Friedman, F.B., *Practical Guide to Environmental Management* (4th ed) (1992, Environmental Law Institute, Washington) at 45. Other possible risk reduction steps (see p. 48) include measures requiring employers (1) to conduct hazard analyses, establish and implement procedures to accommodate changes in plant equipment and technology; (2) to set up a management system; (3) to understand and correct hazards involved in the use, storage, manufacturing, handling and movement of highly hazardous materials; (4) to communicate that information to employees, etc. See also Orts, E.W. and Deketelaere, K., *Environmental Contracts* (2001, Kluwer Law International, London) at 391–4.

127   Orts and Deketelaere, above note 127 at 393.

128   Compulsory insurance for environmental damage is widely under discussion. See, for example, Lockett, N., *Environmental Liability Insurance* (1996, Cameron May, London) at 12–13.

section 21 company the establishment thereof is complicated and expensive, while the procedure for the establishment of a close corporation or a trust is less complicated. The establishment of a trust is subjected to the least formalities and would be the most efficient form for a rehabilitation fund.[129]

Another alternative to conventional insurance cover is the use of mutual funding within particular industrial sectors. The ability to act quickly may be essential in some instances of environmental damage. In contrast to civil liability, which requires a lengthy legal process before obtaining compensation, joint compensation schemes can gather funds in advance. Financing could thus be readily available for emergency remedial action or to reimburse early restoration work. Moreover, the burden of damage may be more readily shouldered by collective rather than individual action. If the cost of cleaning up a particular incident is high, it may not be possible to recover all the costs from a liable party with limited financial resources. A joint compensation system would help provide additional resources needed for carrying out the restoration.[130] The advantage of such a scheme is that decisions about targeting clean-up funds are uncoupled from whether blame can be attributed against a particular polluter.[131] However, environmental protection should not, in principle, depend on policies which rely on grants of aid and place the burden of combating pollution on the community.

Outsurance could provide significant protection against the liability for environmental damage. The problems of extended time scales and the risk of insolvency of polluting firms, mean that there is a high risk that, at the time the damage is to be remedied, there will be nobody capable of meeting the liability. A company which is performing an activity which could seriously damage or detrimentally affect the environment should have appropriate coverage with adequate limits. One way to ensure that potential liabilities are adequately underwritten and that risk is spread widely across the industrial sector would be to insist upon mandatory environmental insurance. However, this carries severe disadvantages. Insurers are either obliged to provide cover to all, with only limited selectivity as to risks, or they become surrogate regulators, refusing cover or raising premiums to those whose activities – in the eyes of the insurers, but not necessarily the state's regulators – carry high risks and who are thereby forced out of business. Under mandatory insurance, insurers assume responsibility for setting standards and operators who succeed in obtaining cover may in practice and under certain circumstances be relieved from responsibility for taking all necessary measures for preventing environmental damage.

The most successful system for protection against liability for environmental harm is in the writer's view a combination of all forms discussed above. A company should (be compelled to) implement proper risk management

---

129　See also Burger, T., 'Die Gebruik van 'n Rehabilitasiefonds as Boedelbeplanningsinstrument vir die Sakeman: 'n Kritiese Ontleding' (LLM Dissertation, North-West University, Potchefstroom Campus, 2004).

130　See also Winter, above note 40 at 235.

131　In place of a court apportioning liability there can be a panel to prioritise funding (Winter, above note 40 at 236).

measures and negotiate the financial transfer of the risk by creating (mandatory) rehabilitation trusts and by effecting (mandatory) environmental insurance. By spreading the risk in such a manner, environmental insurance will be more readily available and not expensive as it currently is.

Liability Insurance and the Insolvent Estate[132]

Introduction[133]

Injured or aggrieved persons usually do not receive (full) compensation for environmental damage, even though there is an insurer in the background. Although very seldom, it may happen that the person liable for environmental damage (insured), for the sake of his claims history or insurance record, is not prepared to bring a claim against his liability insurance. In such a case it will benefit the aggrieved person to study the policy provisions. It may be that the terms of the policy make provision for the insurer to pay damages directly to the aggrieved. If the terms of the policy do not provide for this, the aggrieved's only option is to turn to the insured. Another reason why an aggrieved person does not receive compensation for environmental damage is the very relevant instance where the insured juristic person is no longer in existence. This situation often occurs in practice, particularly in instances of 'long-tail' damages.[134] The question is how liability must be established if there is no longer an insured person in existence. There is no solution or explanation readily offered in the sources. The use of mutual funding within particular industrial sectors may be a solution in cases such as these. A joint compensation system would help provide the resources required.

By far the most problems occur in practice in instances where the estate of the insured has been sequestrated.[135] The focus in this part of the discussion will be on this last mentioned situation.[136]

---

132 For a detailed investigation into the legal position as well as a comparison between the Dutch, English and South African systems, see Stander, A.L., 'Skadevergoeding betaalbaar deur die insolvente versekerde in die geval van omgewingsbenadeling' (2004) *South African Mercantile Law Journal* 327.

133 This discussion is relevant irrespective of the definition ultimately given to 'environmental damage' and irrespective of the guidelines formulated for measuring of quantifying ecological damage. As long as it is certain that the insolvent is liable, the following principles will be relevant.

134 These are damages that are caused gradually over a period and the claim is, therefore, brought against the insurer quite some time after the damages had actually arisen.

135 This also includes the liquidation of a company or close corporation.

136 See Stander, above note 133 for a discussion of the legal position in this regard and a comparison between the Dutch, English and South African systems.

With Reference to the Claim for Environmental Damage

As already mentioned above the insolvent's liability for environmental damage, towards the injured is not secured. The Insolvency Act also does not grant any preference with regard to the claim. This means that the injured must participate in the sequestration process as a concurrent creditor. The chances of full or sufficient payment of his damages are extremely small. More often the possibility also exists that the claimant may be liable for contribution.[137] This possibility becomes greater where one has to do with enormous industries or businesses where, besides the liability by virtue of environmental damage, substantial claims against the insolvent estate are usually also the rule. The injured mostly has no recourse.

Should there in the particular instance be an insurer in the background, the question is how this situation affects the injured. If the injured is to recover damages from the insurer via the insolvent estate, it would make no difference to his legal position. Money that was intended to compensate somebody for (environmental or other) damage would be utilised to the benefit of the preferential and concurrent creditors, because the money would have to be paid into the estate and, therefore, form part of the free residue. The preferential and concurrent creditors then indeed enjoy the benefit of the insurance. This is obviously extremely unfair.

Section 156 of the Insolvency Act[138]

However, section 156 of the Insolvency Act provides as follows:

> Whenever any person (hereinafter called the insurer) is obliged to indemnify another person (hereinafter called the insured) in respect of any liability incurred by the insured towards a third party, the latter shall, on the sequestration of the estate of the insured, be entitled to recover from the insurer the amount of the insured's liability towards the third party but not exceeding the maximum amount for which the insurer has bound himself to indemnify the insured.

The effect of this section is that the amount of compensation does not at any stage form part of the insolvent estate. Besides the fact that he may not recover more than that which the insurer had committed himself to, the third party may recover his damages in full, even if other unsecured creditors have to be satisfied with a few cents in the rand.[139] This principle that is expressed in section 156 is based on considerations of public interest.[140] However, the independent cause of

---

137   In the case where the free residue of the estate is not adequate to redeem the sequestration costs.
138   Also applicable in the case of a company or close corporation by virtue of the Companies Act (61 of 1973), section 339 and the Close Corporations Act (69 of 1984), section 66 (respectively).
139   *Woodley v Guardian Assurance Co of SA* 1976 1 SA 758 (W) at 759.
140   Idem.

the claim, the direct action of the third party emanating from section 156, is indeed dependent on the policy agreement between the insured and the insurer. In *Supermarket Haasenback (Pty) Ltd v Santam Insurance Ltd*[141] it is said that:

> (it) ... does not mean that a plaintiff (third party) has an absolute right to recover without having to prove the validity and the enforceability of the contract of insurance.

> I am of the view that [section] 156 can never be interpreted to mean that all the third party has to do is to prove there is a policy and that therefore he must succeed. The section clearly contemplates the existence of an enforceable agreement to indemnify the third party. If it is unenforceable in the hands of the insured because of non compliance with the specific requirements ... it is unenforceable at the instance of the third party.

> ... the agreement by which a third party is indemnified is the fons et origo of the action. Unless this is proved, no right of action resides in the third party.

> It was said that there need not be proof that the insured or anybody else complied with clause 3A(a) because the third party is not bound by the terms and conditions of the policy, as he is not privy to that contract. Certainly this is completely contrary to basic principle. A person who by Act of Parliament is given the right to sue and to recover the amount of the insured's liability to a third party is in my view placed in the shoes of the insured and in no way can this now be interpreted to mean that the terms and conditions of the policy do not apply.

These principles are not contradicted by the Court of Appeal.[142] The Court of Appeal found that section 156 does not result in any right for a plaintiff that stands apart from the terms of the policy. This is correct. It only creates a procedure in terms of which a third party receives preference to recover directly from the insurer and not via the insolvent estate of the insured.

Section 156 has no application where the policy simply obliges the insurer to compensate the insolvent for damage to property.[143] This is only applicable where an insurer is obliged to compensate the insolvent with regard to liability incurred by the insolvent against a third person. It is ideally applicable to claims on the basis of the liability of the insolvent for environmental damage. As clearly discussed in the quotation above, the section also does not give the third party greater rights against the insurer than those that the insured had in terms of the policy. Therefore, the insurer is entitled to oppose the third party's claim by

---

141 1989 SA 790 (W) at 793-794 (emphasis added).
142 *Supermarket Leaseback (Elsburg) (Pty) Ltd v Santam Insurance Ltd* 1991 1 SA 410 (A).
143 Idem.

proving that the insurance contract is unenforceable.[144] The insurer may also make use of a defence it had against the insured,[145] for example that the indemnity was limited to 'loss actually sustained and paid ... in respect of liabilities insured' and that the insolvent had paid nothing to the third party.[146]

In *Canadian Superior Oil Ltd v Concord Insurance Co Ltd (formerly INA Insurance Co Ltd)*,[147] the court found:

> What the third party can recover, however, and whether the third party's claim is of such a kind as is covered by the indemnity conferred upon the insured, are matters which have to be determined by reference to the contract of insurance. If the liability is not of the kind covered by the indemnity provided by the insurer, then, it stands to reason, there will be no liability upon the insurer to the third party. So also, if the liability is of the kind for which the contract of insurance makes provision subject to a condition, the insurer will only be obliged to pay if the condition has been fulfilled.

Apart from that which is referred to above, section 156 contains no reference to the process or the procedure to determine or establish the liability of the insured. Questions such as the following are, therefore, also under discussion: Must the insolvent assist the third party in his direct action against the insurer? If so, is he as insolvent capable to act as such? Does the insolvency legislation not limit his capacity in this regard? Must the liability of the insolvent towards the third party already have been determined before the third party may take any steps in terms of section 156? How must the third party go about matters procedurally in order to bring his action?

In 1991, the Court found in *Gypsum Industries Ltd v Standard General Insurance Co Ltd*[148] that:

> The clear wording of section 156 of the Insolvency Act creates and confers upon the third party a right which did not exist prior to insolvency. Unlike the English statute it does not transfer to, nor vest the existing rights of an insolvent in, the third party ... section 156 eliminates the insolvent estate entirely upon insolvency supervening, and all the concomitant pitfalls and dangers of litigation against an insolvent estate ...

The effect of this provision is that, at the moment of sequestration, an own cause of action arises for the third party and he may now act directly against the insurer. 'Own cause action' in this sense means that the third party does not first have to obtain a judgment against the insolvent estate for the amount that he is now

---

144 *Supermarket Leaseback (Elsburg) (Pty) Ltd v Santam Insurance Ltd* 1989 2 SA 790 (W) 794.

145 *Przybylak v Santam Insurance Ltd* 1992 1 SA 588 (K).

146 *Canadian Superior Oil Ltd v Concord Insurance Co Ltd (formerly INA Insurance Co Ltd)* 1992 4 SA 263 (W) at 274.

147 1992 4 SA 263 (W).

148 1991 1 SA 718 (W).

claiming from the insurer,[149] nor does he have to enter into an agreement with the trustee of the insolvent estate[150] with regard to the claim.[151] In this case the plaintiff brought a claim against the insurer on the basis of two liability policies. There were two insurance policies that a company (insured) had taken out with the insurer specifically to cover its liability towards the plaintiff in the case of a breach of contract. The plaintiff (insurer) had filed a special plea that the claim was premature, as the plaintiff had not yet obtained a judgment against the company. The court had found that the special plea had to be struck out and the insurer was granted leave to file fresh allegations in substitution of the paragraph struck out. With regard to the procedure for the determination of the insured's liability nothing is said.

What is the position where the liability of the insured (insolvent) has not been determined? Ensuing from this question follows an important aspect concerning the role of the insured in such a situation. Is he obliged to provide information in the case arising from section 156? It is not expressly so provided. In this regard, *David Trust and others v Aegis Insurance Co Ltd and others*[152] emphasised four requirements for the application of section 156:

- That the insured is liable towards the third party;
- The quantum of that liability;
- The obligation of the insurer in terms of the policy, to compensate the insured for that liability; and
- The amount that the insurer would have to pay the insured.

The Court found that these four requirements must be proven by the third party (injured).[153] This takes place in one and the same action or procedure. In particular, the burden of proof rests on the third party to prove that the provisions of the policy contract which determine the liability of the insurer are complied with. The insolvent will be subpoenaed as an essential witness in the lawsuit,[154] without any incapacity imposed in terms of insolvency law keeping him from doing so. The action, in other words, no longer affects his insolvent estate in the proprietary sense or otherwise. From this the deduction can be made that the insolvent (insured), by virtue of the effect of section 156, is compelled to provide

---

149   Also see Meskin, above note 112 at 5–9.

150   Or the liquidator of the company or close corporation.

151   *Gypsum Industries Ltd v Standard General Insurance Co Ltd* 1991 1 SA 718 (W). The Court relies on *Woodley v Guardian Assurance Co of SA* 1976 1 SA 758 (W) and *Supermarket Leaseback (Elsburg) (Pty) Ltd v Santam Insurance Ltd* 1989 2 SA 790 (W). However, both cases were argued from the point of departure that the liability of the insured has already been determined. Nevertheless, the author is of the opinion that in *Gypsum Industries* the finding has been correct. Section 156, however, does not give the third party the right to claim any amount in terms of a reinsurance contract which any registered insurer has entered into.

152   2000 3 SA 289 (HCA).

153   At 293.

154   At 304.

information regarding the incident concerned so that the third party (injured) may utilise his direct action. But what if the insured is no longer in existence? This remains a crucial problem.

As far as the quantum of the third party's claim is concerned, it is a requirement that the third party has to set out his particulars in the pleadings carefully. The claim of the third party against the insured is unliquidated because it is a claim for damages. Because the claim of the third party against the insurer in terms of section 156 is the same as his claim against the insured, that claim is also unliquidated.

In *Le Roux v Standard General Versekeringsmaatskappy Bpk*,[155] it was once again confirmed that, in order to succeed in an action against an insurer in terms of section 156, the third party (the injured party and the appellant in this case) would have to prove not only his claim against the insured, but also that the insured would have succeeded in his claim for an indemnity. However, the Court found that there was nothing in the section to indicate that the insurer could not repudiate liability after sequestration or liquidation or that the insurer could not depend on his contractual rights in terms of the policy after sequestration or liquidation.

If the interpretation of section 156 is that the third party obtains a vested right against the insurer upon the sequestration of the insured's estate and this right is not extinguished by the insurer's subsequent (lawful) nullification of the policy on account of the insured's breach of contract,[156] it would mean that the third party obtains in terms of the section a better right against the insurer than what the insured ever had. This would also mean that the insurer would be prevented from depending on his contractual rights should it become apparent that the insured had committed a breach of contract. Such an interpretation would be untenable and could surely never have been the intention of the legislator.

In this case the policy in terms of which the insurer (respondent) indemnified the insured (a company) against liability on the basis of negligence, contained a provision according to which the insured was obliged immediately to forward to the insurer any notice of a claim, warrant, summons or judicial process instituted against the insured in regard to the event that gave rise to the claim. The third party (appellant), as a consequence of certain injuries that he had sustained on the premises of insured,[157] had instituted an action for damages against the insured and had obtained a judgment by default. A month later the insured was liquidated. However, the insured had not forwarded the summons to the insurer (respondent) as required by the policy. The third party (appellant) subsequently on the basis of section 156 instituted an action against the insurer in a local division. Owing to the failure of the insured to submit to the insurer the third party's summons for damages, the insurer repudiated liability by virtue of the policy and alleged that he was not liable to the insured and consequently also not liable to the third party. The Court of Appeal agreed with him.

---

155   2000 4 SA 1035 (HCA).
156   Based on the insured's earlier failure to give notice.
157   A crane fell on him.

This principle may have serious consequences for the third party. This is so because it is generally required from the insured in insurance policies to give notice to the insurer of any circumstance that may give rise to the bringing of a claim within a relatively short period and to require of the insured immediately to send to the insurer a copy of any document or other process of court with which he is served in this regard. If these requirements in terms of this policy are a condition for the liability of the insurer, the insured, and in turn, the third party, may lose cover in terms of the policy if it is not complied with.

The problem is that in practice it will be difficult for the third party to prevent the insured from not complying with his obligations in terms of the policy. The same principle will probably apply where these notices or formalities only have to occur after sequestration and, therefore, have to be carried out by the trustee. The same problem will, therefore, also occur in this instance. It is submitted that, where sequestration supervenes, the duty of the trustee should be to 'forward to the insurer any notices of a claim, warrant, summons or judicial process' within a reasonable time and not immediately.

In *Coetzee v Attorneys' Insurance Indemnity Fund*[158] the third party, Coetzee, suffered serious injuries when he slipped on a wet floor at the house of a friend. This led to a claim against the friend of about one and a half million rand. Coetzee appointed an attorney, one Botha, to bring an action on his behalf. Acting negligently, Botha allowed Coetzee's claim to become prescribed. Coetzee then sued Botha for the sum mentioned above, together with costs. Before the trial was heard, Botha's estate was finally sequestrated (on 9 January 1997).[159] The court

---

158 2003 1 SA 1 (SCA).

159 In the first case the parties agreed that the merits of Coetzee's claim will be decided first and that the quantum of his damages will be decided later. Shortly before the trial date (on 2 September 1997) Coetzee's representatives gave notice to amend the particulars of claim by replacing Botha as defendant with his trustee in insolvency, one Wessels. This led to the need to seek condonation. Hancke J, before whom the trial came (the hearing on the merits lasted from 2–5 September 1997), then suggested that there should be a substitution of defendants to cite, not Wessels (the trustee), but the Attorneys Insurance Indemnity Fund (the Fund), this under section 156 of the Act. By agreement between the parties the Fund became the sole defendant on 3 September 1997. (In the report it is stated that the Fund became defendant in the proceedings by agreement between the parties and in terms of the provisions of section 156. But section 156 says nothing about the procedure.) Merits and quantum having been separated, Hancke J decided on 18 September 1997 in favour of Coetzee on the merits. He also ordered costs against the Fund. Subsequently quantum was agreed. Coetzee, as plaintiff, accepted that the capital amount of his claim was limited to R1m (because the indemnity policy the insured (Botha) had with the Fund limited his claim to R1m), but contended that his recoverable costs were not subjected to the limitation and may be recovered from the Fund (insurer) in addition to the ZAR 1 million. The Fund, on the other hand, contended that its total liability for capital and costs was ZAR 1 million. This dispute came before Lombard J. He also decided in favour of *Coetzee* (*Coetzee v Vrywaringsversekeringsfonds vir Prokureurs*) 2000 2 SA 262 (O)). The Full Bench in *Vrywaringsversekeringsfonds vir Prokureurs v Coetzee* 2001 4 SA 1273

decided in favour of Coetzee on the merits. The court also ordered costs. However, the parties could not agree whether costs were to be included in the R1m limit, or whether they were recoverable additionally to the R1m.

It was decided that the third party could not have a better right than the insured. Liability arises out of the policy, including all its terms and conditions. Therefore, the insurer's liability is limited to the amount stated in the policy, costs included. The insurer's liability should not be increased. A contrary view would be inconsistent with the terms and purpose of section 156.

Conclusion

Section 156 applies to any liability incurred by the insolvent (insured) towards a third party. As said above, section 156 applies not only in the case of a sequestration, but also in the case of a liquidation. It is the writer's view that a person's liability to make good/compensate any environmental damage should be invoked in claims under section 156 of the Insolvency Act. The insolvent may be any person or entity which will in given circumstances be held responsible for environmental damage (or part of it) according to the South African law, as set out above. Furthermore, if the polluter pays principle is elevated to a customary international law principle it will be seen as an inherent component of the South African law. The effect would be that, if the insolvent has taken out a liability policy which is effective at the time of sequestration/liquidation and the insolvent is (in future, probably on the basis of the polluter pays principle) liable to compensate environmental damages, the third party will automatically have a right to invoke the privilege of section 156. The insurer is obliged to compensate because of the liability incurred by the insolvent against a third person. Under discussion is a general liability policy as well as a liability policy for environmental damages.

Section 156 effectively gives a third party a preferential claim in an insolvent estate in that s/he does not join the group of creditors which would normally end up with a dividend, but would get the full amount due subject to the insurer's maximum liability. The effect of section 156 is that the insurer in South African law can, on the basis of the section, never make an extinctive payment[160] to the insolvent estate. The reason is that section 156 in this situation eliminates the insolvent and the insolvent estate. An Act of Parliament gives the right to sue and to recover the amount of the insured's liability towards a third party, who is now placed in the shoes of the insured. The insured and the insolvent estate are eliminated. The insured is incapable of disposing of the claim against the insurer. This claim is also non-attachable. At the moment of sequestration an own cause of action arises for the third party and he now act directly against the insurer. For instances where there is more than one injured and the total amount of

---

(O) reversed this decision. It is the appeal against that decision which is now discussed.

160   Without any further liability.

compensation due exceeds the insured amount, the principle of proportionality will probably apply.

No procedure such as that an injured who institutes a legal claim against the insurer is only competent to do so if he take care that the insured is also called timeously in the action, but it is logical that the insured does have a role to play in the whole matter. On the basis of *David Trust and others v Aegis Insurance Co Ltd and others*,[161] the insolvent may be subpoenaed as an essential witness in the case, without his being prevented from doing so by any incapacity imposed upon him by insolvency law. The action no longer affects his insolvent estate in a proprietary sense or otherwise. From this it may be deduced that the insolvent (insured), on the basis of the effect of section 156, is compelled to provide information regarding the relevant incident so that the injured (third party) may utilise his direct action.

It is not stated in section 156 that the rights of the insolvent (insured) are transferred to the third party, irrespective of whether liability to the third party has been incurred before or after the sequestration of the estate of the insured. In the writer's view that is in fact the legal position. Section 156 also applies with regard to liability incurred after sequestration.

It is submitted that a provision should be included in section 156 that the injured/aggrieved may also without submission of a claim by the insured, require payment if the insured is a juristic person which no longer exists. There is no such provision in section 156. This in the writer's opinion offers a good solution to the problem where a juristic person in the running of its business has incurred liability but no longer exists.

---

161   2000 3 SA 289 (HCA).

Chapter 14

Reducing Collateral Damage in Franchisor Insolvency

Jenny Buchan

Introduction

> Although the franchise relationship may appear unremarkable on the
> surface, it has in fact a highly distinctive structure. Unlike either an
> employment relation or an ordinary independent contractual relation, the
> franchise relationship is characterised by the fact that franchisees own the
> bulk of the capital assets of the franchise and franchisors retain the right to
> determine how franchisees will use those assets.[1]

This structure poses challenges for insolvency law. The franchisee of the insolvent
franchisor is a newcomer on the insolvency scene, and, like many newcomers, it is
yet to establish its place. The franchisee is important because it effectively
occupies the role that providers of labour (employees and contractors) and finance
capital (shareholders and secured lenders) occupy in a traditional business model.
In addition to providing labour and finance capital directly to the franchisor by way
of working in the franchise and paying an initial franchise fee and other sums,[2]
franchisees take on the hiring and financing risks associated with establishing their
own business. However, if the franchisor becomes insolvent, the franchisee of an
insolvent franchisor struggles for recognition amongst the established classes of
stakeholder.

The legal and contractual arrangements that create a franchise system are
oriented towards permitting the franchisor to exercise maximum control over its
assets (which include the franchisees) and the minimum exposure to risk. But:

> When it comes to companies going bust, the insolvency of a franchise is
> usually about as shambolic as you can get. Of all insolvency matters, the
> most difficult is the failure of a franchise group ... There are always

---

1   See Hadfield, G.K., 'Problematic Relations: Franchising and the Law of Incomplete
     Contracts' (1990) 42 *Stanford Law Review* 927 at 991.
2   See Table 14.3 below.

problems with the Franchise Code,[3] always leasing problems and unforeseen third party issues.[4]

Sometimes franchisors do fail.[5] The failure impacts on their franchisees.[6] Important questions for insolvency policy are: should franchisees be specifically recognised as unique stakeholders in the franchisor's insolvency and, if so, what form should that recognition take? This chapter explores the legal consequences that flow for franchisees when a franchisor becomes insolvent and the way the Australian insolvency regime currently deals with the franchisees. It identifies specific legal issues that will need to be considered as debate about legal policy in this area progresses. In this chapter, only franchisees of failed corporate franchisors will be considered because 74 percent of Australian franchisors are corporations,[7] and all but one of the 62 failed franchisors and master franchisors on the author's database of failed franchisors are corporate entities.

This chapter is set out in four parts. The first describes the twenty-first century franchise and examines the specific legal environment that regulates franchised businesses in Australia. The second identifies the role of the franchisee in the franchise system, while the third looks at the current approaches taken in Australian law to protecting franchisees' interests. The final part summaries the challenges that franchisor insolvency poses for the law and draws some conclusions.

Twenty-First Century Franchising

Franchising is a method of expanding a business via a network. It may be used by any business that is capable of replicating some or all of its operations.

> The franchise is the agreement or licence between two parties which gives a person (the franchisee) the rights to market a product or service using

---

3   Franchising Code of Conduct ('FCC') issued under the Trade Practices (Industry Codes – Franchising) Regulations 1998, as authorised by the Trade Practices Act 1974 (Cth).

4   See Binning, D., Code Wars – a liquidator's worst fears (Australian Financial Review Special Report, 29 June 2006) at 13, quoting David Cowling, insolvency partner with law firm Clayton Utz.

5   See Buchan, J., When the franchisor fails (January 2006, CPA Australia) identifies some Australian franchisors and master franchisors that failed between 1990 and 2005. This is available at: <www.cpaaustralia.com.au/cps/rde/xchg/SID-3F57FEDF-7E0E2EC1/cpa/hs.xsl/726_17547_ENA_HTML.htm> (last viewed 31 May 2007).

6   The author has an unpublished database of 3,124 franchisees that have been affected by the insolvency of 62 franchisors in Australian between 1990 and 2006.

7   See Frazer, L. et al., 'Franchising Australia 2004' (Griffith University, Brisbane), Question D18 at 69–70.

the trademark of another business (the franchisor).[8] The franchisee has the rights to market the product or service using the operating methods of the franchisor. The franchisee has the obligation to pay the franchisor certain fees and royalties in exchange for these rights. The franchisor has the obligation to provide these rights and generally support the franchisee.[9]

Franchising is thought to have been:

born in France [in] the Middle Ages, between the 10th and 12th centuries, by the granting of liberties and privileges accorded by the lords, benefiting specific populations, defined by territory.[10]

Manufacturers sowed the seeds for modern franchising. In 1930s France:

the Roubaix Woollen Mills set up a chain of stores. They were independent retailers (trading as Pingouin Wools) that would be linked under a contract guaranteeing them product and territorial exclusivity. In the USA, the resurgence of franchising was motivated by the need for manufacturers to invent new distribution methods because proprietary sales were illegal under American Antitrust legislation. The Marketing Director of General Motors worked with the company's lawyers on a new kind of contract to avoid breaching the antitrust legislation.[11]

Thus, the modern franchise was born. Franchising became increasingly popular throughout the latter part of the twentieth century and is now a clearly identifiable and growing part of the economy of many countries where it operates. At least 56 countries have a franchise sector mature enough to support an industry association.[12] A universally recognised brand such as McDonalds is an example of the global success of the franchise model. It could be said that franchising, as a contributor towards the:

---

8   FCC, section 4 states that: 'franchisor includes the following: (a) a person who grants a franchise; (b) a person who otherwise participates in a franchise as a franchisor; (c) a sub franchisor in its relationship with a sub franchisee; (d) a master franchisee in a master franchise system; (e) a master franchisee in its relationship with a franchisee'.

9   Pricewaterhouse Coopers, 'Economic Impact of Franchised Businesses' (2004, International Franchise Association Educational Foundation) at iii.

10   'La Fédération de la Franchise', available at: <www.franchise-fff.com/index.php> (last viewed 31 May 2007).

11   Idem.

12   Argentina, Australia, Austria, Belgium, Brazil, Bulgaria, Canada, Chile, China, Colombia, Czech Republic, Denmark, Dominican Republic, Ecuador, Egypt, England, Finland, France, Germany, Greece, Hong Kong, Hungary, India, Indonesia, Northern Ireland, Ireland, Israel, Italy, Japan, Kazakhstan, South Korea, Latvia, Malaysia, Mexico, The Netherlands, New Zealand, Peru, Philippines, Poland, Portugal, Russia, Singapore, Slovenia, South Africa, Spain, Sweden, Switzerland, Taiwan, Thailand, Turkey, the Ukraine, Uruguay, the United States, Venezuela, Yugoslavia and Zimbabwe.

spectacular increase in foreign direct investment (FDI) as well as other forms of international private capital flows since the mid 1980s, is a manifestation of the 'globalization' or integration of (the) world economy.[13]

Estimated sales through franchise systems are: USD 1.53 trillion in the United States,[14] GBP 13 billion in the United Kingdom, the Yen equivalent of USD 142 billion in Japan, USD 5 billion in Malaysia and AUD 111.2 billion for the 2004–2005 financial year in Australia.[15]

Franchisees choose to become a franchisee rather than establishing a stand alone business for a number of reasons, including their inexperience in business. As a stand alone start up business, the franchisee may not have the credibility to negotiate a lease with one of the large shopping centre owners or to obtain the benefits of economies of scale which franchising offers. People wanting to own a small to medium sized business choose franchising because, in the words of one Australian liquidator:

> the start up costs for a similar business in the same industry that is not a franchise are remarkably dearer, unless the person already has a strong knowledge in a particular field.[16]

But franchisor failure, and its cost, remains largely the subject of anecdote and speculation. Despite its objective of calculating the financial contribution that franchise businesses contribute to the American economy, the cost of franchisor and franchisee failure was not considered in the Economic Impact of Franchised Businesses Report.[17]

At the same time as franchising is being embraced, public attitudes to bankruptcy are changing.

> Economic recessions in the late 1980s and early 1990s caused dramatic increases in the number of bankruptcy filings (in the USA). This era has

---

13 Information available at: <web.worldbank.org/WBSITE/EXTERNAL/TOPICS/TRADE/0 (last viewed 31 May 2007).

14 In the United States, 50 per cent of all retail sales are conducted through a franchise. Bou, A. et al., 'Insolvency in International Franchise Relationships', paper delivered in September 2004 at International Bar Association ('IBA') Conference in Chapter 2.

15 IBIS World (2006), Franchising in Australia (IBIS World Industry Report, Melbourne).

16 Telephone interview with the author on 6 December 2004.

17 Economic Impact of Franchised Businesses (EIFB) conducted by PriceWaterhouse Coopers for the International Franchise Association ('IFA') in 2004 to calculate the financial contribution that franchise businesses contribute to the American economy. The IFA reportedly committed nearly USD 500,000 to underwrite the research. The report is a staggering achievement; the double sided page printed version being 4 cm thick.

witnessed a marked change in the attitude towards bankruptcy. No longer is bankruptcy considered the last desperate act of a financially defeated person or entity. Bankruptcy is now viewed as a viable business option and financial planning tool.[18]

This attitude to personal bankruptcy and to its corporate equivalent, insolvency is both global and pragmatic. Franchisors are business people and are not exempt.

Franchise Contracts

For this part of the chapter, the focus will be on the franchisor and its individual franchisee. The franchise agreement is the key contract that describes the parties' rights and obligations for the duration of the franchise.

> The role of the (franchise) contract is to provide the framework, procedures and the points of departure for fair contract negotiation and adjustment over time. This approach allows for the self-regulation of the parties, providing greater creativity and efficiency than formalistic interpretation by courts.[19]

The range and function of contracts that may be entered into between the franchisor or master franchisee and their subsidiaries, and the franchisee, are described in Table 14.1 below.

However, '... franchising is problematic for contract law'.[20] The traditional view of contracts is that the contract records the parties' negotiated agreement. The parties are presumed to have discussed all important issues and provided for them. In the absence of bad faith (for which the franchisee may have common law remedies), unconscionable conduct or misleading or deceptive conduct by the franchisor (for which the franchisee can access legislated solutions),[21] the express

---

18   See Freed, K., Gurnick, D. and Honesty, E., 'Bankruptcy Issues', unpublished paper delivered at International Franchise Association 29th Annual Legal Symposium (1996) at 2.

19   See Spencer, E., 'Standard Form and Relational Aspects of Franchise Contracts', paper delivered at the International Society of Franchising 20th Conference (2006, Palm Springs CA), at 21, quoting Sciarra, S., 'Franchising and Contract of Employment: Notes on a Still Impossible Assimilation', in Joerges, C. (ed.), *Franchising and the Law: Theoretical and Comparative Approaches in Europe and the United States* (1991, Nomos, Baden-Baden) at 265.

20   Hadfield, above note 1 at 929.

21   Trade Practices Act 1974 (Cth), section 51AC; Industrial Relations Act 1996 (NSW), section 106 gives the Industrial Relations Commission the power to declare contracts void or varied if the contract was an unfair contract at the time it was entered into or that it subsequently became an unfair contract because of any conduct of the parties, any variation of the contract or any other reason.

terms of the contract will govern the relationship between franchisor and franchisee.

While the relational contract model is arguably the contract model that best explains the legal basis of the franchise relationship, the franchisee signs a standard form franchise agreement that leaves no room for negotiation.[22] A relational contract attempts to document and provide for a 'continuing process between people whose interests include maintaining business relations'.[23]

> Two firms that are intimately bound up with each other because of the nature of their business will tend to behave in a less strictly contractual way than they would do if they had a choice of firms to contract with.[24]

This is true of franchising where the franchisor and the franchisee are bound together by the franchise but the franchisor must retain flexibility to experiment and develop the business.

The franchise agreement places a franchisee in a position of great dependence on the franchisor. Spencer states:

> The inherent dynamic in franchisor/franchisee relationship ... involved maintaining the franchisee in a subordinate position. This increases the franchisee's motivation to provide assurances of performance, among them taking on risk ... Despite being overburdened with risk, because of the standard form (franchise agreement) the franchisee is faced with the choice of accepting the contract terms or giving up on the deal entirely.[25]

There is an overwhelming sameness in franchise agreements that fit broad categories, such as 'retail store' or 'home based business'. This is predictable as the interests the franchisors seek to protect are similar.

Moving on from the issue of whether the franchisee has entered a truly relational contract or a standard form contract, a further challenge for franchising is the common law doctrine of privity of contract. This may impact heavily on the franchisee if the franchisor becomes insolvent. The common law doctrine of privity of contracts provides that, as a general rule, only the parties to a contract can acquire legally enforceable rights or acquire legally enforceable obligations under it. Thus:

---

22 The franchisor may agree to small changes in the franchise agreement for a franchisee taking on a new concept, or for franchisees that are very early to the system when the franchise agreement is not yet fully evolved. Depending again on the system, a master franchise agreement or a national master franchise agreement will typically be more genuinely negotiable.

23 See Seddon, N. and Ellinghaus M.F., *Cheshire and Fifoot's Law of Contract* (8th ed) (2002, LexisNexis Butterworths, Chatswood NSW) at 1124, quoting Williamson.

24 Ibid., at 1126.

25 Spencer, above note 19 at 25.

a stranger to a contract cannot in a question with either of the contracting parties take advantage of provisions of the contract, even where it is clear from the contract that some provision in it was intended to benefit him.[26]

Most franchisors operate through several legal entities, each having a different role. The franchisee may only have a contractual relationship with the franchisor, but may have no privity of contract with, say, its landlord. The contractual commitments that the franchisee enters thus fall into three categories, of which examples are provided in columns A, B and C in Table 14.1.

Table 14.1   Contractual Commitments of Franchisee

A: Contracts between franchisee and franchisor	B: Contracts between franchisee and third parties, related to the franchisor	C: Contracts between franchisee and third parties unrelated to the franchisor
Franchise Agreement	Supplier agreements	Franchise agreement with national or master franchisee
Licence to use franchisor's intellectual property	Licence to use Intellectual property	Vehicle leases
Sub-licence to use intellectual property	Agreement to provide shop fitting services	Equipment leases
Sub-lease or licence of premises	Lease, sub-lease or licence of premises	Lease, sub-lease or licence of premises[27]
Finance arrangements[28]	Finance arrangements[29]	Finance arrangements – secured over real property or shares owned by franchisee before its involvement to become a franchisee
Licence to use system software		Employment contracts with the franchisee's employees
Options to develop future territories		Supplier contracts

Source: Own Information.

26   *Scruttons Ltd v Midland Silicones Ltd* [1962] AC 446 at 474 (per Lord Reid), cited in Khoury, D. and Yamouni, Y., *Understanding Contract Law* (6th ed) (2003, LexisNexis Butterworths, Chatswood NSW) at 244.

27   Frazer, above note 7 at 66 states that in Australia, 69 per cent of franchisees operate from specific commercial sites with 25 per cent from mobile bases and 24 per cent being home based.

28   Ibid., which also found that 29 per cent of Australian franchisors provide finance to franchisees, with the most popular being direct finance supplied by the franchisor (59 per cent).

29   Ibid., further finding that, of the franchisors providing finance in Australia, 4.9 per cent did so through a company related to the franchisor.

Table 14.1 helps demonstrate how the franchise model is applied in different franchise systems. For instance, the franchisee may enter a financing contract with a franchisor, a franchisor-related entity or a third party. In the contracts listed in columns B and C of Table 14.1, there is no privity of contract between the franchisee and the franchisor. This contributes to the lack of uniform outcomes for franchisees in franchisor failure.

The Franchise System

The twenty-first century franchisor is a combination of several discrete but interconnected businesses. No two franchise networks are structured in exactly the same way. A franchisor will think of the whole network of interconnected entities as 'the franchise'. The legal system, on the other hand, interprets the franchise as a number of separate legal entities, each with its own creditors, debtors, assets and liabilities. In addition to the franchisor, there could be, for instance:

- a public listed parent company that owns the franchisor; for example, Ansett Airlines (in liquidation), wholly owned Traveland Pty Ltd, that was the franchisor of 270 Traveland travel agencies;
- a proprietary, limited liability company that will be the franchisor on the franchise agreements, for example Traveland Pty Ltd, one of 39 subsidiaries of the former Ansett Airlines;
- the intellectual property used by the franchisees may be owned by the franchisor or a related entity. For example, the owner of the trademarks in the successful Australian Bakers Delight franchise is Bakers Delight Holdings Ltd, although the identity of the franchisor is not clear from the website;
- the head leases on the franchisees' premises may be in the name of the franchisor or of a company related to the franchisor, for example the Bakers Delight website states that 'the lease is held by Baker's Delight who then grants franchisees the right to occupy the premises on the same terms and conditions as were originally negotiated'. Searches of the New South Wales Department of Lands records reveal that the Bakers Delight entities that holds the head leases are, depending on the premises in question Baker's Delight (N.S.W.) Pty Ltd, Bakers Delight Holdings Ltd, or Baker's Delight Holdings Pty Ltd. The Australian Securities and Investments Commission ('ASIC') records reveal that, in addition to the above, there are five other Bakers Delight companies,[30] each presumably having a role in the Bakers Delight franchise system across Australia.

The picture may be made more complex by the addition of further franchisor owned entities. In Australia, it is not possible to determine their relationship to the franchise system or what their role is from the public record. They could be, for example a Franchisor Construction Pty Ltd that may be the

---

30   These are: Baker's Delight (S.A.) Pty Ltd, Baker's Delight (Vic) Pty Ltd, Baker's Delight (Qld) Pty Ltd, Bakers Delight (ACT) Pty Ltd and Bakers Delight (W.A.) Pty Ltd.

supplier of shop designs and fit-outs, a Franchisor Supplies Pty Ltd supplying stock to the franchisees and a Franchisor Finance Pty Ltd which may supply finance to franchisees.

There are several ways the basic franchise model can be expanded on, including the franchisor appointing national franchisees who are known as the international master for a specific country and have the responsibility of establishing the franchise there. This means the international master contracts with franchisees in their country, the only contract linking the franchisor to the country is the international master franchise agreement.

Assets in the Franchise System

The results in an Australian survey,[31] where franchisors reported their level of agreement with a series of statements shown in Table 14.2 indicated that more than 50 per cent of franchisor respondents thought the assets owned by their individual franchisees could be used in a different business without incurring high adaptation costs. It is suggested that if the answers of retail franchisees with high sunk costs in premises and licensing of intellectual property were analysed separately, the number that would 'strongly agree' would be much higher.

Table 14.2   Survey of Assets in a Franchise System

'The assets (eg building, vehicle, equipment etc) owned by your individual franchisees are specific to this franchise and could only be used in a different business by incurring high adaptation costs'[32]									
Strongly disagree		Tend to disagree		Undecided		Tend to agree		Strongly agree	
60	23.1 %	79	30.4%	14	5.4%	64	24.6%	43	16.5%

Source: Survey Data.

Table 14.3 breaks down the monetary cost of each of the 'assets' acquired by an actual retail non-food franchisee establishing its business in suburban Sydney, New South Wales. In this case, the franchisor was established in 2000. A franchise agreement was entered into in 2004, at the end of which year the franchisor entered insolvency proceedings. In that case, the assets could only be used in another business if the landlord was prepared to grant a new lease to the franchisee operating as a non-franchised business after the franchisor became insolvent.

---

31   Survey conducted by Lorelle Frazer in 1996.
32   See Frazer, L., 'Franchise Fees Australian Survey Results' (1996, University of Southern Queensland) at 25.

Table 14.3   The Monetary Cost of Assets

Item paid by Franchisee	Cost	Relevant Contract	Payment made to:	Outcome for Franchisee in Franchisor's Insolvency
Initial franchise fee paid to secure rights for 5 years	AUD 60,000 plus additional AUD 20,000 training	Franchise agreement	Franchisor in full before commencing business	Franchisee no right to claim
Sunk fit-out costs	AUD 99,000	Disclosure document	Franchisor for paying on to independent shop fitter	Lease (in franchisor's name) was disclaimed by administrator appointed 29 October 2004. Landlord would only negotiate with franchisee for a continued lease or licence agreement if franchisee gave up entire value of fit-out. All sums lost.
Franchisor's fit-out supervision	AUD 25,000	Franchise agreement	Franchisor as a 25 per cent fee on top of invoiced fit-out cost	Service fully performed by franchisor; franchisee no right to claim
Inventory/stock	AUD 45,000	Supplier agreements	Supplier	Return or sell, depending on terms of supply
Security deposit on franchisor's head lease	Bank guarantee for three months' rent (approximately AUD 15,000)	Franchise agreement	Provided direct to landlord	After a drawn out argument with landlord, agreed to be released – no damage suffered
Monthly premises rental	Approximately AUD 4,000 pm	Lease between franchisor and landlord. Sublease/licence between franchisor and franchisee	Franchisor for forwarding to landlord	Franchisee debtor of franchisor
Training costs	AUD 20,000	Franchise agreement	To general revenue of franchisor or franchisor related company on day paid	No claim possible
Other costs	AUD 6,000	Franchise agreement	Paid to franchisor up front	No claim possible
Options to open 3 future franchisee owned stores at AUD 20,000 per option	AUD 60,000	Agreement between franchisor and franchisee	Paid to franchisor up front	No claim possible

Source: Own Data.

Interests in Real Property 'Most franchise systems operate from specific commercial sites (69 per cent)'.[33] This implies the need for agreements in relation to occupation of those specific sites. The different methods by which franchisees become entitled to occupy premises in Australia are shown in Table 14.4. As is shown in the right hand column, the nature of the franchisee's tenure will play a significant role in the outcome for the franchisee of a franchisor's insolvency.

Personal Property The grant of the franchise is personal property for the franchisee. The additional personal property the franchisee invests in may include, for example a vehicle, a lawnmower and trailer, trading stock, stationery, cash registers and the shop fit.

Intellectual Property A franchise system is replete with intellectual property. Much of the initial franchise fee paid by the franchisee is attributed to buying the licence to use the franchisor's intellectual property. This money is paid in full before the franchisee starts trading. Most Australian franchisors charged an initial fee of AUD 35,000 in 2004, with the range being AUD 0 to AUD 400,000.[34] Typically, full payment is required before the franchisee starts trading. For example, in the franchise system that Table 14.3 is based on, a franchise fee of AUD 80,000 (including AUD 20,000 for training) was paid to secure the grant by the franchisor:

> To the Franchisee who accepts an exclusive right to operate the franchised business within the territory and a non exclusive right to use the franchise system the marks and the intellectual property in the operation by the franchisee of the franchised business for the term at the premises from the commencement date.

The 'term' was the 'Period ending on the earlier of the following:

- Five (5) years from the Commencement Date;
- When the Lease expires of is terminated and is not renewed; or
- When the occupation licence expires or is terminated and is not renewed.[35]

---

33   Frazer, above note 7 at 66.
34   Ibid., at 24.
35   Danoz Directions Franchise Agreement dated 9 February 2004, Schedule Item 11. The franchise system failed, giving the landlord the right to terminate the lease which had been granted to the franchisor.

Table 14.4   Franchisee Interests in Real Property

				Australian Premises Occupancy Outcomes for Franchisee if Franchisor Insolvent					
Premises Owner	Head Lessee	Sub-Tenant with Sub-Lease	Licence	Law permits Franchisor's Interest to be registered on the Title	Law permits Franchisee's Interest to be registered on the Title	Franchisee has Privity of Contract with Landlord	Franchisor's Insolvency will affect Franchisee's Right to Tenure	Liquidator entitled to disclaim Head Lease	Franchisee may retain Tenure, if Franchisor Insolvent
Independent Entity	Franchisor	Franchisee	N/A	Yes	Yes	No	Yes	Yes	No
Independent Entity	Franchisor	N/A	Franchisee	Yes	No	No	Yes	Yes	No
Independent Entity	Master Franchisee	Franchisee	N/A	No, Franchisor not involved	Yes	No	No	No	Yes
Independent Entity	Master Franchisee	N/A	Franchisee	No, Franchisor not involved	No	No	Not Directly	Not Directly	No
Independent Entity	Franchisee	N/A	N/A	N/A	Yes	Yes	No	No	Yes
Independent Entity	No Formal Tenancy Arrangement	N/A	N/A	N/A	No	Yes	No	N/A	N/A
Franchisor	Master Franchisee	Franchisee	N/A	Yes, as Owner	Yes	No	Yes	Yes	Maybe
Franchisor	Master Franchisee	N/A	Franchisee	Yes, as Owner	No	No	Yes	Yes	No
Franchisor	Franchisee	N/A	N/A	Yes, as Owner	Yes	Yes	Yes	Yes	Maybe
Franchisor	No Formal Tenancy Arrangement	N/A	N/A	Yes, as owner	No	No	Yes	Yes	No
Franchisor-related Entity	Master	Francisee	N/A	N/A	Yes	No	Not Directly	Maybe	Maybe
Franchisor-Related Entity	Master Franchisee	N/A	Franchisee	N.A	No	No	Not Directly	Not Directly	Maybe
Franchisor-Related Entity	Franchisee	N/A	N/A	N/A	Yes	Yes	No	N/A	Yes
Franchisee	Franchisor	N/A	Franchisee	Yes	N/A	N/A	No	Yes	Yes

Source: Own Data.

Goodwill Goodwill is an asset that accumulates in both the franchisor's business and the franchisees'. The Australian Taxation Office is attracted to the interpretation of the concept of goodwill by reference to site, name and personal goodwill.[36] In relation to franchisees, it says, there are 'possible viewpoints on the question whether a franchisee can own goodwill ...'.[37] 'The judgment of the Full Federal Court of Australia in the appeal of *Krakos Investments Pty Ltd v Federal Commissioner of Taxation*[38] is relevant. *Ranoa Pty Ltd v BP Oil Distribution Ltd & Anor*[39] and *Federal Commissioner of Taxation v Just Jeans Pty Ltd*[40] could be said to be authority for the view that in the absence of a specific contractual provision to the contrary on the termination of a franchise, the benefit of the goodwill remains in the franchisor. There is an alternative argument that, depending on the terms of the franchise agreement and lease arrangements, the franchisee, with the franchisor's consent, can dispose of the goodwill in the franchised business 'in whole or in part'.[41] Steinberg and Lescatre also discuss goodwill in United States franchise systems in considerable depth.[42]

People It has often been said that the most important assets of a business are its people. Apart from its own employees, the key people in a franchise system are the franchisor, master franchisees and the franchisees and their employees. There were approximately 600,000 people employed directly in the Australian franchise sector in 2004.[43] Peter and Sandra in a 'Spud Milligan's' franchise are an example of first time franchisees:

> ... neither ... had any experience in conducting a business. The ... Peter had spent most of his life in the public service and had latterly been a purchasing officer for various health related goods used in the public hospital system. Sandra had worked as a bus driver.
>
> In 1995 Peter, then aged about 46 years, was retrenched and received about [AUD] 225,000 as severance pay. He had been taking a business training course for some time at a university and upon retrenchment, completed most of that course. (Peter and Sandra) decided between them that they would try to buy a business that they could manage and which would allow them to work together, produce an income to support their family and give them an interest.[44]

---

36   Australian Taxation Office Pre-Ruling Consultative Document titled 'PCD Capital Gains: Goodwill' (8 November 1995).
37   Ibid., at 1.
38   95 ATC 4369; (1995) 30 ATR 506.
39   (1989) 91 ALR 251.
40   87 ATC 4373; 18 ATR 775.
41   Above note 36 at 4.
42   See Steinberg, P. and Lescatre, G., 'Beguiling Heresy: Regulating the Franchise Relationship' (2004) 109 *Pennsylvania State Law Review* 105 at 216–26.
43   Frazer, above note 7 at 8.
44   *Neilson Investments (Qld) P/L & Ors v Spud Mulligan's P/L & Ors* [2002] QSC 258.

To illustrate how crucial people are to franchisors, 48 per cent of Australian franchisors list the 'lack of suitable franchisees' as their equal greatest hindrance to growth.[45]

Role of the Franchisee

As an independent business person (or, usually, proprietary limited company), the franchisee can develop a business with a head start over non-franchised new businesses as the franchisee should benefit from the expertise of the franchisor in every aspect of the business. The franchisee plays a very prominent role in creating local awareness of a franchisor's brand.

Source of Labour

The franchisee occupies the role the employees or contractors would occupy in a traditional business model. McDonalds recognises this when it states:

> Owner/operators are as golden as the golden arches. The unique relationship we have with our independent franchisees represents perhaps our most important strength.[46]

In Australia, 'McDonalds employs more than 56,000 people in 730 restaurants Australia wide'.[47] When McDonalds states that it 'employs' 56,000 people, it is not speaking in the strictly legal sense, but in a marketing sense of there being 56,000 people who service the brand. This figure includes more than an estimated 38,000 people who are McDonalds' franchisees and the franchisees' employees. A typical McDonalds in Australia can employ 80 to 100 staff.[48]

The franchisee itself is never an 'employee' of the franchisor in the way the law recognises employees. This fact is clearly stated in all franchise agreements. For example, a standard clause to put the relationship beyond ambiguity is:

> The Franchisee shall not ... represent itself as being the Franchisor nor a partner employee or representative (other than an independent franchisee) of the Franchisor. Nothing in this agreement shall operate so as to

---

45   Frazer, above note 7 at 28. Also identified by 48 per cent of franchisors as a hindrance were the franchisees' ability to access finance and increased competition in the marketplace.

46   See McDonalds Corporation 2005 Summary Annual Report at 12, available at: <mcd.mobular.net/mcd/90/14/34/> (last viewed 31 May 2007).

47   Information from company website at: <www.mcdonalds.com.au> (last viewed 31 May 2007).

48   Above note 15 at 22.

constitute the Franchisee a partner, employee or joint venturer of the Franchisor.[49]

Furthermore, the way in which the common law views the distinction between franchisees and employees is interesting, as Ward suggests:

> Importantly, Australian common law only recognises individuals as employees. As neither a body corporate nor a partnership will be recognised as an employee, it is only that class of smaller franchise operated by a sole trader which may (potentially) be classified as an employee.[50]

The relationship between franchisee and franchisor is different in many respects from that between employee and employer.[51] For example:

- The employee does not make a sunk capital investment in the employer's brand; the franchisee does.
- The employee does not hire its own workforce; the franchisee is an employer itself.
- The employee does not bear any of the employer's financial or other business risk; the franchisee does bear some of the franchisor's risk.
- The employee has leave entitlements; the franchisee does not.
- The employee does not have an opportunity to make a capital gain from their employment; the franchisee may make a capital gain from the sale of their business.

The franchisor would have to employ a significant workforce to develop businesses under its brand itself if it were not for the franchisees. However, if the franchisor becomes insolvent, the franchisees do not enjoy any of the special recognition that employees enjoy in Australia and other countries. Table 14.5 sets out a comparison of the recognition given to a range of stakeholders in insolvency.[52]

---

49 Mail Boxes Etc Australian Individual Franchise Agreement, clause 20.1.
50 See Ward, P., 'Can Franchisees Be treated as employees?', paper delivered at the 22nd Annual IBA/IFA Joint Seminar (May 2006).
51 See Buchan, J., 'Is there a Basis for Equating Franchisees with Employees in Priority Ranking on the Insolvency of Franchisors?', paper delivered at the International Society of Franchising 20th Conference (2006, Palm Springs CA), considers this issue in depth.
52 The data that Tables 14.5 and 14.6 are based on was created from a survey conducted for the author by the IBA, which distributed it by email to all members of its 'Creditors Rights' and 'International Franchising' committees. Legal practitioners and law academics from the following countries responded: Argentina, Australia, Belgium, British Virgin Islands, Canada, Colombia, Denmark, England, Finland, France, Germany, Greece, India, Ireland, South Korea, Mexico, the Netherlands, New Zealand, Nigeria, Spain, Sweden, Switzerland, Syria, United Kingdom, United States of America and Vietnam. The data provides an indication of variations across

Source of Development Finance

Much of the money the franchisee invests to buy its business occupies the role that would otherwise be occupied by the franchisor raising capital from debt and equity. If this money were not provided by franchisees, the franchisor would have to source it elsewhere. In addition to financing the development and promotion of the franchisor's brand, the franchisee finances its own business. The finance a franchisee needs to establish a retail business in Australia is outlined in Table 14.3. In Australia 12 per cent of franchisors report difficulties in obtaining franchisor expansionary capital as a hindrance to growth of their franchise system.[53] Thus, the availability of a source of capital in the form of franchisees equity capital and their access to personal debt capital is of high value to franchisors.

Risk Sharing between Franchisor and Franchisee

A franchisee bears all risk for its own performance, plus some of the risk associated with the franchisor failing. Table 14.4 illustrates risk sharing in the area of premises leasing.

On signing the franchise agreement, the franchisee agrees to be controlled.

> Together, the standard form and relational characteristics of the contract synerginistically deprive the franchise contract of the essential element of bargained-for-exchange. The interaction of the two qualities means that the franchisor can manage risk through contract design and drafting and contractual risk-shifting. The franchisee, however, cannot manage risk through contract. The franchisee must accept the risk assigned to him by the contract or decline to enter the relationship altogether.[54]

---

jurisdictions. The responses have not been objectively verified and should be regarded as indicative only. As the author's franchisor insolvency research progresses, specific information will be sought about what informs the recognition of the parties in each jurisdiction.

53 Frazer above note 7 at 28–29.
54 See Spencer E., 'Standard Form and Relational Aspects of Franchise Contracts', paper delivered at the International Society of Franchising 20th Conference (2006, Palm Springs CA), at 15.

Table 14.5 Stakeholders Recognised in Business Failure Laws

Country	Legal System	Stakeholders Recognised in Insolvency Systems							
		Creditor	Debtor	Employee	Government Agency	Liquidator	Shareholder	Franchisee	Other
Australia	Common Law	X	X	X	X	X	X		
Belgium	Civil	X		X		X			
British Virgin Islands	Common Law	X	X	X	X	X	X		
Canada	Common law/Civil	X	X	X	X	X	X	X	
Colombia	Civil	X		X	X				
Denmark	Civil	X		X		X			
England	Common Law	X	X	X	X	X	X		
Finland	Civil	X	X	X		X			Contracting parties in long-term contracts
France	Civil	X	X	X	X	X			
Germany	Civil	X		X		X			
Greece	Civil	X	X	X	X	X	X		
India	Common Law	X	X	X	X	X	X		
Northern Ireland	Common Law	X	X	X	X	X	X		
Ireland	Common Law	X	X	X	X	X	X		
Mexico	Civil	X		X	X				
The Netherlands	Civil	X	X	X	X	X	X		Directors, supervisory judges, lessees
New Zealand	Common Law	X	X	X	X	X	X		
Nigeria	Common Law	X	X	X	X	X	X		
Scotland	Civil/Common Law	X	X	X	X	X	X		
South Korea	Civil	X	X	X	X	X	X		
Spain	Civil	X		X	X		X		
Sweden	Civil	X	X	X	X	X			
Switzerland	Civil	X	X	X	X	X	X		
Syria	Civil	X	X		X		X	X	
United States	Common Law	X	X	X	X	X	X		
Vietnam	Civil	X	X	X	X	X	X	X	

Protection of Franchisees' Interests under Australian Law

The franchisee has access to a number of possible legal actions against its franchisor. These include bringing a common law action for breach of contract, or a statute based action. While the franchisor is solvent, the franchisee or the Australian Competition and Consumer Commission ('ACCC') is able to issues proceedings under Parts IVA, in particular section 51AC [55] (unconscionable conduct provisions), or V, including section 52[56] (fair trading provisions) of the Trade Practices Act 1974 (Cth) ('TPA').

A recognition of the franchisee as a vulnerable business consumer has led to the enactment of mandatory pre contract disclosure requirements in several countries, including Australia,[57] and voluntary disclosure requirements in others.[58] In Australia, the primary regulatory response to the franchisee as a distinct and vulnerable business consumer has been that, with few exceptions,[59] franchisors have to comply with the FCC.[60] Failure to comply is a breach of the TPA. At State level, franchisees may seek redress under state legislation, such as the Fair Trading Act 1987 (NSW),[61] Contracts Review Act 1980 (NSW)[62] and the Industrial Relations Act 1996 (NSW).[63]

The FCC fails to provide any legislative protection for a franchisee once the franchisor becomes insolvent. Once a company becomes insolvent, its assets pass

---

55   Trade Practices Act 1974 (Cth), section 51AC (Unconscionable conduct in business transactions) provides a non-exclusive list of 10 examples of conduct that the court may conclude is unconscionable in a business to business transaction. *Australian Competition & Consumer Commission v Simply No-Knead (Franchising) Pty Ltd* [2000] FCA 1365 provides an example of a franchisor prosecuted under both sections 51AC and 51AD, TPA.

56   Trade Practices Act 1974 (Cth), section 52 (Misleading or deceptive conduct) states that: (1) A corporation shall not, in trade or commerce, engage in conduct that is misleading or deceptive or is likely to mislead or deceive. Cases arguing section 52 include *Sanders v Glev Franchises Pty Ltd* [2002] FCA 1332; *Miba v Nescor Industries* [1996] 834 FCA 1 (17 September 1996); *Australian Competition & Consumer Commission v Trayling* [1999] FCA 1133; *Otrava Pty Ltd & Ors v Mail Boxes Etc (Australia) Pty Ltd; Mail Boxes Etc (Australia) Pty Ltd v Otrava Pty Ltd & Ors* [2004] NSWSC 1066.

57   Including Australia, Belgium, Canada, France, Germany, Italy, Mexico, South Korea, the United Kingdom and the United States.

58   Including New Zealand.

59   Australia: Trade Practices (Industry Codes – Franchising) Regulations 1998, section 5(3).

60   Above note 3.

61   Or comparable consumer protection legislation in every state and territory.

62   For example *Burger King Corporation v Hungry Jack's Pty Limited* [2001] NSWCA 187.

63   Although the right to an action under section 106 was denied in *McDonald's Australia Holdings Ltd & Anor v Industrial Relations Commission of NSW & 2 Ors* [2005] NSWCA 286.

to the legal control of the administrator or liquidator whose role is regulated under the Corporations Act 2001 (Cth). The FCC is thought by the ACCC (although this has not been tested in court) to bind an administrator, but it does not bind the liquidator.[64]

Regardless of the solvency of 'the franchisor' the franchisee may also able to sue a wide range of people associated with the insolvent franchisor; including the franchisor company's directors under section 75B of the Trade Practices Act (Cth).[65]

Insolvency Policy

In Australia, insolvency is regulated by the Federal Government with personal insolvency being governed by the Bankruptcy Act 1966 (Cth), while corporate insolvency rules are set out in the Corporations Act 2001 (Cth).[66] The general policy objective of the insolvency provisions in the Corporations Act 2001 (Cth) is to allow for an assessment of whether the company can be rescued, and for the orderly winding up and ultimate deregistration of insolvent companies. The basic components of the legislative corporate insolvency scheme in Australia are:

> A company may enter voluntary administration,[67] the procedure designed to resolve a company's future direction quickly. In a voluntary administration the independent voluntary administrator (appointed by the company, a chargee or by a liquidator) takes full control of the company to try to work out a way to save either the company or its business. If it is not possible to save the company or its business, the aim is to administer the affairs of the company in a way that results in a better return to creditors than they would have received if the company had been placed

---

64   Memorandum sent by the ACCC to members of the Insolvency Practitioners Association of Australia (19 December 2005), in which the ACCC states that the appointment of an administrator does not of itself terminate or constitute a repudiation of the franchise agreement. Copy available at: <www.ipaa.com.au/pdfs/ V2%20Release%20for%20distribution%20to%20IPAA.pdf> (last viewed 31 May 2007).

65   Trade Practices Act 1974 (Cth), section 75B (Interpretation) states: (1) A reference in this Part to a person involved in a contravention of a provision of Part IV, IVA, IVB, V or VC, or of section 75AU or 75AYA, shall be read as a reference to a person who: (a) has aided, abetted, counselled or procured the contravention; (b) has induced, whether by threats or promises or otherwise, the contravention; (c) has been in any way, directly or indirectly, knowingly concerned in, or party to, the contravention; or (d) has conspired with others to effect the contravention. (2) [omitted].

66   See Keay, A. and Murray, M., *Insolvency: Personal and Corporate Law and Practice* (4th ed) (2002, LawBook Company, Sydney) at 17–18, cited in Murray, M., Submission CAP 10 (31 August 2002) at 2.

67   Corporations Act 2001 (Cth), Part 5.3A.

straight into liquidation.[68] 'Voluntary administration commences when an administrator is appointed[69] and usually terminates on the execution by the company of a deed of company arrangement or a resolution by the creditors that the company should be wound up. Typically the period of time that a company will be in administration is around four to five weeks.[70]

A corporation being operated by a voluntary administrator or liquidator is given some protection; creditors cannot enforce any judgments or orders they may have obtained[71] and other legal proceedings may not be brought or pursued against the corporation without the leave of the court.[72]

Although the voluntary administration process is capable of resulting in a franchisor being rescued, the process, from the perspective of a franchisee:

> really only serves to protect directors by putting up endless barriers to accountability.[73]

A liquidator's experience in 2006 is:

> I am only guessing, but very few (franchisor) companies survive the administration, whereas many franchise systems would survive in a new company set-up.[74]

The problem in voluntary administrations, as in liquidations, is that the franchisee is not a stakeholder in the process, which generally runs through the following sequence:

---

68   ASIC Voluntary Administration: a guide for creditors, available at: <www.asic.gov.au> (last viewed 31 May 2007). For an example, see *Wallace-Smith v Thiess Infraco (Swanston) Pty Ltd* [2005] FCAFC 49.

69   Corporations Act 2001 (Cth), section 437A.

70   See Murray, M., *Keay's Insolvency: Personal and Corporate Law and Practice* (5th ed) (2005, LawBook Company, Sydney) at 466.

71   Corporations Act 2001 (Cth), sections 468(4) and 500(1). An example of the insolvency regime's effect on franchisees is provided by the collapse of the Cut Price Deli franchise. Giugni, D. et al. wrote: 'The effect of the Cut Price Deli collapse was that its unsecured creditors would become entitled only to a small distribution in respect of their outstanding debts. That category included those franchisees who had obtained prior judgments against the franchisor while those with proceedings still outstanding received nothing'. (Giugni, D. et al., 'Factors in Franchise Failure: Lessons from the Cut Price Deli Litigation', paper presented at the 12th Annual Society of Franchising Conference (March 1998)).

72   Ibid., sections 471B and 500(2).

73   Interview conducted by the author on 28 September 2006 with a former franchisee of a now insolvent franchisor.

74   Interview conducted by the author on 28 September 2006 with a Sydney based liquidator who has been appointed to a number of franchisor insolvencies. This raises the question of what happened to the franchisees of the insolvent franchisor?

- If a corporation is insolvent,[75] an application may be made to the Court to appoint a liquidator.[76]
- Once the liquidation has commenced, the liquidator is the only person empowered to dispose of company property.
- The assets of the corporation are realised and the proceeds distributed by the liquidator proportionately to those creditors who are able to prove debts in the corporate insolvency.[77]
- Once the creditors have been paid, the surplus assets of the corporation (if any) are distributed to its members, also on a proportional basis'.[78].

The insolvency regime in Australia generally tends to favour creditors over shareholders. Creditors are paid out in insolvency according to priorities. Some have security for the money owed them and are entitled to sell the security to recover the debt. Entitlements due to employees are given special treatment in insolvency legislation.[79] The reason generally put forward for prioritising debts due to employees is that employees are particularly vulnerable if their employer becomes bankrupt or insolvent. The priority was introduced into insolvency legislation for social welfare reasons 'to ease the financial hardship caused to a relatively poor and defenceless section of the community by the insolvency of their employer'.[80] However:

> the effect of the (employee) priority is to deprive other unsecured creditors of their claim to a share of the available assets. Included in that class of unsecured creditors may be small traders who were substantially dependent upon the insolvent for their business and persons who were in an employee-like relationship with the insolvent but who are classified (in a strict legal sense) as independent contractors. There, creditors may be as vulnerable as employees in the event of bankruptcy or liquidation but enjoy no protection.[81]

Even more vulnerable than the independent contractors mentioned by the Australian Law Reform Commission, are franchisees. As can be seen from Table 14.5, insolvency regimes the world over give special recognition to creditors and employees, but almost uniformly exclude franchisees as stakeholders. The independent contractor is free to look for a new contract. The franchisee is likely to

---

75   Corporations Act 2001 (Cth), section 95A.
76   Ibid., section 459P.
77   Some creditors may be granted priority by the Corporations Act 2001 for some of the moneys owed to them.
78   Subject to any provisions in the constitution of the corporation that may provide for preferential treatments of certain classes of shareholders. See also Australian Law Reform Commission Report on Insolvency (2002) in Chapter 32.
79   Corporations Act 2001 (Cth), section 558 (Debts due to employees).
80   Australian Law Reform Commission General Insolvency Inquiry (1988) at paragraph 722, quoting the Cork Report, paragraph 1428.
81   Ibid., at paragraph 723.

be contract bound to remain in the franchise relationship while the administrator or liquidator initially explores options for the future of the system and then pursues the best option for the creditors. This can take months. For example; the insolvency of the Traveland franchisor is described as a tragedy in four acts by Sykes.[82] He recounts:

> Act I. 24 September 2001 ... saw the parent company; Ansett's administrators sell Traveland to a dot.com company that had not previously been involved in the travel industry, Internova Travel for [AUD] 500,000. At this stage Traveland had 104 branches and 750 staff. Internova Travel (incorporated specifically for the Traveland purchase) bought the money-losing business with borrowed money, without tying down its potential partners and financiers.

> Act II. 28 September 2001 saw the Australian Investment Corporation of Western Samoa (AIC) buy half of Internova Travel for [AUD] 500,000. ... the half a million (Australian dollars) AIC put up seems to have disappeared straight down the insatiable maw of Traveland in wages and other costs.

> Act III. 8 October 2001. Financial Options Group Inc (FOGI), a company owned by the two Sydney entrepreneurs who controlled AIC, paid [AUD] 2 million for the balance of Traveland. Possession of the business passed on 8 October but settlement was not required until 24 October. The money was not paid and on 26 November 2001 Internova Travel's directors put it into administration, which quickly turned into liquidation. The Australian Securities and Investment Commission put FOGI into liquidation on 18 February 2002.

> Act IV. 23 December 2001. FOGI's liquidator sold Traveland to Travelworld for [AUD] 250,000. Travelworld now has all Traveland's staff and licenses ... Finally, Traveland was vanishing like the Cheshire cat.

Throughout the drama recounted by Sykes, there is little mention of the estimated 270 to 285 Traveland franchisees. The Traveland business was an asset in the Ansett insolvency. The Traveland Franchise Council was of the view that franchisees did not have grounds for terminating franchise agreements. This was a view shared by a Melbourne Queen's Counsel who was consulted by one of the franchisees:

---

82   See Sykes, T., 'Pierpont Column' (*Australian Financial Review*, 9–10 March 2002) at 12.

> We'd just renewed the franchise agreements on our four outlets for five
> years when the franchisor's administrator was appointed. We went to see
> a QC to see if we could get out of the agreements and there was no way.[83]

According to a former franchisee, the purchasers of Traveland knew nothing about travel or franchising. Once it became obvious to the franchisees that the new owners of the Traveland brand did not have the expertise to run a franchised chain of travel agents, the franchisees moved in several directions:

- 20 franchisees switched to UTAG Travel;
- Several franchisees switched to Harvey World Travel;
- 150 Traveland franchisees joined Travelworld;
- One franchisee became an employee of another agency, having lost so much that he could not continue as a franchisee;
- At least three franchisees re-branded as independent travel agents; but
- The fate of the approximately 100 other former Traveland franchisees is unknown.[84]

At no stage were the franchisees offered the opportunity of buying the franchisor. It should be noted that a liquidator does not appear to have an obligation to sell assets of the failed franchisor to the purchaser who would be the most suitable from the franchisees' perspective, nor to a purchaser who is well motivated towards the franchisees. Theoretically, there is nothing to stop a liquidator selling the franchisor's business to a direct competitor of the franchisor. That direct competitor may elect not to buy the franchise agreements but, instead, to simply buy the brand and shelve it.

Franchisor Insolvency

The franchise business model has evolved outside the insolvency regime. Franchisees, through their contractual arrangements with franchisors, may be categorised as creditors, debtors, assets or liabilities. Table 14.6 illustrates the approaches some countries take to franchisees in franchisor insolvency. In Australia, between 1990 and early 2006, more than 62 franchisors were under administration or became insolvent. Some 45 of these failures occurred after the FCC had been enacted to provide protection for franchisees as small business consumers.

The ACCC considers:

> the most common cause of franchising problems can be broken down
> into two broad categories: firstly scams masquerading as legitimate

---

83   See Buchan, J. et al., 'The Domino Effect: How Ansett Airlines' Failure Impacted on Traveland Franchisees', paper presented at the Academy of World Business and Management Development Conference (2006) at 1906.

84   Above note 5 at 19.

franchise investments, and secondly, genuine systems experiencing severe pressures from expanding too quickly of from structural flaws not sorted out in the early phases of the business. Regardless of the cause, once things go wrong, it is the franchisee that is predominantly the loser.[85]

The outcome of franchisor failure for individual franchisees depends on:

- how individual franchise agreements address franchisor administration or insolvency (usually they are silent on the issue);
- the decisions the liquidator takes in relation to disclaiming onerous contracts;
- whether a suitably qualified buyer can be found for the franchise network;
- how the franchise network is structured (levels and nature of delegation, allocation of risk, ownership of the assets that make up the franchisor etc.); and
- the individual franchisee's negotiating ability.

The importance of dealing with the franchise issue in insolvency is underlined by Bou, who states:

> As an economy develops, more and more of its wealth is likely to be contained in or controlled by contracts. As a result, the treatment of contracts is of overriding importance in insolvency. There are two overall difficulties in developing legal policies in that regard. The first difficulty is that, unlike all other assets of the insolvent estate, contracts are usually tied to liabilities of claims. A second difficulty is that contracts are of many types. The include simple contracts for sale of goods, short term or long term leases of land or of personal property; and immensely complicated contracts for franchises.[86]

Thus, the franchise agreement is a classic example of an unresolved treatment of contracts. Rohrbacher has identified a third, fundamental difficulty in developing legal policies around contract based property rights:

> For executory contracts in bankruptcy, the debtor's right to performance is treated as property, but the debtor's obligation to perform is treated as contract.[87]

---

85   See Samuel, G. (Chairman of the ACCC), 'Code not the culprit in failed franchises' (*The Australian*, 22 August 2006).

86   See Bou, A. et al., 'Insolvency in International Franchise Relationships', paper presented at the International Bar Association Conference (2003, San Francisco) at 16.

87   See Rohrbacher, B., 'More equal than others: defending property-contract parity in bankruptcy' (2005) 114(5) *Yale Law Journal* 1099 in note 35.

Table 14.6   **Possible Categorisation of Franchisees in Franchisor Insolvency**

Country	Possible Categorisation of Franchisees in Franchisor Insolvency						
	Asset	Liability	Creditor	Debtor	Franchisee	Other	Don't Know
Australia	X			X			
Belgium			X	X			
British Virgin Islands							X
Canada	X		X	X	X	X	
Colombia						X	
Denmark	X		X	X	X	X	
England			X	X			
Finland			X	X	X		
France					X	X	
Germany		X	X	X	X		
Greece	X	X	X	X			
India			X	X		X	
Northern Ireland			X	X			
Ireland							X
Mexico			X		X		
The Netherlands					X		
New Zealand			X	X	X		X
Nigeria	X	X	X	X			
Scotland	X	X	X	X	X		
South Korea	X	X	X	X			
Spain			X				
Sweden			X	X		X	
Switzerland			X	X	X		
Syria	X				X		
United States						X	
Vietnam							

The Franchise Agreement is the starting point for the courts, liquidators and administrators to determine rights in insolvency. The weakness in individual franchise agreements is that they contemplate and provide for the failure of the franchisee but are, almost without exception, silent about the possible failure of the franchisor.[88]

In addition to governing the relationship between franchisor and franchisee, the contract governs the relationship between the administrator or liquidator and the franchisee. The Corporations Act 2001 (Cth) and the Bankruptcy Act 1966 (Cth) allow the liquidator, but not an administrator,[89] to disclaim onerous contracts.[90] This includes franchise agreements, leases, supplier contracts, and other contracts that affect the existence and viability of the franchisees' businesses.

For example, in the case of the failure of Jatora Pty Ltd (in liquidation), the Australian master franchisee for Canadian-based Kernel's Popcorn, the report to creditors, filed by the liquidator pursuant to section 439A of the Corporations Act 2001 (Cth), dated 11 April 2005, stated:

> there were 24 Kernels Extraordinary Popcorn stores, of which 20 operated pursuant to franchise agreements. The (franchisor) company was the lessor of (all) franchisee stores ... it was necessary for me to disclaim all of the company's leases.

The liquidator may also disclaim franchise agreements. The franchisee does not have a reciprocal right to disclaim the agreement.

Categorisation of Franchisee in Franchisor Insolvency

Whilst insolvency procedures (both voluntary administration and liquidation) recognise specific categories of stakeholder, the franchisee's situation does not fit logically and cleanly within any of the categories. Franchisees are in a unique position. They are in a relationship of dependence with the franchisor. At the same time, they are conducting an independent business which involves assuming liabilities and entering contracts in relation to the franchisee business.

88	See Buchan, J., 'Franchisor failure in Australia – impact on franchisees and potential solutions', paper presented at the International Society of Franchising Conference (2005, London).

89	An administrator has the powers granted under, Corporations Act 2001 (Cth), sections 437A and 442A-F. These include the power to sell company property but not the power to disclaim onerous contracts. See also *Tolcher v National Australia Bank* (2004) 22 ACLC 397 at 401.

90	Corporations Act 2001 (Cth), section 568(1) (Disclaimer by liquidator; application to Court by party to contract) states: (1) Subject to this section, a liquidator of a company may at any time, on the company's behalf, by signed writing disclaim property of the company that consists of (8 property types listed in legislation) ... (1A). A liquidator cannot disclaim a contract (other than an unprofitable contract or a lease of land) except with the leave of the Court.

A number of practical issues compound the franchisees legal impotence in relation to the liquidation:

- The franchisee may be anywhere in the world, and will not, in most cases, be located near the franchisor's head office, or in the city where the liquidator is based;
- The franchisees have no representative body like a trade union that can argue their position;
- Franchisees are required to continue operating their business while the administrator or liquidator meets with creditors or seeks a buyer for the franchisor (franchisees are thus stretched for time).

So, how is the franchisee categorised in insolvency?

Franchisee as Debtor   In almost all franchise systems, the franchisee owes relatively small amounts of money to the franchisor, as royalties, cost of stock, advertising levy and other routine sums, and is likely to be categorised as a debtor in relation to these sums.

Franchisee as Creditor   Unless a franchisee is a creditor, there is virtually no room in Australia's insolvency regime for it to have a voice in the franchisor's insolvency, far less a share of the insolvent's estate. There are three categories of activity that might place a franchisee into the position of being a creditor in a franchisor's insolvent estate. These are:

- In a minority of franchise systems the franchisee is remunerated by commission. In these systems, the franchisee makes the sale but the franchisor supplies the products or services direct to the customer. The customer pays the franchisor and the franchisor pays the franchisee. In travel agency franchises, for example, part of the franchisor's revenue stream is from the sale of airline tickets. If the airline is the ultimate holding company for the franchisor (as Ansett airlines was for the Traveland franchisees) it will owe the travel agent franchisee commission on airline ticket sales; and
- The franchisee may be a creditor if, for example, goods that were supplied by the franchisor are returned under warranty by the franchisee's customers.

However, the sums of money owed to the franchisee as a creditor under the above arrangements are bound to be a relatively small proportion of the franchisees' total investment.

- The third instance is when the franchisee may be a creditor of the franchisor, the 'big ticket item', for moneys payable by the franchisor pursuant to a concluded dispute between franchisee and franchisor. Where the conclusion has been that the franchisor owes the franchisor settlement money, the sums could be substantial. In Australia, disputes between franchisors and franchisees are resolved by negotiation or mediation as well as in court. The mediation mechanism is established as the preferred method of franchise dispute resolution in Part 4 of the FCC.

Although 'around 75 per cent of mediations conducted through the OMA result in a binding settlement that both parties are prepared to live with ...',[91] the disadvantage of a mediated settlement, if the franchisor becomes insolvent, is that it is likely to be recorded in a contract. Unless the settlement included a requirement that the franchisor provide security for the settlement moneys, the franchisee will be an unsecured creditor for that sum. Franchisees that have already secured a judgment may secure a small payment.[92]

The franchisee is in a much worse position than traditional suppliers of capital and labour. Suppliers of capital are recognised as creditors in insolvency. Shareholders understand the risks they run as shareholders, and the benefits from the increase in value of their shares and the receipt of dividends. Traditional suppliers of labour (employees and contractors) have the freedom to leave the failed business and seek alternative work.

Franchisee as Potential Litigant   If franchisees are contemplating litigation, or have not yet had their case heard, they may be forestalled by the rule that, on the administrator or liquidator being appointed, a stay is automatically applied that prevents any action or civil proceedings being begun or continued against the company without the leave of the court being obtained.[93]

> There are often franchisees who will not mutiny against the franchisor, no matter what level of provocation exists. Most systems contain, amongst the franchisees, family members, franchisees on 'special deals' or who believe they are on special deals, and some that are financially bound to the franchisor.[94]

There is also anecdotal evidence that, rather than risk making their franchisor financially vulnerable, some franchisees make a conscious decision not to litigate potential claims against their franchisors. Essentially, franchisees do not want their franchisor to fail and are often the last to hear when the franchisor does fail.[95]

---

91   Office of the Mediation Officer website at: <www.mediationadviser.com.au/> (last viewed 31 May 2007). The mediation adviser is appointed pursuant to FCC, Part 4.

92   Above note 71.

93   Murray, above note 70 at 283 and 487. The relevant legislation is contained in the Corporations Act 2001 (Cth), sections 440D and 471(2). See *Ibbco Trading Pty Ltd v HIH Casualty and General Insurance Ltd* (2001) 19 ACLC 1093.

94   Interview with Australian franchise lawyer/mediator (August 2006).

95   The author has interviewed former franchisees who say that while the franchisor's employees knew something was amiss because of company gossip or late pay, the franchisees did not find out until after the administrator was appointed, and then, only from the media.

Consequences for Franchisee of Franchisor's Insolvency

In deciding to invest their labour and capital in the franchise, franchisees assume that the franchisor will deliver on its promises, and they take for granted that it will remain solvent. The ripple effect of the failure of a franchisor on its franchisees can be significant. The effect on each specific franchisee will depend on a number of variables such as the nature of the franchise business, the saleability of the franchise network, the amount of sunk investment the franchisee has made, the location of the business (home based, mobile or retail premises based), the amount of debt the franchisee has, the length of time the franchisee has been operating the franchise and the nature of third party contracts the franchisee has entered into.

The franchisees' problems start with the franchise agreement:

> ... the troublesome issue in executory contracts is not that property and contracts are treated so differently but that debtors and creditors are. The current property-contract distinction allows debtors to enjoy greater rights than they have outside bankruptcy as compared to the other party to the contract. The issue, simply stated, is this: The debtor's right to performance enters bankruptcy as property of the estate and is treated as property, but the debtor's obligation to perform becomes the nondebtor party's claim, which is treated as contractual. This 'reduction of a property right to an ordinary claim' disregards nondebtor's nonbankruptcy entitlements and expectations.[96]

During the period of administration or insolvency, the franchisee's ongoing rights to performance of the franchisor obligations contained in the franchise agreement depend on the administrator or liquidator. The franchisee may lose the right to access the franchisor's intellectual property and it typically has no contractual or statutory rights to distinguish it from other contracting parties. The franchisee has liabilities to third parties (for example franchisee's suppliers and franchisees' employees) that are dependant on, but not contingent on, the franchisors continued solvency.

This also appears to be the case in the United States, despite the fact that:

> ... the Congress actually has gone a short distance towards property-contract parity by enacting [section] 365(n) [of the Bankruptcy Code] ... Section 365(n), which 'permits a licensee of intellectual property to retain its rights despite rejection of an executory contract', gives the nondebtor party (ie franchisee) back its property right ... Thus, if the trustee assumes the contract, the nondebtor party performs as normal. If, however, the trustee rejects the contract, the nondebtor party can choose either to take damages (its typical contractual remedy) or to retain its rights under the contract.[97]

---

96   Rohrbacher, above note 86 at 1099 in note 35.
97   Ibid., in notes 207–209.

Because of the complex structure of the franchise network, and the degree of dependence the franchisee has on the franchisor,[98] this is not a total solution where the non-debtor party is a franchisee. One American franchising practitioner has confirmed the difficulties that exist in writing:

> If the franchisor fails … a franchisor can assign its rights under a franchise agreement to a buyer of all or a portion of the bankrupt franchisor's franchise network. A franchisor can also 'reject' a franchise agreement – terminating the franchisor's obligations to perform in the future. (This is) really the tip of the iceberg regarding the impact a bankruptcy may have on the franchisor-franchisee relationship.[99]

The greatest cost for a franchisee establishing as a retail franchisee is likely to be the premises fit out costs. If the liquidator disclaims the lease, the franchisee will lose the value of these sunk costs unless it is able to negotiate a new lease. Even then, the franchisee may find the lack of the power of the brand, or the bargaining power a group has with a supplier, may mean the franchisee is not able to trade successfully as an independent. To quote an example:

> James Rixon was a franchisee in the failed (Australian master franchisee owned) Kernel's Popcorn chain. He sold his business at a loss nine months after his franchisor went into administration in 2005 … Rixon, a shop-fitter by trade, renegotiated a lease with his landlord, formed direct relationships with his suppliers and got together with other Kernel's Popcorn franchisees to trade under a new brand, Pop n Go, when his franchisor failed. But the business was not as profitable as he would have liked. Rixon says he did not have the marketing expertise to run the operations without a franchisor, so he got out.[100]

There are two contract claims that a franchisee of an insolvent franchisor may be able to bring; either a claim that the franchise agreement has been fundamentally breached or a claim against the liquidator for unjust enrichment. To mount either action would severely tax an individual franchisee's resources, therefore litigation would be best undertaken by a group of disenfranchised franchisees.

Frustration or Fundamental Breach of the Franchise Agreement 'Events may occur after a contract has been made which makes its performance pointless, more

---

98   See the situation for James Rixon, Kernel's popcorn franchisee, below. A similar experience is reported by the franchisee whose details are tabulated in Table 14.3. In this case, following the franchisor's failure in 2004, the former franchisee closed the store in 2006 as the business was not viable.

99   See Reiss, D.H., Article in 'Franchise Law Insider' (In-house publication of Kolmes & Lofstrom LLP, Los Angeles CA).

100   Walker, J., 'It pays to have a Plan B' (*Business Review Weekly*, 16–22 March 2006) at 57.

difficult or more costly, or even impossible. Such events may result in the termination of the contract by operation of law, on the basis that it has been frustrated'.[101] The common law action for frustration or fundamental breach is basically the same in Australia as in Canada. In Canada, in *Magnetic Marketing Ltd v Print Three Franchising Corp. et al.*,[102] the plaintiff franchisee sought rescission of its franchise agreement based upon fundamental breach. It also sought the return of the franchise fee, royalty fees and advertising fees paid to the franchisor. In considering the issue of fundamental breach and the numerous alleged breaches of the franchise agreement by the franchisor, the Court found that the franchisee had obtained substantially what it had bargained for under the franchise agreement, and accordingly the Court found that there was no 'fundamental breach of the agreement'.[103] Goldman explains this particular decision stating:

> Whether a fundamental breach argument has any chance of success is fact dependent. The greater the benefit that the franchisee has already received from being part of the franchised system, the less likely that the franchisor's bankruptcy will be found to have fundamentally breached the franchise agreement.[104]

Unjust Enrichment Also available to franchisees, though not tested in Australian courts in a franchisee situation, is the right to embark on litigation against the liquidator, or against the directors of the failed franchisor. This action could take the form of an equitable action claiming unjust enrichment. To succeed in an unjust enrichment plea 'a restitutionary claim based on unjust enrichment depends upon the plaintiff establishing the following elements:

- Benefit or enrichment (defendant franchisor/director/liquidator) has been enriched by the receipt of a benefit – in the case of the franchisor, up front fee that was charged for the right to conduct a franchise for say, five years, but the franchisor became insolvent after one year – 4/5 of the initial franchise fee would be a starting point);
- At the plaintiff's expense;
- Unjust factor (unjust to allow the defendant to retain the benefit); and
- There are no bars to the restitutionary claim (no other consideration barring the claim, such as a subsisting valid and enforceable contract between the parties).

To succeed in a restitutionary claim all these elements must be satisfied. In the first instance, the plaintiff must prove elements one to three on the balance of

---

101 Seddon and Ellinghaus, above note 23 at 881.
102 (1991) 38 CPR (3d) 540.
103 See Goldman, S.H., 'Tackling Troublesome Insolvency Issues for Franchisees' (8 October 2003) at 11, copy available at: <www.goldmanrosen.com/pdf/franchiseesinsolvency1.pdf> (last viewed 31 May 2007).
104 Ibid., at 12.

probabilities. In many cases this would be sufficient. Generally speaking it is up to the defendant (liquidator) to raise the issue of a bar to restitution. Then the plaintiff must prove element four. If, on the balance of probabilities, the court is not satisfied that there is no bar to a restitutionary claim, then the plaintiff fails.[105]

The use of an unjust enrichment action could be considered by franchisees that recently paid a franchise fee but derived very little benefit prior to the franchisor's failure. The pool of money available to the liquidator to pay creditors is artificially expanded by the franchise fee, thus it is arguable that the liquidator has been 'unjustly enriched'. This was pleaded by a group of franchisees in Ontario, Canada in one of the Country Style Food Services cases.[106] There, the franchisees did not act quickly or cohesively enough to succeed; the comments about unjust enrichment did not form part of the decision, but the court did not rule out unjust enrichment as a possible cause of action by the court for future franchisor insolvency cases.

> In reorganization, where the objective of the proceedings is to enable the debtor (franchisor) to survive and continue its affairs to the extent possible, the continuation of contracts (franchise agreements and leases of premises that are sub-let to franchisees) that are beneficial or essential to the debtors' business and contribute value to the estate may be crucial to the success of the proceedings.[107]

The Challenges for Insolvency Policy: A Summary of the Problems

In theory, insolvency would give all legitimate stakeholders a right to have their interests taken into account. When insolvency involves a franchise system the insolvency model locates a key stakeholder, the franchisees, in the wrong place in the insolvency model. The franchisee has no legal right to influence the outcome of either the administration or the liquidation of the franchisor. The franchise agreement is an 'asset' or a 'liability' and, the franchisees have no rights beyond those contained in the franchsie agreement. Currently, every concession secured by

---

105   See Davenport, P. and Harris, C., *Unjust Enrichment* (1997, The Federation Press, Annandale NSW) at 34.

106   *Country Style Food Services Cases: Country Style Food Services Inc. v. 1304271 Ontario Ltd* (Ontario Superior Court of Justice, Chapnik J., Judgment of 11 February 2003); *In the matter of the Companies Creditors Arrangement Act., RSC 1985 C c-36, as amended AND In the matter of the Courts of Justice Act RSO 1990 c-43, as amended AND in the matter of a plan of compromise or arrangement of Country Style Food Services Inc, Country Style Food Services Holdings Inc, Country Style Realty Limited, Melody Farms Specialty Foods and Equipment Limited, Buns Master Bakery Systems Inc and Buns Master Bakery Realty Inc* (15 April 2002, Court of Appeal for Ontario Docket M28458, unreported decision), referred to by Coltraine, C., 'Franchisees: Insolvency and Restructuring', paper delivered at Toronto conference (June 2003).

107   Bou, above note 86 at 16.

franchisees in relation to every contractual commitment will be as a result of their ability as negotiators.

Commentators (academic and judicial) in the United States observe:

> Franchisees may reasonably believe that they will own their own business and reap the benefits of the goodwill – reputational and locational – created by the franchisees' hard work. The founder of Dunkin' Donuts noted: "Franchising gives people a sense of ownership". That the 'ownership' is illusory is irrelevant: The very survival of franchising is dependent upon conveying a sense of ownership without the attributes of ownership; the sense of contractual obligation without the mutual obligations contracts traditionally entail.[108]

> The underlying recognition is that a relational contract is of an ongoing, and often relatively open-ended, character; and that it is in society's interest to accord to each party to a contract of this kind, reasonable security for the protection of his or her justified expectations.[109]

> [However, none of the current approaches to redressing the overt power imbalance,] satisfactorily strikes at the heart of the problem: the incompleteness of the contracts that structure such a complex relationship (franchisor/franchisee), one which requires high levels of commitment to protect large sunk investments.[110]

Prospective franchisees, with all the care and diligence in the world, do make a decision during the negotiation process that they will proceed with the venture. In making this decision, they decide they can trust the franchisor. There is so much weight against the franchisee in the standard form franchise agreements that they must be making this decision. Then, under the dynamic of that resolution to trust, they modify their position in negotiations, and sign the franchise agreement.[111]

The necessarily incomplete relational contract (franchise agreement) implicitly acknowledges that there will be issues that arise during the course of the franchise relationship that have not been considered. The franchisee believes they will be addressed when they arise and they often are. Some incomplete contracts provide a procedure for resolution of unknowns; others address them as and when they arise. The law presumes that franchisees and franchisors have privity of contract with each other.[112] However, in many franchise systems there are third

---

108   Steinberg and Lescatre, above note 52 at at 229.
109   *Dymocks Franchise Systems v Bilgola Enterprises Ltd* 8 TCLR 612 at 630 (per Hammond J.).
110   Hadfield, above note 1 at 929.
111   Interview with Australian franchise lawyer and mediator (August 2006).
112   The FCC requires the franchisor to make disclosure, but only requires limited information about the other franchisor controlled entities that the franchisee must do business with.

party contracts that are just as important to the viability of the franchisees business as the franchise agreement is. The ongoing commitments that a franchisee has under these third party contracts are not contingent on the franchisors remaining solvent. The franchisee in Table 14.3 (and the other 16 franchisees in the same system) was not a creditor of the franchisor and was a debtor to the extent of the monthly royalty and the rent which is ultimately owed to the landlord. This is not a strong negotiating position in relation to the franchisor's liquidator. Of the estimated total money outlaid by the franchisee in Table 14.3 (excluding professional advice and bank charges):

- A pro-rated amount of the AUD 60,000 (initial franchise fee) could be the subject of an equitable claim for unjust enrichment. Any action would need to be approved by the court;[113]
- AUD 99,000 is 'sunk' costs, spent on fit out. Depending on how portable the items purchased were, some may have second hand value. Others (e.g. shop window and flooring) would have become part of the land owner's real property;
- AUD 25,000 charged by the franchisor for supervising the fit out is deemed earned as soon as the fit out is complete;
- AUD 45,000 inventory is returned to suppliers or sold or thrown away by the franchisee, depending on the relevant terms of trade;
- AUD 15,000 bank guarantee provided by the franchisee to guarantee the franchisor's obligations under the head lease. Depending on the landlord's attitude towards the franchisee as a replacement tenant and the amount of rent the now insolvent franchisor owes, this guarantee may be called up by the landlord or, as in the case described in Table 14.3, used to support the replacement lease to the former franchisee;
- AUD 26,000 training costs and other amounts deemed earned by the franchisor pursuant to the franchise agreement. No claim possible;
- AUD 60,000 to secure options to 'own' three future territories. This, also, is potentially the subject of a claim for unjust enrichment.

As the franchisor is insolvent, the franchisee may issue proceedings against any solvent directors of the franchisor.

The focus of all current regulation of franchising is on pre contractual disclosure and provisions enabling a franchisee to file an action for unconscionable or misleading conduct. When the franchisor becomes insolvent, none of the protections afforded to the franchisee are of any relevance.

The law does not currently recognise that administrators and liquidators owe a duty of care to the franchisees. If it did, franchisees would be included in discussions about the suitability of a proposed purchaser of the franchisor.

Controlling property interests in and related to the franchise will enable the franchisor to:

---

113 Corporations Act (2001) Cth, sections 440D (Stay of proceedings for company under administration) and 471B (Stay of proceedings and suspension of enforcement process for company in liquidation).

- Build the franchisor's business;
- Grant lesser property rights to franchisees;
- Bundle sets of rights for granting to franchisees at different levels in the system (e.g. master franchisees will be granted different property rights to individual franchisees; franchisees in overseas jurisdictions may be granted different bundles of rights); and
- Offer the property as security for loans.

A final, and significant, challenge is that raised by Rohrbacher in his analysis of the property-contract lack of parity in bankruptcy. He states:

> Improving the bankruptcy system is important because property and contractual rights are keys to the smooth functioning of our economic enterprises.[114]

Conclusion

Franchisees of insolvent franchisors are a significant item of 'collateral damage' when a franchisor becomes insolvent. However, solutions to the problem are not clear cut. The actual cost of franchisor failure is unknown. This suggests much more empirical research is required before any definitive solutions are proposed to this emerging challenge.

Solutions that may be considered include:

- Doing nothing;
- Requiring franchisees to insure against their franchisor's insolvency;[115]
- Making one set of 'rules' for franchisees that make no significant sunk investment and a separate set of 'rules' for franchisees that are required to make a significant sunk investment. Then, provide rights in insolvency for the latter;
- Implying terms into all franchise agreements to give franchisees rights if the franchisor fails. For example there could be a right, but not an obligation, for franchisees to be released from the franchise agreements if the franchisor becomes insolvent. The consequential problem that would not be resolved is that rights in the franchise agreement this would not release franchisees from third party commitments such as rental guarantees, leases or licenses to occupy premises or supplier arrangements, which may be equally burdensome;

---

114 Rohrbacher, above note 87 at 1099 in note 35.

115 The author is not aware of any such insurance but theoretically the risk and potential loss are measurable so the possibility of insurance should not be ruled out. A specific issue that would have to be taken into account is that sometimes franchisees do not realise they are in a franchise. For example, in *Australian Competition & Consumer Commission v Ewing* [2004] FCA 5, the franchisees in Synergy in Business thought they were licensees until the court found they were franchisees and deserved the protection of the Franchising Code of Conduct.

- Requiring franchisors to provide their own security deposits for retail premises, or permit franchisees to be the lessees;
- Requiring franchisors to hold sums like the AUD 60,000 option for future sites fee in Table 14.3 on trust for the franchisees until they options are exercised; or
- Imposing a statutory duty of care on liquidators towards franchisees.

Practitioners and academics will identify further challenges and solutions that have not been raised in this chapter. Employees and finance providers enjoy rights in both administration and insolvency, yet, franchisee that replace the traditional employees and finance providers have no rights. Lawyers in all 26 countries where practitioners were surveyed for this chapter report that their countries have national business failure laws.[116] There is no consistency, and in most jurisdictions, no provision for, franchisees of insolvent franchisors. Consumer protection laws are incapable of providing a complete solution – this is a job for business failure laws.

It is suggested that the issue is too widespread and too complex to be dealt with efficiently on a case by case basis. It is difficult to see how this situation could be addressed in Australia other than through amendments to insolvency legislation.

---

116   Above note 52.

Index

actio legis Aquiliae, 347, 349
addictio, 9
administration, 14, 24, 28-29, 31-32, 35-38, 40, 42, 46-47, 50-51, 53, 56, 58-59, 84-85, 88-89, 92-102, 105-114, 116-133, 174-176, 179-180, 182, 237, 240-241, 249, 252-254, 256-257, 263, 278, 280, 286-287, 385-386, 388-390, 392, 395-396, 398, 400, 402
administrator, 88-89, 94-97, 99-103, 106, 109, 111-131, 133, 240, 262, 305, 317, 327, 376, 385-386, 388-389, 392-395
  see also insolvency practitioner, liquidator, nominee, receiver, trustee (in bankruptcy)
affiliated companies, 177
ancillary proceedings, see proceedings
Antarctica, 339
Argentina, 310, 369, 381
Asian Development Bank (ADB), 214, 222, 232-233
asset management companies (AMC), 220-222, 228, 234-235
assets, see property
Australia, 23, 31, 33-34, 39-40, 51-52, 54, 66, 83-84, 88-89, 93-106, 108, 110, 113, 115-123, 125-131, 133, 295, 306, 312, 314-316, 334, 368-370, 373-374, 377, 379-382, 384-385, 387, 389, 392-393, 397, 402
Australian Competition and Consumer Commission (ACCC), 384-385, 389-390
Australian Securities and Investments Commission (ASIC), 115, 124, 131
Austria, 66, 77, 306, 369
Authentic Consent Model, 63
auxiliary proceedings, see proceedings
balance sheet, 220, 223-224
banking, 20, 23, 29, 33, 64, 101, 251, 258, 261, 264
Bank of England, 136, 215, 217

banking, 211-213, 215-216, 218-233, 235
banking crisis, 218, 221, 223
bankrupt, 3-5, 7, 12, 15, 19-20, 24-25, 30-31, 65, 135, 142, 153-158, 213, 270-271, 284, 288, 299, 305-306, 314, 316, 320-321, 323-324, 335, 351, 387, 396
bankruptcy, 3-8, 10-20, 24-26, 29, 31-32, 36, 40, 43, 46, 50, 53, 58, 61-62, 64-68, 77-78, 112, 135-137, 140-142, 144, 146-165, 168-170, 270, 273, 277, 281, 284, 288, 290, 295-296, 302, 305-309, 311-312, 315, 318, 320-323, 326, 328, 330-331, 341, 350-354, 370-371, 387, 390, 395-397, 401
Basel Committee, 211-212, 215, 218, 229-233
Belgium, 66, 229, 312, 369, 381, 384
Bermuda, 306
Board of Trade, 14
bona fide, see insolvency principles
bona vacantia, 352-353
borrower, 213, 215, 217, 219-221, 223, 231, 237, 248-249, 251, 258, 260, 342-343
  see also debtor
borrowing, see financing
Botswana, 66, 270-271, 288-289, 291-292
Brazil, 306-307, 312, 369
British Virgin Islands, 54
Bulgaria, 37, 369
business, 3-4, 7, 18, 20-26, 30, 34-35, 48, 61, 63-64, 68, 71, 76-79, 86, 94, 97, 99, 102, 105, 108-109, 111-112, 115, 117-119, 126, 135-137, 139, 141-144, 148, 150, 152, 155, 157, 161, 165, 242-244, 247, 249, 252, 257-263, 338, 340-341, 343, 351-353, 356-357, 359, 366-372, 375-377, 379-382, 384-385, 387-390, 392-396, 398-402

see also close corporation,
company, firm
business cycle, 64

Canada, 23, 37, 54, 66, 168, 170, 216,
227, 229, 305-306, 308, 312, 321,
323, 325, 327, 333, 354, 369, 381,
384, 397, 398
capital, 105, 295-300, 304, 321, 328,
341, 351, 364, 367, 370, 381-382,
394, 395
central bank, 218, 223-224, 228, 233-234
centre of main interests (COMI), 52, 55-
56, 58-59, 173-176, 178-183
cessio bonorum, 135
Chapter 7, 73, 90, 94-95, 147, 169
Chapter 11, 24-26, 37, 52, 84-86, 90, 93-
95, 99, 105, 112-113, 118, 122,
326-328
Chapter 13, 170
charge, 238-241, 243-247, 250, 252, 256,
259, 262, 338, 350-353, 355
fixed, 21-22, 237-239, 242-244,
246-248, 259-260
floating, 21-23, 88, 93, 102, 107,
124, 238-242, 244-247, 250, 253,
256, 259-260, 318
qualifying, 88, 93-95, 98-103, 109,
115
see also security
chargeholder (chargee), 107, 109, 113-
116, 119-120, 122, 239-240, 259,
385
Chile, 306, 369
China, 212, 215, 217, 222, 306, 311,
320-321, 330, 369
choice of forum, 38, 40, 42, 46, 49, 53
choice of law, 36, 38-41, 46, 53, 58, 60
claims, 3-4, 7, 10, 14, 23-24, 28, 30-33,
36, 42-45, 47-48, 50-53, 57, 65, 68,
70, 72, 74, 78, 84, 91, 105, 187-189,
193, 199, 223, 228-229, 239-240,
246-247, 257, 271-273, 278-281,
285-288, 290-293, 295-298, 300-
315, 317-322, 325-326, 330, 332-
335, 347, 349-350, 353, 355, 358-
366
claw-back, 153
close corporation, 351, 352, 356, 358,
359, 362
see also business, company, firm

coercive measures/powers, 190
collective
agreements, 303-304, 332-333
bargaining, 267, 273, 281, 298, 300,
327
process, 83
redundancies, 268
satisfaction, 28
Colombia, 306, 369, 381
comity, 38-39, 43, 51
commencement (of proceedings), 83-87,
90, 92-94, 98-100, 103-104, 178
commercial morality, 30, 34
common pool problem, 61, 69, 76, 79
Commonwealth, 7, 8, 23, 151
communication, 192-195, 204, 208
Companies House, 115, 237, 249
company (corporation), 7-8, 11, 20, 22,-
25, 31-32, 34, 37, 40, 46, 48, 62, 68,
77-79, 83, 85-89, 92-103, 105, 107-
109, 111-118, 120-124, 126-131,
175-176, 178, 180-183, 237-243,
246, 249-258, 260-261, 263, 295-
299, 305, 307-308, 310, 312-316,
324, 326, 328-329, 332, 342, 346-
347, 351-352, 354, 356-359, 362-
363, 368-369, 373-374, 376, 380,
384-388, 392-394, 400
see also business, close corporation,
firm
composition, 141, 145-146, 148, 151,
161, 185-186, 193, 197-198, 202-
206, 208
concurrent proceedings, see proceedings
conflict of laws, see private international
law
constructive destruction, 61
consumer, 136-145, 148-151, 152, 156-
157, 159, 161, 167-170, 337
contract
employment, 274, 276, 279, 289-
290, 297-298, 300
privity of, 372-374, 399
service, 279-280, 283
convention
direct 55
indirect, 54
cooperation, 31, 45, 49, 51, 53, 57, 67,
71, 75, 185, 188, 193-194, 197, 207,
267, 269, 298
coordination, 185, 187-188, 193-194

Cork Committee, 23-24, 107, 108
Cork Report, 4, 87, 107
Corporate (Company) Voluntary
    Arrangement, 24, 85, 128
corporate groups, 177, 181, 184
Corporations and Markets Advisory
    Committee (CAMAC), 92, 99, 106,
    110, 116, 119, 122, 127
cost-effective(ness), see insolvency
    principles
Council of Europe, 52, 55
County Court Administration Order
    (CCAO), 142
countries
    developed, 298-299, 330
    developing, 212, 222, 225-226, 235
    see also economies
credit, 61-62, 76, 85, 100, 122, 135-136,
    138-140, 145, 150, 152, 157, 160,
    162, 164-165, 168-169, 213-214,
    230-232, 234, 296-297, 304, 310-
    311, 313, 318, 325, 332
creditor, 4-6, 9-11, 13-14, 16, 19-23, 28,
    30, 32, 37, 41, 48, 50, 57, 63-66,
    68-69, 71-76, 78-79, 89-90, 98,
    100-102, 107, 110-111, 119, 121-
    122, 124, 129, 136, 148, 150-151,
    153, 160, 164-166, 174, 177-178,
    180, 186-188, 190, 192-194, 196-
    208, 212, 225, 229, 237, 239-240,
    246-248, 253-254, 256-257, 259,
    261-263, 270-271, 278-280, 283,
    285-288, 295, 297-302, 304-309,
    310-312, 314-316, 318, 320-321,
    330, 374, 385-387, 389, 392-395,
    398
    see also lender
credit markets, 157
Creditors' Bargain Model, 63
creditors' meeting, 113, 118-119, 120-
    121, 123-125, 128-129
crystallisation, 22, 244, 246
Czech Republic, 66, 306, 369

debenture, 88, 101-102, 109, 238, 245-
    247, 263
Debt Arrangement Scheme (DAS), 143-
    144, 149, 162-163, 165, 167-168
Debt Management Arrangement (DMA),
    142, 144, 163
Debt Relief Order (DRO), 144, 164

debt, 61-64, 68-71, 75, 87, 136, 138-139,
    141-143, 145-146, 148-150, 154,
    156, 160-169, 203, 212, 215-216,
    222, 233, 237-243, 245-250, 256,
    258-263
debt financing, see financing
debtor, 3-6, 9-11, 13-14, 16-23, 25-26,
    28-34, 36-38, 40-42, 44-47, 48, 50,
    52, 55-59, 61-67, 69-71, 73, 76-79,
    90-95, 100, 104, 138-170, 173-176,
    178-180, 182-183, 186-190, 192,
    202-203, 205-208, 212, 374, 389,
    395, 398
    see also borrower
debtor-in-possession, 112
Deed of Company Arrangement, 89,
    128, 316
default, see insolvency related problems
Denmark, 66, 151, 188, 369, 381
deposit insurance, 228-229
depositors, 212, 216, 223-226, 228, 229
development
    agencies, 340
    sustainable, 336, 340-341, 344, 346,
    351
director, 7, 22, 26, 31, 62, 65, 87-89, 93-
    94, 98-100, 103, 105, 109, 112-115,
    120, 127-128, 130-131, 147, 157,
    299, 309-310, 315-317, 321-322,
    333-334, 340, 356
    see also shadow directorship
discharge, 4-6, 11, 13, 139-152, 154,
    156-158, 161-162, 165
distribution, 3-5, 7, 10, 12, 15, 27, 29-30,
    32, 34, 45-47, 52-53, 62-63, 111,
    121, 129-130, 240, 300
dividend, 149-150, 160, 164, 194
Dominican Republic, 369

ecological damage, 337-339, 358
    see also environmental damage,
    environmental harm
economic distress, see insolvency related
    problems
economies
    developed, 212
    transitional, 211-212, 216, 220, 226,
    232
    see also countries
Ecuador, 369
efficiency, see insolvency principles

Egypt, 66, 369
employee, 23, 25, 33, 62, 118, 247, 263,
    267-271, 273-286, 288-292, 295-
    317, 319-326, 329-330, 333-334,
    367, 373, 379-381, 387, 389, 394-
    395, 402
    claims, 295-296, 298, 301, 305-315,
    317, 320, 333
    protection, 267, 269-275, 280-282,
    289, 291-292, 296-297, 300-306,
    308-315, 317, 319, 321, 327, 330-
    331, 333
    see also worker
employer, 267-269, 271-284, 286, 288-
    292, 298-299, 302-303, 308, 311-
    313, 316-317, 319-321, 323, 325-
    332, 340, 356
employment, 267-268, 272-285, 288-
    293, 367, 381
enforcement (of judgments), 4-5, 24, 40,
    42-43, 46, 49-50, 53-55, 57-58, 60,
    63, 70-71, 73, 75-76, 143, 151, 164,
    166, 213-214, 221, 233, 250, 262
England (and Wales), 3-4, 11-12, 14, 18,
    30, 37-41, 52, 54, 58, 65-67, 87,
    135-138, 140-144, 146-150, 152-
    154, 156, 159, 161-163, 165, 168-
    169, 369, 381, 306
    see also Great Britain, United
    Kingdom

environmental
    costs, 337
    damage, 335-347, 349-350, 352-
    354, 356-360, 365
    harm, 337, 339, 341, 348, 351, 354,
    357
    protection, 340-342, 348, 357
    see also ecological damage
equal pay, 268
equity, 71, 74, 78, 154
equity financing, see financing
Eritrea, 54
establishment, 56-57, 179
Estonia, 307
Europe, 268, 271
European Community, 12, 174-175, 178,
    182, 186
European Convention on Certain
    Aspects of Bankruptcy (Istanbul
    Convention), 186

European Court of Justice, 179
European Insolvency Regulation, 55-56,
    58, 115, 151, 173-183, 185-193,
    195-205, 207-208
European Union, 24, 151, 165, 178, 181,
    185-186, 188, 191, 207-208, 228,
    268-269, 271-273, 282, 285, 289,
    303, 342, 344-345
execution (of judgments), 4-5, 11, 196
exequatur, 189
externality, 336-337
extraterritoriality, 39

factoring, see financing
failure, see insolvency related problems
Federal Deposit Insurance Corporation
    (FDIC), 211-212, 216, 225, 227,
    229
financial difficulties, see insolvency
    related problems
financial distress, see insolvency related
    problems
financial failure, see insolvency related
    problems
financing
    borrowing, 8, 22
    debt, 20
    equity, 20, 382
    factoring, 238, 249, 251, 258, 262
    invoice discounting, 248-249, 251,
    258
    leasing, 252, 257, 259
    lending, 8, 214-216, 218, 220, 223,
    230-231, 233, 237, 242-243, 248,
    251-254, 257-259, 261, 263
    liquidity, 218, 223, 235
    overdraft, 20, 242, 248, 251-254,
    257-259, 262-263
    receivables, 248-252, 254, 256-258,
    262
Financial Services Authority, 169
Finland, 369, 381
firm, 62, 64-69, 72-75, 77, 91, 295-300,
    304, 306-307, 313, 315-316, 320-
    321, 323-326, 333
    see also business, close corporation,
    company
'first come, first served', see insolvency
    principles
fixed charge, see charge
floating charge, see charge

foreign main proceedings, see
proceedings
foreign non-main proceedings, see
proceedings
forum shopping, 48
France, 66, 173-175, 179-180, 216, 229,
317, 369, 381, 384
franchise, 367-372, 374-377, 379-382,
385-386, 388-390, 392-401
fee, 367, 377, 397-398
franchisee, 367-377, 379-382, 384-390,
392-402
franchisor, 367-377, 379-382, 384-386,
388-390, 392-401
fraud, 5, 12, 16
freedom of association, 267
fresh start, 139, 145-146, 152, 156-158

game theory, 68, 70
Germany, 37, 66, 180, 229, 296, 307,
320, 324-325, 329-330, 369, 381,
384
globalization, 27, 269
going concern, 67, 71, 73, 97-98, 111-
112, 268-277, 282, 292
goods, see property
goodwill, see property
Great Britain, 54
see also England, Scotland, United
Kingdom
Greece, 66, 369, 381
guarantee
fund, 296, 302, 304-305, 307-315,
318, 320-321, 325-327, 331-333
institution, 272
insurance, 296

habitual residence, 176
Harmer Committee, 108, 130
harmonization (of laws), 36, 55
hire purchase, 252, 259, 262
holding companies, 181, 184
Hong Kong, 306, 369
Hungary, 306, 369

immovable, see property
impaired loans, 216, 219, 220
imprisonment for debt, 11, 13, 15-16, 18
incorporation, 176, 178-180, 183
indebtedness, see insolvency related
problems

India, 307, 369, 381
Individual Voluntary Arrangement, 136,
141
Indonesia, 66, 306, 369
infamia, 11
informal work-out, 67
information asymmetry, 86, 298
INSOL, 137-138, 140-141, 145-146,
150, 152, 156, 161-162, 167, 170
insolvency, 3, 8, 11, 14-15, 17, 20, 23-
26, 28-69, 72-73, 75-79, 83-85, 87-
94, 97-101, 103-104, 106-110, 112-
113, 115, 118-119, 122, 128, 132,
135-140, 142, 144, 146-147, 150-
151, 155, 157-159, 161-163, 165-
168, 185-188, 190-196, 202,-205,
207-208, 211, 214, 219-226, 228-
229, 233, 237-239, 241-242, 246,
249, 256-260, 262-263, 267-273,
275-281, 283-284, 287-288, 290-
291, 293, 295, 296-317, 319-323,
325-326, 329, 332-334, 350, 352-
354, 357, 361-362, 364, 366-368,
371, 375, 377, 381-382, 385-390,
392-395, 398, 401-402
insolvency (*de facto*), 90
insolvency officeholder, see insolvency
practitioner
insolvency practitioner, 15, 26, 30, 49,
141, 160, 163, 242, 258, 260, 262-
263
see also administrator, liquidator,
nominee, receiver, trustee (in
bankruptcy)
insolvency principles
bona fide (good faith), 90, 102
cost-effective(ness), 139, 150, 159-
160
efficiency, 47, 63, 65, 72-73, 98,
109, 139, 150, 159, 216, 221, 301,
304, 306, 310, 311
'first come, first served', 70, 75
pari passu, 30, 279, 286-287, 300,
308, 310, 320
plurality, 33, 42, 44
territoriality, 42-47, 49, 51-52, 205
unity, 31, 42, 47, 174, 187-188,
207-208
universalism (universality), 42, 45-
49, 51-52, 174, 186
insolvency related problems

default, 213, 220, 257
economic distress, 61, 64
failure, 136, 140, 150, 162
financial difficulties, 77, 86, 92, 99, 103
financial distress, 61, 63-64, 68-69, 72-74, 76-79, 295-298, 304, 307, 312, 321, 324, 326, 333
financial failure, 28, 34-35
indebtedness (over-), 4-5, 9, 11-12, 15, 136-139, 142, 145-146, 149, 164, 168
insolvent, 213, 216, 220, 224-228, 233, 237, 242, 254, 263, 268, 271-273, 275-279, 281, 283, 285-288, 290-292, 295-296, 298, 304, 307, 309, 313, 315-316, 321, 323, 325, 328, 335, 350-354, 356, 358-362, 365-368, 372, 375, 381, 384-387, 389-390, 393-394, 396-397, 400-402
liquidity problems, 218, 223
insolvent trading, 127-128
insurance, 33-34, 55, 212, 218, 224-226, 228-229, 296, 302, 305, 308, 311-314, 317, 320, 329, 331-333, 335, 341, 356-362, 364
fund, 305, 313, 317, 329
see also guarantee fund
intellectual property, see property
interdependent proceedings, see proceedings
Internal Market, 188, 193
International Court of Justice, 345
International Financial Reporting Standards, 214, 232
International Labour Organisation, 271-273, 277-278, 280-281, 285, 287-288, 290-291
International Monetary Fund, 135, 211, 212, 217-219, 222, 230, 232-233
invoice discounting, see financing
involuntary filing, 90
Ireland, 66, 179, 182, 313, 369, 381
Israel, 37, 306, 369
Italy, 66, 229, 319-320, 369, 384

Japan, 43, 54, 66, 212, 229, 232, 234, 306, 315, 331, 369, 370
jurisdiction, 5, 18, 36, 39-40, 42, 45-46, 50-52, 54-55, 57-58, 60, 83, 85, 93-

94, 103, 106, 115, 127, 153, 174-175, 177-182, 189-190, 192, 212, 214, 217, 296-300, 304-307, 311-313, 322, 334, 341, 355, 382

Kaldor-Hicks efficiency, 63
Kazakhstan, 369
Kenya, 37
Korea, 66

Latin America, 66, 212
Latvia, 369
Law and Economics, 61, 63, 69, 79
Law Merchant, 4, 12
leasing, see financing
lender, 139-140, 157, 164, 241-243, 245, 248, 251, 258-263, 297, 340, 342, 367
liability, 335, 341
see also creditor
lending, see financing
lex concursus, 186, 189, 191, 207
lex fori, 191
concursus, 191
concursus secundi, 196
limited liability, 7-8, 11, 19
liquidation, 25, 29-30, 32, 36-37, 39-40, 43, 46, 50, 59, 61-62, 67-68, 85-86, 90, 95-101, 103, 108, 112, 116, 127, 129-133, 135, 139, 141, 143, 145, 185, 188, 192, 195-208, 219, 225-229, 233, 235, 238, 240, 275, 278, 284, 301-302, 305, 307, 310, 316, 318, 321, 334-335, 350, 356, 358, 363, 365
liquidator, 89, 93-99, 185, 187-208, 219-221, 240, 276-277, 280, 284-285, 290, 292, 335, 351-352, 362, 368, 370, 385-390, 392-398, 400
provisional, 89, 93-95
see also administrator, insolvency practitioner, receiver, trustee (in bankruptcy)
liquidity, 64, 74
liquidity financing, see financing
liquidity problems, see insolvency related problems
loan portfolio, 215-216, 220-221, 224-225, 228
locus standi (standing), 196, 207, 339
lodgement (of claims), 199

London Stock Exchange, 37
Luxembourg, 229

main proceedings, see proceedings
Malaysia, 222, 306, 369, 370
market
    place 3-4, 62, 74
    value, 338, 353
Mexico, 54, 306, 310, 369, 381, 384
minimum capital ratio, 212
moral hazard, 218, 230, 234, 309, 325, 330
moratorium, 24, 29, 32, 37, 50, 56, 85, 87, 105, 112
mortgage, see security
movable, see property

Namibia, 267, 270-271, 281, 284, 287, 292
Netherlands (The), 66, 190, 193, 197-198, 201, 203, 205, 229, 369, 381
New Zealand, 23, 54, 66, 248, 369, 381, 384
nexum, 9
No Income No Assets (NINA), 144, 149, 159, 163-167
nominee, 141, 153, 160
    see also administrator, insolvency practitioner, liquidator, receiver, trustee (in bankruptcy)
non-performing loan (NPL), 211-212, 214-222, 226, 228, 230, 232-235
Northern Ireland, 369
Norway, 66, 306

Organisation for Economic Cooperation and Development (OECD), 296, 298, 306, 311, 320, 330, 344-345
Official Assignee, 14
Official Receiver, 65, 142, 146-147, 150, 155-157, 159, 163-164
option (share-), 74-77
overdraft, see financing
over-indebtedness, see insolvency related problems

Paraguay, 66
parallel proceedings, see proceedings
Pareto efficiency, 63
pari passu, see insolvency principles
partnership, 7-8

pension, 296-299, 304-305, 308, 313, 321, 323-333
    assets, 298, 324
    benefits, 298, 327
    fund, 297, 324-325, 327-328, 330
    income, 298, 326
    law, 299
Peru, 369
Philippines (The), 216, 369
plurality, see insolvency principles
Poland, 54, 66, 369
polluter pays principle, 335-337, 344-345, 347-350, 365
Portugal, 66, 369
preference, 113, 278-280, 285-288, 290-293, 305, 308, 310-311, 359-360
preservation (protective) measures, 178
priority, 30, 33-44, 45, 48, 53, 62, 74, 91, 100, 104, 112, 122, 228-229, 231, 239-241, 245-248, 257, 296, 298, 300-302, 304-311, 313-320, 323, 328, 333
    super-priority, 296, 306-307, 309-310, 315
prisoner's dilemma, 61, 70, 72, 75-79
private international law, 29, 36, 53, 58-60, 192
private ordering, 33
proceedings
    ancillary (auxiliary), 50, 51, 53
    concurrent, 185, 188, 194
    foreign main 56-57
    foreign non-main, 56-57
    interdependent, 192, 207
    main, 173-174, 182, 185-192, 194-208
    parallel, 50
    secondary, 185-188, 190-208
    territorial, 190, 197
profit, 61
property
    assets, 3-7, 10, 12, 15-16, 21-22, 24, 61-74, 76, 136-137, 141-142, 146, 148-149, 152-154, 156, 161-164, 167, 174, 176-178, 182, 185, 187-198, 202, 204-207, 239-247, 249-252, 257-259, 262-263, 271-272, 278, 280, 285, 291, 297, 299, 303-306, 308-310, 314, 317-320, 323-324, 326, 328-332, 367, 374-375, 379, 384, 387, 389-390

goods, 4, 12, 20-21, 27-28, 33, 56, 247, 337-338, 343
goodwill, 259, 379, 399
immovable, 21, 191, 350
intellectual, 373-375, 377, 395
movable, 21
receivables, 248-254, 256-259, 262, 264
shares, 74
Protected Trust Deed (PTD), 136, 142, 165
public international law, 341
purchase money loan security, see security

qualifying charge, see charge
quasi-security
retention of title, 206, 241, 259
set-off, 65
see also security

race
to collect, 63, 70, 72
to the bottom, 270
realisation (of assets), 190
receivables, see property
receivables financiers, 249, 251, 253, 256, 262, 264
receivables financing, see financing
receiver (and manager), 23, 101-102, 107, 111, 115-116, 123, 224-225, 228-229, 240-241, 247, 249-250, 262
see also administrator, insolvency practitioner, liquidator, nominee, trustee (in bankruptcy)
receivership, 19, 21-24, 26, 67, 73-74, 111, 113, 116, 237, 246, 249, 251-253, 256-257, 263, 321-322
recognition (of judgments), 36, 39-40, 42-44, 46-47, 49, 53-58, 60, 104, 189, 192
reconstruction, 109
see also rehabilitation, reorganisation, rescue, restructuring
recuperação da empresa, 307
registered office, 175-177, 182-183
registration, 7, 21, 176, 182
rehabilitation, 5, 23-24, 38, 62, 65-66, 68, 139, 145, 161, 356, 358

see also reconstruction, reorganisation, rescue, restructuring
relation back doctrine, 31
relief, 198
remedy, 4-5, 11, 14, 32, 43, 62, 70
reorganization, 29, 32, 34, 36-40, 46, 50, 59, 61, 77-78, 85, 90, 92, 97, 100, 103, 118, 135, 193, 195, 198, 206
see also reconstruction, rehabilitation, rescue, restructuring
rescue, 3, 5, 18, 20, 23-26, 83-88, 92, 94, 97-100, 103-106, 109-110, 112-113, 117, 122, 128, 130, 132-133, 135, 137, 186, 188, 197, 202-206, 208, 240-241, 260-263
see also reconstruction, rehabilitation, reorganisation, restructuring
rescue culture, 83, 87
restitutionary claim, 397
restructuring, 61-62, 64-66, 68, 73, 77-79, 185, 220, 225, 233, 296, 302, 305, 307, 319, 329-330
see also reconstruction, rehabilitation, reorganisation, rescue
retention of title, see quasi-security
retrenchment, 276-279
rights
in personam, 46
in rem, 46, 190, 197, 206
risk, 28, 144, 148, 177, 213, 217, 232, 295-299, 301, 304-305, 310-311, 315, 324-329, 332, 335, 347, 349, 351, 356-357, 367, 372, 381-382, 390, 394, 401
Romania, 54, 306
Roman Law, 9, 11-12
Russia, 306, 369

scheme of arrangement, 141, 161
Scotland, 14, 18, 66, 135-138, 140-144, 146-150, 152-155, 157-163, 165-166, 168, 306
see also Great Britain, United Kingdom
Scottish Individual Voluntary Arrangement (SIVA), 143, 159, 161-162, 168
secondary proceedings, see proceedings

security, 20-22, 65, 70, 88-89, 101-102,
213, 239-240, 242, 244, 248, 251,
254, 256-258, 260-263, 271, 278,
342, 352-353, 355
mortgage, 223, 271
purchase money loan security, 21
statutory lien, 70
see also quasi-security
sequestration, 29, 31, 40, 43, 46, 50, 136,
141-142, 144, 146, 148-149, 151,
153-156, 158, 160, 162-163, 165-
167, 169, 275-276, 278-280, 283-
288, 290-292, 335, 350, 356, 359,
361, 363-366
Serbia and Montenegro, 54
see also Yugoslavia
services, 27-28, 33, 37, 56, 247, 249,
271, 276, 280, 292
set-off, see quasi-security
shadow directorship, 248, 260
see also director
shareholder, 7-8, 87, 92, 228, 269, 340,
367, 387, 394
shares, see property
Singapore, 306, 369
Slovakia, 66, 306
Slovenia, 369
social
costs, 336, 337
dumping, 269, 278, 293
rights, 267-268, 270
security, 267-268, 269, 270, 272,
292, 301, 302, 304, 307, 311, 313
solvency, 90
South Africa, 23, 54, 66, 270-271, 273,
275, 277-278, 281-282, 285, 288-
289, 292-293, 306, 310, 336, 342-
344, 346, 348, 369
South African Development Community
(SADC), 267-271, 273, 278, 292-
293
South East Asia, 212
South Korea, 222, 234, 369, 381, 384
Spain, 66, 216, 229, 306, 369, 381
stakeholder, 62, 66-67, 83, 86-87, 94,
97-98, 261, 263, 367-368, 381, 386-
387, 392, 398
state sovereignty, 43
statutory lien, see security
statutory seat, 175-176, 178-180, 183

stay (of process), 186, 188, 195-202,
204, 206-208, 394
summary warrants, 166
supervisory judge, 189, 192
suspect period, 31
Sweden, 66, 69, 212, 229, 232, 306, 324-
325, 332, 369, 381
Switzerland, 66, 224, 228-229, 306, 369,
381

Taiwan, 369
territorial proceedings, see proceedings
territoriality, see insolvency principles
Thailand, 214, 306, 369
trade union, 276, 281-282, 293
trustee, 276-277, 284, 286, 290, 335,
350-354, 362, 364
in bankruptcy, 5, 146, 152, 305
see also administrator, insolvency
practitioner, liquidator, nominee,
receiver
Turkey, 216, 369
Twelve Tables, 9, 11

UNCITRAL, 28-36, 52-55, 57-59, 135,
137, 151, 301-302, 307
Model Law, 29, 52-59, 151
unemployment, 268, 276, 279-280, 288
insurance, 302, 320
unequal bargaining, 298
unfair dismissal, 273-275, 277, 314, 319
Ukraine (The), 369
United Kingdom, 5, 7-8, 11, 14-15, 18-
20, 22-26, 84-85, 87-89, 93-133,
136, 139, 157, 165, 179, 215, 222,
228-229, 296, 314, 328-329, 370,
381, 384
see also England, Great Britain,
Scotland
United Nations Economic Commission
for Europe (UNECE), 345
United States, 7-8, 11, 15-21, 23-27, 35-
39, 45, 47, 51, 54, 66, 70, 73, 83-84,
87, 89-95, 98-100, 103-105, 113,
122, 137-138, 147, 156, 168-170,
212, 214-216, 218, 220, 222, 224-
225, 227-229, 232, 296, 306, 309-
310, 312, 318, 323-326, 328-329,
342, 369-371, 379, 381, 384, 395,
399
unity, see insolvency principles

universalism, see insolvency principles
universality, see insolvency principles
unjust enrichment, 396-398, 400
Uruguay, 369

Venezuela, 306, 369
Vietnam, 306, 381
Virgós-Schmit Report, 189-190, 192-
    204, 206
voidable transaction, 31, 38-39
voluntary administration, 84-85, 88, 92-
    93, 95-100, 103, 105-111, 116-118,
    122-125, 127-128, 130-133, 385

winding up, 95-98, 103, 111, 116, 128,
    130, 187, 196-198, 203, 205, 240,
    246, 275-276, 280, 283, 385

worker, 270-272, 274-275, 280-282,
    295-303, 305-306, 308, 310-312,
    315, 317, 319-322, 324, 326, 332
    see also employee
workplace democracy, 267
World Bank, 27-28, 34-35, 135, 222,
    230, 232-233, 300-301, 307, 310,
    321
wrongful trading, see insolvent trading

Yugoslavia, 369
see also Serbia and Montenegro

Zaire, 66
Zimbabwe, 66, 369

UNIVERSITY OF WOLVERHAMPTON
LEARNING & INFORMATION SERVICES